A SANSKRIT READER

WITH NOTES AND SANSKRIT-ENGLISH VOCABULARY

CHARLES ROCKWELL LANMAN

Kaveri Books

New Delhi-110002

Edition 2016

ISBN 978-81-7479-176-4 (PB)

Published by

Kaveri Books

4832/24, Ansari Road

New Delhi - 110 002 (India)

Tel.: 011-2328 8140, 2324 5799

E-mail: info@kaveribooks.com,

kaveribooks@gmail.com

Website: www.kaveribooks.com

Laser Typesetting by : Tamalika Computers, Delhi

PRINTED IN INDIA

PREFACE.

The results of comparative philology are now so generally incorporated into our modern classical grammars, lexicons, and text-books, that even a slight knowledge of Sanskrit, if it be accurate so far as it goes, is of great service to the classical teacher in making his instruction interesting and effective. As independent disciplines, moreover, Sanskrit and comparative philology, and the literatures and religions of India, are constantly gaining in importance, so that, for example, Sanskrit is now taught at all but one of the twenty universities of the German Empire.

The design of this work, then, is twofold. In the first place, it is to serve as an introduction to these subjects for the students of our colleges and universities. The excellent Chrestomathy of Boehtlingk has no vocabulary; and few persons can be expected to buy the costly dictionary of Williams or that of Boehtlingk and Roth, at the outset, when they are uncertain whether Sanskrit will be of sufficient interest or use to them to warrant their continuing its study. What the beginner needs is an elementary work comprehending both text and vocabulary in a single volume. And accordingly, this Reader is meant to furnish ample material for about fifty weeks' reading, in a course of three hours a week, and, with the text, the appropriate lexical apparatus. The Reader is made as a companion-volume to Whitney's *Sanskrit Grammar*, and these two books supply all that is needed for the first year's study.

This Reader is designed, in the second place, to render a knowledge of Sanskrit accessible to the classical teachers of high-schools, academies, and colleges. These teachers, if they pursue this study at all, usually do so without the aid of an instructor. And it is especially *the requirements of unaided private study* that I have taken constant pains to meet. I state this fact thus explicitly, because, both here at Cambridge, and during my connection with the Johns Hopkins University (where the plan for this work was formed), numerous inquiries for such a book have been addressed to me by persons very remote from any of the higher institutions of learning.

If, incidentally, this work should help to correct some of the false notions which are prevalent respecting the relations of Sanskrit to other languages of the Indo-European family, and to save the literature from undue depreciation and from exaggerated praise, it will have served a worthy object.

So cumbrous or so meagre have been hitherto the appliances for acquiring even a moderate knowledge of Sanskrit, that classical students, when seeking such knowledge as an auxiliary to their special work, have found the labor discouragingly great. These students unquestionably have a legitimate and sufficient reason for undertaking Sanskrit, and I venture to hope that the difficulties of the beginning (see p. xv) have been so materially lessened that they will now find even a modicum of Sanskrit well worth the trouble of attainment.

In making my selections[1] from the various Sanskrit writings, I have had two practical aims in view: first, to provide abundant material for thorough drill in the language of the classical period; and, secondly, to furnish a brief introduction to the works of the Vedic period, Mantra, Brāhmana, and Sūtra. Accordingly I have not sought to give any thing new, but rather that which is best suited for beginners. The easy Nala is the Xenophon's Anabasis of Sanskrit students, and quotations from it appear very often in the grammars. And the first five chapters here given form a complete story. For an elementary reader, the Hitopadeça is unrivalled, and to leave it out would have been an inexcusable omission, unless, indeed, its place were taken by the Panchatantra. From this latter work I attempted to prepare some selections; but the text is in so unsatisfactory a condition, that I relinquished the plan. And so, although the Hitopadeça has been printed very often, I have given a considerable part[2] of it here, choosing the fables on the ground of their intrinsic excellence and their interest as originals of well-known occidental stories.[3] For similar reasons the six tales from the Kathā-sarit-sāgara were selected. On account of their easy style and simple narrative, they furnish admirable matter for exercise in rapid reading. The selections from "Manu" are so made as to illustrate some of the most important and interesting matters of Hindu custom and belief.[4]

Among the Vedic hymns (or Mantra-material) are, first, some of the easiest[5]; then some taken on account of their poetic[6] or dramatic[7] merit, or

[1] These include 68 pages of classical Sanskrit and 37 pages of Vedic Sanskrit.

[2] Nineteen fables: there are forty-three in all.

[3] See the introductions to the fables in the Notes.

[4] Compare the table of contents. The text-selections are intended to be mutually illustrative as far as may be. Thus the passage 64^{8} ff. is given for its interesting bearing on Rigveda x.18.7 (86^{17}), the verse which was appealed to as scriptural authority for the practice of widow-burning. Compare also the notes on 28^{23}, 57^{3}, and 65^{9} ff., with those on 65^{6}, 91^{16}, and 97^{2} respectively.

[5] Such are selections xxxi. (Rigveda i.1), xxxiii., xxxviii., xxxix., xli., xlv., xlvi., and lix.

[6] Selection xxxii. is the best.

[7] Selections xxxv., xxxvii., and lvi. are in dramatic form (see WHITNEY, page xviii), and are among the most difficult.

their ethical interest[1]; and finally some taken because of their historical importance.[2] For the most part, a repetition of the hymns given by DELBRUECK and by BOEHTLINGK in their Chrestomathies has been avoided. The Brāhmana pieces are chosen in such a way as to show the relation of this kind of literature to the hymns or Mantras.[3] The selections from the Grihya-sūtras are the two most interesting chapters of Indian private antiquities, the wedding and the burial service. These texts are, to a certain extent, rubrics, and prescribe that numerous specified stanzas of the Rigveda be repeated at these ceremonials. Care has therefore been taken that all the stanzas here cited by their first words should be given in full among the selections from the hymns.[4]

Concerning the text, little need be said. It would have been either folly or idle pretense to make elaborate text-studies for the short extracts of which the Reader is composed.[5] I have accordingly contented myself, in the main, with reprinting the text of the best editions. Misprints have of course been corrected, and I have endeavored to make the orthography conformable to the best standard[6] and consistent throughout.[7] Of some slight emendations, due mention will be made in the Notes. For the Nala, I followed the edition of BUEHLER in his *Third Book of Sanskrit*[8]; for the Hitopadeça, the text of BOEHTLINGK in the second edition of his Chrestomathy,[8] and MUELLER; for the Kathā-sarit-sāgara, BROCKHAUS; and for "Manu," LOISELEUR DESLONGCHAMPS. I regret that the results of the studies of BUEHLER, BURNELL, HOPKINS, and JOLLY on the text of "Manu" are not yet available.

[1] Such are the Varuna-hymns, selections xliii.–xlv.

[2] Such are the hymns for the dead and the wedding-hymn; likewise selection xxxvii., and selection xxxvi. (which contains the Sāvitrī). Selection lxii. is the Maitrāyanī version of the Hiranya-garbha hymn, Rigveda x. 121, and is given partly in order that those who possess copies of the Rigveda may study the two versions comparatively.

[3] Thus the Brāhmana selections lxvi., lxvii., lxviii., and lxxii. stand in connection with the Mantra selections lvi., xlvii., lxii., and xlvi. respectively.

[4] The stanzas required for the wedding ceremonial are given in selections lviii., lvii., and lv. From this the student will see why there are some selections consisting of only one or two stanzas. The burial-stanzas are from Rigveda x. 9, 14, 16, 17, 18, 53, 154, and 155 (selections xlix. ff.), and i. 97 (selection xxxiv.). This last hymn is mere trash, and would not have been included among the texts, had not Açwalāyana (at iv.6.18) prescribed that it be used as a burial-hymn; but I could not allow room for the "Sun-hymns" (sāuryāṇi) and the "Blessings" (svasty-ayanāni), which are also mentioned at iv.6.18.

[5] See A. WEBER, *Indische Studien*, ii. 151.

[6] Especially in the use of *anusvāra* and of the nasal mutes, of b and of ç. I have written cch where WHITNEY (see § 227) writes ch.

[7] But some of the interesting orthographical peculiarities of the Maitrāyanī Sanhitā I have allowed to stand.

[8] See the "Brief List," page xvii.

It is a pleasant duty to acknowledge my thanks to BOEHTLINGK, who, in a way no less generous than unexpected, volunteered to look over all the proofs of the classical part of the text. For the well-established and well-edited Vedic texts, such help was of course not needed.

For the Rigveda, AUFRECHT's second edition was made the standard. For the selections from the Maitrāyaṇī Sanhitā, I am indebted to the kindness of its editor,[1] DR. LEOPOLD VON SCHROEDER, of Dorpat. The extracts from the Brāhmanas naturally follow the editions of WEBER and AUFRECHT. The chapters from Açwalāyana are a reprint from STENZLER's edition, with some unimportant typographical licenses.

The vocabulary, it is almost needless to say, is based on the great Lexicon of BOEHTLINGK AND ROTH. I should of course deviate from it only with the utmost circumspection; but I trust that I have not followed it slavishly.

As for the extent of the vocabulary, it is designed to be complete for the text given in the Reader, and also, it may be added, for the text in the Appendix to the Grammar.

It is proper to mention here several matters touching the general plan of the vocabulary. It is not a mere list of the actually occurring Sanskrit words with their English equivalents. So far as possible, it aims to do with thoroughness two things:

First, as regards the *forms*, To enable the student to trace every word back to its root, by giving references to WHITNEY's chapters (xvi. and xvii.) on word-formation, and by giving the root itself, and, in the case of secondary and tertiary derivatives, the intermediate forms, even when these do not occur in the text at all. Thus, for the complete explanation of **mithyopacāra** (p. 217), are given, first, **mithyā́**, then the older form thereof, **mithuyā́**,[2] then the adjective **míthu** from which the adverb is derived, and finally the root **mith**, although neither the adverbs nor the adjective nor any verbal form of the root occurs in the text. In like manner, **car + upa** is given solely on account of **upacāra**.

Secondly, as regards the *meanings*, To enable the student to trace every signification back to the radical idea, by giving not only the meaning required for translating a particular passage, but also, if this is a secondary or tertiary or later meaning, the intermediate meanings, and in their logical order of development. Thus the only meanings of the word **pāda**, as it

[1] He gave them to me in manuscript, before he himself began printing.

[2] By looking out the reference to 1112e (under **míthu**), the student will have his attention drawn to the peculiar form and accent of the adverb and will find the explanation thereof.

occurs in the text of this Reader, are 'foot' or 'leg,' in ten passages, and 'verse of a three-versed stanza,' in one passage (60[12]). The history and uses of the word may be clearly understood from BOEHTLINGK AND ROTH. The original meaning 'foot' was extended to that of 'leg'; then specialized to the meaning 'limb of a quadruped'; then generalized to the meaning 'quarter' (as, conversely, the English word *quarter* is specialized to the meaning 'fourth part of a quadruped, including a leg,' e.g., in *quarter of beef*); once more it is specialized to the meaning 'quarter of a four-versed stanza,' i.e. 'verse'; and then, at last, the use of the word is illogically extended, and it is made to denote a verse of even a three-versed stanza. To have given the meanings 'foot, leg, verse,' in three words, and perhaps in the order 'verse, leg, foot,' would have sufficed, it is true, for the purpose of making a translation; but such translation demands of the student only the most thoughtless and mechanical labor. On the other hand, by indicating briefly the development and connection of meanings, the attention of the student is directed to the processes which are constantly going on in the life and growth of language; and thus, although Sanskrit is a dead language, the *study* of Sanskrit may be made a study of life and growth.

The illustration of the transitions of meaning by analogies from the English and other familiar tongues would, it seemed to me, greatly increase the interest and usefulness of the vocabulary. And so, considerable space has been devoted to this matter. Thus under **vyāma** (p. 254, top), 'a stretch-out,' i.e. 'a fathom,' are adduced the closely parallel English *fathom*, from Anglo-Saxon *fæðm*, 'the extended arms,' and also ὀργυιά and French *toise*, both meaning 'fathom,' and of common origin respectively with ὀρέγω and Latin *tendere*, 'stretch.'[1]

In a book intended partly for persons whose chief interest in Sanskrit is from the side of its relations to the classical languages and to our mother-tongue, etymological comparisons are plainly called for. Accordingly, the kindred words from the Greek, Latin, Anglo-Saxon, and English have been given,[2] and always along with their meanings. It is hoped that these comparisons, presenting, as they do, many familiar words with which the learner can associate what is new and strange, will prove a useful aid to the memory. Etymology is a subject in which there is large room for reasonable

[1] For other parallels, compare, for example, **ābharaṇa, barhis, bhavana, vaṅça, varṇa.** Sometimes the understanding of the parallelism depends on a knowledge of the etymology of an English word; thus under root **nud + vi**, are adduced the English *di-vert*, *dis-port*, and *s-port*, and a reference to SKEAT's dictionary or to WEBSTER's may be necessary for the student, in order to find how these words are parallel in specialization and metaphor. On this subject in general, compare CURTIUS, *Grundzüge*[5], pp. 111–116, and BRINKMANN, *Die Metaphern*, Bonn, 1878.

[2] To give them without their meanings and without showing the connection of ideas is, for an elementary book, a useless task.

difference of opinion on matters of detail, and on such matters well-recognized authorities often disagree. I have tried to use the standard works of reference in the light of the best and latest etymological criticism at my command, and to distinguish with care between what is certain and what is mere conjecture. In the revision of the greater part of my manuscript for the press, I had the benefit of KLUGE's valuable dictionary.[1] His acceptance of the current comparisons has often given me assurance, and his sober judgment has often confirmed me in scepticism or silence on doubtful points. In the numerous cases where the undoubtedly allied words are too many to be given in full, I have usually selected those forms which were the simplest or the most interesting, or those whose kinship was clearest.[2]

These comparisons include only genuinely cognate words, as distinguished from borrowed words; the latter have as a rule been excluded, or, if given, have been characterized as borrowings.[3] Thus ἕνος, Latin *sen-ex*, and English *sen-green* are given on page 266, all as genuine cognates of **sana**; the words *senate*, *senator*, *senatorial*, *senescent*, *senile*, *senility*, *senior*, *sire*, *sir*, *seigniorage*, etc., are not mentioned, because they are not genuine English cognates, but only more or less ancient borrowings or more or less direct derivatives from the Latin.[4] So under the root **sṛp** (p. 276) are given Latin *serpens* and *reptilis*, and it would be superfluous to add the borrowed English *serpent* and *reptile*.

The accents of all words have been regularly marked in the headings of the articles, so far as the accents are known from the occurrence of the words in any accentuated texts of the literature.[5] But in addition to these words, the verb-forms immediately following the root have been uniformly accented, according to the rules, except in a few doubtful cases; and a number of compounds occurring on the pages of Nala have been accented,

[1] Entitled *Etymologisches Wörterbuch der deutschen Sprache.* Strassburg, Karl J. Trübner. 1883. Royal 8°. Price 10 Mark 50 Pfennige.

[2] Thus under **sana** (p. 266) might have been given, in addition to Latin *senex*, the words *senior, senectus, senīlis, senesco, senātor, senātus*, etc.; but these are readily suggested by *senex*.

[3] Thus the interesting compound *sene-schal* is added under **sana**, not as a genuine English cognate, but as a borrowing through the French from Continental Germanic, where its first member is indeed a genuine cognate.

[4] Compare note [2], above.

[5] For these accents I have relied on BOEHTLINGK's *Sanskrit-Wörterbuch in Kürzerer Fassung* as far as it has appeared, i.e. to the end of **bh**, and for the rest of the alphabet, on the great thesaurus of BOEHTLINGK AND ROTH. There are many words accented in more than one way (e.g., **rājyá, rājyà, rā́jya, ā́sana, āsaná, dáridra, daridra, dāíva, dāivá, bhūtí, bhū́ti, vṛṣṭí, vṛ́ṣṭi, veṇú, vé̄ṇu**); such have generally been left unmarked; but of a few common words like **mánu, dvipád, paçú, pāpá**, and **matí**, the prevailing accent is given, especially, if (as in the case of **bhṛtí** or **pātrí**) the other accent is rare, or (as in the case of **çúṣka**) not authenticated.

according to the rules, in order to make more tangible the difference between homonymous determinatives and possessives.[1]

What form should be given to the headings of articles is often a question. For denominative verbs, I have chosen the stem-form (e.g., **mantraya** rather than **mantray**); to this is prefixed the root-sign (√), merely in order to catch the eye; the sign must not be understood as meaning that such stems are in any wise co-ordinate with roots. The stems of the perfect active participle and of the primary comparatives are given as ending in **vāṅs** and **yāṅs**, but without any implication that these are theoretically better than the weaker forms. Roots with medial or final **ar** or **ṛ** are given in the latter form, and so are the stems in **ar** or **ṛ**.[2]

The synopses of conjugational forms which follow each verbal root are based on the collections, still in manuscript, made by Professor WHITNEY.[3] These were placed at my disposal by him with the greatest kindness. They include all the verb-forms cited by the St. Petersburg Lexicon and BOEHTLINGK's Abridgment, as occurring in the actual literature, besides very extensive gleanings made independently by Professor WHITNEY from texts represented in the Lexicon,[4] and from others published since its completion,[5] or even not yet published.[6] In the description and classification of the forms, I have followed WHITNEY. It often happens that there are several forms in actual use for the same tense; in such cases, the commonest one has been given, or else the one prescribed by the Hindu Root-book (*dhātu-pāṭha*), or sometimes more than one form. Although in the case of many roots the aorist is confined almost exclusively to the Vedic language, I have nevertheless given the aorist in such cases in order to fill out the conjugational scheme, since this seemed desirable from a pedagogical point of view. For pedagogical reasons, also, the secondary conjugations have been for the most part omitted. Many roots which are conjugated regularly in only one voice show forms of the other voice in the Epos, especially where the metre demands them. It is very difficult to say just how far such forms should be included, and my course in accepting or rejecting them has been, I fear, not wholly consistent.

The Notes, which form the third part of this work, will be issued as soon as is practicable. It is designed that they shall be as brief as possible, but shall render ample assistance in the interpretation of difficult passages and

[1] Compare **bhīmaparākramá** and **bhīmá-parākrama**, p. 206.

[2] See WHITNEY, §§ 107 and 108, and compare § 370.

[3] See *Proceedings of the American Oriental Society* for May, 1882, p. xiii.

[4] For example, the Çatapatha and Aitareya Brāhmaṇas.

[5] Especially GARBE's edition of Apastamba's Çrauta Sūtra, and VON SCHROEDER's Maitrāyaṇī.

[6] The Jaiminīya Brāhmaṇa.

the explanation of allusions to the antiquities of India. The plan includes also concise literary introductions to the various selections.

An open acknowledgment of my thanks is due to the printers of the vocabulary, Messrs. J. S. Cushing & Co. They have performed their part with such intelligence, accuracy, and skill as to merit most cordial recognition.

In conclusion, I desire to make public expression of my gratitude to my honored teacher, Professor William Dwight Whitney, for his constant interest in this undertaking and for his generous aid. I can only hope that the book may do something to further the cause in which he has labored long and devotedly, and that it may help to enlarge the scope of classical teaching, to quicken the interest in the history of our mother-tongue, and to make Sanskrit study among us increasingly fruitful.

C. R. L.

Hollis Hall, Harvard College,
Cambridge, Massachusetts,
December, 1883.

CONTENTS

(C). From the Kathā-sarit-sāgara

* For detailed synopsis, aeo Notes.

INTRODUCTORY SUGGESTIONS.

It is chiefly at the beginning that the difficulties of Sanskrit present themselves. The variety of forms, the strange alphabet, the peculiarities of word and sentence combination, — all these simultaneously confront the student at the very outset. Accordingly, the plan followed with my classes, and for which provision is here made, is to distribute these difficulties over the first few weeks of the course. The common paradigms of nouns and verbs should first be learned. These are given by the Grammar in transliteration. The reading of the first four pages of the Nala in Roman letters should then be taken up. The Reader gives these in transliteration on an inset conveniently facing the same text in *nāgarī* letters. The student may thus become familiar with the *form* and *sound* of the vocables, without being embarrassed by the alphabet and the running together of the words. Next, the same familiar text should be read aloud over and over again in *nāgarī* letters. I am convinced that the easiest way to master the alphabet is to read frequently in it words which one already knows. The next step will be the reading of pages five to nine without the help of a transliteration, but with the aid given by the typographical separation of the words, which has been carried out so far as is practicable, though in violation of Indian usage. Finally, from this point on, the reading may be continued without other help for the difficulties of euphonic and graphic combination than is offered by the notes.

After finishing the Nala, the student should take up the Hitopadeça. Selections xvii., xx., and xi. are very easy and are good to begin with. The remaining short ones from vi. to xxi. may then follow in order; and finally the long selections ii. to v.

It is recommended that the student use the stories from the Kathā-sarit-sāgara for exercise in rapid reading, as soon as he has acquired a fair vocabulary from what precedes. The passages from "Manu" may be read as they stand.

Of the Vedic selections, the easiest are numbers xxxi. (Rigveda i. 1), xxxiii., xxxviii., xxxix., xli., xlv., xlvi., and lix.; and it is advisable to read these first and in the order here mentioned. Selection xxxii., as being one of poetic merit and not over-hard, may next be taken up, and after it, the Varuna-hymns, selections xliii.-xliv.; then the hymns in dramatic form, selections xxxv., xxxvii., and lvi.

After these, selections xxxvi., xl., xlii., xlvii., xlviii., liv., and lxii. may be rapidly read. There will then remain the selections for the burial-service, xlix.–liii., lvii., lx., lxi., and xxxiv., and those for the wedding, lviii., lvii., and lv. These may properly be read last, in order that they may be fresh in the mind when reading the Sūtras, where constant reference is made to them.

The Brāhmana pieces may be read in the order in which they are printed; but selections lxvi., lxvii., lxviii., and lxxii. ought not to be taken up, unless selections lvi., xlvii., lxii., and xlvi. have previously been studied.

It is very undesirable to attempt to read the Sūtra chapters until one is familiar with the burial and wedding stanzas just mentioned. It is advisable to write out a translation of these chapters, and to insert therein each *mantra* in its proper place, writing out the original of the *mantra* in full, and its translation, the latter also in metre, if possible.

Since the synopses following each verbal root in the vocabulary represent the great mass of all the forms in actual use (rather than those simply prescribed by the grammarians), and so correspond to the "principal parts" of the Latin and Greek verbs, the student should make it his duty to learn the synopsis for each root when he first meets verbal forms of that root in the text.

Attention is called to the explanations and abbreviations (pages 289–294); these should be looked over carefully before using the vocabulary.

A BRIEF LIST OF BOOKS FOR STUDENTS OF SANSKRIT.

THIS list has a purely practical aim,[1] and is restricted to a few of the more important and useful books and[2] to such as are neither rare nor out of print. It includes (*a*) a grammar, (*b*) readers, (*c*) dictionaries, (*d*) classical works, books for the study (*e*) of the Rigveda and its literature, and (*f*) of the Atharvaveda, and last (*g*) some books on antiquities and the history of the literature and the religions of India.

1. **Whitney**, William Dwight. A Sanskrit Grammar, including both the classical language, and the older dialects, of Veda and Brahmana. Leipzig, Breitkopf and Härtel. London, Trübner & Co. 1879. 8°. Price (bound in cloth) 12 shillings.

This may be had in Boston of Ginn, Heath, and Co. The work exists also in a German translation, which may be had of the Leipzig publishers.

2. **Bühler**, Georg. Third Book of Sanskṛit. With a glossary by Vishnu P. Shastri Pandit. Second edition. Bombay. 1877. 12°. 128 pages of text and 97 of glossary. Price 9 annas.

This book can be procured from Trübner & Co. in London (price 3 shillings). It contains the entire Story of Nala (26 chapters), Daçaratha's Death (Rāmāyana, ii. 63–64), and four stories from the Panchatantra. For beginners, the typography proves troublesome and the glossary too meagre; but the little volume is inexpensive and contains excellent material for easy and rapid reading, and so is highly to be recommended to those who have finished the classical part of this Reader and wish to continue their Sanskrit. For such students the glossary would be quite sufficient.

3. **Böhtlingk**, Otto. Sanskrit-Chrestomathie. Zweite, gänzlich umgearbeitete Auflage. St. Petersburg. 1877. Large 8°. 372 pages. Price 4 Mark 80 Pfennige.

This work and the two following are publications of the Russian Imperial Academy, and should be ordered through the Academy's agent, Leopold Voss, of Leipzig. The volume contains selections from the Veda (Mantra, Brāhmana, and Sūtra), from the Mahā-bhārata, Rāmāyana, Vishnu-purāna, Kathā-sarit-sāgara, Hitopadeça, "Manu's Laws," and Pānini's Grammar, and from various other books; a rich collection of proverbs; the Vedānta-sāra, a philosophical treatise, in text and translation; and the entire drama, Ratnāvali. The Vedic hymns are all translated in the volume mentioned below, no. 15; and the notes show where many of the other selections may be found translated. Like all publications of the Academy, this is sold at an extremely low price. Since the book has no vocabulary, the student will at this point need to get a dictionary.

[1] Hence the prices are included. Both the Mark and the shilling may be reckoned as a quarter of a dollar. The prices given with the titles are publishers' prices. To these prices, except when given in dollars, should be added the duty, which is 25 per cent. The books will cost the American purchaser somewhat more or less according to his facilities for obtaining foreign books.

[2] With perhaps one exception, no. 18, which can, however, be had of second-hand dealers.

4. **Böhtlingk,** Otto. Sanskrit-Wörterbuch in kürzerer Fassung. St. Petersburg. 1879–. 4°.

To be ordered through Voss (see above). Parts I. to IV. have appeared, and reach to the end of bh; they cover 1167 pages, i.e. nigh two-thirds of the whole, and cost 34 Mark 80 Pfennige. The rest may be expected in the course of 1885. The manuscript is ready as far as varṇa. The work is an abridgment of the following.

5. **Böhtlingk,** Otto, **and** Rudolph **Roth.** Sanskrit-Wörterbuch. St. Petersburg. 1855–1875. Seven volumes. 4°. Price 177 Mark 90 Pfennige.

To be ordered through Voss (see above). This work, which is often called the "St. Petersburg Lexicon," is by far the most important production of Sanskrit scholarship. To such as wish to make any special study of the language and literature, it is absolutely indispensable.

6. **Williams,** Monier. A Sanskṛit-English Dictionary, etymologically and philologically arranged, with special reference to Greek, Latin, Gothic, German, Anglo-Saxon, and other cognate Indo-European languages. London and New York, Macmillan and Co. 1872. 4°. 1186 pages. Price 94 shillings 6 d. in England, or $24 in the United States.

This is the only dictionary of Sanskrit into English which approaches completeness. It is in one compact and handy volume and is very convenient for reading works of the classical period. Unfortunately, the common meanings of a word are not distinguished from those which are seldom or never found. All Sanskrit words are given in transliteration, and the roots and more important words in *nāgarī* letters also.

7. **Williams,** Monier. S'akuntalā, a Sanskṛit drama in seven acts, by Kālidāsa. Second edition. London and New York, Macmillan and Co. 1876. 8°. 339 pages. Price 21 shillings in England, or $5.25 in the U.S.

This gives literal English translations of all the metrical passages, explanatory notes, and the Sanskritization of the Prakrit passages, and all on the same page with the text of this, the most famous of the plays.

8. **Kielhorn,** Franz, **and** Georg **Bühler.** Panchatantra. Edited with notes. Bombay. 1868. 8°.

The work constitutes numbers IV., III., and I. of the "Bombay Sanskrit Series." Number IV. (comprehending book I.) appeared in a second edition in 1873. The book may be had of Trübner & Co., London. The price of the entire work is 8 shillings; but the first book may be had separately for 3 shillings. The Panchatantra is easy and entertaining reading. It has been admirably translated into German by Benfey: Pantschatantra. Leipzig, F. A. Brockhaus. 1859. 2 vols. 8°. Price 24 Mark. The translation is accompanied by a very valuable history of fable-literature.

9. **Delbrück,** Berthold. Vedische Chrestomathie. Mit Anmerkungen und Glossar. Halle, Buchhandlung des Waisenhauses. 1874. 8°. Price 3 Mark.

This contains 47 hymns from the Rigveda. Of these, only five are repeated in this Reader. Both text and glossary are in transliteration. On account of the small price of the book, its mention may prove useful to such as do not wish to buy the two complete editions following (numbers 11 and 12).

10. **Windisch,** Ernst. Zwölf Hymnen des Rigveda. Mit Sāyaṇa's Commentar. Text. Wörterbuch zu Sāyaṇa. Appendices. Leipzig, S. Hirzel. 1883. 8°. Price 5 Mark.

This gives the text, and the comment of the great scholiast, both in *nāgarī* letters. The text is printed with the genuine accentuation (as in this Reader). The book serves a useful purpose as introduction to the native Hindu or traditional exegesis of the Veda. The vocabulary does not cover the hymns themselves; but seven of the twelve hymns are translated in the little book mentioned below, no. 15.

11. **Aufrecht,** Theodor. Die Hymnen des Ṛigveda. Herausgegeben. Zweite Auflage. Bonn, Adolph Marcus. 1877. 2 volumes. 8°. Price 20 Mark.

The entire *sanhita* text is given in transliteration, and extracts from the *pada* text at the foot of each page. The exceedingly valuable appendix contains lists of the poets, divinities, and metres, and a complete table of first lines of every stanza, with references to the concordant texts of other Vedas.

12. **Müller, F. Max.** The Hymns of the Rigveda, in the Samhita and Pada texts, reprinted from the editio princeps. Second edition. London, Trübner & Co. 1877. 2 volumes. 8°. Price 32 shillings.

This edition gives the two texts complete on parallel pages and in *nāgarī* letters. The names of the poets, divinities, and metres are given at the beginning of each hymn.

13. **Grassmann,** Hermann. Wörterbuch zum Rig-veda. Leipzig, F. A. Brockhaus. 1873[–1875]. 8°. Price 30 Mark.

This is not only a dictionary, but also a complete concordance to the Rigveda. It is a work of wonderful industry, method, clearness, and accuracy. Aside from the St. Petersburg Lexicon, this dictionary stands next in importance, for Vedic students, after the Vedic text itself.

14. **Grassmann,** Hermann. Rig-veda. Uebersetzt und mit kritischen und erläuternden Anmerkungen versehen. Leipzig, F. A. Brockhaus. 1876. 1877. 2 volumes. 8°. Price 24 Mark.

This translation is entirely in metre, except for a few corrupt or difficult hymns. The student can almost invariably see just what word Grassmann intended as the rendering of any given word of the text. This work is especially useful as giving a convenient general view of the contents of the Rigveda, and as enabling the student to grasp easily many matters touching the metres, the arrangement, and the textual condition of the original.

15. **Geldner,** Karl, **und** Adolf **Kägi.** Siebenzig Lieder des Rigveda. Uebersetzt. Mit Beiträgen von R. Roth. Tübingen. H. Laupp'sche Buchhandlung. 1875. 12°. Price 3 Mark.

Thirty-six of the seventy hymns of which this book gives metrical translations were later incorporated by Böhtlingk into his Chrestomathy (no. 3, above).

16. **Aufrecht,** Theodor. Das Aitareya Brāhmaṇa. Mit Auszügen aus dem Commentare von Sāyaṇācārya und anderen Beilagen herausgegeben. Bonn, Adolph Marcus. 1879. 8°. Price 11 Mark.

This Brāhmana belongs to the Rigveda. The text is in transliteration. The translation of Haug (London, Trübner & Co. 1863) would be of help; but it is inaccurate and hard to get. A good many passages are translated in volumes I., II., and V. of Muir (below, no. 26). Using these as an introduction, and the St. Petersburg Lexicon for help in hard places, an advanced student can make good progress with this text.

17. **Stenzler,** Adolf Friedrich. Indische Hausregeln. Sanskrit und deutsch herausgegeben. I. Açvalāyana. Erstes Heft. Text. Leipzig. 1864. 8°. Price 2 Mark. —Zweites Heft. Uebersetzung. 1865. Price 3 Mark.

Published by the German Oriental Society, in volumes III. and IV. of the Abhandlungen für die Kunde des Morgenlandes. To be ordered through the Society's agent, F. A. Brockhaus, in Leipzig. These are the Grihya-sūtras belonging to the Rigveda.

18. **Roth, R., und Whitney,** W. D. Atharva Veda Sanhita. Herausgegeben. Erster Band. Text. Berlin, Ferd. Dümmler. 1856. Royal 8°. Price 28 Mark 50 Pfennige.

This is the most important and interesting of the Vedas, after the Rik. It is full of magic incantations and other products of curious superstitions.

19. **Garbe,** Richard. Vaitâna Sûtra. The Ritual of the Atharvaveda. Edited with critical notes and indices. London, Trübner & Co. 1878. 8°. Price 5 shillings.

20. **Garbe,** Richard. Vaitâna Sûtra. Das Ritual des Atharvaveda. Aus dem Sanskrit übersetzt und mit Anmerkungen versehen. London, Trübner & Co. 1878. 8°. Price 5 shillings.

Since this is the only Çrauta-sūtra published with translation, and since it is to be had easily and cheaply, it is recommended as an introduction to the works of this class.

21. **Weber,** Albrecht. The history of Indian Literature. Translated from the second German edition by John Mann and Theodor Zachariae. Second edition. London, Trübner & Co. 1878. 8°. Price 10 shillings 6 pence.

This is a systematic treatise covering both the Vedic and the classical Sanskrit literature. It gives abundant and practical bibliographical information. As a guide and as a work of reference it is of the utmost value.

22. **Zimmer,** Heinrich. Altindisches Leben. Die Cultur der vedischen Arier. Nach den Saṁhitā dargestellt. Berlin, Weidmannsche Buchhandlung. 1879. 8°. Price 10 Mark.

Under the different categories — geography, climate, minerals, plants, animals, agriculture, commerce, dress, food, amusements, family relations, art, etc. — the Vedic texts touching these subjects are discussed, and the results deducible from them are put together in a very readable and pleasant way.

23. **Kägi,** Adolf. Der Rigveda. Die älteste Literatur der Inder. Zweite, umgearbeitete und erweiterte, mit vollständigem Sach- und Wortregister versehene Auflage. Leipzig, Otto Schulze. 1881. 12°. Price 4 Mark.

This contains an account of the Vedic writings in general, descriptions of the gods in language agreeing closely with the actual words of the original as cited in the notes, and sketches of some of the more important phases of Vedic life and thought. The numerous notes are highly useful as a guide to the already extensive literature of these subjects. and point out many interesting parallels of custom, belief, and expression to be found in biblical and classical antiquity.

24. **Barth,** Auguste. The religions of India. Authorized translation by Rev. J. Wood. London, Trübner & Co. 1882. 8°. Price 16 shillings.

The subject is treated in five chapters corresponding to the five grand phases of religious development in India: the Vedic religion; Brahmanism (ritual, philosophic speculation, decline); Buddhism; Jainism; and Hinduism (the sects and their great deities, Vishnuism and Çivaism, reforming sects, cultus). The copious references to the literature of the subjects in hand add greatly to the value of the work.

25. **Oldenberg,** Hermann. Buddha; his life, his doctrine, his order. Translated from the German by William Hoey. London, Williams and Norgate. 1882. 8°. Price 18 shillings.

Oldenberg has recently finished editing (in five volumes) the Vinaya Piṭakam, one of the most important among the Buddhist sacred books. He has a wide and deep knowledge of the original Pāli sources, and in his use of them he is guided by rare critical acumen and good common-sense. His account of Buddha's life, doctrine, and order contains the best results of his studies and they are presented in an extremely attractive form.

26. **Muir,** John. Original Sanskrit texts on the origin and history of the people of India, their religions and institutions. Collected, translated, and illustrated. London, Trübner & Co. 1872–1874. 5 volumes. 8°.

The first four volumes have appeared in a second edition, and the second volume in a third edition. The third volume costs 16 shillings. The price of each of the others is 21 shillings. The first volume discusses the origin of caste. The fifth is devoted to the cosmogony, mythology, religious ideas, life, and manners of the Indians in the Vedic age.

EXPLANATIONS AND ABBREVIATIONS.

CITATIONS.

All numbers below 107 refer to the text of this Reader, which is cited by page and line; thus, 79² means page 79, line 2. When still more precise reference is needed, the first half of a line is designated by ª and the second by ᵇ.

All numbers above 107 refer to the sections of Whitney's Grammar. Observe, however, that reference is occasionally made to grammar-sections preceding § 107, and that the word "Whitney" is then prefixed to the number to show that the Grammar is meant. The grammar-sections sometimes have subdivisions unmarked by letters or numbers. In referring to these, a small superior number is used, and designates the (typographical) paragraph as counted from the last lettered or numbered subsection. Thus 330⁶ refers to the paragraph beginning "Pl.: nom.-voc. masc."; 371¹² begins with "From stṛ come"; 1222³, with "The accent of derivatives"; 1222c2², with "In the Brāhmaṇas."

SIGNS.

The root-sign (√) is prefixed to roots and quasi-roots to catch the eye or as an abbreviation. It is also set before denominative verb-stems, although these are of course in no sense roots.

The plus-sign (+) is set before prepositions with which verbs appear in composition and before certain other elements used as prefixes.

A star (*) signifies that the word or stem or root to which it is prefixed does not actually occur in that form.

A half-parenthesis on its side (‿) is used to show that two vowels, which, for the sake of clearness, are printed with hiatus in violation of the rules of euphonic combination, should be combined according to those rules.

A hyphen is sometimes used to avoid the repetition of an element of a compound; thus in the article loka, p. 235, para- stands for para-loka.

In Greek words, the old palatal spirant yod is represented by *j*, pronounced of course as English *y*. A very few Slavic and Lithuanian words occur, in which the actual or original nasalization of a vowel is denoted by an inverted comma, thus, *ę*, *ą*. Anglo-Saxon *æ* has the sound of *a* in *man*.

ABBREVIATIONS.

It is hoped that most of these, if not all, will be found self-explaining. To preclude any misunderstanding, however, a complete list of the abbreviations is given below, p. 293.

But certain abbreviations and words are used in an arbitrary way and require more explanation than is given in the list.

When both the letters, *m.* and *n.*, follow a stem, they mean that it shows both masculine and neuter case-forms.

An "etc." following a reference that stands after a certain definition signifies that the word is of common occurrence in that meaning.

The abbreviation [do.] is used to avoid repetition of identical items in the square brackets at the end of articles; for examples, see the three words following **abhivāda**, p. 119.

The etymological cognates are usually introduced by the conventional "cf."; this implies that the words which the reader is bidden to "compare" are akin. The fact that two related words are compared implies as a rule only that they are radically akin, and not that their formative suffixes are identical. Thus with **anta** is compared English *end*, although this corresponds strictly only to the Sanskrit secondary derivative **antya**. So **asthan**, *ὀστέον*, and *os* are radically identical, though not of entirely parallel formation.

On the other hand, where it is desired to call attention, not to radically kindred words, but to words analogous only in metaphor or in transfer of meaning, the brief phrase, "for mg, cf.," is used; and this is to be understood as standing for the phrase, "for a parallelism in the development of meaning, compare," or, "for an analogous instance of transition of meaning, compare."

Specially important references to the Grammar are marked by the word "see": thus under **nārāyaṇá** (p. 181), special attention is called to § 1219, which shows that this word is a simple patronymic of **nára**, and is not what the text (at 57[6]) says it is, a compound of **nārá** + **áyana**.

GENERAL ARRANGEMENT OF THE VOCABULARY.

The order of the articles is strictly and solely alphabetical (see below). Respecting words whose alphabetic place changes with their inflection, the following remarks may be made for beginners.

All nouns, whether they be substantives or adjectives, are given under the stem. In order to know the stem, a preliminary study of the more important paradigms and rules of euphonic combination is necessary. Thus the nom. sing. **rājā** must be looked for under **rājan**, and the acc. sing. **nāma** under **nāman** (Whitney, 424); but **nalo**, as standing for **nala-s** (175a, 330), must be looked for under **nala**. The stems in **ṛ** or **ar** are entered in the form **ṛ**. The stems of the perf. act. ppl. and of the primary comparatives are given as ending in **vāṅs** and **yāṅs**. The stems in **at** or **ant** are given in the fuller form, **ant**, and similarly those in **mant** and **vant**; and the feminines of these and of the **in**-stems are not given, since they are always made in **antī** or **atī**, **matī**, **vatī**, **inī**.

All verb-forms must be sought under the root. Thus **āsīt** will be defined only under the root 1 **as** (636), and not in the alphabetic place which the augment gives it, under long **ā**. Likewise prepositional compounds of verbs will be found under the roots (see 1076), and not in the alphabetic place under the preposition. The beginner is advised to make himself thoroughly familiar with the list of prepositions (1077) at the outset.

Of the verbal adjectives and nouns (Whitney, chapter xiii., p. 307 ff.), only the gerundives (in **ya**, **tavya**, and **anīya**) have been given regularly in alphabetic place. The participles in **ta** and **na** are usually given under the roots; but in some cases, where they have assumed a distinctly adjectival or substantival coloring or have an inconveniently large variety of meanings and uses, they are treated at length in alphabetic place; such, for example, are **ṛta**, **kṛta**, **gata**, **jāta**, **nivṛtta**, **bhūta**, **sthita**, **hita**, etc. Gerunds with **a-** or **su-** (e.g. **a-citvā**) are of course treated in alphabetic place.

Such adverbs as are merely case-forms of substantive or adjective stems, are generally to be sought for under those stems. Those from pronominal stems (e.g. **kim**, **tad**, **yad**) receive separate treatment.

The pronouns of the first and second person would require a dozen different articles apiece if all their forms were given alphabetically. The same is true to a greater or less extent of the other pronouns. The student should therefore learn, as early as possible, the forms given at 491, 495, 499b, 501 (especially ayam: asāu is less important), 504, and 509. The uses of sa-s, etc., eṣa-s, etc., and ayam, etc., are given under ta, etad, and idam respectively.

As for compounds, they are given with completeness for the Vedic selections, and with great freedom for the remaining texts, especially for the Nala. The meaning of such as are lacking can be easily learned by looking out their component parts.

THE ALPHABETIC ORDER.

The order of the letters is given by Whitney at § 5 (compare § 7); but several matters which are frequent occasions of stumbling, may be noticed here.

The *visarga* has the first place after the vowels. Thus antaḥ-pura (for antar + pura) stands next after anta, p. 116, and not after antardhāna. But the *visarga* which is regarded as equivalent to a sibilant and exchangeable with it (Whitney, 7[2]), stands in the alphabetic place of the sibilant. Thus the *visarga* of adhaḥ-çāyin, as equivalent to ç (172), brings this word just before adhas (p. 115, top), and not between adha and adhanya.

The sign ṅ, as representing "the *anusvāra* of more independent origin" (Whitney, 73[3]), has its place before all the mutes etc. (Whitney, 5). Thus in aṅç-a, the ṅ represents a nasalization of the radical vowel, and the word comes immediately after a. So haṅsa comes just after ha, p. 284; daṅç and daṅṣṭrin, at the beginning of the letter d.

The sign ṁ, as representing an assimilated m, is differently placed, according to its phonetic value. On the one hand, if ṁ, as product of a m assimilated to a semivowel, sibilant, or h (see 213c, d), represent a nasal semivowel or *anusvāra*, then its place is like that of ṅ. Thus saṁyatendriya follows sa, and saṁhita comes just before sakacchapa (p. 263), and puṁs before puṭa (p. 191).

On the other hand, if, for instance, as product of a m assimilated to a guttural, the sign ṁ represent guttural ñ, then its place is that of ñ; and a similar rule applies to all the other cases under 213b. Thus saṁkaṭa and saṁkalpa follow sagara, and saṁgama follows sañga, p. 264; so saṁcaya (whose ṁ = ñ) follows sajya; and saṁtati (whose ṁ = n) follows sant, p. 266.

Vedic ḻ is placed after ḍ, and ḻh after ḍh.

THE CONTENTS OF THE SEPARATE ARTICLES.

Homonyms, unless differentiated by accent, are distinguished by a prefixed number (cf. añga, vayas); similarly homonymous roots (cf. kṛ).

References to the Grammar in square brackets *immediately after* a declinable stem refer to some peculiarity of declension. Occasionally, typical cases of stems are given. Thus under dṛç are given the nom. and acc. sing. and instr. dual; from these, the other cases (dṛk-ṣu, dṛç-ā, etc., dṛg-bhis, etc.) are easily known.

Each root is followed by a synopsis of its conjugational forms, so far as they actually occur in the literature. The finite forms are given in the third person singular of the indicative, and in the order in which they are treated in the Grammar, namely, present, perfect, aorist, and future; then follow the past participle, the infinitive, and the two gerunds (e.g. āptá, ā́ptum; āptvā́, -ā́pya: observe the alternation of the accents); then follow in order the third sing. present indicative of the passive, intensive, desiderative, and causative, so far as they seemed of importance for the users of this Reader.

Meanings which are synonymous or nearly so, are separated by commas; those which differ considerably from each other, are separated by semicolons or by full-faced dashes and figures (—1., etc.). The colon is often used to show that several meanings which follow it and are separated by semicolons are co-ordinate with each other. Thus on p. 268, under samīpa —2b., the meanings "before," "near," "hard by," and "by" are co-ordinate, and are equivalent to "in the presence *or* neighborhood of"; cf. suvarcas.

The arrangement for matter in heavy brackets at the end of articles is: in the case of primary derivatives, first, the root from which the word comes, with reference, if necessary, to the section giving the suffix of derivation; second, cognate words from allied languages; and third, words showing a development of meaning analogous to that shown by the Sanskrit word or illustrative of it. If the derivation of a simple word is not given, it is because it is unknown or too uncertain to be worth mentioning. In the case of secondary derivatives, the primary is given, with a reference to the section showing its treatment. The analysis of compounds is often indicated by a hyphen; but if one member ends and the next begins with a vowel or diphthong, the latter member is given in square brackets at the end of the article; cf. nalopākhyāna.

Where words of different languages are given together, separated only by commas, the definition given after the last applies to them all; or, if no definition is given, the English word in italics at the end is both a cognate and a definition of all at the same time; for examples, see ákṣa ('axle'), aṣṭa, ūrṇa.

The references to the Grammar may seem too numerous; but they are really a device for avoiding the frequent repetition of explanations which would otherwise have to be given in full. It would take half a dozen lines to explain the etymology of manmatha, for instance; but the references to 1148.4 and 1002b make this needless; cf. the references under daridra, çiçu, sunva.

It often happens that the statement in the section referred to does not directly cover the point aimed at in citing it; but a moment's thought will show what is meant. Thus under saṁkrānti, the two references to be compared mean that the derivative suffix is ti, and that before it the root-vowel suffers the same peculiar change that is seen in the past participle. Under saṁyatendriya reference is made to 1298, which states that possessive descriptives "are very much more common than [simple] descriptives of the same form." The real point of the reference is plainly, not to bring out this fact, but to show the beginner in what category of compounds this word belongs. So 1290 states that "other compounds with adverbial prior members are quite irregularly accented"; but the section is cited, e.g., under sadha-māda, to indicate that this is a descriptive compound (see the heading of the preceding right-hand page, 441) in which the first member is an adverbial element with the function (cf. 1289) of an adjective. Many roots form verb-stems in aya, but without causative signification; this is briefly indicated by the reference 1041[2]. In the case of secondary derivatives in vant, mant, tā, and tva, a simple reference to one of the sections treating of these endings (1233, 1235, 1237, 1239) is put instead of a repetition of the primitive.

LIST OF ABBREVIATIONS.

a. . . . . adjective.
abl. . . . . ablative.
acc. . . . . accusative.
acct . . . . . . accent.
act. . . . . active, actively.
adj. . . . . . . adjective, adjectively.
adv. . . . . . . adverb, adverbial.
advly . . . . . adverbially.
aor. . . . . . . aorist.
AS. . . . . Anglo-Saxon.
assev. . . . . . asseverative.
B. . . . . Brāhmaṇa.
beg. . . . . . . beginning.
caus. . . . . . . causative.
cf. . . . . compare.
colloq. . . . . . colloquial.
comp. . . . . . comparative.
conj. . . . . . . conjunction.
correl. . . . . . correlative.
cpd, cpds . . . compound, compounds.
dat. . . . . . . dative.
denom. . . . . denominative.
deriv., derivs . derivative, derivatives.
desid. . . . . . desiderative.
e.g. . . . . for example.
encl. . . . . . . enclitic.
Eng. . . . . . . English.
equiv. . . . . . equivalent.
esp. . . . . . . especially, especial.
etc. . . . . and so forth.
excl. . . . . . . exclamation.
f., fem. . . . . feminine.
ff. . . . . and the following.
fig. . . . . figuratively, figurative.
fr. . . . . from.
fut. . . . . future.
gen. . . . . . . genitive.
Ger. . . . . . . German.
Goth. . . . . . Gothic.
grd . . . . gerund.
grdv. . . . . . . gerundive.
Hdt. . . . . . . Herodotus.
ident. . . . . . identical.
i.e. . . . . that is.
imf. . . . . . . imperfect.
impers. . . . . impersonally, impersonal.
imv. . . . . . . imperative.
ind. . . . . indicative.
indecl. . . . . . indeclinable.
indef. . . . . . indefinite.
inf . . . . infinitive.
instr. . . . . . . instrumental.
intens. . . . . . intensive.
interr. . . . . . interrogative.
intrans. . . . . intransitive, intransitively.
irreg. . . . . . . irregularly, irregular.
Lat. . . . . Latin.
lit. . . . . literally, literal.
loc. . . . . locative.
m., masc. . . . masculine.
MBh. . . . . . . Mahābhārata.
met. . . . . . . metaphorically, metaphor.
mg, mgs . . . . meaning, meanings.
mid. . . . . . . middle.
N. . . . . note.
n., neut. . . . . neuter.
nom. . . . . . . nominative.
num. . . . . . . numeral.
opp. . . . . opposed, opposite.
opt. . . . . optative.
orig. . . . . . . originally, original.
pass. . . . . . . passive, passively.
pcl. . . . . particle.
perf. . . . . . . perfect.
pers. . . . . . . person, personal.
pl. . . . . plural.
poss. . . . . . . possibly.
ppl. . . . . participle.
prep. . . . . . . preposition.
pres. . . . . . . present.
prob. . . . . . . probably, probable.
pron. . . . . . . pronoun, pronominal.
prop. . . . . . . properly.
q.v. . . . . which see.
reg. . . . . regularly, regular.
ṚV. . . . . Rigveda.
S. . . . . Sūtra.
s. . . . . singular.
sc. . . . . scilicet.
sing. . . . . . . singular.
Skt. . . . . Sanskrit.
subst. . . . . . . substantive, substantively.
superl. . . . . . superlative.
s.v. . . . . sub voce.
trans. . . . . . . transitive, transitively.
U.f. . . . . uncombined form *or* forms.
vbl . . . . verbal.
V. . . . . Vedic, Veda.
voc. . . . . vocative.
w. . . . . with.

For abbreviations of titles, see next page.

ABBREVIATIONS OF TITLES.

See also pages 315–16, 332, 340, 359, 398, 402.

RV.	Rigveda Saṁhitā.	AB.	Āitareya Brāhmaṇa.
SV.	Sāmaveda "	ÇB.	Çatapatha "
AV.	Atharvaveda "	PB.	Pañcaviṅça or Tāṇḍya Br.
MS.	Māitrāyaṇī "	TA.	Tāittirīya Āraṇyaka.
TS.	Tāittirīya "	AGS. . . .	Açvalāyana Gṛhya-sūtra.
VS.	Vājasaneyi "	ÇGS. . . .	Çāṅkhāyana "
K.	Kāṭhaka.	PGS. . . .	Pāraskara "

JASB. . . . Journal of the Asiatic Society of Bengal.
JA. . . . . . Journal Asiatique.
JRAS. . . . Journal of the Royal Asiatic Society.
JAOS. . . . Journal of the American Oriental Society.
PAOS. . . . Proceedings " " "
ZDMG. . . . Zeitschrift der Deutschen Morgenländischen Gesellschaft.

AJP. . . . . American Journal of Philology — ed. B. L. Gildersleeve.
Ind. Ant. . . Indian Antiquary — ed. James Burgess.
ISt. . . . . . Indische Studien — ed. Albrecht Weber.
KZ. . . . . . Zeitschrift für vergleichende Sprachforschung — ed. A. Kuhn.

ASL. . . . . History of Ancient Sanskrit Literature, by Max Müller.
BI. . . . . . Bibliotheca Indica — publ. by the Asiatic Society of Bengal.
BR. . . . . . Böhtlingk and Roth's Sanskrit-Wörterbuch — see *Brief List*, p. xviii, no. 5.
GKR. . . . . Geldner, Kaegi, and Roth's Siebenzig Lieder — see p. xix, no. 15.
HIL. . . . . History of Indian Literature, Weber — see p. xx, no. 21.
IA. . . . . . Indische Alterthumskunde, by Christian Lassen.
ILuC. . . . . Indiens Literatur und Cultur, Schroeder — see p. 359, § 100.
OLSt. . . . . Oriental and Linguistic Studies, Whitney — see p. 359, § 100.
VP. . . . . . Viṣṇu Purāṇa — Bombay text; or Wilson's translation, ed. 1 or ed. 2 (F. Hall).

SBE. . . . . Sacred Books of the East — transl. by various scholars and ed. F. Max Müller.

Vol.		Vol.	
i.	Upaniṣads. 1.	xv.	Upanisads. 2.
ii.	Laws. 1. Āpastamba, Gāutama.	xxiii.	Avesta. 2. Yashts, etc.
iv.	Avesta. 1. Vendidād.	xxv.	Manu.
vii.	Laws. Viṣṇu.	xxvi.	Çatapatha Brāhmaṇa. 2.
x.	Dhammapada, etc.	xxix.	Gṛhya-sūtras. 1. ÇGS., AGS., PGS.
xii.	Çatapatha Brāhmaṇa. 1. See p. 356, N. 9.	xxx.	Gṛhya-sūtras. 2.
xiv.	Laws. 2. Vasiṣṭha, Bāudhāyana.	xxxi.	Avesta. 3. Yasna, etc.

Bergaigne . La religion védique — see p. 359, § 100.
Kaegi . . . . Der Rigveda — see p. 352, § 70.
Ludwig . . . Der Rigveda — see p. 359, § 100.
Muir . . . . Original Sanskrit Texts — see p. xx, no. 26.
Si-yu-ki . . . Buddhist Records of the Western World. Transl. by S. Beal, London, 1884.
Zimmer. . . . Altindisches Leben — see p. xx, no. 22.

The Vocabulary will often serve as an index to the Notes.

PART I.

THE SANSKRIT TEXT.

Transliterated Text of Sanskrit Reader.

[Page 1.]

atha nalopākhyānam.

bṛhadaçva uvāca.

āsīd rājā, nalo nāma, vīrasenasuto balī,
upapanno guṇāir iṣṭāi, rūpavān, açvakovidaḥ.
atiṣṭhan manujendrāṇām mūrdhni devapatir yathā,
upary upari sarveṣām āditya iva tejasā;
brahmaṇyo, vedavic, chūro, niṣadheṣu mahīpatiḥ,
akṣapriyaḥ, satyavādī, mahān akṣāuhiṇīpatiḥ;
īpsito naranārīṇām, udāraḥ, saṁyatendriyaḥ,
rakṣitā, dhanvināṁ çreṣṭhaḥ, sākṣād iva manuḥ svayam.
tathāivāsīd vidarbheṣu bhīmo, bhīmaparākramaḥ,
çūraḥ, sarvaguṇāir yuktaḥ, prajākāmaḥ, sa cāprajaḥ.
sa prajārthe paraṁ yatnam akarot, susamāhitaḥ.
tam abhyagacchad brahmarṣir, damano nāma, bhārata.
taṁ sa bhīmaḥ, prajākāmas, toṣayām āsa, dharmavit,
mahiṣyā saha, rājendra, satkāreṇa, suvarcasam.
tasmāi prasanno damanaḥ sabhāryāya varaṁ dadāu.

[Page 3.]

tato 'ntarikṣago vācaṁ vyājahāra nalaṁ tadā:
hantavyo 'smi na te, rājan; kariṣyāmi tava priyam;
damayantīsakāçe tvāṁ kathayiṣyāmi, nāiṣadha,
yathā tvad anyam puruṣaṁ na sā maṅsyati karhi cit.
evam uktas tato haṅsam utsasarja mahīpatiḥ.
te tu haṅsāḥ samutpatya vidarbhān agamaṅs tataḥ.
vidarbhanagarīṁ gatvā, damayantyās tadāntike
nipetus te garutmantaḥ, sā dadarça ca tān gaṇān.
sā, tān adbhutarūpān vāi dṛṣṭvā, sakhigaṇāvṛtā,
hṛṣṭā grahītuṁ khagamāṅs tvaramāṇopacakrame.
atha haṅsā visasṛpuḥ sarvataḥ pramadāvane.
ekāikaças tadā kanyās tān haṅsān samupādravan.
damayantī tu yaṁ haṅsaṁ samupādhāvad antike,
sa, mānuṣīṁ giraṁ kṛtvā, damayantīm athābravīt:
damayanti, nalo nāma, niṣadheṣu mahīpatiḥ,
açvinoḥ sadṛço rūpe; na samās tasya mānuṣāḥ.
tasya vāi yadi bhāryā tvam bhavethā, varavarṇini,
saphalaṁ te bhavej janma, rūpaṁ cedaṁ, sumadhyame.
vayaṁ hi devagandharvamānuṣoragarākṣasān
dṛṣṭavanto; na cāsmābhir dṛṣṭapūrvas tathāvidhaḥ.
tvaṁ cāpi ratnaṁ nārīṇāṁ, nareṣu ca nalo varaḥ;
viçiṣṭāyā viçiṣṭena saṁgamo guṇavān bhavet.
evam uktā tu haṅsena damayantī, viçām pate,

[Page 2.]

kanyāratnaṁ, kumārāṅç ca trīn udārān, mahāyaçāḥ,
damayantīṁ, damaṁ, dāntaṁ, damanaṁ ca suvarcasam,
upapannān guṇāiḥ sarvāir, bhīmān, bhīmaparākramān.
damayantī tu rūpeṇa, tejasā, yaçasā, çriyā,
sāubhāgyena ca, lokeṣu yaçaḥ prāpa, sumadhyamā.
atha tāṁ, vayasi prāpte, dāsīnāṁ samalaṁkṛtam
çataṁ, çataṁ sakhīnāṁ ca, paryupāsac, chacīm iva.
tatra sma·rājate bhāimī, sarvābharaṇabhūṣitā,
sakhīmadhye, 'navadyāṅgī, vidyut sāudāmanī yathā,
atīva rūpasampannā, çrīr ivāyatalocanā.
na deveṣu, na yakṣeṣu, tādṛg rūpavatī kva cit,
mānuṣeṣv api cānyeṣu, dṛṣṭapūrvātha vā çrutā,
cittapramāthinī bālā devānām api sundarī.
nalaç ca naraçārdūlo, lokeṣv apratimo bhuvi,
kandarpa iva rūpeṇa mūrtimān abhavat svayam.
tasyāḥ samīpe tu nalam praçaçaṅsuḥ kutūhalāt,
nāiṣadhasya samīpe tu damayantīm punaḥ punaḥ.
tayor adṛṣṭakāmo 'bhūc chṛṇvatoḥ satataṁ guṇān;
anyonyam prati, kāunteya, sa vyavardhata hṛcchayaḥ.
açaknuvan nalaḥ kāmaṁ tadā dhārayituṁ hṛdā,
antaḥpurasamīpasthe vana āste raho gataḥ.
sa dadarça tato haṅsāñ jātarūpapariṣkṛtān;
vane vicaratāṁ teṣām ekaṁ jagrāha pakṣiṇam.

[Page 4.]

abravīt tatra taṁ haṅsam: tvam apy evaṁ nale vada.
tathety uktvāṇḍajaḥ kanyāṁ vidarbhasya, viçām pate,
punar āgamya niṣadhān, nale sarvaṁ nyavedayat.
iti nalopākhyāne prathamaḥ sargaḥ.

---

bṛhadaçva uvāca.

damayantī tu, tac chrutvā vaco haṅsasya, bhārata,
tataḥ prabhṛti na svasthā nalam prati babhūva sā.
tataç cintāparā, dīnā, vivarṇavadanā, kṛçā,
babhūva damayantī tu, niḥçvāsaparamā tadā.
ūrdhvadṛṣṭir, dhyānaparā, babhūvonmattadarçanā,
pāṇḍuvarṇā kṣaṇenātha, hṛcchayāviṣṭacetanā.
na çayyāsanabhogeṣu ratiṁ vindati karhi cit.
na naktaṁ, na divā çete, hā heti rudatī punaḥ.
tato vidarbhapataye damayantyāḥ sakhījanaḥ
nyavedayat tām asvasthāṁ damayantīṁ nareçvare.
tac chrutvā nṛpatir bhīmo damayantīsakhīgaṇāt,
cintayām āsa tat kāryaṁ sumahat svāṁ sutām prati.
sa samīkṣya mahīpālaḥ svāṁ sutām prāptayāuvanām,
apaçyad ātmanā kāryaṁ damayantyāḥ svayaṁvaram.
sa saṁnimantrayām āsa mahīpālān viçām patiḥ:
anubhūyatām! ayaṁ, vīrāḥ, svayaṁvara iti, prabho.

I.

॥ अथ नलोपाख्यानम् ॥

बृहदश्व उवाच ।

आसीद् राजा नलो नाम वीरसेनसुतो बली ।
उपपन्नो गुणैर् इष्टै रूपवान् अश्वकोविदः ॥ १ ॥
अतिष्ठन् मनुजेन्द्राणां मूर्ध्नि देवपतिर् यथा ।
उपर्य् उपरि सर्वेषाम् आदित्य इव तेजसा ॥ २ ॥
ब्रह्मण्यो वेदविच् छूरो निषधेषु महीपतिः ।
अक्षप्रियः सत्यवादी महान् अक्षौहिणीपतिः ॥ ३ ॥
ईप्सितो नरनारीणाम् उदारः संयतेन्द्रियः ।
रक्षिता धन्विनां श्रेष्ठः साक्षाद् इव मनुः स्वयम् ॥ ४ ॥
तथैवासीद् विदर्भेषु भीमो भीमपराक्रमः ।
शूरः सर्वगुणैर् युक्तः प्रजाकामः स चाप्रजः ॥ ५ ॥
स प्रजार्थे परं यत्नम् अकरोत् सुसमाहितः ।
तम् अभ्यगच्छद् ब्रह्मर्षिर् दमनो नाम भारत ॥ ६ ॥
तं स भीमः प्रजाकामस् तोषयामास धर्मवित् ।
महिष्या सह राजेन्द्र सत्कारेण सुवर्चसम् ॥ ७ ॥
तस्मै प्रसन्नो दमनः सभार्याय वरं ददौ ।

कन्यारत्नं कुमारांश् च त्रीन् उदारान् महायशाः ॥८॥
दमयन्तीं दमं दान्तं दमनं च सुवर्चसम् ।
उपपन्नान् गुणैः सर्वैर् भीमान् भीमपराक्रमान् ॥९॥
दमयन्ती तु रूपेण तेजसा यशसा श्रिया ।
सौभाग्येन च लोकेषु यशः प्राप सुमध्यमा ॥१०॥
अथ तां वयसि प्राप्ते दासीनां समलंकृतम् ।
शतं शतं सखीनां च पर्युपासच् छचीम् इव ॥११॥
तत्र स्म राजते भैमी सर्वाभरणभूषिता ।
सखीमध्ये ऽनवद्याङ्गी विद्युत् सौदामनी यथा ॥१२॥
अतीव रूपसंपन्ना श्रीर् इवायतलोचना ।
न देवेषु न यक्षेषु तादृग् रूपवती क्व चित् ॥१३॥
मानुषेष्व् अपि चान्येषु दृष्टपूर्वाथ वा श्रुता ।
चित्तप्रमाथिनी बाला देवानाम् अपि सुन्दरी ॥१४॥
नलश् च नरशार्दूलो लोकेष्व् अप्रतिमो भुवि ।
कन्दर्प इव रूपेण मूर्तिमान् अभवत् स्वयम् ॥१५॥
तस्याः समीपे तु नलं प्रशशंसुः कुतूहलात् ।
नैषधस्य समीपे तु दमयन्तीं पुनः पुनः ॥१६॥
तयोर् अदृष्टकामो ऽभूच् छृण्वतोः सततं गुणान् ।
अन्योन्यं प्रति कौन्तेय स व्यवर्धत हृच्छयः ॥१७॥
अशक्नुवन् नलः कामं तदा धारयितुं हृदा ।
अन्तःपुरसमीपस्थे वन आस्ते रहो गतः ॥१८॥
स ददर्श ततो हंसाञ् जातरूपपरिष्कृतान् ।
वने विचरतां तेषाम् एकं जग्राह पक्षिणम् ॥१९॥

ततो ऽन्तरिक्षगो वाचं व्याजहार नलं तदा ।
हन्तव्यो ऽस्मि न ते राजन् करिष्यामि तव प्रियम् ॥२०॥
दमयन्तीसकाशे त्वां कथयिष्यामि नैषध ।
यथा त्वद् अन्यं पुरुषं न सा मंस्यति कर्हि चित् ॥२१॥
एवम् उक्तस् ततो हंसम् उत्ससर्ज महीपतिः ।
ते तु हंसाः समुत्पत्य विदर्भान् अगमंस् ततः ॥२२॥
विदर्भनगरीं गत्वा दमयन्त्यास् तदान्तिके ।
निपेतुस् ते गरुत्मन्तः सा ददर्श च तान् गणान् ॥२३॥
सा तान् अद्भुतरूपान् वै दृष्ट्वा सखिगणावृता ।
हृष्टा ग्रहीतुं खगमांस् त्वरमाणोपचक्रमे ॥२४॥
अथ हंसा विससृपुः सर्वतः प्रमदावने ।
एकैकशस् तदा कन्यास् तान् हंसान् समुपाद्रवन् ॥२५॥
दमयन्ती तु यं हंसं समुपाधावद् अन्तिके ।
स मानुषीं गिरं कृत्वा दमयन्तीम् अथाब्रवीत् ॥२६॥
दमयन्ति नलो नाम निषधेषु महीपतिः ।
अश्विनोः सदृशो रूपे न समास् तस्य मानुषाः ॥२७॥
तस्य वै यदि भार्या त्वं भवेथा वरवर्णिनि ।
सफलं ते भवेज् जन्म रूपं चेदं सुमध्यमे ॥२८॥
वयं हि देवगन्धर्वमानुषोरगराक्षसान् ।
दृष्टवन्तो न चास्माभिर् दृष्टपूर्वस् तथाविधः ॥२९॥
त्वं चापि रत्नं नारीणां नरेषु च नलो वरः ।
विशिष्टाया विशिष्टेन संगमो गुणवान् भवेत् ॥३०॥
एवम् उक्ता तु हंसेन दमयन्ती विशां पते ।

अब्रवीत् तत्र तं हंसं त्वम् अप्य् एवं नले वद ॥३१॥
तथेत्य् उक्त्वाण्डजः कन्यां विदर्भस्य विशां पते ।
पुनर् आगम्य निषधान् नले सर्वं न्यवेदयत् ॥३२॥

॥ इति नलोपाख्याने प्रथमः सर्गः ॥१॥

बृहदश्व उवाच ।

दमयन्ती तु तच् छ्रुत्वा वचो हंसस्य भारत ।
ततः प्रभृति न स्वस्था नलं प्रति बभूव सा ॥१॥
ततश् चिन्तापरा दीना विवर्णवदना कृशा ।
बभूव दमयन्ती तु निःश्वासपरमा तदा ॥२॥
ऊर्ध्वदृष्टिर् ध्यानपरा बभूवोन्मत्तदर्शना ।
पाण्डुवर्णा क्षणेनाथ हृच्छयाविष्टचेतना ॥३॥
न शय्यासनभोगेषु रतिं विन्दति कर्हिचित् ।
न नक्तं न दिवा शेते हा हेति रुदती पुनः ॥४॥
ततो विदर्भपतये दमयन्त्याः सखीजनः ।
न्यवेदयत ताम् अस्वस्थां दमयन्तीं नरेश्वरे ॥५॥
तच् छ्रुत्वा नृपतिर् भीमो दमयन्तीसखीगणात् ।
चिन्तयामास तत् कार्यं सुमहत् स्वां सुतां प्रति ॥६॥
स समीक्ष्य महीपालः स्वां सुतां प्राप्तयौवनाम् ।
अपश्यद् आत्मना कार्यं दमयन्त्याः स्वयंवरम् ॥७॥
स संनिमन्त्रयामास महीपालान् विशां पतिः ।
अनुभूयताम् अयं वीराः स्वयंवर इति प्रभो ॥८॥

श्रुत्वा तु पार्थिवाः सर्वे दमयन्त्याः स्वयंवरम् ।
अभिजग्मुस् ततो भीमं राजानो भीमशासनात् ॥९॥
हस्त्यश्वरथघोषेण पूरयन्तो वसुंधराम् ।
विचित्रमाल्याभरणैर् बलैर् दृश्यैः स्वलंकृतैः ॥१०॥
तेषां भीमो महाबाहुः पार्थिवानां महात्मनाम् ।
यथार्हम् अकरोत् पूजां ते ऽवसंस् तत्र पूजिताः ॥११॥
एतस्मिन्न् एव काले तु सुराणाम् ऋषिसत्तमौ ।
अटमानौ महात्मानाव् इन्द्रलोकम् इतो गतौ ॥१२॥
नारदः पर्वतश् चैव महाप्राज्ञौ महाव्रतौ ।
देवराजस्य भवनं विविशाते सुपूजितौ ॥१३॥
ताव् अर्चयित्वा मघवा ततः कुशलम् अव्ययम् ।
पप्रच्छानामयं चापि तयोः सर्वगतं विभुः ॥१४॥

नारद उवाच ।

आवयोः कुशलं देव सर्वत्र गतम् ईश्वर ।
लोके च मघवन् कृत्स्ने नृपाः कुशलिनो विभो ॥१५॥

बृहदश्व उवाच ।

नारदस्य वचः श्रुत्वा पप्रच्छ बलवृत्रहा ।
धर्मज्ञाः पृथिवीपालास् त्यक्तजीवितयोधिनः ॥१६॥
शस्त्रेण निधनं काले ये गच्छन्त्य् अपराङ्मुखाः ।
अयं लोको ऽक्षयस् तेषां यथैव मम कामधुक् ॥१७॥
क्व नु ते क्षत्रियाः शूरा न हि पश्यामि तान् अहम् ।
आगच्छतो महीपालान् दयितान् अतिथीन् मम ॥१८॥

एवम् उक्तस् तु शक्रेण नारदः प्रत्यभाषत ।
शृणु मे मघवन् येन न दृश्यन्ते महीक्षितः ॥१९॥
विदर्भराज्ञो दुहिता दमयन्तीति विश्रुता ।
रूपेण समतिक्रान्ता पृथिव्यां सर्वयोषितः ॥ २० ॥
तस्याः स्वयंवरः शक्र भविता नचिराद् इव ।
तत्र गच्छन्ति राजानो राजपुत्राश् च सर्वशः ॥ २१ ॥
तां रत्नभूतां लोकस्य प्रार्थयन्तो महीक्षितः ।
काङ्क्षन्ति स्म विशेषेण बलवृत्रनिषूदन ॥ २२ ॥
एतस्मिन् कथ्यमाने तु लोकपालाश् च साग्निकाः ।
आजग्मुर् देवराजस्य समीपम् अमरोत्तमाः ॥ २३ ॥
ततस् ते शुश्रुवुः सर्वे नारदस्य वचो महत् ।
श्रुत्वैव चाब्रुवन् हृष्टा गच्छामो वयम् अप्य् उत ॥ २४ ॥
ततः सर्वे महाराज सगणाः सहवाहनाः ।
विदर्भान् अभिजग्मुस् ते यतः सर्वे महीक्षितः ॥ २५ ॥
नलो ऽपि राजा कौन्तेय श्रुत्वा राज्ञां समागमम् ।
अभ्यगच्छद् अदीनात्मा दमयन्तीम् अनुव्रतः ॥ २६ ॥
अथ देवाः पथि नलं ददृशुर् भूतले स्थितम् ।
साक्षाद् इव स्थितं मूर्त्या मन्मथं रूपसंपदा ॥ २७ ॥
तं दृष्ट्वा लोकपालास् ते भ्राजमानं यथा रविम् ।
तस्थुर् विगतसंकल्पा विस्मिता रूपसंपदा ॥ २८ ॥
ततो ऽन्तरिक्षे विष्टभ्य विमानानि दिवौकसः ।
अब्रुवन् नैषधं राजन्न् अवतीर्य नभस्तलात् ॥ २९ ॥
भो भो नैषध राजेन्द्र नल सत्यव्रतो भवान् ।

अस्माकं कुरु साहाय्यं दूतो भव नरोत्तम ॥ ३० ॥

॥ इति नलोपाख्याने द्वितीयः सर्गः ॥ २ ॥

बृहदश्व उवाच ।

तेभ्यः प्रतिज्ञाय नलः करिष्य इति भारत ।
अथैतान् परिपप्रच्छ कृताञ्जलिर् उपस्थितः ॥ १ ॥
के वै भवन्तः कश् चासौ यस्याहं दूत ईप्सितः ।
किं च तद् वो मया कार्यं कथयध्वं यथातथम् ॥ २ ॥
एवम् उक्ते नैषधेन मघवान् अभ्यभाषत ।
अमरान् वै निबोधास्मान् दमयन्त्यर्थम् आगतान् ॥ ३ ॥
अहम् इन्द्रो ऽयम् अग्निश् च तथैवायम् अपां पतिः ।
शरीरान्तकरो नृणां यमो ऽयम् अपि पार्थिव ॥ ४ ॥
त्वं वै समागतान् अस्मान् दमयन्त्यै निवेदय ।
लोकपाला महेन्द्राद्याः समायान्ति दिदृक्षवः ॥ ५ ॥
प्राप्तुम् इच्छन्ति देवास् त्वां शक्रो ऽग्निर् वरुणो यमः ।
तेषाम् अन्यतमं देवं पतित्वे वरयस्व ह ॥ ६ ॥
एवम् उक्तः स शक्रेण नलः प्राञ्जलिर् अब्रवीत् ।
एकार्थं समुपेतं मां न प्रेषयितुम् अर्हथ ॥ ७ ॥
कथं नु जातसंकल्पः स्त्रियम् उत्सहते पुमान् ।
परार्थम् ईदृशं वक्तुं तत् क्षमन्तु महेश्वराः ॥ ८ ॥

देवा ऊचुः ।

करिष्य इति संश्रुत्य पूर्वम् अस्मासु नैषध ।

न करिष्यसि कस्मात् त्वं व्रज नैषध माचिरम् ॥ ९ ॥
बृहदश्व उवाच ।
एवम् उक्तः स देवैस् तैर् नैषधः पुनर् अब्रवीत् ।
सुरक्षितानि वेश्मानि प्रवेष्टुं कथम् उत्सहे ॥ १० ॥
प्रवेक्ष्यसीति तं शक्रः पुनर् एवाभ्यभाषत ।
जगाम स तथेत्य् उक्त्वा दमयन्त्या निवेशनम् ॥ ११ ॥
ददर्श तत्र वैदर्भीं सखीगणसमावृताम् ।
देदीप्यमानां वपुषा श्रिया च वरवर्णिनीम् ॥ १२ ॥
अतीव सुकुमाराङ्गीं तनुमध्यां सुलोचनाम् ।
आक्षिपन्तीम् इव प्रभां शशिनः स्वेन तेजसा ॥ १३ ॥
तस्य दृष्ट्वैव ववृधे कामस् तां चारुहासिनीम् ।
सत्यं चिकीर्षमाणस् तु धारयामास हृच्छयम् ॥ १४ ॥
ततस् ता नैषधं दृष्ट्वा संभ्रान्ताः परमाङ्गनाः ।
आसनेभ्यः समुत्पेतुस् तेजसा तस्य धर्षिताः ॥ १५ ॥
प्रशशंसुश् च सुप्रीता नलं ता विस्मयान्विताः ।
न चैनम् अभ्यभाषन्त मनोभिस् त्व् अभ्यपूजयन् ॥ १६ ॥
अहो रूपम् अहो कान्तिर् अहो धैर्यं महात्मनः ।
को ऽयं देवो ऽथ वा यक्षो गन्धर्वो वा भविष्यति ॥ १७ ॥
न तास् तं शक्नुवन्ति स्म व्याहर्तुम् अपि किं चन ।
तेजसा धर्षितास् तस्य लज्जावत्यो वराङ्गनाः ॥ १८ ॥
अथैनं स्मयमानं तु स्मितपूर्वाभिभाषिणी ।
दमयन्ती नलं वीरम् अभ्यभाषत विस्मिता ॥ १९ ॥
कस् त्वं सर्वानवद्याङ्ग मम हृच्छयवर्धन ।

प्राप्तो ऽस्य् अमरवद् वीर'ज्ञातुम् इच्छामि ते ऽनघ" ॥२०॥
कथम् आगमनं चेह कथं चासि न लक्षितः ।
सुरक्षितं हि मे वेश्म राजा चैवोग्रशासनः ॥२१॥
एवम् उक्तस् तु वैदर्भ्या नलस् तां प्रत्युवाच ह ।
नलं मां विद्धि कल्याणि देवदूतम् इहागतम् ॥२२॥
देवास् त्वां प्राप्तुम् इच्छन्ति शक्रो ऽग्निर् वरुणो यमः ।
तेषाम् अन्यतमं देवं पतिं वरय शोभने ॥२३॥
तेषाम् एव प्रभावेन प्रविष्टो ऽहम् अलक्षितः ।
प्रविशन्तं न मां कश् चिद् अपश्यन् नाप्य् अवारयत् ॥२४॥
एतदर्थम् अहं भद्रे प्रेषितः सुरसत्तमैः ।
एतच् छ्रुत्वा शुभे बुद्धिं प्रकुरुष्व यथेच्छसि ॥२५॥

॥ इति नलोपाख्याने तृतीयः सर्गः ॥३॥

बृहदश्व उवाच ।

सा नमस्कृत्य देवेभ्यः प्रहस्य नलमब्रवीत् ।
प्रणयस्व यथाश्रद्धं राजन्किं करवाणि ते ॥१॥
अहं चैव हि यच्चान्यन्ममास्ति वसु किं चन ।
तत्सर्वं तव विश्रब्धं कुरु प्रणयमीश्वर ॥२॥
हंसानां वचनं यत्तु तन्मां दहति पार्थिव ।
त्वत्कृते हि मया वीर राजानः संनिपातिताः ॥३॥
यदि त्वं भजमानां मां प्रत्याख्यास्यसि मानद ।

विषमग्निं जलं रज्जुमास्थास्ये तव कारणात् ॥४॥
एवमुक्तस्तु वैदर्भ्या नलस्तां प्रत्युवाच ह ।
तिष्ठत्सु लोकपालेषु कथं मानुषमिच्छसि ॥५॥
येषामहं लोककृतामीश्वराणां महात्मनाम् ।
न पादरजसा तुल्यो मनस्ते तेषु वर्तताम् ॥६॥
विप्रियं ह्याचरन्मर्त्यो देवानां मृत्युमृच्छति ।
त्राहि मामनवद्याङ्गि वरयस्व सुरोत्तमान् ॥७॥
विरजांसि च वासांसि दिव्याश्चित्राः स्रजस्तथा ।
भूषणानि च मुख्यानि देवान्प्राप्य तु भुङ्क्ष्व वै ॥८॥
य इमां पृथिवीं कृत्स्नां संक्षिप्य ग्रसते पुनः ।
हुताशमीशं देवानां का तं न वरयेत्पतिम् ॥९॥
यस्य दण्डभयात्सर्वे भूतग्रामाः समागताः ।
धर्ममेवानुरुध्यन्ति का तं न वरयेत्पतिम् ॥१०॥
धर्मात्मानं महात्मानं दैत्यदानवमर्दनम् ।
महेन्द्रं सर्वदेवानां का तं न वरयेत्पतिम् ॥११॥
क्रियतामविशङ्केन मनसा यदि मन्यसे ।
वरुणं लोकपालानां सुहृद्वाक्यमिदं शृणु ॥१२॥
नैषधेनैवमुक्ता सा दमयन्ती वचो ऽब्रवीत् ।
समाप्लुताभ्यां नेत्राभ्यां शोकजेनाथ वारिणा ॥१३॥
देवेभ्यो ऽहं नमस्कृत्य सर्वेभ्यः पृथिवीपते ।
वृणे त्वामेव भर्तारं सत्यमेतद्ब्रवीमि ते ॥१४॥
तामुवाच ततो राजा वेपमानां कृताञ्जलिम् ।
दौत्येनागत्य कल्याणि कथं स्वार्थमिहोत्सहे ॥१५॥

कथं ह्यहं प्रतिश्रुत्य देवतानां विशेषतः ।
परार्थे यत्नमारभ्य कथं स्वार्थमिहोत्सहे ॥१६॥
एष धर्मो यदि स्वार्थो ममापि भविता ततः ।
एवं स्वार्थं करिष्यामि तथा भद्रे विधीयताम् ॥१७॥
ततो बाष्पाकुलां वाचं दमयन्ती शुचिस्मिता ।
प्रत्याहरन्ती शनकैर्नलं राजानमब्रवीत् ॥१८॥
उपायो ऽयं मया दृष्टो निरपायो नरेश्वर ।
येन दोषो न भविता तव राजन्कथं चन ॥१९॥
त्वं चैव हि नरश्रेष्ठ देवाश्चेन्द्रपुरोगमाः ।
आयान्तु सहिताः सर्वे मम यत्र स्वयंवरः ॥२०॥
ततो ऽहं लोकपालानां संनिधौ त्वां नरेश्वर ।
वरयिष्ये नरव्याघ्र नैवं दोषो भविष्यति ॥२१॥
एवमुक्तस्तु वैदर्भ्या नलो राजा विशां पते ।
आजगाम पुनस्तत्र यत्र देवाः समागताः ॥२२॥
तमपश्यंस्तथायान्तं लोकपाला महेश्वराः ।
दृष्ट्वा चैनं ततो ऽपृच्छन्वृत्तान्तं सर्वमेव तम् ॥२३॥
कच्चिद्दृष्टा त्वया राजन्दमयन्ती शुचिस्मिता ।
किमब्रवीच्च नः सर्वान्वद भूमिपते ऽनघ ॥२४॥

नल उवाच ।

भवद्भिरहमादिष्टो दमयन्त्या निवेशनम् ।
प्रविष्टः सुमहाकक्षं दण्डिभिः स्थविरैर्वृतम् ॥२५॥
प्रविशन्तं च मां तत्र न कश्चिद्दृष्टवान्नरः ।
ऋते तां पार्थिवसुतां भवतामेव तेजसा ॥२६॥

सख्यश्चास्या मया दृष्टास्ताभिश्चाप्युपलक्षितः ।
विस्मिताश्चाभवन्सर्वा दृष्ट्वा मां विबुधेश्वराः ॥ २७ ॥
वर्ण्यमानेषु च मया भवत्सु रुचिरानना ।
मामेव गतसंकल्पा वृणीते सा सुरोत्तमाः ॥ २८ ॥
अब्रवीच्चैव मां बाला आयान्तु सहिताः सुराः ।
त्वया सह नरव्याघ्र मम यत्र स्वयंवरः ॥ २९ ॥
तेषामहं संनिधौ त्वां वरयिष्यामि नैषध ।
एवं तव महाबाहो दोषो न भवितेति ह ॥ ३० ॥
एतावदेव विबुधा यथावृत्तमुदाहृतम् ।
मया शेषे प्रमाणं तु भवन्तस्त्रिदशेश्वराः ॥ ३१ ॥

॥ इति नलोपाख्याने चतुर्थः सर्गः ॥ ४ ॥

बृहदश्व उवाच ।

अथ काले शुभे प्राप्ते तिथौ पुण्ये क्षणे तथा ।
आजुहाव महीपालान्भीमो राजा स्वयंवरे ॥ १ ॥
तच्छ्रुत्वा पृथिवीपालाः सर्वे हृच्छयपीडिताः ।
त्वरिताः समुपाजग्मुर्दमयन्तीमभीप्सवः ॥ २ ॥
कनकस्तम्भरुचिरं तोरणेन विराजितम् ।
विविशुस्ते नृपा रङ्गं महासिंहा इवाचलम् ॥ ३ ॥
तत्रासनेषु विविधेष्वासीनाः पृथिवीक्षितः ।
सुरभिस्रग्धराः सर्वे प्रमृष्टमणिकुण्डलाः ॥ ४ ॥
तत्र स्म पीना दृश्यन्ते बाहवः परिघोपमाः ।

आकारवन्तः सुश्लक्ष्णाः पञ्चशीर्षा इवोरगाः ॥ ५ ॥
सुकेशान्तानि चारूणि सुनासाक्षिभ्रुवाणि च ।
मुखानि राज्ञां शोभन्ते नक्षत्राणि यथा दिवि ॥ ६ ॥
दमयन्ती ततो रङ्गं प्रविवेश शुभानना ।
मुष्णन्ती प्रभया राज्ञां चक्षूंषि च मनांसि च ॥ ७ ॥
तस्या गात्रेषु पतिता तेषां दृष्टिर्महात्मनाम् ।
तत्र तत्रैव सक्ताभून्न चचाल च पश्यताम् ॥ ८ ॥
ततः संकीर्त्यमानेषु राज्ञां नामसु भारत ।
ददर्श भैमी पुरुषान्पञ्च तुल्याकृतीनथ ॥ ९ ॥
तान्समीक्ष्य ततः सर्वान्निर्विशेषाकृतीन्स्थितान् ।
संदेहादथ वैदर्भी नाभ्यजानान्नलं नृपम् ॥ १० ॥
यं यं हि ददृशे तेषां तं तं मेने नलं नृपम् ।
सा चिन्तयन्ती बुद्ध्याथ तर्कयामास भाविनी ॥ ११ ॥
कथं हि देवाञ्जानीयां कथं विद्यां नलं नृपम् ॥ १२ ॥
एवं संचिन्तयन्ती सा वैदर्भी भृशदुःखिता ।
श्रुतानि देवलिङ्गानि तर्कयामास भारत ॥ १३ ॥
देवानां यानि लिङ्गानि स्थविरेभ्यः श्रुतानि मे ।
तानीह तिष्ठतां भूमावेकस्यापि न लक्षये ॥ १४ ॥
सा विनिश्चित्य बहुधा विचार्य च पुनः पुनः ।
शरणं प्रति देवानां प्राप्तकालममन्यत ॥ १५ ॥
वाचा च मनसा चैव नमस्कारं प्रयुज्य सा ।
देवेभ्यः प्राञ्जलिर्भूत्वा वेपमानेदमब्रवीत् ॥ १६ ॥
हंसानां वचनं श्रुत्वा यथा मे नैषधो वृतः ।

पतित्वे तेन सत्येन देवास्तं प्रदिशन्तु मे ॥१७॥
वचसा मनसा चैव यथा नाभिचराम्यहम् ।
तेन सत्येन विबुधास्तमेव प्रदिशन्तु मे ॥१८॥
यथा देवैः स मे भर्ता विहितो निषधाधिपः ।
तेन सत्येन मे देवास्तमेव प्रदिशन्तु मे ॥१९॥
यथेदं व्रतमारब्धं नलस्याराधने मया ।
तेन सत्येन मे देवास्तमेव प्रदिशन्तु मे ॥२०॥
स्वं चैव रूपं कुर्वन्तु लोकपाला महेश्वराः ।
यथाहमभिजानीयां पुण्यश्लोकं नराधिपम् ॥२१॥
निशम्य दमयन्त्यास्तत्करुणं परिदेवितम् ।
यथोक्तं चक्रिरे देवाः सामर्थ्यं लिङ्गधारणे ॥२२॥
सापश्यद्विबुधान्सर्वानस्वेदान्स्तब्धलोचनान् ।
हृषितस्रग्रजोहीनान्स्थितानस्पृशतः क्षितिम् ॥२३॥
छायाद्वितीयो म्लानस्रग्रजःस्वेदसमन्वितः ।
भूमिष्ठो नैषधश्चैव निमेषेण च सूचितः ॥२४॥
सा समीक्ष्य तु तान्देवान्पुण्यश्लोकं च भारत ।
नैषधं वरयामास भैमी धर्मेण पाण्डव ॥२५॥
विलज्जमाना वस्त्रान्ते जग्राहायतलोचना ।
स्कन्धदेशे ऽसृजत्तस्य स्रजं परमशोभनाम् ॥२६॥
वरयामास चैवैनं पतित्वे वरवर्णिनी ।
ततो हा हेति सहसा मुक्तः शब्दो नराधिपैः ॥२७॥
देवैर्महर्षिभिस्तत्र साधु साध्विति भारत ।
विस्मितैरीरितः शब्दः प्रशंसद्भिर्नलं नृपम् ॥२८॥

दमयन्तीं तु कौरव्य वीरसेनसुतो नृपः ।
आश्वासयद्वरारोहां प्रहृष्टेनान्तरात्मना ॥२९॥
यत्त्वं भजसि कल्याणि पुमांसं देवसंनिधौ ।
तस्मान्मां विद्धि भर्तारमेवं ते वचने रतम् ॥३०॥
यावच्च मे धरिष्यन्ति प्राणा देहे शुचिस्मिते ।
तावत्त्वयि भविष्यामि सत्यमेतद्ब्रवीमि ते ॥३१॥
दमयन्तीं तथा वाग्भिरभिनन्द्य कृताञ्जलिः ।
. . . . ॥३२॥
तौ परस्परतः प्रीतौ दृष्ट्वा त्वग्निपुरोगमान् ।
तानेव शरणं देवाञ्जग्मतुर्मनसा तदा ॥३३॥
वृते तु नैषधे भैम्या लोकपाला महौजसः ।
प्रहृष्टमनसः सर्वे नलायाष्टौ वरान्ददुः ॥३४॥
प्रत्यक्षदर्शनं यज्ञे गतिं चानुत्तमां शुभाम् ।
नैषधाय ददौ शक्रः प्रीयमाणः शचीपतिः ॥३५॥
अग्निरात्मभवं प्रादाद्यत्र वाञ्छति नैषधः ।
लोकानात्मप्रभांश्चैव ददौ तस्मै हुताशनः ॥३६॥
यमस्त्वन्नरसं प्रादाद्धर्मे च परमां स्थितिम् ।
अपां पतिरपां भावं यत्र वाञ्छति नैषधः ॥३७॥
स्रजश्चोत्तमगन्धाढ्याः सर्वे च मिथुनं ददुः ।
वरानेवं प्रदायास्य देवास्ते त्रिदिवं गताः ॥३८॥
पार्थिवाश्चानुभूयास्य विवाहं विस्मयान्विताः ।
दमयन्त्याश्च मुदिताः प्रतिजग्मुर्यथागतम् ॥३९॥
गतेषु पार्थिवेन्द्रेषु भीमः प्रीतो महामनाः ।

विवाहं कारयामास दमयन्त्या नलस्य च ॥४०॥
अथ तत्र यथाकामं नैषधो द्विपदां वरः ।
भीमेन समनुज्ञातो जगाम नगरं स्वकम् ॥४१॥
अतीव मुदितो राजा भ्राजमानोऽंशुमानिव ।
अरञ्जयत्प्रजा वीरो धर्मेण परिपालयन् ॥४२॥
ईजे चाप्यश्वमेधेन ययातिरिव नाहुषः ।
अन्यैश्च बहुभिर्धीमान्क्रतुभिश्चाप्तदक्षिणैः ॥४३॥
पुनश्च रमणीयेषु वनेषूपवनेषु च ।
दमयन्त्या सह नलो विजहारामरोपमः ॥४४॥
जनयामास च नलो दमयन्त्यां महामनाः ।
इन्द्रसेनं सुतं चापि इन्द्रसेनां च कन्यकाम् ॥४५॥
एवं स यजमानश्च विहरंश्च नराधिपः ।
ररक्ष वसुसंपूर्णां वसुधां वसुधाधिपः ॥४६॥

॥ इति नलोपाख्याने पञ्चमः सर्गः ॥५॥

॥ अथ हितोपदेशः ॥

II.

श्रुतो हितोपदेशोऽयं पाटवं संस्कृतोक्तिषु ।
वाचां सर्वत्र वैचित्र्यं नीतिविद्यां ददाति च ॥
अजरामरवत्प्राज्ञो विद्यामर्थं च चिन्तयेत् ।
गृहीत इव केशेषु मृत्युना धर्ममाचरेत् ॥

सर्वद्रव्येषु विद्यैव द्रव्यमाहुरनुत्तमम् ।
अहार्यत्वादनर्घ्यत्वादक्षयत्वाच्च सर्वदा ॥
विद्या शस्त्रं च शास्त्रं च द्वे विद्ये प्रतिपत्तये ।
आद्या हास्याय वृद्धत्वे द्वितीयाद्रियते सदा ॥
यन्नवे भाजने लग्नः संस्कारो नान्यथा भवेत् ।
कथाच्छलेन बालानां नीतिस्तदिह कथ्यते ॥
मित्रलाभः सुहृद्भेदो विग्रहः संधिरेव च ।
पञ्चतन्त्रात्तथान्यस्माद्ग्रन्थादाकृष्य लिख्यते ॥

अस्ति भागीरथीतीरे पाटलिपुत्रनामधेयं नगरम् । तत्र सर्वस्वामिगुणोपेतः सुदर्शनो नाम नरपतिरासीत् । स भूपतिरेकदा केनापि पठ्यमानं श्लोकद्वयं शुश्राव ।

अनेकसंशयोच्छेदि परोक्षार्थस्य दर्शकम् ।
सर्वस्य लोचनं शास्त्रं यस्य नास्त्यन्ध एव सः ॥
यौवनं धनसंपत्तिः प्रभुत्वमविवेकता ।
एकैकमप्यनर्थाय किं पुनस्तु चतुष्टयम् ॥

इत्याकर्ण्यात्मनः पुत्राणामनधिगतशास्त्राणां नित्यमुन्मार्गगामिनां शास्त्राननुष्ठानेनोद्विग्नमनाः स राजा चिन्तयामास ।

को ऽर्थः पुत्रेण जातेन यो न विद्वान्न धार्मिकः ।
काणेन चक्षुषा किं वा चक्षुःपीडैव केवलम् ॥
अजातमृतमूर्खाणां वरमाद्यौ न चान्तिमः ।
सकृद्दुःखकरावाद्यावन्तिमस्तु पदे पदे ॥

किं च । स जातो येन जातेन याति वंशः समुन्नतिम् ।

परिवर्तिनि संसारे मृतः को वा न जायते ॥

अपरं च । वरमेको गुणी पुत्रो न च मूर्खशतैरपि ।
एकश्चन्द्रस्तमो हन्ति न च तारागणैरपि ॥
यस्य तस्य प्रसूतो ऽपि गुणवान्पूज्यते नरः ।
धनुर्वंशविशुद्धो ऽपि निर्गुणः किं करिष्यति ॥
हा हा पुत्रक नाधीत्त सुगतैतासु रात्रिषु ।
तेन त्वं विदुषां मध्ये पङ्के गौरिव सीदसि ॥

तत्कथमिदानीमेते मम पुत्रा गुणवन्तः क्रियन्ताम् । यच्चोच्यते । यदभावि न तद्भावि भावि चेन्न तदन्यथा ।
इति चिन्ताविषघ्नो ऽयमगदः किं न पीयते ॥

एतत्कार्याक्षमाणां केषां चिदालस्यवचनम् ।
न दैवमिति संचिन्त्य त्यजेदुद्योगमात्मनः ।
अनुद्योगेन कस्तैलं तिलेभ्यः प्राप्तुमर्हति ॥

अन्यच्च । उद्योगिनं पुरुषसिंहमुपैति लक्ष्मीर्
दैवेन देयमिति कापुरुषा वदन्ति ।
दैवं निहत्य कुरु पौरुषमात्मशक्त्या
यत्ने कृते यदि न सिध्यति को ऽत्र दोषः ॥
यथा ह्येकेन चक्रेण रथस्य न गतिर्भवेत् ।
एवं पुरुषकारेण विना दैवं न सिध्यति ॥

तथा च । पूर्वजन्मकृतं कर्म तद्दैवमिति कथ्यते ।
तस्मात्पुरुषकारेण यत्नं कुर्यादतन्द्रितः ॥
उद्यमेन हि सिध्यन्ति कार्याणि न मनोरथैः ।
न हि सुप्तस्य सिंहस्य प्रविशन्ति मुखे मृगाः ॥

मूर्खो ऽपि शोभते तावत्सभायां वस्त्रवेष्टितः ।
तावच्च शोभते मूर्खो यावत्किं चिन्न भाषते ॥

एतच्चिन्तयित्वा स राजा पण्डितसभां कारितवान् । राजोवाच । भो भोः पण्डिताः । श्रूयताम् । अस्ति कश्चिदेवंभूतो विद्वान्यो मम पुत्राणां नित्यमुन्मार्गगामिनामनधिगतशास्त्राणामिदानीं नीतिशास्त्रोपदेशेन पुनर्जन्म कारयितुं समर्थः ।

यतः । काचः काञ्चनसंसर्गाद्धत्ते मारकतीं द्युतिम् ।
तथा सत्संनिधानेन मूर्खो याति प्रवीणताम् ॥

उक्तं च । हीयते हि मतिस्तात हीनैः सह समागमात् ।
समैश्च समतामेति विशिष्टैश्च विशिष्टताम् ॥

अत्रान्तरे विष्णुशर्मनामा महापण्डितः सकलनीतिशास्त्रतत्त्वज्ञो बृहस्पतिरिवाब्रवीत् । देव । महाकुलसंभूता एते राजपुत्राः । तन्मया नीतिं ग्राहयितुं शक्यन्ते ।

यतः । नाद्रव्ये निहिता का चित्क्रिया फलवती भवेत् ।
न व्यापारशतेनापि शुकवत्पाठ्यते बकः ॥

अन्यच्च । अस्मिंस्तु निर्गुणं गोत्रे नापत्यमुपजायते ।
आकरे पद्मरागाणां जन्म काचमणेः कुतः ॥

अतो ऽहं षण्मासाभ्यन्तरे तव पुत्रान्नीतिशास्त्राभिज्ञान्करिष्यामि । राजा सविनयं पुनरुवाच ।

कीटो ऽपि सुमनःसङ्गादारोहति सतां शिरः ।
अश्मापि याति देवत्वं महद्भिः सुप्रतिष्ठितः ॥

तदेतेषामस्मत्पुत्राणां नीतिशास्त्रोपदेशाय भवन्तः प्रमाणम् । इत्युक्त्वा तस्य विष्णुशर्मणो बहुमानपुरःसरं पुत्रान्समर्पित-

वान् । अथ प्रासादपृष्ठे सुखोपविष्टानां राजपुत्राणां पुरस्तात्प्रस्तावक्रमेण स पण्डितो ऽब्रवीत् ।

काव्यशास्त्रविनोदेन कालो गच्छति धीमताम् ।
व्यसनेन तु मूर्खाणां निद्रया कलहेन वा ॥

तद्भवतां विनोदाय काककूर्मादीनां विचित्रां कथां कथयामि । राजपुत्रैरुक्तम् । आर्य । कथ्यताम् । विष्णुशर्मोवाच । शृणुत यूयम् ! संप्रति मित्रलाभः प्रस्तूयते ।

III.

अहमेकदा दक्षिणारण्ये चरन्नपश्यम् । एको वृद्धव्याघ्रः स्नातः कुशहस्तः सरस्तीरे ब्रूते । भो भोः पान्थाः । इदं सुवर्णकङ्कणं गृह्यताम् । तद्वचनमाकर्ण्य भयात्को ऽपि तत्पार्श्वे न भजते । ततो लोभाकृष्टेन केन चित्पान्थेनालोचितम् । भाग्येनैतत्संभवति । किं त्वस्मिन्नात्मसंदेहे प्रवृत्तिर्न विधेया । यतः ।

अनिष्टादिष्टलाभे ऽपि न गतिर्जायते शुभा ।
यत्रास्ति विषसंसर्गो ऽमृतं तदपि मृत्यवे ॥

किं तु सर्वत्रार्थार्जने प्रवृत्तिः संदेह एव । तथा चोक्तम् ।

न संशयमनारुह्य नरो भद्राणि पश्यति ।
संशयं पुनरारुह्य यदि जीवति पश्यति ॥

तन्निरूपयामि तावत् । प्रकाशं ब्रूते । कुत्र तव कङ्कणम् । व्याघ्रो हस्तं प्रसार्य दर्शयति । पान्थो ऽवदत् । कथं मारात्मके त्वयि विश्वासः । व्याघ्र उवाच । शृणु रे पान्थ । प्रागेव यौ-

वनदशायामतिदुर्वृत्त आसम् । अनेकगोब्राह्मणमनुष्यवधान्मे पुत्रा अनेकशो मृता दाराश्च । सांप्रतं निर्वंशो ऽस्मि । ततः केनापि धार्मिकेणाहमुपदिष्टः । दानधर्ममाचरतु भवानिति । तदुपदेशादिदानीमहं स्नानशीलो दाता वृद्धो गलितनखदन्तो दयावांश्च कथं न विश्वासभूमिः । उक्तं च ।

इज्याध्ययनदानानि तपः सत्यं क्षमा दमः ।
अलोभ इति मार्गो ऽयं धर्मस्याष्टविधः स्मृतः ॥
तत्र पूर्वश्चतुर्वर्गो दम्भार्थमपि सेव्यते ।
उत्तरश्च चतुर्वर्गो नामहात्मसु विद्यते ॥

मम चैतावाल्ँ लोभविरहो येन स्वहस्तगतमपि सुवर्णकङ्कणं यस्मै कस्मै चिद्दातुमिच्छामि । तथापि व्याघ्रो मानुषं खादतीति लोकप्रवादो दुर्निवारः । यतः ।

गतानुगतिको लोकः कुट्टनीमुपदेशिनीम् ।
प्रमाणयति नो धर्मे यथा गोघ्नमपि द्विजम् ॥

मया च धर्मशास्त्राण्यधीतानि । शृणु ।

मरुस्थल्यां यथा वृष्टिः क्षुधार्ते भोजनं तथा ।
दरिद्रे दीयते दानं सफलं पाण्डुनन्दन ॥
प्राणा यथात्मनो ऽभीष्टा भूतानामपि ते तथा ।
आत्मौपम्येन सर्वत्र दयां कुर्वन्ति साधवः ॥

अपरं च । प्रत्याख्याने च दाने च सुखदुःखे प्रियाप्रिये ।
आत्मौपम्येन पुरुषः प्रमाणमधिगच्छति ॥

अन्यच्च । मातृवत्परदारांश्च परद्रव्याणि लोष्टवत् ।
आत्मवत्सर्वभूतानि यः पश्यति स पश्यति ॥

त्वं च दुर्गतः। तेन तत्तुभ्यं दातुं सयत्नो ऽहम्। तथा चोक्तम्।

दरिद्रान्भर कौन्तेय मा प्रयच्छेश्वरे धनम्।
व्याधितस्यौषधं पथ्यं नीरुजस्तु किमौषधैः॥

अन्यच्च। दातव्यमिति यद्दानं दीयते ऽनुपकारिणे।
देशे काले च पात्रे च तद्दानं सात्त्विकं स्मृतम्॥

तदत्र सरसि स्नात्वा सुवर्णकङ्कणमिदं प्रतिगृहाण। ततो जातविश्वासो यावदसौ सरः स्नातुं प्रविष्टस्तावदेव महापङ्के निमग्नः पलायितुमक्षमः। पङ्के पतितं दृष्ट्वा व्याघ्रो ऽवदत्। अहह। महापङ्के पतितो ऽसि। अतस्त्वामुत्थापयामि। इत्युक्त्वा शनैः शनैरुपगम्य तेन व्याघ्रेण धृतः स पान्थो ऽचिन्तयत्।

न धर्मशास्त्रं पठतीति कारणं
न चापि वेदाध्ययनं दुरात्मनः।
स्वभाव एवात्र तथातिरिच्यते
यथा प्रकृत्या मधुरं गवां पयः॥

किं च। अवशेन्द्रियचित्तानां हस्तिस्नानमिव क्रिया।
दुर्भगाभरणप्रायो ज्ञानं भारः क्रियां विना॥

तन्न मया भद्रं कृतं यदत्र मारात्मके विश्वासः कृतः। तथा ह्युक्तम्। नखिनां च नदीनां च शृङ्गिणां शस्त्रपाणिनाम्।
विश्वासो नैव कर्तव्यः स्त्रीषु राजकुलेषु च॥

अपरं च। सर्वस्य हि परीक्ष्यन्ते स्वभावा नेतरे गुणाः।
अतीत्य हि गुणान्सर्वान्स्वभावो मूर्ध्नि वर्तते॥

अन्यच्च। स हि गगणविहारी कल्मषध्वंसकारी
दशशतकरधारी ज्योतिषां मध्यचारी।

विधुरपि विधियोगाद्ग्रस्यते राहुणासौ
लिखितमपि ललाटे प्रोज्झितुं कः समर्थः ॥

इति चिन्तयन्नेव तेनासौ व्याघ्रेण व्यापादितः खादितश्च ।

IV.

अस्ति मगधदेशे चम्पकवती नामारण्यानी । तस्यां चिरान्महता स्नेहेन मृगकाकौ निवसतः । स च मृगः स्वेच्छया भ्राम्यन्पुष्टाङ्गः केन चित्सृगालेनावलोकितः । तं दृष्ट्वा सृगालोऽचिन्तयत् । आः । कथमेतन्मांसं सुललितं भक्षयामि । भवतु । विश्वासं तावदुत्पादयामि । इत्यालोच्योपसृत्याब्रवीत् । मित्र । कुशलं ते । मृगेणोक्तम् । कस्त्वम् । जम्बुको ब्रूते । क्षुद्रबुद्धिनामा जम्बुकोऽहम् । अत्रारण्ये मित्रबन्धुहीनो मृतवदेकाकी निवसामि । इदानीं भवन्तं मित्रमासाद्य पुनः सबन्धुर्जीवलोकं प्रविष्टोऽस्मि । अधुना मया तवानुचरेण सर्वथा भवितव्यम् । मृगेणोक्तम् । एवमस्तु । ततोऽस्तं गते सवितरि भगवति मरीचिमालिनि मृगस्य वासभूमिं प्रति मृगजम्बुकौ गतौ । तत्र चम्पकवृक्षशाखायां सुबुद्धिनामा काको मृगस्य चिरमित्रं निवसति । तौ दृष्ट्वा काकोऽवदत् । सखे चित्राङ्ग । कोऽयं द्वितीयः । मृगो ब्रूते । जम्बुकोऽयमस्मत्सख्यमिच्छन्नागतः । काको ब्रूते । मित्र । अकस्मादागन्तुना सह विश्वासो नैव युक्तः । तन्न भद्रमाचरितम् । तथा चोक्तम् ।

अज्ञातकुलशीलस्य वासो देयो न कस्य चित् ।
मार्जारस्य हि दोषेण हतो गृध्रो जरद्गवः ॥

इत्याकर्ण्य स जम्बुकः सकोपमाह। मृगस्य प्रथमदर्शनदिने भवानप्यज्ञातकुलशील एवासीत्। तद्भवता सह कथमद्य यावदेतस्य स्नेहानुवृत्तिरुत्तरोत्तरं वर्धते।

यत्र विद्वज्जनो नास्ति श्लाघ्यस्तत्राल्पधीरपि।
निरस्तपादपे देश एरण्डो ऽपि द्रुमायते॥

अन्यच्च। अयं निजः परो वेति गणना लघुचेतसाम्।
उदारचरितानां तु वसुधैव कुटुम्बकम्॥

यथा चायं मृगो मम बन्धुस्तथा भवानपि। मृगो ऽब्रवीत्। किमनेनोत्तरोत्तरेण। सर्वैरेकत्र विश्रम्भालापैः सुखमनुभवद्भिः स्थीयताम्। यतः।

न कश्चित्कस्य चिन्मित्रं न कश्चित्कस्य चिद्रिपुः।
व्यवहारेण मित्राणि जायन्ते रिपवस्तथा॥

काकेनोक्तम्। एवमस्तु। अथ प्रातः सर्वे यथाभिमतदेशं गताः। एकदा निभृतं सृगालो ब्रूते। सखे मृग। एतस्मिन्नेव वनैकदेशे सस्यपूर्णं क्षेत्रमस्ति। तदहं त्वां तत्र नीत्वा दर्शयामि। तथा कृते सति मृगः प्रत्यहं तत्र गत्वा सस्यं खादति। अथ क्षेत्रपतिना तद्दृष्ट्वा पाशास्तत्र नियोजिताः। अनन्तरं पुनरागतो मृगस्तत्र चरन्पाशैर्बद्धो ऽचिन्तयत्। को मामितः कालपाशादिव व्याधपाशात्त्रातुं मित्रादन्यः समर्थः। अत्रान्तरे जम्बुकस्तत्रागत्योपस्थितो ऽचिन्तयत्। फलितं तावदस्माकं कपटप्रबन्धेन। मनोरथसिद्धिरपि बाहुल्यान्मे भविष्यति। एतस्योत्कृत्यमानस्य मांसासृगनुलिप्तान्यस्थीनि मयावश्यं प्राप्तव्यानि। स च मृगस्तं दृष्ट्वोल्लसितो ब्रूते। सखे। छिन्धि ता-

वन्मम बन्धनम् । सत्वरं त्रायस्व माम् । यतः ।

आपत्सु मित्रं जानीयाद्युद्धे शूरमृणे शुचिम् ।
भार्यां क्षीणेषु वित्तेषु व्यसनेषु च बान्धवान् ॥

अपरं च । उत्सवे व्यसने चैव दुर्भिक्षे शत्रुसंकटे ।
राजद्वारे श्मशाने च यस्तिष्ठति स बान्धवः ॥

जम्बुकः पाशं मुहुर्मुहुर्विलोक्याचिन्तयत् । दृढबन्धनबद्धो ऽस्ति तावदयं मृगः । ब्रूते च । स्नायुनिर्मिताः पाशाः । तदद्य भट्टारकवारे कथमेतान्दन्तैः स्पृशामि । मित्र । यदि नान्यथा मन्यसे तदा प्रभाते यत्त्वयोच्यते तन्मया कर्तव्यम् । इत्युक्त्वा तत्समीप आत्मानमाच्छाद्य स्थितः सः । अनन्तरं स काकः प्रदोपकाले मृगमनागतमवलोक्येतस्ततो ऽन्विष्य तथाविधं दृष्ट्वोवाच । सखे । किमेतत् । मृगेणोक्तम् । अवधीरितसुहृद्वाक्यस्य फलमेतत् । तथा चोक्तम् ।

सुहृदां हितकामानां यः शृणोति न भाषितम् ।
विपत्संनिहिता तस्य स नरः शत्रुनन्दनः ॥

काको ब्रूते । स सृगालः क्व । मृगेणोक्तम् । मन्मांसार्थी तिष्ठत्यत्रैव । काको ब्रूते । मित्र । उक्तमेव मया पूर्वम् ।

अपराधो न मे ऽस्तीति नैतद्विश्वासकारणम् ।
विद्यते हि नृशंसेभ्यो भयं गुणवतामपि ॥
परोक्षे कार्यहन्तारं प्रत्यक्षे प्रियवादिनम् ।
वर्जयेत्तादृशं मित्रं विषकुम्भं पयोमुखम् ॥

दीर्घं निःश्वस्य । अरे वञ्चक । किं त्वया पापकर्मणा कृतम् । यतः ।

संलापितानां मधुरैर्वचोभिर्मिथ्योपचारैश्च वशीकृतानाम्।
आशावतां श्रद्दधतां च लोके किमर्थिनां वञ्चयितव्यमस्ति॥

अन्यच्च। उपकारिणि विश्रब्धे शुद्धमतौ यः समाचरति पापम्।
तं जनमसत्यसंधं भगवति वसुधे कथं वहसि॥

दुर्जनेन समं सख्यं प्रीतिं चापि न कारयेत्।
उष्णो दहति चाङ्गारः शीतः कृष्णायते करम्॥

अथ वा स्थितिरियं दुर्जनानाम्।

प्राक्पादयोः पतति खादति पृष्ठमांसं
कर्णे कलं किमपि रौति शनैर्विचित्रम्।
छिद्रं निरूप्य सहसा प्रविशत्यशङ्कः
सर्वं खलस्य चरितं मशकः करोति॥

तथा च। दुर्जनः प्रियवादी च नैतद्विश्वासकारणम्।
मधु तिष्ठति जिह्वाग्रे हृदये तु हलाहलम्॥

अथ प्रभाते स क्षेत्रपतिर्लगुडहस्तस्तं प्रदेशमागच्छन्काकेनावलोकितः। तमालोक्य काकेनोक्तम्। सखे मृग। त्वमात्मानं मृतवत्संदर्श्य वातेनोदरं पूरयित्वा पादान्स्तब्धीकृत्य तिष्ठ। यदाहं शब्दं करोमि तदा त्वं सत्वरमुत्थाय पलायिष्यसि। मृगस्तथैव काकवचनेन स्थितः। ततः क्षेत्रपतिना हर्षोत्फुल्ललोचनेनावलोकितः। तथाविधं मृगमवलोक्यासौ आः स्वयंमृतो ऽयमित्युक्त्वा मृगं बन्धनान्मोचयित्वा पाशान्संवरितुं सयत्नो बभूव। ततः कियद्दूरे ऽन्तरिते क्षेत्रपतौ स मृगः काकस्य शब्दं श्रुत्वा ससंभ्रमः समुत्थाय पलायितः। तमुद्दिश्य तेन क्षेत्रपतिना प्रकोपात्क्षिप्तलगुडेन सृगालो व्यापादितः। तथा

चोक्तम् । त्रिभिर्वर्षैस्त्रिभिर्मासैस्त्रिभिः पक्षैस्त्रिभिर्दिनैः ।
अत्युग्रपुण्यपापानामिहैव फलमश्नुते ॥

अतो ऽहं ब्रवीमि ।

भक्ष्यभक्षकयोः प्रीतिर्विपत्तेरेव कारणम् ।
सृगालात्पाशबद्धो ऽसौ मृगः काकेन रक्षितः ॥

V.

अस्ति भागीरथीतीरे गृध्रकूटनाम्नि पर्वते महान्पर्कटीवृक्षः । तस्य कोटरे दैवदुर्विपाकाद्गलितनयनो जरद्गवो नाम गृध्रः प्रतिवसति । अथ कृपया तज्जीवनाय तद्वृक्षवासिनः पक्षिणः स्वाहारात्किं चित्किं चिद्ददति । तेनासौ जीवति । अथ कदा चिद्दीर्घकर्णनामा मार्जारः पक्षिशावकान्भक्षयितुं तत्रागतः । ततस्तमायान्तं दृष्ट्वा पक्षिशावकैर्भयार्तैः कोलाहलः कृतः । तच्छ्रुत्वा जरद्गवेनोक्तम् । को ऽयमायाति । दीर्घकर्णो गृध्रमवलोक्य सभयमाह । हा हतो ऽस्मि । अधुनातिसंनिधानेन पलायनमप्यशक्यम् । तद्यथा भवितव्यं तथा भवतु । एतत्समीपमुपगच्छामि । इत्यालोच्योपसृत्याब्रवीत् । आर्य । त्वामभिवन्दे । गृध्रो ऽवदत् । कस्त्वम् । सो ऽब्रवीत् । मार्जारो ऽहम् । गृध्रो ब्रूते । तद्दूरमपसर । नो चेद्धन्तव्यो ऽसि मया । मार्जारो ऽवदत् । श्रूयतां तावदस्मद्वचनम् । ततो यद्यहं वध्यस्तदा हन्तव्यः । यतः ।

जातिमात्रेण कश्चित्किं वध्यते पूज्यते क्व चित् ।
व्यवहारं परिज्ञाय वध्यः पूज्यो ऽथ वा भवेत् ॥

गृध्रो ब्रूते । ब्रूहि । कीदृग्व्यापारवान् । सो ऽवदत् । अहमत्र गङ्गातीरे नित्यस्नायी निरामिषाशी ब्रह्मचर्येण चान्द्रायणव्रतमाचरंस्तिष्ठामि । युष्मांश्च धर्मज्ञानरतान्विश्वासभूमयः पक्षिणः सर्वे सर्वदा ममाग्रे स्तुवन्ति । अतो भवद्भ्यो विद्यावयोवृद्धेभ्यो धर्मं श्रोतुमिहागतः । भवन्तश्चैतादृशा धर्मज्ञा यन्मामतिथिं हन्तुमुद्यताः । गृहस्थस्य धर्मश्चैष समुदीरितः ।

अरावप्युचितं कार्यमातिथ्यं गृहमागते ।
छेत्तुमप्यागते छायां नोपसंहरते द्रुमः ॥

किं च । यद्यन्नं नास्ति तदा प्रीतिवचसाप्यतिथिः पूज्यः । यतः ।

तृणानि भूमिरुदकं वाक्चतुर्थी च सूनृता ।
एतान्यपि सतां गेहे नोच्छिद्यन्ते कदा चन ॥

अन्यच्च । बालो वा यदि वा वृद्धो युवा वा गृहमागतः ।
तस्य पूजा विधातव्या सर्वत्राभ्यागतो गुरुः ॥

अन्यच्च । निर्गुणेष्वपि सत्त्वेषु दयां कुर्वन्ति साधवः ।
न हि संहरते ज्योत्स्नां चन्द्रश्चाण्डालवेश्मनि ॥

अन्यच्च । अतिथिर्यस्य भग्नाशो गृहात्प्रतिनिवर्तते ।
स दत्त्वा दुष्कृतं तस्मै पुण्यमादाय गच्छति ॥

अन्यच्च । उत्तमस्यापि वर्णस्य नीचो ऽपि गृहमागतः ।
पूजनीयो यथायोग्यं सर्वदेवमयो ऽतिथिः ॥

गृध्रो ऽवदत् । मार्जारा हि मांसरुचयो भवन्ति पक्षिशावकाश्चात्र निवसन्ति । तेनैवं ब्रवीमि । मार्जारो ऽप्येवं श्रुत्वा भूमिं स्पृष्ट्वा कर्णौ स्पृशति ब्रूते च । मया धर्मशास्त्रं श्रुत्वा वीतरागेणेदं दुष्करं व्रतं चान्द्रायणमध्यवसायितम् । यतः पर-

स्परं विवदमानानामपि धर्मशास्त्राणामहिंसा परमो धर्म इत्यत्रैकमत्यम् । यतः ।

सर्वहिंसानिवृत्ताश्च नराः सर्वसहाश्च ये ।
सर्वस्याश्रयभूताश्च ते नराः स्वर्गगामिणः ॥

अन्यच्च । एक एव सुहृद्धर्मो निधने ऽप्यनुयाति यः ।
शरीरेण समं नाशं सर्वमन्यद्धि गच्छति ॥

किं च । यो ऽत्ति यस्य यदा मांसमुभयोः पश्यतान्तरम् ।
एकस्य क्षणिकी प्रीतिरन्यः प्राणैर्विमुच्यते ॥

अपि च । मर्तव्यमिति यद्दुःखं पुरुषस्योपजायते ।
शक्यस्तेनानुमानेन परो ऽपि परिरक्षितुम् ॥ शृणु

पुनः । स्वच्छन्दवनजातेन शाकेनापि प्रपूर्यते ।
अस्य दग्धोदरस्यार्थे कः कुर्यात्पातकं महत् ॥

एवं विश्वास्य स मार्जारस्तरुकोटरे स्थितः । ततो दिनेषु गच्छत्सु पक्षिशावकानाक्रम्य कोटरमानीय प्रत्यहं खादति । अथ येषामपत्यानि खादितानि तैः शोकार्तैर्विलपद्भिरितस्ततो जिज्ञासा समारब्धा । तत्परिज्ञाय मार्जारः कोटरान्निःसृत्य पलायितः । पश्चात्पतत्रिभिरितस्ततो निरूपयद्भिस्तत्र तरुकोटरे शावकास्थीनि प्राप्तानि । अनन्तरं चानेनैव शावकाः खादिता इति निश्चित्य मिलित्वा तैः पक्षिभिः स गृध्रो व्यापादितः । अतो ऽहं ब्रवीमि ।

अज्ञातकुलशीलस्य वासो देयो न कस्य चित् ।
मार्जारस्य हि दोषेण हतो गृध्रो जरद्गवः ॥

VI.

अस्ति वाराणस्यां कर्पूरपटो नाम रजकः । स चैकदा निर्भरं प्रसुप्तः । तदनन्तरं द्रव्याणि हर्तुं तद्गृहं चौरः प्रविष्टः । तस्य प्राङ्गणे गर्दभो बद्धस्तिष्ठति कुक्कुरश्चोपविष्टः । तं चौरमवलोक्य गर्दभः श्वानमाह । तव तावदयं व्यापारः । तत्किमिति त्वमुच्चैः शब्दं कृत्वा स्वामिनं न जागरयसि । कुक्कुरो ब्रूते । माम। नियोगस्यास्य चर्चा किं त्वया कर्तव्या। त्वमेव जानासि यथाहमेतस्याहर्निशं गृहरक्षां करोमि । यतो ऽयं चिरान्निर्वृतो ममोपयोगं न जानाति तेनाधुना ममाहारदाने ऽपि मन्दादरः । विना विधुरदर्शनं स्वामिनो ऽनुजीविषु मन्दादरा भवन्ति । गर्दभो ब्रूते । शृणु रे बर्बर ।

याचते कार्यकाले यः स किंभृत्यः स किंसुहृत् । कुक्कु-
रो ब्रूते । भृत्यान्संभावयेद्यस्तु कार्यकाले स किंप्रभुः ॥
किं च । आश्रितानां भृतौ स्वामिसेवायां धर्मसेवने ।
पुत्रस्योत्पादने चैव न सन्ति प्रतिहस्तकाः ॥

ततो गर्दभः सकोपमाह । आः । पापीयांस्त्वं यः स्वामिकार्योपेक्षां करोषि। भवतु। यथा स्वामी जागर्ति तथा मया कर्तव्यम् ।
यतः । पृष्ठतः सेवयेदर्कं जठरेण हुताशनम् ।
स्वामिनं सर्वभावेन परलोकममायया ॥

इत्युक्त्वा स अतीव चीत्कारं कृतवान् । ततः स रजकस्तेन चीत्कारेण प्रबुद्धो निद्राविमर्दकोपादुत्थाय गर्दभं लगुडेन ताडयामास । अतो ऽहं ब्रवीमि ।

पराधिकारचर्चां यः कुर्यात्स्वामिहितेच्छया ।

स विषीदति चीत्कारात्ताडितो गर्दभो यथा ॥

VII.

अस्त्युत्तरापथे ऽर्बुदशिखरनाम्नि पर्वते महाविक्रमो नाम सिंहः । तस्य पर्वतकन्दरमधिशयानस्य केसराग्रं मूषिकः कश्चिच्छिनत्ति । स सिंहः केसराग्रं लूनं बुद्ध्वा कुपितो विवरान्तर्गतं मूषिकमलभमानो ऽचिन्तयत् । किं विधेयमत्र । भवतु । एवं श्रूयते ।

क्षुद्रशत्रुर्भवेद्यस्तु विक्रमान्न स नम्यते ।
तं निहन्तुं पुरस्कार्यः सदृशस्तस्य सैनिकः ॥

इत्यालोच्य तेन ग्रामं गत्वा दधिकर्णनामा बिडालो मांसाद्याहारेण संतोष्य प्रयत्नादानीय स्वकन्दरे धृतः । ततस्तद्भयान्मूषिको बहिर्न निःसरति । तेनासौ सिंहो ऽक्षतकेसरः सुखं स्वपिति । मूषिकशब्दं यदा यदा शृणोति तदा तदा सविशेषं तं बिडालं मांसाहारदानेन संवर्धयति । अथैकदा स मूषिकः क्षुधा पीडितो बहिः संचरंस्तेन मार्जारेण प्राप्तो व्यापादितः खादितश्च । अनन्तरं स सिंहो यदा कदा चिदपि मूषिकशब्दं न शुश्राव तदोपयोगाभावात्तस्य बिडालस्याहारदाने मन्दादरो बभूव । अतो ऽहं ब्रवीमि ।

निरपेक्षो न कर्तव्यो भृत्यैः स्वामी कदा चन ।
निरपेक्षं प्रभुं कृत्वा भृत्यः स्याद्दधिकर्णवत् ॥

VIII. IX.

कस्मिंश्चित्तरौ वायससदंपती निवसतः । तयोश्चापत्यानि त-

रुकोटरावस्थितकृष्णसर्पेण खादितानि। ततः पुनर्गर्भवती वायसी ब्रूते। स्वामिन्। त्यज्यतामयं तरुः। अत्र यावत्कृष्णसर्पस्तावदावयोः संततिः कदा चिदपि न भविष्यति। यतः।

दुष्टा भार्या शठं मित्रं भृत्यश्चोत्तरदायकः।
ससर्पे च गृहे वासो मृत्युरेव न संशयः॥

वायसो ब्रूते। प्रिये। न भेतव्यम्। वारं वारं मयैतस्य महापराधः सोढः। इदानीं पुनर्न क्षन्तव्यः। वायस्याह। कथमनेन बलवता कृष्णसर्पेण सार्धं भवान्विग्रहीतुं समर्थः। वायसो ब्रूते। अलमनया चिन्तया। यतः।

यस्य बुद्धिर्बलं तस्य निर्बुद्धेस्तु कुतो बलम्।
वने सिंहो बलोन्मत्तः शशकेन निपातितः॥

वायस्याह। कथमेतत्। वायसः कथयति। अस्ति मन्दरनाम्नि पर्वते दुर्दान्तो नाम सिंहः। स च सर्वदा पशूनां वधं विदधान एवास्ते। ततः सर्वैः पशुभिर्मेलकं कृत्वा स सिंहो विज्ञप्तः। देव। किमर्थं सर्वपशुवधः क्रियते। वयमेव भवदाहारार्थं प्रत्यहमेकैकं पशुमुपढौकयामः। सिंहेनोक्तम्। यद्येतदभिमतं भवतां तर्हि भवतु। ततः प्रभृति प्रत्यहमेकैकं पशुमुपकल्पितं भक्षयन्नास्ते। अथ कदा चित्कस्यापि वृद्धशशकस्य वासरः प्राप्तः। ततः सो ऽचिन्तयत्।

त्रासहेतोर्विनीतिस्तु क्रियते जीविताशया।
पञ्चत्वं चेद्गमिष्यामि किं सिंहानुनयेन मे॥

तन्मन्दं मन्दमुपगच्छामि। ततः सिंहो ऽपि क्षुधा पीडितः कोपात्तमुवाच। कुतस्त्वं विलम्ब्यागतो ऽसि। शशको ऽब्र-

वीत् । नाहमपराद्धः । पथि सिंहान्तरेण बलाद्धृतस्तस्याग्रे पुनरागमनाय शपथं कृत्वा स्वामिनं निवेदयितुमत्रागतो ऽस्मि । सिंहः सकोपमाह । सत्वरं गत्वा मां दर्शय । क्वासौ दुरात्मा तिष्ठति । ततः शशकस्तं गृहीत्वा गम्भीरकूपसमीपं गतः । अत्रागत्य पश्यतु स्वामीत्युक्त्वा तस्मिन्कूपजले तस्यैव प्रतिबिम्बं दर्शितवान् । ततो ऽसौ दर्पाध्मातस्तस्योपर्यात्मानं निक्षिप्य पञ्चत्वं गतः। अतो ऽहं ब्रवीमि। यस्य बुद्धिर्बलं तस्येत्यादि।

वायसी ब्रूते। श्रुतं मया। कर्तव्यतां ब्रूहि। वायसो ऽवदत्। प्रिये। आसन्ने सरसि राजपुत्रः सततमागत्य स्नाति। तस्मिन्प्रस्तरे तदङ्गादवतारितं कनकसूत्रं चञ्च्वा धृत्वानीयास्मिन्कोटरे धरिष्यसि। अथ कनकसूत्रानुसरणप्रवृत्तैः राजपुरुषैः कोटरे निरूप्यमाणे कृष्णसर्पो द्रष्टव्यो व्यापादयितव्यश्च। अथ कदा चित्स्नातुं प्रविष्टे राजपुत्रे वायस्या तदनुष्ठितम्। तथानुष्ठिते तद्वृत्तम्। अतो ऽहं ब्रवीमि।

उपायेन हि तत्कुर्याद्यन्न शक्यं पराक्रमैः।
काक्या कनकसूत्रेण कृष्णसर्पो निपातितः॥

X.

अस्ति नर्मदातीरे पर्वतोपत्यकायां विशालः शाल्मलीतरुः। तत्र निर्मितनीडक्रोडे पक्षिणः सुखेन वर्षास्वपि निवसन्ति। अथ नीलपटैरिव जलधरपटलैरावृते नभस्तले धारासारैर्महती

वृष्टिर्बभूव। ततो वानरांस्तरुतले ऽवस्थिताञ्छीतार्तान्कम्पमानानवलोक्य पक्षिभिरुक्तम्। भो भो वानराः। श्रूयताम्।

अस्माभिर्निर्मिता नीडाश्चञ्चुमात्राहृतैस्तृणैः।
हस्तपादादिसंयुक्ता यूयं किमवसीदथ॥

तच्छ्रुत्वा वानरैर्जातामर्षैरालोचितम्। अहो। निर्वातनीडगर्भावस्थिताः सुखिनः पक्षिणो ऽस्मान्निन्दन्ति। तद्भवतु। तावद्वृष्टेरुपशमः। अनन्तरं शान्ते पानीयवर्षे तैर्वानरैर्वृक्षमारुह्य सर्वे नीडा भग्नाः। तेषां पक्षिणामण्डानि चाधः पतितानि। अतो ऽहं ब्रवीमि।

विद्वानेवोपदेष्टव्यो नाविद्वांस्तु कदा चन।
वानरानुपदिश्याज्ञान्स्थानभ्रंशं ययुः खगाः॥

XI.

अस्ति हस्तिनापुरे कर्पूरविलासो नाम रजकः। तस्य गर्दभो ऽतिभारवाहनाद्दुर्बलो मुमूर्षुरिवाभवत्। ततस्तेन रजकेनासौ व्याघ्रचर्मणा प्रच्छाद्यारण्यसमीपे सस्यक्षेत्रे मोचितः। ततो दूरादवलोक्य व्याघ्रबुद्ध्या क्षेत्रपतयः सत्वरं पलायन्ते। स च सुखेन सस्यं चरति। अथैकदा केनापि सस्यरक्षकेण धूसरकम्बलकृततनुत्राणेन धनुष्काण्डं सज्जीकृत्यावनतकायेनैकान्ते स्थितम्। तं च दूरे दृष्ट्वा गर्दभः पुष्टाङ्गो गर्दभीयमिति मत्वा शब्दं कुर्वाणस्तदभिमुखं धावितः। ततस्तेन सस्यरक्षकेण गर्दभो ऽयमिति ज्ञात्वा लीलयैव व्यापादितः। अतो ऽहं ब्रवीमि।

सुचिरं हि चरन्मौनं श्रेयः पश्यत्यबुद्धिमान् ।
द्वीपिचर्मपरिच्छन्नो वाग्दोषाद्गर्दभो हतः ॥

XII.

कदा चिद्वर्षास्वपि वृष्टेरभावात्तृषार्तो गजयूथो यूथपतिमाह । नाथ । को ऽप्युपायो ऽस्माकं जीवनाय नास्ति । अस्त्यत्र क्षुद्रजन्तूनां निमज्जनस्थानम् । वयं च निमज्जनाभावादन्धा इव क्व यामः किं वा कुर्मः । ततो हस्तिराजो नातिदूरं गत्वा निर्मलं ह्रदं दर्शितवान् । ततस्तत्तीरावस्थिताः शशका गजयूथपादाहतिभिर्बहवश्चूर्णिताः । अनन्तरं शिलीमुखो नाम शशकः सर्वानाहूय चिन्तयामास । अनेन गजयूथेन पिपासाकुलितेन प्रत्यहमेवात्रागन्तव्यम् । अतो विनङ्क्ष्यत्यस्मत्कुलम् । अथ विजयो नाम वृद्धशशको ऽवदत् । मा विषीदत । प्रतीकारो मया कर्तव्यः । इति प्रतिज्ञाय चलितः । गच्छता च तेनालोचितम् । कथं मया गजयूथपनिकटे गत्वा वक्तव्यम् । यतः । स्पृशन्नपि गजो हन्ति जिघ्रन्नपि भुजंगमः ।
हसन्नपि नृपो हन्ति मानयन्नपि दुर्जनः ॥

अतो ऽहं पर्वतशिखरमारुह्य यूथनाथमभिवादयामि । तथानुष्ठिते सति यूथनाथ उवाच । कस्त्वम् । कुतः समायातः । स ब्रूते । दूतो ऽहं भगवता चन्द्रेण प्रेषितः । यूथपतिराह । कार्यमुच्यताम् । विजयो वदति । शृणु गजेन्द्र ।
उद्यतेष्वपि शस्त्रेषु दूतो वदति नान्यथा ।
सदैवावध्यभावेन यथार्थस्य हि वाचकः ॥

तदहं तदाज्ञया ब्रवीमि । शृणु । यदेते शशकाश्चन्द्रसरोरक्षकास्त्वया निःसारितास्तन्न युक्तं कृतम् । यतो रक्षकास्ते शशका मदीया अत एव लोके मे शशाङ्क इति प्रसिद्धिः । एवमुक्तवति दूते स यूथपतिर्भयादिदमाह । इदमज्ञानतः कृतम् । पुनर्न गमिष्यामि । दूत उवाच । तदत्र सरसि भगवन्तं चन्द्रमसं प्रकोपात्कम्पमानं प्रणम्य प्रसाद्य च गच्छ । ततस्तेन रात्रौ नीत्वा तत्र जले चञ्चलं चन्द्रप्रतिबिम्बं दर्शयित्वा स यूथपतिः प्रणामं कारितः । देव । अज्ञानादेवानेनापराधः कृतस्तत्क्षम्यतामित्युक्त्वा तेन शशकेन स यूथपतिः प्रस्थापितः । अतो ऽहं ब्रवीमि ।

व्यपदेशेन महतां सिद्धिः संजायते परा ।
शशिनो व्यपदेशेन वसन्ति शशकाः सुखम् ॥

XIII.

अस्ति सृगालः कश्चित्स्वेच्छया नगरोपान्ते भ्रमन्नीलसंधानभाण्डे निपतितः । पश्चात्तत उत्थातुमसमर्थः प्रातरात्मानं मृतवत्संदर्श्य स्थितः । अथ नीलीभाण्डस्वामिनासावुत्थाप्य दूरे नीत्वा परित्यक्तः । ततो ऽसौ वनं गत्वात्मानं नीलवर्णमवलोक्याचिन्तयत् । अहमिदानीमुत्तमवर्णः । तदात्मनः किमुत्कर्षं न साधयामि । इत्यालोच्य सृगालानाहूय तेनोक्तम् । अहं भगवत्या वनदेवतया स्वहस्तेनारण्यराज्ये सर्वौषधिरसेनाभिषिक्तः । पश्यत मम वर्णम् । तदद्यारभ्यास्मदाज्ञयास्मिन्नरण्ये व्यवहारः कार्यः । सृगालाश्च तं विशिष्टवर्णमवलोक्य साष्टाङ्गपातं प्रणम्योचुः । यथाज्ञापयति देवः । ततो ऽनेन क्रमेण

सर्वेष्वरण्यवासिष्वाधिपत्यं तस्य बभूव। ततस्तेन सिंहव्याघ्रादीनुत्तमपरिजनान्प्राप्य सृगालानवलोक्य लज्जमानेनावज्ञया दूरीकृताः स्वज्ञातयः। ततो विषण्णान्सृगालानवलोक्य वृद्धसृगालेन केन चित्प्रतिज्ञातम्। मा विषीदत। एवं चेदनेनानीतिज्ञेन वयं मर्मज्ञाः परिभूताः। तद्यथायं नश्यति तन्मया विधेयम्। यतो ऽमी व्याघ्रादयो वर्णमात्रविप्रलब्धाः सृगालमज्ञात्वा राजानममुं मन्यन्ते तद्यथायं परिचीयते तथा कुरुत। तत्र चैवमनुष्ठेयं यथा वदामि। यदा सर्वे संध्यासमये तत्संनिधाने महारावमेकदा करिष्यथ ततस्तं शब्दमाकर्ण्य स्वभावात्तेनापि शब्दः कर्तव्यः। यतः।

यः स्वभावो हि यस्य स्यात्तस्यासौ दुरतिक्रमः।
श्वा यदि क्रियते भोगी तत्किं नाश्नात्युपानहम्॥

ततः शब्दाद्विज्ञाय व्याघ्रेण हन्तव्यः। तथानुष्ठिते सति तद्वृत्तम्। तथा चोक्तम्।

छिद्रं मर्म च वीर्यं च विजानाति निजो रिपुः।
दहत्यन्तर्गतश्चैव शुष्कवृक्षमिवानलः॥

अतो ऽहं ब्रवीमि।

आत्मपक्षं परित्यज्य परपक्षे च यो रतः।
स परैर्हन्यते मूढो नीलवर्णसृगालवत्॥

XIV. XV. XVI.

अस्ति मगधदेशे फुल्लोत्पलाभिधानं सरः। तत्र चिरात्संकटविकटनामानौ हंसौ निवसतः। तयोर्मित्रं कम्बुग्रीवनामा

कूर्मः प्रतिवसति । अथैकदा धीवरैरागत्य तत्रोक्तं यदद्यास्माभिरत्रोषित्वा प्रातः कूर्ममत्स्यादयो व्यापादयितव्याः । तदाकर्ण्य कूर्मो हंसावाह । सुहृदौ । श्रुतो ऽयं धीवरालापः । अधुना किं मया कर्तव्यम् । हंसावाहतुः । ज्ञायतां तावत् । पश्चाद्यदुचितं तत्कर्तव्यम् । कूर्मो ब्रूते । मैवं यतो दृष्टव्यतिकरो ऽहमत्र । तथा चोक्तम् ।

अनागतविधाता च प्रत्युत्पन्नमतिश्च यः ।
द्वावेतौ सुखमेधेते यद्भविष्यो विनश्यति ॥

तावाहतुः । कथमेतत् । कूर्मः कथयति । पुरैतस्मिन्नेव सरस्येवंविधेष्वेव धीवरेषूपस्थितेषु मत्स्यत्रयेणालोचितम् । तत्रानागतविधाता नामैको मत्स्यः । तेनोक्तम् । अहं तावज्जलाशयान्तरं गच्छामि । इत्युक्त्वा स ह्रदान्तरं गतः । अपरेण प्रत्युत्पन्नमतिनाम्ना मत्स्येनाभिहितम् । भाविन्यर्थे प्रमाणाभावात्कुत्र मया गन्तव्यम् । तदुत्पन्ने कार्ये यथाकार्यमनुष्ठेयम् । ततो यद्भविष्येणोक्तम् ।

यदभावि न तद्भावि भावि चेन्न तदन्यथा ।
इति चिन्ताविषघ्नो ऽयमगदः किं न पीयते ॥

ततः प्रातर्जालेन बद्धः प्रत्युत्पन्नमतिर्मृतवदात्मानं संदर्श्य स्थितः । ततो जालादपसारितः स्थलादुत्प्लुत्य गम्भीरं नीरं प्रविष्टः । यद्भविष्यश्च धीवरैः प्राप्तो व्यापादितः । अतो ऽहं ब्रवीमि । अनागतविधातेत्यादि ।

तद्यथाहमन्यह्रदं प्राप्नोमि तदद्य विधीयताम् । हंसावाहतुः । जलाशयान्तरे प्राप्ते तव कुशलम् । स्थले गच्छतस्ते को वि-

धिः । कूर्मो ब्रूते । यथाहं भवद्भ्यां सहाकाशवर्त्मना यामि स उपायो विधीयताम् । हंसौ ब्रूतः । कथमुपायः संभवति । कच्छपो वदति । युवाभ्यां चञ्चुधृतं काष्ठमेकं मया मुखेनावलम्बितव्यम् । अतो भवतोः पक्षबलेन मयापि सुखं गन्तव्यम् । हंसौ ब्रूतः । संभवत्येष उपायः । किं तु ।

उपायं चिन्तयेत्प्राज्ञस्तथापायं च चिन्तयेत् ।
पश्यतो बकमूर्खस्य नकुलैर्भक्षिता बकाः ॥

कूर्मः पृच्छति । कथमेतत् । तौ कथयतः । अस्त्युत्तरापथे गृध्रकूटो नाम पर्वतः । तत्रैव रेवातीरे न्यग्रोधपादपे बका निवसन्ति । तस्य वटस्याधस्ताद्विवरे सर्पस्तिष्ठति । स च बकानां बालापत्यानि खादति । ततः शोकार्तानां बकानां प्रलापं श्रुत्वा केन चिद्वृद्धबकेनोक्तम् । भोः । एवं कुरुत यूयम् । मत्स्यानानीय नकुलविवरादारभ्य सर्पविवरं यावत्पङ्क्तिक्रमेणैकैकशो मत्स्यान्धत्त । ततस्तदाहारवर्त्मना नकुलैरागत्य सर्पो द्रष्टव्यः स्वभावद्वेषाद्व्यापादयितव्यश्च । तथानुष्ठिते सति तद्वृत्तम् । अथ नकुलैर्वृक्षोपरि पक्षिशावकानां रावः श्रुतः । पश्चात्तैर्वृक्षमारुह्य शावकाः सर्व एव खादिताः । अत आवां ब्रूवः । उपायं चिन्तयेदित्यादि ।

आवाभ्यां नीयमानं त्वां दृष्ट्वा लोकैः किं चिद्वक्तव्यमेव । तदाकर्ण्य यदि त्वमुत्तरं ददासि तदा तव मरणं भविष्यति । तत्सर्वथात्रैव स्थीयताम् । कूर्मो वदति । किमहमज्ञः । न किमपि मया वक्तव्यम् । तत एवमनुष्ठिते सत्याकाशे नीयमानं कूर्ममालोक्य सर्वे गोरक्षकाः पश्चाद्धावन्ति वदन्ति च ।

अहो महदाश्चर्यम्। पक्षिभ्यां कूर्मः समुह्यते। तत्र कश्चिदाह। यद्ययं कूर्मः पतति तदात्रैव पक्त्वा खादितव्यः। को ऽपि निगदति। गृहं नेतव्यः। कश्चिद्वदति। सरसः समीपे पक्त्वा भक्षितव्यः। तत्परुषवचनमाकर्ण्य स कूर्मः क्रोधाद्विस्मृतसंस्कारो ऽवदत्। युष्माभिर्भस्म भक्षितव्यम्। इति वदन्नेव काष्ठात्पतितो गोरक्षकैर्व्यापादितः। अतो ऽहं ब्रवीमि।

सुहृदां हितकामानां न करोतीह यो वचः।
स कूर्म इव दुर्बुद्धिः काष्ठाद्भ्रष्टो विनश्यति॥

XVII.

अस्ति गौतमारण्ये महातपा नाम मुनिः। तेनाश्रमसंनिधाने मूषिकशावकः काकमुखाद्भ्रष्टो दृष्टः। ततो दयालुना तेन मुनिना नीवारकणैः स संवर्धितः। तं च मूषिकं खादितुमनुधावन्बिडालो मुनिना दृष्टः। पश्चात्तपःप्रभावात्तेन मुनिना मूषिको बलिष्ठो बिडालः कृतः। स बिडालः कुक्कुराद्बिभेति। ततो ऽसौ कुक्कुरः कृतः। कुक्कुरस्य व्याघ्रान्महद्भयम्। तदनन्तरं स व्याघ्रः कृतः। अथ व्याघ्रमपि तं मूषिकनिर्विशेषं पश्यति मुनिः। अतः सर्वे तत्रस्था जनास्तं व्याघ्रं दृष्ट्वा वदन्ति। अनेन मुनिना मूषिको ऽयं व्याघ्रतां नीतः। एतच्छ्रुत्वा स व्याघ्रः सव्यथो ऽचिन्तयत्। यावदनेन मुनिना जीवितव्यं तावदिदं मम स्वरूपाख्यानमकीर्तिकरं न पलायिष्यते। इति समालोच्य मुनिं हन्तुं समुद्यतः। ततो मुनिना तस्य चिकीर्षितं ज्ञात्वा पुनर्मूषिको भवेत्युक्त्वा मूषिक एव कृतः। अतो ऽहं ब्रवीमि।

नीचः श्लाघ्यपदं प्राप्य स्वामिनं लोप्तुमिच्छति ।
मूषिको व्याघ्रतां प्राप्य मुनिं हन्तुं गतो यथा ॥

XVIII.

अस्ति मालवविषये पद्मगर्भाभिधानं सरः । तत्रैको वृद्धबकः सामर्थ्यहीनस्तथोद्विग्नमिवात्मानं दर्शयित्वा स्थितः । स च केन चित्कुलीरेण दूरादेव पृष्टः । किमिति भवानाहारपरित्यागेन तिष्ठति । बकेनोक्तम् । मत्स्या मम जीवनहेतवः । ते चात्रावश्यमेव कैवर्तैर्व्यापादयितव्या इति नगरोपान्ते पर्यालोचना मयाकर्णिता । तदितो वर्तनाभावादस्मन्मरणमुपस्थितम् । इति ज्ञात्वाहमाहारे ऽपि मन्दादरः कृतः । तच्छ्रुत्वा सर्वैर्मत्स्यैरालोचितम् । इह समये तावदुपकारक एवायमुपलक्ष्यते ऽस्माकम् । तदयमेव यथाकर्तव्यं पृच्छ्यताम् । तथा चोक्तम् ।

उपकर्त्रारिणा संधिर्न मित्रेणापकारिणा ।
उपकारापकारौ हि लक्ष्यं लक्षणमेतयोः ॥

मत्स्या ऊचुः । भो बक । अस्माकं कुत्र रक्षणोपायः । बको ब्रूते । अस्ति रक्षणहेतुर्जलाशयान्तरम् । तत्राहमेकैकशो युष्मान्नयामि । मत्स्यैरपि भयादुक्तम् । एवमस्तु । ततो ऽसौ दुष्टबकस्तान्मत्स्यानेकैकान्नीत्वा कस्मिंश्चिद्देशे खादित्वा पुनरागत्य वदति । ते मया जलाशयान्तरे स्थापिताः । अनन्तरं कुलीरस्तमुवाच । भो बक । मामपि तत्र नय । ततो बको ऽप्यपूर्वकुलीरमांसार्थी सादरं तं नीत्वा स्थले धृतवान् । कुलीरो ऽपि

मत्स्यकङ्कालाकीर्णां भूमिं दृष्ट्वाचिन्तयत् । हा हतो ऽस्मि मन्दभाग्यः । भवतु । इदानीं समयोचितं व्यवहरामि । यतः ।

तावद्भयात्तु भेतव्यं यावद्भयमनागतम् ।
आगतं तु भयं दृष्ट्वा प्रहर्तव्यमभीतवत् ॥

अपरं च । अयुद्धे हि यदा पश्येन्न किंचिद्धितमात्मनः ।
युध्यमानस्तदा प्राज्ञो म्रियते रिपुणा सह ॥

इत्यालोच्य स कुलीरस्तस्य बकस्य ग्रीवां चिच्छेद । स बकः पञ्चत्वं गतः । अतो ऽहं ब्रवीमि ।

भक्षयित्वा बहून्मत्स्यानुत्तमाधममध्यमान् ।
अतिलौल्याद्बकः कश्चिन्मृतः कर्कटकग्रहात् ॥

XIX.

अस्ति देवीकोट्टनगरे देवशर्मा नाम ब्राह्मणः । तेन विषुवत्संक्रान्तौ सक्तुपूर्णशरावः प्राप्तः । ततस्तमादायासौ भाण्डपूर्णकुम्भकारमण्डपिकैकदेशे शय्यानिक्षिप्तदेहः सन्रात्रावचिन्तयत् । यद्यहमिमं सक्तुशरावं विक्रीय दश कपर्दकान्प्राप्नोमि तदा तैरिह समये शरावांस्ततो घटादीनुपक्रीय विक्रीयानेकधा वृद्धैर्धनैः पुनः पुनः पूगवस्त्रादिकमुपक्रीय लक्षसंख्यानि धनान्युत्पाद्य विवाहचतुष्टयं करोमि । ततस्तासु पत्नीषु याधिकरूपवती तस्यामधिकानुरागं करोमि । अनन्तरं जातेर्ष्यास्तत्सपत्न्यो यदा द्वंद्वं कुर्वन्ति तदा कोपाकुलो ऽहं ताः पत्नीर्लगुडेनेत्थं ताडयामि । इत्यभिधायोत्थाय तेन लगुडः क्षिप्तः । अतः सक्तुशरावश्चूर्णितो भाण्डानि च बहूनि भग्ना-

नि । ततो भाण्डभङ्गशब्देनागतकुम्भकारेण तद्दृष्ट्वा स ब्राह्मणस्तिरस्कृतो मण्डपिकागर्भाद्बहिष्कृतः । अतो ऽहं ब्रवीमि ।

अनागतवतीं चिन्तां कृत्वा यस्तु प्रहृष्यति ।
स तिरस्कारमाप्नोति भग्नभाण्डो द्विजो यथा ॥

XX.

अस्ति गौतमारण्ये प्रस्तुतयज्ञः कश्चिद्ब्राह्मणः । स च यज्ञार्थं ग्रामान्तराच्छागमुपक्रीय स्कन्धे कृत्वा गच्छन्धूर्तत्रयेणावलोकितः । ततस्ते धूर्ता यद्येष छागः केनाप्युपायेन प्राप्य खाद्यते तदा मतिप्रकर्षो भवतीत्यालोच्य प्रान्तरे वृक्षत्रयतले ब्राह्मणस्य वर्त्मन्युपविश्य स्थिताः । तत्रैकेन धूर्तेन स ब्राह्मणो गच्छन्नभिहितः । भो ब्राह्मण । किमिति त्वया कुक्कुरः स्कन्धेनोह्यते । ब्राह्मणो ब्रूते । नायं श्वा । यज्ञच्छागो ऽयं । अनन्तरं पुनर्द्वितीयेन क्रोशमात्रावस्थितेन तदेवोक्तम् । तदाकर्ण्य ब्राह्मणस्तं छागं भूमौ निधाय मुहुर्मुहुर्निरीक्ष्य पुनः स्कन्धे कृत्वा दोलायमानमतिश्चलितः । तदनन्तरं पुनर्गच्छन्स ब्राह्मणस्तृतीयेन धूर्तेनोक्तः । भो ब्राह्मण । किमिति कुक्कुरं स्कन्धेन भवान्वहति । तदाकर्ण्य निश्चितमेवायं कुक्कुर इति मत्वा छागं त्यक्त्वा स्नात्वा स्वगृहं ययौ । स छागो तैर्धूर्तैर्नीत्वा भक्षितः । अतो ऽहं ब्रवीमि ।

आत्मौपम्येन यो वेत्ति दुर्जनं सत्यवादिनम् ।
स तथा वञ्च्यते धूर्तैर्ब्राह्मणश्छागतो यथा ॥

XXI.

अस्त्युज्जयिन्यां माठरो नाम ब्राह्मणः। तस्य ब्राह्मणी बालापत्यस्य रक्षार्थं ब्राह्मणमवस्थाप्य स्नातुं गता। अथ ब्राह्मणस्य कृते राज्ञः श्राद्धं दातुमाह्वानमागतम्। तच्छ्रुत्वा ब्राह्मणः सहजदारिद्र्यादचिन्तयत्। यदि सत्वरं न गच्छामि तदान्यः कश्चिच्छ्राद्धं ग्रहीष्यति। उक्तं च।

आदानस्य प्रदानस्य कर्तव्यस्य च कर्मणः।
क्षिप्रमक्रियमाणस्य कालः पिबति तद्रसम्॥

किं तु बालकस्यात्र रक्षको नास्ति। तत्किं करोमि। यातु। चिरकालपालितमिमं पुत्रनिर्विशेषं नकुलं बालकरक्षार्थमवस्थाप्य गच्छामि। तथा कृत्वा स तत्र गतः। ततस्तेन नकुलेन बालकसमीपमागच्छता कृष्णसर्पो दृष्टो व्यापादितश्च। अथासौ नकुलो ब्राह्मणमायान्तमवलोक्य रक्तविलिप्तमुखपादः सत्वरमुपागम्य तस्य चरणयोर्लुलोठ। ततो ऽसौ ब्राह्मणस्तं तथाविधं दृष्ट्वा मम पुत्रो ऽनेन भक्षित इत्यवधार्य व्यापादितवान्। अनन्तरं यावदसावुपसृत्य पश्यति ब्राह्मणस्तावद्बालकः सुस्थः सर्पश्च व्यापादितस्तिष्ठति। ततस्तमुपकारकमेव नकुलं निरूप्य विभावितकृत्यः संतप्तचेताः स परं विषादमगमत्। अतो ऽहं ब्रवीमि।

यो ऽर्थतत्त्वमविज्ञाय क्रोधस्यैव वशं गतः।
स तथा तप्यते मूढो ब्राह्मणो नकुलाद्यथा॥

॥ अथ कथासरित्सागरः ॥

XXII.

अत्रान्तरे स राजापि पुत्रकः सत्यसंगरः ।
विवेश विन्ध्यकान्तारं विरक्तः स्वेषु बन्धुषु ॥
भ्रमन्नवाप तत्रासौ बाहुयुद्धैकतत्परौ ।
पुरुषौ द्वौ ततस्तौ स पृष्टवान्कौ युवामिति ॥
मयासुरसुतावावां तदीयं चास्ति नौ धनम् ।
इदं भाजनमेषा च यष्टिरेते च पादुके ॥
तन्निमित्तेन युद्धं नौ यो बली स हरेदिति ।
एतत्तद्वचनं श्रुत्वा हसन्प्रोवाच पुत्रकः ॥
कियदेतद्धनं पुंसस्ततस्तौ समवोचताम् ।
पादुके परिधायैते खेचरत्वमवाप्यते ॥
यष्ट्या यल्लिख्यते किं चित्सत्यं संपद्यते हि तत् ।
भाजने यो य आहारश्चिन्त्यते स स तिष्ठति ॥
तच्छ्रुत्वा पुत्रको ऽवादीत्किं युद्धेनास्त्वयं पणः ।
धावन्बलाधिको यः स्यात्स एवैतद्धरेदिति ॥
एवमस्त्विति तौ मूढौ धावितौ सो ऽपि पादुके ।
अध्यास्योदपतद्व्योम गृहीत्वा यष्टिभाजने ॥
अथ दूरं क्षणाद्गत्वा ददर्श नगरीं शुभाम् ।
आकर्षिकाख्यां तस्यां च नभसो ऽवततार सः ॥

———

XXIII.

अर्थैः संचयवानर्थान्प्राप्नोति कियदद्भुतम् ।
मया पुनर्विनैवार्थं लक्ष्मीरासादिता पुरा ॥
गर्भस्थस्यैव मे पूर्वं पिता पञ्चत्वमागतः ।
मन्मातुश्च तदा पापैर्गोत्रजैः सकलं हृतम् ॥
ततः सा तद्भयाद्गत्वा रक्षन्ती गर्भमात्मनः ।
तस्थौ कुमारदत्तस्य पितृमित्रस्य वेश्मनि ॥
तत्र तस्याश्च जातो ऽहं साध्व्या वृत्तिनिबन्धनम् ।
ततश्चावर्धयत्सा मां कृच्छ्रकर्माणि कुर्वती ॥
उपाध्यायमथाभ्यर्थ्य तया किं चन दीनया ।
क्रमेण शिक्षितश्चाहं लिपिं गणितमेव च ॥
वणिक्पुत्रो ऽसि तत्पुत्र वाणिज्यं कुरु सांप्रतम् ।
विशाखिलाख्यो देशे ऽस्मिन्वणिक्चास्ति महाधनः ॥
दरिद्राणां कुलीनानां भाण्डमूल्यं ददाति सः ।
गच्छ याचस्व तं मूल्यमिति माताब्रवीच्च माम् ॥
ततो ऽहमगमं तस्य सकाशं सो ऽपि तत्क्षणम् ।
इत्यवोचत्क्रुधा कं चिद्वणिक्पुत्रं विशाखिलः ॥
मूषको दृश्यते यो ऽयं गतप्राणो ऽत्र भूतले ।
एतेनापि हि पण्येन कुशलो धनमर्जयेत् ॥
दत्तास्तव पुनः पाप दीनारा बहवो मया ।
दूरे तिष्ठतु तद्वृद्धिस्त्वया ते ऽपि न रक्षिताः ॥
तच्छ्रुत्वा सहसैवाहं तमवोचं विशाखिलम् ।
गृहीतो ऽयं मया त्वत्तो भाण्डमूल्याय मूषकः ॥

इत्युक्त्वा मूषकं हस्ते गृहीत्वा संपुटे च तम् ।
लिखित्वास्य गतो ऽभूवमहं सो ऽप्यहसद्वणिक् ॥
चणकाञ्जलियुग्मेन मूल्येन स च मूषकः ।
मार्जारस्य कृते दत्तः कस्य चिद्वणिजो मया ॥
कृत्वा तांश्चणकान्पिष्टान्गृहीत्वा जलकुम्भिकाम् ।
अतिष्ठं चत्वरे गत्वा छायायां नगराद्बहिः ॥
तत्र श्रान्तागतायाम्भः शीतलं चणकांश्च तान् ।
काष्ठभारिकसंघाय सप्रश्रयमदामहम् ॥
एकैकः काष्ठिकः प्रीत्या काष्ठे द्वे द्वे ददौ मम ।
विक्रीतवानहं तानि नीत्वा काष्ठानि चापणे ॥
ततः स्तोकेन मूल्येन क्रीत्वा तांश्चणकांस्ततः ।
तथैव काष्ठिकेभ्यो ऽहमन्येद्युः काष्ठमाहरम् ॥
एवं प्रतिदिनं कृत्वा प्राप्य मूल्यं क्रमान्मया ।
काष्ठिकेभ्यो ऽखिलं दारु क्रीतं तेभ्यो दिनत्रयम् ॥
अकस्मादथ संजाते काष्ठच्छेदे ऽतिवृष्टिभिः ।
मया तद्दारु विक्रीतं पणानां बहुभिः शतैः ॥
तेनैव विपणीं कृत्वा धनेन निजकौशलात् ।
कुर्वन्वाणिज्यं क्रमशः संपन्नो ऽस्मि महाधनः ॥
सौवर्णो मूषकः कृत्वा मया तस्मै समर्पितः ।
विशाखिलाय सो ऽपि स्वां कन्यां मह्यमदात्ततः ॥
अत एव च लोके ऽहं प्रसिद्धो मूषकाख्यया ।
एवं लक्ष्मीरियं प्राप्ता निर्धनेन सता मया ॥

XXIV.

तथा च पूर्वं राजाभूत्तपस्वी करुणापरः ।
दाता धीरः शिबिर्नाम सर्वसत्त्वाभयप्रदः ॥
तं वञ्चयितुमिन्द्रो ऽथ कृत्वा श्येनवपुः स्वयम् ।
मायाकपोतवपुषं धर्ममन्वपतद्द्रुतम् ॥
कपोतः स भयाद्गत्वा शिबेरङ्कमशिश्रियत् ।
मनुष्यवाचा श्येनो ऽथ स तं राजानमब्रवीत् ॥
राजन्भक्ष्यमिदं मुञ्च कपोतं क्षुधितस्य मे ।
अन्यथा मां मृतं विद्धि कस्ते धर्मस्ततो भवेत् ॥
ततः शिबिरुवाचैनमेष मे शरणागतः ।
अत्याज्यस्तद्ददाम्यन्यन्मांसमेतत्समं तव ॥
श्येनो जगाद यद्येवमात्ममांसं प्रयच्छ मे ।
तथेति तत्प्रहृष्टः सन्स राजा प्रत्यपद्यत ॥
यथा यथा च मांसं स्वमुत्कृत्यारोपयन्नृपः ।
तथा तथा तुलायां स कपोतो ऽभ्यधिको ऽभवत् ॥
ततः शरीरं सकलं तुलां राजाध्यरोपयत् ।
साधु साधु समं त्वेतद्दिव्या वागुदभूत्ततः ॥
इन्द्रधर्मौ ततस्त्यक्त्वा रूपं श्येनकपोतयोः ।
तुष्टावक्षतदेहं तं राजानं चक्रतुः शिबिम् ॥
दत्त्वा चास्मै वरानन्यांस्तावन्तर्धानमीयतुः ॥

XXV.

पुराभूद्गौतमो नाम त्रिकालज्ञो महामुनिः ।

अहल्येति च तस्यासीद्भार्या रूपजिताप्सराः ॥
एकदा रूपलुब्धस्तामिन्द्रः प्रार्थितवान्रहः ।
प्रभूणां हि विभूत्यन्धा धावत्यविषये मतिः ॥
सानुमेने च तं मूढा वृषस्यन्ती शचीपतिम् ।
तच्च प्रभावतो बुद्ध्वा तत्रागाद्गौतमो मुनिः ॥
मार्जाररूपं चक्रे च भयादिन्द्रो ऽपि तत्क्षणम् ।
कः स्थितो ऽत्रेति सो ऽपृच्छदहल्यामथ गौतमः ॥
एसो ठिओ खु मज्जाओ इत्यपभ्रष्टवक्रया ।
गिरा सत्यानुरोधिन्या सा तं प्रत्यब्रवीत्पतिम् ॥
सत्यं त्वज्जार इत्युक्त्वा विहसन्स ततो मुनिः ।
सत्यानुरोधक्लृप्तान्तं शापं तस्यामपातयत् ॥
पापशीले शिलाभावं भूरिकालमवाप्नुहि ।
आ वनान्तरसंचारिराघवालोकनादिति ॥
दत्तशापो यथाकामं तपसे स मुनिर्ययौ ।
अहल्यापि शिलाभावं दारुणं प्रत्यपद्यत ॥

XXVI.

ततः कदा चिदध्यास्त वसन्तसमयोत्सवे ।
देवीकृतं तदुद्यानं स राजा सातवाहनः ॥
विहरन्स चिरं तत्र महेन्द्र इव नन्दने ।
वापीजले ऽवतीर्णो ऽभूत्क्रीडितुं कामिनीसखः ॥
असिञ्चत्तत्र दयिताः सहेलं करवारिभिः ।
असिच्यत स ताभिश्च वशाभिरिव वारणः ॥

अथैका तस्य महिषी राज्ञः स्तनभरालसा ।
शिरीषसुकुमाराङ्गी क्रीडन्ती श्रममभ्यगात् ॥
सा जलैरभिषिञ्चन्तं राजानमसहा सती ।
अब्रवीन्मोदकैर्देव परिताडय मामिति ॥
तच्छ्रुत्वा मोदकान्राजा द्रुतमानाययत्तदा ।
ततो विहस्य सा राज्ञी पुनरेवमभाषत ॥
राजन्नवसरः को ऽत्र मोदकानां जलान्तरे ।
उदकैः सिञ्च मा त्वं मामित्युक्तं हि मया तव ॥
संधिमात्रं न जानासि माशब्दोदकशब्दयोः ।
न च प्रकरणं वेत्सि मूर्खस्त्वं कथमीदृशः ॥
इत्युक्तः स तया राज्ञ्या शब्दशास्त्रविदा नृपः ।
परिवारे हसत्यन्तर्लज्जाक्रान्तो झटित्यभूत् ॥
परित्यक्तजलक्रीडो वीतदर्पश्च तत्क्षणम् ।
जातावमानो निर्लक्ष्यः प्राविशन्निजमन्दिरम् ॥
ततश्चिन्तापरो मुह्यन्नाहारादिपराङ्मुखः ।
चित्रस्थ इव पृष्टो ऽपि नैव किं चिदभाषत ॥
पाण्डित्यं शरणं वा मे मृत्युर्वेति विचिन्तयन् ।
शयनीयपरिन्यस्तगात्रः संतापवानभूत् ॥
अकस्मादथ राज्ञस्तां दृष्ट्वावस्थां तथाविधाम् ।
किमेतदिति संभ्रान्तः सर्वः परिजनो ऽभवत् ॥
ततो ऽहं शर्ववर्मा च ज्ञातवन्तौ क्रमेण ताम् ।
अत्रान्तरे च स प्रायः पर्यहीयत वासरः ॥
प्रातरावामगच्छाव वासवेश्म महीपतेः ॥

तत्र सर्वस्य रुद्धे ऽपि प्रवेशे कथमप्यहम् ।
प्राविशं मम पश्चाच्च शर्ववर्मा लघुक्रमम् ॥
उपविश्याथ निकटे विज्ञप्तः स मया नृपः ।
अकारणं कथं देव वर्तसे विमना इति ॥
तच्छ्रुत्वापि तथैवासीत्स तूष्णीं सातवाहनः ।
शर्ववर्मा ततश्चेदमद्भुतं वाक्यमब्रवीत् ॥
श्रुतिमन्तं मां कुर्विति प्रागुक्तं देव मे त्वया ।
तेनाहं कृतवानद्य स्वप्नमाणवकं निशि ॥
स्वप्ने ततो मया दृष्टं नभसश्च्युतमम्बुजम् ।
तच्च दिव्येन केनापि कुमारेण विकासितम् ॥
ततश्च निर्गता तस्माद्दिव्या स्त्री धवलाम्बरा ।
तव देव मुखं सा च प्रविष्टा समनन्तरम् ॥
इयद्दृष्ट्वा प्रबुद्धो ऽस्मि सा च मन्ये सरस्वती ।
देवस्य वदने साक्षात्संप्रविष्टा न संशयः ॥
एवं निवेदितस्वप्ने शर्ववर्मणि तत्क्षणम् ।
मामस्तमौनः साकूतमवदत्सातवाहनः ॥
शिक्ष्यमाणः प्रयत्नेन कालेन कियता पुमान् ।
अधिगच्छति पाण्डित्यमेतन्मे कथ्यतां त्वया ॥
मम तेन विना ह्येषा लक्ष्मीर्न प्रतिभासते ।
विभवैः किं नु मूर्खस्य काष्ठस्याभरणैरिव ॥
ततो ऽहमवदं राजन्वर्षैर्द्वादशभिः सदा ।
ज्ञायते सर्वविद्यानां मुखं व्याकरणं नरैः ॥
अहं तु शिक्षयामि त्वां वर्षषट्केन तद्विभो ।

श्रुत्वैतत्सहसा सेर्ष्यं शर्ववर्मा किलावदत् ॥
सुखोचितो जनः क्लेशं कथं कुर्यादियच्चिरम् ।
तदहं मासषट्केन देव त्वां शिक्षयामि तत् ॥
श्रुत्वैवैतदसंभाव्यं तमवोचमहं रुषा ।
षड्भिर्मासैस्त्वया देवः शिक्षितश्चेत्ततो मया ॥
संस्कृतं प्राकृतं तद्वद्देशभाषा च सर्वदा ।
भाषात्रयमिदं त्यक्तं यन्मनुष्येषु संभवेत् ॥
शर्ववर्मा ततोऽवादीन्न चेदेवं करोम्यहम् ।
द्वादशाब्दान्वहाम्येष शिरसा तव पादुके ॥
इत्युक्त्वा निर्गते तस्मिन्नहमप्यगमं गृहम् ।
राजाप्युभयतः सिद्धिं मत्वा शस्तो बभूव सः ॥
शर्ववर्मा च वीहस्तः प्रतिज्ञां तां सुदुस्तराम् ।
पश्यन्सानुशयः सर्वं स्वभार्यायै शशंस तत् ॥
सापि तं दुःखितावोचत्संकटेऽस्मिंस्तव प्रभो ।
विना स्वामिकुमारेण गतिरन्या न दृश्यते ॥
तथेति निश्चयं कृत्वा पश्चिमे प्रहरे निशि ।
शर्ववर्मा निराहारस्तत्रैव प्रस्थितोऽभवत् ॥
सोऽपि वातैकभक्षः सन्कृतमौनः सुनिश्चयः ।
प्राप स्वामिकुमारस्य शर्ववर्मान्तिकं क्रमात् ॥
शरीरनिरपेक्षेण तपसा तत्र तोषितः ।
प्रसादमकरोत्तस्य कार्त्तिकेयो यथेप्सितम् ॥
आगत्य शर्ववर्माथ कुमारवरसिद्धिमान् ।
चिन्तितोपस्थिता राज्ञे सर्वा विद्याः प्रदत्तवान् ॥

प्रादुरासंश्च तास्तस्य सातवाहनभूपतेः ।
तत्क्षणं किं न कुर्याद्धि प्रसादः पारमेश्वरः ॥

XXVII.

एवं गुणाढ्यवचसा साथ सप्तकथामयी ।
स्वभाषया कथा दिव्या कथिता काणभूतिना ॥
तथैव च गुणाढ्येन पैशाच्या भाषया तया ।
निबद्धा सप्तभिर्वर्षैर्ग्रन्थलक्षाणि सप्त सा ॥
मैतां विद्याधरा हार्षुरिति तामात्मशोणितैः ।
अटव्यां मष्यभावाच्च लिलेख स महाकविः ॥
तथा च श्रोतुमायातैः सिद्धविद्याधरादिभिः ।
निरन्तरमभूत्तच्च सवितानमिवाम्बरम् ॥
गुणाढ्येन निबद्धां च तां दृष्ट्वैव महाकथाम् ।
जगाम मुक्तशापः सन्काणभूतिर्निजां गतिम् ॥
पिशाचा ये ऽपि तत्रासन्नन्ये तत्सहचारिणः ।
ते ऽपि प्रापुर्दिवं सर्वे दिव्यामाकर्ण्य तां कथाम् ॥
प्रतिष्ठां प्रापणीयैषा पृथिव्यां मे बृहत्कथा ।
अयमर्थो ऽपि मे देव्या शापान्तोक्तावुदीरितः ॥
तत्कथं प्रापयाम्येनां कस्मै तावत्समर्पये ।
इत्येवाचिन्तयत्तच्च स गुणाढ्यो महाकविः ॥
अथैको गुणदेवाख्यो नन्दिदेवाभिधः परः ।
तमूचतुरुपाध्यायं शिष्यावनुगतावुभौ ॥

तत्काव्यस्यार्पणस्थानमेकः श्रीसातवाहनः ।
रसिको हि वहेत्काव्यं पुष्पामोदमिवानिलः ॥
एवमस्त्विति तौ शिष्यावन्तिकं तस्य भूपतेः ।
प्राहिणोत्पुस्तकं दत्त्वा गुणाढ्यो गुणशालिनौ ॥
स्वयं च गत्वा तत्रैव प्रतिष्ठाने पुराद्बहिः ।
कृतसंकेत उद्याने तस्थौ देवीविनिर्मिते ॥
तच्छिष्याभ्यां च गत्वा तत्सातवाहनभूपतेः ।
गुणाढ्यकृतिरेषेति दर्शितं काव्यपुस्तकम् ॥
पिशाचभाषां तां श्रुत्वा तौ च दृष्ट्वा तदाकृती ।
विद्यामदेन सासूयं स राजैवमभाषत ॥
प्रमाणं सप्त लक्षाणि पैशाचं नीरसं वचः ।
शोणितेनाक्षरन्यासो धिक्पिशाचकथामिमाम् ॥
ततः पुस्तकमादाय गत्वा ताभ्यां यथागतम् ।
शिष्याभ्यां तद्गुणाढ्याय यथावृत्तमकथ्यत ॥
गुणाढ्यो ऽपि तदाकर्ण्य सद्यः खेदवशो ऽभवत् ।
तत्त्वज्ञेन कृतावज्ञः को नामान्तर्न तप्यते ॥
सशिष्यश्च ततो गत्वा नातिदूरं शिलोच्चयम् ।
विविक्तरम्यभूभागमग्निकुण्डं व्यधात्पुरः ॥
तत्राग्नौ पत्त्रमेकैकं शिष्याभ्यां साश्रु वीक्षितः ।
वाचयित्वा स चिक्षेप श्रावयन्मृगपक्षिणः ॥
नरवाहनदत्तस्य चरितं शिष्ययोः कृते ।
ग्रन्थलक्षं कथामेकां वर्जयित्वा तदीप्सिताम् ॥
तस्मिंश्च तां कथां दिव्यां पठत्यपि दहत्यपि ।

परित्यक्ततृणाहाराः शृण्वन्तः साश्रुलोचनाः ॥
आसन्नभ्येत्य तत्रैव निश्चला बद्धमण्डलाः ।
निखिलाः खलु सारङ्गवराहमहिषादयः ॥
अत्रान्तरे स राजाभूदस्वस्थः सातवाहनः ।
दोषं चास्यावदन्वैद्याः शुष्कमांसोपभोगजम् ॥
आक्षिप्तास्तन्निमित्तं च सूपकारा बभाषिरे ।
अस्माकमीदृशं मांसं ददते लुब्धका इति ॥
पृष्टाश्च लुब्धका ऊचुर्नातिदूरे गिरावितः ।
पठित्वा पत्रमेकैकं को ऽप्यग्नौ क्षिपति द्विजः ॥
तत्समेत्य निराहाराः शृण्वन्ति प्राणिनो ऽखिलाः ।
नान्यतो यान्ति तेनैषां शुष्कं मांसमिदं क्षुधा ॥
इति व्याधवचः श्रुत्वा कृत्वा तानेव चाग्रतः ।
स्वयं स कौतुकाद्राजा गुणाढ्यस्यान्तिकं ययौ ॥
ददर्श तं समाकीर्णं जटाभिर्वनवासतः ।
प्रशान्तशेषशापाग्निधूमिकाभिरिवाभितः ॥
अथैनं प्रत्यभिज्ञाय सबाष्पमृगमध्यगम् ।
नमस्कृत्य च पप्रच्छ तं वृत्तान्तं महीपतिः ॥
सो ऽपि स्वं पुष्पदन्तस्य राज्ञे शापादिचेष्टितम् ।
ज्ञानी कथावतारं तमाचख्यौ भूतभाषया ॥
ततो गणावतारं तं मत्वा पादानतो नृपः ।
ययाचे तां कथां तस्माद्दिव्यां हरमुखोद्गताम् ॥
अथोवाच स तं भूपं गुणाढ्यः सातवाहनम् ।
राजन्षड्ग्रन्थलक्षाणि मया दग्धानि षट्कथाः ॥

लक्ष्मेकमिदं त्वस्ति कथैका सैव गृह्यताम् ।
मच्छिष्यौ तव चात्रैतौ व्याख्यातारौ भविष्यतः ॥
इत्युक्त्वा नृपमामन्त्र्य त्यक्त्वा योगेन तां तनुम् ।
गुणाढ्यः शापनिर्मुक्तः प्राप दिव्यं निजं पदम् ॥
अथ तां गुणाढ्यदत्तामादाय कथां बृहत्कथां नाम्ना ।
नृपतिरगान्निजनगरं नरवाहनदत्तचरितमयीम् ॥
गुणदेवनन्दिदेवौ तत्र च तौ तत्कथाकवेः शिष्यौ ।
क्षितिकनकवस्त्रवाहनभवनधनैः संविभेजे सः ॥
ताभ्यां सह च कथां तामाश्वास्य स सातवाहनस्तस्याः ।
तद्भाषयावतारं वक्तुं चक्रे कथापीठम् ॥
सा च चित्ररसनिर्भरा कथा विस्मृतामरकथा कुतूहलात् ।
तद्विधाय नगरे निरन्तरां ख्यातिमत्र भुवनत्रये गता ॥

॥ इति कथासरित्सागरे ऽष्टमस्तरङ्गः ॥

XXVIII.

॥ अथ मानवधर्मशास्त्रम् ॥

आसीदिदं तमोभूतमप्रज्ञातमलक्षणम् ।
अप्रतर्क्यमविज्ञेयं प्रसुप्तमिव सर्वतः ॥५॥ ॥ अध्या० १ ॥
ततः स्वयंभूर्भगवानव्यक्तो व्यञ्जयन्निदम् ।
महाभूतादि वृत्तौजाः प्रादुरासीत्तमोनुदः ॥६॥
यो ऽसावतीन्द्रियग्राह्यः सूक्ष्मो ऽव्यक्तः सनातनः ।
सर्वभूतमयो ऽचिन्त्यः स एव स्वयमुद्बभौ ॥७॥

सो ऽभिध्याय शरीरात्स्वात्सिसृक्षुर्विविधाः प्रजाः ।
अप एव ससर्जादौ तासु बीजमवासृजत् ॥८॥
तदण्डमभवद्धैमं सहस्रांशुसमप्रभम् ।
तस्मिञ्जज्ञे स्वयं ब्रह्मा सर्वलोकपितामहः ॥९॥
आपो नारा इति प्रोक्ता आपो वै नरसूनवः ।
ता यदस्यायनं पूर्वं तेन नारायणः स्मृतः ॥१०॥
यत्तत्कारणमव्यक्तं नित्यं सदसदात्मकम् ।
तद्विसृष्टः स पुरुषो लोके ब्रह्मेति कीर्त्यते ॥११॥
तस्मिन्नण्डे स भगवानुषित्वा परिवत्सरम् ।
स्वयमेवात्मनो ध्यानात्तदण्डमकरोद्द्विधा ॥१२॥
ताभ्यां स शकलाभ्यां च दिवं भूमिं च निर्ममे ।
मध्ये व्योम दिशश्चाष्टावपां स्थानं च शाश्वतम् ॥१३॥
अग्निवायुरविभ्यस्तु त्रयं ब्रह्म सनातनम् ।
दुदोह यज्ञसिद्ध्यर्थमृग्यजुःसामलक्षणम् ॥२३॥
लोकानां तु विवृद्ध्यर्थं मुखबाहूरुपादतः ।
ब्राह्मणं क्षत्रियं वैश्यं शूद्रं च निरवर्तयत् ॥३१॥
अहोरात्रे विभजते सूर्यो मानुषदैविके ।
रात्रिः स्वप्नाय भूतानां चेष्टायै कर्मणामहः ॥६५॥
पित्र्ये रात्र्यहनी मासः प्रविभागस्तु पक्षयोः ।
कर्मचेष्टास्वहः कृष्णः शुक्लः स्वप्नाय शर्वरी ॥६६॥
दैवे रात्र्यहनी वर्षं प्रविभागस्तयोः पुनः ।
अहस्तत्रोदगयनं रात्रिः स्याद्दक्षिणायनम ॥६७॥
ब्राह्मस्य तु क्षपाहस्य यत्प्रमाणं समासतः ।

एकैकशो युगानां तु क्रमशस्तन्निबोधत ॥६८॥
चत्वार्याहुः सहस्राणि वर्षाणां तु कृतं युगम् ।
तस्य तावच्छती संध्या संध्यांशश्च तथाविधः ॥६९॥
इतरेषु ससंध्येषु ससंध्यांशेषु च त्रिषु ।
एकापायेन वर्तन्ते सहस्राणि शतानि च ॥७०॥
यदेतत्परिसंख्यातमादावेव चतुर्युगम् ।
एतद्द्वादशसाहस्रं देवानां युगमुच्यते ॥७१॥
दैविकानां युगानां तु सहस्रं परिसंख्यया ।
ब्राह्ममेकमहर्ज्ञेयं तावती रात्रिरेव च ॥७२॥

भूतानां प्राणिनः श्रेष्ठाः प्राणिनां बुद्धिजीविनः ।
बुद्धिमत्सु नराः श्रेष्ठा नरेषु ब्राह्मणाः स्मृताः ॥९६॥
ब्राह्मणेषु च विद्वांसो विद्वत्सु कृतबुद्धयः ।
कृतबुद्धिषु कर्तारः कर्तृषु ब्रह्मवेदिनः ॥९७॥

वेदो ऽखिलो धर्ममूलं स्मृतिशीले च तद्विदाम् ।
आचारश्चैव साधूनामात्मनस्तुष्टिरेव च ॥६॥ ॥अध्या॰ २॥
श्रुतिस्मृत्युदितं धर्ममनुतिष्ठन्हि मानवः ।
इह कीर्तिमवाप्नोति प्रेत्य चानुत्तमं सुखम् ॥९॥
श्रुतिस्तु वेदो विज्ञेयो धर्मशास्त्रं तु वै स्मृतिः ।
ते सर्वार्थेष्वमीमांस्ये ताभ्यां धर्मो हि निर्बभौ ॥१०॥
यो ऽवमन्येत ते मूले हेतुशास्त्राश्रयाद्द्विजः ।
स साधुभिर्बहिष्कार्यो नास्तिको वेदनिन्दकः ॥११॥
वेदः स्मृतिः सदाचारः स्वस्य च प्रियमात्मनः ।
एतच्चतुर्विधं प्राहुः साक्षाद्धर्मस्य लक्षणम् ॥१२॥

वैदिकैः कर्मभिः पुण्यैर्निषेकादिर्द्विजन्मनाम् ।
कार्यः शरीरसंस्कारः पावनः प्रेत्य चेह च ॥२६॥
गार्भैर्होमैर्जातकर्मचौडमौञ्जीनिबन्धनैः ।
बैजिकं गार्भिकं चैनो द्विजानामपमृज्यते ॥२७॥
स्वाध्यायेन व्रतैर्होमैस्त्रैविद्येनेज्यया सुतैः ।
महायज्ञैश्च यज्ञैश्च ब्राह्मीयं क्रियते तनुः ॥२८॥
प्राङ्नाभिवर्धनात्पुंसो जातकर्म विधीयते ।
मन्त्रवत्प्राशनं चास्य हिरण्यमधुसर्पिषाम् ॥२९॥
नामधेयं दशम्यां तु द्वादश्यां वास्य कारयेत् ।
पुण्ये तिथौ मुहूर्ते वा नक्षत्रे वा गुणान्विते ॥३०॥
मङ्गल्यं ब्राह्मणस्य स्यात्क्षत्रियस्य बलान्वितम् ।
वैश्यस्य धनसंयुक्तं शूद्रस्य तु जुगुप्सितम् ॥३१॥
शर्मवद्ब्राह्मणस्य स्याद्राज्ञो रक्षासमन्वितम् ।
वैश्यस्य पुष्टिसंयुक्तं शूद्रस्य प्रैष्यसंयुतम् ॥३२॥
स्त्रीणां सुखोद्यमक्रूरं विस्पष्टार्थं मनोहरम् ।
मङ्गल्यं दीर्घवर्णान्तमाशीर्वादाभिधानवत् ॥३३॥
चतुर्थे मासि कर्तव्यं शिशोर्निष्क्रमणं गृहात् ।
षष्ठे ऽन्नप्राशनं मासि यद्वेष्टं मङ्गलं कुले ॥३४॥
चूडाकर्म द्विजातीनां सर्वेषामेव धर्मतः ।
प्रथमे ऽब्दे तृतीये वा कर्तव्यं श्रुतिचोदनात् ॥३५॥
गर्भाष्टमे ऽब्दे कुर्वीत ब्राह्मणस्योपनायनम् ।
गर्भादेकादशे राज्ञो गर्भात्तु द्वादशे विशः ॥३६॥
प्रतिगृह्येप्सितं दण्डमुपस्थाय च भास्करम् ।

प्रदक्षिणं परीत्याग्निं चरेद्भैक्षं यथाविधि ॥४८॥
भवत्पूर्वं चरेद्भैक्षमुपनीतो द्विजोत्तमः ।
भवन्मध्यं तु राजन्यो वैश्यस्तु भवदुत्तरम् ॥४९॥
व्यत्यस्तपाणिना कार्यमुपसंग्रहणं गुरोः ।
सव्येन सव्यः स्प्रष्टव्यो दक्षिणेन च दक्षिणः ॥७२॥
अध्येष्यमाणं तु गुरुर्नित्यकालमतन्द्रितः ।
अधीष्व भो इति ब्रूयाद्विरामो ऽस्त्विति चारमेत् ॥७३॥
ब्राह्मणः प्रणवं कुर्यादादावन्ते च सर्वदा ।
स्रवत्यनोंकृतं पूर्वं परस्ताच्च विशीर्यते ॥७४॥
अकारं चाप्युकारं च मकारं च प्रजापतिः ।
वेदत्रयान्निरदुहद्भूर्भुवः स्वरितीति च ॥७६॥
त्रिभ्य एव तु वेदेभ्यः पादं पादमदूदुहत् ।
तदित्यृचो ऽस्याः सावित्र्याः परमेष्ठी प्रजापतिः ॥७७॥
एतदक्षरमेतां च जपन्व्याहृतिपूर्विकाम् ।
संध्ययोर्वेदविद्विप्रो वेदपुण्येन युज्यते ॥७८॥
ऊर्ध्वं प्राणा ह्युत्क्रामन्ति यूनः स्थविर आयति ।
प्रत्युत्थानाभिवादाभ्यां पुनस्तान्प्रतिपद्यते ॥१२०॥
अभिवादनशीलस्य नित्यं वृद्धोपसेविनः ।
चत्वारि तस्य वर्धन्ते आयुर्विद्या यशो बलम् ॥१२१॥
अभिवादात्परं विप्रो ज्यायांसमभिवादयन् ।
असौ नामाहमस्मीति स्वं नाम परिकीर्तयेत् ॥१२२॥
नामधेयस्य ये के चिदभिवादं न जानते ।
तान्प्राज्ञो ऽहमिति ब्रूयात्स्त्रियः सर्वास्तथैव च ॥१२३॥

भोःशब्दं कीर्तयेदन्ते स्वस्य नाम्नो ऽभिवादने ।
नाम्नां स्वरूपभावो हि भोभाव ऋषिभिः स्मृतः ॥१२४॥
आयुष्मान्भव सौम्येति वाच्यो विप्रो ऽभिवादने ।
अकारश्चास्य नाम्नो ऽन्ते वाच्यः पूर्वाक्षरः प्लुतः ॥१२५॥
यो न वेत्त्यभिवादस्य विप्रः प्रत्यभिवादनम् ।
नाभिवाद्यः स विदुषा यथा शूद्रस्तथैव सः ॥१२६॥
ब्राह्मणं कुशलं पृच्छेत्क्षत्रबन्धुमनामयम् ।
वैश्यं क्षेमं समागम्य शूद्रमारोग्यमेव च ॥१२७॥
अवाच्यो दीक्षितो नाम्ना यवीयानपि यो भवेत् ।
भोभवत्पूर्वकं त्वेनमभिभाषेत धर्मवित् ॥१२८॥
परपत्नी तु या स्त्री स्यादसंबन्धा च योनितः ।
तां ब्रूयाद्भवतीत्येवं सुभगे भगिनीति च ॥१२९॥
मातुलांश्च पितृव्यांश्च श्वशुरानृत्विजो गुरून् ।
असावहमिति ब्रूयात्प्रत्युत्थाय यवीयसः ॥१३०॥
ब्राह्मस्य जन्मनः कर्ता स्वधर्मस्य च शासिता ।
बालो ऽपि विप्रो वृद्धस्य पिता भवति धर्मतः ॥१५०॥
अध्यापयामास पितॄन्शिशुराङ्गिरसः कविः ।
पुत्रका इति होवाच ज्ञानेन परिगृह्य तान् ॥१५१॥
ते तमर्थमपृच्छन्त देवानागतमन्यवः ।
देवाश्चैतान्समेत्योचुर्न्याय्यं वः शिशुरुक्तवान् ॥१५२॥
अज्ञो भवति वै बालः पिता भवति मन्त्रदः ।
अज्ञं हि बालमित्याहुः पितेत्येव तु मन्त्रदम् ॥१५३॥

षट्त्रिंशदाब्दिकं चर्यं गुरौ त्रैवेदिकं व्रतम् ।

तदर्धिकं पादिकं वा ग्रहणान्तिकमेव वा ॥१॥ ॥अध्या° ३॥
वेदानधीत्य वेदौ वा वेदं वापि यथाक्रमम् ।
अविप्लुतब्रह्मचर्यो गृहस्थाश्रममावसेत् ॥२॥
तं प्रतीतं स्वधर्मेण ब्रह्मदायहरं पितुः ।
स्रग्विणं तल्प आसीनमर्हयेत्प्रथमं गवा ॥३॥
गुरुणानुमतः स्नात्वा समावृत्तो यथाविधि ।
उद्वहेत द्विजो भार्यां सवर्णां लक्षणान्विताम् ॥४॥
सर्वान्परित्यजेदर्थान्स्वाध्यायस्य विरोधिनः ।
यथा तथाध्यापयंस्तु सा ह्यस्य कृतकृत्यता ॥१७॥ अध्या° ४॥
क्लृप्तकेशनखश्मश्रुर्दान्तः शुक्लाम्बरः शुचिः ।
स्वाध्याये चैव युक्तः स्यान्नित्यमात्महितेषु च ॥३५॥
वैणवीं धारयेद्यष्टिं सोदकं च कमण्डलुम् ।
यज्ञोपवीतं वेदं च शुभे रौक्मे च कुण्डले ॥३६॥
नेक्षेतोद्यन्तमादित्यं नास्तं यान्तं कदा चन ।
नोपसृष्टं न वारिस्थं न मध्यं नभसो गतम् ॥३७॥
न लङ्घयेद्वत्सतन्त्रीं न प्रधावेच्च वर्षति ।
न चोदके निरीक्षेत स्वं रूपमिति धारणा ॥३८॥
मृदं गां दैवतं विप्रं घृतं मधु चतुष्पथम् ।
प्रदक्षिणानि कुर्वीत प्रज्ञातांश्च वनस्पतीन् ॥३९॥
वाय्वग्निविप्रमादित्यमपः पश्यंस्तथैव गाः ।
न कदा चन कुर्वीत विण्मूत्रस्य विसर्जनम् ॥४८॥
मूत्रोच्चारसमुत्सर्गं दिवा कुर्यादुदङ्मुखः ।
दक्षिणाभिमुखो रात्रौ संध्ययोश्च यथा दिवा ॥५०॥

न वारयेद्गां धयन्तीं न चाचक्षीत कस्य चित् ।
न दिवीन्द्रायुधं दृष्ट्वा कस्य चिद्दर्शयेद्बुधः ॥५९॥
सामध्वनावृग्यजुषी नाधीयीत कदा चन ।
वेदस्याधीत्य वाप्यन्तमारण्यकमधीत्य च ॥१२३॥
ऋग्वेदो देवदैवत्यो यजुर्वेदस्तु मानुषः ।
सामवेदः स्मृतः पित्र्यस्तस्मात्तस्याशुचिर्ध्वनिः ॥१२४॥
नाधर्मश्चरितो लोके सद्यः फलति गौरिव ।
शनैरावर्तमानस्तु कर्तुर्मूलानि कृन्तति ॥१७२॥
यदि नात्मनि पुत्रेषु न चेत्पुत्रेषु नप्तृषु ।
न त्वेव तु कृतो ऽधर्मः कर्तुर्भवति निष्फलः ॥१७३॥
धर्मं शनैः संचिनुयाद्वल्मीकमिव पुत्तिकाः ।
परलोकसहायार्थं सर्वभूतान्यपीडयन् ॥२३८॥
नामुत्र हि सहायार्थं पिता माता च तिष्ठतः ।
न पुत्रदारं न ज्ञातिर्धर्मस्तिष्ठति केवलः ॥२३९॥
एकः प्रजायते जन्तुरेक एव प्रलीयते ।
एको ऽनुभुङ्क्ते सुकृतमेक एव च दुष्कृतम् ॥२४०॥
मृतं शरीरमुत्सृज्य काष्ठलोष्टसमं क्षितौ ।
विमुखा बान्धवा यान्ति धर्मस्तमनुगच्छति ॥२४१॥
तस्माद्धर्मं सहायार्थं नित्यं संचिनुयाच्छनैः ।
धर्मेण हि सहायेन तमस्तरति दुस्तरम् ॥२४२॥
प्राणस्यान्नमिदं सर्वं प्रजापतिरकल्पयत् ।
स्थावरं जङ्गमं चैव सर्वं प्राणस्य भोजनम् ॥२८॥ अध्या० ५॥
चराणामन्नमचरा दंष्ट्रिणामप्यदंष्ट्रिणः ।

अहस्ताश्च सहस्तानां शूराणां चैव भीरवः ॥२९॥
कुर्याद्घृतपशुं सङ्गे कुर्यात्पिष्टपशुं तथा ।
न त्वेव तु वृथा हन्तुं पशुमिच्छेत्कदा चन ॥३७॥
यावन्ति पशुरोमाणि तावत्कृत्वो ह मारणम् ।
वृथापशुघ्नः प्राप्नोति प्रेत्य जन्मनि जन्मनि ॥३८॥
मां स भक्षयितामुत्र यस्य मांसमिहाद्म्यहम् ।
एतन्मांसस्य मांसत्वं प्रवदन्ति मनीषिणः ॥५५॥

नास्ति स्त्रीणां पृथग्यज्ञो न व्रतं नाप्युपोषितम् ।
पतिं शुश्रूषते येन तेन स्वर्गे महीयते ॥१५५॥
पाणिग्राहस्य साध्वी स्त्री जीवतो वा मृतस्य वा ।
पतिलोकमभीप्सन्ती नाचरेत्किं चिदप्रियम् ॥१५६॥
कामं तु क्षपयेद्देहं पुष्पमूलफलैः शुभैः ।
न तु नामापि गृह्णीयात्पत्यौ प्रेते परस्य तु ॥१५७॥
आसीता मरणात्क्षान्ता नियता ब्रह्मचारिणी ।
यो धर्म एकपत्नीनां काङ्क्षन्ती तमनुत्तमम् ॥१५८॥

एवं गृहाश्रमे स्थित्वा विधिवत्स्नातको द्विजः ।
वने वसेत्तु नियतो यथावद्विजितेन्द्रियः ॥१॥ ॥अध्या० ६॥
वसीत चर्म चीरं वा सायं स्नायात्प्रगे तथा ।
जटाश्च बिभृयान्नित्यं श्मश्रुलोमनखानि च ॥६॥
ग्रीष्मे पञ्चतपास्तु स्याद्वर्षास्वभ्रावकाशिकः ।
आर्द्रवासास्तु हेमन्ते क्रमशो वर्धयंस्तपः ॥२३॥

वनेषु तु विहृत्यैवं तृतीयं भागमायुषः ।
चतुर्थमायुषो भागं त्यक्त्वा सङ्गान्परिव्रजेत् ॥३३॥

आश्रमादाश्रमं गत्वा हुतहोमो जितेन्द्रियः ।
भिक्षाबलिपरिश्रान्तः प्रव्रजन्प्रेत्य वर्धते ॥ ३४ ॥
ब्रह्मचारी गृहस्थश्च वानप्रस्थो यतिस्तथा ।
एते गृहस्थप्रभवाश्चत्वारः पृथगाश्रमाः ॥ ८७ ॥
एकैकं ह्रासयेत्पिण्डं कृष्णे शुक्ले च वर्धयेत् ।
उपस्पृशंस्त्रिषवणमेतच्चान्द्रायणं स्मृतम् ॥ २१६ ॥ अध्या° ११ ॥
एतमेव विधिं कृत्स्नमाचरेद्यवमध्यमे ।
शुक्लपक्षादि नियतश्चरंश्चान्द्रायणं व्रतम् ॥ २१७ ॥
शुभाशुभफलं कर्म मनोवाग्देहसंभवम् ।
कर्मजा गतयो नृणामुत्तमाधममध्यमाः ॥ ३ ॥ ॥ अध्या° १२ ॥
तस्येह त्रिविधस्यापि त्र्यधिष्ठानस्य देहिनः ।
दशलक्षणयुक्तस्य मनो विद्यात्प्रवर्तकम् ॥ ४ ॥
परद्रव्येष्वभिध्यानं मनसानिष्टचिन्तनम् ।
वितथाभिनिवेशश्च त्रिविधं कर्म मानसम् ॥ ५ ॥
पारुष्यमनृतं चैव पैशुन्यं चापि सर्वशः ।
असंबद्धप्रलापश्च वाङ्मयं स्याच्चतुर्विधम् ॥ ६ ॥
अदत्तानामुपादानं हिंसा चैवाविधानतः ।
परदारोपसेवा च शारीरं त्रिविधं स्मृतम् ॥ ७ ॥
मानसं मनसैवायमुपभुङ्क्ते शुभाशुभम् ।
वाचा वाचा कृतं कर्म कायेनैव च कायिकम् ॥ ८ ॥
शरीरजैः कर्मदोषैर्याति स्थावरतां नरः ।
वाचिकैः पक्षिमृगतां मानसैरन्त्यजातिताम् ॥ ९ ॥
यद्याचरति धर्मं स प्रायशोऽधर्ममल्पशः ।

तैरेव चावृतो भूतैः स्वर्गे सुखमुपाश्नुते ॥२०॥
यदि तु प्रायशो ऽधर्मं सेवते धर्ममल्पशः ।
तैर्भूतैः स परित्यक्तो यामीः प्राप्नोति यातनाः ॥२१॥
यामीस्ता यातनाः प्राप्य स जीवो वीतकल्मषः ।
तान्येव पञ्च भूतानि पुनरभ्येति भागशः ॥२२॥
एता दृष्ट्वास्य जीवस्य गतीः स्वेनैव चेतसा ।
धर्मतो ऽधर्मतश्चैव धर्मे दध्यात्सदा मनः ॥२३॥
सत्त्वं रजस्तमश्चैव त्रीन्विद्यादात्मनो गुणान् ।
यैर्व्याप्येमान्स्थितो भावान्महान्सर्वानशेषतः ॥२४॥
यत्कर्म कृत्वा कुर्वंश्च करिष्यंश्चैव लज्जते ।
तज्ज्ञेयं विदुषा सर्वं तामसं गुणलक्षणम् ॥३५॥
येनास्मिन्कर्मणा लोके ख्यातिमिच्छति पुष्कलाम् ।
न च शोचत्यसंपत्तौ तद्विज्ञेयं तु राजसम् ॥३६॥
यत्सर्वेणेच्छति ज्ञातं यन्न लज्जति चाचरन् ।
येन तुष्यति चात्मास्य तत्सत्त्वगुणलक्षणम् ॥३७॥
तमसो लक्षणं कामो रजसस्त्वर्थ उच्यते ।
सत्त्वस्य लक्षणं धर्मः श्रैष्ठ्यमेषां यथाक्रमम् ॥३८॥
येन यांस्तु गुणेनैषां संसारान्प्रतिपद्यते ।
तान्समासेन वक्ष्यामि सर्वस्यास्य यथाक्रमम् ॥३९॥
देवत्वं सात्त्विका यान्ति मनुष्यत्वं च राजसाः ।
तिर्यक्त्वं तामसा नित्यमित्येषा त्रिविधा गतिः ॥४०॥
त्रिविधा त्रिविधैषां तु विज्ञेया गौणिकी गतिः ॥
अधमा मध्यमाग्र्या च कर्मविद्याविशेषतः ॥४१॥

स्थावराः कृमिकीटाश्च मत्स्याः सर्पाः सकच्छपाः।
पशवश्च मृगाश्चैव जघन्या तामसी गतिः ॥४२॥
हस्तिनश्च तुरंगाश्च शूद्रा म्लेच्छाश्च गर्हिताः।
सिंहा व्याघ्रा वराहाश्च मध्यमा तामसी गतिः ॥४३॥
चारणाश्च सुपर्णाश्च पुरुषाश्चैव दाम्भिकाः।
रक्षांसि च पिशाचाश्च तामसीषूत्तमा गतिः ॥४४॥
झल्ला मल्ला नटाश्चैव पुरुषाः शस्त्रवृत्तयः।
द्यूतपानप्रसक्ताश्च जघन्या राजसी गतिः ॥४५॥
राजानः क्षत्रियाश्चैव राज्ञां चैव पुरोहिताः।
वादयुद्धप्रधानाश्च मध्यमा राजसी गतिः ॥४६॥
गन्धर्वा गुह्यका यक्षा विबुधानुचराश्च ये।
तथैवाप्सरसः सर्वा राजसीषूत्तमा गतिः ॥४७॥
तापसा यतयो विप्रा ये च वैमानिका गणाः।
नक्षत्राणि च दैत्याश्च प्रथमा सात्त्विकी गतिः ॥४८॥
यज्वान ऋषयो देवा वेदा ज्योतींषि वत्सराः।
पितरश्चैव साध्याश्च द्वितीया सात्त्विकी गतिः ॥४९॥
ब्रह्मा विश्वसृजो धर्मो महानव्यक्त एव च।
उत्तमां सात्त्विकीमेतां गतिमाहुर्मनीषिणः ॥५०॥
श्वसूकरखरोष्ट्राणां गोऽजाविमृगपक्षिणाम्।
चण्डालपुल्कसानां च ब्रह्महा योनिमृच्छति ॥५५॥
हिंस्रा भवन्ति क्रव्यादाः कृमयोऽभक्ष्यभक्षिणः।
परस्परादिनः स्तेनाः प्रेता ऽन्यस्त्रीनिषेविणः ॥५९॥
धान्यं हृत्वा भवत्याखुः कांस्यं हंसो जलं प्लवः।

मधु दंशः पयः काको रसं श्वा नकुलो घृतम् ॥ ६२॥
छुच्छुन्दरिः शुभान्गन्धान्पत्त्रशाकं तु बर्हिणः ।
श्वावित्कृतान्नं विविधमकृतान्नं तु शल्यकः ॥ ६५ ॥
स्त्रियो ऽप्येतेन कल्पेन हृत्वा दोषमवाप्नुयुः ।
एतेषामेव जन्तूनां भार्यात्वमुपयान्ति ताः ॥ ६९ ॥
वेदाभ्यासस्तपो ज्ञानमिन्द्रियाणां च संयमः ।
अहिंसा गुरुसेवा च निःश्रेयसकरं परम् ॥ ८३॥
प्रवृत्तं कर्म संसेव्य देवानामेति साम्यताम् ।
निवृत्तं सेवमानस्तु भूतान्यत्येति पञ्च वै ॥ ९०॥
या वेदबाह्याः स्मृतयो याश्च काश्च कुदृष्टयः ।
सर्वास्ता निष्फलाः प्रेत्य तमोनिष्ठा हि ताः स्मृताः ॥ ९५॥
उत्पद्यन्ते च्यवन्ते च यान्यतो ऽन्यानि कानि चित् ।
तान्यर्वाक्कालिकतया निष्फलान्यनृतानि च ॥ ९६॥
अज्ञेभ्यो ग्रन्थिनः श्रेष्ठा ग्रन्थिभ्यो धारिणो वराः ।
धारिभ्यो ज्ञानिनः श्रेष्ठा ज्ञानिभ्यो व्यवसायिनः ॥१०३॥

XXIX. XXX.

एकोना विंशतिर्नार्यैः क्रीडां कर्तुं वने गताः ।
विंशतिर्गृहमायाताः शेषो व्याघ्रेण भक्षितः ॥
समादिशत्पिता पुत्रं लिख लेखं ममाज्ञया ।
न तेन लिखितो लेखः पितुराज्ञा न खण्डिता ॥

XXXI. RIGVEDA I. 1.

अ॒ग्निमी॑ळे पु॒रोहि॑तं य॒ज्ञस्य॑ दे॒वमृ॒त्विज॑म् ।
होता॑रं रत्न॒धात॑मम् ॥१॥
अ॒ग्निः पूर्वे॑भि॒रृषि॑भि॒रीड्यो॒ नूत॑नैरु॒त ।
स दे॒वाँ एह व॑क्षति ॥२॥
अ॒ग्निना॑ र॒यिम॑श्नव॒त्पोष॑मे॒व दि॒वे दि॑वे ।
य॒शसं॑ वी॒रव॑त्तमम् ॥३॥
अग्ने॒ यं य॒ज्ञम॑ध्व॒रं वि॒श्वतः॑ परि॒भूरसि॑ ।
स इद्दे॒वेषु॑ गच्छति ॥४॥
अ॒ग्निर्होता॑ क॒विक्र॑तुः स॒त्यश्चि॒त्रश्र॑वस्तमः ।
दे॒वो दे॒वेभि॒रा ग॑मत् ॥५॥
यद॒ङ्ग दा॒शुषे॒ त्वमग्ने॑ भ॒द्रं क॑रि॒ष्यसि॑ ।
तवेत्तत्स॒त्यम॑ङ्गिरः ॥६॥
उप॑ त्वाग्ने दि॒वे दि॑वे॒ दोषा॑वस्तर्धि॒या व॒यम् ।
नमो॒ भर॑न्त॒ एम॑सि ॥७॥
राज॑न्तमध्व॒राणां॑ गो॒पामृ॒तस्य॒ दीदि॑विम् ।
वर्ध॑मानं॒ स्वे दमे॑ ॥८॥
स नः॑ पि॒तेव॑ सू॒नवेऽग्ने॑ सूपाय॒नो भ॑व ।
सच॑स्वा नः स्व॒स्तये॑ ॥९॥

XXXII. RIGVEDA I. 32.

इन्द्रस्य नु वीर्याणि प्र वोचं यानि चकार प्रथमानि वज्री ।
अहन्नहिमन्वपस्ततर्द प्र वक्षणा अभिनत्पर्वतानाम् ॥ १ ॥
अहन्नहिं पर्वते शिश्रियाणं त्वष्टास्मै वज्रं स्वर्यं ततक्ष ।
वाश्रा इव धेनवः स्यन्दमाना अञ्जः समुद्रमव जग्मुरापः ॥ २ ॥
वृषायमाणोऽवृणीत सोमं त्रिकद्रुकेष्वपिबत्सुतस्य ।
आ सायकं मघवादत्त वज्रमहन्नेनं प्रथमजामहीनाम् ॥ ३ ॥
यदिन्द्राहन्प्रथमजामहीनामान्मायिनाममिनाः प्रोत मायाः ।
आत्सूर्यं जनयन्द्यामुषासं तादीत्ना शत्रुं न किला विवित्से ॥ ४ ॥
अहन्वृत्रं वृत्रतरं व्यंसमिन्द्रो वज्रेण महता वधेन ।
स्कन्धांसीव कुलिशेना विवृक्णाहिः शयत उपपृक्पृथिव्याः ॥ ५ ॥
अयोद्धेव दुर्मद आ हि जुह्वे महावीरं तुविबाधमृजीषम् ।
नातारीदस्य समृतिं वधानां सं रुजानाः पिपिष इन्द्रशत्रुः ॥ ६ ॥
अपादहस्तो अपृतन्यदिन्द्रमास्य वज्रमधि सानौ जघान ।
वृष्णो वध्रिः प्रतिमानं बुभूषन्पुरुत्रा वृत्रो अशयद्व्यस्तः ॥ ७ ॥
नदं न भिन्नममुया शयानं मनो रुहाणा अति यन्त्यापः ।
याश्चिद्वृत्रो महिना पर्यतिष्ठत्तासामहिः पत्सुतःशीर्बभूव ॥ ८ ॥
नीचावया अभवद्वृत्रपुत्रेन्द्रो अस्या अव वधर्जभार ।
उत्तरा सूरधरः पुत्र आसीद्दानुः शये सहवत्सा न धेनुः ॥ ९ ॥
अतिष्ठन्तीनामनिवेशनानां काष्ठानां मध्ये निहितं शरीरम् ।
वृत्रस्य निण्यं वि चरन्त्यापो दीर्घं तम आशयदिन्द्रशत्रुः ॥ १० ॥
दासपत्नीरहिगोपा अतिष्ठन्निरुद्धा आपः पणिनेव गावः ।

अपां बिलमपिहितं यदासीद्वृत्रं जघन्वाँ अप तद्ववार ॥११॥
अश्व्यो वारो अभवस्तदिन्द्र सृके यत्त्वा प्रत्यहन्देव एकः ।
अजयो गा अजयः शूर सोममवासृजः सर्तवे सप्त सिन्धून् ॥१२॥
नास्मै विद्युन्न तन्यतुः सिषेध न यां मिहमकिरद्ध्रादुनिं च ।
इन्द्रश्च यद्युयुधाते अहिश्चोतापरीभ्यो मघवा वि जिग्ये ॥१३॥
अहेर्यातारं कमपश्य इन्द्र हृदि यत्ते जघ्नुषो भीरगच्छत् ।
नव च यन्नवतिं च स्रवन्तीः श्येनो न भीतो अतरो रजांसि ॥१४॥
इन्द्रो यातो ऽवसितस्य राजा शमस्य च शृङ्गिणो वज्रबाहुः ।
सेदु राजा क्षयति चर्षणीनामरान्न नेमिः परि ता बभूव ॥१५॥

XXXIII. RIGVEDA I. 50.

उदु त्यं जातवेदसं देवं वहन्ति केतवः ।
दृशे विश्वाय सूर्यम् ॥१॥
अप त्ये तायवो यथा नक्षत्रा यन्त्यक्तुभिः ।
सूराय विश्वचक्षसे ॥२॥
अदृश्रमस्य केतवो वि रश्मयो जनाँ अनु ।
भ्राजन्तो अग्नयो यथा ॥३॥
तरणिर्विश्वदर्शतो ज्योतिष्कृदसि सूर्य ।
विश्वमा भासि रोचनम् ॥४॥
प्रत्यङ्देवानां विशः प्रत्यङ्ङुदेषि मानुषान् ।
प्रत्यङ्विश्वं स्वर्दृशे ॥५॥
येना पावक चक्षसा भुरण्यन्तं जनाँ अनु ।

त्वं वरुण पश्यसि ॥ ६ ॥
वि द्यामेषि रजस्पृथ्वहा मिमानो अक्तुभिः ।
पश्यञ्जन्मानि सूर्य ॥ ७ ॥
सप्त त्वा हरितो रथे वहन्ति देव सूर्य ।
शोचिष्केशं विचक्षण ॥ ८ ॥
अयुक्त सप्त शुन्ध्युवः सूरो रथस्य नप्त्यः ।
ताभिर्याति स्वयुक्तिभिः ॥ ९ ॥

XXXIV. RIGVEDA I. 97.

अप नः शोशुचदघमग्ने शुशुग्ध्या रयिम् ।
अप नः शोशुचदघम् ॥ १ ॥
सुक्षेत्रिया सुगातुया वसूया च यजामहे ।
अप नः शोशुचदघम् ॥ २ ॥
प्र यद्भन्दिष्ठ एषां प्रास्माकासश्च सूरयः ।
अप नः शोशुचदघम् ॥ ३ ॥
प्र यत्ते अग्ने सूरयो जायेमहि प्र ते वयम् ।
अप नः शोशुचदघम् ॥ ४ ॥
प्र यदग्नेः सहस्वतो विश्वतो यन्ति भानवः ।
अप नः शोशुचदघम् ॥ ५ ॥
त्वं हि विश्वतोमुख विश्वतः परिभूरसि ।
अप नः शोशुचदघम् ॥ ६ ॥
द्विषो नो विश्वतोमुखाति नावेव पारय ।

अप नः शोशुचदघम् ॥७॥
स नः सिन्धुमिव नावयाति पर्षा स्वस्तये ।
अप नः शोशुचदघम् ॥८॥

XXXV. RIGVEDA I. 165.

कया शुभा सवयसः सनीळाः समान्या मरुतः सं मिमिक्षुः ।
कया मती कुत एतास एतेऽर्चन्ति शुष्मं वृषणो वसूया ॥१॥
कस्य ब्रह्माणि जुजुषुर्युवानः को अध्वरे मरुत आ ववर्त ।
श्येनाँ इव ध्रजतो अन्तरिक्षे केन महा मनसा रीरमाम ॥२॥
कुतस्त्वमिन्द्र माहिनः सन्नेको यासि सत्पते किं त इत्था ।
सं पृच्छसे समराणः शुभानैर्वोचेस्तन्नो हरिवो यत्ते अस्मे ॥३॥
ब्रह्माणि मे मतयः शं सुतासः शुष्म इयर्ति प्रभृतो मे अद्रिः ।
आ शासते प्रति हर्यन्त्युक्थेमा हरी वहतस्ता नो अच्छ ॥४॥
अतो वयमन्तमेभिर्युजानाः स्वक्षत्रेभिस्तन्व१ः शुम्भमानाः ।
महोभिरेताँ उप युज्महे न्विन्द्र स्वधामनु हि नो बभूथ ॥५॥
क्व१ स्या वो मरुतः स्वधासीद्यन्मामेकं समधत्ताहिहत्ये ।
अहं ह्यु१ग्रस्तविषस्तुविष्मान्विश्वस्य शत्रोरनमं वधस्नैः ॥६॥
भूरि चकर्थ युज्येभिरस्मे समानेभिर्वृषभ पौंस्येभिः ।
भूरीणि हि कृणवामा शविष्ठेन्द्र क्रत्वा मरुतो यद्वशाम ॥७॥
वधीं वृत्रं मरुत इन्द्रियेण स्वेन भामेन तविषो बभूवान् ।
अहमेता मनवे विश्वश्चन्द्राः सुगा अपश्चकर वज्रबाहुः ॥८॥
अनुत्तमा ते मघवन्नकिर्नु न त्वावाँ अस्ति देवता विदानः ।

न जायमानो नशते न जातो यानि करिष्या कृणुहि प्रवृद्ध ॥९॥
एकस्य चिन्मे विभ्व१स्त्वोजो या नु दधृष्वान्कृणवै मनीषा ।
अहं ह्यू१ग्रो मरुतो विदानो यानि च्यवमिन्द्र इदीश एषाम् ॥१०॥
अमन्दन्मा मरुत स्तोमो अत्र यन्मे नरः श्रुत्यं ब्रह्म चक्र ।
इन्द्राय वृष्णे सुमखाय मह्यं सख्ये सखायस्तन्वे तनूभिः ॥११॥
एवेदेते प्रति मा रोचमाना अनेद्यः श्रव एषो दधानाः ।
संचक्ष्या मरुतश्चन्द्रवर्णा अच्छान्त मे छदयाथा च नूनम् ॥१२॥
को न्वत्र मरुतो मामहे वः प्र यातन सखीँरच्छा सखायः ।
मन्मानि चित्रा अपिवातयन्त एषां भूत नवेदा म ऋतानाम् ॥१३॥
आ यद्दुवस्याद्दुवसे न कारुरस्माञ्चक्रे मान्यस्य मेधा ।
ओ षु वर्त्त मरुतो विप्रमच्छेमा ब्रह्माणि जरिता वो अर्चत् ॥१४॥
एष व स्तोमो मरुत इयं गीर्मान्दार्यस्य मान्यस्य कारोः ।
एषा यासीष्ट तन्वे वयां विद्यामेषं वृजनं जीरदानुम् ॥१५॥

XXXVI. RIGVEDA III. 62.

तत्सवितुर्वरेण्यं भर्गो देवस्य धीमहि ।
धियो यो नः प्रचोदयात् ॥१०॥
देवस्य सवितुर्वयं वाजयन्तः पुरंध्या ।
भगस्य रातिमीमहे ॥११॥
देवं नरः सवितारं विप्रा यज्ञैः सुवृक्तिभिः ।
नमस्यन्ति धियेषिताः ॥१२॥

XXXVII. RIGVEDA IV. 42.

मम द्विता राष्ट्रं क्षत्रियस्य विश्वायोर्विश्वे अमृता यथा नः ।
क्रतुं सचन्ते वरुणस्य देवा राजामि कृष्टेरुपमस्य वव्रेः ॥१॥
अहं राजा वरुणो मह्यं तान्यसुर्याणि प्रथमा धारयन्त ।
क्रतुं सचन्ते वरुणस्य देवा राजामि कृष्टेरुपमस्य वव्रेः ॥२॥
अहमिन्द्रो वरुणस्ते महित्वोर्वी गभीरे रजसी सुमेके ।
त्वष्टेव विश्वा भुवनानि विद्वान्समैरयं रोदसी धारयं च ॥३॥
अहमपो अपिन्वमुक्षमाणा धारयं दिवं सदन ऋतस्य ।
ऋतेन पुत्रो अदितेरृतावोत त्रिधातु प्रथयद्वि भूम ॥४॥
मां नरः स्वश्वा वाजयन्तो मां वृताः समरणे हवन्ते ।
कृणोम्याजिं मघवाहमिन्द्र इयर्मि रेणुमभिभूत्योजाः ॥५॥
अहं ता विश्वा चकरं नकिर्मा दैव्यं सहो वरते अप्रतीतम् ।
यन्मा सोमासो ममदन्यदुक्थोभे भयेते रजसी अपारे ॥६॥
विदुष्टे विश्वा भुवनानि तस्य ता प्र ब्रवीषि वरुणाय वेधः ।
त्वं वृत्राणि शृण्विषे जघन्वान्त्वं वृताँ अरिणा इन्द्र सिन्धून् ॥७॥

XXXVIII. RIGVEDA IV. 52.

प्रति ष्या सूनरी जनी व्युच्छन्ती परि स्वसुः ।
दिवो अदर्शि दुहिता ॥१॥
अश्वेव चित्रारुषी माता गवामृतावरी ।
सखाभूदश्विनोरुषाः ॥२॥
उत सखास्यश्विनोरुत माता गवामसि ।

उतोषो वस्व ईशिषे ॥३॥
यावयद्द्वेषसं त्वा चिकित्वित्सूनृतावरि ।
प्रति स्तोमैरभुत्स्महि ॥४॥
प्रति भद्रा अदृक्षत गवां सर्गा न रश्मयः ।
ओषा अप्रा उरु ज्रयः ॥५॥
आपप्रुषी विभावरि व्यावर्ज्योतिषा तमः ।
उषो अनु स्वधामव ॥६॥
आ द्यां तनोषि रश्मिभिरान्तरिक्षमुरु प्रियम् ।
उषः शुक्रेण शोचिषा ॥७॥

XXXIX. RIGVEDA V. 24.

अग्ने त्वं नो अन्तम उत त्राता शिवो भवा वरूथ्यः ॥१॥
वसुरग्निर्वसुश्रवा अच्छा नक्षि द्युमत्तमं रयिं दाः ॥२॥
स नो बोधि श्रुधी हवमुरुष्या णो अघायतः समस्मात् ॥३॥
तं त्वा शोचिष्ठ दीदिवः सुम्नाय नूनमीमहे सखिभ्यः ॥४॥

XL. RIGVEDA V. 40.

स्वर्भानोरध यदिन्द्र माया अवो दिवो वर्तमाना अवाहन् ।
गूळ्हं सूर्यं तमसापव्रतेन तुरीयेण ब्रह्मणाविन्दद्त्रिः ॥६॥
मा मामिमं तव सन्तमत्र इरस्या द्रुग्धो भियसा नि गारीत् ।
त्वं मित्रो असि सत्यराधास्तौ मेहावतं वरुणश्च राजा ॥७॥
ग्राव्णो ब्रह्मा युयुजानः सपर्यन्कीरिणा देवान्नमसोपशिक्षन् ॥

अत्रिः सूर्यस्य दिवि चक्षुराधात्स्वर्भानोरप माया अघुक्षत ॥८॥

XLI. RIGVEDA VII. 55.

अमीवहा वास्तोष्पते विश्वा रूपाण्याविशन् ।
सखा सुशेव एधि नः ॥१॥
यदर्जुन सारमेय दतः पिशङ्ग यच्छसे ।
वीव भ्राजन्त ऋष्टय उप स्रक्वेषु बप्सतो नि षु स्वप ॥२॥
स्तेनं राय सारमेय तस्करं वा पुनःसर ।
स्तोतॄनिन्द्रस्य रायसि किमस्मान्दुच्छुनायसे नि षु स्वप ॥३॥
त्वं सूकरस्य दर्दृहि तव दर्दर्तु सूकरः ।
स्तोतॄनिन्द्रस्य रायसि किमस्मान्दुच्छुनायसे नि षु स्वप ॥४॥
सस्तु माता सस्तु पिता सस्तु श्वा सस्तु विश्पतिः ।
ससन्तु सर्वे ज्ञातयः सस्त्वयमभितो जनः ॥५॥
य आस्ते यश्च चरति यश्च पश्यति नो जनः ।
तेषां सं हन्मो अक्षाणि यथेदं हर्म्यं तथा ॥६॥
सहस्रशृङ्गो वृषभो यः समुद्रादुदाचरत् ।
तेना सहस्येना वयं नि जनान्स्वापयामसि ॥७॥
प्रोष्ठेशया वह्येशया नारीर्यास्तल्पशीवरीः ।
स्त्रियो याः पुण्यगन्धास्ताः सर्वाः स्वापयामसि ॥८॥

XLII. RIGVEDA VII. 56.

क ईं व्यक्ता नरः सनीळा रुद्रस्य मर्या अधा स्वश्वाः ॥१॥

नकिर्ह्येषां जनूंषि वेद ते अङ्ग विद्रे मिथो जनित्रम् ॥२॥
अभि स्वपूभिर्मिथो वपन्त वातस्वनसः श्येना अस्पृध्रन् ॥३॥
एतानि धीरो निण्या चिकेत पृश्निर्यदूधो मही जभार ॥४॥
सा विट्सुवीरा मरुद्भिरस्तु सनात्सहन्ती पुष्यन्ती नृम्णम् ॥५॥
यामं येष्ठाः शुभा शोभिष्ठाः श्रिया संमिश्ला ओजोभिरुग्राः ॥
उग्रं व ओज स्थिरा शवांस्यधा मरुद्भिर्गणस्तुविष्मान् ॥७॥
शुभ्रो वः शुष्मः क्रुध्मी मनांसि धुनिर्मुनिरिव शर्धस्य धृष्णोः ॥
सनेम्यस्मद्युयोत दिद्युं मा वो दुर्मतिरिह प्रणङ्नः ॥९॥
प्रिया वो नाम हुवे तुराणामा यत्तृपन्मरुतो वावशानाः ॥१०॥

XLIII. RIGVEDA VII. 86.

धीरा त्वस्य महिना जनूंषि वि यस्तस्तम्भ रोदसी चिदुर्वी ।
प्र नाकमृष्वं नुनुदे बृहन्तं द्विता नक्षत्रं पप्रथच्च भूम ॥१॥
उत स्वया तन्वा३ सं वदे तत्कदा न्व१न्तर्वरुणे भुवानि ।
किं मे हव्यमहृणानो जुषेत कदा मृळीकं सुमना अभि ख्यम् ॥
पृच्छे तदेनो वरुण दिदृक्षूपो एमि चिकितुषो विपृच्छम् ।
समानमिन्मे कवयश्चिदाहुरयं ह तुभ्यं वरुणो हृणीते ॥३॥
किमाग आस वरुण ज्येष्ठं यत्स्तोतारं जिघांससि सखायम् ।
प्र तन्मे वोचो दूळभ स्वधावो ऽव त्वानेना नमसा तुर इयाम् ॥
अव द्रुग्धानि पित्र्या सृजा नो ऽव या वयं चकृमा तनूभिः ।
अव राजन्पशुतृपं न तायुं सृजा वत्सं न दाम्नो वसिष्ठम् ॥५॥
न स स्वो दक्षो वरुण ध्रुतिः सा सुरा मन्युर्विभीदको अचित्तिः ।

अस्ति ज्यायान्कनीयस उपारे स्वप्नश्चनेदनृतस्य प्रयोता ॥६॥
अरं दासो न मीळ्हुषे कराण्यहं देवाय भूर्णये ऽनागाः ।
अचेतयदचितो देवो अर्यो गृत्सं राये कवितरो जुनाति ॥७॥
अयं सु तुभ्यं वरुण स्वधावो हृदि स्तोम उपश्रितश्चिदस्तु ।
शं नः क्षेमे शमु योगे नो अस्तु यूयं पात स्वस्तिभिः सदा नः ॥

XLIV. RIGVEDA VII. 88.

प्र शुन्ध्युवं वरुणाय प्रेष्ठां मतिं वसिष्ठ मीळ्हुषे भरस्व ।
य ईमर्वाञ्चं करते यजत्रं सहस्रामघं वृषणं बृहन्तम् ॥१॥
अधा न्वस्य संदृशं जगन्वानग्नेरनीकं वरुणस्य मंसि ।
स्व१र्यदश्मन्नधिपा उ अन्धो ऽभि मा वपुर्दृशये निनीयात् ॥
आ यद्रुहाव वरुणश्च नावं प्र यत्समुद्रमीरयाव मध्यम् ।
अधि यदपां स्नुभिश्चराव प्र प्रेङ्ख ईङ्खयावहै शुभे कम् ॥३॥
वसिष्ठं ह वरुणो नाव्याधादृषिं चकार स्वपा महोभिः ।
स्तोतारं विप्रः सुदिनत्वे अह्नां यान्नु द्यावस्ततनन्यादुषासः ॥४॥
क्व१ त्यानि नौ सख्या बभूवुः सचावहे यदवृकं पुरा चित् ।
बृहन्तं मानं वरुण स्वधावः सहस्रद्वारं जगमा गृहं ते ॥५॥
य आपिर्नित्यो वरुण प्रियः सन्त्वामागांसि कृणवत्सखा ते ।
मा त एनस्वन्तो यक्षिन्भुजेम यन्धि ष्मा विप्रः स्तुवते वरूथम् ॥
ध्रुवासु त्वासु क्षितिषु क्षियन्तो व्य१स्मत्पाशं वरुणो मुमोचत् ।
अवो वन्वाना अदितेरुपस्थाद्यूयं पात स्वस्तिभिः सदा नः ॥

XLV. RIGVEDA VII. 89.

मो षु वरुण मृन्मयं गृहं राजन्नहं गमम् ।
मृळा सुक्षत्र मृळय ॥१॥
यदेमि प्रस्फुरन्निव दृतिर्न ध्मातो अद्रिवः ।
मृळा सुक्षत्र मृळय ॥२॥
क्रत्वः समह दीनता प्रतीपं जगमा शुचे ।
मृळा सुक्षत्र मृळय ॥३॥
अपां मध्ये तस्थिवांसं तृष्णाविदज्जरितारम् ।
मृळा सुक्षत्र मृळय ॥४॥
यत्किं चेदं वरुण दैव्ये जनेऽभिद्रोहं मनुष्या३श्चरामसि ।
अचित्ती यत्तव धर्मा युयोपिम मा नस्तस्मादेनसो देव रीरिषः ॥

XLVI. RIGVEDA VIII. 14.

यदिन्द्राहं यथा त्वमीशीय वस्व एक इत् ।
स्तोता मे गोषखा स्यात् ॥१॥
शिक्षेयमस्मै दित्सेयं शचीपते मनीषिणे ।
यदहं गोपतिः स्याम् ॥२॥
धेनुष्ट इन्द्र सूनृता यजमानाय सुन्वते ।
गामश्वं पिप्युषी दुहे ॥३॥
न ते वर्तास्ति राधस इन्द्र देवो न मर्त्यः ।
यद्दित्ससि स्तुतो मघम् ॥४॥
यज्ञ इन्द्रमवर्धयद्यद्भूमिं व्यवर्तयत् ।

चक्राण ओपशं दिवि ॥५॥
वावृधानस्य ते वयं विश्वा धनानि जिग्युषः ।
ऊतिमिन्द्रा वृणीमहे ॥६॥
व्य१न्तरिक्षमतिरन्मदे सोमस्य रोचना ।
इन्द्रो यदभिनद्वलम् ॥७॥
उद्गा आजदङ्गिरोभ्य आविष्कृण्वन्गुहा सतीः ।
अर्वाञ्चं नुनुदे वलम् ॥८॥
इन्द्रेण रोचना दिवो दृळ्हानि दृंहितानि च ।
स्थिराणि न पराणुदे ॥९॥
अपामूर्मिर्मदन्निव स्तोम इन्द्राजिरायते ।
वि ते मदा अराजिषुः ॥१०॥
त्वं हि स्तोमवर्धन इन्द्रास्युक्थवर्धनः ।
स्तोतृणामुत भद्रकृत् ॥११॥
इन्द्रमित्केशिना हरी सोमपेयाय वक्षतः ।
उप यज्ञं सुराधसम् ॥१२॥
अपां फेनेन नमुचेः शिर इन्द्रोदवर्तयः ।
विश्वा यदजय स्पृधः ॥१३॥
मायाभिरुत्सिसृप्सत इन्द्र द्यामारुरुक्षतः ।
अव दस्यूँरधूनुथाः ॥१४॥
असुन्वामिन्द्र संसदं विषूचीं व्यनाशयः ।
सोमपा उत्तरो भवन् ॥१५॥

XLVII. RIGVEDA VIII. 85.

वृत्रस्य त्वा श्वसथादीषमाणा विश्वे देवा अजहुर्ये सखायः ।
मरुद्भिरिन्द्र सख्यं ते अस्त्वथेमा विश्वाः पृतना जयासि ॥७॥
त्रिः षष्टिस्त्वा मरुतो वावृधाना उस्रा इव राशयो यज्ञियासः ।
उप त्वेमः कृधि नो भागधेयं शुष्मं त एना हविषा विधेम ॥८॥
तिग्ममायुधं मरुतामनीकं कस्त इन्द्र प्रति वज्रं दधर्ष ।
अनायुधासो असुरा अदेवाश्चक्रेण ताँ अप वप ऋजीषिन् ॥

XLVIII. RIGVEDA VIII. 91.

अग्ने घृतस्य धीतिभिस्तेपानो देव शोचिषा ।
आ देवान्वक्षि यक्षि च ॥१६॥
तं त्वाजनन्त मातरः कविं देवासो अङ्गिरः ।
हव्यवाहममर्त्यम् ॥१७॥
प्रचेतसं त्वा कवे ऽग्ने दूतं वरेण्यम् ।
हव्यवाहं नि षेदिरे ॥१८॥
नहि मे अस्त्यघ्न्या न स्वधितिर्वनन्वति ।
अथैतादृग्भरामि ते ॥१९॥
यदग्ने कानि कानि चिदा ते दारूणि दध्मसि ।
ता जुषस्व यविष्ठ्य ॥२०॥
अग्निमिन्धानो मनसा धियं सचेत मर्त्यः ।
अग्निमीधे विवस्वभिः ॥२२॥

XLIX. RIGVEDA X. 9.

आपो हि ष्ठा मयोभुवस्ता न ऊर्जे दधातन ।
महे रणाय चक्षसे ॥१॥
यो वः शिवतमो रसस्तस्य भाजयतेह नः ।
उशतीरिव मातरः ॥२॥
तस्मा अरं गमाम वो यस्य क्षयाय जिन्वथ ।
आपो जनयथा च नः ॥३॥

L. RIGVEDA X. 14.

परेयिवांसं प्रवतो महीरनु बहुभ्यः पन्थामनुपस्पशानम् ।
वैवस्वतं संगमनं जनानां यमं राजानं हविषा दुवस्य ॥१॥
यमो नो गातुं प्रथमो विवेद नैषा गव्यूतिरपभर्तवा उ ।
यत्रा नः पूर्वे पितरः परेयुरेना जज्ञानाः पथ्या३ अनु स्वाः ॥२॥
प्रेहि प्रेहि पथिभिः पूर्व्येभिर्यत्रा नः पूर्वे पितरः परेयुः ।
उभा राजाना स्वधया मदन्ता यमं पश्यासि वरुणं च देवम् ॥७॥
सं गच्छस्व पितृभिः सं यमेनेष्टापूर्तेन परमे व्योमन् ।
हित्वायावद्यं पुनरस्तमेहि सं गच्छस्व तन्वा सुवर्चाः ॥८॥
अपेत वीत वि च सर्पतातोऽस्मा एतं पितरो लोकमक्रन् ।
अहोभिरद्भिरक्तुभिर्व्यक्तं यमो ददात्यवसानमस्मै ॥९॥
अति द्रव सारमेयौ श्वानौ चतुरक्षौ शबलौ साधुना पथा ।
अथा पितॄन्सुविदत्राँ उपेहि यमेन ये सधमादं मदन्ति ॥१०॥
यौ ते श्वानौ यम रक्षितारौ चतुरक्षौ पथिरक्षी नृचक्षसौ ।

ताभ्यामेनं परि देहि राजन्त्स्वस्ति चास्मा अनमीवं च धेहि ॥
उरूणसावसुतृपा उदुम्बलौ यमस्य दूतौ चरतो जनाँ अनु ।
तावस्मभ्यं दृशये सूर्याय पुनर्दातामसुमद्येह भद्रम् ॥१२॥

LI. RIGVEDA X. 16.

मैनमग्ने वि दहो माभि शोचो मास्य त्वचं चिक्षिपो मा शरीरम् ।
यदा शृतं कृणवो जातवेदोऽथेमेनं प्र हिणुतात्पितृभ्यः ॥१॥
शृतं यदा करसि जातवेदोऽथेमेनं परि दत्तात्पितृभ्यः ।
यदा गच्छात्यसुनीतिमेतामथा देवानां वशनीर्भवाति ॥२॥
सूर्यं चक्षुर्गच्छतु वातमात्मा द्यां च गच्छ पृथिवीं च धर्मणा ।
अपो वा गच्छ यदि तत्र ते हितमोषधीषु प्रति तिष्ठा शरीरैः ॥
अजो भागस्तपसा तं तपस्व तं ते शोचिस्तपतु तं ते अर्चिः ।
यास्ते शिवास्तन्वो जातवेदस्ताभिर्वहैनं सुकृतामु लोकम् ॥४॥
अव सृज पुनरग्ने पितृभ्यो यस्त आहुतश्चरति स्वधाभिः ।
आयुर्वसान उप वेतु शेषः सं गच्छतां तन्वा जातवेदः ॥५॥
यत्ते कृष्णः शकुन आतुतोद पिपीलः सर्प उत वा श्वापदः ।
अग्निष्टद्विश्वादगदं कृणोतु सोमश्च यो ब्राह्मणाँ आविवेश ॥६॥
अग्नेर्वर्म परि गोभिर्व्ययस्व सं प्रोर्णुष्व पीवसा मेदसा च ।
नेत्त्वा धृष्णुर्हरसा जर्हृषाणो दधृग्विधक्ष्यन्पर्यङ्खयाते ॥७॥
इममग्ने चमसं मा वि जिह्वरः प्रियो देवानामुत सोम्यानाम् ।
एष यश्चमसो देवपानस्तस्मिन्देवा अमृता मादयन्ते ॥८॥
क्रव्यादमग्निं प्र हिणोमि दूरं यमराज्ञो गच्छतु रिप्रवाहः ।

इहैवायमितरो जातवेदा देवेभ्यो हव्यं वहतु प्रजानन् ॥९॥
यो अग्निः क्रव्यात्प्रविवेश वो गृहमिमं पश्यन्नितरं जातवेदसम्।
तं हरामि पितृयज्ञाय देवं स घर्ममिन्वात्परमे सधस्थे ॥१०॥
यो अग्निः क्रव्यवाहनः पितॄन्यक्षदृतावृधः।
प्रेदु हव्यानि वोचति देवेभ्यश्च पितृभ्य आ ॥११॥
उशन्तस्त्वा नि धीमह्युशन्तः समिधीमहि।
उशन्नुशत आ वह पितॄन्हविषे अत्तवे ॥१२॥
यं त्वमग्ने समदहस्तमु निर्वापया पुनः।
कियाम्ब्वत्र रोहतु पाकदूर्वा व्यल्कशा ॥१३॥
शीतिके शीतिकावति ह्लादिके ह्लादिकावति।
मण्डूक्या३ सु सं गम इमं स्व१ग्निं हर्षय ॥१४॥

LII. RIGVEDA X. 17.

त्वष्टा दुहित्रे वहतुं कृणोतीतीदं विश्वं भुवनं समेति।
यमस्य माता पर्युह्यमाना महो जाया विवस्वतो ननाश ॥१॥
अपागूहन्नमृतां मर्त्येभ्यः कृत्वी सवर्णामददुर्विवस्वते।
उताश्विनावभरद्यत्तदासीदजहादु द्वा मिथुना सरण्यूः ॥२॥
पूषा त्वेतश्च्यावयतु प्र विद्वाननष्टपशुर्भुवनस्य गोपाः।
स त्वैतेभ्यः परि ददत्पितृभ्योऽग्निर्देवेभ्यः सुविदत्रियेभ्यः ॥३॥
आयुर्विश्वायुः परि पासति त्वा पूषा त्वा पातु प्रपथे पुरस्तात्।
यत्रासते सुकृतो यत्र ते ययुस्तत्र त्वा देवः सविता दधातु ॥४॥
पूषेमा आशा अनु वेद सर्वाः सो अस्माँ अभयतमेन नेषत्।

स्वस्तिदा आघृणिः सर्ववीरो ऽप्रयुच्छन्पुर एतु प्रजानन् ॥५॥
प्रपथे पथामजनिष्ट पूषा प्रपथे दिवः प्रपथे पृथिव्याः ।
उभे अभि प्रियतमे सधस्थे आ च परा च चरति प्रजानन् ॥

LIII. RIGVEDA X. 18.

परं मृत्यो अनु परेहि पन्थां यस्ते स्व इतरो देवयानात् ।
चक्षुष्मते शृण्वते ते ब्रवीमि मा नः प्रजां रीरिषो मोत वीरान् ॥
मृत्योः पदं योपयन्तो यदैत द्राघीय आयुः प्रतरं दधानाः ।
आप्यायमानाः प्रजया धनेन शुद्धाः पूता भवत यज्ञियासः ॥२॥
इमे जीवा वि मृतैराववृत्रन्नभूद्भद्रा देवहूतिर्नो अद्य ।
प्राञ्चो अगाम नृतये हसाय द्राघीय आयुः प्रतरं दधानाः ॥३॥
इमं जीवेभ्यः परिधिं दधामि मैषां नु गादपरो अर्थमेतम् ।
शतं जीवन्तु शरदः पुरूचीरन्तर्मृत्युं दधतां पर्वतेन ॥४॥
यथाहान्यनुपूर्वं भवन्ति यथ ऋतव ऋतुभिर्यन्ति साधु ।
यथा न पूर्वमपरो जहात्येवा धातरायूंषि कल्पयैषाम् ॥५॥
आ रोहतायुर्जरसं वृणाना अनुपूर्वं यतमाना यति ष्ठ ।
इह त्वष्टा सुजनिमा सजोषा दीर्घमायुः करति जीवसे वः ॥६॥
इमा नारीरविधवाः सुपत्नीराञ्जनेन सर्पिषा सं विशन्तु ।
अनश्रवो ऽनमीवाः सुरत्ना आ रोहन्तु जनयो योनिमग्रे ॥७॥
उदीर्ष्व नार्यभि जीवलोकं गतासुमेतमुप शेष एहि ।
हस्तग्राभस्य दिधिषोस्तवेदं पत्युर्जनित्वमभि सं बभूथ ॥८॥
धनुर्हस्तादाददानो मृतस्यास्मे क्षत्राय वर्चसे बलाय ।

अत्रैव त्वमिह वयं सुवीरा विश्वा स्पृधो अभिमातीर्जयेम ॥९॥
उप सर्प मातरं भूमिमेतामुरुव्यचसं पृथिवीं सुशेवाम् ।
ऊर्णम्रदा युवतिर्दक्षिणावत एषा त्वा पातु निर्ऋतेरुपस्थात् ॥
उच्छ्वञ्चस्व पृथिवि मा नि बाधथाः सूपायनास्मै भव सूपवञ्चना ।
माता पुत्रं यथा सिचाभ्येनं भूम ऊर्णुहि ॥११॥
उच्छ्वञ्चमाना पृथिवी सु तिष्ठतु सहस्रं मित उप हि श्रयन्ताम् ।
ते गृहासो घृतश्चुतो भवन्तु विश्वाहास्मै शरणाः सन्त्वत्र ॥१२॥
उत्ते स्तभ्नामि पृथिवीं त्वत्परीमं लोगं निदधन्मो अहं रिषम् ।
एतां स्थूणां पितरो धारयन्तु तेऽत्रा यमः सादना ते मिनोतु ॥
प्रतीचीने मामहनीष्वाः पर्णमिवा दधुः ।
प्रतीचीं जग्रभा वाचमश्वं रशनया यथा ॥१४॥

LIV. RIGVEDA X. 33.

कुरुश्रवणमावृणि राजानं त्रासदस्यवम् ।
मंहिष्ठं वाघतामृषिः ॥४॥
यस्य मा हरितो रथे तिस्रो वहन्ति साधुया ।
स्तवै सहस्रदक्षिणे ॥५॥
यस्य प्रस्वादसो गिर उपमश्रवसः पितुः ।
क्षेत्रं न रण्वमूचुषे ॥६॥
अधि पुत्रोपमश्रवो नपान्मित्रातिथेरिहि ।
पितुष्टे अस्मि वन्दिता ॥७॥
यदीशीयामृतानामुत वा मर्त्यानाम् ।

जीवेदिन्मघवा मम ॥८॥
न देवानामति व्रतं शतात्मा चन जीवति ।
तथा युजा वि वावृते ॥९॥

LV. RIGVEDA X. 40. 10.

जीवं रुदन्ति वि मयन्ते अध्वरे दीर्घामनु प्रसितिं दीधियुर्नरः ।
वामं पितृभ्यो य इदं समेरिरे मयः पतिभ्यो जनयः परिष्वजे ॥

LVI. RIGVEDA X. 52.

विश्वे देवाः शास्तन मा यथेह होता वृतो मनवै यन्निषद्य ।
प्र मे ब्रूत भागधेयं यथा वो येन पथा हव्यमा वो वहानि ॥१॥
अहं होता न्यसीदं यजीयान्विश्वे देवा मरुतो मा जुनन्ति ।
अहरहरश्विनाध्वर्यवं वां ब्रह्मा समिद्भवति साहुतिर्वाम् ॥२॥
अयं यो होता किरु स यमस्य कमप्यूहे यत्समञ्जन्ति देवाः ।
अहरहर्जायते मासि मास्यथा देवा दधिरे हव्यवाहम् ॥३॥
मां देवा दधिरे हव्यवाहमपम्लुक्तं बहु कृच्छ्रा चरन्तम् ।
अग्निर्विद्वान्यज्ञं नः कल्पयाति पञ्चयामं त्रिवृतं सप्ततन्तुम् ॥
आ वो यक्ष्यमृतत्वं सुवीरं यथा वो देवा वरिवः कराणि ।
आ बाह्वोर्वज्रमिन्द्रस्य धेयामथेमा विश्वाः पृतना जयाति ॥५॥
त्रीणि शता त्री सहस्राण्यग्निं त्रिंशच्च देवा नव चासपर्यन् ।
औक्षन्घृतैरस्तृणन्बर्हिरस्मा आदिद्धोतारं न्यसादयन्त ॥६॥

LVII. RIGVEDA X. 53.

तन्तुं तन्वन्रजसो भानुमन्विहि ज्योतिष्मतः पथो रक्ष धिया कृतान्।
अनुल्बणं वयत जोगुवामपो मनुर्भव जनया दैव्यं जनम् ॥६॥
अश्मन्वती रीयते सं रभध्वमुत्तिष्ठत प्र तरता सखायः।
अत्रा जहाम ये असन्नशेवाः शिवान्वयमुत्तरेमाभि वाजान् ॥८॥

LVIII. RIGVEDA X. 85. 36, 24–26, 32–33, 27, 43–47.

गृभ्णामि ते सौभगत्वाय हस्तं मया पत्या जरदष्टिर्यथासः।
भगो अर्यमा सविता पुरंधिर्मह्यं त्वादुर्गार्हपत्याय देवाः ॥३६॥
प्र त्वा मुञ्चामि वरुणस्य पाशाद्येन त्वाबध्नात्सविता सुशेवः।
ऋतस्य योनौ सुकृतस्य लोकेऽरिष्टां त्वा सह पत्या दधामि ॥२४॥
प्रेतो मुञ्चामि नामुतः सुबद्धाममुतस्करम्।
यथेयमिन्द्र मीढ्वः सुपुत्रा सुभगासति ॥२५॥
पूषा त्वेतो नयतु हस्तगृह्याश्विना त्वा प्र वहतां रथेन।
गृहान्गच्छ गृहपत्नी यथासो वशिनी त्वं विदथमा वदासि ॥२६॥
मा विदन्परिपन्थिनो य आसीदन्ति दंपती।
सुगेभिर्दुर्गमतीतामप द्रान्त्वरातयः ॥३२॥
सुमङ्गलीरियं वधूरिमां समेत पश्यत।
सौभाग्यमस्यै दत्त्वायाथास्तं वि परेतन ॥३३॥
इह प्रियं प्रजया ते समृध्यतामस्मिन्गृहे गार्हपत्याय जागृहि।
एना पत्या तन्वं१ सं सृजस्वाधा जिव्री विदथमा वदाथः ॥२७॥
आ नः प्रजां जनयतु प्रजापतिराजरसाय समनक्त्वर्यमा।

अदुर्मङ्गलीः पतिलोकमा विश शं नो भव द्विपदे शं चतुष्पदे॥
अघोरचक्षुरपतिघ्न्येधि शिवा पशुभ्यः सुमनाः सुवर्चाः।
वीरसूर्देवकामा स्योना शं नो भव द्विपदे शं चतुष्पदे ॥४४॥
इमां त्वमिन्द्र मीढ्वः सुपुत्रां सुभगां कृणु।
दशास्यां पुत्राना धेहि पतिमेकादशं कृधि ॥४५॥
सम्राज्ञी श्वशुरे भव सम्राज्ञी श्वश्र्वां भव।
ननान्दरि सम्राज्ञी भव सम्राज्ञी अधि देवृषु ॥४६॥
समञ्जन्तु विश्वे देवाः समापो हृदयानि नौ।
सं मातरिश्वा सं धाता समु देष्ट्री दधातु नौ ॥४७॥

LIX. RIGVEDA X. 137.

उत देवा अवहितं देवा उन्नयथा पुनः।
उतागश्चक्रुषं देवा देवा जीवयथा पुनः ॥१॥
द्वाविमौ वातौ वात आ सिन्धोरा परावतः।
दक्षं ते अन्य आ वातु परान्यो वातु यद्रपः ॥२॥
आ वात वाहि भेषजं वि वात वाहि यद्रपः।
त्वं हि विश्वभेषजो देवानां दूत ईयसे ॥३॥
आ त्वागमं शंतातिभिरथो अरिष्टतातिभिः।
दक्षं ते भद्रमाभार्षं परा यक्ष्मं सुवामि ते ॥४॥
त्रायन्तामिह देवास्त्रायतां मरुतां गणः।
त्रायन्तां विश्वा भूतानि यथायमरपा असत् ॥५॥
आप इद्वा उ भेषजीरापो अमीवचातनीः।

आपः सर्वस्य भेषजीस्तास्ते कृण्वन्तु भेषजम् ॥६॥
हस्ताभ्यां दशशाखाभ्यां जिह्वा वाचः पुरोगवी ।
अनामयित्नुभ्यां त्वा ताभ्यां त्वोप स्पृशामसि ॥७॥

LX. RIGVEDA X. 154.

सोम एकेभ्यः पवते घृतमेक उपासते ।
येभ्यो मधु प्रधावति तांश्चिदेवापि गच्छतात् ॥१॥
तपसा ये अनाधृष्यास्तपसा ये स्वर्ययुः ।
तपो ये चक्रिरे महस्तांश्चिदेवापि गच्छतात् ॥२॥
ये युध्यन्ते प्रधनेषु शूरासो ये तनूत्यजः ।
ये वा सहस्रदक्षिणास्तांश्चिदेवापि गच्छतात् ॥३॥
ये चित्पूर्व ऋतसाप ऋतावान ऋतावृधः ।
पितॄन्तपस्वतो यम तांश्चिदेवापि गच्छतात् ॥४॥
सहस्रणीथाः कवयो ये गोपायन्ति सूर्यम् ।
ऋषीन्तपस्वतो यम तपोजाँ अपि गच्छतात् ॥५॥

LXI. RIGVEDA X. 155.

परीमे गामनेषत पर्यग्निमहृषत ।
देवेष्वक्रत श्रवः क इमाँ आ दधर्षति ॥५॥

LXII. MAITRAYANI SANHITA II. 13. 23.

हिरण्यगर्भः समवर्तताग्रे भूतस्य जातः पतिरेक आसीत् ।

स दाधार पृथिवीं द्यामुतेमां कस्मै देवाय हविषा विधेम ॥१॥
यः प्राणतो निमिषतश्च राजा पतिर्विश्वस्य जगतो बभूव ।
ईशे यो अस्य द्विपदश्चतुष्पदः कस्मै देवाय हविषा विधेम ॥२॥
य ओजोदा बलदा यस्य विश्व उपासते प्रशिषं यस्य देवाः ।
यस्य छायामृतं यस्य-मृत्युः कस्मै देवाय हविषा विधेम ॥३॥
यस्येमे विश्वे गिरयो महित्वा समुद्रं यस्य रसया सहाहुः ।
दिशो यस्य प्रदिशः पञ्च देवीः कस्मै देवाय हविषा विधेम ॥
येन द्यौरुग्रा पृथिवी च दृढा येन स्वः स्तभितं येन नाकः ।
यो अन्तरिक्षं विममे वरीयः कस्मै देवाय हविषा विधेम ॥५॥
य इमे द्यावापृथिवी तस्तभाने अधारयद्रोदसी रेजमाने ।
यस्मिन्नधि विततः सूर एति कस्मै देवाय हविषा विधेम ॥६॥
आपो ह यन्महतीर्विश्वमायन्गर्भं दधाना जनयन्तीरग्निम् ।
ततो देवानां निरवर्ततासुः कस्मै देवाय हविषा विधेम ॥७॥

LXIII. MAITRAYANI SANHITA I. 5. 12.

यमो वा अम्रियत । ते देवा यम्या यममपाब्रुवन् । तां यदपृच्छन्त्साब्रवीदद्यामृतेति । ते ऽब्रुवन्न वा इयमिममित्थं मृष्यते रात्रीं सृजावहा इति । अहर्वाव तर्ह्यासीन्न रात्रिः । ते देवा रात्रिमसृजन्त । ततः श्वस्तनमभवत् । ततः सा तममृष्यत । तस्मादाहुरहोरात्राणि वावाघं मर्षयन्तीति ।

LXIV. MAITRAYANI SANHITA I. 10. 13.

प्रजापतेर्वा एतज्ज्येष्ठं तोकं यत्पर्वताः । ते पक्षिण आ-

सन्। ते परापातमासत यत्र यत्राकामयन्त। अथ वा इयं तर्हि शिथिरासीत्। तेषामिन्द्रः पक्षानच्छिनत्। तैरिमामदृंहत्। ये पक्षा आसंस्ते जीमूता अभवन्। तस्मादेते सददि पर्वतमुप प्लवन्ते। योनिर्ह्येषामेषः।

LXV. MAITRAYANI SANHITA II. 1. 12.

ऐन्द्राबार्हस्पत्यं हविर्निर्वपेद्यो राष्ट्रीयो नेव प्रस्तिङ्नुयात्। अदितिर्वै प्रजाकामौदनमपचत्। सोच्छिष्टमाश्नात्। तं वा इन्द्रमन्तरेव गर्भं सन्तमयस्मयेन दाम्नापौम्भत्। सो ऽपोब्धो ऽजायत। तं वा एतेन बृहस्पतिरयाजयदैन्द्राबार्हस्पत्येन। तस्य तद्दाम स्वयमेव व्यपद्यत। स इमा दिशो वज्रेणाभिपर्यावर्तत। यो राष्ट्रीयो नेव प्रस्तिङ्नुयात्तमेतेन याजयेदैन्द्राबार्हस्पत्येन। परितो हि वा एष पाप्मना। अथैष न प्रस्तिङ्नोति। बृहस्पतये निरुप्यते इन्द्राय क्रियते सर्वत एवैनं मुञ्चति। वज्रेणेमा दिशो ऽभिपर्यावर्तते।

LXVI. TAITTIRIYA SANHITA II. 6. 6.

अग्नेस्त्रयो ज्यायांसो भ्रातर आसन्। ते देवेभ्यो हव्यं वहन्तः प्रामीयन्त। सो ऽग्निरबिभेदित्थं वाव स्य आर्तिमारिष्यतीति। स निलायत। सो ऽपः प्राविशत्। तं देवताः प्रैषमैच्छन्। तं मत्स्यः प्राब्रवीत्। तमशपद्धिया धिया त्वा वध्यासुर्यो मा प्रावोच इति। तस्मान्मत्स्यं धिया धिया घ्नन्ति। शप्तो हि। तमन्वविन्दन्। तमब्रुवन्नुप न आ वर्तस्व हव्यं नो

वहेति। सो ऽब्रवीद्वरं वृणै यदेव गृहीतस्याहुतस्य बहिःपरिधि स्कन्दात्तन्मे भ्रातॄणां भागधेयमसदिति। तस्माद्यद्गृहीतस्याहुतस्य बहिःपरिधि स्कन्दति तेषां तद्भागधेयम्।

LXVII. AITAREYA BRAHMANA III. 20.

इन्द्रो वै वृत्रं हनिष्यन्सर्वा देवता अब्रवीदनु मोप तिष्ठध्वमुप मा ह्वयध्वमिति। तथेति। तं हनिष्यन्त आद्रवन्। सो ऽवेन्मां वै हनिष्यन्त आ द्रवन्ति हन्तेमान्भीषया इति। तानभि प्राश्वसीत्। तस्य श्वसथादीषमाणा विश्वे देवा अद्रवन्। मरुतो हैनं नाजहुः प्रहर भगवो जहि वीरयस्वेत्येवैनमेतां वाचं वदन्त उपातिष्ठन्त। तदेतदृषिः पश्यन्नभ्यनूवाच वृत्रस्य त्वा श्वसथादिति। सो ऽवेदिमे वै किल मे सचिवा इमे माकामयन्त हन्तेमानस्मिन्नुक्थ आ भजा इति। तानेतस्मिन्नुक्थ आभजत्।

LXVIII. AITAREYA BRAHMANA III. 21.

इन्द्रो वै वृत्रं हत्वा सर्वा विजितीर्विजित्याब्रवीत्प्रजापतिमहमेतदसानि यत्त्वमहं महानसानीति। स प्रजापतिरब्रवीदथ को ऽहमिति। यदेवैतदवोच इत्यब्रवीत्। ततो वै को नाम प्रजापतिरभवत्। को वै नाम प्रजापतिः। यन्महानिन्द्रो ऽभवत्तन्महेन्द्रस्य महेन्द्रत्वम्।

LXIX. ÇATAPATHA BRAHMANA II. 2. 2.

द्वया वै देवाः। देवा अहैव देवाः। अथ ये ब्राह्मणाः शुश्रुवां-

सो ऽनूचानास्ते मनुष्यदेवाः । तेषां द्वेधा विभक्त एव यज्ञः । आहुतय एव देवानां दक्षिणा मनुष्यदेवानां ब्राह्मणानां शुश्रुवुषामनूचानानाम् । आहुतिभिरेव देवान्प्रीणाति दक्षिणाभिर्मनुष्यदेवान्ब्राह्मणाञ्छुश्रुवुषो ऽनूचानान् । त एनमुभये देवाः प्रीताः सुधायां दधति ॥६॥

LXX. ÇATAPATHA BRAHMANA II. 2. 2.

तस्य वा एतस्याग्न्याधेयस्य सत्यमेवोपचारः । स यः सत्यं वदति यथाग्निं समिद्धं तं घृतेनाभिषिञ्चेदेवं हैनं स उद्दीपयति तस्य भूयो भूय एव तेजो भवति श्वः श्वः श्रेयान्भवति । अथ यो ऽनृतं वदति यथाग्निं समिद्धं तमुदकेनाभिषिञ्चेदेवं हैनं स जासयति तस्य कनीयः कनीय एव तेजो भवति श्वः श्वः पापीयान्भवति । तस्मादु सत्यमेव वदेत् ॥१९॥ तदु हाप्यरुणमौपवेशिं ज्ञातय ऊचुः स्थविरो वा अस्यग्नी आ धत्स्वेति । स होवाच ते मैतद्ब्रूथ वाचंयम एवैधि न वा आहिताग्निनानृतं वदितव्यं न वदञ्जातु नानृतं वदेत्तावत्सत्यमेवोपचार इति ॥२०॥

LXXI. ÇATAPATHA BRAHMANA X. 4. 3.

एष वै मृत्युर्यत्संवत्सरः । एष हि मर्त्यानामहोरात्राभ्यामायुः क्षिणोति । अथ म्रियन्ते । तस्मादेष एव मृत्युः । स यो हैतं मृत्युं संवत्सरं वेद न हास्यैष पुरा जरसो ऽहोरात्राभ्यामायुः क्षिणोति । सर्वं हैवायुरेति ॥१॥ एष उ एवान्तकः । एष हि मर्त्यानामहोरात्राभ्यामायुषो ऽन्तं गच्छति । अथ म्रियन्ते ।

तस्मादेष एवान्तकः । स यो हैतमन्तकं मृत्युं संवत्सरं वेद न हास्यैष पुरा जरसो ऽहोरात्राभ्यामायुषो ऽन्तं गच्छति । सर्वं हैवायुरेति ॥२॥ ते देवा एतस्मादन्तकान्मृत्योः संवत्सरात्प्रजापतेर्बिभयां चक्रुर्यद्वै नो ऽयमहोरात्राभ्यामायुषो ऽन्तं न गच्छेदिति ॥३॥ त एतान्यज्ञक्रतूंस्तेनिरे ऽग्निहोत्रं दर्शपूर्णमासौ चातुर्मास्यानि पशुबन्धं सौम्यमध्वरम् । त एतैर्यज्ञक्रतुभिर्यजमाना नामृतत्वमानशिरे ॥४॥ ते हाप्यग्निं चिक्यिरे । ते ऽपरिमिता एव परिश्रित उप दधुरपरिमिता यजुष्मतीरपरिमिता लोकंपृणा यथेदमप्येतर्ह्येक उपदधति । इति देवा अकुर्वन् । इति ते ह नैवामृतत्वमानशिरे ॥५॥ ते ऽर्चन्तः श्राम्यन्तश्चेरुरमृतत्वमवरुरुत्समानाः । तान्ह प्रजापतिरुवाच न वै मे सर्वाणि रूपाण्युप धत्थाति वैव रेचयथ न वाभ्यापयथ तस्मान्नामृता भवथेति ॥६॥ ते होचुस्तेभ्यो वै नस्त्वमेव तद्ब्रूहि यथा ते सर्वाणि रूपाण्युपदधामेति ॥७॥ स होवाच षष्टिं च त्रीणि च शतानि परिश्रित उप धत्त षष्टिं च त्रीणि च शतानि यजुष्मतीरधि षट्त्रिंशतमथ लोकंपृणा दश च सहस्राण्यष्टौ च शतान्युप धत्ताथ मे सर्वाणि रूपाण्युप धास्यथाथामृता भविष्यथेति । ते ह तथा देवा उप दधुः । ततो देवा अमृता आसुः ॥८॥ स मृत्युर्देवानब्रवीदित्थमेव सर्वे मनुष्या अमृता भविष्यन्त्यथ को मह्यं भागो भविष्यतीति । ते होचुर्नातो ऽपरः कश्चन सह शरीरेणामृतो ऽसद्यदैव त्वमेतं भागं हरासा अथ व्यावृत्य शरीरेणामृतो ऽसद्यो ऽमृतो ऽसद्विद्यया वा कर्मणा वेति । यद्वै तदब्रुवन्विद्यया वा कर्मणा वेत्येषा

हैव सा विद्या यदग्निरेतदु हैव तत्कर्म यदग्निः ॥९॥ ते य एवमेतद्विदुर्ये वैतत्कर्म कुर्वते मृत्वा पुनः सं भवन्ति । ते संभवन्त एवामृतत्वमभिसं भवन्ति । अथ य एवं न विदुर्ये वैतत्कर्म न कुर्वते मृत्वा पुनः सं भवन्ति त एतस्यैवान्नं पुनः पुनर्भवन्ति ॥१०॥

LXXII. ÇATAPATHA BRAHMANA XII. 7. 3.

इन्द्रस्येन्द्रियमन्नस्य रसं सोमस्य भक्षं सुरयासुरो नमुचिरहरत् । सो ऽश्विनौ च सरस्वतीं चोपाधावच्छेपानो ऽस्मि नमुचये न त्वा दिवा न नक्तं हनानि न दण्डेन न धन्वना न पृथेन न मुष्टिना न शुष्केण नार्द्रेणाथ म इदमहार्षीदिदं म आ जिहीर्षथेति । ते ऽब्रुवन्नस्तु नो ऽत्राप्यथा हरामेति । सह न एतदथा हरतेत्यब्रवीत् । इति तावश्विनौ च सरस्वती च अपां फेनं वज्रमसिञ्चन्न शुष्को नार्द्र इति । तेनेन्द्रो नमुचेरासुरस्य व्युष्टायां रात्रावनुदित आदित्ये न दिवा न नक्तमिति शिर उदवासयत् । तस्मादेतदृषिणाभ्यनूक्तमपां फेनेनेति ।

LXXIII. NIRUKTA II. 16.

अतिष्ठन्तीनामनिविशमानानामित्यस्थावराणां काष्ठानां मध्ये निहितं शरीरं मेघः । शरीरं शृणातेः शम्नातेर्वा । वृत्रस्य निण्यं निर्णामं विचरन्ति विजानन्त्याप इति । दीर्घं द्राघतेः । तमस्तनोतेः । आशयदाशेतेः । इन्द्रशत्रुरिन्द्रो ऽस्य शमयिता वा शातयिता वा तस्मादिन्द्रशत्रुः । तत्को वृत्रः । मेघ इति नैरु-

क्ताः । त्वाष्ट्रो ऽसुर इत्यैतिहासिकाः । अपां च ज्योतिषश्च मिश्रीभावकर्मणो वर्षकर्म जायते । तत्रोपमार्थेन युद्धवर्णा भवन्ति । अहिवत्तु खलु मन्त्रवर्णा ब्राह्मणवादाश्च । विवृध्या शरीरस्य स्रोतांसि निवारयां चकार । तस्मिन्हते प्रसस्यन्दिर आपः । तदभिवादिन्येषर्ग्भवति ।

LXXIV. AÇVALAYANA'S GRIHYASUTRA I. 5, 7, 8.

कुलमग्रे परीक्षेत ये मातृतः पितृतश्चेति यथोक्तं पुरस्तात् ।१। बुद्धिमते कन्यां प्रयच्छेत् ।२। बुद्धिरूपशीललक्षणसंपन्नामरोगामुपयच्छेत ।३। दुर्विज्ञेयानि लक्षणान्यष्टौ पिण्डान्कृत्व ऋतमग्रे प्रथमं जज्ञ ऋते सत्यं प्रतिष्ठितम् । यदियं कुमार्यभिजाता तदियमिह प्रतिपद्यताम् । यत्सत्यं तद्दृश्यतामिति पिण्डानभिमन्त्र्य कुमारीं ब्रूयादेषामेकं गृहाणेति ।४। क्षेत्राच्चेदुभयतःसस्याद्गृह्णीयादन्नवत्यस्याः प्रजा भविष्यतीति विद्याद्गोष्ठात्पशुमती वेदिपुरीषाद्ब्रह्मवर्चस्विन्यविदासिनो ह्रदात्सर्वसंपन्ना देवनात्कितवी चतुष्पथाद्द्विप्रव्राजिनीरिणादधन्या श्मशानात्पतिघ्नी ।५। ॥५॥

अथ खलूच्चावचा जनपदधर्मा ग्रामधर्माश्च तान्विवाहे प्रतीयात् ।१। यत्तु समानं तद्वक्ष्यामः ।२। पश्चादग्नेर्दृषदमश्मानं प्रतिष्ठाप्योत्तरपुरस्तादुदकुम्भं समन्वारब्धायां हुत्वा तिष्ठन्प्रत्यङ्मुखः प्राङ्मुख्या आसीनाया गृभ्णामि ते सौभगत्वाय हस्तमित्यङ्गुष्ठमेव गृह्णीयाद्यदि कामयीत पुमांस एव मे पुत्रा जायेरन्निति ।३। अङ्गुलीरेव स्त्रीकामः ।४। रोमान्ते हस्तं साङ्गुष्ठ-

मुभयकामः ।५। प्रदक्षिणमग्निमुदकुम्भं च त्रिः परिणयं जपति

अमो ऽहमस्मि सा त्वं सा त्वमस्यमो ऽहम् ।
द्यौरहं पृथिवी त्वं सामाहमृक्त्वम् ॥
तावेहि विवहावहै प्रजां प्रजनयावहै ।
संप्रियौ रोचिष्णू सुमनस्यमानौ जीवेव शरदः शतम् ॥

इति ।६। परिणीय परिणीयाश्मानमारोहयति

इममश्मानमारोहाश्मेव त्वं स्थिरा भव ।
सहस्व पृतनायतो ऽभितिष्ठ पृतन्यतः ॥

इति ।७। वध्वञ्जला उपस्तीर्य भ्राता भ्रातृस्थानो वा द्विर्लाजानावपति ।८। त्रिर्जामदग्न्यानाम् ।९। प्रत्यभिघार्य हविः ।१०। अवत्तं च ।११। एषो ऽवदानधर्मः ।१२।

अर्यमणं नु देवं कन्या अग्निमयक्षत ।
स इमां देवो अर्यमा प्रेतो मुञ्चातु नामुतः स्वाहा ॥
वरुणं नु देवं कन्या अग्निमयक्षत ।
स इमां देवो वरुणः प्रेतो मुञ्चातु नामुतः स्वाहा ॥
पूषणं नु देवं कन्या अग्निमयक्षत ।
स इमां देवः पूषा प्रेतो मुञ्चातु नामुतः स्वाहा ॥

इत्यविच्छिन्दत्यञ्जलिं स्रुचेव जुहुयात् ।१३। अपरिणीय शूर्पपुटेनाभ्यात्मं तूष्णीं चतुर्थम् ।१४। ओप्योप्य हैके लाजान्परिणयन्ति तथोत्तमे आहुती न संनिपततः ।१५। अथास्यै शिखे विमुञ्चति यदि कृते भवत ऊर्णास्तुके केशपक्षयोर्बद्धे भवतः ।१६। प्र त्वा मुञ्चामि वरुणस्य पाशादिति ।१७। उत्तरामुत्तरया ।१८। अथैनामपराजितायां दिशि सप्त पदान्यभ्युत्क्रामयति

इष एकपदी ऊर्जे द्विपदी
रायस्पोषाय त्रिपदी मायोभव्याय चतुष्पदी
प्रजाभ्यः पञ्चपदी ऋतुभ्यः षट्पदी
सखा सप्तपदी भव सा मामनुव्रता भव।
पुत्रान्विन्दावहै बहूंस्ते सन्तु जरदृष्टयः॥

इति।१९। उभयोः संनिधाय शिरसी उदकुम्भेनावसिच्य।२०। ब्राह्मण्याश्च वृद्धाया जीवपत्न्या जीवप्रजाया अगार एतां रात्रीं वसेत्।२१। ध्रुवमरुन्धतीं सप्त ऋषीनिति दृष्ट्वा वाचं विसृजेत जीवपत्नी प्रजां विन्देयेति।२२।॥७॥

प्रयाण उपपद्यमाने पूषा त्वेतो नयतु हस्तगृह्येति यानमारोहयेत्।१। अश्मन्वती रीयते सं रभध्वमित्यर्धर्चेन नावमारोहयेत्।२। उत्तरेणोत्क्रमयेत्।३। जीवं रुदन्तीति रुदत्याम्।४। विवाहाग्निमग्रतोऽजस्रं नयन्ति।५। कल्याणेषु देशवृक्षचतुष्पथेषु मा विदन्परिपन्थिन इति जपेत्।६। वासे वासे सुमङ्गलीरियं वधूरितीक्षकानीक्षेत।७। इह प्रियं प्रजया ते समृध्यतामिति गृहं प्रवेशयेत्।८। विवाहाग्निमुपसमाधाय पश्चादस्यानडुहं चर्मास्तीर्य प्राग्ग्रीवमुत्तरलोम तस्मिन्नुपविष्टायां समन्वारब्धायामा नः प्रजां जनयतु प्रजापतिरिति चतसृभिः प्रत्यृचं हुत्वा समञ्जन्तु विश्वे देवा इति दध्नः प्राश्य प्रतिप्रयच्छेदाज्यशेषेण वानक्ति हृदये।९। अत ऊर्ध्वमक्षारालवणाशिनौ ब्रह्मचारिणावलंकुर्वाणावधःशायिनौ स्यातां त्रिरात्रं द्वादशरात्रम्।१०। संवत्सरं वैक ऋषिर्जायत इति।११।

चरितव्रतः सूर्याविदे वधूवस्त्रं दद्यात् ।१२। अन्नं ब्राह्मणेभ्यः ।१३। अथ स्वस्त्ययनं वाचयीत ।१४। ॥८॥

LXXV. AÇVALAYANA'S GRIHYASUTRA IV. 1—6.

आहिताग्निं चेदुपतपेत्प्राच्यामुदीच्यामपराजितायां वा दिश्युदवस्येत् ।१। ग्रामकामा अग्नय इत्युदाहरन्ति ।२। आशंसन्त एनं ग्राममाजिगमिषन्तो ऽगदं कुर्युरिति ह विज्ञायते ।३। अगदः सोमेन पशुनेष्ट्येष्ट्वावस्येत् ।४। अनिष्ट्वा वा ।५। संस्थिते भूमिभागं खानयेद्दक्षिणपूर्वस्यां दिशि दक्षिणापरस्यां वा ।६। दक्षिणाप्रवणं प्राग्दक्षिणाप्रवणं वा ।७। प्रत्यग्दक्षिणाप्रवणमित्येके ।८। यावानुद्बाहुकः पुरुषस्तावदायामम् ।९। व्याममात्रं तिर्यक् ।१०। वितस्त्यवाक् ।११। अभित आकाशं श्मशानम् ।१२। बहुलौषधिकम् ।१३। कण्टकिक्षीरिणस्त्विति यथोक्तं पुरस्तात् ।१४। यत्र सर्वत आपः प्रस्यन्देरन्नेतदादहनस्य लक्षणं श्मशानस्य ।१५। केशश्मश्रुलोमनखानि वापयन्तीत्युक्तं पुरस्तात् ।१६। विगुल्फं बर्हिराज्यं च ।१७। दधन्यत्र सर्पिरानयन्ति ।१८। एतत्पित्र्यं पृषदाज्यम् ।१९। ॥१॥

अथैतां दिशमग्नीन्नयन्ति यज्ञपात्राणि च ।१। अन्वञ्चं प्रेतमयुजो ऽमिथुनाः प्रवयसः ।२। पीठचक्रेण गोयुक्तेनेत्येके ।३। अनुस्तरणीम् ।४। गाम् ।५। अजां वैकवर्णाम् ।६। कृष्णामेके ।७। सव्ये बाहौ बद्ध्वानुसंकालयन्ति ।८। अन्वञ्चो ऽमात्या अधोनिवीताः प्रवृत्तशिखा ज्येष्ठप्रथमाः कनिष्ठजघन्याः ।९। प्राप्यैवं भूमिभागं कर्तोदकेन शमीशाखया त्रिः प्रसव्यमायतनं

परिव्रजन्प्रोक्षत्यपेत वीत वि च सर्पतात इति ।१०। दक्षिणपूर्व उद्धतान्त आहवनीयं निदधाति ।११। उत्तरपश्चिमे गार्हपत्यम् ।१२। दक्षिणपश्चिमे दक्षिणम् ।१३। अथैनमन्तर्वेदीध्मचितिं चिनोति यो जानाति ।१४। तस्मिन्बर्हिरास्तीर्य कृष्णाजिनं चोत्तरलोम तस्मिन्प्रेतं संवेशयन्नुत्तरेण गार्हपत्यं हृत्वाहवनीयमभिशिरसम् ।१५। उत्तरतः पत्नीम् ।१६। धनुश्च क्षत्रियाय ।१७। तामुत्थापयेद्देवरः पतिस्थानीयो ऽन्तेवासी जरद्दासो वोदीर्ष्व नार्यभि जीवलोकमिति ।१८। कर्ता वृषले जपेत् ।१९। धनुर्हस्तादाददानो मृतस्येति धनुः ।२०। उक्तं वृषले ।२१। अधिज्यं कृत्वा संचितिमचित्वा संशीर्यानुप्रहरेत् ।२२। ॥२॥

अथैतानि पात्राणि योजयेत् ।१। दक्षिणे हस्ते जुहूम् ।२। सव्य उपभृतम् ।३। दक्षिणे पार्श्वे स्फ्यं सव्ये ऽग्निहोत्रहवणीम् ।४। उरसि ध्रुवां शिरसि कपालानि दत्सु ग्राव्णः ।५। नासिकयोः स्रुवौ ।६। भित्त्वा चैकम् ।७। कर्णयोः प्राशित्रहरणे ।८। भित्त्वा चैकम् ।९। उदरे पात्रीम् ।१०। समवत्तधानं च चमसम् ।११। उपस्थे शम्याम् ।१२। अरणी ऊर्वोः ।१३। उलूखलमुसले जङ्घयोः ।१४। पादयोः शूर्पे ।१५। छित्त्वा चैकम् ।१६। आसेचनवन्ति पृषदाज्यस्य पूरयन्ति ।१७। अमा पुत्रो दृषदुपले कुर्वीत ।१८। लौहायसं च कौलालम् ।१९। अनुस्तरण्या वपामुत्खिद्य शिरोमुखं प्रच्छादयेदग्नेर्वर्म परि गोभिर्व्ययस्वेति ।२०। वृक्का उद्धृत्य पाण्योरादध्यादति द्रव सारमेयौ श्वानाविति दक्षिणे दक्षिणं सव्ये सव्यम् ।२१। हृदये हृदयम् ।२२। पिण्डौ चैके ।२३। वृक्कापचार इत्येके ।२४। सर्वां यथाङ्गं विनिक्षिप्य च-

मेणा प्रच्छाद्योममग्ने चमसं मा वि जिह्वर इति प्रणीताप्रणयनमनुमन्त्रयते ।२५। सव्यं जान्वाच्य दक्षिणाग्नावाज्याहुतीर्जुहुयादग्नये स्वाहा कामाय स्वाहा लोकाय स्वाहानुमतये स्वाहेति ।२६। पञ्चमीमुरसि प्रेतस्यास्माद्वै त्वमजायथा अयं त्वदधि जायतामसौ स्वर्गाय लोकाय स्वाहेति ।२७। ॥३॥

प्रेष्यति युगपदग्नीन्प्रज्वालयतेति ।१। आहवनीयश्चेत्पूर्वं प्राप्नुयात्स्वर्गेलोक एनं प्रापदिति विद्याद्रात्स्यत्यसावमुत्रैवमयमस्मिन्निति पुत्रः ।२। गार्हपत्यश्चेत्पूर्वं प्राप्नुयादन्तरिक्षलोक एनं प्रापदिति विद्याद्रात्स्यत्यसावमुत्रैवमयमस्मिन्निति पुत्रः ।३। दक्षिणाग्निश्चेत्पूर्वं प्राप्नुयान्मनुष्यलोक एनं प्रापदिति विद्याद्रात्स्यत्यसावमुत्रैवमयमस्मिन्निति पुत्रः ।४। युगपत्प्राप्तौ परामृद्धिं वदन्ति ।५। तं दह्यमानमनुमन्त्रयते प्रेहि प्रेहि पथिभिः पूर्व्येभिरिति समानम् ।६। स एवंविदा दह्यमानः सहैव धूमेन स्वर्गं लोकमेतीति ह विज्ञायते ।७। उत्तरपुरस्तादाहवनीयस्य जानुमात्रं गर्तं खात्वावकां शीपालमित्यवधापयेत्ततो ह वा एष निष्क्रम्य सहैव धूमेन स्वर्गं लोकमेतीति ह विज्ञायते ।८। इमे जीवा वि मृतैराववृत्रन्निति सव्यावृतो व्रजन्त्यनवेक्षमाणाः ।९। यत्रोदकमवहद्भवति तत्प्राप्य सकृदुन्मज्ज्यैकाञ्जलिमुत्सृज्य तस्य गोत्रं नाम च गृहीत्वोत्तीर्यान्यानि वासांसि परिधाय सकृदेनान्यापीड्योदग्दशानि विसृज्यासत आ नक्षत्रदर्शनात् ।१०। आदित्यस्य वा दृश्यमाने प्रविशेयुः ।११। कनिष्ठप्रथमा ज्येष्ठजघन्याः ।१२। प्राप्यागारमश्मानमग्निं गोमयमक्षतांस्तिलानप उ-

पस्पृशन्ति ।१३। नैतस्यां रात्र्यामन्नं पचेरन् ।१४। क्रीतोत्पन्नेन वा वर्तेरन् ।१५। त्रिरात्रमक्षारालवणाशिनः स्युः ।१६। द्वादशरात्रं वा महागुरुषु दानाध्ययने वर्जयेरन् ।१७। दशाहं सपिण्डेषु ।१८। गुरौ चासपिण्डे ।१९। अप्रत्तासु च स्त्रीषु ।२०। त्रिरात्रमितरेष्वाचार्येषु ।२१। ज्ञातौ चासपिण्डे ।२२। प्रत्तासु च स्त्रीषु ।२३। अदन्तजाते ।२४। अपरिजाते च ।२५। एकाहं सब्रह्मचारिणि ।२६। समानग्रामीये च श्रोत्रिये ।२७। ॥४॥

संचयनमूर्ध्वं दशम्याः कृष्णपक्षस्यायुजास्वेकनक्षत्रे ।१। अलक्षणे कुम्भे पुमांसमलक्षणायां स्त्रियम् ।२। अयुजो ऽमिथुनाः प्रवयसः ।३। क्षीरोदकेन शमीशाखया त्रिः प्रसव्यं परिव्रजन्प्रोक्षति शीतिके शीतिकावतीति ।४। अङ्गुष्ठोपकनिष्ठिकाभ्यामेकैकमस्थ्यसंह्रादयन्तो ऽवदध्युः ।५। पादौ पूर्वं शिर उत्तरम् ।६। सुसंचितं संचित्य पवनेन संपूय यत्र सर्वत आपो नाभिस्यन्देरन्नन्या वर्षाभ्यस्तत्र गर्ते ऽवदध्युरुप सर्प मातरं भूमिमेतामिति ।७। उत्तरया पांसूनवकिरेत् ।८। अवकीर्योत्तराम् ।९। उत्ते स्तभ्नामीति कपालेनापिधायाथानवेक्षं प्रत्याव्रज्याप उपस्पृश्य श्राद्धमस्मै दद्युः ।१०। ॥५॥

गुरुणाभिमृता अन्यतो वापक्षीयमाणा अमावास्यायां शान्तिकर्म कुर्वीरन् ।१। पुरोदयादग्निं सहभस्मानं सहायतनं दक्षिणा हरेयुः क्रव्यादमग्निं प्र हिणोमि दूरमित्यर्धर्चेन ।२। तं चतुष्पथे न्युप्य यत्र वा त्रिः प्रसव्यं परियन्ति सव्यैः पाणिभिः सव्यानूरूनाघ्नानाः ।३। अथानवेक्षं प्रत्याव्रज्याप उपस्पृश्य केश-

श्मश्रुलोमनखानि वापयित्वोपकल्पयीरन्नवान्मणिकान्कुम्भानाचमनीयांश्च शमीसुमनोमालिनः शमीमयमिध्मं शमीमय्यावरणी परिधींश्चानडुहं गोमयं चर्म च नवनीतमश्मानं च यावत्यो युवतयस्तावन्ति कुशपिञ्जूलानि ।४। अग्निवेलायामग्निं जनयेदिहैवायमितरो जातवेदा इत्यर्धर्चेन ।५। तं दीपयमाना आसत आ शान्तरात्रादायुष्मतां कथाः कीर्तयन्तो माङ्गल्यानीतिहासपुराणानीत्याख्यापयमानाः ।६। उपरतेषु शब्देषु संप्रविष्टेषु वा गृहं निवेशनं वा दक्षिणाद्द्वारपक्षात्प्रक्रम्याविच्छिन्नामुदकधारां हरेत्तन्तुं तन्वन्रजसो भानुमन्विहीत्योत्तरस्मात् ।७। अथाग्निमुपसमाधाय पश्चादस्यानडुहं चर्मास्तीर्य प्राग्ग्रीवमुत्तरलोम तस्मिन्नमात्यानारोहयेदा रोहतायुर्जरसं वृणाना इति ।८। इमं जीवेभ्यः परिधिं दधामीति परिधिं परिदध्यात् ।९। अन्तर्मृत्युं दधतां पर्वतेनेत्युत्तरतो ऽश्मानमग्नेः कृत्वा परं मृत्यो अनु परेहि पन्थामिति चतसृभिः प्रत्यृचं हुत्वा यथाहान्यनुपूर्वं भवन्तीत्यमात्यानीक्षेत ।१०। युवतयः पृथक्पाणिभ्यां दर्भतरुणकैर्नवनीतेनाङ्गुष्ठोपकनिष्ठिकाभ्यामक्षिणी आज्य पराच्यो विसृजेयुः ।११। इमा नारीरविधवाः सुपत्नीरित्यञ्जाना ईक्षेत ।१२। अश्मन्वती रीयते सं रभध्वमित्यश्मानं कर्ता प्रथमो ऽभिमृशेत् ।१३। अथापराजितायां दिश्यवस्थायाग्निनानडुहेन गोमयेन चाविच्छिन्नया चोदकधारयापो हि ष्ठा मयोभुव इति तृचेन परीमे गामनेषतेति परिक्रामत्सु जपेत् ।१४। पिङ्गलो ऽनड्वान्परिणेयः स्यादित्युदाहरन्ति

।१५। अथोपविशन्ति यत्राभिरंस्यमाना भवन्त्यहतेन वाससा प्रच्छाद्य ।१६। आसते ऽस्वपन्त ओदयात् ।१७। उदित आदित्ये सौर्याणि स्वस्त्ययनानि च जपित्वान्नं संस्कृत्याप नः शोशुचदघमिति प्रत्यृचं हुत्वा ब्राह्मणान्भोजयित्वा स्वस्त्ययनं वाचयीत ।१८। गौः कंसो ऽहतं वासश्च दक्षिणा ।१९। ॥६॥

GEBRÜDER UNGER, BERLIN, SW.

PART II.

NOTES.

SELECTION I.

The Story of Nala and Damayantī.

§ 1. The trend of Aryan migration in India has been from the extreme northwest to the south-east, across the region drained by the Indus and its affluents, and called the Panjāb or Land of the Five Rivers; and again south-east, down the valleys of the Jumna and Ganges. One prominent group of Aryan immigrant tribes was that of the Kosalas, Videhas, and Magadhas, who settled in the *lower* valley of the Ganges, *east* of its confluence with the Jumna, in the districts now named Oudh and Behar, the Palestine of Buddhism.

§ 2. Another group of tribes had their home on the upper Indus, in the northwest of the Panjāb. Theirs was the religion and civilization of which the Vedas are the monument. Later we find them advancing south-eastward, and establishing themselves on the *upper* course of the Jumna and Ganges, in Madhya-deça, The Mid-Land. Foremost among them are the tribes of the Bhāratas, the Kurus, and the Panchālas. Here arose the system of Brahmanism; here the simple nature-religion of the Vedas developed into a religion of priests and sacrifices; here the Bhāratas attained a kind of religious primacy and the lustre of a great name, although gradually merging their tribal individuality with that of kindred tribes; here were fought the battles of the Bhāratas; and here, to ever-ready listeners, in school or forest-hermitage, at a sacrifice or a burial, were told the tales of these battles and their heroes. These are the tales that form the nucleus of the Great-Bhārata-Story (**mahā-bhārata‿ākhyāna**, or, more briefly), the Mahā-bhārata.

§ 3. These tales were probably first circulated in prose, until some more clever teller put them into simple and easily-remembered metrical form. The date of these first simple epics we do not know. They may well have existed several centuries before our era; but neither their language nor the notices of the Greeks afford any satisfactorily direct evidence upon the subject. Around this nucleus have been grouped additions, — historical, mythological, and didactic, — until the Great-Bhārata, as we now have it, contains over one hundred thousand distichs, or about eight times as much as the Iliad and Odyssey together.

§ 4. Only about one-fifth of the whole poem is occupied with the principal story. This, in the briefest possible summary, is as follows. The two brothers, Dhritarāshtra and Pāndu (**dhṛta-rāṣṭra, pāṇḍu**), were brought up in their royal home of Hastinā-pura, about sixty miles north-east of modern Delhi. Dhritarāshtra, the elder, was blind, and so Pāndu became king, and had a glorious reign. He had five sons, chief of whom were Yudhishthira, Bhīma, and Arjuna. They are called Pāndavas, and are the types of honor and heroism. Dhritarāshtra's hundred sons, Duryodhana and the rest, are usually called the Kuru princes, and are represented as in every way bad. After Pāndu's death, his sons are brought up with their cousins. The kingdom devolved on Dhritarāshtra, who in turn made his nephew Yudhishthira the heir apparent.

§ 5. Yudhishthira's exploits aroused the ill-will of his cousins, and, to escape their plots, the Pāndu princes went away to the king of Panchāla, whose daughter, Draupadī, became their common wife. In view of this strong alliance with the Panchālas, Dhritarāshtra thought it best to conciliate the Pāndus. So he divided the kingdom, and gave Hastinā-pura to his sons, and to his nephews a district to the south-west, where they built Indra-prastha, the modern Delhi. Here the Pāndavas and their people lived happily under king Yudhishthira.

§ 6. On one occasion Dhritarāshtra held a great assembly of princes at his capital. The Pāndavas were invited and came. Yudhishthira was challenged to play with Duryodhana, and accepted. The dice were thrown for Duryodhana by his uncle Çakuni. Yudhishthira loses everything — wealth, kingdom, brothers, wife. A compromise, however, is made, by which the Pāndavas give up their part of the kingdom for twelve years, and agree to remain incognito for a thirteenth. With Draupadī, they retire to the Kāmyaka forest, on the Saraswatī.

§ 7. For twelve years the Pāndu princes dwell in the wood. Many legends are told to divert and console them in their exile; and these stories, with the description of the forest-life of the princes, combine to make up the third or 'Forest-book,' the **vana-parvan**, which is one of the longest in the whole poem.

§ 8. The thirteenth year arrived and passed. "Then in the fourteenth the Pāndavas demanded back their possessions, but received them not. From this arose the conflict. They overthrew the ruling house, slew prince Duryodhana, and then, although losing most of their warriors, they got back again their kingdom." MBh. i.61.51=2280. Thus ended the Bhārata, doubtless, in its oldest and simplest form.

§ 9. The poem, as we now have it, spins out the story of the combat through several books and through thousands of distichs. At length Yudhishthira is crowned in Hastinā-pura, and Bhīshma, the leader of the Kurus, although mortally wounded, instructs him, for about twenty thousand distichs, on the duties of kings and on other topics, and then dies. In the seventeenth book, the Pāndus renounce the kingdom, and in the next, the last, they ascend to heaven with Draupadī.

§ 10. The Nala-episode illustrates very well how loose is the connection of the episodes in general with the main thread of the Bhārata. The story of Nala is one of those inserted in the third book (above, § 7), and its setting is as follows. Arjuna had gone to the heaven of Indra to get from him divine weapons. The other Pāndavas, remaining in the forest with Draupadī, lament their brother's absence and the loss of their kingdom. Meantime the fierce and stout-armed Bhīma addresses his brother Yudhishthira, and offers to go out and slay their deceitful cousins. Yudhishthira counsels Bhīma to wait till after the thirteenth year, and is trying to calm his impetuous brother, when suddenly there arrives a mighty sage, Brihadaçwa. The holy man is received with honor and with the customary guest's-dish of milk and honey. When he is seated, Yudhishthira sits by him, bewails his sad lot, and asks, "Hast thou ever seen or heard of a man more luckless than I am? I believe there never was one more unhappy." "On this point," replies the sage, "I will tell thee a story of a king who was even more luckless than thou. King Nala was once cheated out of his kingdom by a false dice-player, and dwelt in the forest, and neither slaves, chariot, brother, nor friend was left him; but thou art surrounded by heroes, brothers, and friends, and oughtest not to grieve." Thereupon Yudhishthira begs him to relate the story at length. Accordingly, to console the king, and to show him that there is hope of regaining his kingdom, just as Nala regained his, Brihadaçwa begins as in the extract given in the Reader (1[3]).

§ 11. Chapter 1. Nala was a prince of Nishadha. Damayantī was the lovely daughter of Bhīma, the king of Vidarbha. By the miraculous interposition of swans, the prince and princess become mutually enamored.

§ 12. Chap. 2. Bhīma accordingly holds a swayamvara ('self-choice') for her. The neighboring kings are invited, and she is permitted to choose for herself her husband from them. The chief gods hear of it and determine to go also. On their way, they meet Nala, who is bound on the same errand.

§ 13. Chap. 3. The gods request Nala to sue for them. Reluctantly consenting, he enters the chamber of the princess and tells how the gods desire her hand.

§ 14. Chap. 4. Damayantī refuses to listen to the arguments in favor of the gods. She desires that the swayamvara be held in the usual form, and that the gods be present, and informs Nala that she intends to show openly her preference for him. All this Nala reports to the gods.

§ 15. Chap. 5. The gods and kings assemble. The four chief gods assume the appearance of Nala. Unable to distinguish the real Nala, the princess, distressed, prays to the gods, and they, in answer, resume their proper forms and peculiar attributes (see 14[12] n.). Thereupon she chooses Nala. The kings express their sorrow, and the gods their delight. The gods give Nala the magic power of having fire and water whenever he wishes, and a wonderful skill in cookery. The wedding-feast is celebrated. Nala returns to Nishadha with his bride. They live happily, and have a son and daughter. — Here the extract in the Reader ends.

§ 16. Chapters 6–26. These tell of Nala's misfortunes, and their final happy issue. He loses everything, even his kingdom, by gambling, and wanders, hungry and half naked, in the forest. He is transformed into a dwarf, and becomes charioteer of Rituparna, king of Oudh. Damayantī, at her father's in Kundina, is led by certain tidings to suspect that Nala is at Oudh. By way of stratagem, she holds out hopes of her hand to Rituparna, if he will drive from Oudh to Kundina, some five hundred miles, in a single day, knowing well that only Nala's skill in horsemanship (see 1[4]) is equal to this task. Rituparna gets Nala to drive him thither through the air. Nala receives as reward perfect skill in dicing. His wife recognizes him by his magical command of fire and water, and by his cooking. He resumes his true form, plays again, and wins back all he had lost, and lives happy ever after.*

§ 17. When Brihadaçwa had finished the story of Nala, Yudhishthira, pleased, asked him for perfect skill in dicing; and the hermit, granting him his prayer, departed.

§ 18. This story is unquestionably one of the oldest and most beautiful episodes of the Mahā-bhārata. It was extremely popular in India; and to this is due the fact that it escaped the bad influence of Vishnuism, whose adherents have worked over the vast epic, changing and interpolating, and always for the worse.

* The student may read the entire story in any of the numerous translations — by Milman, Bopp, Rückert, and others. The most easily obtained is the very spirited English rendering of Edwin Arnold, in his *Indian Idylls*, Boston, Roberts Brothers, 1883, $1.00.

§ 19. Even the Nala, especially in the first chapter, has suffered much from later hands; but on the whole it is one of the least corrupted episodes. Its antiquity is shown by the simplicity of manners implied in its incidents — the prince, for example, cooks his own food, — by the character of Indra (cf. 14^{22} N.), and in other ways. See Holtzmann's *Indische Sagen*, Stuttgart, 1854, p. xiv. Bruce has attempted to reject definite passages throughout the poem, and has published, at St. Petersburg in 1862, a text of the Nala, reduced from 983 to 522 distichs.

§ 20. The story begins at iii.53.1 (folio 58 b) of the Bombay edition of 1877, and at iii. 2072 of the Calcutta edition of 1834.

§ 21. THE METRE. The stanza (çloka) or distich consists of four octosyllabic verses (pāda). The first and second pādas form together a half-çloka or a line, divided at the middle by the caesura: likewise the third and fourth. The more important rules follow.

a. Odd pādas end usually with a first epitrite, ⏑———, or antispast, ⏑——⏑.
b. Even pādas end in a diiambus, ⏑—⏑—, or second paeon, ⏑—⏑⏑.

So the type of the half-çloka is ○○○○ | ⏑——⏓ ‖ ○○○○ | ⏑—⏑⏓. But
c. In no pāda may the syllables 2, 3, 4 form a tribrach, ⏑⏑⏑, or anapaest, ⏑⏑—;
d. Nor, in the even pādas, an amphimacer, —⏑—.

NOTES TO PAGE 1.

LINE 1. **atha**, see p. 114, s.v. **atha** 3. —**nalopākhyāna-m**, nom.s.n. (see 330) of **nalopākhyāna**: this last is a compound stem, see s.v., p. 180: its analysis is indicated in the manner mentioned at p. 292, paragraph 2, end: the second member is **upākhyāna**, as given in the square brackets, p. 180: its initial, **u**, has evidently combined with the final vowel of the first member to **o**: according to the important rule 127, that final must have been an *a*-vowel (**a** or **ā**), and, since there is no stem **nalā**, the first member must be **nala**: since this logically determines the second member, i.e. distinguishes the 'Nala-episode' from all other episodes, the compound is to be classed as a determinative, see 1262.

2. **bṛhadaçva**, u.f. **bṛhadaçva-s** (175b), nom.s.m. of **bṛhád-açva**, see s.v., p. 202: as shown in the square brackets, the first member of the cpd is **bṛhánt**, which, by 1249a, enters into composition in its weak form **bṛhát**: by the law of regressive assimilation (159, the most important rule of Sanskrit phonetics), the **t** becomes **d**. The combination **bṛhad-açvá**, with the accent on the ultima, means 'a great hórse'; the same combination, with the acct of the prior member, is a secondary adjective cpd, and means 'having great horses': here the secondary adjective is used as a substantive, '(man) having great horses, i.e. Greát-horse': see 1293^2 and cf. the difference between *a great heárt* and Bunyan's *Mr. Greát-heart*. For the ligature **çv**, see Whitney 13^6. —**uvāca**, √**vac**, p. 236, perf. act. 3d sing., see 800e. —For the connection of this line with the story, see p. 298, § 10.

3^a. **āsīd**, u.f. **āsīt**, by the law of regressive assimilation, just mentioned: as was said at p. 290, paragraph 8, the meaning must be sought under √1 **as**, p. 122: the form is imf. 3d sing., 636. —**rājā**, see p. 290, paragraph 7, and for declension, 424. —**nalo**, u.f. **nala-s**, 175a: declension, 330. Nominatives in **as** are extremely common, and so of course is the change of **as** to **o**. —**nāma**, acc.s.n. (424) of **nāman**, see s.v. 3.

3^b. **vīrasena-suto**, u.f. **-suta-s**, 175a: the word is a dependent noun-cpd and = **vīrasenasya sutas**, see 1264: the stem **vīrá-sena** (see s.v.) is itself also a cpd, and of the same kind as **bṛhád-açva**. —**balī**, see 440.

4^a. **upapanno**, u.f. upa-panna-s (175a), √pad+upa, p. 186. As a prepositional cpd, this must be sought under the root, not under the preposition — read p. 290, paragraph 8. For the form panna, see 957d: lit., it has only an indefinite past sense, not a passive sense, see 952^2. —**guṇāir**, u.f. guṇāis, 174: declension, 330. —**iṣṭāi**, u.f. iṣṭāis, which becomes iṣṭāir (174 again) before the following sonant initial; and since this is r, the final r is dropped — see 179: iṣ-ṭá is ppl. of √1 iṣ, 953: the t of ta becomes ṭ by progressive assimilation (197), which is far less common than regressive assimilation. —The half-line means, 'endowed with (desired, i.e. desirable *or*) excellent virtues.' For the use of the instr., see 278.

4^b. **rūpavān**, see 452 and 453, and cf. 447. For rū, cf. Whitney 10d. —**açvakovidaḥ**, u.f. açvakovidas, 170a, an extremely common change. Nala's skill in the manege is a point of prime importance in the story — see p. 299, § 16.

5^a. **atiṣṭhan**, u.f. atiṣṭhat (161) is 3d s. imf. act. of √sthā, 742. [The a is augment, 585: ti is reduplication (for t, see 590c; for i, 660): the i alters s to ṣ (180 and 184c), and this ṣ involves the conversion of th to ṭh (197 — cf. iṣṭa). Orig. sthā belonged to the reduplicating class (671 — cf. *ἵ-στη-μι, ἵ-στη-s, ἵ-στη-σι*), but has been transferred (749) to the commonest of all classes, the a-class, and is inflected as if the stem were tiṣṭha, i.e. as if we had in Greek *ἵ-στω, ἵ-στεις, ἵ-στει.*] —**manujendrāṇām**, gen.pl. of manujendra: after the lingual r, the n of the ending is changed to lingual ṇ — see 189 and 190a: for the cǒmbination of manuja+indra, see 127; for dr, Whitney 14.

5^b. **mūrdhni**, loc.s. of mūrdhan, 424: for rdh, see Whitney 14. —**devapatir**, u.f. devapatis, 174: declension, 339. —**yathā**, see s.v. 4. —'He (stood, i.e.) was at the head of princes, as Indra (sc. is at the head of gods)': i.e. "He was as much superior to other princes as Indra to other gods.' "As handsome as Indra" was a proverbial expression.

6^a. **upary**, u.f. upari, 129: the word is repeated for emphasis, 1260: 'above, above,' i.e. 'far above.' —**sarveṣām**, gen.pl. of sarva, 522 and 524: for construction, see s.v. upari and 1130 end.

6^b. **āditya**, u.f. ādityas, 175b. —**tejasā**, 414: as referring to the sun, it means 'splendor,' and as referring to Nala, it has the transferred mg, 'majesty': the instr., prop. the 'with'-case, is here best rendered by 'by,' i.e. 'in virtue of.' —The force of atiṣṭhat extends through the çloka or distich. 'He was far above all in majesty, as the sun (is) in splendor.'

7^a. **vedavic chūro**, u.f. vedavit çūras: the final t is changed to the palatal c, before the palatal sibilant ç (regressive assimilation, 203), and the sibilant ç is also changed to the mute ch, 203: the same changes appear in paryupāsac chacīm, 2^7, abhūc chṛṇvatoḥ, 2^{18}, hṛcchayaḥ, 2^{19}, and tac chrutvā, 4^6, 4^{16}: vedavit is nom.s.m. of vedavid (391), the d being changed to t (159) before the s of the case-ending, which last, however, is dropped — see 150.

7^b. **niṣadheṣu**, 'among the Nishadhans' or 'in Nishadha'. —**mahīpatiḥ**, u.f. mahīpatis, 170a: declension, 339.

—It is not known where Nishadha was. Vidarbha, the modern Berar, is at the headwaters of the Taptī, between Nagpore and the Nizam's Kingdom, and about five hundred miles from Oudh. The general run of the story makes it highly probable that Nishadha was between Berar and Oudh. From chapter ix., it would seem to have been north of Oujein (ujjayinī). From an allusion in the Çatapatha-brāhmana, ii.3.2, Weber thinks it is in the south (i.e. from Madhyadeça). These premises give some ground for the inference that Nishadha was in the valley of the Sind, which traverses Gwalior State, Central India. On the Sind is Narwār; and local tradition connects this place with "King Nala" in a story whose leading features bear a striking resemblance to those of our poem. Finally, Nala is said, chap. xv., to have reached Oudh on the tenth day after quitting Damayantī, and this time suits the distance — some two hundred miles — very well.

8[a]. **akṣapriyaḥ**, u.f. **akṣapriyas**, 172: for kṣ, cf. Whitney 13 end. — **satyavādī**, nom.s., 440. — As a dependent cpd (1265), akṣapriya may mean, 1. 'dice-beloved, lucky at gaming,' or, 2. 'dice-loving, friend of dice, fond of gaming': on the whole, mg 2 is perhaps to be preferred.

8[b]. **mahān**, nom.s., 450b.

9. See **īpsita**, which is ppl. (1037) of the desid. — **nara-nārī**, declension, 364: for ṇ, cf. 1[5a] N. end: nārī, see under **nāra**: for use of case, 296b. — **udāraḥ**, 172 again, like akṣapriyaḥ, 1[8], and çreṣṭhaḥ and manuḥ, next line, etc. etc. — **saṁyatendriyaḥ**, read p. 291, paragraph 6: **saṁyata**, √**yam**, 954d.

10. **rakṣitā**, 373. — **dhanvin-ām**, 440. — **sākṣād**, u.f. **sākṣāt**, 159. — **manu-ḥ**, 341. — Render 'as it were, Manu himself, in visible presence.'

11. **tathāivāsīd**, u.f. **tathā eva āsīt**, 127, 126, 159: see **tathā**, mg 3. — **bhīmáparākrama**, possessive form of the descriptive cpd **bhīma-parākramá**: see references in vocab.

12. **sarva-guṇāir**, u.f. **sarva-guṇāis**, 174, cf. 1[4a] N.: for mg, see **sarva** 2b: a descriptive cpd, 1279. — **yuktaḥ**, u.f. **yukta-s** (170d), ppl. (953, 219 and 217) of √**yuj**: see √**yuj** 4, 'yoked with' (hence instr., 278), and so 'possessed of'. — **prajákāmaḥ**, observe accent and references in vocab. — **sa cāprajaḥ**, u.f. **sas ca aprajas**, 176a (as exception to 170c): for **sa-s**, 495: **ca**, though coalescing with **aprajas** in euphony (126) and in print, is really an enclitic and so belongs w. **sa**: 'and yet he (sc. was) childless.'

13. **akarot**, 3d s. imf. of √1**kṛ**, 714. — 'He (in the matter of, i.e.) for the sake of children made the greatest effort,' i.e. he performed pious rites, etc.; or else, 'He had the matter of children greatly at heart, all intent (upon it).'

14. **tam**, 495, 274a. — **abhy-agacchad**, √**gam**+**abhi**, see references after pres. form **gacchati** in vocab.: this is 3d s. imf., 742. Respecting the spelling **cch**, see Preface, p. v. note 6. — **brahmarṣi-r**: for **r**, 174: declension, 339: formation, see references in vocab. There were three kinds of Rishis (see **ṛṣi**): the **rājarṣi**, or prince who adopted a life of devotion; the **devarṣi**, or sage who was also a demigod, as Nārada; and the **brahmarṣi**, or priestly sage.

— **Bhārata**, like **rājendra**, **kāunteya**, **viçām pate**, **prabho**, **mahārāja**, **rājan**, **pāndava**, **kāuravya**, etc., is an interjected vocative, addressed by Brihadaçwa, the narrator, to Yudhishthira, see p. 298, § 10.

15. **sa**, see p. 291, paragraph 1, and vocab., s.v. **ta** 4. — **toṣayām āsa**, periphrastic perf. of caus. of √**tuṣ**, 1070, 1071a: the auxiliary is the 3d s. perf. (800a) of √**as**, 'be.' — **dharma-vit**, nom.s.m., declined like **veda-vit**, 1[7].

16. **mahiṣyā**, instr. (364) of **mahiṣī**. — **suvarcas-am**: declension, 418: goes with **tam**. — **15–16**. 'Along with his queen, Bhīma, desiring children (and) knowing his duty, gratified him (tam, Damana), the glorious, with hospitality.'

17. **tasmāi**, 495. — **pra-sanno**, √**sad**+**pra**, cf. **upa-panno**, 1[4] N. — **sabhāryāya**, dat.s.m. with **tasmāi**, 'to him having an accompanying wife, i.e. to him and his wife': observe that **bhāryā** shortens its final **ā** in composition, 334[2]. — **dadāu**, √**dā**, 'give,' 800e.

NOTES TO PAGE 2.

1. **kumārāṅç ca**, u.f. **kumārān ca** (208), or rather, **kumārāṅs ca** (170c); for the so-called "inserted sibilant" is in the acc.pl. a historic survival, the original ending having been **ns**. — **trīn**, 482c. — **mahā-yaçās** (418) goes with **damanas**.

2. **damayantīm**, 364.

3. Cf. 1[4] and 1[11] and notes.

4. **tejas-ā**, 414: so **yaças-ā**. — **çriy-ā**, stem **çrí**, 351.

5. **prāpa**, 3d s. perf. √**āp**+**pra**, 783c[2], 800a. — **4–5**. 'Fair-waisted D. won fame among men by her beauty, majesty, fame, grace, and comeliness.' — Reprehensible tautology.

6. **tām**, 495. — **vayas-i prāpte**, loc. absolute, 303b: **prāpta**, ppl. of √**āp**+**pra**. — **dāsīnām**, 295 end.

7. paryupāsac chacīm, u.f. pary-upa‿āsat çacīm, see 1[7a] N.: āsat, 3d s. impf. of a-class (742 — augment 585) fr. √ās; this is reg. of the root-class, 628, and mid. voice. —6–7. Lit. 'Now, her marriageable age having come, of slaves an adorned hundred, and a hundred of friends sat around her (tām), as (they do) around Çacī.'

8. rājate, √rāj, 735. —sarva‿ābharaṇa-bhūṣitā, 'adorned with all (her) jewels,' a dependent cpd (1265), whose first member, sarvābharaṇa, is itself a cpd, like sarva-guṇa, see 1[12] N.

9. sakhī-madhye, see madhya 1. —anavadyāñgī, initial elided, 135: the cpd is the possessive form of a descriptive, 1297–8. —vidyut, 391. The Hindu epos often likens maiden beauty to the brilliantly flashing lightning of the rain-cloud.

10. rūpa-sampannā goes with bhāimī. —U.f. çrī-s (174) iva āyata-locanā, 'like long-eyed Çrī.'

11. U.f. tādṛk, nom.s.f. —rūpavatī, nom.s.f. of rūpavant, 452.

12. U.f. mānuṣeṣu (120) api ca anyeṣu dṛṣṭa-pūrvā (sc. āsīt) atha vā çrutā. api ca continues the force of the preceding negatives, 'nor also.' —For dṛṣṭa-pūrva, see reference in vocab.: dṛṣ-ṭa, ppl. of √dṛç, 218. —atha vā, see atha 6. —çrutā = çruta-pūrvā, 1316[3].

—Omission of copula (asi, asti, smas, santi, āsīt, 'art, is, are, was,' etc., 636) is extremely common; esp. so w. past pples, which thus do duty as finite verbs — cf. 3[19] N., 7[6-7] N. So also in German.

13. citta-pramāthinī; fem., 438, 440 end. —devānām, 1316, first example. —Lines 11–13 belong together: 'Neither among gods nor Yakshas (sc. was) such a beauty seen before or heard of, nor also among other beings, (namely) mortals': bālā is added in apposition to the subject.

14. nalaç, 170c. —bhuvi, 351.

15. kandarpa, 175b. —mūrtimān, 453. —abhavat, 742. —'In beauty he was like K. himself incarnate *or* having bodily form' — w. pregnant mg, since K. is said to be 'bodiless,' an-añga.

16. U.f. tasyās, 495. —pra-çaçaṅsuḥ, 3d pl. perf. (800a) of √çaṅs+pra, p. 254: subject indef., 'they' or 'messengers.'

17. punaḥ punaḥ, u.f. punar punar, 178.

18. tayor, 495. —'bhūc chṛṇvatoḥ, u.f. abhūt çṛṇvatos, see 1[7a] N.: abhūt, 829: çṛṇv-at-os, loc. du., 447, of pres. ppl., 705, of √çru, 710.

19. anyonyam, see vocab. —kāunteya, see 1[14] N. end. —vy-avardhata, √vṛdh+vi, 742.

20. a-çak-nuv-an, negatived pres. ppl., 705 (cf. 697[3] and 129[2]), of √çak. —dhārayitum, inf., 1051[6], of √dhṛ, whose pres. is made from a caus. stem, 1041, 1042b. —hṛd-ā, 391.

21. antaḥpura-, read p. 291, paragraph 4. —vana, u.f. vane, 133. —ās-te, 612. —gata-s, ppl. of √gam, 954d. —'Stays in a wood near the harem, having gone secretly.'

22. dadarça, 3d s. perf. √dṛç, strong stem dadarç, weak dadṛç, 792, 793c, 800. —haṅsāñ, 202[2]. —parişkṛtān, ppl. of √1 kṛ +pari, 1087d, 180. —'Gold-adorned' = 'of golden plumage'.

23. vi-caratām, gen. pl. of pres. ppl. of √car+vi. —teṣām, 495. —jagrāha, 3d s. perf. of √grah, 590b, 800.

NOTES TO PAGE 3.

1. vācam etc., see under vāc. —vy-ā-jahāra, 590b, 800.

2. Lines 2–4 are the words of the bird. —asmi, 636. —te, enclitic, and tava, are gen.s. of 2d pers. pron., 491: use of case, 296b. —rājan, 424. —kariṣyāmi, 933. —See priya 2a.

3. tvām, 491, object of kathayiṣyāmi, fut. of denom. stem kathaya, 933. —Supply tathā as correl. of yathā na, 'ut non', next line.

4. See yathā 6. —tvad, 491, abl. w. anya, 292b. —maṅsyati, 933, √man, mg 4.

5. ut-sa-sarj-a, √srj+ud, 800.

6. te must be from ta, 495, since the enclitic te (491) could not stand at beg. of verse. —sam-ut-pat-ya, gerund of √pat+sam-ud, 990. Note how the gerund, as instr. of accompaniment of a verbal noun

(read 989), gets its mg: 'with a flying,' i.e. 'flying' or 'having flown.' —vidarbhān, 274a. —agamaṅs, u.f. agaman, 208, aor. of √gam, 846.

7. ga-tvā, gerund again, 991: the root, gam, shows the same form as in the ppl. ga-ta, 954d. —U.f. tadā antike.

8. nipetus, √pat+ni, 800d, 794c. —dadarça, 2[22] N.

9. dṛṣ-ṭvā, √dṛç, 991, 218. —U.f. sakhigaṇa‿āvṛtā, 'surrounded by (her) friend-crowd,' 1265: sakhi- is demanded by the metre, instead of sakhī-, p. 300, § 21*d:* ā-vṛtā, ppl. of √1 vṛ+ā.

10. hṛṣ-ṭā, ppl. of √hṛṣ, 197. —grahītum, inf., 968, 972[3]: used here with verb of motion (√kram — see 981[3]), Latin, 'subiit captum'. —khagamāṅs, u.f. -ān, 208; but the s is here a true historic survival, cf. 2[1] N. —U.f. tvaramāṇā upa-, 127: √tvar, 741: upa-ca-kram-e, √kram+upa, 590b, 800a, 3d s. mid.

11. See √sṛp+vi, and 800.

12. ekāikaças refers to both subject and object — 'singulae (puellae) singulos (anseres).' —sam-upa‿adravan, √dru, 742.

13. sam-upa‿adhāvat, √dhāv, 742. — antike, 'in the presence, i.e. near,' is superfluous with 'ran on unto.'

14. kṛ-tvā, √1 kṛ, mg 3, and 991. —abravīt, 3d s. imf. of √brū, w. acc. of person, 274b. —13–14. Observe that the relative clause comes first, w. incorporated antecedent, 'ad quem anserem D. accurrit, is . . . dixit': cf. 512, and vocab. ya 4.

15. With mahīpatis supply asti, 'there is a prince . . .': cf. 2[12] N. end.

16. The first half-line goes w. line 15: supply santi in the second. —The two genitives are explained at 296b.

—The caesura, be it observed, here marks the beginning of a new clause. This is often the case. So 3[2, 8, 18, 21], 5[6], etc.

17. bhāryā, predicate nom. —U.f. bhavethās, 177, 738. —var-, voc.s., 364, fem., 440 end.

18. bhavej, u.f. bhavet, 202, 738. — janma, 424. —U.f. rūpam ca idam, 'pulcritudoque haec'. —'Fruitful (of good) would be thy birth, and this beauty (of thine),' i.e. it would then prove a fortunate thing that thou wast born and art so beautiful.

19. For the long cpd, see 1247 I[2]: divide -mānuṣa-uraga-, 127: the whole is object of dṛṣṭa-vant-as (supply smas, 'sumus' — 2[12] N. end), which is exactly like the Eng. '(are) having seen' = 'have seen': read 959 and 960. —In the later mythology, the serpents are divine beings with human face, whose beauty is often praised: cf. 13[1].

20. U.f. na ca asmābhis (491), 'neque a nobis.' —dṛṣṭapūrvas, supply āsīt and see N. to 2[12]. —tathāvidhas, substantively, of course: '(a man) of such sort'.

21. U.f. tvam ca api, supply asi, as in 2[12] N. —nārīṇām, 364, in vocab. under nāra. —nalo, supply asti, as in 2[12] N.

22. U.f. viçiṣṭāyās, 177, gen.s.f., ppl. of √çiṣ+vi. —For use of instr., 284. —'Eximiae cum eximio congressus.' —For saṁgama, read p. 291 ¶ 7.

23. For viçām pate, 'O prince', s.v. viç 2, see 1[14] N. end.

Notes to Page 4.

1. abravīt, see 3[14] N. —nale, 304a. — 'Do thou speak so to Nala also' (sc. as thou hast to me). The api ought to follow nale.

2. See iti, mg 2, and tathā, mg 2. — uktvā, √vac, 991: the root shows same weak form as in ppl., 954b — cf. 217.

3. ā-gam-ya, 990. —nale, as in line 1. —See √1 vid+ni: imf. 3d s. of caus., 1042a, cf. 1043. —2–3. 'The bird, saying "Yes" to the maid (274b) of Vidarbha, ..., communicated all to Nala.'

4. See iti, mg 2e. —In this poem, adhyāya (not sarga) is the proper word for 'chapter.'

6. For tac chrutvā, see N. to 1[7a]: tat, 495: çru-tvā, 991. —bhārata, see N. to 1[14] end.

7. prati, here used as a true "preposition", or rather postposition, connecting nalam with svasthā — see 1123. —babhūva, √bhū, 789a.

8. U.f. tatas, 170c. —For an explanation of the nature of these and the following long cpds, look up the references under them in vocab.

9. niḥçvāsa-, read p. 291 ¶ 4.

10. unmatta-darçanā, 1299: for un-, 161.

11. U.f. kṣaṇena atha. —The complete analysis of the long word is indicated by references in vocab.

12. First cpd, see 1253a. —vindati, √2 vid.

13. çete, √1 çī, 629. —U.f. "hā hā" iti. —See √rud and 619. —See punar 2.

15. asvasthām: observe the use, common in Skt., of a predicate adj. or subst. instead of subordinate clause: thus, 'announced D. as ill', where we should say, 'announced that she was ill': so 4^{19} kāryam. —nareçvare (like nale, $4^{1.8}$) is loc. w. nyavedayat and in logical apposition w. the dat. vidarbhapataye, despite the difference of case.

16. See N. to 4^{6}. —Observe how the idea of 4^{14b} is here put in one cpd.

17. cint-, see N. to 1^{15}. —'Considered this important matter (in respect to, i.e.) concerning his daughter.'

18. See √īkṣ and 992. —prāp-, see 1308. —'Considering his daughter who had reached nubility,' i.e. taking fully into account the fact of her marriageability (though he knew it well enough before).

19. apaçyad, 759, 760.6. —See ātman 3, and 514. 'Saw D's swayamvara requiring to be instituted by himself, saw that he must hold D's sw.'; cf. N. to 4^{15}.

20. Periphrastic perf. of denom. mantraya+saṁ-ni, 1070, 1071a.

21. anubh- is 3d s. pres. imv. pass., √bhū +anu, 771.4. —ayam, read p. 291 ¶ 1, and see 501. —iti marks the four preceding words as the precise words of Bhīma's invitation: 'Let this swayamvara be heard *or* taken notice of, O heroes, i.e. Understand ye that one will take place here.' —prabho, 341, see 1^{14} N. end. —Observe that we have ⏑ ⏑ — ⏑ — as the first half of the first pāda, a not infrequent irregularity.

NOTES TO PAGE 5.

1. sarve, 524, cf. 495.

2. abhijagmus, √gam+abhi, 590b, 794d. —For abl., see 291^{2}.

3. The aggregative cpd hasty-açva-ratha (1252) makes w. ghoṣa a genitively dependent cpd (1264): hasti for hastin, $1249a^{2}$. —pūrayantas (√1 pṛ), agrees w. subject of preceding clause.

4. Divide, vicitramālya+ābharaṇa, as descriptive, 1280b. —balāis, 279. —'(They came) . . . with troops, splendid (and) well adorned with variegated-garland-ornaments.'

5. teṣām (495) pārth-, objective gen. w. pūjām.

6. akarot, 1^{13} N. —te begins new clause —see 3^{16} N. —U.f. avasan, 135, 208, √3 vas.

7. U.f. etasmin, 210, 499b: see vocab. under etad. —'The two best of the Rishis (1264) of the gods': the verb is in line 10.

8. See √aṭ and 741. —U.f. mahātmānāu, 134. —gatāu, 954d.

9. U.f. ca eva, 127, see eva, end. —mahā- stands in adverbial relation to -prājña ('greatly, i.e. very, wise'), since the whole is a descriptive *adjective* cpd — see 1279.

10. Third pers. dual, perf. mid., √viç, 800a. —See sú 2, inseparable prefix.

11-12. U.f. tāu, 495. —arc-, gerund from caus. stem of √ṛc, 1051^{7}. —papraccha, 590, 794c. —U.f. anāmayam ca api. —-gata (like -bhūta, see 6^{7} N., and 1273c) is a mere means of turning sarva- [=sarvatra] into attributive form: so also in sarvatragatam, line 14, which should be printed as a cpd, and means, like sarvagatam, 'under all circumstances, i.e. in all their goings and doings.' Amend vocab. accordingly.

—'Saluting them, Maghavan then asked after the welfare unbroken and also diseaseless of them two under all circumstances — he, the mighty one': i.e. (cf. the principle explained 4^{15} N.) 'asked if it had gone constantly well with them and if they had been entirely free from sickness.'

14-15. āvayos, 491. —Copulas omitted — 2^{12} N. —'Of us two (there is) welfare O god, under all circumstances, O lord: and in the whole (kṛtsne) world, O Maghavan, the princes (are) prosperous, O mighty one.'

18-20 are prefatory to the question proper in line 21[a]: 'The princes (proleptic nom. independent) . . . , who (509) go to death by the sword (280) . . . , — this (501) imperishable world, i.e. heaven, (is — cf. 2[12] N. end) granting every wish of them, just as (yathā‿eva) of me (it grants every wish).' The idea is, Since the brave warriors can here obtain their every wish, why do they not come up?

21. 'Where now (are) those princes, heroes?' —Observe caesura: cf. 3[16] N.

22. **āgacchatas, √gam+ā,** 741, 447, agrees w. **tān.**

NOTES TO PAGE 6.

2. çṛṇu, 710, 703. —**me,** 491, 297b. —**dṛçyante,** 768, 771.

3. Supply **asti,** 'there is' (a daughter)... —See **iti,** mg 2 f. —**√çru+vi.**

4. Ppl. of **√kram+sam-ati** (955a) 'having excelled = excelling.'

5. tasyās, 495. —**bhavitā,** 944.

7. See **bhūta** 2, and reference, 1273c, and cf. 5[12] N. —Pres. ppl. of denom. stem **arthaya+pra,** 1068.

8. kāṅkṣanti governs **tām.**

9. 'While this (499b) is being told' (pres. ppl. pass. of **kathaya,** 1068, cf. 1052a), loc. absolute, 303b. —Study references under **sāgnika.** an important kind of cpd: lit. 'having an accompanying (**sa-**) Agni', where **sa-** is equiv. to an adj. Others in line 13.

10. √gam+ā, cf. 5[2] N.

11. √çru, 3d pl. perf., 800b.

12. U.f. **çrutvā eva ca abruvan** (632) **hṛṣṭās.** —**gacchāmas:** for tense, 777a.

13. mahārāja, see 1[14] N. end.

14. yatas, supply **āsan,** 'were.'

15. kāunteya, see 1[14] N. end.

17. path-i, loc.s., 433. —**dadṛçus,** 2[22] N. —**sthitam,** superfluous, see **sthita** 2.

18. 'In reality almost, the god of love, present (see **sthita** 3) with definite shape, (by reason of beauty =) so handsome was he.' Cf. 2[16] N.

20. tasthus, 590c, 794f, 800c. —**√smi+vi.**

21. viṣṭabhya, √stabh+vi, 185, 992.

22. rājann, 210: see 1[14] N. end. —**√tṛ +ava,** 992[2], 242.

23. U.f. **bhos,** see 176a. —**bhavān,** see **bhavant** and 456, and supply **asti,** 514.

NOTES TO PAGE 7.

1. 'Do thou (714) assistance of us' (491). Observe caesura.

4. √jñā, 989. —U.f. **kariṣye,** 133, 933. —'Nala, promising them "I will do (the assistance)", . . .'.

5. etān, 499b. —**√sthā+upa,** 954c.

6-7. Now review declension of pronouns — very frequent hereabouts: interrogatives, **ke, kas, kim,** 504; demonstratives, **tad,** 495, **ayam** and **asau,** 501; personal, **aham, mayā, asmān,** and **vas, tvam, tvām,** 491.

Note frequent omission (2[12] N.) of copula: u.f. **ke bhavantas (santi,** 514)? **kas ca asāu (asti), yasya aham īpsitas (asmi) dūtas? kim ca (asti) tad vas mayā kāryam** ('mihi faciendum')? —**yasya dūtas,** 'as messenger *to* whom.' —**kath-,** 1068, 1043.4.

8[a]. See 303b[4].

9. √budh+ni, 739. —'Know us as gods, i.e. know that we are gods' — cf. 4[15] N. —See **artha.**

10. U.f. **aham indras (asmi), ayam agnis ca (asti), tathā eva ayam apām patis (asti).** —**ayam,** 'this one here', with a gesture of introduction. —**apām,** see **ap.** 'Lord of waters' is Varuṇa.

11. nṛṇām, gen.pl. of **nṛ,** 371[5]. —U.f. **yamas ayam (asti).**

12. 'Announce us as assembled' — cf. 4[15] N.

The last three lines (13-15) of Indra's speech contain in oratio recta the message which he wishes Nala to deliver.

13. Lit. 'The world-protectors, having Great-Indra as first, i.e. Great-Indra and the other world-protectors': for this important kind of cpd, study 1302c 1, and **ādi** in vocab. —**√yā+sam-ā,** 611. —See reference under **didṛkṣu.**

14. 'The gods seek (**√1 iṣ,** 608) to win (**√āp,** 968) thee.'

15. 'Choose thou', √2 vṛ, 1043.4.

17. 'Me, come hither (sam-upa-itam, √i) for one and the same purpose.' —Inf. of √2 iṣ+pra, 1051.

18–19. 'Pray how can (√sah+ud) a man who is in love say (√vac, 968) such a thing to a woman (striyam 366, 274b) for another?'

20. ūcus, √vac, perf., see references.

21. saṁ-çru-tya, 992. —For loc., 304a.

Notes to Page 8.

1. kar-, 933. —Observe caesura.

4. veç-, object of praveṣṭum, which is inf. of √viç+pra, 218.

5. U.f. pra-vekṣyasi (√viç, fut., 932, 218) iti . . . eva abhy-.

6. √gam. —See iti, mg 2.

7. Third word is vāidarbhīm. —See √1 vṛ+sam-ā.

8. √dīp, intens. 1000, 1002a, 1016. —vapuṣ-ā, 414.

10. √kṣip+ā, 752.5.

11. Join tasya w. kāmas, and tām w. dṛṣṭvā. —√vṛdh, 800.

12. See satya 3. —cik-, √1 kṛ, desid., 1027, 1028b. —√dhṛ, 1070, 1071a.

13. √bhram+sam, 955a.

14. √pat+sam-ud, 794c. —√dhṛṣ.

16. U.f. na ca enam, see ena and 500.

18. U.f. kas ayam (asti)? —For rest of line, see atha 6 and 948^2 end.

19. √çak, $697^{1,3}$. —See √hṛ+vy-ā: inf. —See 1 ka 2c and 507.

20. Nom.pl.fem. of lajjāvant, 452^3.

21–22. 'Then to him smiling, Damayantī — with a smile addressing — unto the hero Nala spake, amazed.'

Notes to Page 9.

1. U.f. prāptas (√āp) asi, 636. —'Thou art having come like a god, i.e. thou camest invisibly?' Observe caesura. —√jñā, w. gen. te, 'get acquainted with thee.'

2. U.f. ca iha (āsīt). Caesura. —U.f. asi na lakṣitas (ppl. of lakṣaya), 'wast thou not noticed.'

3. Caesura. —U.f. ca eva ugra-.

5. viddhi = ἴσθι: see √1 vid 2 and 617.

6–7. Cf. $7^{14,15}$. —çobh-, voc.s.fem.

8. U.f. praviṣṭas aham (asmi), √viç.

9. √viç, 752.5. —See 1 ka 2d and 507. —U.f. apaçyat, na api avār- (√1 vṛ caus.).

10. preṣitas (asmi), √2 iṣ.

11. √1 kṛ+pra, 2d s. impv. mid. 714.

14. From here on, the use of virāma with a final consonant to prevent its combining in print with a following initial is given up. Thus in nalamabravīt, we allow the a, which — if unannulled by virāma — is inherent in the nāgarī sign for ma, to serve as the first letter of abravīt. Cf. 9^4 with the identical 10^2.

See 992 for the two cpd gerunds.

15. √nī+pra, 739: for ṇ, 192a. —See √1 kṛ 2, 714, 578.

16. U.f. yat (202) ca anyat (161) mama asti: see √1 as 2. —'For both I and what other good soever I have —'

17. 'That all (is) thine.' —kuru, 714. —īçvara = Nala.

18. Explained at 512a, q.v.

19. √pat+saṁ-ni, pass. ppl. of *causative*, hence long ā, 1051.

20. √khyā+praty-ā, 932: 948^2 examples.

Notes to Page 10.

1. āsthāsye, √sthā+ā, 932. —Suicide by hanging etc. is referred to: so also Pañchatantra iv. fable 2.

2. Identical with 9^4.

3. √sthā 5: loc. (741), absolute, 303b. —'The gods being present, how seekest thou a man (as husband, in preference)?'

4–5. As at $3^{13,14}$ (see N.), the relative clause comes first, with incorporated antecedent: lit. 'Of what world-creating noble lords I (am) not equal to the foot-dust (instr., see 281a), let thy mind on those be busied' (√vṛt 4, 739). More natural to us would seem teṣu lokakṛtsu īçvareṣu mahātmasu. "He's not as good as the dust on my feet" was prob. a proverbial expression of reproach: so Mālavikā, act i.

6. U.f. hi ācaran, pres. ppl. —devānām limits vipriyam, 296 b. —ṛcchati, see √ṛ.

7. √trā, 617. —Cf. 2^9 N. and 7^{15} N.

8. See tathā 3. Nala tells her (lines 8–9) what she may enjoy if she chooses a god.

9. devān prāpya, √āp, 992, 'by obtaining gods (in wedlock).' —bhuñkṣva, √2 bhuj, 689.

10. U.f. yas: its antecedent is tam. —imām, 501. —√kṣip, 992. —See punar 3.

12-13. Explained 291^2. —yasya limits only daṇḍa-, not the whole cpd, 1316. Yama is meant here.

16-17. kriyatām (770c) varaṇam, 'let a choice be made'. —yadi manyase, √man 3. —suhṛdvākyam. —çṛṇu, 6^2 N.

19. √plu+sam-ā, past ppl., instr. dual. —See atha 4. —See vāri and 339.

21. √2 vṛ, 718. —Declension of bhartṛ, 373. —satyam etad bravīmi, see satya 3.

22. √vip, 741. —kṛtāñjalim, here fem., 346, 344.

23. āgatya, √gam, 992. —U.f. iha utsahe: see √sah+ud 2.

NOTES TO PAGE 11.

1. U.f. hi aham. —For gen., 297a.

2. See √rabh+ā 2. —katham, epanalepsis.

3. U.f. eṣas (176a) dharmas (sc. asti), forms a clause. —bhavitā, 944. See 949^2 near end.

4. See √1 dhā+vi 5 and 770b.

6. See √1 hṛ+praty-ā.

7. 'Here is a safe means (seen—in the mind, i.e.) thought out by me.'

8. bhavitā = bhaviṣyati, line 12.

9-10. U.f. tvam ca eva . . . devās ca . . . āyāntu (√yā, 611): verb agrees w. nearest subject. Observe caesura in 10. With yatra supply asti.

11. For saṁnidhi (ṁ = n), read p. 291 ¶ 7.

12. var- governs tvām. —U.f. na evam.

14. U.f. punar, 178. —End, supply āsan.

15. U.f. tam apaçyan (208) tathā āyāntam (619).

16. U.f. ca enam, 500.

17. For kaccid (kat cid, 202), see kad.

18^a. 'And what did she say to us all?'

20. U.f. bhavadbhis, 456. —See √diç +ā. —niv-, with praviṣṭas.

21. 'Guarded (vṛ-tam) by warders' (daṇḍibhis).

22. U.f. na kas cid (1 ka 2d) dṛṣṭavān (sc. asti) naras, see 959, 960, this example.

NOTES TO PAGE 12.

1. U.f. sakhyas (364) ca asyās (501) . . . tābhis ca api . . . —Copula twice omitted.

2. U.f. sarvās, nom.fem. —vib-, voc.

3. 'While ye are being described by me,' 303b.

4. √2 vṛ, 718. —sur-, voc. —Cf. 10^{21}.

5. In the words āyāntu to bhavitā, line 8, Nala repeats substantially D's plan (11^{9-12}), but in oratio recta. Hiatus (113) is allowed at the caesura; otherwise bālā (unless it had lost a final s, 177) would coalesce with the following initial. Cf. 16^{11} N.

8. mah-, voc. —bhavitā, 11^8 N. —See iti 5.

9-10. U.f. etāvad (nom.n., 453). udāhṛtam (√hṛ, sc. asti) mayā, full stop. —'For the rest, ye (are) an authority, O gods': i.e. it's your affair alone now.

13. The three substantives are locatives absolute with prāpte, $303b^3$.

14. √hū+ā: w. 782 cf. 643b. —For loc., 304.

16. √gam+sam-upa‿ā, 1080. —For acc., dam-, 271a.

18. U.f. viviçus (cf. 5^{13} N.) te nṛpās . . . acalam.

19. U.f. āsaneṣu . . āsīnās, 619^3.

20^b. The cpd is a possessive form (1301) of a descriptive cpd, 1280b.

NOTES TO PAGE 13.

1. Second word is suçlakṣṇāḥ. —'Like the five-headed serpents'—because the hand is quinquepartite. Cf. 3^{19} N.

5. √muṣ, 724: fem. irreg., $449c^3$: 'beguiling'—cf. κλέπτειν νόον. —prabhayā, 364. —cakṣūṅṣi, 414 end.

6-7. U.f. teṣām dṛṣṭis, . . . patitā, . . . saktā (√sañj) abhūt (829)—caesura: na ca (dṛṣṭis teṣām) paçyatām cacāla.

8. 'While the names are being announced'—loc. absolute, 303b, pres. ppl. of pass. of denom. kīrtaya+sam.

9. See atha 4. —See p. 299, § 15.

10. √īkṣ+sam, 992. —See sthita 4.

11. U.f. saṁdehāt (ṁ = n, p. 291 ¶ 7) . . na abhy-ajānāt, √jñā, 730^2, 725.

12. See ya 5. —See √man, 704e. — 'For whichever she saw of them, him she thought (to be) king N.'

13. U.f. buddhyā, 339. —tark-, cf. 1[15] N.

14. Optatives (577) of √jñā, 721, and √1 vid, 616.

17–18. 'What marks of the gods [(are) my heard ones (296b) =] I have heard of from old men, these I do not notice as (being of, i.e.) belonging to even one (ekasya api) of those standing here (iha) on the ground (bhūmāu).'

19. √3 ci+vi-nis, 992. —√car+vi, 1051.

20. 'Thought (it) an arrived-time, i.e. thought that the time had arrived (cf. note to 4[15]) for refuge (of the) to the gods.'

22. prā- is predicate adj. w. bhū-tvā, 991. See √bhū. —U.f. vepamānā idam.

23. 'As surely as N. (was) chosen by me on hearing . . :' see yathā 4.

Notes to Page 14.

1. patitve, 'in marriage,' goes with vṛtas. —See satya 2 and 280 end. —U.f. tam = Nala.

2. U.f. na abhicarāmi.

4. 'Ordained (as my, i.e.) to be my husband'—√1 dhā+vi 3, and 954c.

6. 'As this ceremony (vrata) was undertaken by me (in the =) for the winning of Nala . .'. —√rabh+ā: rabh-ta = rabdha, 160.

8. √1 kṛ 3, 714: should be mid. See p. 209, § 15.

9. See yathā 6. —√jñā+abhi, 721.

10. √4 çam, 992. —U.f. tad.

11. √1 kṛ, 800f.

12–13. 'She saw (apaçyat) all the gods, free from sweat (asvedān), unwinking, having unwithered garlands and free from dust, standing (see sthita 1) without touching (asprçatas) the ground.' The "unwinking eyes" are a survival of the old Vedic conception of the gods that "neither slumber nor sleep." The other marks of anthropomorphic divinity are natural enough. The opposites of all five attributes are ascribed to Nala, besides a shadow.

14. U.f. mlānasrak, nom.s.m., 391. —rajaḥ-sveda- (1252), in instr. relation, forms a cpd (1265) w. sam-anv-itas, √i.

15. 'And (ca eva) the Nishadhan, . . line 14 . ., (was) made recognizable, (by) standing on the ground, and (ca) by winking.'

17. √2 vṛ, 1070. —pāṇḍava, see 1[14] N. end.

18. See √grah 1. —Cf. 2[10].

21. 'The cry "Ah, ah" (hā hā‿iti — cf. 4[13]) was uttered (√muc).'

22–23. Same construction. 'The cry "Bravo" was uttered (īritas, √īr) by . . . praising (√çaṅs) N.' —Note the generous magnanimity of the gods.

Notes to Page 15.

1. kāuravya, see 1[14] N. end.

2. √çvas+ā, caus. imf. —U.f. antarātmanā.

3. See yad 3: correl. in line 4.

4[a]. Cf. 9[5] and N.

4[b]. 'Delighted (√ram 3) with such (see evam, end) words of thine' (as thou hast spoken in choosing me). Loc., 303.

5. See yāvant 2. —See √dhṛ 6.

6[a]. √bhū, construed prop. w. loc. of thing (e.g. dāne), means 'be in *or* on' (e.g. giving), i.e. 'devoted to' (charity): here the construction seems extended in like mg to a person. 'So long will I be devoted to thee' — tvayi. —Line 6[b] = 10[21b].

7–8. See vāc (391) and nand+abhi. A line, containing the principal verb with Nala as subject, seems lacking.

9–10. √prī 3. —U.f. tu agni-: see -purogama. —See √gam 5. —'But the two, mutually pleased, beholding Agni and the others, perceived those very gods as their refuge, i.e. perceived that the gods had been good to them.'

11–12. vṛte, 303b. —U.f. nalāya aṣṭāu (483[3]) . . dadus (800c). —The four gods give each two gifts, and, besides, one gift in common, a couple of children (mithunam, 19). It is by his exercise of the supernatural powers now given to Nala that Damayantī in the sequel (chap. 23) recognizes her lost and transformed husband. In passing through a low door-way, he does not stoop — the lintel rises; when he wants fire and water for cooking, they come at his wish; and he seasons the food exquisitely.

13-14. U.f. **gatim ca an-**, 'and a most excellent gait': this includes the ability to pass through the low door-way, as above. —√prī 2, 760.5.

15. The god of fire and the god of the waters (18) give N. magic power over their respective elements — see above and p. 299, § 15. —U.f. **pra-adāt** (√1 dā, 829) **yatra**.

16. U.f. **lokān ātmaprabhān** (208) **ca eva**: 'places-in-heaven, having his (the Fire-god's) splendor, *or* a splendor of their own' (heaven has "no need of the sun, neither of the moon, to shine in it"): this amounts, perhaps, to 'hopes of future blessedness'; but the Hindus make a deal of loose talk about 'worlds' (lokās).

17. U.f. **yamas tu**. —**anna-rasam**, 'subtle taste for food' — as the sequel shows — see above: vocab. wrong.

18. With **apām patir** supply **prādāt** and see 7^{11} N.

19. U.f. **srajas ca ut-**.

20. U.f. **evam pra-dāya** (992) **asya** (501), explained 297a.

21-22. Construe, **anu-bhūya vivāham asya damayantyāç ca**: 'learning of the wedding, i.e. that it would take place duly' — they went back home.

NOTES TO PAGE 16.

1. √1 kṛ, caus., 1070, 1045.

2. **uṣya**, √3 vas, irreg. (990^2) for **uṣitvā**.

4. U.f. **bhrājamānas añçumān**: after elision (**bhrājamāno 'ñçumān**), the anuswāra belongs to the **o**, and so — in nāgarī — has to be put over the **o** and to the left of the avagraha.

6. U.f. **īje** (√yaj) **ca api**. —Yayāti was an ancient king, whose piety is celebrated even in the Rigveda, where the gods are besought to bless the sacrificer with their presence, as in old time they did for Yayāti. His story is told MBh. i., chap. 75.

7. U.f. **anyāis ca bahubhis, dhīmān, kratubhis ca āptadakṣiṇāis**: the second **ca** seems superfluous.

8. U.f. **punar** (178) **ca . . . upavaneṣu** (126).

9. √hṛ+vi, cf. 3^1 N. and 16^{12}.

10. √jan, 1070, 1045: w. loc., 'begat upon (the body of) D.'

11. Observe hiatus at the caesura — cf. 12^5 N. —By penance the great ascetics could become as gods and thrust even Indra from his throne. The anxious god's most effectual means to defend himself from the power of their austerities was to seduce them by sending a nymph so lovely that they could not resist her charms. 'Indra's weapon' (**indrasenā**, see vocab.) is therefore a very complimentary name for Nala's daughter. To name her brother, a corresponding masculine was formed, which has, of course, no other than grammatical appropriateness.

12. U.f. **viharan ca**, 208.

SELECTIONS II.-XXI.

FROM THE HITOPADEÇA, THE 'BOOK OF GOOD COUNSEL.'

§ 22. The first book ever printed in Sanskrit was Kālidāsa's 'Seasons' (ṛtusaṁhāra), edited by Sir Wm. Jones, and printed in Bengalī letters in 1792. The first Sanskrit book ever printed in Nāgarī letters was the Hitopadeça. It was edited by Carey, and printed at Serampore in 1803. The publication was undertaken, said Henry T. Colebrooke, "to promote and facilitate the study of the ancient and learned language of India in the College of Fort William." It was chosen as the first for this purpose because of its easy style and intrinsic interest and because two English translations of it existed, one by Wilkins (Bath, 1787), and the other by Jones (London, 1799). To pedagogical reasons, accordingly, may be assigned in great part, the importance of this work: it has become important in the West, because the text is so well suited for tyros in Sanskrit; and in the Orient, because of the intrinsic value of its contents.

§ 23. The book belongs to the ethico-didactic class of literature, and is what the Hindus call a nīti-çāstra or 'cónduct-work.' The term nīti (see this in the vocabulary) came to have special reference to the conduct of kings in their domestic life and in their foreign relations; a nīti-çāstra is, accordingly, a 'Prince's handbook of political and social ethics,' a kind of 'Mirrour for Magistrates.' The Hitopadeça consists of mingled verse and prose. The verses are mostly proverbs and maxims — often of the choicest practical wisdom; and their validity is proved, illustrated, and enforced by the fables, which are in prose.

§ 24. The frame in which the work is set is simple and meagre. The sons of King Sudarçana of Pāṭaliputra[1] (Patnā) are ignorant and vicious. He therefore convokes the wise men and asks if any one is able to reform the princes. Viṣṇuçarman offers to do so, and accordingly takes them in charge, and relates to them the stories which make up the body of the collection.

§ 25. The Hitopadeça is not an original work, but, rather, an excellent compilation of ancient material. The time of its composition has not been even approximately determined. The palm-leaf MS. brought by Mr. Cecil Bendall from Nepāl was written in the year 493 of the Nepāl era or A.D. 1373. And Professor Peterson's[2] old paper MS. from Jeypore is of about the same age. At present we can hardly say more than that the work is at least 500 years old. In the working over of the material, the metrical portions would naturally be changed less, on the whole, than the prose; and in fact, many of the proverbs can be traced back in their identical form to works of antiquity. And travellers report that just such proverbs are current to-day in the talk of the lower classes of India.

The author or editor of this collection of fables, according to the colophon[3] of the Jeypore MS., was named Nārāyaṇa, and his patron and publisher was the prince Dhavalacandra.

§ 26. The sources of this compilation are expressly said (end of the preface, 17^8) to be "the Pañcatantra and another work." The first part of this statement is borne out by the fact that, out of forty-three fables in the Hitopadeça, twenty-five are found also in the Pañcatantra. The latter work, as its name implies, consists of five books; while the Hitopadeça is divided into four, whose titles are given in the preface, 17^7. The correspondence is as follows. The first book of the Pañcatantra answers in its frame-work to the second of the Hitopadeça and the second of the Pañcatantra to the first of the Hitopadeça. Five stories from the third book of the Pañcatantra, along with seven from the first, are scattered through the last two books of the Hitopadeça. From the fourth book of the Pañcatantra only one story, "The ass in the tiger-skin," appears in the Hitopadeça; and from the fifth book, only three. It thus appears that, in the main, only the first three books of the Pañcatantra were drawn upon by the author of the Hitopadeça; and Somadeva, in his Kathā-sarit-sāgara (chapters 60–64, much of whose substance is from the Pañcatantra, i.–iii.), has followed a similar course.

§ 27. What the "other work" is we can hardly say with entire certainty. In it ought to be found together — if the statement of the preface is accurate — at least

[1] From this point the spelling of proper names will no longer be anglicized.

[2] See Preface to his Hitopadeça, p. i, ii, v.

[3] Peterson's ed., p. 161: cf. p. iv, v.

the eighteen fables of the Hitopadeça which do not occur in the Pañcatantra. Had the preface said "other works," the problem would be easier. Thus the story of the two giants, iv. 9, may be traced to the Mahā-bhārata, and the prototypes of other single stories are doubtless to be found in one and another ancient collection. Professor Peterson[1] thinks that the "other work" is the Nītisāra of Kāmandaka. The identification deserves further study.

§ 28. The contents of the Pañcatantra have been made the subject of one of the most important contributions to the literary history of the world by the late Professor Benfey. His principal results were published in his *Pantschatantra* (1859, see above, p. xviii, no. 8), and in his introduction to Bickell's edition of the *Kalilag und Damnag* (1876). The latter contains, pages VI–X, a brief résumé of these results. The summary given by Keith-Falconer (1885, see p. 315) is a systematic and lucid account of the history of the fables, and is the one most to be commended to English-speaking students. Some of the most important items follow.

A. The Indian original. In the sixth century of our era, there existed in India a Buddhist Sanskrit work, in thirteen chapters, treating of the conduct of princes.[2] Its doctrines were inculcated in the form of beast-fables, or stories in which animals play the part of human beings.

B. This Indian original was translated by a Persian physician named Barzōī, into the Pehlevī, the literary language of Persia, by command of the Sassanian king, Khosru Anūshīrvān, called The Just (531–579 A.D.).

§ 29. **C1.** Both the Indian original and its Pehlevī version are irrecoverably lost; but from the latter were made two very notable translations. The first was into Syriac, made about 570 A.D., and called *Kalilag and Damnag* after the two jackals, Karaṭaka and Damanaka, who figured prominently in the introduction of the Sanskrit original. A single notice of this version had been preserved in a catalogue of Syriac writings made by Ebed-jesus (died 1318), and published by Assemani at Rome in 1725. A Chaldean bishop, Georgius Ebed-jesus Khayyāth, on his way to the ecumenical council in 1870, stumbled upon a manuscript of this Syriac version in the episcopal library at Mardīn. Through the mediation of Ignazio Guidi in Rome, and by a wonderful combination of lucky accidents and persistent efforts, the existence of "the lost manuscript" was made known to the eager inquirers in Europe,[3] and at last published in text and German translation by Bickell.

§ 30. **C2.** The second translation from the Pehlevī was the *Kalilah and Dimnah* or *Fables of Pilpay* in Arabic, made by Abd-allah ibn al-Moqaffa, a Persian convert to Islam, who lived under the caliph al-Mansor and died about 760. This version was published, though not in the best recension, by Silvestre de Sacy at Paris in 1816, and an English translation of it was given by the Rev. Wyndham Knatchbull, Oxford, 1819.

According to the Arabic introduction, Dabshelim (deva-çarman) was the first king of the Indian Restoration after the fall of the governor appointed by Alexander

[1] See his Introduction, p. 29, 43, Notes, p. 3. The Nītisāra was edited by Rājendralāla Mitra, in the Bibliotheca Indica, vol. iv.

[2] Such was Benfey's conclusion. It was questioned by Weber, *Indische Streifen*, iii. 437. Barzōī's Pehlevī version (B.) may have been based on several *different* works—among them a Pañcatantra. Indeed, from the second chapter of the Arabic Kalilah and Dimnah, 'The mission of Barzōī' (Knatchbull, pages 40–41; cf. Keith-Falconer, p. xxi), and from other evidence (Keith-Falconer, p. liv f), this is the much more probable view.

[3] The story of the discovery is told by Benfey, in Bickell's book, pages XII–XXIII, as also in various periodicals there cited, p. XXII note, e.g. *London Academy* for Aug. 1, 1871.

at the close of his campaign in the Panjāb, B.C. 326. When firmly established, Dabshelim gave himself over to every wickedness. To reclaim the king, a Brahman philosopher takes up his parable, as did Nathan before David, and at last wins him back to virtue. The wise man is called in Arabic *bid-bah*[1] and in Syriac *bid-vag*. These words are satisfactorily traced by Benfey, through the Pehlevī, to the Sanskrit **vidyā-pati**, 'master of sciences.' Accordingly, *bidbah*, which has become Bidpai or Pilpay in our modern books, is not really a proper name, but an appellative, applied to a 'Chief Pandit' or 'Court-scholar' of an Indian prince.

The Arabic version is of prime importance, since from it have flowed other versions, which have been of the utmost influence in shaping the literature of the Middle Ages.

§ 31. **D.** These versions are: **1.** The Later Syriac, made in the tenth or eleventh century, edited by Wright, and translated by Keith-Falconer; **2.** the Greek one, made about 1080, by Symeon Seth, a Jewish physician; **3.** the Persian, made some fifty years later, by Nasr Allah of Ghaznī; **4.** the Hebrew, ascribed to Rabbi Joel, and probably made before 1250, and published, with French translation, at Paris in 1881, by Joseph Derenbourg; **5.** the old Spanish, made from the Arabic in 1251, and published at Madrid in 1860 by Gayangos.

§ 32. **E.** Of the descendants in the fifth degree from the original, only two need be mentioned: **3.** The Persian *Anwār-i Suhailī* or 'Lights of Canopus,' a simplified recast of Nasr Allah's, made about 1494 by Husain Wāiz al-Kāshifī. English translations of this have been published by Eastwick and by Wollaston, see below. **4.** The *Directorium humanae vitae*, made from the Hebrew about 1270 by John of Capua, and printed about 1480.

§ 33. **F.** From John of Capua's version flowed the famous 'Book of examples of the ancient sages,' *Das bůch der byspel der alten wysen*. It was made at the instance of Duke Eberhard im Bart, whose name and motto, EBERHART GRAF Z[U] WIRTENBERG ATTEMPTO, appear as an acrostic in the initials of the first sections. It was first printed about 1481, and has since been admirably edited by W. L. Holland, Stuttgart, 1860. Holland used, besides three manuscripts, two printed editions *sine loco et anno*, and enumerates 17 dated editions that appeared between 1483 and 1592. Four dated editions appeared at Ulm between 1483 and 1485! The great number of editions of the work and their rapid succession are the best proof of its importance as a means of instruction and amusement in the fifteenth and sixteenth centuries.

Another offshoot from the *Directorium* is the Italian version of A. F. Doni, entitled *La moral filosophia*, and printed at Venice[2] in 1552. This is of special interest, because from it came (**G**) the English translation of Sir Thomas North, London, 1570.

It may here be added that La Fontaine, in the second edition of his Fables (1678), which contains eleven books, says[3] that he owed the largest part of his new material (books vii–xi) to Pilpay, the Indian sage. The edition of Henri Regnier (Paris, Hachette, 1883–85, 3 vols.) gives abundant references to the sources of each fable, and is especially to be commended to those who would compare the well-known French offshoots with the Indian originals.

[1] See Benfey, in Bickell, p. XLIII f.
[2] With wood-cuts. Harvard College has a copy.
[3] *Avertissement* prefixed to book vii, Regnier ii. 81.

§ 34. From Benfey's investigations it appears that the truest extant representative of the Indian original is the Syriac version, *Kalilag and Damnag*. Next to the Syriac stands the *Buch der Beispiele*, which, besides, is in language remarkable for its dignity, strength, and beauty; upon this latter version, moreover, are based almost all the printed ones previous to 1644. To the German version almost exclusively, therefore, is Europe indebted for the wide-spread knowledge of this cycle of literature from the last part of the fifteenth to the middle of the seventeenth century.

§ 35. After this account of the direct descendants of the Indian original in the Occident, it remains to speak of the history of that original in India, and of its sources. Whether Barzōī translated from one work of thirteen chapters (cf. § 28) or from several independent works, the fact remains that the originals of all of his sections may be certainly identified on Indian ground save three:[1] five, namely, form the Pañcatantra; two other sections figure as a supplement to the first book of a later recension of the Pañcatantra; and yet other sections, three in number, appear in the Mahā-bhārata.

The first three books of the Pañcatantra (above, § 26) were recast by Somadeva about 1070 A.D., in his Kathā-sarit-sāgara, chapters 60–64. Somadeva's abstract of these three books shows that they had the same form then as at the time of the Pehlevī translation (570). As representatives of the Indian original, the offshoots of the Pehlevī version surpass even the Indian offshoots. These latter, as respects their truthfulness in reflecting the Indian original, are arranged by Benfey as follows: first, the recension of the Indian original used by Somadeva; second, the one on which the Southern Pañcatantra (of Dubois) is based; third, the one from which the Hitopadeça is made; and last, the one from which proceed the common Sanskrit recensions of the Pañcatantra.

§ 36. At the time when Barzōī made his Pehlevī version, Buddhism was already on the decline in India, and Brahmanism regaining its lost supremacy. It was not to be expected on the one hand that the Brahmans would allow a work of such great artistic merit as the original *Mirrour for Magistrates* to be lost and forgotten, nor, on the other, that they would preserve it without transforming its whole spirit, which was that of fanatical hatred for Brahmanism. They have, therefore, omitted or transformed such parts as showed most Buddhist animus, leaving, however, many marks uneffaced which betray its Buddhist origin.

In one other way, too, the original was modified. In most of its sections a doctrine was inculcated by means of a single fable or story, and only a sparing use was made of inserted apologues. But gradually the means became an end; into the main story were inserted others, and others still into these, until the main story became a mere frame, and the result was comparable to a set of Chinese boxes.[2]

§ 37. Respecting the sources of the Indian original only a general statement can be made. There were current among the Buddhists, fables and parables which they ascribed to Buddha, and whose sanctity they sought to increase by identifying the best character in any story with Buddha himself in a former birth. Hence the tales were called *Jātakas* or 'Birth-stories.' There is evidence of the existence of a collection with that name as early as the Council of Vesālī, about 380 B.C.; and in

[1] Of the remaining three, one is shown by its spirit of deadly hatred towards the Brahmans to be the work of Buddhists, and the other two are in Benfey's judgment genuinely Indian.

[2] Pedagogical reasons forbade the retention of this arrangement, except by way of specimen. Thus selection ix is boxed into viii, and xv and xvi into xiv.

the fifth century after Christ the Jātakas were put into the form in which they now appear in the Sutta-piṭaka. They are distinguished for quaint humor and gentle earnestness, and teach the duty of tender sympathy with animals and even of courtesy to them. With these stories may be identified many if not all of the fables of the Hitopadeça.

§ 38. The relation of the earliest Greek and Indian fables has been the subject of much discussion. Wagener tried to show that the Greeks derived their apologues from the Hindus; Weber, that the Hindus got many from the Greeks. Correspondences there undoubtedly are; but the difficulty is that the earliest forms of the fables — which would furnish the only safe basis for comparison — are irrecoverably lost. Aesop and his fables are mentioned by Plato and others as very well known: but whether he was a Phrygian, a Jew, or an Egyptian is matter of dispute; and even the Μυθίαμβοι Αἰσώπειοι of Babrius (ca. 100 A.D.), which tradition offers us as the oldest extant collection, are removed some 700 years from the traditional date of Aesop. The collection on which the common modern fable-books are based was made by the Byzantine monk Maximus Planudes, ca. 1325.

At all events, the oldest extant documentary collections of Greeks or of Buddhists are much later than Alexander's invasion; and considering the intercourse of the Greeks with India after that event, it is quite possible that the influence and borrowing were in both directions.

§ 39. We have seen how, under the New Persian Dynasty, and afterwards under the Caliphs, with the spread of Islam, the Indian stories were carried over western Asia and all southern and western Europe. But this is not all. The pious pilgrims to India from China took home with them Buddhist apologues, which were translated into Chinese, and wandered then to Korea and Japan. They have since been translated from Chinese into French by Stanislas Julien (*Les Avadânas*, Paris, 1859). Among the Mongols, too, Benfey has discovered many of these apologues; and through the Mongols during their supremacy these stories came to the Slavic peoples, and even to the Finns and Samoyeds.

§ 40. BIBLIOGRAPHY. First the titles of some books cited often below.

[1. Pāli.] The Jātaka, together with its commentary, being tales of the anterior births of Gotama Buddha. For the first time edited in the original Pāli, by V. Fausböll. London, Trübner & Co., 1877–.

Buddhist birth stories; or Jātaka tales. Translated by T. W. Rhys Davids. London, Trübner & Co., 1880. Vol. 1 (the only one) goes to Jātaka 40. It contains very useful lists of books illustrating the history and migrations of Buddhist tales.

[2. Sanskrit.] Pantschatantra: Fünf Bücher indischer Fabeln, Märchen und Erzählungen. Aus dem Sanskrit übersetzt mit Einleitung und Anmerkungen von Theodor Benfey. Leipzig, Brockhaus, 1859. 2 volumes. See p. xviii, no. 8. This work is cited as "Benfey."— The fables are cited by the numbers of Benfey and Kosegarten.

[3. Old Syriac version.] Kalilag und Damnag. Alte syrische Uebersetzung des indischen Fürstenspiegels. Text und deutsche Uebersetzung von Gustav Bickell. Mit einer Einleitung von Theodor Benfey. Leipzig, Brockhaus, 1876.

[4. Arabic.] Kalila and Dimna, or the fables of Bidpai. Translated from the Arabic. By the Rev. Wyndham Knatchbull. Oxford, 1819.

Calila und Dimna, oder die Fabeln Bidpai's. Verdeutscht von Ph. Wolff. Stuttgart, 1839. 2 vols.

[5. Later Syriac version.] Kalilah and Dimnah or the fables of Bidpai: being an account of their literary history, with an English translation of the later Syriac version of the same, and notes. By I. G. N. Keith-Falconer. Cambridge University Press, 1885. Price 7 shillings 6 pence.

[6. Persian.] The Anvár-i Suhailí; or, the lights of Canopus; being the Persian version of the fables of Pilpay · ·: literally translated into prose and verse. By Edward B. Eastwick. Hertford, 1854. There is another translation by A. N. Wollaston, London, 1877.

[7. Latin.] Directorium huma ne vite alias parabo|le antiquorū sapientū.| By John of Capua. (Sine loco et anno, gothic type, folio, 82 leaves, quaint wood-cuts.) Copy in Harvard College Library. Printed about 1480. Joseph Derenbourg is now publishing a critical edition of this work, with notes, Paris, Vieweg, 1887–.

[8. German.] Das Buch der Beispiele der alten Weisen. Herausgegeben von Dr. W. L. Holland. Stuttgart, 1860.

§ 41. THE LITERARY HISTORY of the Indian apologues has often been treated. So by Silvestre de Sacy, Loiseleur Deslongchamps, H. H. Wilson (*Works*, London, 1864, iv. 1–159), Lancereau (in his Pantchatantra, Paris, 1871), Max Müller (On the migration of fables, *Chips*, London, 1875, iv. 145–209), Rhys Davids (Introduction to his translation of the Jātakas, London, 1880), J. Schoenberg (in the very readable introduction to his German translation of the Hitopadeça, Vienna, 1884). Keith-Falconer's account is on the whole the best (§ 40).

The French translation of the Hitopadeça by É. Lancereau (Paris, Maisonneuve, 1882) is especially useful on account of the full and convenient references to the books where the analogues of the different fables may be found. This book is intended by the citation "Lancereau."

§ 42. EDITIONS AND TRANSLATIONS. The most accessible text edition is that of Professor Peter Peterson (Bombay, Government Central Book Depot, 1887. Price 1 rupee 10 annas). It contains an introduction most helpful for reading the text in course. It forms no. xxxiii of the Bombay Sanskrit Series. The text edition used most often as a standard of reference is that of Schlegel and Lassen (Bonn, 1829).

A literal English version has been given by Fr. Pincott (London, W. H. Allen, 1880). A cheap reprint of Wilkins's translation appeared in Henry Morley's Universal Library (London and New York, Routledge, 1885).

§ 43. METRES. Aside from the common çloka — see p. 300, § 21 — there occur in this book several other metres requiring description. The following five are monoschematic — i.e. the stanza consists of one metrical scheme four times repeated. The first two are simple and natural iambic-choriambic rhythms and are common in the Veda. The name **vasanta-tilakā** means 'Grace of the spring-time'; **mālinī**, 'Garlanded'; **rathoddhatā** seems to mean 'Car-proud.'

a. ⏓ –́ ⏑ –́ | –́ ⏑ ⏑ –́ | ⏑ –́ ⏑ –́ — **jagatī**, 22[11].
b. ⏓ –́ ⏑ –́ | –́ ⏑ ⏑ –́ | ⏑ –́ ⏑ — **triṣṭubh**, 26[1].
c. – –́ ⏑ –́ | ⏑́ ⏑ ⏑ | –́ ⏑ ⏑ –́ | ⏑ –́ – — **vasanta-tilakā**, 18[14], 26[8].
d. ⏑́ ⏑ ⏑ | ⏑́ ⏑ ⏑ | –́ – ‖ –́ ⏑ –́ | –́ ⏑ –́ | – — **mālinī**, 22[22].
e. –́ ⏑ –́ | ⏑́ ⏑ ⏑ –́ | ⏑ –́ ⏑ –́ — **rathoddhatā**, 56[11].

The **triṣṭubh** is simply a catalectic form of the **jagatī**; but the catalexis gives the new cadence a trochaic effect instead of iambic. The rhythm of the **vasanta-tilakā** is closely analogous to that of the **triṣṭubh**. The **rathoddhatā** is essentially similar to a **jagatī** without its anacrusis.

§ 44. THE **āryā** METRE is based on the number of morae — not on the number of syllables. See Whitney, §§ 76–79. A light syllable counts as one mora; a heavy syllable, as two. In general, the **āryā**-foot consists of four morae. These appear either as two heavy syllables, or with one heavy one at the beginning or at the middle or at the end, or as four light syllables. In each half-stanza, a caesura occurs at the end of the third foot, and the eighth or last foot of each half-stanza is catalectic. The sixth foot of the first half-stanza must be an amphibrach, ⏑ – ⏑, and that

Thus:
– –
– ⏑⏑
⏑ – ⏑
⏑⏑ –
⏑⏑ ⏑⏑

of the second must be a single light syllable. No odd foot may be an amphibrach. The metre occurs at 26^8 and 56^5 to 56^{10}. The scheme is:

— — | — — | — — ‖ — — | — — | ⏑ — ⏑ | — — | —
— — | — — | — — ‖ — — | — — | ⏑ | — — | —.

Applying this scheme, for example, to 56^{5-6}, we have, with the proper resolutions:

⏑⏑ — | ⏑ — ⏑ | — — ‖ — — | ⏑⏑ — | ⏑ — ⏑ | — — | —
⏑⏑ ⏑⏑ | — ⏑⏑ | ⏑⏑ — ‖ ⏑⏑ — | ⏑⏑ — | ⏑ | ⏑⏑ ⏑⏑ | —.

Notes to Page 16.

Line 16. Selection II. Preface and introduction to the Hitopadeça. U.f. saṁskṛta‿ukti, 'cultivated expression.'

17. See √1dā. —ca belongs to nītiv-.

19. gṛh-, 956^4. —iva, 'as if.' —Join mṛt- w. gṛh-.

Notes to Page 17.

1. 'Just wisdom (is) the best thing, they say' (√ah).

2. 'By reason of' the qualities denoted by the three ablatives, 291^2.

3. 'The knowledge (of) weapons and the knowledge (of) books (are) two kinds-of-knowledge (for acquisition =) that one may acquire.'

4. 'The first (is) for laughter — is ridiculous.' This dative is explained at 287 mid.: similar uses 17^{15}, 20^{14}. —√dṛ + ā.

5–6. U.f. yad nave · · · na anyathā · · · tad iha. —'Since ornamentation put upon an unburned dish does not change, therefore to children (297a) nīti is communicated etc.,' i.e. as one decorates a dish *before* burning it, in order to have the result permanent, so worldly wisdom should be taught to children while they are still young. Cf. Horace, Epist. i.2.67–70. —See iha.

8. U.f. tathā anyasmāt granthāt. **7–8.** 'Friend-acquisition · · · is delineated (by the author) drawing (his materials) from · · ·.' See page 311, § 26.

9. The Rāmāyaṇa (i.36–44 = 37–45) and MBh. (iii. chap's 106–109) tell why and how Bh. brought the Ganges down from heaven. See also M. Williams, *Indian Wisdom*, p. 363. —'Town having P. as name,' 1302. In Buddhist books it is called Pāṭali-gāma, 'Trumpet-flower Village.' Wilson thinks Pāṭali-putra is a mere corruption of Pāṭali-pura, 'Trumpet-flower City.' This certainly accords well with the K'usumo-pulo (Skt. Kusuma-pura, 'Flower-City') of the Chinese Buddhist pilgrims — see Beal, *Si-yu-ki*, ii.83–85. The Kathā-sarit-sāgara (chap. iii.) gives a legend telling how the town was founded by a king Putraka and his wife Pāṭalī. This is perhaps an invention suggested by the corrupted form.

—The site of P. is discussed at length in Cunningham's *Archaeological Survey of India Reports*, viii.1–34 and Note prefixed to the vol. See also Journ. As. Soc. of Bengal, xiv.[1]137f, with map.

10. Divide thus, sarva-svāmiguṇa; not sarvasvāmi-guṇa: upeta, √i + upa. —King S. need not be regarded as a historical person.

11. çuçrāva, √çru, 793a, 800b.

12–13. Construe yasya na asti (see √1as2) çāstram, andha eva (see this) sas (asti): -ucchedi and darçakam are attributive adjectives to çās-, and loc- is in apposition w. çās-.

15. 'One by itself, even (api), is harmful (17^4n.); but how much more (kim4) all four together!'

16–17. See iti 2 and ākarṇaya. —'The king, distressed (udvignamanās, 418) by the shaster-neglect (-ananuṣṭhānena) of his (ātmanas) sons, who did not study books (see 1308^2) · · ·'.

18. See 1ka 1. 'What profit (is there) with a son born, i.e. in the birth of a son, who · · ·'.

—Observe the use of the ppl. where we use a verbal noun: this is common in Sanskrit, e.g. 17^{22}, 25^{12}, 38^{23}, and also in Latin, e.g. *post conditam urbem*.

19^b is the answer to **19^a**.

20. 'Of (the three,) an unborn (i.e. no son at all), a dead one, and (1253a) a fool, · · · ': see 2vara. —See ca5.

21. U.f. **duḥkhakarāu** (supply **stas**) **ādyāu**.

22. See ca3. —**jāto**, lit. '(is) born'; pregnantly, 'is born in reality or to some noble purpose.'

NOTES TO PAGE 18.

1. Respecting the metempsychosis, see 65^9 to 68^5 and notes. —**vā** marks the rhetorical question as a rejoinder to an objector's statement. —**jāyate**, lit. 'is born,' √**jan**, refers to the mere physical fact of issuing from the womb.

—Render the proverb: 'He (alone) is born in reality, by whose birth (see 17^{18}N.) his family attains to distinction: or (if you object to that), who, in the circling round of existence, when dead, does not come out of some womb again?'—True, every one does so issue; but the fact *by itself* has no noble significance.

—The entire point lies in the antithesis between the mg of **jāyate** and the pregnant sense of **jāto**. Such pregnant uses of a word are common in gnomic poetry: so 21^{23}, 22^5.

2. 'The best thing is one good son; but (ca5) not with even hundreds of fools (is there any profit).' The ellipsis—though harsh and condemnable—is made clear by such phrases as that at 17^{13} and the others under 1ka 1.

3^b. Supply **tamo hanyate**.

4^a. See ta3. For gen., 296b. —'Though born (of whomsoever =) of humble parentage.'

5. See √1kṛ6. —Note the puns in **vañçaviçuddhas** and **nirguṇas**, which words thus stand in covert and playful contrast w. **yasya tasya prasūtas** and **guṇavān**.

6. U.f. **na adhīta** (see √i+adhi) · **etāsu**.

7. See vidvāns. —See go. —√sad2.

8 end. Passives, 770c, 769. —U.f. **yad ca ucyate**, explained under ya2.

9. 'What is not to be, that will not be: if it is to be, then it will not be otherwise': the do-nothing argument or ignava ratio. —See ced: **na**, if it belonged to the protasis, would precede **ced**.

10. 'This · · remedy, embraced-in-the-words (= **iti**) "What · · · otherwise,"—why is it not drunk?' —√1pā, 770b.

—Lines 9–10 are in apposition w. **yad** (end of 8), and contain the "sloth-talk" condemned in line 11.

12. 'One should not give up his exertion (**udyogam**), thinking, "Fate (will do or prevent all)."'

14. Metre, **vasanta-tilakā**, p. 316, § 43. —U.f. **upa‿eti lakṣmīs**.

16. √**han+ni**, 992^2. —**kuru**, 714. —**ātma-** has the force of a possessive of the *second* person here. cf. ātman3.

17. The loc. absolute expresses one condition, and **yadi na sidhyati** a second.

20–21. The collective result of a man's words and thoughts and deeds is his **karman**: this alone exists after death and is a powerful determinant of his course in the next birth. —**kuryāt**, cf. 25^{21}N.

23. **suptasya**, 954b.

NOTES TO PAGE 19.

1. See tāvant2.

2. See tāvant2. —U.f. **kim cid na**.

3. **kār-**, made (959) from the past pass. ppl. of the *caus.* of √1kṛ, 1051^3.

4. See √çru3 and 770a. —**asti kaç cid**, 'is there anyone · · · ?' see ya1.

5. **putrāṇām** limits **punarjanma**. —Cf. 17^{16}.

7. **dhatte**, √1dhā9, 668.

9. **hīyate**, cf. **pīyate**, 18^{10} and N.

11. See atra1. —Long cpd is analyzed at 1248^2.

—**Viṣṇuçarman**, if not the name of a real person, is chosen as a reminder of the synonymous **Viṣṇugupta**, an epithet of **Cāṇakya**, the wise and famous minister of **Candragupta** = Σανδρόκυπτος or Σανδράκοττος.—See Benfey, Pantch. i.31, and Böhtlingk, Indische Sprüche, 2d ed., no. 7061. Cf. above, p. 311, § 24.

13. U.f. **tad**, 161. —Explained √çak A1.

14. U.f. **na adravye**. —**nihitā**, 954c.

15. Pass. of *caus.* of √paṭh, 1052a.

16. U.f. asmin (208) tu · · na apatyam.

20. U.f. -sañgāt, 'by sticking to · ·,' 291[2].

22. 'You (are) an authority for · ·.'

23. For gen., 297a. —sam-arpitavān, like kāritavān, 19[3]N.: √ṛ+sam, 1042d.

Notes to Page 20.

2. 'By way of introduction.'

3. See √gam2.

5. 'Tale of the crow, tortoise, and so forth' (-ādi 2), not given in this Reader.

7. √stu+pra (770a)—cf. prastāva.

8. Selection III. The old tiger and the traveller. Hitopadeça, book i., fable 2.—The *motif* of this tale is feline hypocrisy (whether of tiger or of cat), and appears again in selection v., as also in Pañcatantra, iii.2, Kalilag und Damnag, p. 65f, MBh.v. 160.15–43 = 5421–49, Jātaka, i. p. 460, no. 128. Cf. 21[23]N.

—aham, namely, the Pigeon-king, who tells this story to dissuade his followers from taking the rice with which a snare was baited. —carann, 210. —See eka3. —The ablution and sacred grass were intended as outward symbols of inward piety. A pretender to virtue is called 'one who acts like a cat,' see Manu iv.195.

11. Observe the impersonal construction (999), which will now be extremely frequent. Logical subject in instr., 282. —See √kṛṣ+ā and √loc+ā.

12. See kim4. —asminn, 210.

13[a]. 'In getting even a desirable (object) from an undesirable (source)'—e.g. bracelet from tiger.

14. Observe caesura and exact order of original. —mṛtyave, '(is) deadly,' 17[4]N.

16–17. Nothing venture, nothing have. —Join na w. paçyati (16). Both gerund-clauses are conditional.

18. U.f. tad. —See tāvant 3a.

19. pra-sārya, 1051 and [5].

20. U.f. prāk eva, 'formerly.' w. emphasis: eva, as much as to say, 'not now, of course'—preliminary hint at a general reformation of character.

Notes to Page 21.

1. Note how Brahmans are distinguished from men: so 95[1]. —U.f. -vadhāt me, 'from my killing · ·, because I killed.'

2. Another me need not be expressed with putrās and dārās: whose they are is clear from nirvaṅço 'smi.

3. upadiṣṭas: the upadeça consisted of the three words marked by iti.

4. U.f. -upadeçāt, 'in accordance with (his) advice,' 291.

5. kathaṁ na, sc. asmi.

6. Cpd, 1253a: 2d member, adhyayana.

7. See iti 3. —"The noble eight-fold (aṣṭavidha) path" is a favorite Buddhist topic. Buddha defines it in the famous "Sermon at Benares." —See smṛta3.

8. See tatra 1: 'among those (eight things).'

9. U.f. na a-mahātmasu, emphatic litotes.

10. U.f. ca etāvān, 206. —See gata4.

11–12. See ya5. —See tathā4. —'The common saying, "vyāghro · · khādati" is · ·.'

13–14. Third word is kuṭṭanīm. —See pramāṇaya. —Cow-slaying is a heinous offence (64[3]), coordinated with man-slaying, 21[1]. —A dvija's 'second *or* spiritual (61[15]) birth' is when he is invested with the sacred girdle, Manu ii.169.

—'The world keeps on in the old ruts, and does not, in a question of right, take as authority a bawd who gives good advice as (quickly as it does) a Brahman, even if he be a cow-killer.' People heed the social position of the adviser rather than the real character of the adviser or the intrinsic value of the advice.

15. adhītāni, √i+adhi: cf. 20[11]N.

16[b]. 'So (is) food (in =) to a hungry man.'

17. 'To a poor man (304a) is given a fruitful gift,' i.e. fruitful is the gift given to a poor man—cf. 22[4] and St. Luke vi.33–35. —Observe that the logically important idea is often put in a grammatically subordinate word.

18. See ātman3 and √liṣ+abhi. —Cf. Dhammapada, stanza 129, and SBE. x.36.

20. Note the use or the omission of ca

according to the convenience of the metre: so 22[18], 26[1,2], 32[4,5].

— Lines 18–21 are positive forms of the Golden Rule: cf. St. Luke vi.31; interesting negative forms appear at MBh.v.39.72–73 = 1517–18, at the beginning of the *Διδαχὴ τῶν δώδεκα ἀποστόλων*, in the Confucian Analects xv.23, Legge's edition, and in the Babylonian Talmud (Story of Hillel).

22. mātṛvat = mātaram iva: similarly the rest. — The accusatives are objects of the first paçyati (√1 paç6).

23. Second paçyati, pregnantly, cf. 18[1]N. — This proverb, along with the one quoted by the cat at 29[5], is quoted in substance by the hypocritical cat in the tale of the 'Cat as Judge,' Kalilag, p. 66. Cf. 20[8]N.

NOTES TO PAGE 22.

2[b]. U.f. pra-yaccha (747) īçvare, 304a.

3. See 1ka 1. The idea is identical with that in St. Luke v.31.

4. dātavyam (999) iti, 'with the thought "It ought to be given (impers.), *i.e.* giving is a duty."'

5[a]. Words used pregnantly, cf. 18[1]N.

6. √grah+prati, 722 end.

7. U.f. yāvat asāu (= pānthas) · · · tāvat · · ni-magnas (√majj).

9. See atas 1. — √sthā+ud, 233a, caus. 1042d.

11. Metre, jagatī, p. 316, § 43. — 'The fact that "He reads the law-books" is not a ground for a judgment' that the reader — be he man or tiger — has a good and harmless nature.

13. 'Just the inherent nature here (atra) is the surpassingly predominant thing (√ric +ati) so

14. 'as by nature cows' (361c) milk is sweet.' — Religious study will not change the bad inborn nature of a man or a tiger any more than sugar would turn sour milk back into sweet milk again. Compare lines 20–21.

15. 'Of those having uncontrolled senses and mind, the (religious) action is like the bathing of elephants,' i.e. is mere external action and without significance as an index of character. One might infer from their frequent ablutions that the elephants were very religiously minded. Cf. 36[6]N.

16. 'Knowledge, without action (to correspond), is a burden, like · · ·.'

17. Explained under yad2.

18. Use of ca, 21[20]N. — Instead of -pāṇīnām, we have, for sake of metre, -pāṇinām, as if from -pāṇin.

19. See eva. — Note that the gen. and loc. here express the same relation. So the dat. and loc. above, lines 4–5.

20. √īkṣ+pari, 'are considered' (namely, by wise people) = 'should be considered': so Mālavikā i.17, kāraṇa-kopās, 'are (only) cause-angry' = 'should not be angry without a cause.' Cf. 41[18]N.

21. √i+ati, 992. — See guṇa2, and note the difference between that and svabhāva.

22. Metre, mālinī, p. 316, § 43.

NOTES TO PAGE 23.

1. 'Even yonder (asāu) moon (sky-wandering, etc., p. 22) is eclipsed (grasyate) · · ·.' The demon Rāhu got a part of the drink of immortality — cf. 32[12]N. The Sun and Moon betrayed him to Viṣṇu, who cut off his head. The head, grown immortal, avenges itself on Sun and Moon by swallowing them at times. Cf. introd. to selection xl.

2. 'Who is able to wipe out (√uñch)?' The Hindus thought that every one's destiny was written on his brow, although invisible to human eye. Like enough the sutures of the skull, which look very similar to the written characters of some Indian alphabets, gave rise to this belief. Now-a-days, writing materials are placed beside the new-born babe in the lying-in room, in order that Vidhātṛ may write the child's destiny on its forehead. See Shib Chunder Bose, The Hindoos as they are, 2d ed., p. 25.

4. SELECTION IV. The deer and the crow, and the jackal. Hitopadeça, book i., fable 3. — In the Indian fables, the jackal plays the rôle which the fox plays in the European; see Pañc. book iii., stanza 73 ed. Kosegarten, = 76 ed. Bombay.

5. bhrāmyan, 763.

7. U.f. etad. —bhavatu, see this under √bhū.

8. 'I'll first get his confidence.' —U.f. upa-sṛtya, 992.

11. ā-sādya, grd of *caus.*

12. adhunā etc., explained at 999.

13. astaṁ gate etc., loc. absolute.

17–18. 'This (ayam) is the jackal, (who is) come seeking (icchann) · · ·.'

19. See √yuj5.

20. '(Is) not to be given to any one (gen. 297a) whose · · ·.'

21. The story which is announced in this line, and which the crow tells to serve as the "example" to the saw of line 20, is inserted in the original between this line and ity ākarṇya (24[1]), but is here taken out for the sake of continuity and given separately as selection v. — cf. p. 29 end.

NOTES TO PAGE 24.

1. iti refers to the story in selection v. —√ah. —mṛgasya, subjective gen. w. -darçana-. —U.f. bhavān api, 'you (= the crow) too' — no less than I (the jackal) now.

2–3. U.f. adya yāvat (see yāvant 3) etasya (= mṛgasya) sneha‿anuvṛttis.

5. Ppl. of √2as+nis forms possessive cpd w. pādape, see 1299. —U.f. deçe, 133.

6. '"ayam · · vā" is the gaṇanā of · ·,' i.e. only the small-minded take into account or stop to ask whether or not a man belongs to their own party or race.

7. See eva. —The proverb expresses a truth that underlies the doctrine of free-trade.

9. U.f. kim (see 1ka 1) anena (501) ut-. —Join anu-bhavadbhis (741) w. sarvāis.

10. sthīyatām, see √sthā3; imv. pass., 770b, used impers., 999. 'Let all remain in one place, enjoying pleasure by means of familiar conversations.'

11. 'No one is any one's friend, no one any one's foe' — i.e. by nature; we must have actual dealings (vyavahāra) with each other to bring out the friendship or enmity.

14. U.f. etasmin eva vana‿ekadeçe = (see 1316) etasya eva vanasya ekadeçe, cf. 33[5]N.

16. tathā · · sati, read 303b[4] and cf. √1as3.

18. U.f. baddhas, 160. —mām, object of trātum. —Join itas (= asmāt) with vyādha-pāçāt.

19. (ko) mitrād anyas, 'who other than my friend = who but him.'

20. U.f. ā-gatya upa-sthitas. —See denom. √phala.

21–22. U.f. etasya (= mṛgasya) utkṛt-yamānasya (√kṛt) māṅsa‿asṛg-anuliptāni asthīni (431) mayā · ·.

23. √las+ud, cf. 162. —chinddhi, √chid, 689. —See tāvant 3b.

NOTES TO PAGE 25.

2. U.f. · · jānīyāt (730, 721 — 'one may recognize'), yuddhe çūram, ṛṇe çucim.

3. bhāryām, 'a true wife,' one who has really taken her husband "for richer for poorer." —√2kṣi.

4–5. A friend in *need* (as well as in joy) is a friend indeed.

6–7. 'Firm-bond-bound indeed (see tāvant 5) is this deer.' The jackal 'thought' this — he did not say it aloud.

7. -nirmitās, √1mā+nis. —Properly, the Hindus designated the days as first, second, third, etc. of the lunar half-month — see tithi. For the (comparatively modern) names of the days as governed successively (like those of our week) by the seven planets, see JAOS. vi.176–7.

8. etān = pāçān: cf. the ecclesiastical prohibition of meat on Fridays. —End, see √man1.

9. U.f. yad tvayā ucyate, tad · ·, 'what you say, that I'll do.'

10. See sthita 4.

11. U.f. mṛgam anāgatam (cf. 4[15]N.) ava-lokya, itas tatas anv-iṣya, tathāvidh-am dṛṣṭvā, uvāca. Note how the gerunds mark each the end of its clause; so 26[16].

12. avadhīrita-, under the denom. √avadhīraya. 'This is the result of rejected friend-words = (17[18]N.) of rejecting them.'

15. 'His trouble is near' (√1dhā+saṁ-ni).

18–19. 'The fact that "I've done no wrong" — that is not a ground of confidence (cf. 22[11]); for there is (√2vid3), from the malicious, danger even for the good:' although — having done to the bad no wrong calling for revenge — they might fairly expect to be let alone.

21. √vṛj, 'one should shun' — subject indefinite: this is very common, when the 3d pers. optative is used; e.g. 18[21], 26[5], 30[17].

Notes to Page 26.

1-2. Metre, triṣṭubh, p. 316, § 43. — Note use of ca — cf. 21[20]N. — √lap+sam, pass. ppl. of *caus.* — See çrad and 668. — The four genitives refer to arthinām. — See kim3. — Line 2[b], 'Is there a to-be-practised-deceit of the needy, i.e. ought they to be deceived?'

3-4. Metre, āryā, p. 316, § 44. — 'Who perpetrates wrong upon (loc.) · · ·.' — U.f. a-satyasaṁdham. — bhag-, voc. s. *fem.*

5. See 2sama 2. — kār-, see √1kṛ, *caus.* end, and 25[21]N.

6. U.f. ca aṅgāras: see ca1b end.

7. atha vā = 'or rather, to express myself more to the point, — this (iyam) is the way (sthitis) of scoundrels.'

8. Metre, vasanta-tilakā, p. 316, § 43.

9. 'In your ear pleasantly something beautiful he gently hums (√ru).'

10. Gerund of √rūpaya+ni.

12. Anacoluthon: 'a scoundrel, though (see ca 6) saying pleasant things, — that is not a ground of confidence (= 25[18b]):' i.e. 'a scoundrel may say · ·; but that's no reason for trusting him.'

14. U.f. laguḍa-hastas (1303[2]) tam · · āgacchan · · ava-.

16. See √dṛç+sam and √1pṛ. Note how the three gerunds mark each the end of its clause: cf. 25[11]N. — See √sthā4.

17. utthāya, 233a; gerund.

17-18. 'The deer waited just so as the crow said.'

18. U.f. harṣa‿utphulla-locanena, 'having joy-expanded eyes, his eyes wide open with joy.'

19. asāu = the farmer.

19-20. Note the position of the gerunds as a help to the correct phrasing.

20. U.f. bandhanāt, 290; not acc.

21. 'The farmer having withdrawn,' √i+antar.

22-23. See diç+ud. 'The jackal was killed by the farmer, throwing the cudgel at him in anger.'

Notes to Page 27.

1-2. 'One reaps the fruit · · right here on earth, (with =) after three · · ·, (or) three days,' i.e. sooner or later.

3. In the *original*, the fables always begin with the moral, which is then repeated at the end, in abbreviated form, with the introductory words, 'Therefore I say.' This arrangement is retained, e.g., 32[10]-33[7].

4. See 1181a end.

5. 'Trap-caught (from the jackal, 291 =) by his plots.'

6. Selection V. The blind vulture, the birdlings, and the cat. Hitopadeça, book i., fable 4. — Cf. 20[8]N., 21[23]N.

— The Vulture-peak, Pāli Gijjhakūṭa, is near Rājagṛha, and famous as a sojourn of Buddha.

7. 'From the evil issue of fate = as hard fate would have it.'

8. Instr., 280 end.

9. U.f. sva‿āhārāt. — See 1ka 2d and 1260. — √1dā, 668.

10. Use of inf., 981[3].

11. U.f. tam ā-yāntam, 619.

12. See 1idam near end: 'τίς δ' οὗτος ἔρχεται;'

14. U.f. api: the idea is, 'To say nothing of my disappointment at not getting the young birds to eat, I'm so very near the vulture that *even escape is impossible.*'

15. Same phrase at 23[8].

17. U.f. dūram apasara (classical pres. imv. √sṛ+apa): no ced, han- (163).

20. 'Is any one ever punished (or) honored on account of mere rank?'

Notes to Page 28.

2. The lunar penance is described 65[5-8].

3. U.f. ācaran tiṣṭhāmi, see √sthā4. — U.f. yuṣmān (= vulture, respectful plural) object of stuvanti. — dharma-jñāna-ratān, see √ram3.

5-6. 'And you (it seems, are) such (etādṛçās, q.v.) a jurisconsult that you (have) undertaken (√yam+ud) to slay me—a guest! ?'

6. U.f. eṣas (see etad) refers forward here! On the duty of hospitality, see Manu iii. 99f. —√īr+sam-ud.

7. 'To an enemy (arāu, 304) even, ·· should be shown.' So Plautus says, Trin. 679 and Rud. 438, that one does not withhold fire and water even from a foe.

8. U.f. chettum api āg- ·· na up-, 'even (in the case of one =) from one come to hew (it) down ···.'

10b. 'And joyous *or* kind (sūnṛtā, as adj., omitted in vocab.) words as a fourth thing.'

11. U.f. na uc-, √chid+ud, 202.

13b. See √gam+abhy-ā, and guru3.

14. Render loc. by 'towards.' —Cf. 21[19].

15. cāṇḍ-, loc. as in 28[8].

16-17. yasya limits gṛhāt and refers to tasmāi (and to a tasmāt, understood w. ā-dāya). —sa = atithis. —dat-tvā, 991 cf. 955c. —See √gam1.

21. First evam, 'so,' namely as at 27[17].

21-22. Touching the feet (Nala xxiv.) or the head (Manu viii.114) was a kind of ordeal used in solemn asseverations in order to call down harm on the one touched in case of falsehood; at Hitopadeça, p. 122[5] = book iv., fable 11 (cf. Pañc. book i., fable 11), touching the ground and ears seems to be a sign of detestation for a suggestion just made. Here the touching seems to partake of both significations.

23. U.f. -rāgeṇa idam ··· adhy-avasāyitam, √sā.

Notes to Page 29.

1-2. U.f. iti atra āika-: see atra1. 'The law-books, though contradicting (√vad+vi) ··, have unanimity on this point, "ahiṅsā paramo dharmas:"' ahiṅsā is a cardinal virtue among Buddhists.

3. See nivṛtta. —See ya3.

4. svarga-: for lingual ṇ, see 193.

5. 'There is just one friend, virtue, who ··:' cf. 63[18]N. and [18]; also 21[23]N.

6. U.f. sarvam anyad hi (163) 'for all else' (but virtue).

7-8. See ya6, 2antara3, and √muc+vi.

9-10. See iti2a and çakya3. —Lit. 'What sorrow (of a =) in a man arises at ···, by this forming-of-a-conception ····' we should expect tad-anumānena as cpd, 'by forming a conception of this (sorrow).' If we will think how we should feel if we were in our enemy's place and about to die, it is possible that we may spare even *his* life.

11-12. √1pṛ+pra, 770c. —kaḥ kuryāt (714), rhetorical question, cf. 18[1]N.

13. vi-çvāsya, grd of *caus.*, 1051 and [8].

15. U.f. yeṣām ··, tāis ·· vi-lapadbhis.

16. √rabh, 160. —U.f. koṭarāt.

18. -asthīni, 431. —U.f. "anena (= gṛdhreṇa) eva ·· khāditās" iti niçcitya, √3ci+nis.

21-22. The story winds up with the distich given p. 23 end, cf. N.

Notes to Page 30.

1. Selection VI. The ass, the dog, and the thief. Hitopadeça, book ii., fable 3.—Weber thinks that the attribution of stupidity to the ass in the Sanskrit fables is wholly un-Indian and due to foreign (western) influences.

4. çvānam, 427. —āha, 801a. —See tāvant5. —See iti2b.

5. See √3gṛ and 1020, and cf. 30[16].

6. māma, Böhtlingk's suggestion; MSS. read mama. —jānāsi, 730.

7. See yathā7. —etasya (= rajakasya) limits gṛha-, 1316. —See yatas2: correl. tena. —See √1vṛ+nis.

8. Second mama (gen., 297a) depends on -dāne, 1316.

12. U.f. sam-bhāvayet (caus.) yas tu kār-, 'who honors them (only) in the time for action, i.e. waits till he is in a strait before he treats them well.'

13. See √çri+ā. —Caesura here divides a cpd; this is very unusual.

15. U.f. pāpīyān (208,464) tvam (sc. asi).

16. Explained under yathā6.

17-18. U.f. sevayet, subject indef., cf. 25[21]N. —U.f. a-māyayā.

20. U.f. -kopāt, abl. 291. 'Because of anger at ···, he got up (992) and beat (√taḍ, 1070) ···.'

22 and 31[1]. U.f. para‿adhikāra- ··· -icchayā. —See √sad+vi.

NOTES TO PAGE 31.

2. SELECTION VII. The lion, the mouse, and the cat. Hitopadeça, book ii., fable 4.

3. See √1çī+adhi, 629, and 619.

4. buddhvā, 991, 160. —**4–5.** 'Not catching the hole-hidden mouse · · ·.'

6. U.f. bhavet yas tu, vikramāt na · ·, lit. 'Who is a · ·, he is not subdued by might,' with a play on the name of the lion.

8–9. Note position of gerunds, each marking the end of its clause. 'A cat was kept (dhṛtas) by him (tena), · · reflecting, · · going, · · satisfying, · · bringing.' —māṅsa‿ādi-āhāra, 'flesh-etc.-food.'

9 end. U.f. tad-bhayāt, 'from fear of it (i.e. the cat).'

10. √sṛ+nis, Epic present, 734. —U.f. asāu.

13. U.f. saṁcaran, 208.

14. See kadā end.

15. See 17^{11}N. —U.f. tadā (correl. of yadā) upayoga‿abhāvāt tasya · ·: the gen. depends (297a) on -dāne (1316); cf. 30^{8}N.

18. 'A servant, making (= if he made) · ·, would be *or* fare (syāt, 636) like D.'

19. SELECTION VIII. The crows and the serpent. Hitopadeça, book ii., fable 10. — It is told by Damanaka to Karaṭaka (see p. 312, § 29), and into it is inserted the story of the lion, the old hare, and the well (selection ix., see 32^{12}N.), told by the crow to the crow-hen.

—Selection viii. answers to Pañcatantra, book i., fable 6, which is told in like manner by Damanaka. He makes the crow and crow-hen ask a jackal for advice, and the latter tells them the inserted story of the heron, the fishes, and the crab (= selection xviii.). Damanaka then finishes his story about the crows (= selection viii.), and further enforces its moral by the story of the lion (selection ix.). The *motif* of selection viii. is analogous to that of selection xvi., cf. 39^{8}N. — A few references for further comparison:

Old Syriac version. Kalilag, p. 12, 13.
Arabic. Knatchbull, p. 113, 115. Wolff, i.40, 44.
Later Syriac version, p. 23–26.
Anvār-i Suhailī, book i., story 11.
Directorium, Cap. II., p. 7 and p. 9 of signature c.
Buch der Beispiele, p. 35^{3}, 36^{16}.
Benfey, i.167 f; ii.57. Lancereau, p. 332.

—U.f. kasmin cid tarāu · · · apatyāni.

NOTES TO PAGE 32.

1. 'By a tree-hollow-abiding-black-serpent' — see √sthā+ava.

2. tyajyatām, 771.4.

3. U.f. tāvat āvayos (491): see kadā.

4–5. U.f. bhṛtyas ca ut-. —ca, cf. 21^{23}N. —mṛtyus is predicate. —See eva.

6. etasya = sarpasya.

7. soḍhas, √sah, 954, 222^{3}, 224b. —āha, 801a. —anena, 501.

9. See alam w. instr.: anayā, 501.

10. Knowledge is power. 'Whose is wit, might is his; but of a witless one, whence is the might?' Repeated at the end, 33^{7}, as a *quod erat demonstrandum*.

11. Just as before (23^{21}, see N.), this line announces the tale which serves as an "example" to the aphorism of line 10.

12. SELECTION IX. The lion, the old hare, and the well. Hitopadeça, book ii., fable 11. — See 31^{19}N.

—Selection ix. answers to Pañcatantra, book i., fable 8. The Buddhist version, the Banyan Deer Jātaka, has deep moral significance as showing the beauty of self-sacrifice and the excellence of loving "all things, both great and small." This Jātaka is mentioned by name and illustrated on the bas-reliefs of the tope or *Stupa of Bharhut*, Cunningham, plate xxv, dating from 200 B.C. or earlier. In the Sanskrit forms, the Jātaka has developed into a simple story that shows how the weak animals get the better of a powerful tyrant, not by force, but by cunning. Somadeva gives the story at lx.91–107. Compare further

Pāli. Jātaka, no. 12: translation, i. p. 205.
Old Syriac version. Kalilag, p. 14.
Arabic. Kalila. Knatchbull, p. 117. Wolff, i.46.
Later Syriac version, p. 27.
Anvār-i Suhailī, book i., story 14.
Directorium, Cap. II., p. 10 of signature c.
Buch der Beispiele, p. 37^{1}.
Benfey, i.179; ii.62. Lancereau, p. 333.

—The first three phrases of this line (12) are specimens of the regular conventional way of introducing the fables. —The mythical mount Mandara was used by the gods as a churning-stick when they churned the ocean to get the drink of immortality — cf. 23[1]N. In this book, a real hill may be intended, namely Mandara, a little south of Bhāgalpur, on the Ganges, east of Magadha.

14. See √dhā+vi5 and √ās3. — Note that the gerund **kṛtvā** goes with the logical subject of the sentence.

15. See √jñā+vi, *caus.*, and 1042d².

17. 'If that is agreeable to you · · ·.'

18. √kḷp+upa, caus. — See √ās3.

20–21. See hetu, ced, 1kal, and anunaya. — "I would put on my good behavior, if I thought I had any chance of my life."

Notes to Page 33.

1. U.f. apa-rāddhas (√rādh) · · dhṛtas · · agre. — See 2antara 4.

2. Note use of acc. w. caus., 'to cause my master to know:' so mām, next line.

4. tam = siṅham. — gṛhītvā, see √grah1, and 254³.

5. U.f. "paçyatu svāmī" iti uktvā. — tasmin kūpa-jale = tasya kūpasya jale, cf. 24[14]N. — tasya (= siṅhasya) eva, 'his own.'

6. darç-, 959, from caus. — U.f. asāu (= siṅhas) darpa‿ā-dhmātas (√dham) tasya (= pratibimbasya) upari ('upon') · · ·.

7–8. 'Therefore I say (the proverb) having yasya buddhir balaṁ tasya as its beginning,' 32[10]N. See ity-ādi.

9. The main story of the crows and the serpent is here resumed: cf. 31[19]N.

10. See √sad+ā. — ā-gatya, 992.

11. √tṛ+ava, ppl. of *caus.* — U.f. cañcvā dhṛtvā, ānīya, · · ·.

12. ni-rūpyamāṇe, loc. absolute, *pass.* ppl. of denom.

13. Gerundives have future force.

14. 'That (plan) was carried out; that being done, that (predicted result of the plan) took place:' see under √sthā+anu2, and cf. 303b⁴.

16. U.f. kuryāt ('one may do'), yad na · · ·.

18. Selection X. The birds and the apes. Hitopadeça, book iii., fable 2. — This story corresponds to Pañcatantra, book i., fable 18, which is itself only a subsidiary form of fable 17. This latter is given by Somadeva lx. 205–210. Compare Jātaka, no. 321 (vol. iii.), and further

Old Syriac version. Kalilag, p. 28.
Arabic. Kalila. Knatchbull, p. 150. Wolff, i. 91.
Later Syriac version, p. 55.
Anvār-i Suhailī, book i., story 24.
Directorium, Cap. II., p. 1, 2 of signature E.
Buch der Beispiele, p. 55[13].
Benfey, i.269–271; ii.112 and 111.

19. 'In the interior of constructed (√mā +nis) nests.'

20. 'The sky being covered (ā-vṛte) with cloud-veils, as it were with dark-garments, · · ·.'

Notes to Page 34.

1–2. U.f. avasthitān (203) çītārtān kampamānān · ·: 'by the birds, seeing · ·, it was said.'

3. 'We have constructed nests with straws brought hither (-āhṛtāis) by the beak-merely' (see mātrā 2, and references).

4. 'Endowed with hands, feet, and so forth (see ādi 2), why are you in distress (√sad+ava)?'

6. U.f. tāvat (see tāvant3) vṛṣṭes upaçamas, 'now there is a stopping of the rain.' — Better perhaps, without the punctuation-bar after bhavatu: 'So let there be for a while a stopping of the rain,' i.e. 'wait till the rain stops a bit and we'll see about it.'

8. bhagnās, √bhañj, 957c. — U.f. aṇḍāni ca adhas.

10. U.f. vidvān eva upa-: caesura; na avidvān tu.

11. U.f. · · upadiçya ajñān · ·, yayus (√yā, 800c).

12. Selection XI. The ass in the tiger-skin. Hitopadeça, book iii., fable 3. — This story corresponds to Pañcatantra, book iv., fable 7, which has been worked over by Somadeva, lxii.19–23. Its oldest Hindu form is the Lion-skin Jātaka. It seems to have been lacking in the Pehlevī version. Plato makes Socrates say, "Since I have put on the lion's skin, I must not be faint of heart" — Kratylos, 411A. The tale appears in the Chinese Avadānas, vol. ii., p. 59, no. 91. Compare also

Pāli. Jātaka, no. 189 (vol. ii.); transl., i. p. v.
Fab. Aesop., Ὄνος λεοντῆν φέρων, no. 336, ed. [Halm.
Lucian, Piscator, § 32.
La Fontaine, book v., no. 21; Regnier, i. p. 431.
Benfey, i.462–3; ii.308.

13–14. 'By the washerman, covering (him) with a tiger-skin, that one (asāu = gardabhas) was let loose · · ·.' —pracchādya, see √1chad + pra, and 227. —See √muc, and 1051³.

15. See buddhi2.

16. See √car3. —**16–18.** The instr. is logical subject of the impers. pass. sthitam: see sthita2 end, and 999. —'Having a-gray-blanket-made body-cover (1293), i.e. having covered himself with a gray blanket.' —U.f. sajjī-kṛtya (992), avanata-kāyena (√nam), ekānte.

18–19. 'The ass, seeing · ·, thinking "gardabhī iyam," making (714, ppl.) · ·, ran · · ·.'

20. See iti 2a end.

NOTES TO PAGE 35.

1–2. See √car3. —See çreyāṅs and 464. —-paricchannas, √1chad, 957d.

3. SELECTION XII. The elephant, the hares, and the moon. Hitopadeça, book iii., fable 4.

—This story corresponds to Pañcatantra, book iii., fable 1, and is given by Somadeva at lxii.29–44. It is unquestionably of Hindu rather than Greek origin, since it turns on the Hindu belief that there is a hare in the moon (36³N.). Compare

Old Syriac version. Kalilag, p. 63–65.
Arabic. Knatchbull, p. 223. Wolff, i.192.
Later Syriac version, p. 135–137.
Anvār-i Suhailī, book iv., story 4.
Directorium, Cap. V., p. 10–11 of signature H.
Buch der Beispiele, p. 104²³.
Benfey, i.348; ii.226. Lancereau, p. 337.

—U.f. varṣāsu api, vṛṣṭes abhāvāt, tṛṣā‿ārtas · · āha.

5–6. 'And we, who from want of bathing are almost blind,—where shall we go, or · · ?'

7–8. U.f. tattīra‿avasthitās · · -āhatibhis bahavas cūrṇitās, 'were crushed in great numbers by the (blows, i.e.) tread of · · ·.'

9–10. ā-hūya, gerund. —See √ākulaya. —U.f. eva atra āgant-, see √gam + ā end. —vinaṅkṣyati, see √1naç.

11. viṣīdata, see √sad, and 185.

13. 'How shall I speak · · ?' —See yūthapa.

14. spṛçann, etc., 210. —See √ghrā.

16–17. See √las3 and √sthā + anu, end.

19. ucyatām, 769.

20–21. 'Even when the weapons are raised (udyateṣu, √yam), an envoy speaks not falsely; álways, because he is inviolable (sadā eva avadhya-), he is, surely, the speaker of pure-truth.'

NOTES TO PAGE 36.

1–2. The moon-god's message goes from yad ete to prasiddhis. —See yad2. —'As for the fact that these hares, · · ·, by thee have been driven away (√sṛ + nis, caus. pass.), therein not rightly (see √yuj5) hast thou done.'

3. See prasiddhi, and cf. çaça, çaçāṅka, and çaçin. The Jātaka tells how the rabbit offered up its own life for Çakra and how Çakra in grateful recognition placed the hare's image in the moon's disk as an enduring memorial of the self-sacrifice—see Jātaka, no. 316, vol. iii., p. 51, and S. Beal, *Si-yu-ki*, ii. p. 60.

4. U.f. bhayāt idam (= τάδε, see idam) āha: idam (= 'my misdeed, just mentioned') · · ·.

5–6. See atra1. —pra-ṇamya, 192a. —See √gam 1.

6–7. tena (çaçakena), · · nītvā, etc. See √1kṛ, *caus.* —Here the elephant is made to worship the moon; but Pliny, *Nat. Hist.* viii.1, gives a curious belief about the voluntary moon-worship and religious ablutions of elephants. Fa-hian, the Chinese Buddhist pilgrim, chap. xxiii., records a like story, Beal, *Si-yu-ki*, i. p. li.

8–9. The rabbit is the elephant's spokesman: deva, 'O (moon-)god.' —U.f. ajñānāt eva anena (= gajena) · ·; tad kṣamyatām. —pra-sthāpitas, 1042d, 1051³.

12. SELECTION XIII. The blue jackal. Hitopadeça, book iii., fable 7.

—This story corresponds to Pañcatantra,

book i., fable 10. It is not found in the Arabic version nor in Somadeva, and so was probably not a part of the Indian original — Benfey, i. p. 223. But cf. Jātaka, no. 188. The *motif* is similar to that of the fable of the whitewashed jackdaw among the doves, Κολοιὸς καὶ περιστεραί, *Fabulae Aesopicae collectae*, ed. C. Halm, no. 201b. See La Fontaine, book iv., fable 9, Regnier, i.298f.

—svecchayā · · bhraman: same phrase, w. the other form (763), at 23^5.

13. tatas (= bhāṇḍāt, 1098), see tatas 1.

13–14. 'Kept pretending to be dead:' see √dṛç + sam, caus., and sthita4.

14–15. U.f. -svāminā asāu (= sṛgālas) utthāpya (1051^6, 1042d). The two gerunds go with the logical subject, -svāminā.

15–16. Note how the gerunds, gatvā, avalokya, mark each the end of its little clause.

16. uttama-varṇas, w. double mg., 'of the best color' (royal purple), and 'of the highest caste' (cf. 28^{18}). —See ātman2, and note how it is used as reflexive of all three persons — here '*my*self.'

17–19. Construe: aham (asmi) abhiṣiktas (√sic) -devatayā aranya-rājye sarva‿oṣadhi-rasena.

19–20. U.f. adya ārabhya (see √rabh + ā3) asmad-ājñayā asmin · · ·. 'By our command conduct must be made = you must do as I command.'

20. viçiṣṭa-varṇam, 1299.

21. U.f. pra-ṇamya (192a) ūcus (800e). —yathā ājñāpayati devas, 'as the king commands' (sc. so will we do), is a common response in the drama.

NOTES TO PAGE 37.

1. U.f. araṇya-vāsiṣu. — tasya, pred. poss. gen., see √bhū.

1–3. Construe: svajñātayas dūrīkṛtās avajñayā tena, · · (see -ādi) prāpya, · · avalokya, · · ·.

3. vi-ṣaṇṇān, √sad, 185, 189.

4–6. U.f. evam ced anena anītijñena · · ·, tad yathā ayam · ·; 'if thus by this · · (we're treated with contempt), then that this one · ·:' see √1dhā + vi5 end. — naçyati: for mode, see $581c^2$ and cf. yathā6.

6. amī, 501. — varṇamātra-vipralabdhās, 'fooled by (his) mere color,' see mātrā2, and √labh + vi-pra.

7. amum, 501. — See √3ci + pari and 770a.

6–8. yatas · · kuruta: the sentence is constructed like the sentence evam · · vidheyam, lines 4–6.

8. See √sthā + anu2.

9–10. tatas · · tena‿api çabdas kartavyas, 'Then he too will raise a howl.'

11. U.f. syāt, tasya asāu (= svabhāvas). —'What inherent-nature anyone (yasya) may have, that (nature — asāu) of him is hard to overcome:' see ya6.

12. U.f. tad kim na açnāti. 'If a dog (427) is made well-fed, i.e. put on good rations, will he not then gnaw a shoe?'

13. 'He'll be killed by (some) tiger, recognizing (him) by his howl.' — tathā etc., cf. 33^{14} and N. and references: for sati, see √1as3.

16. 'And (consumes) destroys, as (does) a hidden fire (antargatas analas) a dry tree.'

18–19. ca, used loosely to connect ratas with the logically, but not grammatically, coordinate parityajya. — See √ram3. —mūḍhas, see 223^4. —-vat, see 1107.

20. SELECTION XIV. The two geese and the tortoise. Hitopadeça, book iv., fable 2.

—This story appears in the Pañcatantra, book i., fable 13, and is given by Somadeva, lx.169–177. The Pāli form of the fable is probably the oldest, and corresponds in moral and incident with the Chinese form, *Avadānas*, vol. i., no. xiv. The Aesopian form, Χελώνη καὶ ἀετός, Babrius, no. 115 of Schneidewin's ed. (cf. no. 419 of Halm's collection), differs in both these respects. Compare

Pāli. Jātaka, no. 215 (vol. ii.); transl., i. p. viii.
Old Syriac version. Kalilag, p. 24.
Arabic. Knatchbull, p. 146. Wolff, i.85.
Later Syriac version, p. 49.
Anvār-i Suhailī, book i., story 23.
Directorium, Cap. II., p. 10 of signature D.
Buch der Beispiele, p. 52^7.
Benfey, i.239; ii.90. Lancereau, p. 340.
La Fontaine, book x., fable 2. Regnier, iii. p. 12f.

21. mitram, nom. neuter: the name-adj., kamb-, agrees in gender with kūrmas.

NOTES TO PAGE 38.

1–2. yad, untranslatable, like *ὅτι*, introducing a direct quotation: cf. *οἱ δὲ εἶπον ὅτι ἱκανοί ἐσμεν;* so St. Luke viii.49, etc. —U.f. adya asmābhis atra uṣitvā (see √3vas). —Lit. 'Now once by fishers, going there, it was said, "By us, staying (over night to-day=) over this night here, to-morrow the tortoises, fishes, and so forth shall be killed."'

4. āhatus, 801a. —See tāvant 3b. 'Let the facts be ascertained first; afterwards, what is fitting (yad ucitam, √uc), · · ·.'

5. U.f. mā evam. —'For I (am) having a seen disaster here = (1308) have seen a · · ·.'

7–8. For the three names, see vocab. The third is of a kind with which Bühler compares the early Christian name 'Quodvult-dea,' and the Puritan 'Fight-the-battle-of-faith,' etc. —U.f. dvāu · · edhete (√edh). —'Both Forethought and who (is) Readywit, these two · · :' the yas merely fills out the metre, see ya3.

9. SELECTION XV. The three fishes. Hitopadeça, book iv., fable 3.

—This story corresponds to Pañcatantra, book i., fable 14; see Benfey, ii. p. 137 and 91. Very similar is book v., fable 6. Somadeva gives a version at lx.179. An excellent version occurs in the MBh. xii.137. 1=4889. Cf. also

Pāli. Jātaka, no. 114, vol. i.
Old Syriac version. Kalilag, p. 15.
Arabic. Knatchbull, p. 121. Wolff, i. 54.
Later Syriac version, p. 31.
Anvār-i Suhailī, book i., story 15.
Directorium, Cap. II., p. 12 of signature c.
Buch der Beispiele, p. 39^{37}.

9–10. U.f. purā etasmin eva · · evaṁvidheṣu · · upasthiteṣu (303b) -trayeṇa.

11. tatra = teṣu matsyeṣu, see tatra 1.

12. See 2antara4.

13–14. See √1dhā+abhi. —'In a matter (still) future, from lack of anything to judge by, where shall I go?' = since the danger is vague and uncertain, I'll keep still for the present. —See √pad+ud.

16–17. Explained in notes to p. 18, lines 9–10.

18. See √dṛç+sam, and cf. 36^{13-14}.

19. U.f. apa-sāritas (pass. of *caus.*) · · ut-plutya.

21. U.f. -ityādi refers to lines 7 and 8 above. Cf. note to 33^{7-8}.

22. SELECTION XIV., continued. 'Therefore (tad), this to-day (tad adya) must be brought about, that I reach (yathā prāpnomi) · · :' cf. passages cited under yathā6 end.

23. prāpte, 'reached = in reaching,' see 17^{18}N. Similarly gacchatas te, 'of you, going = of your going.'

NOTES TO PAGE 39.

1. U.f. bhavadbhyām saha. See vartman.

3. kāṣṭham is subject of avalamb-.

5. 'That is an expedient; but —.'

6. 'A wise man should consider the (expedient *or*) advantage (of a certain course), and likewise the (inexpedient *or*) disadvantage of it he should consider.' Note the etymology of upāya and apāya, and the contrast.

7ª. Gen. absolute, 300^{2}.

8. SELECTION XVI. The herons, the serpent, and the ichneumons. Hitopadeça, book iv., fable 5.

—This story corresponds to Pañcatantra, book i., fable 20. Cf. also introduction to selection viii., 31^{19}. Somadeva gives the story very briefly at lx.235. Cf. also

Old Syriac version. Kalilag, p. 30.
Anvār-i Suhailī, book i., story 26.
Buch der Beispiele, p. 57^{34}.

9. Since this Vulture-peak is placed near the Nerbudda, we can hardly identify it with the one famed in Buddhist story (27^{5}N.), which was near the Ganges.

13–14. U.f. · · ānīya, · · ārabhya (see √rabh+ā 3), · · yāvat (see yāvant 3), pañkti-krameṇa · · dhatta (668).

15. svabhāva-dveṣāt: the enmity of ichneumons and serpents was proverbial: "They fight like cats and dogs;" cf. Pañcatantra, p. 110^{22}f, ed. Kosegarten, = book ii., p. 7^{11}f, ed. Bombay; and selection xxi.

15–16. tathā etc. = 37^{18}: cf. 33^{14}N.

17. U.f. tāis (= nakulāis) · · ā-ruhya, · · sarve · · ·.

18. āvām, 491. —Cf. 33[7-8]N.

19. SELECTION XIV., concluded. —See eva2 near mid.

20. uttaraṁ dā: cf. uttara-dāyaka, 32[4].

21. U.f. sarvathā atra eva. —See kim3.

22. U.f. evam anuṣṭhite sati, 303b[4].

NOTES TO PAGE 40.

1. sam-uhyate, √vah, 769, 252. —āha, 801a.

2. U.f. tadā, atra eva paktvā, khād-, 'Then he shall be eaten, with a cooking (of him) right here' = we'll cook and eat him on the spot. Note that the gerund, as simple instr. of accompaniment of an action-noun, is generally the adjunct of the logical subject of the clause, although the latter (as here) is not always expressed.

4. vismṛta-saṁskāras, 1299.

5. vadann eva, cf. cintayann eva, s.v. eva2.

7–8. Construe: yas na karoti iha vacas suhṛdām · ·, sas etc. —bhraṣṭas, √bhraṅç. —With line 7, cf. 25[14].

9. SELECTION XVII. The hermit, and the mouse that was changed to a tiger. Hitopadeça, book iv., fable 6.

—This story, and the one at MBh. xii.116. 1 = 4254, are ultimately identical with Pañcatantra, book iii., fable 12 (Benfey, ii. p. 262, 281), although very different from their prototype and inferior to it. Benfey traces the connection in a most interesting way, i. p. 373. To his references, add Somadeva, lxii.125, Kalilag, p. 72, Later Syriac, p. 149, Beispiele, p. 116.

9–10. U.f. tena āç- · · · dṛṣṭas, 'he saw.'

11–12. khāditum (981[3]) anu-dhāvan: inf. hantum used similarly, 40[21], 41[2].

12. tapaḥ-prabhāvāt: the austerities of the holy men gave them supernatural powers, cf. 16[11]N.

13. biḍālas, predicate. See √1kṛ9. —kukkurāt, 292a: so vyāghrāt, next line. —See √bhī and 643b.

15. 'Looks upon even the tiger as a mouse.'

17–18. See √nī. —yāvat etc., see 999.

19. U.f. svarūpa_ākhyānam, 'report about my true-nature.'

20. See √yam + sam-ud. —See √1kṛ, desid.

20–21. U.f. "punar mūṣikas bhava" iti uktvā. —See eva.

NOTES TO PAGE 41.

3. SELECTION XVIII. The heron, the fishes, and the crab. Hitopadeça, book iv., fable 7.—See note to 31[19].

—The story occurs in the Pañcatantra, book i., fable 7. Somadeva has it at lx.79. The Buddhist form appears in the Jātaka. A hypocrite is called 'one who acts like a heron,' Manu iv.196 (cf. 20[8]N.).

Pāli. Jātaka, no. 38; translation, i. p. 317.
Old Syriac version. Kalilag, p. 12.
Arabic. Kalila. Knatchbull, p. 113. Wolff, i.41.
Later Syriac version, p. 24.
Anvār-i Suhailī, book i., story 12.
Directorium, Cap. II., p. 8 of signature c.
Buch der Beispiele, p. 35[16].
Benfey, i.174; ii.58. Lancereau, p. 344.
La Fontaine, book x., fable 3. Regnier, iii. p. 18.
Arabian Nights: Night 717 (Weil, iii.914).

4. U.f. tathā ud-vignam iva, 'so, as if terrified.' See √dṛç, caus., and cf. sthita4.

5. pṛṣṭas, 220. —See iti 2b.

7–8. U.f. te ca atra avaçyam eva. 'And these here very surely · · will be killed: I heard (√ākarṇaya) a plan to that effect (iti).'

8–9. See itas3. —U.f. -abhāvāt asmad-maraṇam. —kṛtas, 'am made = have become.'

10–11. See iha and tāvant4. —'This (heron, ayam) appears to be actually (eva) our benefactor; therefore let him be asked (√prach, 768) · · ·.'

13–14. U.f. upakartrā ariṇā saṁdhis. 'Alliance (is proper—cf. 22[20]N.) with a foe who does us a service, not with a friend who injures us (apakāriṇā—cf. 39[6]N.); surely service and injury are to be considered as the essential characteristic of these two.' The fact that one is *called* foe and the other friend is of no account. —lakṣyam agrees with predicate.

18–19. U.f. kasmin cid deçe, 'in a certain place.' —sthāpitās, 1051[3], 1042d.

20–21. U.f. bakas api apūrva-kulīra-māṅsa_arthī · · kulīras api: the api's may be rendered by 'and' or 'but,' as the sense requires — cf. api5.

NOTES TO PAGE 42.

1. -ākīrṇām, √3kṛ+ā.

3. 'One should *fear* danger (bhayāt, 292a) so long (only) as the danger is future.'

5–6. U.f. paçyet na kim cid hitam (163). —mriyate, 773. —'Surely, if one sees not any salvation for himself (in a non-fight =) without a fight, then · · ·.'

9ᵇ is one copulative cpd adj., utta-, 1257.

11. SELECTION XIX. The Brahman and his jar. Hitopadeça, book iv., fable 8. Count not your chickens before they be hatched.

—This story corresponds to Pañcatantra, book v., fable 9. The history and literature of the fable are treated at length by Max Müller, *Chips*, iv.145–209.

—The tale recurs in the *Arabian Nights*, Night 716 (Weil, iii.910): and the Barber's story of his fifth brother, Night 166 (Weil, i.540: Lane, chap. V.) is essentially similar. Ultimately dependent on the Indian original are Grimm's Lazy Heinz and Haggard Liese, *Märchen*, no's 164 and 168. Compare also

Old Syriac version. Kalilag, p. 53.
Arabic. Kalila. Knatchbull, p. 269. Wolff, ii.3.
Later Syriac version, p. 170.
Anvār-i Suhaili, book vi., story 2.
Directorium, Cap. VII., p. 7 of signature K.
Buch der Beispiele, p. 130[14].
Benfey, i.499; ii.345. Lancereau, p. 345.
La Fontaine, b'k vii., fable 10. Regnier, ii.145,495.

—For -çarman in names, see 59[18] and N., and see viṣṇuçarman in vocab.

11–12. The feasts of the winter and summer solstices (corresponding to Christmas and Midsummer), originated in the worship of the sun at his 'entrance' (saṁkrānti) upon his 'north-course' and his 'south-course' respectively, and were celebrated with lavish alms-giving, as appears from the Pañcatantra, book ii., fable 2 (where Kosegarten, 119[1], reads uttarāyaṇa-, and the Bombay ed., 14[21], reads dakṣiṇāyana-: see this last in vocab.).

—The vernal equinox was also the occasion of great festivities, whence, doubtless, the fulness of the Brahman's jar. This feast survives as the *Holī* or Indian Carnival — described by H. H. Wilson, *Works*, ii.222–43.

12–14. U.f. tatas tam (= çarāvam) ā-dāya, asāu (devaçarmā), çayyā-nikṣipta+dehas (1297) san (redundant, √las3), rātrāu acintayat. —The long cpd: 'in a dish-filled-pot-maker's-shed-part (ekadeçe).'

14–17. Construe: yadi aham, imam · · vikrīya, · · prāpnomi, tadā (introduces verb of apodosis, karomi) tāis (= kapardakāis) · · çarāvān tatas ghaṭa‿ādīn upakrīya vikrīya, anekadhā vṛddhāis · · · -ādikam upakrīya, · · utpādya, · · karomi. As a help to the correct phrasing, note that the interjected adverbial clauses end each with its gerund. —tatas, line 15, 'then,' equiv. to 'and': 'dishes and jars and so forth.'

17–18. U.f. tāsu · · yā adh-, tasyām · ·: 'who among those wives (is) most beautiful, on her I bestow · · ·.'

18–20. 'Thereupon, when her co-wives (tat-sapatnyas), jealous, quarrel, then I (will) beat them so' (ittham, said while he throws the cudgel to show how). —U.f. abhidhāya utthāya.

NOTES TO PAGE 43.

1–2. 'By the potter, (who came =) who was brought by the noise of the breaking of the pots, seeing that, the Brahman, scolded (see tiras), was expelled (bahiṣ-) · · ·.'

5. SELECTION XX. The Brahman with the goat, and the three rogues. Hitopadeça, book iv., fable 10.

—This story occurs in the Pañcatantra, book iii., fable 3, and, as usual, in a more elaborate and better form. Somadeva has it at lxii.62. Of the frequent imitations, *Gesta Romanorum*, Cap. 132 = 124 (see ed. of H. Oesterley, p. 486 and 733) may be mentioned. Compare also

Old Syriac version. Kalilag, p. 67.
Arabic. Kalila. Knatchbull, p. 233. Wolff, i.205.
Later Syriac version, p. 141.
Anvār-i Suhaili, book iv., story 7.
Directorium, Cap. V., p. 2 of signature I.
Buch der Beispiele, 109[21].
Benfey, i.355; ii.238. Lancereau, p. 363.

6. U.f. grāma‿antarāt (202) · · gacchan.

7–9. U.f. · · dhūrtās "yadi eṣas (176a) chāgas (227) *supply* asmābhis, kena api upāyena (tam chāgam) prāpya, khādyate, tadā ·· bhavati" iti ālocya, ·· upaviçya, sthitās (see sthita4).

10–11. abhi-hitas, see √1dhā. —See iti 2b. —U.f. skandhena uhyate, 769 and 252.

12. tad eva, 'just that' = 'the same thing.'

14. dolāyamāna-: Grierson, Bihār Peasant Life, p. 45, gives a good picture of the dooly.

16. U.f. "niççitam eva ayam k-" iti matvā.

17. snātvā, to remove the supposed impurity arising from touching a dog. —yayāu, 800c. —Read cchāgas for -go.

19–20. See √1vid4. —vañcyate, pass. of caus. —chāgatas, see 1098c[3].

Notes to Page 44.

1. Selection XXI. The Brahman and his faithful ichneumon. Hitopadeça, book iv., fable 13.

—This story corresponds to Pañcatantra, book v., fable 2. It is undoubtedly of Buddhistic origin — Beal, *Academy*, Nov. 1882, p. 331. It is discussed by Benfey, i.479, who gives a Mongol version and a Tamil imitation. Somadeva has the story at lxiv.3. Lancereau mentions numerous versions and imitations, p. 366. Especially famous is a parallel story, which is told of Llewellyn the Great and his faithful hound Gellert, and goes back to 1205. It is familiar to English readers through the well-known ballad of Wm. R. Spencer. A highly interesting English version is found in *Ye Seven Wyse Maysters of Rome*, printed by Wynkyn de Worde, in 1520, reprinted London 1885, ed. G. L. Gomme, p. 28. Compare also

Old Syriac version. Kalilag, p. 54.
Arabic. Kalila. Knatchbull, p. 268. Wolff, ii.1.
Later Syriac version, p. 169.
Anvār-i Suhailī, book vi., story 1.
Directorium, Cap. VII., p. 8 of signature K.
Buch der Beispiele, p. 131[14].
Benfey, i.479; ii.326. Lancereau, p. 366.

—Through ujjayinī ran the prime meridian of Hindu astronomers.

2–3. 'For (see kṛte) the Br., from the king, a call to offer a çrāddha came.' —çrāddha, see p. 402.

4. sahaja-dāridryāt, 'from connate poverty = a born beggar as he was.'

6–7. 'Of receiving, · · ·, quickly, (if it is) not done, Time drinks the juice of it:' i.e. if you have anything to receive or give or a deed to do, do it quickly or it'll not be worth doing.

9. U.f. cira-kāla-pālitam · · -rakṣārtham.

11. Natural enemies — cf. 39[15]N.

12–13. U.f. asāu · · āyāntam. —'Having blood-smeared snout-and-paws.'

14. See √dhṛ + ava: his conclusion was "mama · · bhakṣitas:" anena = nakulena.

15–16. U.f. asāu upasṛtya. —See √sthā4.

16–17. 'Finding out that the ichneumon was his benefáctor, (and) possessing a discovered (√bhū + vi) deed (kṛtyā), i.e. discovering what he had done, with a pained heart (418) · · ·.'

19–20. 'Who, without · · (a-vijñaya), goes to *or* gets under (gatas) the power of passion · · ·.'

SELECTIONS XXII.–XXVII.

Extracts from the Kathā-sarit-sāgara.

§ 45. The work from which the following extracts are taken holds a rather exceptional place in Hindu literary history, inasmuch as its date and authorship are quite definitely known. According to the author's fancy, it unites in itself all stories as does the ocean all rivers, and he therefore calls it the 'Ocean of the Streams of Story' or Kathā-sarit-sāgara. Following out the metaphor, he divides the work into one hundred and twenty-four chapters, called tarañgas or 'billows.' By another division, independent of the one just mentioned, the work is broken into eighteen books, called lambakas, which Brockhaus, without authority, conjectured to mean 'surges.' The work contains about 22,000 distichs, that is, about one-quarter as much as the Mahā-bhārata, and not quite twice as much as the Iliad and Odyssey together. An analysis of its contents is given by H. H. Wilson, *Works*, vol. iv. 109–159.

§ 46. BIBLIOGRAPHY. The following discussions connected with the literary history of this work should be mentioned.

Fitzedward Hall, the Vāsavadattā, Calcutta, 1859, Introduction, pages 22, 23.

George Bühler, On the Vṛihatkathā of Kshemendra, *Indian Antiquary*, i.302f, Bombay, 1872. Cf. Weber's Remarks, ibidem, ii.57.

George Bühler, Detailed Report of a tour in search of Sanskrit MSS. made [in 1875] in Kaçmīr etc., published at Bombay in 1877 as an Extra Number of the *Journal* of the Bombay Branch of the Royal Asiatic Society, with vol. xii. Preliminary reports had appeared in the *Ind. Ant.*, v.27f, and vi.264f.

George Bühler, Ueber das Zeitalter des Kaçmīrischen Dichters Somadeva, *Sitzungsberichte* der phil.-hist. Classe der Kais. Akademie der Wiss., cx.545f, Vienna, 1885.

Sylvain Lévi, La Bṛihatkathāmañjarī de Kshemendra, *Journal Asiatique*, 8.vi.397f, vii.178f. Vol. vi. contains chapters 1–8 in text and translation.

The text has been edited by H. Brockhaus, Leipsic, 1839, 1862, and 1866. A complete translation has been given by C. H. Tawney, Calcutta, 1880–84.

§ 47. The concluding verses of the work were printed from new and trustworthy manuscript material by Bühler.[1] From them it appears that the author was named Soma, i.e. Somadeva, and was the son of the virtuous Brahman Rāma. Somadeva says that he made this collection of stories to please the queen Sūryavatī, and gives some of the facts relating to the royal house of Kaçmīr then regnant. These facts are supplemented and confirmed by the Rājataraṅginī or 'Chronicles of Kaçmīr,' written by Kalhaṇa, about 1148–1157 A.D.[2] Combining these sources, Bühler reaches conclusions which may here be summarized briefly.

§ 48. In the year 79, i.e. 4079, of loka-kāla,[3] Saṁgrāmarāja, a descendant of Sātavāhana (or Çāta-), succeeded to the throne of Kaçmīr. This was A.D. 1003. He was followed in 1028 by his son Ananta. Anantadeva is described as weak-minded, rash, and impetuous, but as brave even to fool-hardiness. He married Sūryavatī, daughter of the king of Jālandhar (jālaṁdhara). She brought him entirely under her power, and induced him, in 1063, to abdicate in favor of his son Kalaçadeva. He soon repented his hasty step and got control of the government again. Meantime, Kalaça abandoned himself to every vice, and, in rage, his parents determined to punish him, and give over the kingdom to his eldest son Harṣa. In fact, Ananta retired with his court to Vijayakṣetra, the modern Bījbahār, in [41]55 = A.D. 1079, and after two years of feud with Kalaça, took his own life in 1081, leaving the power in the hands of Kalaça, who held it till 1089, when he was succeeded by Harṣa. Sūryavatī burned herself on the funeral pile of her husband Ananta. Now since, according to Somadeva, Kalaça was king when the work was finished, and since it was written for Sūryavatī, the date of the composition must fall between Ananta's first abdication and his wife's death, i.e. between 1063 and 1081 A.D.

§ 49. The real source of the Kathā-sarit-sāgara is stated by Somadeva[4] to be the Bṛhat-kathā or 'Great Narration' of Guṇāḍhya. This work, according to Bühler,[5] goes back to the first or second century of the Christian era; but no manuscript of it has yet been published. On the other hand, important evidence of its general character and contents is afforded by the two works that have flowed from

[1] *Ueber das Zeitalter* etc., pages 547–549.

[2] Bühler's *Report*, p. 52f; *Zeitalter*, p. 554, 557.

[3] The popular calendar (*loka-kāla*) of Kaçmīr is counted from a date corresponding to 3076 B.C. The era is connected — in some real or fanciful way — with Ursa Major (*saptarṣayas* — see *ṛṣi*2), and so is called the Saptarshi era. It is still in use. In giving a date, the hundreds and thousands are ucually omitted. See *Report*, pages 59–60.

[4] See Kathā-sarit-sāgara, i.3 and cxxiv.250, and Reader 56[5].

[5] *Report*, p. 47. Cf. Wilson, l.c., p. 119f.

it, the Bṛhat-kathā-mañjarī and the Kathā-sarit-sāgara. Each is a recast of Guṇāḍhya's original. The former was made by Kṣemendra Vyāsa-dāsa, a contemporary of Somadeva. Its date is not far from the year 1037 A.D., and it is therefore some thirty or forty years prior to Somadeva's work.[1] Both Kṣemendra and Somadeva distinctly assert that they translated from an original in the **pāiçācī bhāṣā** or 'Goblin dialect'; and internal evidence[2] confirms their assertions, and, further, makes it certain that each worked independently of the other. But Somadeva seems to have been well aware of the faults of his predecessor, and his work is a decided improvement upon that of Kṣemendra, whose recast is only about one-third as long as Somadeva's, and sacrifices poetic merit in the effort to be brief.

§ 50. Although Somadeva was a Brahman, there are yet many remaining traces of the Buddhist character of his original, and even direct allusions[3] to the Buddhist Birth Stories occur. Indeed, Weber maintained[4] that Guṇāḍhya was a Buddhist. The name **pāiçācī bhāṣā** seems to have covered a number of Low Prākrit dialects[5] spoken by the most ignorant and degraded classes in many different parts of India. In one of these dialects the Bṛhat-kathā is actually written.

§ 51. It remains — partly by way of introduction to selection xxvii. — to complete and summarize the half-mythical account there given of the origin of the stories.

In a retired spot on the Himālayan peak Kāilāsa, the god Çiva, to please his wife Pārvatī, was telling her (Kathā-sarit-sāgara, i.48) the adventures of the Seven Fairy Kings. Unfortunately, he was overheard by his Gaṇa or attendant (see **gaṇa**), Puṣpadanta. Puṣpadanta foolishly told the tale to his wife, and she recited it in turn to Pārvatī. This made it appear that Çiva had palmed off upon her an old story. Even on learning the truth, she was still exceedingly enraged, and cursed Puṣpadanta to be born as a mortal. She also inflicted the same curse on the Gaṇa Mālyavant who interceded for him.

At their entreaty, however, she set a limit (**anta**) to the curse of each, speaking (i.59) to this effect: "There is a Yakṣa named Supratīka, who, cursed to become a mortal, is living in the Vindhya as a Piçāca, under the name of Kāṇabhūti. When thou, Puṣpadanta, shalt see him, and tell him the tale which thou overheardest Çiva telling me, then thou shalt be released from thy curse. When Kāṇabhūti shall have told it to thee, Mālyavant, he shall be released. And when thou, Mālyavant, shalt have published it to the world, thou shalt be free also."

§ 52. Puṣpadanta, accordingly, is born as Vararuci or Kātyāyana, meets Kāṇabhūti, narrates to him the seven stories of adventure in seven hundred thousand stanzas (ii.26), and is released.

Kāṇabhūti, meantime, remained in the Vindhya, waiting the coming of Mālyavant. The latter is duly born as a Brahman (vi.19, 20), with the name Guṇāḍhya, at Supratiṣṭhita (vi.8) in Pratiṣṭhāna.[6] This is identified with Paiṭhān on the Godāvarī (vi.72), about 150 miles from Bombay, east by north. After travelling in the Deccan, Guṇāḍhya returns to the splendid royal city of Supratiṣṭhita (vi.24) and is appointed a minister (vi.70) of Sātavāhana, the king of whom the story in selec-

[1] Lévi, *Journ. As.*, 8.vii.218–220.

[2] *Ind. Ant.*, i.308–309. *Journ. As.*, 8.vi.413.

[3] E.g., at lxxii.120, to the Boar Jātaka. See Weber, *Indische Streifen*, ii.367.

[4] *Ind. Ant.*, ii.57.

[5] For the views of the Hindus and others concerning these dialects, see Muir, *Orig. Sanskrit Texts*, ii³.43f, esp. p. 48 and 50. Cf. also Jacobi, Ausgewählte Erzählungen in Māhārāshṭrī, Einl. § 2, § 15.

[6] Its Prākrit form is Païṭṭhāna; this is the ΠΑΙΘΑΝΑ of the Περίπλους and the Βαίθανα of Ptolemy. See McCrindle, *Ancient India as described by Ptolemy*, pages 175–6, and J. Burgess, *Arch. Survey of Western India*, iii. (Bīdar, etc.) p. 55.

tion xxvi. is related. In consequence of a wager with his colleague Çarvavarman (52^{3}), Guṇāḍhya forswears the use of Sanskrit, Prākrit, and the local vernacular. Since he knows no other language, he is forced to keep silence, and so to give up his position as minister. With two pupils he retires to the Vindhya, and, falling in with a host of Piçācas (vii.26), learns their dialect. In this he addresses Kāṇabhūti, who exists himself at the time as a Piçāca. Kāṇabhūti tells the tales in 'his own dialect' (svabhāṣayā, 53^{4}), i.e. Pāiçācī, to Guṇāḍhya. The hearer writes them down in Pāiçācī, and with his own blood, since he had no ink by him. Kāṇabhūti is then released.

Guṇāḍhya, in order to "publish the stories to the world," sends the manuscript to Sātavāhana. The king, puffed up by his newly-acquired knowledge of Sanskrit grammar (52^{23}), rejects the stories on account of their dialect. Guṇāḍhya, overcome with grief, reads aloud to his two pupils six hundred thousand distichs and casts the manuscript, leaf by leaf, into the fire, while the beasts stand about in a circle and listen with tears in their eyes.[1] One hundred thousand couplets Guṇāḍhya keeps, because they especially pleased his pupils. At last the king hears of the strange proceeding, comes, and takes what is left,[1] namely the Bṛhat-kathā. The pupils expounded the poem to the king and he composed the first book or lambaka, called Kathāpīṭha (56^{10}N.), to serve as a general introduction to the rest, after Guṇāḍhya had ascended to heaven (56^{4}), released.[2]

[1] Compare the stories of Orpheus and of the Sibyl.

[2] According, then, to Somadeva (and to Kṣemendra, as well, *Ind. Ant.*, i.307), the παράδοσις of the stories is, in turn, from

1. Çiva, to
2. Puṣpadanta (= Vararuci, Kātyāyana),
3. Supratīka (= Kāṇabhūti),
4. Mālyavant (= Guṇāḍhya),
5. Sātavāhana, and
6. The world.

NOTES TO PAGE 45.

LINE 2. SELECTION XXII. King Putraka and the seven-league boots. Kathā-sarit-sāgara, Taraṅga iii.45.—Kṣemendra gives the tale in his Bṛhat-kathā-mañjarī, at ii.48. Tawney, i.14, adduces many parallels, among them, Grimm's Fairy Tales, no. 197, The Crystal Ball. See also Jātaka, no. 186 (vol. ii.); transl., i. p. xvi.f.

2–3. See aṭra 1. —King Putraka's uncles had bribed assassins to kill him. By a greater bribe and a promise to go far away, the king induces the murderers to spare his life: this in explanation of the "meantime," the "promise," the "Vindhya," and the "disgust." —For Putraka, see 17^{9}N. —See √raj + vi.

4–5. The sense-divisions do not correspond with the metrical divisions here as they do in the Epos. U.f. bhraman ava‿āpa asāu -ekatatparāu puruṣāu dvāu; tatas tāu etc. —see iti2.

6. U.f. maya‿asura-sutāu āvām sc. svas.

8. 'On account of this (is) our fighting. Who (is) mighty (= proves to be the stronger), he may take it.' —Brockhaus reads tannimittam—against the metre.

9. U.f. etad tad-vacanam ·· pra‿uvāca.

10. U.f. ·· puṁsas (394)? tatas samavocatām (see √vac, and 854 and 847 end).

11. U.f. pari-dhāya ('by putting on') ·· ava‿āpyate.

12. U.f. yad (162) likhyate: see ya5.

13. See ya5. —'Is thought of.'

14. avādīt, √vad, 898, 899c. Aorists are not very uncommon in this poem, though very few have been met before in this Reader. See 826. —U.f. kim yuddhena? astu ayam paṇas. See 1ka 1.

15. U.f. sas eva etad (= dhanam) haret (163).

16. See under iti2. —mūḍha, 223^{4}.

17. U.f. adhy-āsya, ud-apatat vyoma.

19. √tṛ + ava, with abl.

Notes to Page 46.

1. Selection XXIII. Story of Mousey, the thrifty merchant. Kathā-sarit-sāgara, Taraṅga, vi.28. — It is introduced as a story which Guṇāḍhya hears on his return to Supratiṣṭhita — see p. 333, § 52. It may be called a kind of pendant to selection xix. It is identical with the Cullaka-seṭṭhi Jātaka, no. 4(vol.i.), transl., i.p.168.

2. 'By me, utterly without (vinā eva) capital, wealth was gained' (√sad+ā, caus.).

4. **man-mātus**, abl., 'from my mother:' **man-**, 161, 494.

5. **tad-bhayāt**: **tad-** (494) = **tebhyas**, i.e. **gotrajebhyas**. —See **garbha**3.

7. 'And there was I born, (as the =) to be the means of support of that excellent woman.'

8. See √vṛdh, caus. —**kurvatī**, 714[5].

9–10. U.f. **atha abhy-arthya**. —See √çak B 1. —Lit., 'And then by her, the sad one, having entreated a teacher, I was gradually made to learn writing and ciphering somewhat.'

13. For gen. w. √dā, 297a.

15–16. **agamam**, 846. —**so 'pi** marks beg. of new clause and is little more than a ὁ δὲ with **viçākhilaḥ**. —'Thus (i.e. as follows, lines 17–20) spake (854) to a certain · ·.'

17–18. See 1 **idam**, near end. —**panyena**, appositive to **etena**.

19. **punar**: the antithesis is between a dead mouse and good hard cash.

—The Roman *dēnārius* had long been known to the Hindus. The borrowed word appears, e.g., in an inscription of the time of Kumāra Gupta (ca. 430 A.D., *Ind. Ant.* xv.192), given by Gen. Cunningham, *Arch. Survey of India Reports*, iii. 54–56.

20. See √sthā7. —**te 'pi** (sc. **dīnārās**), 'even the principal.'

22. **tvattas**, 1098a.

Notes to Page 47.

1–2. Construe: **asya sampuṭe** (see this) **tam** (='mouse') **likhitvā, gato 'bhuvam** (829) **aham, so 'pi ahasat**.

3–4. **-yugmena**, instr. of price, 281b: **mūl-**, appositive. —**mārj-** depends on **kṛte**; and the other genitives go w. **dattas**, 297a.

7–8. Construe: **aham çrāntāgatāya -saṁghāya adām** (829) **ambhas**, etc.

9–10. **dve dve**, see **dva**: 'two apiece,' 1260. —U.f. **vikrītavān** (960) **āpaṇe**.

11–12. See **tatas**5: the second is a mere stop-gap. —See √hṛ+ā.

13–14. **mayā**, logical subject of **kṛītam**: **tebhyas**, abl.

15–16. Loc. absolute. —The rains made the roads impassable for the wood-men. —**paṇ-**, 486b. —**çatāis**, 281b.

19–20. 'A golden mouse was sent (1042d) by me, making (it), to that V.; and he gave (**adāt**) · · ·.'

21–22. See √sidh+pra. —U.f. **lakṣmīs iyam**. —**satā**, 'being.'

Notes to Page 48.

1. Selection XXIV. King Çibi, the falcon, and the dove. Kathā-sarit-sāgara, Tar. vii.88. — This story is famous, old, and widespread. It is of distinctly Buddhistic origin and character — see S. Beal, *Si-yu-ki*, i. p. 125 and note. Benfey, Pañcatantra, i. p. 388 f, gives a great many Buddhist and other parallels. It occurs in the Jātaka as no. 499 (vol. iv.). It is frequently figured on Buddhist sculptures: so on the tope of Amarāvatī — see James Fergusson, *Tree and Serpent Worship*,[2] plate lxxxiii. 1, and p. 225, and plate lx. left, and p. 194; also on the great Javan temple of Bōrō Boudour. The Amarāvatī tope dates from about the beginning of our era — see J. Burgess, *Arch. Survey of Southern India* (Amarāvatī, etc.), p. 12, 101.

—In the Cariya-piṭaka, Pāli text, ed. Morris, p. 77, Çibi appears as an incarnation of the Future Buddha. Sakka, in the form of a blind old beggar, asks him for one of his eyes, and he gladly gives up both of them. This is represented in a mural painting of a cave at Ajaṇṭā — J. Burgess, *Cave Temples of India*, p. 315. Beal gives a Chinese version of the story in his *Buddhist Literature in China*, p. 31–41. And the tale occurs in Mohammedan forms with Moses in place of Çibi, and Michael and Gabriel in place of Indra and Dharma (or Agni).

—In Sanskrit works the Çibi-story is common. We find it in the Southern Pañcatantra, French version by J.-A. Dubois, p. 173. It occurs three times in the MBh. It is told at iii.130.21 = 10557, of Uçīnara, the father of Çibi (translated by P. E. Foucaux, *Le MBh., Onze épisodes*, p. 231); at iii.197.1 = 13274, of Çibi himself; and at xiii.32.3 = 2046, of Vṛṣadarbha, the son of Çibi.

— Çibi Āuçīnara is the traditional author of RV. x.179.1, and seems to be the heros eponymos of a clan that dwelt between the Indus and Akesines. See Zimmer, *Altindisches Leben*, p. 130, 431.

1. King Suçarman, having been deceived by a Gaṇa in the form of a Brahman, says, "This is no Brahman, but a god come to deceive me; for such things are constantly happening in this world; and so (**tathā ca** — introducing the following story as a similar instance), in old times, there was (**abhūt**) a king, etc."

2. U.f. **sarva-sattva‿abhaya-pradas**, 'giving a feeling of safety to all creatures:' see 29¹N.

3–4. The inf. denotes purpose: cf. 987 w. 982. — 'Indra himself, having taken on · · ·, pursued (**anv-apatat**) Dharma' — see **dharma3**.

5. U.f. **añkam açiçriyat**: see √**çri3**; for aorist, 859³, 864.

7. 'This (is my) proper food. Surrender (758) to me (297a) · · ·.'

8. For Indra and the reader, who know the secret of the dove's real nature, there is a play upon the word **dharmas**.

9–10. U.f. **enam** (274b) · · **a-tyājyas**; **tad** ('therefore') **dadāmi anyad** · · **tava** (297a).

11. See **evam**. — **ātma-**, see 18¹⁶N. — See 747.

13. See **yathā5**. — √**kṛt+ud**. — **aropayat**, 1042e end.

15–16. See √**ruh+adhi**. — U.f. " · · **tu etad**" **divyā vāk ud-abhūt**. '"That indeed ís equal"', referring to the promise contained in line 10, **etat-samam**.

18–19. U.f. **tuṣṭāu akṣ-** (pred. adj.) · · **dattvā** (991, 955c) **ca** · · **anyān tāu** · · **īyatus** (783b²).

20. SELECTION XXV. Story of Ahalyā. Kathā-sarit-sāgara, Tar. xvii.137. — Çacī is a pattern of wifely virtue, but Indra does not requite her with equal fidelity. His amours are as notorious as those of Zeus. Indra is invoked with the words **ahalyāyāi jāra**, as early as the ÇB. (iii.3.4¹⁸). He is reproached for his affair with Ahalyā, at MBh. v.12.6 = 373; and this is narrated at length in the Rāmāyaṇa, i.48 Schlegel, or i.49 Gorresio. His attempt upon Ruci is told at MBh. xiii. 40.16 = 2262, excerpted by Muir, *Texts*, i².466. Later books smooth over these immoralities by interpreting them allegorically — see Müller, *Ancient Skt. Lit.*, p. 529. — So Holtzmann, ZDMG. xxxii.302 (cf. 294); Muir, *Texts*, iv².48.

NOTES TO PAGE 49.

2. U.f. **-lubdhas** (√**lubh**) **tām**. — See √**arthaya+pra**, 959 and 960.

3. Construe: **matis pra-**, **vibhūti-andhā**, **dhāvati aviṣaye**.

4–5. U.f. **sā anu-mene** (794e) · ·; **tad** ('that occurrence') **ca prabhāvatas** (1098, 291²) **buddhvā** (160), **tatra agāt** · ·.

6–7. See √**1kṛ3**. — See **sthita4**.

8–9. 'She answered her husband with a speech, (provincially ambiguous, i.e.) ambiguous on account of its dialect, (but yet) having some regard for (verbal) truth, "This is, of course, a cat *or* my lover"' — see **majjāo**. Gāutama takes it in the latter sense and replies **tvaj-jāra**.

11. 'He caused to fall on her a curse, truth-regard-limited' (**-kḷptāntam**), i.e. not an endless curse, but one with a definite limit, because she did not lie outright.

12. The curse. — **ava‿āpnuhi**, 703.

13. The limit — cf. p. 333, § 51. — See **ā4** and 293c. — See **2antara 1**. — 'Until forest-interior-wandering-Rāghava-sight, i.e. till thou seest R. wandering in the wood.' "Rāma removed the guilt of Ahalyā by merely looking at her," says the Viṣṇupurāṇa, iv.4.42.

14. **datta-çāpas**, 1299, 1308. — **yayāu**, 800c.

16. SELECTION XXVI. The king who didn't know his Sanskrit grammar. Kathā-sarit-sāgara, Tar. vi.108–164, omitting 111–112, 124–133a, 154–158, 161–162. — Kṣemendra gives this story in brief at vi.35–52, *Journ. As.*, 8.vi.446. The king is called Sātavāhana; but this is merely the family name of a dynasty that reigned in the north-west of the Deccan in the first and second centuries of our era. See Oldenberg, *Ind. Ant.*, x.225 f. Çarvavarman was a protégé of this family — p. 334, § 52. Somadeva, as we saw, makes Harṣa a descendant of Çātavāhana; and for the last, he adds (vii.13), Çarvavarman wrote the easy grammar called Kātantra — Bühler, *Report*, p. 74.

16–17. Guṇāḍhya, who had been interrupted by Kāṇabhūti, resumes his story here with tatas. — adhy-āsta, 620. — tad, 'that' (garden), whose creation by Durgā (see deva2c), Guṇāḍhya had narrated a little before (vi.84). It was just outside of the capital of Pratiṣṭhāna (p. 333).

19. √tṛ+ava, 957b. — Inf. of purpose.

Notes to Page 50.

2. 'Çirīṣa-delicate-limbed, i.e. having limbs as delicate as a Ç. blossom.' — U.f. abhy-agāt.

4. 'She said "Don't with water (mā udakāis — cf. line 8) pelt me."' He understands it as "With comfits (modakāis) pelt me."

5. ānāyayat, √nī+ā, caus. imf.

7. rājann, 210. — See 2antara 1.

8. The order of the words is inverted to remove the ambiguity. — iti uktam · · tava (297a), 'Thus I said to thee.'

9. 'Knowest thou not the mere (mātrā2) euphonic combination of the mā-word and the udaka-word?'

12. hasati, present ppl., loc. absolute. — -ākrāntas, 955a. — See jhaṭ-iti.

13. 'Having abandoned-water-play,' 1308.

14–15. U.f. pra‿aviçat · · muhyan āhārādi-.

17–18. Construe: "çaraṇam me ('sti) p- vā, mṛtyus vā" iti · ·. — 'Having bed-thrown-limbs,' √2as+pari-ni.

19–20. Construe: parijanas, · · dṛṣṭvā, abhavat sambhrāntas, "kim etad" iti ('saying "What's that?"').

21–23. aham, i.e. Guṇāḍhya. — tām, i.e. avasthām. — pary-ahīyata, 770b. — prātar āvām ('I. and Ç.').

Notes to Page 51.

1–2. sarvasya, subjective gen. w. praveçe, which is loc. absol. w. ruddhe. — See katham. — mama begins new clause. — See paçca.

3–4. Construe: nṛpas vijñaptas (1042d[2]) mayā, upaviçya · ·. — See √vṛt7.

5–6. 'S., tho' he heard it, kept silent (just so, tathā eva, i.e.) nevertheless.' See √1as4. — U.f. tatas ca idam.

7–8. U.f. · · kuru" iti prāk · · tena · · adya · · niçi — see adya.

9–10. See svapna. — U.f. nabhasas cyutam (nom.) — see √cyu4. — See √kas+vi.

11–12. tasmāt = ambujāt. — dhavala‿ambarā, like the one Socrates sees, *Crito* 44.

13. iyat (451) dṛṣṭvā. — See √man 1.

15–16. 'Ç. having thus announced his vision' — see √1vid+ni and 1308. — U.f. asta-māunas · · avadat.

17–18. The question goes to pāṇḍityam. — See √çak B1, pass. of caus. of desid. — kālena: for instr., 281c. Similarly varṣāis, line 21.

19. tena = pāṇḍityena. — eṣā, 'this' that you see about me. — na pratibhāsate = 'sordet.'

20. Observe caesura, and see 1ka 1. 'What pray has a fool to do with power, as it were a block with ornaments?' i.e. he has no more to do · ·, than a block · ·.

21–22. In the introduction to the Pañcatantra, also, the time needed for learning Sanskrit grammar is put at twelve years. — See mukha4.

23. See √çak B1, caus. — tad = grammar.

Notes to Page 52.

2. kuryāt, √1kṛ 1.

5–7. Protasis ends w. ced: tatas begins apodosis; 'then by me are renounced (tyaktam) these three languages which pass current' (√bhū+sam3). See p. 334, § 52. — See tadvat. — Kṣemendra (vi.52) has apabhrança for Somadeva's deçabhāṣā. Both of these terms denote indeed a Prākrit dialect; but, in contrast with the word prākṛtam in this connection, they denote a vernacular of a lower order than prākṛtam.

8-9. U.f. na ced evam · ·, -abdān (276) vahāmi eṣas · ·: eṣas, emphatic, 'I, this one,' 'I, Ç. here, (will) carry · ·.'

10-11. tasminn = Ç. —agamam, 846. —See √man 1.

12. ca vīhastaḥ is Boehtlingk's emendation for cavīhastaḥ.

15. 'Without S., no other way of escape appears.' She is led to look to S. or Kumāra for help, because a kumāra (see this) opened the lotus (51^{19}). — Tawney. Weber conjectured that the war-god Skanda owed his name and existence to Alexander the Great.

18. Caesura. —**19.** prāpa, 783c².

21. 'Showed (√1kṛ 1) favor to him (tasya, 297a), i.e. to Ç.'

22-23. 'Having magic power by K.'s gift.' —See cintitop-: for a like magic, see 45^{18}.

Notes to Page 53.

1-2. U.f. prādus āsan ca tās (sciences) tasya (= dat.) · · tatkṣaṇam. · · · hi (163).

3. Selection XXVII. The pathetic history of the stories. Kathā-sarit-sāgara, Tar. viii. — It forms Kṣemendra's eighth chapter (of only 16 couplets), *Jour. As.*, 8.vi.449. For a general explanation of the Taranga, see p. 333, § 51f.

3-4. 'So, by G's request (vii.113), that tale was told by K. in his own (piçāca) dialect.'

5-6. 'And by G., likewise in (lit. with) that dialect, in (lit. with, 281c) seven years (varṣāis), it (sā) was written down as seven couplet-lacs' (appositively).

7-8. U.f. mā (580) · · hārṣus (882) iti: 'Thinking "Let them not steal it," i.e. Fearing lest they might.'

—Both Somadeva and Kṣemendra state that the stories were written down in blood: S. gives the lack of ink as a reason; K. gives none. But the statement may rest on a popular superstition like the Germanic one which ascribes peculiar virtues to pure spittle (cf. also St. Mark viii.23) and to blood. Life rests in the blood, the "vital fluid"; from it a drink of immortality is made; and with it pacts are made or subscribed (cf. Faust, l. 1383).

—At present (1878), all available information points to a Phoenician-Aramaic origin of the Indian alphabets. Writing was probably introduced not earlier than 400 B.C., and was, certainly, little used in India before 250 B.C. So says Burnell, *Palaeography*,² p. 9. See also Whitney, § 2. The material was the palm-leaf, and in Kaçmīr, birch-bark. Paper was introduced by the Mohammedans, i.e. not till after 1000 A.D. For ink, see maṣī in vocab.

9-10. 'The sky (ambaram) became filled (nirantaram) with S. etc., who came (āyātāis) to listen, [became filled *or* covered] as if (iva) with a canopy.'

12. See √gam4. K. was orig. a yakṣa, see p. 333, § 51. —çāpa-muktas would be better.

15-16. 'I must make my B. famous on earth; and this business (of making it so) was enjoined on (lit. announced to, ud-īritas) me by Durgā when she told how my curse would end (lit. in the declaration, -uktāu, of the end, -anta-).' See p. 333, § 51.

19-20. The two nominatives in l. 19 are in partitive apposition to çiṣyāu · · ubhāu, the subject of ūcatus.

Notes to Page 54.

1. Explained under sthāna6.

4. pra‿ahiṇot, 192c. —dattvā: cf. 991 w. 955c.

6. The garden mentioned at 49^{17} — see N.

7-8. 'That MS. was shown to S. (genitive, 297a²) with the words "This is G's work."' —The gender of the pred. determines that of the subject, eṣā.

11. See pramāṇa. "The length of the poem (700,000 distichs) is a weighty argument in its favor, but —" This is quite in accord with later Hindu taste. As if the 100,000 distichs of the extant MBh. were not enough, the preface (MBh. i.1.106a = 104c) tells us that there was a version of 3,000,000 couplets for the use of the gods. Fortunately their years were lengthened out so as to give them plenty of time to hear it — see

58^8N. The Manes had to get along with a version of 1,500,000. Guṇāḍhya is said (54^{22}, 56^1) to keep only one-seventh of his poem; but even this is an exaggeration (it contains less than 22,000 couplets — p. 331). Similarly Manu is said to have been abridged from 100,000 to 12,000 and then to 4,000. It contains less than 3,000 — strictly, 2685, cf. p. 341, § 56.

18. vivikta-ramya‿, 1257: √vic+vi. — bhūbhāgam, in appos. w. çil-.

19–20. √īkṣ+vi. — √√vac and çru, caus.

23. U.f. tasmin · · paṭhati, loc. absol.

Notes to Page 55.

1–3. These three lines and the preceding line make one sentence; the last word is the subject. — pari-tyakta-, 'having abandoned grass-food, quitting their pasturage.' — U.f. āsan abhyetya (√i+abhy-ā, 992): cf. sametya, line 10.

— Compare the story of Orpheus. In the MBh., iv.39.6 = 1290, horses shed tears. The horses of Achilles lament the death of Patroklos, Il. 17.426: cf. Pliny, *Nat. Hist.*, viii. 42 = 64.

5. See √vad4. — See ja.

8–9. U.f. ūcus · · girāu · · ko 'pi · ·.

14–15. 'He saw him completely (abhitas) overspread (√3kṛ) with tangled locks, (that were) like (iva) the smoke of what was left of the fire of his curse, which was [practically] extinguished' [but still smouldering; for G. was almost, but not quite, released from his ban — p. 334].

— Lit., 'as it were, the smoke-of-extinguished-remaining-curse-fire.' The long cpd receives a fem. pl. ending to conform w. jaṭābhis; but it is a genitively dependent subst. (1264 — not adj.) cpd, whose prior member, praçānta-çeṣaçāpāgni, is a descriptive noun cpd (1280); çeṣa-çāpāgni, again, is a descriptive noun cpd (1280); and çāpa‿agni, finally, is a descriptive noun cpd (1280b), with a bold metaphor. Cf. Kathāsarit-sāgara, xix.104.

18^a. '(The adventures) of himself as P.': there is no objection to this grammatically (cf. τῇ ἐμῇ χειρὶ Παύλου); but G. and P. were never identical — see p. 334. The reading puṣpadantasya ca svaṁ ca would be correct in sense and metre.

19. kathā‿avatāraṁ tam is in apposition w. -ceṣṭitam; 'the adventures (which were that coming down, i.e.) which were the occasion of that coming down of the divine story from heaven to earth.'

20. See gaṇa2. — 'Recognizing him as · ·.' — U.f. pāda‿ānatas, √nam. — See p. 333, § 51.

Notes to Page 56.

1. See idam, end. 'But here are 100,000 (making) one story; take that.' Compare the story of the Sibyl.

3–4. See √mantraya+ā, and pada4.

5–6. Metre, āryā, p. 316, § 44. — U.f. ādāya · · agāt (830) nija-. The long cpd (q.v.) goes w. kathām.

7–8. Metre, as before. — The dual cpd is in the accusative — see √bhaj+saṁ-vi 2. For the long cpd, see 1253a.

9–10. Metre, as before. — 'And with (the help of) those two, King S., having comforted that Kathā, in order to narrate (vaktum) her *or* its descent-to-earth in that (pāiçācī) dialect, composed (cakre) the Kathāpīṭha.' This is the name of the prefatory lambaka; but there is a double mg, 'he made the pedestal of Katha (personified), the next book being called 'head of K.,' Kathāmukha. He consoles (√çvas+ā, gerund of caus.) Kathā or Story, by studying it, and so atoning for the indignity he had offered it, 54^{12}.

11–12. Metre, rathoddhata, p. 316, § 43. — 'And that Story, full of varied beauties, made men forget the stories of the gods [lit. (was) possessing forgotten god-stories], by reason of its interest (kutūhalāt, 291^2). Then (atra3), after accomplishing that in the city, it attained to uninterrupted fame in the three worlds.'

SELECTION XXVIII.

EXTRACTS FROM THE MĀNAVA-DHARMA-ÇĀSTRA.

§ 53. BIBLIOGRAPHICAL. The Manu literature is now very extensive. Only several of the most important and recent works need be mentioned here.

Arthur C. Burnell and Edward W. Hopkins. The ordinances of Manu. Translated from the Sanskrit. With an introduction. London, Trübner & Co. 1884. 8°. Price 12 shillings.

George Bühler. The laws of Manu. Translated with extracts from seven commentaries. [=SBE. vol. xxv.] Oxford, at the Clarendon Press. 1886. 8°. Price 21 shillings. The volume contains an elaborate and valuable introduction.

Julius Jolly. Mānava Dharma-çāstra, the code of Manu. Original Sanskrit text, with critical notes. London, Trübner & Co. May, 1887. 8°. Price 10 shillings 6 pence.

Burnell's introduction contains an argument on the date of our Manu text. Professor Hopkins has summed up and criticised this argument (JAOS. xiii. p. xxviii = PAOS. May, 1885), and concludes that it brings us not one step nearer a solution of the problem.

Bühler's introduction (p. civ-cxviii) gives a learned discussion of the date. Of this, Hopkins makes a résumé (JAOS. xiii. p. cxcviii = PAOS. May, 1887). He finds Bühler's conclusions probable, but does not think them absolutely proved by the proofs adduced.

The text-edition of Loiseleur Deslongchamps (Paris, 1830) is hardly obtainable now. It is safe to say that Jolly's robs all preceding ones of their value, inasmuch as it is the result of far-reaching critical studies. The principal places in which Jolly's text varies from that of the Reader are i.97; ii.11,76, 125; xii.23,37,42,45,90,95,96.

The general theory of the origin of the Laws of Manu was summed up and criticised by Whitney (JAOS. xiii. p. xxx = PAOS. May, 1885). Meantime, however, Bühler's Introduction has put the question in a new light.

The relations of our text to the Mahā-bhārata are ably discussed by Hopkins, JAOS. xi.239-275 (cf. PAOS. Oct., 1883). Here may be found, conveniently assembled, quotations from Manu in the Sūtras and inscriptions, the legendary material about him in the Epic, and a careful discussion of the passages in the Epic which profess to be the declarations of a personal Manu.

By way of calling attention to the interesting subject of the knowledge of the Greeks concerning India, occasional citations are given. The references to Strabo's Γεωγραφικά (of which book xv., chap. 1, §§ 1-73 describe India) follow Casaubon's paging.

The following introduction is in the main a brief abstract of some of the more important points of Bühler's introduction.

§ 54. The native tradition respecting the origin of the Mānava-dharma-çāstra takes the book to be the work of an individual law-giver. In accordance with this tradition, until quite recently, it has been usual for English writers to call the treatise 'The Laws of Manu.' And this designation may still be used, provided only it be used with an intelligent mental reservation, which takes due account of the results of modern criticism. For in the light of critical study, the figure of Manu, as a historical person, fades away; but, on the other hand, we find that Manu as a name is one of the greatest and most reverend of the Hindu antiquity. Questions thus arise: Whence the greatness of this name? What was the real origin of this law-book, and how came it to be called Mānavan?

§ 55. The word mánu originally means simply 'man' (see vocabulary). As we speak of human beings as the 'children of men,' so the Rig-veda speaks of them as the 'offspring of man' (mánu); and in this way arose the conception of a personal Mánu, the father of mankind. He is, in fact, the heros eponymos of the human race.

In the Veda[1] he appears as 'Father Manu, child of the Sun,' as a holy seer, the originator of prayer, praise, and sacrifice, and as the object of the special favor of the gods. In the Brāhmaṇas, Manu is the progenitor of the new race after the flood. That he was regarded as a type of wisdom, is evidenced by the ancient saw, 'Whatever Manu said, that is medicine' (TS.ii.2.10²). And again, that he was an eminent type of goodness appears from the fact that his actions came to be looked upon as

[1] For the Vedic legend of his birth, see 85¹²N. The ancillary books make Manu the author of RV. viii. 27-31. For ancient legends about Manu, see Bühler's *Manu*, p. lvii f; Muir, i².161f, and esp. 181f.

examples highly worthy of imitation. Thus the Veda says (TS.iii.1.9[4]), 'Manu divided his property among his sons'; and this is quoted by Bāudhāyana in his Dharma-sūtra as such an example. Such simple beginnings are entirely natural; but they are also sufficient to show how, with the growth of legal literature, the authors of law-books came to cite all kinds of (supposititious) sayings and doings of Manu as authoritative precedent. For, after the custom of referring to Manu as authority was once started, the oftener he was thus cited, the greater his factitious authority and the temptation to cite him would become. Accordingly, if we examine the four oldest Dharma-sūtras, we find much more frequent reference to Manu in Vasiṣṭha, the latest of them, than in Gāutama, the oldest. And thus, at last, what had been a mere name, a part of the traditional inheritance of the mythical past, attained to greatness as a personal authority and actual law-giver.

§ 56. Before proceeding to our other questions, let us rehearse briefly the native account of the origin of the work. In Sanskrit, the book is entitled **mānava**; and this may mean either 'of Manu' or 'of the Mānavans.' The Hindus say, 'of Manu'; and accordingly the opening stanzas represent the great sages as approaching 'Manu, the son of the Self-existent,' and asking him to declare unto them the law. He accedes; but deems it necessary to go back to a time before the Creation, in order to show how he derives his lineage (Manu i.33), and hence also his authority, directly from the Supreme One, Brahmán. 'He,' says Manu (i.58–60), 'composed this law-book, and taught it to me alone in the beginning; I taught it to Bhṛgu; and Bhṛgu will recite it to you.'

Bhṛgu accordingly takes up Manu's cosmogonical discourse, continues with an account of the Four Ages and of other matters, dwells on the excellence of Manu's Laws, and ends book first with a table of contents of the twelve books of which the treatise consists. And in order that we may not forget that it is all (or all but i. 1–60) put into the mouth of Bhṛgu, we are frequently reminded of the situation by an 'I will next declare' or the like, especially at the beginning of books v. and xii., where Bhṛgu is mentioned by name as the promulgator of the laws in question. In accordance with all this, the work is entitled the Bhṛgu-saṁhitā of the Mānava-dharma-çāstra, and it may conveniently be so designated. It contains 2685 çlokas or 5370 lines; compare 54[11]N.

§ 57. For the incredibility of this native account the reasons are near at hand. First, all the passages involving Bhṛgu as promulgator of the work can be separated from the rest as easily as a picture-frame from the canvas which it surrounds. Indeed, the entire first book is a most palpable later addition. And, more than this, Bhṛgu himself is cited (at iii.16), with three others, as an authority on a disputed point. Clearly, the later editors of the work were nodding here; else they would have expunged this stanza. And who knows how many more of a like sort they may have expunged?

Moreover, against the claim that Manu (to say nothing of the Supreme Spirit), was the author and the first law-giver, the case is equally plain. For the work appeals to the authority of Manu here and there, just as the other works of its class do, thus showing that its earlier editors at least did not pretend that Manu was the author of the whole. Nor was he a law-giver without predecessors or rivals; else we should not find, as we do, divergent opinions of other ancient sages cited along with what purports to be his. Moreover, the work itself (ii.6 = 58[14]f) admits that the law is based on the Veda, the usage of virtuous men, etc.; and it plainly mentions (at iii.232) Dharma-çastras, which must be either contemporaneous, or else earlier than itself.

§ 58. Secondly, then, What was the real origin of the work? The first half of the answer is as follows. The Vedic works, as explained below, fall into the three classes of Saṁhitā, Brāhmaṇa, and Sūtra. Chief among the works of the last class is the Kalpa-sūtra, or 'Ceremony-rules.' No Kalpa work had catholic validity among all Brahman families. On the contrary, many of the most important old families had each its own Kalpa-sūtra. In these clannish differences, doubtless, originated the Caraṇas or 'Schools,' in which Brahman science was cultivated and sacred tradition handed down from generation to generation. Thus among the adherents of the Black Yajur-veda, we find the family of Āpastamba; and, bearing his name, we find not only a Brāhmaṇa, but also a complete Kalpa-sūtra in its three subdivisions of Çrāuta-sūtra or 'Rules for the fire-sacrifices,' Gṛhya-sūtra or 'Domestic usages,' and Dharma-sūtra or 'Sacred law.' The Kalpa-sūtra of Bāudhāyana doubtless had a similar make-up. Good editions of various Gṛhya- and Dharma-sūtras are now accessible in text and translation. They treat[1] of the sacraments, of the duties of a Brahman in the various stages of his life, as student, householder, hermit, beggar, of the duties of a king, of the law of inheritance, and so on.

Now these are the very subjects treated also in the Dharma-çastras. But there is one great difference, the difference of form. The Sūtras are in mingled prose and verse, the latter including both triṣṭubh and anuṣṭubh stanzas; while the Çastras are in the ordinary epic çloka. To a mind acquainted with the veriest rudiments of criticism it is quite clear from their form and language alone that the Çastras are later than the Sūtras — a view which is in entire accord with the stanza ii.6 = 54[18], cited above. The conclusion, then, that the Dharma-çastras, in general, as shown by their contents and form, are the outgrowth, by a very natural process of evolution, from the Dharma-sūtras, is unimpeached.

§ 59. The other half of our answer is that the Mānava-dharma-çāstra, in particular, is a later metrical recast of a lost Mānava-dharma-sūtra: in other words, that it is the 'Law-book of the Mānavans.' This is a particular thesis, quite different from the general conclusion just stated; and, although very widely accepted, it is not universally so. The theory[2] of this connection proceeds as follows. Among the schools of the Black Yajur-veda, especially among those of the Māitrāyaṇīya branch thereof, we find the school of the Mānavans.[3] According to the investigations of Dr. von Schröder,[4] the Māitrāyaṇīya seems to have been one of the oldest and most important of all the schools of the Yajus-period.[5] Of these Māitrāyaṇīyas there are still some representatives surviving in Western India; and their Sūtras are entitled Mānava-sūtras. Manuscripts of the Mānava-çrāuta-sūtra and the Mānava-gṛhya-sūtra are still extant.[6]

§ 60. Unfortunately, the Mānava-dharma-sūtra, the link most important to connect our Bhṛgu-saṁhitā with the Vedic schools, is still missing. The researches

[1] Compare p. 358, § 96f, below.

[2] This theory was broached by Weber (ISt. i.69) and Müller (see SBE. ii. p. xi) in 1849. It was confirmed or elaborated by Johäntgen in 1863, *Das Gesetzbuch des Manu*, p. 100f; by West and Bühler in 1867, see *Digest*[2], p. 27; by Schröder in 1879, *Monatsberichte der Berliner Akad.* for 1879, p. 700, and in 1881, ed. of Māitrāyaṇī-saṁhitā, i. p. XVIII; and finally by Bühler in 1887, in his *Manu*, p. xviii–xlv.

[3] See Caraṇa-vyūha, ISt. iii.258.

[4] In the places just cited.

[5] Compare p. 356, § 90, below.

[6] See ZDMG. xxxvi.442–48, where von Bradke describes some of them, and states their contents.

of von Bradke,[1] too, failed to show any striking correspondences between the Mānava-gṛhya-sūtra and our treatise. But, on the other hand, Bühler has discovered[2] important correspondences between it and the Mānava-çrāddha-kalpa. Moreover, as has been repeatedly pointed out,[3] the Dharma-sūtra of Vasiṣṭha contains a quotation (iv.5–8) which has every appearance of being a veritable fragment of the original Mānava-dharma-sūtra. In this quotation we have, first, the prose rule (5); next, the stanzas which support it (6, 7), and which agree entirely or nearly with Manu v. 41 and 48; and, last, a Vedic passage (8) to support both rule and stanzas. This is the arrangement usual in the Dharma-sūtras. And the prose rule (5) is characterized by the words iti mānavam as a quotation from the Sūtra of a special school; for works valid for all Aryans are not so cited.[4]

§ 61. Other quotations[5] are found in Vasiṣṭha at iii.2, xiii.16, xix.37, and xx.18, in close correspondence respectively with Manu ii.168, iv.117, x.120, and xi.152 of our text, and introduced by the formula, 'And on this point they quote a Mānavan stanza.' From this, one might think that Vasiṣṭha was quoting from our Bhṛgu-saṁhitā. But this inference is barred by the evident posteriority of our text, as shown by its form and by other general considerations, and in particular by the fact that the stanza at xix.37 is in the triṣṭubh metre. We conclude, then, that the Mānava-dharma-sūtra known to Vasiṣṭha closely resembled our text, but was not identical with it.

§ 62. Now granting all that precedes, there is a very strong inherent probability in the conclusion that our Bhṛgu-saṁhitā is a metrical recast of the Dharma-sūtra of the Mānavan school. More than this cannot be said; for it is not a necessary conclusion. Its probability, however, has been greatly increased by the considerations respecting the occasion and method of the recast adduced by Bühler.

§ 63. The occasion was the development (beside the sectarian schools which studied exclusively a single branch of the Veda and the rudimentary works ancillary thereto) of the non-sectarian schools of special sciences, whose teachings claimed validity for all Aryans. In the old Vedic schools, the pupils had to learn the texts of the Mantras and Brāhmaṇas of their sect, and the short ancillary treatises, on ritual, etymology, metre, etc., called Aṅgas or 'Limbs' of the Veda. With the development of these subjects to elaborate disciplines, it became impossible for a student to master them all. He must either content himself with a thorough verbal but unintelligent acquaintance with the texts and short treatises of his own sect; or else he must become a specialist in the ritual, the law, or some other subject, and renounce an extensive knowledge of the sacred texts.

§ 64. That this truly describes the course of things is shown by the present state of learning in India. A good Vāidik is able to recite all the texts of his branch of the Veda. But in order to have an elaborate sacrifice performed, there is need of a Çrotriya specialist, who, though ignorant of the other Aṅgas, is yet a master of the ritual. In the case of two of the Aṅgas, grammar and astronomy, the Vedic schools possess no sectarian text-books of their own. These subjects, it would seem, had been abandoned to the specialists at an early period. For a good while longer the sacred law was cultivated in the Vedic schools, as appears from the existence of

[1] In the ZDMG. xxxvi. 417–77 (1882).
[2] Bühler's *Manu*, p. xl f.
[3] See Bühler, SBE. xiv. p. xviii f and esp. 26; *Manu*, p. xxxi.
[4] See Bühler's *Manu*, p. xxxvii.
[5] See Hopkins, JAOS. xi.242–43; and cf. Bühler, SBE. xiv. p. xviii–xx.

the numerous sectarian manuals on the subject. But even in these (see Bühler, *Manu*, p. lii, p. xxv, N.3) we find mention of persons who know several different law-books, that is, who were specialists in the law. And this fact alone would lead us to infer the existence of special law-schools.

§ 65. Granting the existence of these schools, we have precisely the combination of circumstances which would lead to the production of such a work as our Manu-text. The schools had before them plenty of Sūtra-material, sectarian, of only local validity, unsystematic, and incomplete. In the very nature of things, the schools would tend to be non-sectarian, to widen their influence, and to systematize and complete the work of their predecessors. And this is exactly what they have done in our Manu-text. It is absolutely non-sectarian. As contrasted with its forerunners, it emphasizes the practical rather than the moral side of the law, treating strictly legal topics at much greater length. It shows the signs of being a school-book. And finally, it aims at general validity among all Aryans. This explains the fact that our Manu shows so little correspondence with the texts of the Vedic Mānavan schools. The recast was the work of men whose interest in their subject exceeded their interest in a sect.

§ 66. Finally, the greatness of the name of the legendary and semi-divine Manu suggests the reason why a special law-school should have chosen the Mānavan Dharma-sūtra rather than any other as the basis of their new manual. In constructing a treatise that aspired to universal acceptance, they must *ipso facto* withdraw any claim thereto which rested on the high standing of the Sūtra-original as a sectarian work. The problem then was, in accomplishing this task, to avoid too violent a break with tradition. Had they taken the Gāutama-sūtra, and recast it, waiving for it all claim to general validity on the score of Gāutama's authority, it would indeed have been a bold proceeding to father it upon Vyāsa or Manu or any of the great sages of yore. By choosing the Mānava-sūtra, after their silent waiver on the one hand, they had only, on the other, to interpret its title expressly as meaning 'of Manu,' when, — presto — without the smallest offense to tradition or grammar, they had a name of unsurpassed authority to commend their work to the Aryan world.

§ 67. A great deal of the recast — Bühler, p. lxxiii, thinks one half — cannot have been derived from the Sūtra-original. The entire first book is most clearly such a later addition; and such is likewise the twelfth book, whose classification of actions and existences according to the three guṇas (66^8f) is based on the teachings of the Sāṁkhya, Yogā, and Vedānta systems of philosophy.

What now is the source of these later additions? The Mahā-bhārata offers very many correspondences with our Manu-text. A comparative study of the two works shows that the editors of the latter have not drawn on the former, but rather that both works have drawn upon a common stock of popular metrical maxims (Hopkins, JAOS. xi.268), which embodied much of the traditional legal lore, and were ascribed (as is attested by extant inscriptions) now to one and now to another of the ancient mythical sages — Vyāsa, Manu, and the rest.

§ 68. As for the method of conversion of the Sūtra into our Manu-text, Professor Bühler is of opinion (p. xcii) that it took place at one time, and that our text is not the result of many successive recasts.

§ 69. Coming, finally, to the date of the recast, Professor Bühler concludes

(p. cxiv, cxvii) that it existed in the second century A.D., and was made between that time and circa 100 B.C. General considerations make this conclusion seem far from improbable. Our Manu-text is doubtless the oldest of the class of secondary law-books, like those of Yājñavalkya and Nārada, to which it belongs (p. civ). And again, while it is doubtless posterior to the older portions of the Mahā-bhārata, our Manu-text — in some form or other — is probably prior to the later portions of the great Epic, books xii. and xiii. But we do not know the time of Yājñavalkya nor of the Epic; and at present it seems quite vain to seek for an accurate date.

SYNOPSIS.

NOTES TO PAGE 56.

15. This account of Creation (çlokas 5–13), with others, is given and translated by Muir, iv². 30f. —See idam. —'Darkness'—cf. RV. x.129.3.

16. adhyā-1, i.e. prathamo 'dhyāyaḥ.

17–18. 'He, (himself) not-manifest, making manifest (vy-añjayann) this (universe), the grosser elements and so forth, · · revealed himself' (u.f. prādus āsīt).

19–20. U.f. yas asāū atī- etc., sas · · ud-babhāū.

NOTES TO PAGE 57.

1–2. Join the ablatives w. sisṛkṣus. — U.f. apas · · ādāu. Primeval waters: cf. Muir, iv². 24f; also Strabo, xv.59, p. 713.

3–4. 'That (seed) became a golden (u.f. hāimam) egg, having sun-like splendor (prabhā).' —Brahmán is conceived as too distant to be a father; cf. ZDMG.xxxii.295. —The idea of the mundane egg may be traced to the Veda — cf. 91^{16}. It plays a part in divers Indian cosmogonies: see ÇB. xi.1.6^{1}; Chāndogya Upaniṣad, iii.19 (SBE. i.54); Viṣṇu Purāṇa, i.2.52f (see esp. Wilson's Transl.², i.39f and notes); these passages are given by Muir, iv².24f, 41f. Cf. also Preller, *Griech. Mythol.*, i³.35f; and Pott's *Anti-Kaulen*, 68f.

5–6. 'The waters are called "nārās," (because) the waters are indeed the offspring of the Primal Spirit (nara). Since these were his ancient place of motion (ayana), therefore is he called Nārāyaṇa' ('having the nāra = nārās as his ayana,' 1302). This oft-recurring etymology, as found in MBh. and Purāṇas, is discussed at length by Wilson and Hall in notes to Viṣṇu Purāṇa, i.4.6, Transl.², i.56–8. Cf. Lassen, IA. i².769. For correct derivation, see nārāyaṇa.

7–8. 'What (was) that cause (etc. — see sadasadātmaka), thence-created (was) the Puruṣa, (and) in the world he is called "Brahmán."' Cf. ZDMG. xxxviii.193–4, 206.

9–10. ātmano dhyānāt, 'by his meditation' (291^{2}). —See √1kṛ 10.

11–12. See √1mā + nis. —See díç.

13–14. U.f. -ravibhyas. —See bráhman 3. — U.f. yajña-siddhi-artham ṛc-yajus-sāman-lakṣaṇam. —Cf. AB. v.32.

15–16. The -tas puts the whole aggregative cpd in an ablative relation (1098 b). —The older designation of the second caste was rājanya, which term is used at RV. x.90.12, of which stanza this çloka is a paraphrase. For many other mythical accounts of the origin of the castes, see Muir, i².7–160, esp. p. 10 and p. 159.

18ᵇ. 'Day (is) for performance of works.'

19–20. The dark and light lunar fortnights (= one human month) form respectively the day and night of the Manes; for with them everything is reversed. See ÇB. ii.4.2 or AJP. iii.403. They are fed once a month. —The *older* Greek division of the month was in two fortnights (cf. Hesiod, *Works and Days*, 780): **çukla** = μὴν ἱστάμενος; **kṛṣṇa** = μὴν φθίνων.

21–22. U.f. **ahas tatra** (= **rātry-ahnos**) **udag-ayanam.**

23f. Lit. 'Attend ye to that (**tan**) which is the extent both of a night-and-day of Brahman and of the ages.'

NOTES TO PAGE **58**.

1. See **tu** 4. —Respecting the ages, see Roth, *Ueber den Mythus von den fünf Menschengeschlechtern bei Hesiod und die indische Lehre von den vier Weltaltern*, Tübingen, 1860. The conception of a past golden age is common. The scheme of ages as here presented is post-Vedic (see Roth, p. 24f), and based on the simple descending arithmetical progression, 4, 3, 2, 1. Description of the four ages, MBh. iii.149.11 = 11234, f. Criticism and numerical details: Whitney, JAOS. vi. 152f; Viṣṇu Purāṇa, i.3.10f, Transl.², i.49f; Monier Williams, *Indian Wisdom*, 333. Golden age described by the Brahman Κάλανος, Strabo, xv.64, p. 715.

2–3. 'Four thousand of years, they say, (is) the kṛta yuga (see **kṛtá**). Its morning twilight has just as many hundreds; and its evening twilight is similar.' 400 + 4000 + 400 = 4800.

4–5. **itareṣu**, sc. **yugeṣu**, i.e. the Tretā, Dwāpara, and Kali, which last respectively 3600, 2400, and 1200. Total of all four, 12,000. —See √**vṛt**2.

6–7. See **ādi** 1. —'What is that quadruple-age, just now reckoned up completely, that, consisting of 12,000 (years), is called an age of the gods.' Cf. Whitney, l.c., 154 top.

8–9. **sahasram** etc., cf. Psalm xc.4; II. Peter iii.8. —**brāhmam ekam ahar**: here then are distinguished periods of Brahmán's repose (universal death) and of his activity ("new heavens and a new earth"); see ZDMG. xxxviii.191, § 25.

10–13 = MBh. v.6.1–2 = 109–110, with variants.

14–15. No real difference between **çīla** and **ācāra**. See also Bühler's *Manu*, p. lxvii. —**tad-vidām** = **veda-vidām**. —**ātmanas tuṣṭis** may decide in cases where no rule of morals and no usage is involved. —L. 14 agrees exactly with Gāutama's Dharmaçāstra, i.1–2, except that it is in metrical form.

16–17. **-uditam**, √**vad**. —See √**i**+**pra**.

18–19. Observe that **çruti** and **smṛti** (see these) or 'revelation' and 'tradition' have come to be important technical terms. Concerning their significance, see M. Müller, *Ancient Sanskrit Literature*, 86f. —**dharmaçāstram**, collectively: see Bühler's *Manu*, p. xxv. —U.f. **sarva‿artheṣu am-**.

20–21. **mūle**: Jolly reads **tu‿ubhe**. —U.f. **hetuçāstra‿āçrayāt**, 'from support of *or* relying on **hetuçāstras**.' Such treatises on dialectics are mentioned a number of times in the *Si-yu-ki* (Beal), e.g. ii.218f.

22–23. 'What is agreeable to one's own self'—same as **ātmanas tuṣṭis**. —See **lakṣaṇa** 1 end.

NOTES TO PAGE **59**.

1–2. 'The body-consecration, having the **niṣeka** as its first (rite), is to be performed *etc.*' **Saṁskāra** (see this) is here collective, including the various single sacraments.

—Observe that there are rites for all stages of a Brahman's existence from before his birth till after death. Megasthenes gives an interesting account of the Brahmans (preserved by Strabo, xv.59, p. 712f), and notes that even from the time of conception in the womb (ἤδη εὐθὺς καὶ κυομένους) they are under the care of wise men.

—The **saṁskāras** or 'sacraments.'

1. **garbha‿ādhāna**, 'conception.'
2. **puṁ-savana**, 'male-ceremony.'
3. **sīmanta‿unnayana**, 'hair-parting.'
4. **jāta-karman**, 'birth-ceremony.'
5. **nāma-dheya**, 'name-giving.'
6. **niṣkramaṇa**, 'going out.'
7. **anna-prāçana**, 'rice-feeding.'
8. **cūḍā-karman**, 'tonsure of scalp.'
9. **upanāyana**, 'investiture.'
10. **keçānta**, 'tonsure of beard.'
11. **samāvartana**, 'return from study.'
12. **vivāha**, 'marriage.'

Most of these are described at length, AGS. i.13f or SBE. xxix.179f or 46f or M. Williams, *Indian Wisdom*, 246, 201. Number 2 is done to bring it about that the child prove a male. No. 3 is a consecration of the pregnant woman by the parting of her hair.

3-4. gārbhāis homāis: 'the oblations relating to pregnancy' are involved in sacraments 2 and 3. —The ligation of the girdle accompanies investiture (9). — U.f. **enas apa-mṛjyate.**

5-6. See **vrata**4. —U.f. **ijyayā**, 'offering' to Gods, Rishis, and Manes, while he is a student. —**sutāis**: procreation of sons is a duty. 'A Brahman is born laden with three debts. He owes Veda-study to the Rishis; sacrifice to the Gods; and sons to the Manes.' TS. vi.3.10[5]. — The 'great sacrifices' are five, to the Gods, Beings, Manes, Bráhman, and men: enumerated ÇB. xi.5.6[1] or AGS. iii.1 (= SBE. xxix.217) or Manu iii.69f. —**yajñāis**, such as a certain Soma-ceremony called **jyotiṣṭoma**, says a Scholiast. — U.f. **brāhmī**, 'holy, fit for union with Bráhman.'

7-8. See **prāñc**3. —'Feeding of gold-rubbings, honey, and ghee.' See AGS. i.15.1.

9. kārayet: note that in Manu the prescriptive use of the optative with indefinite subject ('a man' or 'one') is very common.

10. Here the **vā**'s are = **eva** and mean 'just.' — Scholiast.

11-12. Subject, **nāma**. —See √**yuj** + **sam**. —See √**gup**. —"Nomen, omen." This is an old belief: cf. ÇB. iii.6.2[24]. The ÇGS., i.24.4-6, mentions two names, one of which is kept secret by the parents to protect the child from witchcraft. See Stenzler's note to AGS. i.15.8. Cf. Weber's 2d Nakṣatra essay, *Abh. der Berliner Akad.*, 1861, p. 316f.

13-14. The scholiast Kullūka gives as examples: **Çubha-çarman; Bala-varman; Vasu-bhūti; Dīna-dāsa.**

15-16. Sc. **nāma syāt**. —See **āçīrv-**.

17-18. U.f. **yad vā iṣṭam** (see √1 **iṣ**) etc., 'or what passes for auspicious in the family,' sc. **tat kartavyam**. The rules allow some latitude for diversities of customs in families, villages, etc. See 98[16] and note. Cf. Manu viii.46.

21-22. See **garbha** 1. —**garbhāṣṭame** = **garbhād aṣṭame**. —**upanāyanam**. this most important ceremony is described AGS. i.19-22 or SBE. xxix.187f.

NOTES TO PAGE 60.

1. prad-, see 99[1]N. —U.f. **pari_itya** (992).

2-3. bhavatpūrvam, see vocab. The formulae are: **bhavati, bhikṣām dehi; bhikṣām, bhavati, dehi; bhikṣām dehi, bhavati.** Similar distinctions, 61[7]N.

4-5. vyatyasta-pāṇinā (√2**as**), 'by (sc. the pupil) having crossed hands.'

6-7. adhy-eṣyamāṇam (√**i**, 939) etc., 'To (the pupil) about to recite, the teacher should say, "Ho, recite (617)!" and should stop (**ā-ramet**) him with the words . . .'

—India presents a thousand striking and interesting contrasts with the Occident. So especially in her way of handing down lore from age to age. This is described by the RV. Prātiçākhya, chap. xv.; and reported by Weber, ISt. x.128f; Zimmer, 210; Kaegi, *Fleckeisen's Jahrbücher*, 1880, p. 451. Or see SBE. xxix.112f,119f.

8-9. brahmaṇas (see **bráhman** 2) limits **ādāu** and **ante**. —See √1**kṛ**7. —**sravati**, subject **bráhma**. —√1**çṛ** + **vi**.

10-11. a + u + m = om. —**Prajāpati** belongs to the period succeeding the RV., and is later supplanted by Brahman. —**nir-aduhat**, 635. —See **iti** 4. —Compare 57[18].

12-13. adūduhat (856) — see √**duh**, *caus.* —'Extracted one verse of the stanza beginning with "**tad**" (74[14]) from each of the three Vedas.' U.f. **tad iti ṛcas.**

14. etām, sc. **ṛcam.**

16. hi, 'for,' has pertinence only as connecting this **çloka** with 119. —U.f. **sthavire ā-yati** (619), loc. absol.

19. Hiatus, without combination, at caesura: cf. 12[5]N.

20-21. See **param**. —'Saying "I am so-and-so by name," he should announce his name.' —The older one or the one superior in station speaks or salutes first. Thus, when the great Yayāti is falling from heaven and meets in mid-air Aṣṭaka and others, Aṣṭaka asks him, "Who art thou?" but not without excusing himself, as the inferior, for bold incivility in speaking first. — MBh. i.88.10 = 3573. So Od. 3.24:

αἰδὼς δ' αὖ νέον ἄνδρα γεραίτερον ἐξερέεσθαι.

22–23. See **abhivāda**. — **na jānate**, from ignorance of Sanskrit. Cf. Burnell, Introduction, p. xxvii. — **striyas**: thus in the prologue to act iv. of the Çakuntalā, Durvāsas, behind the stage, cries out to the women, **ayam aham, bhoḥ**, 'Ho there, it is I.'

NOTES TO PAGE 61.

1–2. 'The word **bhos** one should repeat (at the end of =) after one's name in salutation. For the use of **bhos** instead of a person's real name is declared by the Rishis (to be the same as) the use of the true form of a person's name.' See **bhobhāva** and **svarūpabhāva**. The **bhos** is of course in lieu of the name of the *person addressed*.

4. 'And the vowel **a** must be pronounced (added) at the end of his name, with the previous syllable protracted' — reading **pūrvākṣaraplutaḥ** (see Bühler). Thus **Devadatta** and **Harabhūte** are to be pronounced **Devadattā3a** and **Harabhūtā3ya** — see Whitney, 78.

7–8. This rule is observed, e.g. in the drama, by the Rishis and the king, Çakuntalā, mid. of act v. For other differences in the modes of address used for or by the different castes, see 60²N.; ÇB. i.1.4¹² (or SBE. xii.28 or Weber's *Ind. Streifen*, i.49). The rule is disregarded in the Epos, e.g. at MBh. i.71.5 = 2899.

Analogous distinctions: E. W. Hopkins, *Mutual relations of the four castes*, 6f; Weber, ISt. x.11f; Manu, viii.88 and 113.

9–10. 'A d- is not to be addressed by name even if he is younger (cf. N. to 60²⁾); but with **bhos** or (some case-form from the stem) **bhavant** a dh- should speak to him (**enam**).' Thus, **bho dīkṣita! idaṁ kuru!** or, **bhavatā yajamānena! idaṁ kriyatām!** For the long adverb, see vocab.

11–12. U.f. "**bhavati**" **iti evam**: see **iti4**.

13–14. U.f. **ṛtvijas**. 'One should say [to those in line 13] "**asāu aham**," rising up to meet (them, even if they are) the younger.'

15–16. The 'second' or 'spiritual birth' of the 'twice-born' (see **dvija**) is the **upanāyana**. The teacher is the spiritual father. See SBE. ii.3,174; xiv.9.

17–18. U.f. **adhy-āpayām āsa** (1042e, 1045) **pitṝn** (see **pitṛ 2**) **çiçus**. — See **ha**.

19–20. 'They, (having arrived-anger =) getting angry, asked the gods about the matter. And the gods, assembling (**sametya**), said (**ūcus**) to them *etc.*'

22. See **iti2f** and 1102a² near end.

23. See **ṣaṭtrinçat** and **ābdika**. The Brahmanical school-term lasted 4½ months, began with the **upākarman** and ended with the **utsarga** — see Bühler's *Manu*, p. xlvi, and note to iv.95. — See **guru4**. — 'The course (**vrata**) in the three Vedas is to be followed, (lasting 36 =) for 36 years.' Twelve years for each Veda (see **véda2**), AGS. i.22.3. This is sober earnest for a Hindu. The idea would make a Greek laugh — cf., e.g., Lucian's Ἑρμότιμος, chap. i.f, and esp. vi.

— Not even mighty Indra can absolve those who fain would know the Veda from the necessity of studying it. See the charming tale of Yavakrīta, MBh. iii.135.15–42 = 10706f, outlined at ZDMG. xxxii.318.

— Caesar's account of the Druids (B.G. vi.14) comes near the truth for the Brahmans in several respects. Magnum ibi numerum versuum ediscere dicuntur. Itaque annos nonnulli vicenos in disciplina permanent. Etc. Cf. also Roth, KZ. xxvi.53.

NOTES TO PAGE 62.

1. See **2antika**: adjectives go w. **vratam**.

2–3. **vedān** (as contrasted w. dual and sing.) = '3 Vedas.' AV. not included. — **yathākramam**, first the Mantras, then the Brāhmaṇas, in order. — Two principal elements characterize the 'course' or **vrata**, viz., study (**adhy-ayana**) and holy living (**brahma-carya**). — **adhi‿itya · · ā-vaset**: cf. Megasthenes, in Strabo, xv.59, p. 712, ἔτη δ' ἑπτὰ (!) καὶ τριάκοντα οὕτως ζήσαντα ἀναχωρεῖν εἰς τὴν ἑαυτοῦ κτῆσιν ἕκαστον etc.

4–5. 'Him (= the student), approved (on account of [280] his =) for doing his duty, · · · he (= the "father," sc. **pitā**) should present with a cow.' — **pitus**, 'from his father,' meaning his spiritual "father," i.e. (61^{15}N.) his teacher, who may also be his natural father.

6-7. See √man+anu. —snātvā, technical, see √snā. He thereby becomes a snātaka. —sam-ā-vṛttas, technical — see sacrament no. 11, p. 346. —savarṇām: οὐκ ἔστι γαμεῖν ἐξ ἄλλου γένους, Strabo, xv.49, p. 707. —lakṣaṇa-, cf. $98^{7,8}$.

8-9. 'Let him give up all affairs which hinder his study (296b), but (be) teaching anyhow (see yathā5); for that is the condition of having done his duty *or* of having attained his end.' —'Teaching anyhow,' i.e. 'maintaining himself as best he can while teaching.'

10-11. çuklāmbaras: Ἰνδοὺς ἐσθῆτι λευκῇ χρῆσθαι καὶ σινδόσι λευκαῖς καὶ καρπάσοις etc., Strabo, xv.71, p. 719. The castes wore clothes of different colors. The priests regularly wore white during religious ceremonies. —See yuj2.

12-13. There is so frequent need of water for ceremonial purification that a Brahman should never be without it (see Bāudhāyana, i.6 and 7, esp. i.7.1, or SBE. xiv.160f); hence the jar. —See vedá — not véda. —'Gold ear-rings:' χρυσοφοροῦντα μετρίως ἐν τοῖς ὠσί, Strabo, xv.59, p. 712.

14-15. U.f. na īkṣeta ud-yantam. —See √sṛj+upa and 23^{1}N. —See gata4.

16-17. See √vṛṣ. —See rūpa 1.

18-19. 'Let him make · · · (to be) standing on the right' — see 99^{1}N. Prad- is an adj.; and is neuter, since sexless things are among the substantives. —Places where four ways meet have been the object of awe and of many superstitions: cf. W. Menzel, *Die vorchristliche Unsterblichkeitslehre*, i.145, 163. —vanaspatīn: for an instance of tree-worship, see Kathā-sarit-sāgara, xx.26. Cf. also J. Fergusson, *Tree and Serpent Worship*, passim.

20. U.f. vāyu-agni-vipram. —apas: a similar respect for the waters (which are divinities — 83^{1}) was shown by the Persians (Hdt. i.138; Strabo, xv.3.16, p. 733) and the Greeks (Hesiod, *Works and Days*, 757). —paçyaṅs, 'facing.'

22-23. If the earth be regarded as a flat surface, under which the sun passes by night in the same plane of motion as by day, the sun will be to the north of the dwellers of Northern India at night, just as it is to the south of them in the day.

The point of the prohibitions is that the parts of shame be not turned to the Sun-god or (as at 62^{20}) any other sacred or venerable thing. The prohibition recurs in very many Sanskrit books (e.g. MBh. xiii.104.75=5029,f; VP. iii.11.10f; for other parallel passages, see SBE. vii.194), and may be traced, with similar ones, back to the AV. (xiii.1.56).

—Entirely identical is the Pythagorean πρὸς ἥλιον τετραμμένος μὴ οὔρει—Frag. philos. Graec., ed. Müllach, i. p. 506. This coincidence, with others, is discussed by L. von Schröder, *Pythagoras und die Inder* (Leipzig, 1884), 31-39. But Weber points out that the same thing occurs in Hesiod, *Works and Days*, 727. Cf. Pliny, *Nat. Hist.* xxviii.6 end=19.

Notes to Page 63.

1-2. ā-cakṣīta, 616. 'Nor let him tell (the fact that she is drinking — √2dhā) to any body' (297a). —U.f. divi in-.

3-4. U.f. -dhvanāu ('at the sound of') ṛg-yajuṣī (1253a) na adhi‿iyīta (616) · · adhi‿itya vā api antam etc. See vā 1 end. —Respecting this and the next çloka (SV. impure), see Muir, iii^{2}.25f, Aufrecht, *Rigveda*^{2}, i. p. xxxviii, and Hopkins's note to Burnell's *Manu*, iv.124.

7-8. See go3. 'Like the earth, iniquity done in the world does not bear fruit at once; but *etc.*' —See √vṛt+ā. —mūlāni: same figure at Proverbs xii.3. —√kṛt. —Cf. MBh. i.80.2=3333,f.

9-10. 'If (punishment falls) not on (the doer) himself, (it falls) on his sons, *etc.*' Cf. the second command of the Mosaic decalogue. —See tu3.

13. Lines 13-20: these and $29^{5,6}$ (=Manu viii.17) are translated by Muir, i^{2}.380; and (with classical parallels) in the same author's *Metrical Translations from Skt. Writers*, p. 26.

17-18. See 2sama2. —vimukhās, very naturally! but the rules also forbid looking around (103^{17}).

21–22. See idam.

23 f. See api 2 beg. — "Thus gazelles eat herbs; tigers eat gazelles; men eat fish; lions eat elephants." — Scholiast.

NOTES TO PAGE 64.

2–3. U.f. kuryāt, 59⁹N. — See saṅga2. — See tu 3.

6–7. U.f. bhakṣayitā (1050, cf. 944) · · · iha admi aham. — '*Me eat* in t'other world will he, whose *meat* in this world eat do I. That the wise declare to be the meatness of meat = That is why meat is called meat.' An example of Hindu etymologies, which are often little better than mere puns — as here, mām sa and māṅsam. Hopkins notes that this is given in varied form, MBh. xiii. 116.35 = 5714. Cf. Whitney, AJP. iii.402; also 94[15].

8–9. See upoṣita. — See √çru, desid. — See yena2. — Cf. Strabo, xv.59, p. 712: ταῖς δὲ γυναιξὶ ταῖς γαμεταῖς μὴ συμφιλοσοφεῖν τοὺς Βραχμᾶνας etc. Notable exceptions to this statement are found in the ancient legends of Māitreyī and Gārgī — SBE. xv. 108,130,136.

10–11. 'Any thing disliked of her husband (296b), displeasing to him.' — It is noteworthy that widow-burning (see p. 382) is quite ignored here. It is not mentioned anywhere in Manu; and the same is true of Yājñavalkya, Nārada, Gāutama, Āpastamba, and most of the others. — Jolly, *Sitzungsberichte der Bairischen Akad.*, 1876, p. 447. He thinks it originated among the lower classes.

12–13. See kāmam, adv. — √2kṣi, caus. — See √grah5. — parasya limits nāma.

14–15. U.f. āsīta (616) ā maraṇāt. — √kṣam.

16–17. evam, 'so,' as described in book iii.

18–19. Prescriptions quite the reverse of those at 62[10].

20–21. U.f. pañcatapās (see vocab.) · · varṣāsu abhrā-. Compare, e.g., the penances of Yayāti after he retires to the forest, MBh. i.86.11 = 3544,f; and those exhibited to Alexander, Strabo, xv.61, p. 714; and see xv.63, p. 715.

22. vihṛtya, √hṛ + vi 2.

NOTES TO PAGE 65.

2. pra-vrajan, technical (see vocab.), describing the pravrājaka.

3. THE ORDERS. See āçrama. Perhaps the best English names are: 1. 'Student,' for brahmacārin; 2. 'Householder,' for gṛhastha; 3. 'Forest-hermit,' for vānaprastha; and 4. 'Ascetic' or 'Pious mendicant,' for yati.

The last is often called 'Beggar' (bhikṣu) or 'Wanderer' (pra- or pari-vrājaka).

5–6. Lit. 'One should diminish one mouthful at a time in the dark fortnight *etc.*,' i.e. 'diminish one's food by one mouthful *etc.*' — See triṣavaṇa. — This, the diminuendo-crescendo form of the lunar fast, is called pipīlikā-madhya or 'ant-middled.'

7–8. 'One should follow the same rule entire, in (case of) the yava-madhyama (see this), intent, performing (caranç) the lunar penance with the bright fortnight first.'

— These are fully described, e.g. by Gāutama, xxvii. (transl. SBE. ii.296f), and by Bāudhāyana, iii.8 (SBE. xiv.303f).

9 f. Cf. below, p. 357, § 90. — For a summary of this schematic exposition of the doctrine of metempsychosis, see *Indian Wisdom*, 280.

9–10. 'Resulting in weal or woe (is our) karman, which originates in mind, voice, and body.' Thus qualified, karman comprehends 'virtuous and sinful thoughts, words and deeds.' — See gati4.

11–12. tasya, sc. karmaṇas. — See api2 beg. — See dehin. — 'One should know that the mind is the prompter in this world (iha) of this (action) which is three-fold [viz. best, worst, and middling, cf. 65[10]] and has three manifestations [viz. as thoughts, words, and deeds, 65[9]], is connected with the body, (and) has ten kinds [3+4+3 kinds, enumerated in çlokas 5, 6, 7].'

17. avidhānatas: hereby are excluded from this category injuries to sacrificial victims when required by the ritual, or to a man when inflicted as a lawful penalty.

19. U.f. manasā eva ayam (lit. 'this one' = 'a man') upa-bhuñkte. See √2bhuj + upa2.

Notes to Page 66.

1. 'And (ca) he [if he does right for the most part and wrong a little] enjoys bliss in heaven, invested (√1vṛ+ā) with those very elements (see bhūta5), *i.e.* with a corporeal body.' —'Those very' before-mentioned at Manu xii.16.

3. 'Deserted by the elements' = 'after death.' — Scholiast.

4–5. See jīva. —See the mention of the five elements, Strabo, xv.59 end, p. 713. —The spirit, after purgation, takes on a human form again. The purgatorial idea is prominent in book xviii. of the MBh.

6–7. 'Considering (dṛṣṭvā) these gatis (which result) from right-doing and from wrong-doing' (1098). —See √1dhā3.

8–9. See sattva2, rajas4, tamas3, and esp. guṇa3, and also ātman5, and mahant2, all technical terms here. —'One should know goodness, passion, and darkness as the ātman's three qualities, with which the mahant constantly pervades all these existent things without exception.' See p. 344, § 67. Line 9 is explained under sthita4.

10–11. ca · · ca: the sense requires 'or · · or.' —'As having the quality of darkness as its attribute:' tāmasam modifies only the prior member, guṇa-; the verbally strict phrase would be tamo-guṇa-lakṣaṇam (cf. line 15).

14–15. 'What (deed) one wishes (to be) known by everybody *etc.*' —jñātam: conjecture of BR. at vi.489. —lajjati, metri gratia, for -te.

18–19. See ya6 and sarva2c. —'But the transmigrations which (a man) enters upon by reason of any (quality of them =) of these qualities, these (of all, *i.e.*) through all this world in order I will briefly state.'

20–23. A summary of the scheme following.

Notes to Page 67.

1–18, çlokas 42–50. Scheme of the nine sets of gatis. On him who is governed by it, each guṇa entails a gati: to wit,

I. tamas, the gati of a beast (42–44);
II. rajas, the gati of a man (45–47);
III. sattva, the gati of a god (48–50).

Each gati is of three kinds:

a. lowest; b. middling; c. highest.

The scheme is not strictly adhered to. In line 1, for instance, 'plants' are put among the beasts; and in 15, the 'Vedas,' among the gods. But we are not surprised to find 'Çūdras' (line 3) among the beasts, and 'Brahmans' (line 13) among the gods (see 94[18]).

6. U.f. tāmasīṣu (sc. gatiṣu) uttamā.

7–8. See jhalla. —√sañj+pra.

11–12. ye merely fills out the verse — see ya3 beg. —'Likewise all Apsarases.' On the Apsarases, see Holtzmann, ZDMG. xxxiii.631f.

17. Technically used words — see vocab.

19–20. 'A Brahman-slayer enters the womb of dogs (çvan), swine, asses, camels, cows, goats (aja), sheep (avi), *etc.*,' in order to be born therefrom as dog, etc.

22–23. U.f. pretās antyastrī-: pronounce, pretāntyastrī-, in violation of 177. —'By stealing grain, one becomes a mouse; · · (by stealing) water, (one becomes) a duck; *etc.*' The same construction runs on to 68[3]. Note that some of the gatis have a special appropriateness.

Notes to Page 68.

4–5. 'Women also in like manner (see kalpa) by stealing would incur guilt. They become mates of these very creatures (mentioned above).'

8–9. See pravṛtta and nivṛtta. —eti, 'one attains to.' —aty-eti etc., 'gets rid of the five elements,' i.e. 'obtains final liberation.'

10–11. 'And whatsoever heterodox philosophies (there are).' See 1ka2b: the first ca = 'and.'

12–13. 'Whatsoever doctrines (yāni kāni cid, sc. çāstrāṇi), differing (anyāni) from this (atas = vedāt), spring up and come to nought, — these (tāni) *etc.*'

14–15. See çreṣṭha and 2vara: and for abl., 292b. —vyava-, 'the resolute' who *practice* what they learn.

---

16. Selections XXIX. and XXX. Two specimens of vakrokti, 'play on words' or

'Calembourg.' Both come from the Subhāṣitārṇava, and are taken by me from Böhtlingk's *Indische Sprüche*, 2d ed., no's 1428 and 6846. Other specimens are no's 4042 and 6389.

16-17. 'Nineteen wives went to the wood to play. Twenty came home. The rest were eaten by a tiger.' —Solution: **ekonā viṅçatir nāryaḥ** = 'wives twenty lacking one' (477a); or, dividing **eko nā** (stem **nṛ**), 'one man (and) twenty wives.'

18-19. U.f. **mama ājñayā.** —Solution: **na tena**, 'not by him,' when joined, gives **natena** (√**nam**), 'by him bending over.'

SELECTIONS XXXI.–LXXV.

Extracts from the Vedic Literature.

§ 70. Selections xxxi. to lxxv. comprise Mantra (or "Veda" in its narrower sense), Brāhmaṇa, and Sūtra. They are taken for the most part from the Rigvedic literature (or "Rigveda" in its broader sense). Professor Kaegi's little work, entitled *Der Rigveda* (2d ed.), and described above, *Brief List*, p. xx, no. 23, is recommended as a most useful introduction to Vedic study, on account of its general excellence, and, in particular, on account of the fulness of its bibliographical details. It is, moreover, now easily accessible in an English version by Dr. Robert Arrowsmith, published by Ginn and Co., Boston, 1886, price $1.65. Kaegi's book will be frequently cited in the sequel, as "Kaegi," with the page-number of the translation first, followed by that of the original in parenthesis. The Note-numbers are alike in both.

§ 71. For grammatical forms peculiar to the Veda, reference to Whitney will be made when needful; but the student should read systematically the sections that describe Vedic noun-inflection and verb-conjugation. For the former subject, the small-print lines of 330, 340, and 342 are important; and for the latter, the paragraphs on the subjunctive, 557-563, 736, 700, and those on the mode-forms of the different aorists, chap. xi. The accent, explained by Whitney, 80-86, is important for the exegesis and otherwise. The accent-rules are given at 92-97, 314-320, 591-598, 1082-86. The notation of the accent is explained at 87-90.

§ 72. The Vedic literature is based on the songs of the early Aryan tribes immigrant into India. These tribes were life-loving, brave, and warlike, and show their nature clearly in their songs. But they were remarkable above all for the strength of their religious instinct. This is a cardinal fact — the prime determinant of the character of the early Indian literature; for that literature is one of prevailingly religious content. The Veda is thus distinguished from the later literature of the Epic and the Classical periods by its contents, and also — no less — by its language and style. But within itself, the Vedic literature (or "Veda" in the broader sense of the word) shows differences which serve to divide it into three great groups.

§ 73. To assign a definite chronological period for each of these groups is neither feasible nor necessary.[1] But it is interesting and quite possible to establish an inner chronologic sequence among the groups themselves and the sub-groups, and even among individual books and parts of books. To the first group belong the ancient songs themselves, which are in metrical form and are known as the Vedic hymns or Mantras. The term "Veda" is often used in a narrower sense to denote them. To the second belong the Brāhmaṇas, the oldest Indo-European prose extant, which presuppose and are dependent on the Mantra-literature. The third group comprehends the Sūtras, collections of brief rules upon liturgical and other subjects, which, in turn, presuppose both of the foregoing groups.

[1] Indeed, to do so would give a very false impression. The periods overlap; and the styles of literature shade off from one into another — so, for example, in the Yajurveda.

§ 74. A great mass of Mantra-material originated and was handed down by memorial tradition orally from generation to generation long before the existence of any such collections of Mantras as have come down to us.[1] The Mantras fall into several different classes. To one belongs the hymn-stanza (ṛc); to another, the sacrificial formula (yájus); and to another, the magic charm (bráhman). From the stock of Mantras of one class — for example, the yájus — a certain collection with definite arrangement became established by popular usage in a certain community, and thus arose a Veda, for example, a Yajurveda — not a certain definite book, but some one of many possible and probable collections of Mantras of a certain definite class. From the same stock of the same class another collection was formed in another community, and thus arose another Veda, for example, another Yajurveda. The period in which the oldest hymns of the Rigveda originated may be set back into the second pre-Christian millennium;[2] but this only on certain general considerations — not as a matter of precise argumentation. Geographically, the early Vedic Aryans may be referred to Kābul and the Panjāb.[3]

§ 75. The Mantras have come down to us, for the most part, in several collections, diverse in form and purpose. There was, besides, more or less Mantra-material which was never embodied in any collection,[4] but of which we find remnants scattered about in various books. The great collections of Mantras are the Rigveda, the Sāmaveda, the Yajurveda, and the Atharvaveda. The text of the Mantras forms what is often called a Saṁhitā. To each Saṁhitā is attached a body of dependent or ancillary works of the Brāhmaṇa and Sūtra groups: so that the oldest Indian books are classed, first, according to the Veda to which they belong; and, secondly, according to their character as Mantra, Brāhmaṇa, or Sūtra. It is to be remembered that "Veda" has a narrower and a broader sense, and that "Rigveda," for instance, may mean either the Rigveda-saṁhitā or also the entire body of works belonging to that Veda.

§ 76. The Saṁhitā of the Rigveda is a historical[5] collection. It consists of 1017 hymns, each containing on an average about ten double lines,[6] so that the text is in volume somewhat less than that of the two Homeric poems together. There is a purely external and mechanical division of the text into 'Eighths,' 'Lessons,'[7] 'Groups,' and 'Stanzas' (aṣṭaka, adhyāya, varga, ṛc); but this need not specially concern us now. Of deep historical significance is the other division into 'Books,' 'Chapters,' 'Hymns,' and 'Stanzas' (maṇḍala, anuvāka, sūkta, ṛc).

§ 77. There are ten 'Books' (literally, 'Circles'). And of these, books ii. to viii. are the so-called "Family-books" — that is, they contain each the hymns ascribed to a single family or clan, in which they doubtless originated, and by which they were handed down as a sacred inheritance. Thus, book ii. contains the hymns of Gṛtsamada and his clan. Those of Viçvāmitra and his tribe follow in book iii.; and then in order those of Vāmadeva (book iv.), Atri (book v.), Bharadvāja (book vi.), Vasiṣṭha (book vii.), and Kaṇva (book viii.). The ninth book is made up of

[1] See Roth's *Atharvaveda in Kaschmir*, p. 9–10.

[2] See Whitney in *The Century Magazine*, 1887, xxxiii. 921; or Kaegi, note 38. Cf. Ludwig, iii. 178f.

[3] See Whitney, l.c., p. 913; Kaegi, note 39; Ludwig, iii. 198f.

[4] The Hindus say that the Vedas are infinite. See Ludwig, iii. 15; Muir, iii². 17.

[5] As distinguished from a liturgical collection — see § 86. Respecting the purpose of the RV. collection, see Roth, KZ. xxvi. 56.

[6] For the number of stanzas, words, and syllables, and for some convenient tabular statements, see Müller, ASL. p. 220f.

[7] There are eight 'Lessons' in each 'Eighth.'

hymns addressed to the deified drink Soma. The tenth comprises hymns ascribed to very different authors;[1] while the first consists of fifteen[2] minor groups, each attributed to some ancient poet-sage.

§ 78. The general history of the text of the Rigveda was touched upon by Professor Roth in a very instructive little essay[3] entitled *Vedische Studien.* Some of his conclusions may be briefly stated. The assembling of the Mantras into a collection was accomplished by the aid of writing.[4] The first Rik collections were probably single books and parts of books, each an aggregation of material of such moderate compass as to be easily handled by a single collector. The small collections were later united into one large collection, which, completed by the addition of books ix. and x., and uniformly edited, constitutes our RV. Saṁhitā.

§ 79. Roth recognizes three stages in the tradition: 1. the oral transmission from the authors to the time of the collectors; 2. the reduction from the oral form to the written form; and 3. the transmission of the written text to us. We may admit that in the last stage the text — carefully preserved as it was, see § 98 — has suffered no very important corruptions. The collectors themselves, however, did not by any means write down the texts precisely as they heard them. The reciters from memory must have recited rhythmically. The collectors (writers — redactors or diaskeuasts) have often destroyed the rhythm by putting the texts into the strait-jacket of the rules of grammar, and especially by writing the words according to the later rules of saṁdhi. To the first stage are to be referred the many mistakes which are ascribable to carelessness in listening,[5] and which may be called blunders of the ear rather than of the eye.

§ 80. That the hymns themselves are of diverse origin, both in respect of place and of time, is probable *a priori* and is shown by internal evidence.[6] Accordingly, if we find, for example, two hymns involving inconsistent conceptions of the same deity or of different deities, this is to be deemed quite natural, inasmuch as they originated among clans dwelling in diverse regions. Moreover, after the aggregation of the small collections into the large one, interpolations and later additions were still made. To discriminate between the different elements that now make up the canonical Vedic text is therefore an important problem.

§ 81. Again, in the course of time, and in part as a result of the wrangling pedantry of narrow teachers, the stock collections became ramified into slightly divergent recensions. These were called çākhās or 'branches,' because so related to each other as are different branches from the same tree-stock. The Çākhās often supply to criticism the various readings for which the classical philologist looks to good and independent manuscripts. The community in which such a Çākhā attained definitive authority was called a caraṇa or 'school.' There once existed, presumably, many branches and schools[7] of the RV. The school of the Çākalas,[8] however, seems

[1] The orthodox Hindu conception of the hymns is that they had existed from eternity; it recognizes no human authors. The Hindus do not call Atri, for example, the "author" of a given hymn, but rather the "Rishi," i.e. the "seer," who was so fortunate as to "see" it the last time it was revealed. — Müller, ASL. p. 95.

[2] Bergaigne, JA. viii.8.263 (= 71).

[3] Published, 1883, in KZ. xxvi. 45–68. See especially p. 52–62.

[4] This is entirely consistent with the facts that the tradition in the schools was oral and by memory, and that the open use of a written text was disgraceful. Compare, e.g., *Sarva-sammata Çikshā*, ed. A. O. Franke, rule 36. But this thesis of Roth is denied by some scholars.

[5] Such as *nā́masā* for *mā́nasā*, etc., Roth, l.c., p. 62.

[6] Cf. Ludwig, iii. p. IX.

[7] See Müller, ASL. p. 368.

[8] See Müller, RV. Prātiçākhya, *Einleitung*, p. 7.

to have gained exclusive predominance, and the extant recension of the RV. Saṁhitā bears their name. The Çākhā of the Bāṣkalas is also mentioned.

§ 82. The manuscripts of the RV. Saṁhitā exhibit almost no diversities of reading; so that, in the absence of çākhā-differences, the criticism of the text has to rest on intrinsic evidence, and on a comparison of the other Saṁhitās, and on a study of the RV. citations in the RV. Brāhmaṇas and Sūtras. Other criteria have been brought to light by the study of the arrangement of the collection. Thus, within each of the books ii.–vii., the hymns addressed to the same deity are grouped together and arranged according to the decreasing number of stanzas of each hymn. The same simple principle goes farther, governing, for example, the order of the groups within a book.[1] Violations of the principle may arouse suspicion as to the originality or genuineness of the passages concerned.

§ 83. The first written form of the text would seem to have been the **saṁhitā-pāṭha** or 'combined reading,' wherein the words are combined according to the more or less artificial rules of grammar.[2] These combinations often admit of several different resolutions. To obviate the resulting uncertainties, there was constructed the **pada-pāṭha** or 'word-reading,' which aims to give each word in its true independent form without reference to any rules of combination. The Pada-text of the published RV. is attributed to Çākalya,[3] and is the oldest conscious exegetical work upon the Veda now known. It is far from infallible.[4] For its secondary use, see § 98N.

§ 84. The Sāmaveda is a Veda of **sā́mans**. A sāman is properly a 'tune'—not a text; but in this connection the word means an ṛc so modified[5] as to be better adapted for chanting, especially during the ceremonies of the Soma-sacrifice. Of the 1549 stanzas of the Sāmaveda, 1474 occur also in the Rigveda.[6] The SV. exhibits many variations from the readings of the RV. Saṁhitā, some of which are of value for the criticism of the latter text.[7] In general, the relations of the SV. to the RV. still present many difficult problems.[8]

§ 85. The Saṁhitā of the Atharvaveda, as compared with that of the RV., represents a lower plane of life and thought, as it is also later in respect of form and language. It contains magic incantations for the warding off of the most diverse malign influences, and prayers and charms for success in the various affairs of life, as love, gaming, quarrels, journeys, and the like. It has a high degree of interest for the student of popular superstitions. The Saṁhitā has come down to us in at least two recensions. The one is called the Pāippalāda Çākhā.[9] The other was published in 1856 by Roth and Whitney.[10] About a sixteenth part of the RV. stanzas occur also — with more or less interesting variants — in books i. to xix. of this text. Shankar P. Pandit of Bombay is now editing the AV. with Sāyaṇa's comment.

§ 86. The Yajurveda belongs to the period[11] of the highly developed ritual, and originated in the sacred and famous Madhyadeça.[12] The Saṁhitās contain the

[1] For details see A. Bergaigne, *Recherches sur l'histoire de la saṁhitā du RV.*, JA. 8.viii.193f (esp. p. 199), and 8.ix.191f. Cf. also Oldenberg, ZDMG. xli.508f; and Bergaigne, JA. 8.x.488f.

[2] This is the text given in the Reader.

[3] See Weber, HIL. p. 32f.

[4] A critical estimate of its exegetical value is given by Roth in the afore-mentioned essay, KZ. xxvi.45–52.

[5] By protraction of vowels, insertion of sundry sounds, repetitions, etc. — Whitney, OLSt. i.13–15.

[6] See Whitney, ISt. ii.347–63.

[7] Whitney, JAOS. xi. p. clxxxiv=PAOS. Oct. 1883.

[8] See Oldenberg's interesting discussion, ZDMG. xxxviii.439–80, and esp. 464–65.

[9] Described by Roth, *Der Atharvaveda in Kaschmir*, Tübingen, 1875.

[10] See *Brief List*, p. xix, no. 18. For bibliography of translations, see Kaegi, note 13.

[11] The civilization of this period is treated with especial fulness in Schröder's *Indiens Literatur und Cultur* — see below, § 100.

[12] Cf. p. 297, § 2: also Schröder, ILuC. p. 163.

formulas (see yajus in vocab.) which accompanied the sacrificial ceremonials, and are, as it were, the hand-books of the **adhvaryus** or priests who did the actual manual labor of the sacrifices.[1] With the growth of ritualism and its spread over a wide extent of territory[2] there naturally grew up many differing usages in connection with the sacrifice, and many centres of ritualistic study.[3] In this wise it happened that the sectarian schools of the Yajurveda were especially numerous and flourishing.

§ 87. The Black Yajurveda. The various schools of this, the older Yajurveda, bear the names of men reputed to be the pupils — directly or indirectly — of Vāiçampāyana, a name great in the Epos. At least five schools[4] possessed special Saṁhitās, of which four are still extant: to wit, the Saṁhitā of the Kaṭhas (Καθαῖοι) or the Kāṭhaka; that of the Kapiṣṭhala-Kaṭhas (Καμβίσθολοι); that of the Māitrāyaṇīyas; and that of the school of Āpastamba, a subdivision of the Tāittirīyas. The one last mentioned, the Tāittirīya Saṁhitā, was the first to be printed in a scholarly edition.[5] The Māitrāyaṇī Saṁhitā has recently been published by Dr. L. von Schröder, Leipzig, 1881–86. The others are still unedited. In all these texts of the old Yajus Saṁhitās, the sacred formulas are commingled with prose passages, explanatory and prescriptive. A single such passage is a **Bráhmaṇa**,[6] 'the dictum of a **brahmán** *or* priest,' 'a priestly discourse.'

§ 88. The White Yajurveda. To remedy this confusion, a new school of Adhvaryus, called the Vājasaneyins, arranged a Saṁhitā of 'clear formulas' (çuklāni yajūṅṣi), i.e. a text in which the formulas or Mantras were separated from the priestly discourses or Brāhmaṇas.[7] Not without some little animus, doubtless, they turned to account the double meaning of **çukla**, 'clear' or 'white,' and fixed the name of "Dark" (**kṛṣṇa**, 'dark' or 'black') upon the mingled or uncleared texts of their older rivals. The Saṁhitā of the White Yajurveda or Vājasaneyi Saṁhitā has come down to us in the recension of the Kāṇvas and in that of the Mādhyaṁdinas,[8] and was published by Weber, Berlin, 1849–52.

§ 89. The separate collections of the formulas naturally suggested a similar treatment of the priestly discourses. In the school of the Vājasaneyins, the result of this treatment was a collection of the formerly detached **Bráhmaṇas**, which collection is itself also called a **Bráhmaṇa**,[9] and is practically an encyclopedic digest of the wisdom of their school.[10]

§ 90. The oldest collection of Mantras, the Rigveda, is in the main the reflex of the life of a vigorous, active, and healthy people — a people that prayed most for length of days, for sturdy sons, abundant cattle, doughty retainers, and victory over their enemies; a people whose religion was a simple worship of the deified powers of nature. But even during the Vedic period, there comes a profound change. The Yajurveda represents a turning-point in the development of the Hindu character. The centre of Vedic life is shifted to Madhyadeça; and here were made the first

[1] Ludwig, iii.27.

[2] Schröder, ILuC. p. 164–65.

[3] Cf. Schröder, ILuC. p. 88–89: also Eggeling, SBE. xii. p. xxv f.

[4] Schröder, *Einleitung* to his ed. of MS., book i. p. IX f. Cf. ILuC. p. 89.

[5] By Weber, as vol's xi. and xii. of ISt., 1871–72.

[6] See this in vocab. and cf. it with *brāhmaṇá*.

[7] See Eggeling, SBE. xii., p. xxvii; also ÇB. xiv. 9.4[33] or SBE. xv.226.

[8] Or Μαδιανδινοί: see HIL. p. 106.

[9] Specifically, the Çatapatha Brāhmaṇa. It was published by Weber, Berlin, 1855. Books i.–iv. have been translated by Eggeling, SBE. xii. and xxvi.

[10] Eggeling, SBE. xii. p. xxii f.

great advances in the arts and institutions of civilization, in trade, and in science. Here also priestly families and warrior-families attained to such importance as to assert their independence of the people, and so bring about the strongly marked class-distinctions that grew into the rigid system of caste. And here, with the waxing power of the priesthood, the old Vedic religion was converted into an infinitely complex system of sacrifices and ceremonies. To this period belongs the belief in metempsychosis — a dreadful and universal reality to the Hindu mind. With the growing tendency of the Hindu character towards introspection comes the system of hermit-life and the asceticism which are so prominent in the Hindu Middle Age, and which in turn led naturally to the habit of theosophic speculation. The sultry air of Ganges-land has relaxed both the physical and the mental fibre of the Hindu, and he has become a Quietist.

§ 91. The Hindu character has been transformed almost beyond recognition. The change is wonderful. It would be also incomprehensible, but for the literature of the Brāhmaṇas.[1] As a whole and by themselves, they are puerile, arid, inane. But as the sole and faithful reflex of an immensely important phase in the development of an ethnic type, they have a great interest — an interest heightened by the fact that the annals of human evolution hardly present another type whose history can be studied through so many centuries in unbroken continuity.

§ 92. The sacerdotal class, ever magnifying its office, has invested the sacrifice with a most exaggerated importance and sanctity. The sacrifice has become the central point of the Brahman's life and thought. About it he has spun a flimsy web of mystery, and in each of its events he sees a hidden symbolism.[2] Everything is not only that which it *is* but also that which it *signifies*. So lost is the Brahman in these esoteric vagaries that to him the line of demarcation between "is" and "signifies" becomes almost wholly obliterated.[3] What we deem the realities of life are as pale shadows. The sacrifice and its events are the real facts, and to fathom their mysteries[4] is omnipotence and salvation.

§ 93. It must not be forgotten that the phases of development represented by the Mantras and Brāhmaṇas are not separated by hard and fast lines. The oldest Yajus texts are of the transition type. They are called Saṁhitās, and contain indeed Mantras in abundance; but the Mantras are mingled with prose passages which are the first Brāhmaṇas. Descriptions of the sacrificial ceremonies, attributions to them of hidden meanings, accounts of their origin, legends to illustrate their efficacy — such are the contents of the older Brāhmaṇas. Conscious philosophic speculation plays a subordinate part: its beginnings we can trace to the RV. Saṁhitā;[5] but the great mass of it is contained in the later Brāhmaṇa literature.

§ 94. In this, the later Brāhmaṇa period, the descriptions of the ritual are relegated to systematic treatises (§ 95); and the theosophic and philosophic passages become more lengthy and important, and receive — as containing material appropriate for the meditations of the ὑλόβιοι or Forest-hermits — the special names of Āraṇyakas[6] or 'Forest-treatises' and Upaniṣads.[7] Some of the best of these have

[1] Characterized by Eggeling, SBE. xii. p. ix f, esp. p. xxii-xxv. Enumerated by Kaegi, note 14 a.

[2] See Oldenberg, *Buddha*, 19(20)f.

[3] A point of prime importance in reading the endless identifications of the Brāhmaṇas.

[4] Hence the constant refrain, *ya evaṁ veda* — cf. 97[1]N.

[5] See selection lxii. and N.

[6] See Deussen, *System des Vedānta*, p. 8; Müller, ASL. 313f; or Kaegi, note 16.

[7] Upaniṣad: lit. 'a sitting at the feet of another,' and then 'the hidden doctrine taught at such a session.'

been handed down by tradition as separate works with separate names; and other tracts of the same general style and contents have been written; but it must be remembered that the original Āraṇyakas and Upaniṣads were integral parts of the digested Brāhmaṇas.[1]

Brahmanical speculation culminates in pessimistic Pantheism, in the doctrine of the misery of all earthly existence, from which we can hope for redemption only through reabsorption into the universal All-in-One. This is the result of Brahmanical thought, on which as a foundation was built up the doctrine and order of Buddha; this the link that unites the Brahmanic and the Buddhistic chains of development.[2]

§ 95. The Brāhmaṇas presuppose a thorough acquaintance with the course and details of the sacrifice, and do not undertake a systematic exposition thereof. But when the ceremonies had grown to tremendous length and complexity, it became necessary to have manuals giving full and orderly directions for the use of the celebrant. Such works are the 'Rules for the sacrifices' or Çrāuta-sūtras, so called because they stand in most intimate relation to the Veda or 'sacred texts' (çruti), and continually cite these texts, and prescribe the manner and the occasions of their employment with the various ceremonies.

§ 96. Usage and observance, crystallized into sacred ceremony, invest the whole life of an Aryan Hindu — nay, even his pre-natal and post-mortem existence. These usages differed considerably in different localities, and in the lesser details among the different families of the same locality. In part, perhaps, to counteract the tendency to diversity, books were made describing the observances recognized as normal in a certain school or community. They are called Gṛhya-sūtras, or 'Rules of domestic usages.' Here, too, as well as in the sacrifice, everything proceeds with the recitation of Mantras; so that these books also attach themselves to certain Vedas or Vedic schools. The legitimate subjects of these Rules are the 'Sacraments' (saṁskāras), and the 'Simple-sacrifices' (pāka-yajñas) of the householder.

§ 97. There is also a third class of Sūtras, called Dharma-sūtras, which prescribe rules for the every-day life of those who would conform to the example of the virtuous. Since they have to do with 'agreement-conduct,' i.e. the 'conduct' (ācāra) which has for its norm the 'agreement' (sam-aya, lit. 'con-vention') of those who know the law, they are also called Sāmayācārika-sūtras. The matters belonging more properly to the Gṛhya-sūtras are sometimes treated also in the Dharma-sūtras. But the legitimate subjects of the latter are far more varied than those of the former. They embrace all sorts of injunctions and restrictions relating to etiquette, to eating and sleeping, to purification and penance, and to the details of the daily life of the student and householder and hermit, and even extend to the duties of the king and to the beginnings of civil and criminal law. In the order of development they are plainly posterior to the Gṛhya-sūtras.

§ 98. As the sacred texts of the Mantras grew in sanctity, their dialect and style of thought became obsolescent. For the transmission of the sacred lore, a learned apparatus became necessary. To preserve the written text of a given 'branch' (çākhā) of the Veda from any change in "one jot or one tittle," by establishing the relations of the saṁhitā and pada pāṭhas (§ 83) of that branch, there were composed the phonetic treatises, which, because attaching each 'to a

[1] See Whitney, AJP. vii.1–2.

[2] The genetic relationship of Buddhism to Brahmanism is admirably sketched by Oldenberg, *Buddha*, Introd., chap's ii.–iii.

(certain) branch' (prati-çākham), are called Prātiçākhyas.[1] These give with the utmost minuteness of detail the rules for the retroversion of the pada to the saṁhitā readings, and thus enable us to establish with great accuracy the text as it was in their day.[2]

§ 99. To preserve the knowledge of the sense of obsolescent words, there were made collections of synonyms and of hard words (γλῶσσαι), called the Nighaṇṭavas, the oldest Vedic Glossary. Upon the Glossary there was written, by the ancient sage Yāska, a comment called Nirukta, which is the oldest extant work of formal Vedic exegesis, but which itself acknowledges a number of predecessors. Among its successors, the most famous is the great commentary of Sāyaṇa[3] Ācārya, ca. 1350 A.D. The Anukramaṇīs are little works which give the divinity, the "seer," and the metre of each hymn of a Saṁhitā.

[1] See Whitney, JAOS. vii.339-40; iv.259-60.

[2] The word-texts were thus converted "from instruments more especially of exegesis, into a complete and efficient apparatus for securing the preservation of textual purity." — L.c. iv.260.

[3] Weber, HIL. p. 41-42.

§ 100. It remains to give a brief bibliography of the literature of the Rigveda Saṁhitā with mention of the principal ancillary works appertaining to it. For the bibliography of the other Saṁhitās, reference may be made to Kaegi, notes 8-26, or to Weber's *History of Indian Literature*.

1. Rigveda. Saṁhitā. a. Text-editions. The first complete edition was issued by Aufrecht, 1861-63, as vol's vi. and vii. of the ISt. Müller's great six-volumed quarto, with the full Saṁhitā and Pada texts, Sāyaṇa's commentary, an index, etc., was begun in 1849 and completed in 1874. Then came the editions mentioned at the beginning of this Reader, in the *Brief List*, no's 11 and 12.

b. Exegesis. The greatest achievements in Vedic exegesis must be ascribed to Roth. They are contained principally in the St. Petersburg Lexicon, *Brief List*, no. 5. Grassmann's Dictionary and his Translation are described in the *List*, no's 13 and 14. Professor Alfred Ludwig of Prague has published a large work in five volumes (Prag, Tempsky, 1876-83), entitled *Der Rigveda*. Vol's i. and ii. contain a translation of the hymns arranged according to deities and subjects. Vol. iii. contains an introduction to the translation, entitled *Die Mantra-litteratur und das alte Indien*. Vol's iv. and v. contain a commentary on the translation.

c. General Works. Abel Bergaigne's work entitled *La religion védique* (Paris, Vieweg, 1878-83. 3 vol's) is a systematic and encyclopedic exposition of the religious and mythological conceptions of the RV. The work of Geldner and Kaegi (*List*, no. 15), and those of Weber, Zimmer, and the rest (no's 21-26), all bear more or less directly on the study of the Veda. Whitney's *Oriental and Linguistic Studies* (New York, Scribner, Armstrong, & Co. 1st series, 1873) contain among other things valuable essays on the history, interpretation, and contents of the RV. Very recently has appeared a book by L. von Schröder, *Indiens Literatur und Cultur in historischer Entwicklung* (Leipzig, 1887), the first third of which is devoted to the Veda, and especially to the period of the Yajurveda.

2. Rigveda. Brāhmaṇas etc. The Āitareya Brāhmaṇa was edited by Aufrecht — see *List*, no. 16. Haug had already published the text with a translation (Bombay, 1863), criticised and corrected by Weber, ISt. ix.177-380.

The Āitareya Āraṇyaka is associated with the Brāhmaṇa of the same name. It has five books and was edited with Sāyaṇa's comment by R. Mitra in the *Bibliotheca Indica*, 1876. See SBE. i. p. xci f.

Āitareya Upaniṣad is the name borne by certain parts of the Āraṇyaka, viz. book ii., chap's 4, 5, 6 — see SBE. i. p. xcvi. The text was edited and translated by Röer, BI., 1849-53. Müller gives another translation, SBE. i.200f.

The Çāṅkhāyana or Kāuṣītaki Brāhmaṇa was edited by Bruno Lindner (Jena, Costenoble, 1887). A translation is soon to follow.

The Kāuṣītaki Brāhmaṇa Upaniṣad was edited (with Çaṁkara's comment) and translated by Cowell, BI., 1861. Another translation, by Müller, SBE. i.271f; introduction, ibidem, p. xcviii.

3. Rigveda. Sūtras etc. Āçvalāyana's Çrāuta-sūtra was edited by R. Vidyāratna, BI., 1874.

Āçvalāyana's Gṛhya-sūtra was edited (with translation) by Stenzler — see *List*, no. 17. English version by Oldenberg, SBE. xxix.

Çāṅkhāyana's Çrāuta-sūtra was edited by Alfred Hillebrandt, BI., 1886.

Çāṅkhāyana's Gṛhya-sutra was edited in 1878 by Oldenberg, ISt. xv.1-166, with translation. English version by Oldenberg, SBE. xxix.

No Dharma-sūtra is certainly known to be attached especially to the RV. Saṁhitā.

The RV. Prātiçākhya was edited by Regnier (JA., 1856-58), and by Müller (Leipzig, 1856-69). Each editor gives a translation.

The Nirukta, with the Nighaṇṭavas, was edited and elucidated by Roth (Göttingen, 1848-52).

The Anukramaṇī of Kātyāyana was edited with valuable accessories by Arthur A. Macdonell in the *Anecdota Oxoniensia*, Oxford, 1886.

NOTES TO PAGE 69.

Selection XXXI. RV. i. 1. Hymn to Agni, the Fire-god. — Translated by Whitney, *Century Magazine*, 1887, xxxiii. 915. Respecting Agni, see Kaegi, p.35(50)f, and N.119f.

— THE METRE is gāyatrī. Each stanza (ṛc) consists of three octosyllabic pādas with iambic cadence — see Kaegi, p.24(34) and N.85. Observe that, if the stanza be a triple one, the strophe usually consists of three stanzas and the hymn of a multiple thereof.

— In respect of frequency, the order of the metres in the RV. is: first the triṣṭubh (about ⅖ of RV.); then the gāyatrī (about ¼); then the jagatī (about ⅛) — see Haskell, JAOS. xi.p.lx = PAOS. May, 1881.

LINES 1–2. īḻe, √īḍ: accentless, 592: for the new letter, see p. 291 ¶ 8, and Whitney, 5 end. — RV.x.2.5 plays on the etymology of ṛtv-íj thus: agnír ·· devā́ṅ ṛtu-çó yajāti. — For superl., 471.

3. pū́rvebhis, 330, Vedic instr.: for r final w. initial ṛ, Whitney, 14 end.

4. U.f. devā́ṅs ā́ ihá. This interesting combination is really the result of a historic survival, and is fully explained at 209. Observe that āṅ, though transliterated with two letters, is a simple nasalized vowel, 209 a. — ā́ ·· vakṣati: position of prefix, 1081; accent of verb form, 1082; √vah, aor. sub., 893[1].

5–6. açnavat, 700: use of mode, 576: subject indefinite. — divé-dive, 1260. — yaçásam, 1151.2a.

7–8. ágne, acct, 314[3]. — ási, acct, 595 a. — Position of clauses, 512a. — Locative, 304 a.

10. ā́ gamat, true aor. subjunctive (836[2]), corresponding to the ind. ágan (833): see 558.

11–12. tvám may be read tuám. Observe that in the Veda, when rhythmically read, hiatus is common — 113[3]. — ágne is at the beg. of a new pāda, 314[3]. — U.f. táva íd tád satyám. — Lit. 'Just what pleasant thing thou wilt (= willest to) do for the pious man, of thee indeed that (is) real *or* unfailing' — *i.e.* 'Whatever blessing thou dost purpose to grant, that thou never failest to bestow.'

13–14. U.f. úpa tvā (491[3]) agne (accentless) ··· ā́ imasi (548[1]), √i+upa‿ā.

15–16. The accusatives are to be taken w. tvā. — We *may* pronounce adhvarā́ṇaām (113[3]), or leave the pāda catalectic. — U.f. gopā́m. — In pāda *c*, we *must* pronounce sué, in order to produce an iambic cadence.

17–18. sá ·· bhava, see ta 2. — U.f. sūnáve ágne: for treatment of the acct in combination, see 135, example 4.

— Observe that — as the metre here shows — pādas *a* and *b* are always independent of each other as regards euphonic combination, and that — as here — the written text, with perverse consistency, always combines them when this is possible.

— sácasvā, pada, sácasva, 248 c. — Pronounce su-astáye.

NOTES TO PAGE 70.

SELECTION XXXII. RV. i. 32. Indra slays the dragon. — Respecting Indra and the natural significance of the myths about his battles, see Kaegi, p. 40(57)f, N.141 f; and Perry, JAOS. xi.117f.

— The "hymn" appears to consist of two separate pieces — see N. to 70[20]. The catenary structure is noticeable in some pairs of stanzas (1–2; 3–4) — see Kaegi, p. 24(34).

— THE METRE is triṣṭubh. The old Vedic triṣṭubh is much more free than that of the classical Sanskrit; but its most important feature, the cadence, is the same — see p. 316, § 43.

For statistics, see Haskell, JAOS. xi.p.lxii = PAOS. May, 1881. For a discussion of its development, see Oldenberg, ZDMG. xxxvii.55f.

1. Pronounce vīríāṇi and (line 3) svaríam, and see Whitney, 84 b. — prá vocam, augmentless aorist (847 end), as improper subjunctive (563), with future mg (576).

2. U.f. áhan (637) áhim; ánu apás tatarda. Note juxtaposition of perf. w. impf. and see 823[2]. — prá abhinat, √bhid, 692.

3. **çiçriyāṇā́m**, 807. —Indra's special attribute is his "beloved thunderbolt," of which the Epos fables much, ZDMG. xxxii. 296.

4. 'Like lowing kine, — flowing suddenly to a sea, down came the waters.' The point of comparison is the noise. —**samudrā́m**, perhaps 'to *a* gathering of water, so as to form one' — not necessarily 'to *the* ocean.'

5ª. Pronounce **avṛṇīta**, 135⁴ (important): in the AV., ii.5.7, the augment is written. Cf. 70¹⁷N. —**sómam**: see Kaegi, p. 72(99), and notes 288–94; also Roth, ZDMG. xxxv. 680f and xxxviii.134f.

5ᵇ. Pronounce **tríkadrukeṣu a-**, and observe that final -u is almost never to be *pronounced* as -v when so written. —Cf. RV. ii.15.1, which seems to consist of reminiscences of the beg. of this hymn.

6. 'The Rewarder took the missile bolt — smóte him, the first-born of dragons.' — **áhan** (593) has for direct object the enclitic **enam**, 'him,' or, more correctly, 'im,' since the English pronoun *hím* loses its *h* when enclitic. The **enam** is then explained by an appositive. So 79⁷.

7–8. U.f. **yád indra áhan** · ·, **ā́t māyínām áminās prá utá** · ·. 'When, O Indra, thou smotest · ·, and (**utá**) thereupon broughtest to nought the wiles of the wily, thereupon bringing forth the sun, the day, the dawn, — then soothly foundest thou no enemy.'

—The first **ā́t** continues the force of **yád** through pāda *b*, as the acct (595a) of **áminās** (√2mi) shows. —Position of **prá**, 1081². — Order in pāda *c* is unnatural: expect 'dawn, sun, (full) day.' —Pronounce **sū́riam**. — **dyā́m**, 361d: vocab., under **dív**. —**uṣā́sam** and **kilā**: see references in vocab.; the prolongations are in the even syllables of the cadence. —**vivitse**, 798a.

9. Pronounce **viańsam**: cf. Whitney, 84a.

10. **kúliçenā**, 248b. —**ví-vṛkṇā**, nom. pl. neut., common in Veda, for -**āni**: √**vraçc**. —**çay-a-te**, transition-form (749) from root-class, for **çe-te** (629).

11. **ā́ hí juhv-é** (alternative form for **juhuv-e**), √**hū+ā**: acct, 595d: subject, Vritra.

12ª. 'He (Vritra) did not escape (√**tṛ**, 899a) the shock of his (Indra's) weapons.'

12ᵇ. 'The (cloud-) rifts he crushed together, who had Indra as his conqueror.' That is, the monster, in his retreat or his fall, crushed into a shapeless mass his already riven cloud-castles. This is forced. If we dared emend the ἅπ. λ. **rujā́nās** to **rujānā́s** (840¹), we might render, 'Broken, he was (then) completely crushed' (998b).

—**índra-çatru**: later books, e.g. ÇBr. i.6. 3¹⁰, lay great stress on the correct accentuation of this word; **indra-çatrú**, 'conqueror of I.,' would be blasphemy. See *Indische Studien*, iv.368; or Roth, *Nirukta*, p. xix.

13ᵇ. U.f. **ā́ asya** · · **jaghāna**, see √**han+ā**. Subject here is Indra.

14. See **vṛ́ṣan**. —See √**bhū**, desid. — **açayat**, 629. —Pronounce **ví-astas**, Whitney, 84a.

15. 'Over him, lying so, crushed like (**ná**) a reed, the waters go, flowing for mankind (lit. the waters of man, flowing, do go).' So Pischel, ZDMG. xxxv.717–24. P. thinks that the original text was **mánorúhānā́ti**, i.e. **mános** (cf. 73¹⁹) **úhānās** (√**vah4**, pres. mid. ppl., 619³) **áti**, and that the author of the pada text divided it wrongly, **máno rúhānās**, changing, of course, **n** to **ṇ**.

—If **mánas**, like **áñjas**, could pass for an instr., we might render '(With a will, i.e.) Lustily rising, the waters overwhelm him.' —**amuyā́**, 'so,' w. a sneer: cf. **átra**, 89⁴N.

16. **pari-átiṣṭhat**, acct, 595a, 1083. — **tā́sām** limits only the first member of the foll. cpd.

17. Note relation of acct and mg in **vṛtráputrā**. —U.f. **índras asyās**: observe the accordance between the written and spoken form here — see 135⁴, and cf. 70⁵ᵃN. —**vádhar**, 'weapon' of V's mother, not of Indra.

18. Translated, 777b. —**dā́nus**, fem., = V's mother. —**çaye**, see 613: similarly **duhe**, 80¹⁶, **īçe**, 92³.

19–20. 'The waters overwhelm V's hidden body, that was put down in the midst of · ·. In long darkness lay (**ā́‿açayat**, 629) he who was vanquished by Indra.'

—Here the narration comes to an end. Stanzas 1–10 form a brief but complete epic. The same general theme is treated again by stanzas 11–14. Rik 15 seems to be a later addition.

21. dāsápatnīs: after I's victory, the waters are called (x.43.8) aryá-patnīs, 'having the Aryans as masters,' or 'having a gracious (god) as master.' — paṇíneva gā́vas (see gó): the rain-giving clouds are often called 'cows.' These are pent up by a malicious demon (Paṇi), and their milk, the refreshing water of heaven, is withheld from man.

Curiously, the natural basis of this simple myth is so far forgotten that the myth itself is here made to furnish a simile for the very phenomenon from which it is the poetic outgrowth.

NOTES TO PAGE 71.

1. 'The orifice of the waters which was closed up — he who slew (805, 209) Vritra opened that.' Waters conceived as if pent up in some mighty cask.

2–3. 'A horse's tail becamest thou then, O Indra, when on his lance he (V.) impaled thee. — As god alone, thou conqueredst · · ·. Thou didst let loose the seven streams (but see saptá) to flow' (lit. 'for flowing,' √sṛ, 970b, 982).

— In fighting with demons, Indra sometimes gets roughly handled for a while (so iv.18.9). Such I conceive to be the situation here. Pāda *a* is the crux. Possibly a magic transformation is intended. V. impales I. on his lance; but straightway the god becomes a great sweeping trail of vapor. Very differently Bergaigne, *Rel. Véd.* iii. 61–62.

— It seems unavoidable to join devá ékas with *c*: cf. i.33.4 and i.165.6 = 73[14]. — Second ájayas begins a new clause: hence acct, 593[2].

4. Explained under yá4: asmāi means Vritra. — ákirad dh-, 163. — Cf. what is said of Yahve at Psalm xviii.13,14.

5. yuyudhāte, 800a. — U.f. utá aparíbhyas (see ápara). — ví jigye, 787. — 'Indra was victor (both for the time) while he and Ahi fought and (utá) for the future.'

6–7. 'What avenger of Ahi sawest thou, Indra, when in the heart of thee having slain (him) fear did come — when nine and ninety streams as an affrighted hawk the skies thou didst cross?' This may refer to a time when — after all the aerial commotion (i.e. Indra's battling) — the rain refused to fall and the uncleared heaven signified Indra's retreat. Reminiscences of this legend occur at TS. ii.5.3: cf. MBh. v.9.27 = 255 and 10.43 = 334,f. — jaghnúṣas, 805.

8–9. See √yā 1 and √sā. — U.f. sás íd u (176b) · · arā́n ná · ·. — Gen., 297c. — Tenses, 823[2].

SELECTION XXXIII. RV. i.50. To Sūrya, the Sun-god. — Respecting Sūrya, see Kaegi, p. 54(76). The hymn is rubricated at 106[3]. It is still used in India, at the Midday Service. It was made the text of a linguistic-mythological comment of 225 pages by W. Sonne, KZ. vol's xii.–xv.!

In the textus receptus, the hymn has 13 stanzas. I have given only 1–9. In the first strophe, stanzas 1–3, the god is mentioned only in the 3d person. In the second strophe, he is addressed in the 2d person; and so also in the third strophe, excepting — as often — the final stanza (9).

— That stanzas 10–13 are later additions is proved by their contents and language and their (differing) metre. This proof is confirmed by the fact that the corresponding passage of the AV., xiii.2.16–24, has only stanzas 1–9; and also by the fact that only 1–9 are prescribed to be used in the ritual — see Bezzenberger's *Beiträge*, viii.198, ZDMG. xxxviii.475, JAOS. xi.p.cxcii = PAOS. May, 1884, and AGS. ii.3.13 and comment, and cf. 87[10]N. Moreover, the addenda are at the end of an anuvāka — cf. JA. 8.viii. 207 = 15.

10. See u2. — jātávedasam, see vocab.: although 'All-possessor' was very likely the primary mg (Whitney, AJP. iii.409), yet the mg 'All-knower' also seems to have been associated with the word early and commonly (Eggeling, SBE. xxvi.p.xxxi). For analogous cases, see hótṛ and yamá in vocab.

In the present — very unusual — application of the epithet to Sūrya,

ὃς πάντ' ἐφορᾷ καὶ πάντ' ἐπακούει,

the latter phase of mg predominates.

11. 'That every man may see the sun, *lit.* for every one for beholding the sun.' See dṛç and read 969, 970a, and 982. – viçvāya, 524[2].

12–13. tyé belongs logically with nákṣatrā[ṇi], but is conformed in gender to tāyávas. – With this simile, cf. RV. x. 189.2. – See yathā4. – yanti, no acct, 595a[2]. – sū́rāya, 'for the sun, i.e. to make way for the sun.' Render:

> Off — like as robbers — slink away
> Yon constellations with their beams
> Before the all-beholding Sun.

14. ádṛçram (834b end) · · ví (1081[2]) — passively, 998b: equiv. to vy-adṛkṣata, 882. – jánāñ, 209.

18–19. See pratyáñc3. – Pronounce devā́naām, 113[3]. – pratyáññ, 210. – Pronounce súar (Whitney, 84b): reg. written súvar in TS. – súar dṛçé, 'a light to behold' (cf. θαῦμα ἰδέσθαι), here equiv. to 'a glorious light.'

20 and **72**[1]. yénā, 509 end. – pāvaka: see ref's in vocab.; this word the redactors persist in miswriting; it is a typical mistake belonging to the second stage of the tradition — see p. 354, § 79, and KZ. xxvi.60.

– jánāñ ánu: if joined w. ppl., render 'stirring *or* busy among (so RV. viii.9.2b) his fellows;' if w. páçyasi (acct, 595a), 'over the peoples thou dost look on busy man.' – Pronounce tuám.

– STROPHE 2, stanzas 4, 5, 6. Some join 6 with 7 — possible, but very hard. It is better to regard 6 as a parenthesis in which the poet turns suddenly from Sūrya to Varuṇa. The latter is the personified vault of heaven, and the sun is naturally his eye (RV. vii.63.1), and to mark the deeds of restless man is his proper function [Kaegi, p.65(90)]. Yénā then refers to súar, and cákṣasā is in explanatory apposition w. yénā. We may render 4, 5, 6 thus:

> Thou goest onward, all-beheld.
> Thou makest light, god Sūria.
> Thou shinest to the end of heaven.
> Turning thy face upon the folk
> Of gods, of men, of all the world,
> Thou risest up, thou glorious light—
> With which, as eye, bright Varuṇa,
> Over the peoples thou dost look,
> To mark the deeds of restless man.

NOTES TO PAGE 72.

2–3. U.f. ví dyā́m (see dív) eṣi, rájas (171[4]) pṛthú, áhā (425d) mímānas (√1mā4: see 661, 655) aktúbhis ('with beams'), páçyan (202[2]). – 'Beholding (in pregnant sense) the generations, i.e. while generations come and go.'

4–5. J. Burgess, *Arch. Survey of Western India, Kāṭhiāwāḍ and Kacch*, p. 216, mentions temple-images of Sūrya with a halo (cf. çociṣkeça) and borne by 'seven steeds,' see plate lxv.2. Cf. Kaegi, N. 205.

6–7. áyukta (834b), 'hath just yoked.' – See 356 and 356[4]. – sváyuktibhis, Sāyaṇa rightly, svakīya-yojanena.

SELECTION XXXIV. RV. i.97. To Agni. See Preface, p. v, note 4. — Rubricated at 106[3]. Recurs AV. iv.33. The refrain or burden, pāda *c*, of each stanza, is a mere repetition of pāda *a* of stanza 1; it has no necessary connection with the rest of each stanza, although it happens to fadge well enough in the first and in the last three.

Grassmann and Ludwig make ápa · · çóçucat of the refrain a 3d s. subjunctive (1008[2]) — 'let him drive · ·'; but this would require an accentless çoçucat.

We may therefore disregard the refrains entirely and group the remaining eight couplets [each consisting of two octosyllabic verses], two and two, into four stanzas of four verses each.

8–11. See √çuc+apa and çuc+ā: ápa · · çóçucat is pres. ppl. of intensive conjugation (1012) — no nasal, 444. – U.f. çuçugdhí ā́, perf. impv. of primary conjugation, 813. – Three instrumentals (line 10), 365.1.

STANZA 1 [made by grouping stanzas 1,2] may be rendered:

> Driving away with flames our sin,
> Agni, bring welfare with thy light.
> [Driving away with flames our sin.]
> With prayer for fertile fields, for wealth,
> And prayer for good, we sacrifice —
> [Driving away with flames our sin.]

12. With prá, supply jā́yeta in *a* and jā́yeran in *b*. – bhánd-iṣṭhas (superl. to bhad-rá, √bhand, 467), 'brightest, luckiest'? – asmā́kāsas, 330 end.

14. **prá yát** sc. **jā́yeran** (760.3), 'that they may be propagated = that offspring may go forth from them' — and so in the other clauses of lines 12 and 14.

— In lines 12 and 14, the yad's seem to introduce final clauses expressing the purpose of **yajāmahe**, line 10. In line 16, Whitney makes **yád** = 'as, just as.' For all the **yád**-clauses, Grassmann seeks principal clauses in the refrains.

Stanzas 3,4 and 5,6. '[We sacrifice,] in order that (offspring may go) forth from the luckiest of them (?); and forth from our patrons; that offspring may go forth from thy patrons, Agni, — forth from us (who are) thine,

'As forth from mighty Agni on all sides go the rays. For thou, O (God) who hast a face on all sides, on all sides dost protect.'

20. Bring us across the (stream of) foes as with a boat.' See **nāú** and √2**pṛ+ati**.

Notes to Page 73.

2. Pronounce **sá naḥ síndhviva nāvā́yā**, w. elision of **-m** and combination: instance of a text-error of the second stage of the tradition — see p. 354, § 79 and KZ. xxvi.61, and cf. 78[7]. — See **tá2** end. — **áti parṣā** (248c), √2**pṛ**, impv. of s-aor., 896.

Selection XXXV. RV. i.165. **Indra and the Maruts.** — Respecting the Maruts and their relations to Indra, see Kaegi, p. 39 (56), and Bergaigne, *La religion védique*, ii. 369f, 392, and esp. the interesting article of Oldenberg, *Ākhyāna-hymnen im RV.*, ZDMG. xxxix.60-65. The hymn is the first of a collection of eight Marut hymns (165–172), concerning whose arrangement, see Oldenberg, l.c. We have here the beginnings of poetry in epic-dramatic form — cf. Preface, p. iv, note 7. This hymn has been admirably translated by Roth, ZDMG. xxiv.302 (or *Siebenzig Lieder*, p. 84); English version by Whitney, *North American Review*, 1871, cxiii.182 = OLSt. i.144. It is also translated with comments by Max Müller, *RV. Sanhita, translated*, etc., i.162f. I give the "story of the hymn" abridged from Roth-Whitney.

Stanzas 1–2. The poet inquires whither the Maruts are going and how they are to be detained at the sacrifice. The implicit answer is 'With praise.' This then is accomplished in the dialogue, where, although greatest glory is given to Indra, the god in turn lauds them generously.

Stanzas 3–4. The Maruts ask why Indra is going alone, without them, his usual companions. — Indra answers evasively that he is on the way to a sacrificial feast.

Stanzas 5–6. The Maruts are eager to go with him. — He retorts that they were not so eager when he went, alone, and slew the dragon.

Stanzas 7–8. The Maruts remind him that they *have* helped him do great things and *can* be most useful allies in the future. — Not inclined to share his glory with them, he boasts again of his exploits.

Stanzas 9–12. The Maruts acknowledge his might this time without reserve and to his satisfaction. — Indra, vaunting himself once more (10), thanks them for their homage (11), and declares that the sight of them delights his heart (12).

Stanzas 13–15. The poet (Agastya) turns to the Maruts directly and asks them to recognize and reward his skill and devotion.

4. √**myakṣ+sam**, perf. (785, 794b) as preterito-present. — Lit. 'With what common course (?) have they kept together? i.e. upon what common journey are they together?'

5. **matí**, Classic **matyā́**, 340. — U.f. **kútas ā́_itāsas** (√i, 330 end) **eté**? **árcanti** (accent-combination, 135[2]) **çúṣmam** — acc. as in ἀγωνίζεσθαι πάλην. — **vasūyā́**, as at 72[10].

7. See **mánas2**. — √**ram4**: read 869, 864, and 856.

8. Pronounce **tuám indra**, as 5 syllables. — **máhinaḥ sánn**, 'being (usually) gay': Roth-Whitney, 'though (else so) blithe'; concessive force doubtful: perhaps they mean a gentle reproach for his slighting their company — 'Why go'st thou alone, and so merry withal?'

9. 'Thou talkest (usually), when going along with (us) moving onward.' — See √**ṛ+sam**. Both ppls are of the root-aorist, 840[3]. — **vocés**, 854. — **harivas**, 454b. — **yát te asmé** (loc. 492[2]), 'which (is) to thee on our score, lit. on us,' i.e. 'which thou hast against us.'

10[a]. **çám**, '(are) a joy,' pred. to all three subst.

10[b]. See **çúṣma2**. —**iyarti**, √**r̥**, 643c. —**prá-bhr̥tas**, '(is) ready,' begins a clause.

11. 'They [men] are making supplication (to me); they are enticing (me) with invocation (**ukthā́**, as instr. s.). These two (**imā́**, 501 end) coursers here are carrying me (*lit.* us) unto (**áccha**) them' (**tā́** = **tā́ni**, 495 end: the good things mentioned in pāda *a*).

12. **vayám**, 'we,' i.e. the few who are conceived as speaking for the whole troop. —See √**yuj3**: cf. 840[3]. —Pronounce **tanúaḥ çúmbh-**: notation explained by Whitney, 90b[2]. See **tanū́** under **tanú** and see √**2çubh**. —The spokesmen designate their 'companions' as 'free' in order to magnify the value of their readiness to follow Indra.

13. U.f. **étān** (not **etā́n**): the Maruts drive a dappled team of does or mares. —See √**yuj**+**upa**: **yujmahe** is a root-class present (612a), used with future mg (777a). —U.f. **nú | índra** (314[3]). —See **1svadhā́3**. —**babhū́tha**, 798b.

14. **kvà syá**, Whitney, 90b[2]: pronounce **kúa siá ·· svadhā́sīd**. —**syá**, 'that' (wish for my company), just mentioned, line 13. They did leave him in the lurch once—see 82[1]N. —U.f. **yád ·· sam-ádhatta**: see √**1dhā**+**sam** and 668.

15. Pada-text **ahám hí ugráḥ**. —See under √**nam**: for gen., see 297c end, and cf. 77[3].

16. **bhū́ri**, acc. n., may be either pl. (340) or sing. —Pischel shows that **asmé** may be used as instr. (or gen.) also. 'With (= in company of) us combined, (and) by our united prowess.' —Pronounce **yújiebhis, pāúṅsiebhis**.

17. **kr̥ṇávāmā** (248c), pres. subjunctive (700) of √**kr̥**, 715. —**krátvā**, Classic **kratunā**, 342. —**maruto**, voc.: the spokesmen call on their companions to bear them witness. But the reading **marúto**, nom., has been suggested. —See **yád4** end. —**vā́çāma**, 614.

18. **vádhīm**, 904a. —**babhūvā́n**, 802.

19. Compare 70[15]N.

20. See **á-nutta** and **ánu-tta** in vocab. —See **ā́3**. —See √**2vid3** and 619[3]. —Either, 'Entirely invincible for thee is surely nothing. Not (one) like thee is found among the gods'; or, 'Entirely granted thee is (the fact) that surely no one (**nákis ·· ná**, double neg. = single) like thee *etc.*' Cf. KZ. xxvi. 611 and JAOS. xiii.p.c = PAOS. May, 1886.

Notes to Page 74.

1. **náçate**: acct, 596 and 597, cf. 89[9]N.; the object (**tvā**) is to be understood from what precedes. —Roth emends to **kariṣyā́ḥ**, see 938.

2. Pronounce **ékasya cin me vibhú astu ójas**. —**yā́** = **yā́ni**. See **nú3**. 'Whatsoever things (I am) having ventured, (those) I will accomplish (subjunctive = fut. ind., 576) wisely (365.1).'

3. This **vídānas** may be referred to √**1vid**. —**cyávam**, 563, 743. —**īçe**, as 1st pers. here. —'What things I may undertake, just I, Indra, am master óf thĕm.'

4. U.f. **ámandat mā marutas st-**, 173a: cf. 74[12]N. —**yád ·· bráhma cakrá**, a subject-clause co-ordinate with **stómas**.

5. **máhyam**, appositive to **me**. —**sákhye**, 343a. —**tanúe tanū́bhis**, 'for myself, by yourselves (vestra sponte), i.e. for me, spontaneously *or* heartily.'

6. See **evá 1** end. —Roth suggests the emendation **ánedyāḥ** (**ánediāḥ**), as nom. pl. m.; or else **anedyaçravā́ḥ**. —U.f. **ā́ iṣas dádhānās**.

7. **saṁ-cákṣiā**, 993a. —**ácchānta** (**cch**, 227), for **a-chānt-s-ta**, 883, 233b. See √**2chad**. —**chadáyāthā** (248c), subjunctive, 1043.2. —'In very truth these (are) appearing good unto me, blameless, putting on glory (and) strength. Ye of shining hue have delighted me, upon looking at (you), O Maruts, and delight ye me now.'

8. See √**mah**. —**prá yātana**, 618. —**sákhīnr**, 209.

9. See √**vat**. —**bhūta**, 835. —**návedās**, 415e, as nom. pl. m.

—The accent-rules for the oblique cases of the pron. root **a** (cf. 502) are simple and entirely natural. Thus:

A. If the form is used adjectively, distinguishing 'thís' thing from others, it is accented (74[9]; 92[3], 79[18]). B. So also if used as an emphatic substantive pron. (83[16], 103[4] asmát).

C. But if used as an unemphatic substantive pron., 'his, her, him, their, them,' it is accentless (83[16], 70[3], 71[14], 74[3], 88[17], and very often). In this case the form cannot stand at beg. of pāda.

10. The á́ has pregnant mg (cf. √çuc+ā and +apa) and goes w. both duvasyát (562[2]) and cakré. —Both verbs depend (595) on yád. —Pronounce mäaniásya. —'When the singer entices (you) hither as to an oblation, (and when) the wisdom of Māna's son has brought us hither —.'

—Roth would expunge one d and read duvasyá́, instr. (365.1) of duvasyá́ (1149[6]), 'with an honoring, i.e. reverently.' The passage is a desperate one.

11. U.f. á́ u sú vartta (irreg., 839) · · áccha. See sú 1 and √vṛt+ā. —imá́ = imā́ni. —arcat, 743.

12. va stómo, u.f. vas stómas, 173a: similar combinations at 79[17], vípras st-; 81[17], ájayas sp-; 87[1]; 92[8]; 74[4]; per contra, 47[11]. —iyám here refers back — see 1 idám. —See gír.

13. U.f. á́ iṣá́ yāsīṣṭa (914[3]) · · vidyá́ma (√2vid, a pres. opt. of the root-class) iṣá́-m. —Pronounce vayá́ām? —'Hither with refreshment come ye. For ourselves as a strengthening may we get refreshment (and) a well-watered dwelling-place.'

—It would seem that the poet Agastya was the son of Māna, of the race of Mandāra. This entire final stanza recurs at the end of hymns 166–168. The awkward repetition of 'refreshment' leads Roth to suspect that the original pāda *d* of the stanza is lost and replaced by the one in the text, which is a stock-verse recurring at the very end of twenty subsequent hymns.

SELECTION XXXVI. RV. iii. 62. To Savitar. — Respecting Savitar, see Kaegi, p. 56(79). The last "hymn" (62) of the third maṇḍala is really a collection of six short hymns to various divinities. Each hymn contains three stanzas, and the triad to Savitar is the fourth of the six.

—The first stanza of this triad is the most celebrated stanza of the RV., and is called the sāvitrí (sc. ṛk), or the gāyatrí κατ' ἐξοχήν. It has held, and holds even now, the most important place in the worship of the Hindus. In the Proceedings of the *International Congress of Orientalists* (1881) *at Berlin*, ii.2.160–187, and in *Religious Thought and Life in India*, p. 399f, Monier-Williams discusses the place of the RV. in the religious services of the Hindus of the present day.

He says that the worshipper must first bathe, then apply ashes to his limbs and forehead, bind his hair, sip pure water, and inhale pure air and retain it in his lungs for a while. The worshipper then utters RV. iii.62.10, which — like the Lord's Prayer among Christians and like the Fātihah among Muhammadans — takes precedence of all other forms of supplication. [Cf. Manu ii.101f.] Later on, the gāyatrī is muttered 108 times with the help of a rosary of Tulsī wood.

—Much has been fabled about the stanza and its virtues. See, for example, Manu ii.77–83. And it recurs frequently in the other Vedas; thus, four times in the VS., twice in the TS., and once in the SV. "No good and sufficient explanation of the peculiar sanctity attaching to this verse has ever been given." — Whitney, reprinted in Kaegi, N.222. The stanza has naturally been imitated a great deal: so even in the RV. (v.82) we find verses run in the same mould. And it is interesting to find the RV. stanzas iii.62.10 (gāyatrī) and v.82.1 repeated in juxtaposition in the Tāittirīya āraṇyaka at i.11.2 and i.11.3. After the pattern of the gāyatrī have been made a good many wooden and halting stanzas: so TA. x.1.5,6.

14–15. dhīmahi, root-aor. opt. mid. (837) of √1dhā — see √1dhā8. See also Whitney in Kaegi, N.222. —yó · · pracodáyāt (1043.2), 'and may he inspire.'

16–17. púraṁdhiā, perhaps 'with exaltation (of spirit).' —īmahe, see √i and reference.

18. náras, nom. pl. of nṛ́.

Notes to Page 75.

Selection XXXVII. RV. iv. 42. Indra contests the supremacy of Varuṇa. — Respecting Varuṇa, see Hillebrandt, *Varuṇa und Mitra*, 1877, and Kaegi, p. 61(85), notes 241f. This hymn has ten stanzas; but the last three have nothing to do with the rest.

— Varuṇa is by far the noblest and loftiest character of the Vedic pantheon, and seems to have held the most prominent position in the earliest period. Later — as appears if we consider the RV. as a whole — the warlike and national god Indra is plainly most prominent. The gradual supersession of Varuṇa by Indra[1] is reflected in a considerable number of passages — among them, this hymn — and especially in x.124.

— In stanzas 1–4 of this hymn, Varuṇa claims the godhead, supreme and from the beginning, in virtue of his creating and sustaining the world. — Indra responds (5–6) by asserting his irresistible might as god of battle. — And the hymn ends with an acknowledgment on the part of the poet (st. 7) of the claims of Indra. This is essentially the interpretation of most of the authorities.[2]

— But the general drift of the hymn has been — no less than its details — the subject of very much discussion and difference of opinion. Bergaigne[3] considers stanzas 1–6 as a monologue of Indra. Barth[4] rejects the theory of the decadence of the Varuṇa-cultus and regards RV. x.124 as one of the few survivals of a class of myths in which Varuṇa is not the god of a smiling and gracious heaven, but a malignant divinity. Finally, Whitney urges that this is not a question of supremacy and subordination, but rather of comparative prominence. — This selection, I confess, is out of place in a Reader.

---

[1] Discussed by Muir, OST. v.116f; and, in connection with RV. x.124, by Hillebrandt, p. 107-111. See also Grassmann's introduction to x.124 and his translation of it.

[2] So GKR., p. 26; Grassmann, Translation; and Hillebrandt, esp. 72(159), 104–105.

[3] La religion védique, iii.142, printed 1877.

[4] The religions of India, p. 18.

1. máma: note that every one of the stanzas 1–6 begins with an emphatic form of the first personal pron. — **dvitā́**, if rendered 'equally,' means 'as well as thou, O Indra, who disputest my sovereignty,' or else 'as well over all creatures as over gods;' but Kern defines **dvitā́** as 'from everlasting' or 'to everlasting:' the mg is uncertain and has been so since the time of the **nighaṇṭavas** (cf. Nirukta, v.3). — Pronounce **rāṣṭrám**. — See **viçvā́yu** in vocab. — Grassmann would emend **yáthā naḥ** to **yátānāḥ**, root-aor. ppl. of √**yat**, 'joining themselves together, united:' 'mine (are) all immortals together.' Otherwise we must take **naḥ** as plural of majesty and equiv. to **máma**.

— 'To me, the ruler, forever (belongs) the sovereignty over all creatures, just as all immortals (are) ours, i.e. our vassals.'

2[b]. Taking **vavrí** in mg 1, 'I am king of the folk's highest cover, i.e. king of heaven,' or else 'I am king of the folk of the highest cover, i.e. king of the folk of heaven, *or* king of the gods.' — GKR. quite otherwise.

3. rā́jā as pred. — **prathamā́**(ni), 'first' in order of time. — See √**dhṛ5**.

5. índro: excellent authorities emend, and read **indra**. — **té urví** (342) etc. are accusatives dual neuter, object of the verbs in next line. — **mahitvā́** (330) 'by might.'

6. sám āirayam, √**īr**, 585. — **dhāráyam̐ ca** makes a new clause, hence acct, 593[2].

7–8. 'I made the dropping rains to stream. I uphold heaven in the place of eternal order. And in accordance with eternal order, the sacred son of Aditi (i.e. Varuṇa) spread out the threefold world.' The sending of rain is a function proper to Varuṇa — cf. Hillebrandt, p. 85–86. In the assignment of *this* stanza the authorities differ and waver most.

9. Pronounce **mā́am · · suáçvās**. — **vṛtā́s**, 'the chosen ones, πρόμαχοι' (√2**vṛ**), or else 'hemmed in, sore beset' (√1**vṛ**2): opinion about equally divided. — √**hū**.

10. maghávā‿ahám índras may make a sentence by itself or be taken appositively with the subject of **kṛṇómi**. — See √**vṛ** and reference.

11. cakaram, 817, 818[2]. — **nákis** begins

new clause. —varate, √1vṛ3, root-aor. subj. (836).

12. mamádan, perf. subj., 810a. —yád ukthā́(ni) sc. mā mamádan. —rájasī, 138a.

13. U.f. vidús (790a) te, 188b: similarly 80[15]. —'All beings have knowledge of thee as such a one (tásya). These things thou proclaimest to Varuṇa, O true one.'

14. Pronounce tuám, both times. —çṛṇviṣe, 699[2] end, see √çru2. 'Tu hostium interfector clues.' —jagh-, 805: cf. 71[1]. —vṛtā́n, √1vṛ2. —ariṇās, 725.

SELECTION XXXVIII. RV. iv. 52. To Uṣas, the Dawn-goddess.—See Kaegi, p. 52(73). The monograph by Brandes, *Ushas og Ushas-hymnerne i Rigveda*, Copenhagen, 1879, gives translations of all the 21 hymns in juxtaposition. Cf. also Easton, JAOS. x.p.lxix = PAOS. Oct. 1873.

—Stanzas 1, 2, 3 (= SV. ii.1075–7) form a strophe. Stanzas 5, 6, 7 seem to form a second. Stanza 4 seems to be an addendum to the prior strophe.

15–16. U.f. syā́, 188a. —√1vas+vi. —svásus, cf. RV. i. 113.3. —práti adarçi (844), note force of práti.

17–18. citrā́ as pred. —mātā́, cf. Hesiod, Theogony, 378–82. —gávām, 361c. The 'kine' are the fleecy morning-clouds, the children of Dawn—cf. Kaegi, note 197. —See ṛtā́van: the idea in Job xxxviii.12[b] or Psalm civ.19[b] is similar. "The sun knoweth his going down."

Bright as a ruddy steed became
The faithful mother of the kine,
Uṣas, the friend of Açvins twain.

19. Note how all three pādas of this stanza begin with utá. —Pronounce sákhāsi, u.f. sákhā asi.

NOTES TO PAGE 76.

1. U.f. utá uṣas (voc.). —vásv-as, 342, 297c. —īçiṣe, 630.

3. práti · · abhutsmahi (√budh), 882 and 155: 'we have awaked with praises to meet thee (tvā)'—vocab. wrong.

4–5. práti adṛkṣata (√dṛç), 879b, 882, 218. —U.f. ā́ uṣás aprās (889).

Gladsome before our eyes appear
Her beams—like herds of kine let loose.
The wide expanse of air she fills.

6–7. ā-paprúṣī, sc. jráyas, or with Sāyaṇa, jagat, 'the world,' 'all': the stems of this perf. ppl. are paprivā́ṅs- and paprúṣ-, cf. 803 and 459. —Pronounce ví āvar (√1vṛ, 831[2], 585[2]). —'According to thy wont, be gracious.'

8–9. dyā́m, see dív. —U.f. ā́‿antárikṣam, sc. tanoṣi (√1tan+ā, 698B). —See priyá3. —Note the radical connection of the assonant words and render by 'radiant ray,' 'effulgent flame,' or the like.

SELECTION XXXIX. RV. v. 24. To Agni. —The stanzas are dvipada, i.e. consist of two pādas, one of 8 and one of 11 or 12 syllables. Most nearly like this hymn in metre is RV. x.172; but the stanzas of RV. viii.12,13,15, and 18 are essentially similar (8+8+12).

—It is very worthy of note that three of the stanzas occur in immediate juxtaposition in the other saṁhitās, and as follows: in the order 1, 2, 4, at SV. ii.457,458,459, at VS. xv. 48[a],48[b],48[c], and at VS. iii.25[a],25[b],26[a] (here stanza 3 follows as 26[b]); and in the order 1,4,2 at TS. i.5.6 and iv.4.4. Finally, to judge from the legend given below, and from the prescriptions of the ritual—of the sacrifice to the Manes, for example—this hymn would appear to be a tṛca or triad of riks (see Sāyaṇa to RV. v.24 and to PB. xiii.12.5).

—Tradition (Kātyāyana) ascribes this hymn and also x.57–60 to the Gāupāyana brothers, Bandhu, Subandhu, Çrutabandhu, and Viprabandhu. In his comments to x. 57–60, Sāyaṇa gives the pertinent legendary material taken from ancient sources; and this, with other matter, is given in translation, in JRAS. NS.ii.441f, by Max Müller, who discusses the legend at length.

—The Bṛhaddevatā says that king Asamāti sent away the four brothers who were his priests, and put in their stead two Brahman wizards. These took shape as doves, bewitched Subandhu, and plucked out his soul. In order to cause the spirit to return, the *three* remaining brothers recited x.58 etc., and 'praised Agni with the dvipada hymn as it is among the Atris,' i.e. in the book of the family of Atri, the fifth. Then Agni gave back to Subandhu his soul, and the brothers, delighted, sang the rest of x.60 (7–12) and laid their hands (cf. 91[2]N.) on the one thus resuscitated.

10. **ágne**, acct, 314[3]. —Pronounce **tuám**. —**bhavā**, 248c: so **uruṣyā́** and **çrudhí**, line 12.

11. **ácchā**, 248a. —**nakṣi**, √2naç, 624. —Superl., 471. —**dās**, 835.

12. **sá**, see **tá2** end. —**nas**, 297b. —**bodhi**, see 839 end: here from √budh, see √budh3. —**çrudhí** for **çrudhí**: aorist impv., 839: acct, 593[2] mid. —**ṇo**, u.f. **nas**, 194. —**aghāyatás**, pres. ppl. ablative, 290: acct, 316, 318a. —See **1sama**.

13. See under **tá2**. —**dīdivas**, √dī, perf. ppl., voc., 462a. —**īmahe**, see √i.

SELECTION XL. RV. v. 40. Indra and Atri, and the sun eclipsed by the demon.—For a critical analysis of the hymn, see Grassmann, Translation, i.190 and esp. 540. Stanzas 6, 7, 8, here given, are quite independent of the rest.

—Ludwig identifies the eclipse here referred to with that of April 20, 1001 B.C., O.S.—see *Sitzungsberichte d. böhmischen Gesell. d. Wiss.*, 1885. His argument is reported by Whitney, JAOS. xiii.p.lxi f = PAOS. Oct. 1885, and by Bergaigne, JA. 8.vi.372f. No fair interpretation of the text furnishes data precise enough for an exact identification.

—Stanzas 6 and 8 are spoken by the poet; stanza 7, by the Sun. The Sun's foe, Súarbhānu (accent!), is 'he who has the sun's beams,' and is later identified with Rāhu, the demon who 'swallows,' 'devours,' or 'seizes' (√2gṛ, √gras—cf. 23[1]N., √grah) the sun or moon, and so causes eclipses. The Sun is in terror, and implores Atri for help: and the latter rescues the orb by prayer and praise.

—Atri's mythical exploit is often mentioned in the Brāhmaṇas (see texts in Ludwig, v.508; and cf. SBE. xxvi.346). Thus the PB., at vi.6.8,11, narrates how, at the request of the gods, Atri restored to brightness the sun, which the demon had smitten with darkness. On this account, it continues, a present of gold, the symbol of brightness, is made to a descendant of Atri at a sacrifice now-a-days.

—Interesting are the Greek ideas about the πάγκοινον τέρας that bringeth to nought men's strength and wisdom—see Pindar's *Fragments* [74], Bergk[4] i.411 f and notes.

14. **ava‿áhan** (593), cf. 70[7] and note.

15. **gūḷhám**, √guh. —**ápa-vrata**, 'having action off, i.e. baffling,' or, as in vocab. —'The sun, hidden · ·, Atri found (**avindat**) by the fourth prayer.'

—Ludwig reasons thus: The other priests had a regular liturgy of three prayers for combating eclipses. On this occasion, these proved ineffectual. Atri knew a fourth, and that brought the sun out. Hence the totality must have been very long. This matter is discussed in full by Whitney, l.c., p. lxv(=xxi). Bergaigne, l.c., p. 383(=14), says it is a mere case of the use of a sacred number plus one—cf. *Rel. védique*, ii.128.

16. **mā́m** (pronounce **mā́am**) **imám**, 'me here, i.e. in this plight;' Sāyaṇa, **īdṛg-avastham**. —U.f. **atre**: the Sun is addressing Atri. —**irasyā́**, 365.1. —**bhiyás-ā**, '(me, who am thine) with fear, i.e. who am thine, (but) sore in terror:' or, the word *may* be taken actively, as the accent (1151.2c) and Sāyaṇa's gloss ('fear-inspiring') suggest, and joined with the subject—'with a frightening.' —**mā́ · · ní gārīt**: √2gṛ; aor., 899a; combination w. **mā́**, 579.

17. Pronounce **tuám mitṛó asi · · tā́ú mehā́vatam**. —**mitró**, 'friend.' —U.f. **tā́ú** (see **tá2** end) **mā ihá avatam**: 'so do ye two help me here, (thou) and V.' With the peculiar omission of **tvám** compare that of **ahám**, 79[10]N. So RV. viii.1.6.

18 and **77[1]**. **brahmā́** = **átris** of next line. —**yuyujānás** (807), see √yuj2. —**kīrí** may rather mean 'praise.' —**upaçíkṣan**, see √çak+upa. —U.f. **cákṣus ā́‿adhāt** (830). —**ápa aghukṣat**, √guh, 920, 916.

NOTES TO PAGE 77.

SELECTION XLI. RV. vii. 55. Magic spells to produce sleep. — Ascribed to Vasiṣṭha. The hymn consists of three parts differing in metre and disconnected in contents. For a general discussion of it, see Colebrooke's *Essays* ²i.27, and Whitney's note, ibid. p. 112; JAOS. iii.336f; and esp. Aufrecht, ISt. iv.337f. Sāyaṇa reports the native traditions about the hymn. Thus:

Vasiṣṭha came by night to the house of Varuṇa — to sleep, say some; to steal grain, say others. He was assailed by the watchdog, which bayed at him, and fain would have bitten him; but he laid the hound asleep with the stanza beginning,

When, silv'ry Sārameya, thou,

and the one following. — Later superstition uses the hymn to quiet uncanny creatures at night: see Rigvidhāna, ii.26.

— FIRST PART. The hymn next preceding this in the RV., vii.54, is to Vāstoṣpati, the Lar familiaris, and consists of three stanzas. The first part of our hymn, vii.55.1, is a mere addition to these three stanzas, and belongs accordingly to vii.54 rather than to vii.55, as appears from the fact that the four stanzas are all recited together in the ceremony of moving into a new house. See ÇGS. iii.4, AGS. ii.9.9, and esp. PGS. iii.4.7 — all in SBE. xxix.; and cf. MS. i.5.13.

The joining of this stanza to hymn 55 is a simple misdivision of which the NT. shows many parallel instances. Thus Mark ix.1 belongs to viii.; chap. ix. should begin with the Transfiguration. A converse misdivision is at AV. vi.63–64 as compared with RV. x.191.

— SECOND PART. Stanzas 2–4 are part of a scene at the entrance to Yama's kingdom or the regions of the blessed. Yama's two watch-dogs (cf. 83¹⁷N. and introd.) guard the pathway and keep out the wicked. Here one of them barks at some who would come in; and these, in turn, protest that they are godly men, and so have a right to enter in peace. See Kaegi, N.274; Zimmer, p. 421.

— THIRD PART. Stanzas 5–8 are the incantations by which the entire household is put to sleep. According to Aufrecht, l.c. (or Zimmer, p. 308), it is while a maid is receiving the visit of her lover; but that seems a little doubtful because we have plurals nas and sáṁ hanmas and vayám, lines 12, 13, 15, and not duals.

With stanzas 5, 6, 7, 8 correspond respectively stanzas 6, 5, 1, 3 of AV. iv.5, and the variants are interesting. The third part has nothing to do with the second; but the diaskeuasts have juxtaposed them because in both a dog is put to sleep.

2–3. vāstoṣpate, see above: for ṣ, see 187. — viçvā for viçvāni, 330. — edhi, 636. — Yāska, Nirukta x.17, says yad yad rūpaṁ kāmayate devatā, tat tad devatā bhavati. Sāyaṇa quotes him from memory thus, yad yad rūpaṁ kāmayante, tat tad devā viçanti.

4–5. See dánt. — vìva, accent!, 128 end: cf. 83¹⁵. U.f. ví iva bhrājante ṛṣṭáyas. — See úpa2. — See √bhas and 678. — 'They (the teeth) shine like spears, in the jaws of the devouring one.' — ní ṣú (188a) svapa is a refrain.

The dog here addressed is partly white and partly reddish brown, as Sāyaṇa rightly observes; and this is in accord with the adj. çabála, 'brinded,' applied to both of them at 83¹⁷.

6–7. punaḥsara: for the mg, see vocab. and cf. Hamlet i.4.51–53. — kím, 'why?'

8. For the genitives, see 297c end, and cf. 73¹⁵. — See √1dṛ and 1010 and 1011. — Probably the swine as a domestic animal is meant here. In that case, this stanza is a later addition to 2 and 3, and is based on a conception of the situation such as the native tradition presents.

10. Quoted at 593², which see.

11. In the Veda, 'complete' is sárva and 'all *or* every' is viçva. Later, viçva dies out and sárva does double duty. In the Veda, the use of sárva in the proper mg of viçva (as here, 77¹⁷, 85²⁰, 91¹) marks the passage as late. See vocab. under sárva.

— ayám etc., 'these here people on all sides, all the people around here.'

—STANZA 5 may be spoken by maid or by lover or by both. With the AV. reading, svápantu asyāi jñātáyaḥ (see 365.3), it must be spoken by the lover. Stanzas 6–8 may be spoken by both.

12–13. nas, expect nāu — see above. — See under yáthā2 and cf. yá2.

14–15. See vṛṣabhá 1. — ténā sahasyènā (248b), 'by (aid of) this mighty one.' — vayám, expect āvám? — √svap + ni, caus., 548.

16–17. nā́rīs, nom. pl., 365.2. — Pāda c may be read as catalectic.

SELECTION XLII. RV. vii. 56. To the Maruts or gods of the storm-winds. — Compare selection xxxv. (73^4) and introduction. The hymn consists of two parts, of which the first, here given, ends with stanza 10. Number 11 is only the fragment of a stanza. The rest (12–25) is in an entirely different metre.

—The metre of the ten stanzas is without doubt a secondary one, being simply a form of the triṣṭubh syncopated at the sixth place, i.e. with the prevailingly light sixth syllable left out (cf. JAOS. xi.p.lxiii = PAOS. May, 1881). Thus,

⏓ –́ ⏑ –́ ⏓ [⏑] ⏑ –́ ⏑ –́ ⏓.

Each of the parts into which the verse is broken is a 'syllable-pentad' or akṣara-pañkti; and each is an independent pāda, since verbs at the beginning of the even pentads are accented, e.g., at vii.34.3^b, 3^d, 4^b, 6^b. A pentad-couplet is sometimes joined with a simply broken but unsyncopated triṣṭubh verse to form a half-stanza or stanza (e.g. i.67.8^{cd}; 70.4^{cd}, 10^{cd}; x.46.1^{gh}); and this fact seems to suggest the derivative character of the pentads.

—The gāyatrī-stanza has 3 verses of 8 syllables; and the strophe has 3 stanzas, a multiple of the number of verses. The pentad-stanza has 4 or 8 verses of 5 syllables; and the hymn has 5, 10, or 20 stanzas, a multiple of the number of syllables. The hymns RV. i.65–70 have each 5 stanzas of 8 pentasyllabic verses; while vii.34A and vii.56A and ix.109 probably consisted originally each of 10 or 20 stanzas of 4 pentasyllabic verses. Compare Bollensen, ZDMG. xxii.572f.

18. U.f. ké īm víaktās · · ádha suáçvās.

NOTES TO PAGE **78**.

1. U.f. nákis hí eṣām: cf. John iii.8, οὐκ οἶδας πόθεν ἔρχεται (τὸ πνεῦμα). — vidre, 790b, 798a.

2. sva-pū́bhis, 'with their (sva-) wings,' taking -pū in the sense of pávana. Pávana, lit. 'a cleaner,' from √pū, sometimes means a 'sieve' or a 'fan.' At 104^{13} (see note), the pávana used to clean or winnow the ashes from the bones of a cremated corpse may perhaps be a 'wing-like winnowing-fan;' and observe that German *Schwinge* means 'winnowing-fan' and 'wing.' — abhí · · vapanta, 'bestrew, cover.' — aspṛdhran, see √spṛdh and 834b end.

—Here the storm-gods are pictured as lusty eagles, each sportively striving with the others for precedence, and spreading his wings over them in turn, to put them down and master them.

—Ludwig interprets, 'They vie in overwhelming each other with their blasts' (pávana has also the mg 'wind'). This view accords with the character of the playful, boisterous, and roaring gods, but not with the conception of them as eagles; and it would seem to require the reading abhí · · vápantaḥ.

—Roth, and after him the vocab., suggests that svapū́ is a 'besom (that raises the dust)': 'they bestrew each other (in sport) with dust.' At best, the line is doubtful.

3. ciketa, 787, √cit3. — See yád2. — The storm-gods are cloud-born, i.e. children of the cloud conceived under the figure of a dapple cow, pṛ́çni. This stanza (4) ought to come immediately after the second.

4. See viç2. — sáhantī, active: the forms are usually middle. — See √puṣ2. — 'The host heroic, with the Maruts (as a part of it *or* as allies), must be ever victorious, displaying deeds of manhood.' Similarly stanza 7. The viṭ seems to mean the Maruts in alliance with Indra (cf. p. 364) or with some mortal protégé (cf. vii.56.23, i.64.13).

5. Lit. 'As to going, the best-going; most adorning themselves with adornment; united with beauty; terrible with strength.' Their abundant ornaments are much spoken of (e.g. v.54.11). Note the radical connection of ójas and ugrá.

6. 'Terrible is your strength; steadfast your power; therefore (ádhā) is a troop, with the Maruts (as allies), mighty.'

7. **krúdhmī**, nom. n. pl., 340. — Pronounce **múnīva** (cf. 73²N.) or **múnir ́iva**. — 'Clear is your whistling. Your hearts are wrathful as the wild onward-rush of a doughty troop.' Otherwise Bergaigne, *Mélanges Renier*, p. 85.

8. **yuyóta**: irreg. impv. (654) of √2yu; accented, as standing at the beg. of a pāda (see above). — **práṇan naḥ**, u.f. **prá-nak** (192a, 161) **nas**: **nak**, for **nak-t**, √2naç, 833, 218³; augmentless aor. as subjunct., w. **mā́**.

9. Classic, **priyā́ṇi nā́māni** (425d). — **huve**: we should expect **huvé**. — U.f. **ā́ yád tṛpán** (3d pl., 848 end: **pada-pāṭha** wrongly **tṛpát**). — See **yád**3 and √vaç2. — We have here an unsyncopated verse — see above. Grassmann emends. — 'I invoke the dear names of you the mighty, in order that they (among you) who desire (our praise) may be gladdened, O Maruts.'

SELECTION XLIII. RV. vii. 86. To Varuṇa. — Respecting Varuṇa, see vocab. and cf. p. 367. The hymn is rendered by GKR., p. 6. The comments of Ludwig, vol.iv.p.88, deserve careful attention.

— The poet is ill and deems his sickness a punishment sent by Varuṇa for some sin. He acknowledges the wisdom of the majestic god; but ventures to approach him with confession of sin and prayer for forgiveness and renewed self-consecration to the divine service. Compare Kaegi, p. 66(92).

10–11. **dhī́rā** = **dhī́rāṇi**. — See **tú**2. — **mahinā́**, poss. like colloquial Eng. 'mightily, *i.e.* very.' — **urv-ī́**, acc.du.f. — **paprā́that**, classed doubtfully as an augmentless reduplicated aor., 869³. — Note how the accent or the lack of accent of the verb-forms affects the exegesis.

— 'Wise in sooth is his nature (with might =) and mighty [? *or* Stable in sooth are the creatures by his might], who propped asunder the two wide worlds, even. He set the great lofty firmament in motion, the stars (*collectively*) for ever [*or* the stars as well, *cf.* 75¹N.]; and he stretched out the earth.' — Biblical parallels, Kaegi, p. 62(86).

12–13. Accent-marks, Whitney, 90b²: **tanúā sám · · nú antár**. — **bhuvāni**, 836¹·³. — See **kím**3. — **abhí khyam**, 847 middle.

— 'And with my (**sváyā**) self I say this (take counsel thus), "When pray am I to be in Varuṇa's presence?" *etc.*'

14. **tád énas**, τὸ ἁμάρτημα, 'the (admitted) sin.' — U.f. **didṛ́kṣu | úpa u emi** — see **u**2 end. Ludwig takes **didṛ́k-ṣu** as loc.pl.m. of **didṛ́ç**, 'seer.' Thus case-form, stem-form (see 1147b), and construction (cf. German *bei Jemand anfragen*) are entirely regular. Others take **didṛ́kṣūpa** for **didṛ́kṣus úpa** (nom.s.m. with elision and crasis, cf. 78¹⁷N.); but the acct is wrong — see vocab.

— 'And unto the wise (√cit, 787, 802) I go to find out by inquiry' (√prach+vi, 970a, 981³).

15. **kaváyaç cid** — not my conscience only. — U.f. **āhus**, 801a. — √2hṛ.

16. 'What was, O Varuṇa, the sin most grievous (lit. principal)?' — See **yád**3. — See √han and 1028 e and f.

17. **prá vocas**, 'tell,' 848³, 847 end. — U.f. **svadhāvas | áva** (135²) **tvā anenā́s námasā turás iyām** (616³). Pronounce, with elision and combination, **turéyām**.

18–19. See √sṛj+ava 3 and 2. — Note prolongations of finals in **sṛjā**, **sṛjā́**, and **cakṛmā́**. — With the second **áva**, supply **sṛja tā́ni**: **yā́** = **yā́ni**. — Pronounce **dā́mano** (425f end), abl. — **Vasiṣṭha**, the seer to whose family all the hymns of this seventh book are ascribed.

20. 'It was not my own will, it was infatuation · ·.' Note how the pronouns conform in gender with the predicates. — 'Liquor, dice' — ancient and perennial sources of crime: cf. Tacitus, *Germania*, xxiv.

NOTES TO PAGE 79.

1. 'The older is in the transgression of the younger. Not even (**caná** 1) sleep itself

(id) excludes wrong.' I, Vasiṣṭha, have not entirely overcome the sins of my youth. Thoughts of malice or impurity trouble even my sleep. — Interpretation doubtful.

2-3. **áram** (not **arám**) **karāṇi**, 'I will serve,' root-aor. subjunctive (836[1]) of √1 kṛ. — **ánāgās**, now that my sin has been, as I hope, forgiven. —'Made the unknowing to know.' —'The wise (man) unto wealth the still wiser (god) doth speed' (√jū).

4-5. **ayám · · stómas**, referring *back* to the hymn just ending — see **idám**. — See √çri+upa. — See **kṣéma2**. — See **u 1** end. — 'Ye gods, O keep us evermore with blessings' — refrain of the Vasiṣṭha-hymns; see Kaegi, note 83c, and Ludwig, iii.129.

SELECTION XLIV. RV. vii. 88. To Varuṇa. — Translated by GKR., p. 10. Like enough stanza 7 is a later addition.

— The poet, forsaken by Varuṇa on account of some sin, calls sadly to mind the by-gone days when he walked so happily with the god, and also the scene when, gliding over the waters with the god of the waters, he received the sacred appointment of Rishi. He asks forgiveness and restoration to divine favor. See Kaegi, p. 68(94). — It is not unnatural that Vasiṣṭha should address himself (cf. Ps. ciii.1) or speak of himself as a third person.

6-7. Pronounce **práy-iṣṭham** and cf. 470[3]. — **īm**, enclitic pron., with which **vṛ́ṣaṇam** is in epexegetical apposition — cf. 70[5]N. — **kárate**, root-aor. subjunctive, 836. — See **vṛ́ṣan3**, and cf. the Hebrew conception of the sun that "rejoiceth as a *strong man* to run a race," Ps. xix.5.

8. **manśi**, √man2, *s*-aor. mid. 1st pers. s., 882. — 'So now, having come (805) to the sight of him, as Agni's face I deem Varuṇa's.' When I contemplate Varuṇa, his face seems to me like blazing fire.

9. **áçmann**, 210, 425c. — **abhí · · ninīyāt** (accentless), put doubtfully as a *present* opt. of the reduplicating class, 651. — 'The light which in heaven [is], and the dark, let the lord unto me bring, a wonder to see.' The beauty of the heaven by night no less than by day was a wonder.

10. **ā́ · · ruhā́va** implies the subject **āvám**, i.e. (**ahám**) **váruṇaç ca**: see 76[17]N. At KZ. xxiii.308 is adduced the AS. parallel, *vit Scilling song āhōfon*, 'we two, Scilling (and I) raised a song.' — See √īr+pra. — See **mádhya3**.

11. **ádhi apā́m snúbhis**, 'ἐπ' (εὐρέα) νῶτα θαλάσσης:' pronounce **sā́nubhis**. — U.f. **preñkhé**. — **prá · · īñkhayāvahāi** (1043.2) is apodosis, as the accent shows. — See **1 çúbh** and **kám**.

12. U.f. **nāví ā́‿adhāt** (829). — Pronounce **su-ápā(s)**.

13. **sudinatvé áhnām** (430a): cf. εἴποτε εὐημερίας ἡμέραν ἐπιτελοίη, 'if ever he makes a *jolly day* of it,' Alkiphron's *Letters*, i.21. — U.f. **yā́t** (see this) **nú dyā́vas** (361d) **tatánan** (810a), **yā́t uṣā́sas** (**tatánan**). Cf. Psalm lxxii.5,7,17.

14. Pronounce **kúa tyā́ni nāu sakhiā́** and see **kvà**. — **sácāvahe**: tense, see 778a; depends on **yád**. — See **yád3**. — Muir compares Psalm lxxxix.49.

15. **jagamā** (248c, 793b), 'I had access to:' we *might* expect **jagámā**, accented, and so co-ordinate with **sác-**. — V's golden house is built (AV. vii.83.1) on the waters:

> **apsú te rājan varuṇa**
> **gṛhó hiraṇyáyo mitáḥ.**

16-17. See explanation under **yá7**. — Pronounce **tuám**. — **kṛṇávat**, 715, 70C. — 'Doeth sins against thee.' — **sákhā te**, '(he is yet) thy friend,' as apodosis to the concessively taken **yás kṛṇávat**. So Ludwig. — See √2bhuj5. — U.f. **yandhí** (617, 212) **sma** (188a, 248a) **vípras** (see 74[12]N.) **stuvaté** (619).

18-19. GKR. transpose pādas *b* and *c*. — **tvāsú**: u.f., as given rightly by the padapāṭha, **tvā** (object of **vanvānās**) **āsú** (loc. pl. fem. 501). 'In these fixed *or* secure dwellings dwelling, thee we (are) beseeching (√van, 713, 705) for grace from the lap of Aditi.' — **ví · · mumocat**, 809, 810a. — Refrain as before, 79[5]N.

NOTES TO PAGE 80.

SELECTION XLV. RV. vii. 89. To Varuṇa. — The hymn has been often translated:

so by Müller, ASL. p. 540; Muir, v.67; GKR. p. 12; Hillebrandt, *Varuṇa und Mitra*, p. 64; Bergaigne, *Religion Védique*, iii.155.

— It is the prayer of a man who is **varuṇa-gṛhīta**, 'seized by Varuṇa, i.e. afflicted with the dropsy.' V. is god of the waters (cf. 7[10]N., 79[15]N.), and the disease is supposed to come from him and as a punishment for sin: see AV. iv.16.7; also AB. vii.15, **atha ha‿āikṣvākaṁ varuṇo jagrāha; tasya ha‿udaraṁ jajñe**; and ÇB. ii.5.2[2]. Cf. Hillebrandt, p. 63–65, 54. Ludwig's interpretation is quite different: see his notes, vol. iv. p. 91.

1–2. **mó**, see u2. — **ṣú**, 188a. — **gṛhám**, Kaegi, note 329: cf. also the AS. poem in Thorpe's *Analecta*, p. 142, entitled *The Grave*, and familiar through Longfellow's translation. — **gamam**, 833, 835: with **mā́**, 579. — **mṛlā́**, 248c, √**mṛḍ**.

3–4. 'When I go, tottering along, like a bag, puffed up, — have mercy.' — √**sphur** implies quick or vigorous motion — see vocab. Here the **iva** is not a particle of comparison; it modifies the mg of the root to that of a languid shake or wabble such as is characteristic of a dropsical person. So **pra-hasan**, 'laughing out;' **pra-hasann iva**, 'smiling.'

— **dhmātás**, 'puffed up' (with wind) or 'bloated' (with serum), has reference not only to the bag, but also to the understood **ahám**. Grassmann, 'schnaufend,' i.e. 'blown, winded, puffing.' Otherwise Bergaigne, iii. 155N. — **adrivas** (454b), always of Indra, except here, and at ix.53.1 (of Soma)! — On this stanza the exegetes differ much.

5–6. **krátvas**, gen., 342. — **dīnátā**, 365.1. — **jagamā**, 79[15]N.

7–8. Line 7 has trochaic cadences. — 'On (me, thy) singer, (though) standing (803) in the midst of water, thirst has got hold' (**avidat**, √2**vid**2). See Horace's description, Odes, ii.2, *Crescit indulgens*, etc.

9–10. See **yád**5. — See 2**idám**. — See **jána**: for loc., 303a. — **dhármā**, 425d. — **yuyopimá**, 793e. — See √**riṣ**: caus. aorist, 1046, 859; augmentless form as subjunctive w. **mā́**, 579.

— 'If we mortals do anything (**kíṁ ca**, neut.) here (that proves to be) an offense (masc.) against the gods, if with folly thy steadfast decrees we have thwarted, do not (cause us to take harm from this sin =) chastise us for this sin.'

— Metre, **jagatī**. This stanza is not a part of the hymn. The stanza is an oft-recurring one — Schroeder, MS. iv. p. 290. Its repetition daily for a year is prescribed at Manu xi.253: cf. Rigvidhāna, ii.29.1. The interesting stanza at RV. iv.54.3 = TS. iv.1.11[1] is probably a reminiscence of this. The AV., at vi.51.3, modernizes **ácittī** (340) **yád** to **ácittyā céd**.

Selection XLVI. RV. viii. 14. To Indra. — Indra and Namuci. — For the introduction to the Namuci-myth, see 81[16]N. For the later forms of the myth, see selection lxxii., p. 97[6]N.

— Division into five strophes of three stanzas is possible. In respect of contents, the first three stanzas and the last three make very good strophes. Stanzas 1, 2, and 3 form a strophe at SV. ii.1184–6; but 5, 7, and 8 form another at 989–91. The hymn is unsymmetrically divided into three at AV. xx.27–29.

11–12. **íçīya**: form, 616; acct, 628; mode, 581b, note the second example. Similar idea at 87[20]f, and often in RV., e.g. viii.19.25,26. — **vásvas**, gen. 342.

13–14. See √**çak** B2 and 1030. — **dítseyam**, 1030; accented at beg. of clause, though not at beg. of pāda, 593[2]. — Note the old mg of **çácī-páti** (vocab.), whence was evolved the later 'Mrs. Might' (see **çácī**).

15–16. U.f. **dhenús te**, 188b: similar combinations at 87[19], 84[15]. — **sūnṛ́tā**, cf. 28[1Cb]N. — **sunvaté**, √1**su**, 705; acct, 318. — 'Kine and horses,' see under **gó** 1. — **pi-py-úṣ-ī**, √**pī**, 802 end, 459. — **duhe**, 613, and 70[18]N.

17–18. 'Nor god nor mortal is a restrainer of thy blessing, when . .'

19. U.f. **yád** ('when') **bhúmim vi-avartayat**: cf. "He taketh up the isles as a very little thing," Isaiah xl.15; also 12.

Notes to Page 81.

1. **cakrāṇás**, √1**kṛ**8, and 807. 'Putting his plume in the heaven = touching the heaven with his plume.' Just so, RV. x. 125.7[d].

2-3. See √vṛdh3 and 807[2]. —ji-gy-úṣ-as (787 —strong stem ji-gī-vā́ṅs) goes also with te. —U.f. indra ā́ vṛṇīmahe (718).

4-5. U.f. ví antárikṣam (Whitney, 90b[2]) atirat (√tṛ). —ábhinat, √bhid, 692. — valám, cf. Indra's epithet, 5[17].

6-7. U.f. úd gā́s (361c) ājat (√aj). — āvíṣ-kṛṇván, 187, 1078.

8-9. dṛḷhā́ni dṛṅhitā́ni ca, '(were) made stable and (were) established,' both from √dṛh. —parā-ṇúde: form of inf., 192a, 970a: use of inf., 982c. — 'Steady, not for thrusting away = so steadfast they may not be moved.' Cf. Ps. xciii.1 or 2; xcvi.10.

10-11. See under √mad 1. —See √rāj+vi and 902.

12-13. Pronounce tuám. —U.f. índra‿ási: acct, 595d. — stotṝṇā́m (acct, 372), objective gen. w. bhadrakṛ́t, which has noun construction rather than verbal.

14-15. U.f. indrám íd keçínā (441). — vakṣatas, 'let them bring,' 893[2]. — See úpa2. —surā́dhasam might be joined with either índram or yajñā́m.

16-17. Namuci-myth. 'With foam of the waters, Namuci's head, O Indra, thou didst cause to fly asunder, when thou wast conquering all thy foes.' It appears to me likely that the natural phenomenon to which this refers is a water-spout ('Trombe') on an inland lake. This fear-inspiring thing may well be personified as a demon. The verb úd avartayas means 'didst cause to move out or fly asunder with a gyratory or centrifugal motion.' This accords well with the facts of the not infrequent phenomenon as seen by unscientific eyes. See Major Sherwill on Bengal waterspouts, JASB. 1860, xxix.366f, with good pictures, and Th. Reye, *Die Wirbelstürme*[2], p. 17f. The line MBh. v.10.37 = 328 seems to favor my view. The whole passage is a reminiscence of the Namuci-myth.

The head of the column is twisted and made to burst asunder and scatter itself (phénena, instr. of accompaniment, lit. 'with foam,' i.e.) in abundant foamy masses. Then, with the dispersion of the column, often comes (Sherwill, 370; Reye, 32) a heavy rain. All this is set forth as gracious Indra's prowess. —U.f. ájayas spṛ́dhas, see 74[12]N.

Bergaigne's discussion, ii.346-7, may be compared and also RV. v.30.7,8 and vi.20.6. —The form of the myth as it appears in the Brāhmaṇas originates in a misconception of the case-relation of phénena (see above), which they take as an instr. of means, i.e. as the weapon by means of which Indra slew Namuci. So Sāyaṇa: phenena vajrībhūtena; see vocab., √sic3. Cf. notes to selection lxxii., p. 97.

18-19. ut-sísṛpsatas (√sṛp) and ā-rúrukṣatas (√ruh), acc.pl.m. of ppl., 1027, 1029. —dyā́m, 361d. — dásyūn̐r, u.f. dásyūn, prop. dásyūṅs, see 209 and b and 338[2]. — See √dhū+ava and 706. — Cf. the legend at Odyssey xi.305-20, and see Eggeling, SBE. xii.286.

20-21. víṣūcīm (408), 'so that it was parted asunder *or* scattered,' as factitive predicate of ví-anāçayas (√1 naç). —See úttara 1. 'Becoming victorious (after *or* as result of) quaffing the Soma.'

Notes to Page 82.

Selection XLVII. RV. viii. 85. 7, 8, 9. Indra and the Maruts, and Vṛtra. —For the corresponding Brāhmaṇa legend, see selection lxvii., p. 94[4]. Cf. also Muir, v.93.

—All three stanzas are addressed to Indra; and might be put in the mouth of the Maruts, were it not for havíṣā, st. 8[d]. If, on the other hand, they are put in the mouth of the worshippers, then úpa ā́‿imas cannot serve as verb to marútas nor govern tvā of st. 8[a]. I therefore suspect that either pāda *b* or *d* of stanza 8 is a foreign intrusion. If it is the former, the original may have contained ánu yanti or the like.

1. See √iṣ. —víçve devā́s, other than the Maruts; for here, presumably, they are not included among the friends who desert Indra; and the Brāhmaṇa says expressly that they do not desert. But at RV. viii.7.31 the contrary is affirmed; cf. p. 364. —ajahus, √2hā (661, 657): its object is tvā.

2. Explanation under átha2. Similarly átha is used after an impv. implying a condition (572^2), at 96^{17}, 97^{10}. —jayāsi, 736. —Half-line, cf. 88^{15}.

3–4. Numerical construction, 486b. — vāvṛdhānā́s (807^2), 'growing strong, rejoicing in strength.' —úpa tvémaḥ (acct!) u.f. úpa tvā ā́‿imas (127, end). —kṛdhí, 839. — 'Thy impetuosity = thee, the impetuous.' —enā́, 502^2.

— 'Thrice sixty Maruts, in their strength rejoicing, (do follow?) thee, like hosts of morning, reverend. Unto thee come we. Grant thou us a blessing.' Etc.

5–6. ā́yudham and ánīkam are best made co-ordinate with vájram. —See ásura2.

SELECTION XLVIII. RV. viii.91. To Agni. — Stanzas 7,8,9 and 13,14,15 form strophes in the SV. The rest of the hymn (16–22), after rejection of one stanza, forms two strophes: 16,17,18 may be safely grouped together; and of the remaining four, I have followed Grassmann in rejecting st. 21, on account of the contents and language. Moreover, the tense of īdhe is proper to a final stanza — cf. Delbrück, *Tempuslehre*, p. 106–7. On the other hand, it must be admitted that stanzas 20 and 21 occur in juxtaposition at MS. ii.7.7, TS. iv.1.10^1, VS. xi.73–4, and elsewhere.

7–8. Four explanations of dhītí. 1. Grassmann, for diti, q.v.; instances of the confusion of dhi and di are adduced. 2. Ludwig, 'durch die künstlichen mittel des ghṛta,' see 2dhītí. 3. Sāyaṇa takes it from √dhā, 'put,' and renders by nidhānāis, 'with the deposits' of ghee. 4. Best taken as 'draughts,' √dhā, 'drink,' see 1 dhītí and reference, and cf. RV. x.115.1.

—tepānā́s, 794e, 807. —vakṣi, √vah, 624: so yákṣi (√yaj); accented, 593^2 middle, cf. 76^{12}, 77^{10}, 78^{11}, 80^{13}, etc.

9–10. táṁ tvā: see examples under tá2. Sāyaṇa renders tám by prasiddham, 'illum;' similarly tā́s, at 83^1, he glosses by tādṛçyas. —ajananta (a-class and mid.!), classic ajanayan. —See mātṛ́: cf. RV. iii.29.1–3.

11–12. Pronounce tuā. —ní ṣedire (185), see √sad+ni2; subject, 'men.' Cf. 88^{17}.

13–14. Pronounce ásti (595d) ághniā. —Perhaps, 'There is no ax (with me) desiring (it), i.e. I have no ax by me, = own none.' —See etādṛ́ç.

—I have no cow from whose milk I might make ghee for an oblation, nor an ax to cut sticks for the sacrificial fire. So I offer thee such as I have, i.e. gathered bits of wood. — 'One should sacrifice, if only a bit of wood,' says tradition: cf. the widow's mites; and see ASL. p.204 and Bhagavad-gītā, ix.26.

15–16. VS., kā́ni kā́ni cid; MS. and TS., yā́ni kā́ni ca; AV., yā́ni kā́ni cid; see 1 ka2d. —√dhā+ā2; ending, 548. —Pronounce yaviṣṭhia: the anomalous ending is solely for the sake of the metre, since yaviṣṭha makes just as good a catalectic diiambus as yaviṣṭhya. 'Youngest,' for he starts into life anew every day.

—In old times Agni would not devour fuel that was not ax-hewn. The Rishi Prayoga, who was too poor to own an ax and had to pick up his wood, made it toothsome for Agni with this stanza, yád agne yā́ni kā́ni ca. So TS. v.1.10^1.

—Note how the other texts make 20 and 21 into two anuṣṭubh stanzas by inserting 21^c in the one and adding 20^c to the other.

17–18. See √idh or indh. —See mánas 1. —idhe, 'I have enkindled,' tense, see above. Perfect used to state a thing to some one who has just seen it transpire.

NOTES TO PAGE 83.

SELECTION XLIX. RV. x.9.1–3. To the Waters. — Rubricated at 105^{21}, funeral service. This hymn in the RV. has nine stanzas; but the first three form a strophe which recurs very often in other texts: so TS., thrice; MS. and VS., twice; K., SV., AV., and TA.

—The Gṛhya-sūtras prescribe the use of this strophe, with the pouring or sprinkling of water, at the wedding-ceremony, ÇGS. i.14, in the choosing of a house-site, AGS. ii.8.12, in the consecration of a new dwelling, ib. ii.9.8, and in certain funeral rites, ib. iv.6. 14 = 105^{21}. Indeed, so frequent is their use that they have a name and are called the "three āpohiṣṭhiya stanzas" — cf. 1215a. The modern Hindus use them daily in their mārjana, see Monier-Williams, as cited at p. 366.

1-2. ṣṭhā, u.f. stha, 188a, 248c. —tā́s, see 829N. —√1 dhā2 and 669. —cákṣase, √cakṣ, 970c. —Lit. 'Bring us to vigor, to great gladness, to behold:' attraction, 982a.

3-4. See √bhaj, caus. —uçatís, fem. ppl., √vaç.

5-6. U.f. tásmāi, the master of the new dwelling. —gamāma, 848[3]. —janáyathā (248c), 'produce, i.e. bring:' for aught the accent shows, it may be co-ordinate with jínvatha (595) or also not (see 594a).

—'For him may we satisfy you, to whose dwelling ye hasten, Waters, and bring us'—whatever that may mean. It seems to have pertinence only as said by officiating priests in performing the above-mentioned consecration.

SELECTION L. RV. x.14.1-2, and 7-12. Funeral-hymn.—Rubricated at 102[1,21], 103[12]—see p. 402. See Whitney's essay, On the Vedic doctrine of a future life, OLSt. i.46-63 (= *Bibliotheca Sacra*, 1859, xvi.404f); also Zimmer, p. 408-22. On immortality as an Indo-European belief, see Kaegi, N. 265 and literature there cited, and N. 283a. On the funeral rites, see introduction to selection lxxv. and literature there cited. Translations of this hymn: Muir, v.292; GKR. p. 146; and Whitney, l.c., p. 58.

—Although maṇḍala x. on the whole is late, it yet contains antique passages; and among these the following seems to belong: so Roth. The hymn contains 16 stanzas, of which 13-16 are palpably later additions. Only 7-12 are actually prescribed by Āçvalāyana for use in the funeral service; but 1 and 2, although not rubricated, are given for their intrinsic interest.

—The passage as it stands consists of an introductory summons to the assembled mourners (1-2); and of an address to the departed (7-8); then, after bidding the mourners disperse (stanza 9), the spokesman implores the favor of the kindly-disposed hounds of Yama, for the departed (11) and for the company (12).

—In stanza 10, on the other hand, these hounds are conceived as ill-disposed creatures standing guard to keep the departed out of bliss—see p. 370; and possibly the stanza which originally belonged with 9 has been displaced by the one in our text. Or is stanza 9 itself the intruder? See Bezzenberger's *Beiträge*, viii.202.

—The stanzas of RV. x.14 recur elsewhere, with more or less interesting variants. Those in the Reader correspond respectively with AV. xviii.1.49,50,54; 3.58; 1.55; 2.11, 12,13. Compare also MS. iv.14.16; ii.7.11; TA. vi.1.1; 4.2; 6.1; 3.1,2. For st. 9, see note thereto, 83[15].

7-8. parā‿iyiváṅsam, √i, 803, 783b[2]. —'Along after (ánu) i.e. unto the mighty heights,' i.e. to the other world. —anupaspaçānám, √1 paç, 807. —vāivasvatám, cf. 85[13]N. So also in the Avesta, Yima is V's son. —'Gatherer of the peoples;' precisely so in the Avesta, Vd. ii.21, Yima makes a gathering (hañjamanem) of mortals. Cf. Ἅιδης ἀγησίλαος, Preller, *Gr. Myth.*[3] i.660, Kaegi, N. 276. —Note that Yama is a king, and not, like Varuṇa (line 12), a god.

—Yama is the first mortal (see yamá in vocab.); the first to reach the other world (AV. xviii.3.13); the leader of the endless train of them that follow him; and so the king of the blessed (see yamá-rājan). The comparison of Yama with the Avestan Yima is very interesting: see Roth, *die Sage von Dschemschid*, ZDMG. iv.417-431; and SBE. iv.p.lxxv., and p.10-21.

—We read at AV. xviii.4.7,

tīrthāís taranti pravā́to mahī́r íti,
By passes pass they to the mighty heights, 'tis said.

This is most interesting as a reminiscence of the same traditional material of which RV. x.14.1 is another outgrowth.

9-10. 'Yamus nobis perfugium primus repperit:' gātúm, q.v., pregnantly, like τόπον at John xiv.2. —eṣā́ gávyūtis, i.e. the gātú, just mentioned. —ápa-bhartavā́ u: the pada-pāṭha reads -tavā́í u (133); form of inf., 972[2]; use of inf., 982c. —For the thought, see an Avestan parallel, Kaegi, N. 270. —yátrā, 248a. —parā‿iyús, 783b[2].

—jajñānás, √jan2, 807, '(their) children,' sc. párā yanti.

11–12. prá‿ihi, 617, see vocab. —The AV. modernizes the forms a little, reading rā́jānāu, mádantāu. —paçyāsi, subjunctive (760.2), w. future mg, as in Homer. —Note the appropriate connection of this stanza with st. 2 and observe the identical pādas.

13–14. The derivation and mg of iṣṭā-pūrtá are discussed most carefully by Windisch, *Festgruss an Böhtlingk*, 1888, p. 115f. —hitvā́ya, √2hā, 993b. —púnar ástam ā́‿ihi, 'Go back home,' as if the soul had come from heaven. Illustrative material in Kaegi, n. 275. Cf. *zu Gott heimkehren* = 'die.' —Pāda *d* is metrically defective: te tanúā, 'with thy (new) body,' is suggested, Kaegi, n. 278, which see; te tanúā suvárcasā is suggested by Sāyaṇa's comment. Cf. the Christian conceptions at Philippians iii.21, I. Cor. xv.40f.

15–16. U.f. ápa‿ita, ví‿ita, ví ca sarpata‿átas. asmāí (accent, 74[9]n.) etám · · áhobhis adbhís · · ví-aktam (√añj). —vī̀ta, acct, 128 end; so vī̀va, 77[5]n. —akran, 831. —Second asmāi, accentless, cf. 74[9]n.

—Pāda *c*. '(A place of rest) adorned with days, with waters, with nights:' i.e. where the delights of earth are found again, the change of day and night, cooling waters, etc. Note the especial mention of waters in the enumeration of the joys of heaven at RV. ix.113.7f, and in the description of the 'Assembly-hall' of Yama Vāivasvata, MBh. ii.8.7 = 317. And observe how very frequent are the allusions to the waters in the mentions of Paradise in the Koran, e.g. xlvii. 10–20; lxxvi.5; xiii.35.

—This pāda at best is bad. It is avoided by the noteworthy, but not very helpful, variants of the Yajurveda. VS. xii.45 reads

> ápeta vī̀ta ví ca sarpatáto
> yé átra sthá purāṇā́ yé ca nū́tanāḥ.
> ádād yamó avasā́nam pṛthivyā́
> ákrann imám pitáro lokám asmāi,

and substantially so read MS., TS., TB. The scholiast to VS. takes this as an address to 'Yama's men.' It *is* a little forced to refer it to the mourners.

17–18. In *this* stanza, these dogs, the offspring of Saramā, are ill-disposed (durvidátra) — see introduction. —Pronounce çuā́nāu. —'Four-eyed:' later this is taken to mean 'with two eyes and two round spots above the eyes.' Note the Parsi custom of having such a dog (cf. Vd. viii.16) view the corpse before exposure — Monier-Williams, *Mod. India*, 173–6, ed. 1878.

—Respecting Saramā, see Kaegi, n. 149. Respecting the dogs, see ib., n. 274, 274a, and Muir, v.294. Homer mentions the 'dog of Hades,' Od. xi.623f, Il. viii.368. Not till later is he called 'many-headed' and Κέρβερος. With Κέρβερος is identified çabála — see Benfey, *Göttingische Nachrichten*, 1877, p. 8f = *Vedica*, i.149f. In Avestan belief (Vd. xiii.9), dogs guard the entrance of the other world. These beliefs are compared, SBE. iv.p.lxxxvii.

19. In this stanza and the following, the dogs are kindly creatures.

Notes to Page 84.

1. Pronounce tā́bhiām. —Verbs, 668.

2–3. U.f. asutṛ́pāu: admits several explanations — see vocab., and Bergaigne, iii. 72. —These messengers go about to conduct to the other world those who have received the summons of Yama. —sū́ryāya, attraction, explained at 982a. —U.f. púnar dātām (839) ásum adyá‿ihá: 'may the two give back again —,' for the mourners have been in the shadow of death.

Selection LI. RV. x. 16. Funeral-hymn, used at the ceremony of cremation. — Rubricated are only stanzas 1–9 and 14 — see p. 402. The rubricated stanzas are translated by Max Müller, ZDMG. ix.p.viiif, and the whole hymn by Zimmer, p. 402. Most of the stanzas are addressed to Agni; but 3, 6, and 7, to the dead man. The hymn has two parts, clearly sundered by the metre.

—In the first, Agni is to burn the corpse, not rudely, but gently, just enough to "make it done." To this end, a sacrificial goat (st. 4) is provided, and (st. 7) the corpse is covered with a caul, in order that Agni may spend his fury on these things and spare the corpse from too severe a burning. The original purpose of this custom may have been different. The Greeks had the custom — see Il. xxiii.165f, Od. xxiv.65f.

Moreover, Agni is to carry up the departed to the Fathers or Manes, who have their seat in the 'fore-heaven' (AV. xviii.2.48, Whitney, OLSt. i.59). Perhaps st. 8–10 did not belong originally to the first part.

—The second part consists of heterogeneous material, vagrant stanzas, having some connection, verbal or logical, real or apparent, with the words or ideas of the first.

—Every stanza of the hymn, save st. 11, appears in the AV., and some elsewhere also, and with interesting variants.

4–5. enam: the minds of all present are so exclusively upon the departed, that the first reference to him may be made by an accentless and gestureless word without unclearness. Similarly asya. —ví dahas, abhí çocas, 743, 579. The AV. reads çūçucas (869). —cikṣipas, 869, 579. —kṛṇávas, 700. —U.f. átha im enam. —prá hiṇutāt: ṇ, 192c; form, 570, 704, cf. 91[5]; mg, 571.

6–7. Pāda *d* = atha devān vaçam neṣyati, 'he shall bring the gods into his control' (cf. RV. x.84.3), i.e. 'win their favor.'

8–9. Note the combination of triṣṭubh and jagatī pādas (11, 12, 12, 11). Pronounce diám. —See dhárman. —apás, óṣadhīṣu, cf. x.58.7. —See hitá2. —çarīrāis, Sāyaṇa, 'çarīra‿avayavāis' ('members').

—For this stanza there is abundant and interesting illustrative material. See Muir, v.298,319; Kaegi, n. 275,275a. Man is a microcosm. Each element in him comes from some element in nature with which it has most affinity and thereto it returns (cf. Eurip. Suppl. 532f). These affinities are pointed out with much detail in ÇB. xiv. 6.2[13].

yatra‿asya puruṣasya mṛtasya‿ agnim vāg apyeti, vātam prāṇaç, cakṣur ādityam, manaç candram, diçaḥ çrotram, pṛthivīm çarīram, ākāçam ātmā‿, oṣadhīr lomāni, vanaspatīn keçā, apsu lohitam ca retaç ca nidhīyate, — kva‿ayam tadā puruṣo bhavati? 'In case the dead man's · · · soul goes to the ether, the hair of his body to the plants, the hair of his head to the trees, and his blood and seminal fluid in the waters are put, what then becomes of this spirit?'

Cf. the formula recited at the slaughter of the sacrificial victim, AB. ii.6.13,

> sūryam cakṣur gamayatāt,
> vātam prāṇam anvavasṛjatāt,
> antarikṣam asum,
> diçaḥ çrotram,
> pṛthivīm çarīram.

Dissolution into the five elements (see bhūta) is later the stereotyped phrase for death (see pañcatva). Cf. the four elements ἐξ ὧν συμπέπηγε τὸ σῶμα, γῆς πυρὸς ὕδατός τε καὶ ἀέρος, Plato, *Timaeus*, p. 82.

—The affinity of the eye and the sun is universally palpable: cf., for example, Plato, *Repub.* 508, ἡλιοειδέστατόν γε οἶμαι [τὸ ὄμμα] τῶν περὶ τὰς αἰσθήσεις ὀργάνων. Not less so is that of breath and wind. Bones and earth, *Timaeus*, 73e; blood and plants, ib.80e. Cf. Darmesteter, SBE. iv.187, who cites Iliad vii.99 and Empedocles, 378–82 (ed. Müllach).

10–11. 'The goat [laid limb by limb on the corpse on the fire] (is thy) portion. Burn it with burning; that let thy heat burn; that, thy flame.' — But deal gently with the dead man. —Note the emphatic position of the last two tám's. —The goat is the animal most fit for sacrifice — see the legend, AB. ii.8. Later, ajá is taken as a-já, the 'unborn' part: so Sāyaṇa; cf. Ludwig, iii.p.435–6; Pañcatantra, book iii., fable 2; MBh. xii.338.3 (= 12820) fol. 255[b]; ISt. i.428.

—Agni has 'dreadful forms' (ghorás tanúas) as well as 'kindly' ones. —See loká 2b and sukṛt. The Hindus regard u as a particle; but it may be part of a word uloká, which combination appears in old texts, and even at the head of a pāda, where u (as enclitic) could not stand.

12–13. See √hu+ā. 'Who, offered to thee, goes freely.' The corpse may have been conceived — now as yielding easily to the devourer, and now as struggling against it. Otherwise Zimmer, p. 403n.

—'Putting on life (as a garment), let him seek after offspring.' Where is to be found expressed the wish for children in the new life? It is repulsive. But that carnal intercourse was by no means excluded from the (doubtless later) ideas of heaven would appear from the material gathered by Muir, v.307–9, esp. from AV. iv.34.2 and xiv.2.32. Add AB. i.22.14, and cf. Zimmer, 413.

—After all, may not çéṣas here mean simply 'those whom we leave behind us,' viz. at the grave (see 63[17,18]), in order to continue the journey of life without them, i.e. 'those who have gone before?' These the dead man is now to rejoin.

—Pāda *d*: cf. 83[14] and n.

14–15. **kṛṣṇáḥ çakunás** is one of ill-omen. —**utá vā**: function of **utá** like that of **átha** in **átha vā**, see **atha**6. —U.f. **agnís tád** (80[15]n.) **viçva‿át**. —See **brāhmaṇá**: no necessary allusion to caste here. —If unclean creatures have done any harm to the corpse, Agni is to remove from it the traces of such imperfections, i.e. 'make it whole.' The 'soma' seems to stand for some purifying sacrifice at which it was used in conjunction with the fire.

16–17. Rubricated at 102[21]. Cutting out the caul of the **anustáraṇī**, the celebrant covers the head and face of the dead man with it, for the purpose mentioned in the introduction. —**góbhis**, see **gó**2: the caul, suet, and fat are meant. —√**vyā**+**pari**: see the orig. mg of √**vyā**. —U.f. **sám prá‿ūrṇuṣva** (712): acct, 1083–84. —See **néd** and references. —√**hṛṣ**, intens., 1012. —**vi-dhakṣyán**, √**dah**, fut. ppl. —Subjunctive form, 1068, cf. 736.

—Lit., then, 'Wind a protection (**várma**) from the fire (abl.) around thyself by means of the caul etc., i.e. envelop thyself with the caul as a protection from the fire [addressed to the dead man, although the celebrant actually does the enveloping]; cover thyself completely with suet and fat: in order that the bold one (Agni), very impatient, may not with his grip firmly clasp thee around, to devour thee.'

18–19. **ví jihvaras**, √**hvṛ**, 858[1], in form and use like **cikṣipas**, line 4. —Pāda *c*: metre faulty; read **eṣá u** or **eṣá íd**? —See √**mad**, *caus.* 2. —This stanza seems to have pertinence only as an accompaniment of the ritual (103[1]). The hymn proper may have ended with st. 7.

20. For **ṇ**, 192c. —**yamárājñas**, cf. 83[8]n.

Notes to Page 85.

1. U.f. **ihá‿evá‿ayám ítaras, jātávedās**, 'Right here is this other one, Jātavedas,' i.e. **agní havya-váhana**, as distinguished from **agní kravya-váhana**. The cremation has now proceeded far enough; so the corpse-consuming Agni is dismissed to the Manes, and the oblation-bearing Agni summoned.

2–3. This continues the thought of st. 9. In the presence of the Manes (who don't mind the heat), the dismissed Agni may burn as fiercely as he likes and drive his flames in or to the highest place. —'Him I remove *or* dismiss (√1 **hṛ**3) to the **pitṛyajñá**:' this Ludwig, v.p.423, takes to be a sacrifice to the gods conducted by the Manes; otherwise vocab. —**invāt**: form, 736; quasi-root **inv**.

4–5. The diaskeuasts have put this stanza here on account of the mention of **kravya-váhana** and the Manes. —**yákṣat**, 893[3], √**yaj**. —U.f. **prá íd u** ··. —'Both to the gods and to the Manes'—so Sāyaṇa, Mahīdhara (to VS. xix.65), and vocabulary under **á**2. But Ludwig (see transl.) says 'to the gods also, from the Manes.'

6–7. See √**vaç**. —**tvā**, the sacred fire. —**ní dhīmahi** (cf. 74[14]) and **sám idhīmahi**, 837. —'Gladly would we set thee down, gladly make burn brightly' (**sám** gives to **idh** this intensive force). The optative does not imply that they do not suit the action to the word. —'Glad, bring thou hither the glad Fathers, to the oblation (982a) to eat' (√**ad**, 970b).

8–9. '*Him* cool thou off (see √1 **vā**+**nis**), i.e. let him whom thou wast consuming cool off again.' And let the burning-place be so cool and moist that even water-plants (pādas *c d*) may grow there.

10–11. Rubricated at 104[11]. —The four words in line 10 may be either voc's s.f. or loc's s.m.n.: accent, indecisive; the **i** before **k** (1222d) favors the first view. —**sám gamas** (active!), 848[3]. —The stanza seems to be meaningless rubbish.

Selection LII. RV. x.17.1–2 and 3–6. Funeral-hymn.—Under x.17 are included divers elements: A. the fragmentary legend of the Children of the Sun (1–2); B. the funeral-hymn proper (3–6); C. a prayer to Sarasvatī (7–9); D. sundry fragments.

—A. Stanzas 1–2. This famous fragment begins a new anuvāka and has nothing to do with the funeral-hymns. It smacks of antiquity; and it has become the nucleus of later legends. Of these, the oldest is that reported by Yāska, in the Nirukta, xii.10; and the next is that of Çāunaka, in the Bṛhaddevatā, vi.33 to vii.2. Ç's version is quoted in full by Sāyaṇa, in his comment to RV. vii.72.2, in order to prove that the Rishi Vasiṣṭha was a relative (first cousin) of the Açvins. Both legends are given in the original and in translation by Muir, v.227–9; also by Kuhn, KZ. i.440–43; L. Myriantheus, *Die Açvins oder arischen Dioskuren*, Munich, 1876, p. 1–4; and in substance by Max Müller, *Lectures*, 2d series, no. xi., p. 501 Am. ed. of 1865 = 528 Eng. ed. of 1873. Late form of legend, VP., b'k iii., chap. 2.

—The verbal exegesis of the two stanzas is beset with uncertainties: see Roth, in the essay cited above (83[8]n.), ZDMG. iv.425; Grassmann, Transl., ii.p.466; Bergaigne, ii. 318; and the very suggestive discussions by Ludwig, iii.332–5 and v.391–2.

—As for their interpretation from the mythological point of view, see Roth, l.c. p.425 (reported by Müller, l.c., p.503 = 530); ISt. xiv.392f; Kuhn, l.c., p.443f; Müller, l.c., p.528 = 556, and 502 = 529; Grassmann, l.c.; Bergaigne, ii.506–7; and esp. Ludwig, iii. 332–5 and v.391–2.

12. U.f. íti_idám. — Note that pariuhyámānā is from the same root as vahatúm. —Tvaṣṭar, a god, gives the wedding; yet it takes place on the earth!

13. yamásya mātā́: proleptically; prop., she who afterwards became Y's mother.

14. kṛtví, 993b. —adadus, 668.

15. U.f. utá_açvínāu abharat yád tád ásīt | ájahāt (2hā 1) u. —dvā́ mith-, 'two pairs' (Yama, Yamī; Açvins): Yāska, 'the two (Y. and Y.) that formed a pair' ('she forsook').

"Tvaṣṭar's making a wedding for his daughter"—
At this news all the world here comes together.
Yama's mother, during her wedding,
The wife of mighty Vivasvant, vanished.

They hid away the immortal from mortals.
Making a like one, they gave her to Vivasvant.
And she bare the two Açvins when that happened,
And left two pairs behind her—Saraṇyū.

— "A braw story, but unco short." The actual text is tantalizingly fragmentary. We can hardly hope to recover the legend with any satisfactory completeness. Yāska gives it thus:

Tvaṣṭar's daughter, Saraṇyū, bare twins (Yama and Yamī) to Vivasvant. She foisted upon him another female of the same appearance (sávarṇām), and, taking on the form of a mare, fled forth. Vivasvant took on the form of a horse, followed her, and coupled with her. From that were born the two Açvins or 'Horse-men.' Of the sávarṇā was born Manu.

That is—Vivasvant, the Sun, and Saraṇyū, were the parents of Yama and Yamī (83[3], 92[14]), the first human pair. But there was a coexisting belief in Manu (see manu in vocab., and cf. SBE. xxv.p.lvii) as the father of mankind. Are not RV. x.17.1–2 the fragment of a legend which attempted to reconcile the two beliefs by fabling a sávarṇā who should give birth to Manu, so that, according to either myth, the human race are the Children of the Sun?

—Yāska *tells* more than does the text; yet we are not sure that he (to say nothing of Çāunaka) *knew* anything more than is contained in the two stanzas. We are therefore not obliged to interpret the stanzas so as to fadge with Yāska's story.

A possible rendering of line 14 is (see Ludwig): 'They disclosed (ἀπεκάλυψαν) the immortal to mortals (*dat.*). Endowing her with visible form, they gave her to V.' Lit. 'making her (to be) sá-varṇa,' i.e. (see 2 sa and 1304c) 'making her (to be) having an accompanying varṇa *or* making her (to be) endowed with external appearance.'

B. Stanzas 3–6. The funeral-hymn proper, addressed esp. to Pūṣan ψυχοπομπός, and rubricated at 103[18]. Respecting Pūṣan, see Kaegi, p. 55(77), and notes 209–12. As sun-god and heavenly herdsman, he knoweth well the ways through the heaven and the spaces, and so is a safe guide to conduct the souls of the dead to the regions of the blessed. Translation by Muir, v.173.

16-17. U.f. **tvā** (= the dead man) **itás cyāvayatu prá** (goes with **cyāv-**, 1081²) **vidvā́n.** — **pári dadat**, 650³.

18-19. **pári pāsati**, √2**pā**, 893². — See **prápatha.** — U.f. **yátra ā́sate** (628). — See **sukŕ̥t.**

20. U.f. **imā́s ā́çās.** — See √1 **vid+anu.** — **sárvās**, see 77¹¹N. — **neṣat**, √**nī**, 893³

NOTES TO PAGE 86.

2-3. **ajaniṣṭa**, 902, √**jan2**; as we say, 'he was "born and bred" there, i.e. is at home.' — 'On the distant-way of ways · · ·: on the distant-way of heaven; *etc.*' No matter how long or where the journey is, P. is at home on it.

— 'Unto the two most wonted places — both to and from, he goes, knowing the way.' The construction is faulty — and yet plain enough: **abhí sadhásthe** harmonizes with **ā́ carati**; but **párā carati** requires **sadhásthebhyas** (abl.).

SELECTION LIII. RV. x.18. Funeral-hymn. — Rubricated, all except the last stanza, in the later ritual — see p. 402. The simple ceremonies originally used are inferrible from the hymn. Very different are those of the later ritual. For illustrations of these differences, see Roth, ZDMG. viii. 471f. The hymn is given, with the concordants and variants of the AV., TB., TA., and VS., and the scholia of Sāyaṇa and Mahīdhara to the concordant passages, by Windisch, in his *Zwölf Hymnen* (see p. xviii, no. 10 of my *Brief List*).

— The hymn has been translated by Roth, ZDMG. viii.467f (reprinted by Zimmer, 404f); Max Müller, ZDMG. ix., appendix; H. H. Wilson, JRAS. xvi.201 f = *Works*, ii.270f; Whitney, *Bibliotheca Sacra*, xvi.409 = OLSt. i.46f; GKR. p. 150; Ludwig, no. 943; Grassmann, no. 844; Rājendralāla Mitra, *Indo-Aryans*, ii.122f; and most of it by Kaegi, 76(105)f. Roth, Whitney, GKR., and Kaegi give "the action" of the hymn.

— The hymn is remarkable for its intrinsic interest and beauty. And it has acquired great notoriety in connection with the discussions of Suttee (= **satī**) or Hindu widow-burning. Properly, **satī** (see **sant** 4) means a 'virtuous wife.' Improperly, but more commonly, it has come to be used of the rite of self-immolation which she practised. See the admirable article *Suttee* in Col. H. Yule's *Anglo-Indian Glossary*, with some forty pertinent extracts.

— That Suttee is an ancient custom appears from many references to it in classical authors. See Cicero, *Tusc. disp.* v.27.78; Propertius, iv.12.15; Plutarch, *Moralia*, p.499; Nicholas of Damascus, fr. 143 = frag. hist. graec., ed. Müller, iii.463; Strabo, xv.30, p. 699; 62, p. 714; and esp. the story in Diodorus Siculus, xix.33-34, according to which the rite is authenticated for 316 B.C. These passages are given in full by J. Grimm, in his masterly essay, *Ueber das Verbrennen der Leichen, Abh. der Berliner Akad.*, 1849, p. 261f = *Kleinere Schriften*, ii.298f. And Peter von Bohlen, in *Das alte Indien* (1830), i.293-302, cites a great deal of interesting pertinent literature.

— The custom was abolished by the British during the administration of Lord William Bentinck, in 1829. The story of the abolition is well told by H. H. Wilson, in his continuation of James Mill's *History of British India*, vol.iii.(= ix.),185-192. For descriptions, statistics, etc., see Parliamentary Doc's, 1821.xviii.; 1823.xvii.; 1824.xxiii.; 1825.xxiv.; and esp. the *Calcutta Review*, 1867, vol. xlvi. p.221-261. Other descriptions in *Quarterly Review*, lxxxix.257f; Shib Chunder Bose, *The Hindoos as they are*, chap. xxi.; *Das Ausland*, for 1857, p. 1057f.

— From Müller's *Essay on Comparative Mythology*, *Chips*, ii.34f, or *Selected Essays*, vol. i. (ed. of 1881), p. 333f, it would appear that the seventh stanza of our hymn had played a great rôle in Hindu history. At any rate, this idea is current, and seems traceable to the *Essay*. Here it is stated that the stanza was purposely falsified by an unscrupulous priesthood, and that a garbled version of it, reading **agnéḥ** for **ágre**, was directly responsible for the sacrifice of thousands of innocent lives. That the author is in error on these points is argued with great detail by Fitzedward Hall, JRAS. NS.iii.183–192. He shows that the misreading can be traced to Raghunandana, ca. 1500 A.D., and no further; and that Suttee was deemed to be amply justified by warrants other than those of the Vedic saṁhitā, which was by no means the ultimate appeal for the mediæval Hindu.

–In the literary discussions of Suttee, on the other hand, the stanza has indeed played a rôle. There is probably no other stanza in the Veda about which so much has been written. It was first cited, in mangled form and as sanction for Suttee, by Colebrooke, in 1794, *On the duties of a faithful Hindu widow, Asiatick Researches*, 1795, iv.209–219 = *Essays*, i.133–140. It was discussed by Wilson, in 1854, in his paper *On the supposed Vaidik authority* for Suttee, JRAS. xvi.201–14 = *Works*, ii.270-92. In answer to this, Rājā Rādhākānta Deva, in 1858, endeavored to adduce good Vedic authority for the rite, JRAS. xvii.209–17 (reprinted in Wilson's *Works*, ii.293–305). The most exhaustive treatment of the various readings of the stanza is that by Hall, l.c. Finally must be mentioned the paper read by Rājendralāla Mitra in 1870, *On the funeral ceremonies* etc., JASB. xxxix.1.241-264 (reprinted in his Introduction to the TA., p. 33–58, and with additions in his *Indo-Aryans*, ii.114–155); see esp. p. 257f (= 50f = 147f).

–The Rigveda gives no warrant for the custom. Çāunaka, in the Bṛhad-devatā, furnishes important positive evidence against it (see *Chips*, ii.37); and likewise Manu, v. 156-8(= 64[10]f, see N.). Cf. Kaegi, N.51.

–The hymn was originally used at a burial which was not preceded by cremation. The situation and action are as follows. The corpse lies on a raised place; and by it is the widow.

STANZAS 1-2. The spokesman adjures Death to remove, and to harm not the living (1); and pronounces for them absolution from impurity (2).

STANZAS 3-4. The conductor of the ceremony dwells with joy on the fact that, thanks to the efficacy of their prayers, they have not joined the company of the dead (3). Now, for the better safety of the survivors, and wishing them long life, he sets a stone near the grave as a symbolic boundary of the domain of Death, as a barrier, so that he may not pass to the space beyond or domain of the living.

STANZAS 5–6. The wish and prayer for long life is here continued.

STANZAS 7–8. The women are now summoned to make their appearance together, and, provided with ointments, 'to go up to the place,' i.e. of course, where the dead man and the widow are (7).

Here we must infer that they adorn the widow (as a sign that she is to re-enter the world of life), and that the dead man's brother (devṛ́, 'levir') then takes her hand in token of the levirate marriage.

The priest then bids her leave her lifeless spouse, and makes solemn declaration of the new relation into which she has entered (8).

STANZA 9. The bow is now taken from the dead man's hand, in order that the power and glory of which the weapon was the symbol may remain with the survivors; and a closing benediction is said for them and for the departed.

STANZAS 10-13. "And now, with gentle action and tender words, the body is committed to the earth."

4–5. √i + anu-parā. –te suás, cf. 55[18]N. –ítara, w. abl., like anya, 3[4]. –devayā́nāt, 'going *or* leading to the gods,' sc. pathás, abl. –U.f. mā́ · · rīriṣas (80[10]N.), mā́ utá. Note how utá follows the repeated portion of the second clause.

6-7. See padá3. –Discussions of √yup, Ludwig, v.514, Whitney, AJP. iii.402, Roth, *Festgruss an Böhtlingk*, 1888, p. 98-99. –āíta, 620. –See √1 dhā7. –√pyā + ā.

6ᵃ. Either 'Clogging Death's foot [by a bundle of brush (kūdī́) or a billet of wood, tied to the corpse's foot], as ye came;' or else, 'Effacing Death's foot-print' [by the same means]. I confess, I incline to the former view. But, whichever way we take padáṁ yop-, the simple symbolism amounts to the same thing. The clog is attached to the foot of the corpse, which represents Death, in order that Death may not get back or find his way back so easily to harm the living. See AV. v.19.12 (explained by Roth, l.c.) in connection with xii.2.29. Roth adduces the device of Hermes, in the Homeric Hymn to Hermes, 80-84.

8-9. U.f. ví mṛtāís (283²) ā‿avavṛtran (√vṛt+vy-ā): Whitney takes the form as a 3d pl. (550¹) impf. mid. of the redup. class, present-stem vavṛt, irreg. like cakṛ (expect vivṛt). —**ábhūt**, 'hath been,' 928. —Pāda *c* refers — not to "mirth in funeral," but rather — to a fresh start on a new stretch of life, in which, leaving the dead behind, they look for much joy.

10-11. Note radical connection of paridhím and dadhāmi. —U.f. mā́‿eṣām nú gāt áparas ('an other'). —'A hundred autumns, numerous, may they live.' Prayers like this are frequent. The love of long life is very clear in the Vedic texts as contrasted with those of the later period. We must not think of 'hundred' as just '99+1.' —See √1 dhā+antar, and note carefully the development of the mg. 'May they hide Death by a mountain, i.e. put a mountain (symbolized by the rock or paridhí) betwixt themselves and Death.' See párvata 2 and 4.

—There is much evidence that the age of a hundred years was deemed entirely normal. This appears from RV. i.89.9. Again, to a question about a funeral lustration, Pāraskara (PGS. iii.10.14,15) prescribes the use of a special answer "in case the departed was not yet a hundred years old." Weber, ISt. xvii.500. SBE. xxix. 356. The 'tenth decade of life' has a name, daçamī (see BR.). In the Jātaka (Fausböll, vol.ii.p.16), the Bodhisat says to his father, when the latter sneezes,

> O Gagga, live a hundred years,
> And twenty others added on. · ·
> Live thou a hundred autumns yet.

See also Bhartṛhari's fine stanza, āyur varṣaçataṁ nṛṇām etc., Vāirāgya-çataka, 50 Bohlen = 107 Telang. — Among Semitic peoples, the sacred age was 120 years; while the pious Egyptian prayed to Osiris that he might live to be 110. — Krall.

—Very interesting are the classical stories of Hindu longevity. Sometimes, according to Onesikritos, they capped a hundred with thirty more — Strabo, xv.34,p.701. The Uttara Kurus are said, MBh. vi.7.11 = 264, to live 1000 or 10,000 years, and to this fable is probably due the report of Megasthenes περὶ τῶν χιλιετῶν Ὑπερβορέων in Strabo, xv.57,p.711 — see McCrindle's Megasthenes, p.79N., or Lassen, IA. i².613.

—Note that years are counted, now by winters, now by autumns, and now by rainy seasons (see hima and varṣa in vocab.), and that these differences correspond in general with differences of habitat of the people. ISt. xvii.232, Zimmer, 371-2.

12-13. U.f. yáthā áhāni, yáthā ṛtávas (see 127²): pronounce yáthā́hāni · · | yáthartáva. —'As a following one deserts not the former one, i.e. as each season lacks not a successor.' —See evá 1: contrast 18¹⁸·¹⁹. —See √kḷp: 'so dispose their lives, i.e. make them move on in the same unbroken way.'

14-15. yáti ṣṭhá (188a), 'quot estis.' —**karati**, true root-aor. subjunctive, 836¹. —**jīváse**, 970c, 982. —'Attain ye to (long-life, ā́yus, i.e.) fulness of days, old age your portion making, one after another, in turn (yátamānās) all of you' (yáti ṣṭhá). Otherwise OLSt. i.53.

16-17. STANZA 7. See introduction, and Kaegi, N.328. —nā́rīs, classical nā́ryas, 365. 2. —See √viç+sam. —Pāda *d*: 'Let the wives ascend to the (raised) place (on which the corpse lies), to begin with' (ágre). — After which, they are to do their errand, see introduction to stanzas 7-8. It does not mean, 'Let them go (away from the bier) up to a sacrificial altar first, i.e. before others;' for this we should expect prathamā́s rather than ágre.

18-19. U.f. úd īrṣva (√īr) nāri · ·. —gatā́sum etám úpa çeṣe, lit. 'With this one whose life is gone liest thou.' —U.f. ā́‿ihi. —'To take the hand' is the essential preliminary of wedding — see 89⁵N. —U.f. didhiṣós táva idám. See 2idám. —**pátyus** (343b) janitvám means 'condition of being jáni of a páti;' and the whole line 19 (see bhū+abhi-sam) means simply 'Thou hast entered into the state of being wife of a spouse (who was) a hand-grasper (and is) thy suitor now.'

—Hillebrandt, at ZDMG. xl.708f, shows plainly that this stanza, RV. x.18.8, belonged originally to the ritual of the human sacrifice. Weber describes the ceremony at ZDMG. xviii.269f = *Indische Streifen*, i.65f. The king's first queen was obliged to lie with the dead victim. The situation is evident from the connection in which RV. x. 18.8 occurs at AV. xviii.3.1–4. She is bidden to rise with our stanza, úd īrṣva nāri — see Çāñkhāyana Çrāuta-sūtra, xvi.13.13.

In this light, the logical connection of pādas *a b* with pādas *c d* becomes clear. She is to forsake the corpse and "come hither" to the king.

> Rise up, woman, to the world of the living.
> Fled is the soul of him with whom thou liest. Come hither.

Quitting the embrace of hateful Death, the queen rises and approaches him who had already once taken her hand in wedlock and now stands waiting for her as a suitor once more. Upon thus resuming her proper relation of wife again, she is greeted with the words:

> To him who grasped thy hand, thy suitor now,
> As wife to husband art thou become related.

—As appears from AGS. iv.2.18 = 102[7], this stanza was at an early date appropriated for the funeral-service, where — as an accompaniment of the levirate marriage — it fits very well (didhiṣú means also 'a second husband'). Regarding leviration, see Kaegi, n.51. Its existence in Vedic times is proved by RV. x.40.2. — Compare also Deuteronomy xxv.5–10.

20. U.f. dhánus hástāt ā-dádānas (668) mṛtásya | asmé (dat., 492[2]) kṣatrā́ya etc. '(I, the spokesman,) taking from the dead man's hand the bow, for us for power ·· i.e. that ours may be the power, glory, might'—. Here the construction breaks off short, but without a jot of unclearness. —Note that the bow is left in his hand till the very last. This was their noblest and chiefest weapon: cf. RV. vi.75; the stories of Arjuna's bow, Gāṇḍiva; and Strabo, xv.66,p.717.

Notes to Page 87.

1. U.f. átra‿evá tvám ('thou,' the departed — sc. jayes); ihá ··. See átra2. The adverbs are contrasted as in εὐδαιμονέστεροί εἰσιν οἱ ἐκεῖ τῶν ἐνθάδε, Plato, *Ap.* 41c. — U.f. víçvās, cf. 74[12]n. —abhímātis, as adj., 'plotting against (us)' — cf. √man+abhi2.

2–3. Addressed to the departed. —The earth, 'a maid soft as wool to a pious man (dákṣiṇāvate) — she shall protect thee from destruction's lap.' —Pāda c has 12 syllables.

4–5. √çvañc+ud: note mg of çvañc and its concinnity with the metaphor of yuvatí. —mā́ ní bādhathās (743): compare the formulae

> sit tibi terra levis!
> ne gravis esse velis!
> tu levis ossa tegas!

etc., cited by J. Grimm, l.c., p. 193 = 214. —asmāi and enam, cf. 84[4]n. —U.f. bhūme. —√1 vṛ+abhi, 712.

6–7. mít-as, nom. pl.: cf. 486b. — gṛhā́sas: cf. 80[1] and n., and Kaegi, n.329. —Pronounce santu átra. —The like beautiful conception of committal to a place of security pervades the Eng. word *bury*, the Old High Ger. *bi-fëlan*, and Goth. *ga-filhan*.

8–9. Pronounce tuát pári: see pári. — U.f. ni-dádhat. —See u and 1122a[2]. — riṣam, 848[3]. —té 'trā, u.f. te | átra: te is accentless (135[2]) and so belongs of course to pāda *c*.

—Pāda *b*: 'And laying down this clod may I not get harm.' This seems to refer to the *glebam in os inicere* (a custom which still accompanies the "earth to earth, ashes to ashes, dust to dust" of Christian burial), and to betray the natural "uncanny feeling at having to do with a corpse." Cf. Kaegi, n.330.

—Pāda *c*. The 'pillar' or 'prop' may be a rude beam or tree, laid over the corpse so as to keep the earth from caving in on it: cf. AV. xviii.2.25,

> "Let not the tree press hard on thee,
> Nor yet the earth, the great, divine."

Sometimes the tree was hollowed out as a coffin (AV. xviii.3.70): cf. the Germanic *Todtenbaum* of sacred oak — Weinhold, *Altnordisches Leben*, 497, 491.

10-11. U.f. áhani | íṣvās · · á dadhus. 'On a fitting day me, as the plume of an arrow, have they set.' — The stanza seems to express the poet's satisfaction at having made a good hymn at the right time and place and with as good skill as a skilful horseman has. Whitney renders,

> They've set me in a fitting day,
> As one the plume sets on the shaft.
> I've caught and used the fitting word,
> As one a steed tames with the rein.

— The stanza is fully discussed, JAOS. xi. p.cxci = PAOS. May, 1884. It is interesting as illustrating the varieties of cumulative evidence that may be brought to bear on the criticism of the Veda. Thus: 1. The stanza is at the end of the hymn and out of connection. 2. It is in a different kind of metre. 3. The metre is bad of its kind. 4. The form íṣvās is bad Vedic — for íṣos; and 5. pratícīm is a late form for pratīcím. 6. The stanza is ignored by Āçvalāyana; and 7. by Sāyaṇa.

SELECTION LIV. RV. x.33.4-9. The aged priest to the young prince. — The hymn has nine stanzas. The first three have nothing to do with the rest. The rest (4-9) forms two tṛca's. This passage has more than common freshness, and also directness of connection with the life of Vedic time. The situation would seem to be somewhat as follows.

— The old priest stood well with the gods, so that the efficacy of his intercession with them was of unusually good repute. Accordingly, the foes of king Kuruçravaṇa had once tried to win the Rishi over to their side and away from his master, Kuruçravaṇa; but in vain. He had remained faithful to the royal family in whose service he long had been.

Now at last king Kuruçravaṇa has passed away, leaving Upamaçravas as his son and heir. And in presence of the young prince, the priest tells with pride and pleasure of the old times, and speaks with regret of the loss of his departed patron.

— Ludwig, iii.182, has called attention to the genealogical series of the RV. These cover oftenest, of course, only three generations, since memory, unaided by records, does not easily go further back. But for preserving that amount of genealogical tradition there was frequent need (Weber, ISt. x.78-88, esp. 82): thus, at the offering to the Manes, the priest has to address by name the father, grandfather, and great-grandfather of the sacrificer; see ÇB. ii.4.2[16] or SBE. xii.365 or OLSt. i.60: similarly at the pravara; cf. ISt. ix.322-3 or x.78-9 or Müller, ASL. 386.

In the present instance, however, we have a series of five at least. Trasadasyu is a prince of the Pūru tribe, and of the *line* of Purukutsa (he is not necessarily the latter's son — RV. vii.19.3), and is often mentioned for his generosity and for the special favors shown him by the gods. The series is

Purukutsa
⋮
Trasadasyu
⋮
Mitrātithi
|
Kuruçravaṇa
|
Upamaçravas.

Compare Bergaigne, JA. 8.vi.373-4, and Kaegi, 80(110), and N.340. The Pūrus were one of several tribes that were ultimately fused together in the famous Kurus — Oldenberg, *Buddha*, 403 = 411.

12-13. āvṛṇi: augment, 585[2]; impf. mid. (725), 1st sing. 'I, the Rishi, preferred king K.' (to his enemies); i.e. I chose to keep him as my master, in order to go out to battle with him, etc. A choice was inevitable. It would appear that priests who sacrificed for many or for a village were despised (Yājñavalkya, i.161,163, Manu, iv. 205). The purohitas marched out with their kings to battle (AGS. iii.12), as did the μάντεις, e.g. to the battle of Plataea (Hdt. ix.33,37), and for similar motives — *μεμισθωμένοι οὐκ ὀλίγου — κατὰ τὸ κέρδος.*

14-15. tisrás, 482c. — stávāi (626, 617), 'I will praise,' sc. tám, meaning Kuruçravaṇa. — sah-, sc. yajñé. — K's horses (*trīga*) still come to fetch the priest in state to the sacrifice.

16-17. yásya: K. is still meant. — ūcúṣe, 803, √vac. — 'Of whom, (namely) of U's father, the words (were) highly pleasing to (me) the intercessor, as a lovely home.' [? The text is awkward and unclear.] Time was, when king K., to offset the overtures of his enemies, had to make very persuasive offers to the priest. No false delicacy restrains the latter now from alluding to these with satisfaction in the presence of his future patron. —The mention of K. as 'father of U.' is peculiar. Somewhat analogous is the Semitic fashion: cf. *Abd-allah*, 'Gott-schalk.'

18–19. **ádhi** goes w. **ihi**, √i, q.v. —U.f. **nápāt · · pitús te** (80[15]N.). —**pitús** limits **vanditá** as a possessive (not objective) genitive. The objective gen. would be **devánām**. —**asmi**: the present does not necessarily imply that K. is still alive.

20. **yád íçīya**, cf. 80[11]N. "Had it depended on me, my maghavan K. should have lived. But —." —But for **utá**, the **vā** would have to follow **mártiānaām**—cf. **atha**6.

Notes to Page 88.

1. U.f. **íd**. —See **maghávan** 1.

2–3. See **vratá** 1. —Passage explained under **caná**2. —'Accordingly, with my yoke-fellow (K.) I have parted'—√vṛt+vi.

Selection LV. RV. x.40.10. "Wedding-stanza."—Rubricated at 100[12] and ÇGS. i. 15.2. Recurs with variants at AV. xiv.1.46. The ritual prescribes that it be recited, if, on the way from the wedding to the groom's home, the bride chance to weep. For such an occasion, its relevance lies solely in the fact that it contains the word 'weep.'

4–5. See √2mā or mī+vi: form made after the model of **nayante**. —**ánu dīdhiyus** (AV. **dīdhyus**), 786[3]. —U.f. **yé idám sameriré** (AV. correctly, **sam-īriré**), 'who have come together here:' **īriré**, perf. of primary conj. (not caus. —vocab. wrong) of √īr. —√svaj+pari, 970a.

—The import of the very obscure (if not hopelessly corrupt) stanza is possibly this. The first half tells what happens at the burial of a wife. While the rest lament aloud, the men show their sorrow for the bereaved husband by pensive silence. The second half contains reflections on the joys of wedlock, whose appositeness is clear, if we assume that they are uttered in the tone of mournful regret. [But cf. ISt. v.200.]

—'They weep for the living one (the widower). They cry aloud at the service. The men thought over the long reach (of his happy wedded life now past).

'A lovely thing for the fathers who have come together here,—a joy to husbands,—are wives to embrace.'

Selection LVI. RV. x.52. The gods install Agni as oblation-bearer.—The *motif* is akin to that of the much superior hymn x.51, given by Böhtlingk (no. 30), and also by GKR. (no. 43), who add a translation of the Brāhmaṇa form of the legend of Agni's hiding (selection lxvi.). The hymn is in dramatic form.

Stanzas 1–2. Agni asks the gods for directions concerning his service at the sacrifice (1); and, with the help of the Açvins and with everything in readiness, he proposes to resume his work (2).

Stanza 3. Some gods raise doubts as to his fitness (pādas *a b*). Others answer that he is ready whenever needed (pāda *c*).

The poet accordingly announces Agni's installation, in narrative form (pāda *d*).

Stanza 4. Agni accepts the office (pādas *a b*); and the gods bid him set about his duties (*c d*).

Stanza 5. Agni promises due performance.

Stanza 6. The poet adds a kind of *envoi* in narrative form.

6–7. **víçve devās**: see **devá** 2b; note accentual unity, 314[4] (JAOS. xi.61). —**çāstána**: acct, 594a; form, 618. —**manávāi**: √man5; form, 713, 700. —**yád** seems superfluous. —See √sad+ni.

—'Teach me (the way) in which, chosen here as **hótṛ**, I am to be minded (= what I am to have in view), when (*sic*) having taken my place. Declare to me (the way) in which your portion, the path by which your oblation, I am to bear unto you.'

8–9. U.f. **áhar-ahar**, 1260. —'Every day, O Açvins, the office of **adhvaryú** (**ádhv-**) is yours.' —U.f. **samít**, nom. s. of **samídh**. —**bhavati**, 'is on hand.' —U.f. **sá‿āhutis**.

10–11. Explained under yá3. As Yama is king of the blessed Fathers (83[8]N.), Yama's hotṛ must be competent to satisfy them at the monthly çrāddha (p. 402). —'Has he (see kám2) grasped (√2ūh+api), i.e. does he know, (that) which the gods take (see √añj +sam4, and Böhtlingk's smaller dictionary, s.v.), i.e. does he know what they like?'— Is he equal to both sets of duties?

—In pāda *c* the objections are met. Agni is born anew every day for the agnihotra (ISt. x.328), at which the gods take their food; and anew every month, when the Manes take theirs.

12–13. Pronounce máām. —See √1 dhā5. —√mluc+apa: 'hidden' in the waters—see 93[16]. —Classic, bahū́ni kṛcchrā́ṇi: see √car3. —kalp- (1043.2), 'let him—.' — Pāda *d* (=RV. x.124.1b): The victims of the animal sacrifice were five, 'man, horse, ox, sheep, goat' (see AV. xi.2.9 or ISt. xiii. 292); and its later surrogate is called 'five-fold' as containing the 'essence' of all these victims (ÇB. i.2.3[3]—see Eggeling's note). But it may be ill-judged to try to attach special significance to these numbers. 'Three' and 'seven' are of course sacred numbers.

14–15. ā́ yakṣi: see √yaj+ā; form, s-aor. mid. 1st sing., 882. At first the gods were mortal (96[3]f). —See yáthā6. —Pronounce bāhuór. —ā́ dheyām, 837[2]. —U.f. átha_imā́s: átha · · jayāti, 'then (if I do), he shall win,' cf. 82[2] and N.

16–17. See 486 for construction. '3339 gods.' —√ukṣ, 585. —ástṛṇan, 725. — U.f. asmāi | ā́t íd hótāram.

NOTES TO PAGE 89.

SELECTION LVII. RV. x.53.6 and 8. Burial and wedding-stanzas.—Rubricated as burial stanzas at 105[9] and 105[18]. The eighth is also used (100[11]) as a wedding-stanza, in case the bride has to embark and disembark on her wedding-journey. See also AB. iii. 38. Interesting variants of the stanza and reminiscences of its traditional material at AV. xii.2.26,27,28[a].

1. tanván (705), see √tan4. The metaphor is frequent. —rájasas appears to be abl. and to refer backwards as well as forwards, i.e. to tanván as well as to ánv-ihi. —Note that rakṣa and Eng. *keep* coincide in having the mgs 'guard' and (as here) 'not quit.'

2. vayata, see √2vā. —See jógū and 352. —mánu, here as the typical originator of prayer, praise, and sacrifice—see vocab., and cf. ÇB. i.5.1[7], manur ha vā agre yajñena_īje; tad anukṛtya_imāḥ prajā yajante. —Note again that janáyā and Eng. *produce* coincide in having the mgs 'generate' and (as here—cf. i.31.17, ā́ vahā dāíviaṁ jánam, and 82[8]) 'fetch along *or* bring to view.'

—STANZA 6 is really a prayer to Agni and his flames to help in the work of devotion. As the immortal messenger (see Muir, v.201) between men and gods, he is to go from earth, traverse the atmosphere (see rájas in vocab.), and pursue his way to the gods through the súar. Here he is to keep to the paths (cf. TS. v.7.7) which are made by the prayers and oblations that go up to the gods,—the devayā́nās or 'god-paths,' as the AB. at iii.38 calls them, on which the gods descend to man. Pāda *c*, continuing the metaphor of *a*, is addressed to Agni's flames; and *d*, to Agni.

Stretching devotion's weft from gloom to light go on.
Keep to the radiant pathways which our prayers have made.
Without a blemish weave ye now the singers' work.
Be Manu thou. Bring to our sight the heavenly race.

3–4. 'It (sc. nadī) flows stony,' the logical predicate being áçmanvatī—cf. ῥέουσι μεγάλοι, Hdt. ii.25; cum flueret lutulentus, Horace, *Sat.* i.4.11. Others, not so well, make áçm- a proper name (die Stein-ach), or refer it to the stream from the press-stones, i.e. the Soma. —Note that √tṛ has special reference to *water*: thus, ava-tṛ, 'go down into the water' (49[19]); ut-tṛ, 'come up out of it;' pra-tṛ, 'advance in crossing it.' —átra, 'thére,' with a sneer: cf. amuyā́, 70[15]N. —yé ásann (636[3]) áçevās, 'qui infelices sint:' not so well the vocab. —úttarema_abhí, see √tṛ+abhy-ud.

—STANZA 8. The situation is perhaps this. A band of men, hotly pursued by their enemies, are in the middle of a stream, which they hope soon to have put betwixt themselves and the foe. They call out to each other encouragingly the words of the stanza. The famous hymn RV. iii.33 involves a situation which is similar (Muir, i[2].338), and, indeed, familiar elsewhere (Hebrews xi.29; Hdt. viii.138).

> The stream is stony. Hold ye well together.
> Your footing keep. On! make your crossing, comrades!
> There let us leave them in a mood unhappy,
> While we go out and on to happy conquests.

SELECTION LVIII. RV. x.85.36, 24–26, 32–33, 27, 43–47. The wedding-hymn. — The stanzas are here given in the order in which they are rubricated at 98[19]f — see p. 398. Their uses in the ritual are discussed by Haas in his treatise on the ancient wedding customs of India, ISt. v.267–412.

— The hymn is called the sūryā-sūkta or "The marriage of Soma and Sūryā," and has received at the hands of Dr. J. Ehni, ZDMG. xxxiii.166–176, a mythological interpretation, briefly summarized in AJP. i.211. The hymn has 47 stanzas, with an appendix given by Aufrecht, *Rigveda*[2] ii.682, and comprises somewhat heterogeneous matter (ISt. v.269). Most of the hymn occurs in AV. xiv.1 and 2, with many variants. Partial concordance:

RV. x.85.	AV. xiv.	RV. x.85.	AV. xiv.
36 =	1.50	27 =	1.21
24 =	1.19,58	43 =	2.40
25 =	1.18	44 =	2.17
26 =	1.20	45	
32 =	2.11	46 =	1.44
33 =	2.28	47	

— Besides the translations of Ludwig and of Grassmann, there is one of hymn and appendix by Weber, ISt. v.177–195. This is followed by one of AV. xiv. (pages 195–217) and of the other wedding-stanzas of the AV. (pages 218–266) — see also Ludwig, iii. p. 469–76. Most of the Reader-stanzas are translated, with explanations, by Zimmer, 311–313. See also Kaegi, 74(102), and notes 317–325.

STANZA 36. Said to the bride by the groom in the very act of taking her hand in token of wedlock.

STANZAS 24–26 and 32–33. Said just before the bride's departure for her new home. Stanzas 24 and 32 are said by a third person; 25, 26, and 33 *may* be put in the mouth of the groom. St. 33 may, as the Sūtra says, be spoken on the way, when people come out of their dwellings to gaze.

STANZA 27. Pādas *a*, *b*, and *c* are said to the bride, and *d* to the couple, on their arrival.

STANZAS 43–47. The groom first prays to Prajāpati on behalf of himself and his bride (43 *a b*), and addresses the latter with good wishes and solemn benedictions (43 *c d*, 44); prays to Indra that the bride may be fruitful (45); bids her hold her own with her new relatives (46); and, finally, beseeches the gods, on behalf of himself and his wife, that they two may dwell in unity (47).

5–6. gṛbhṇā́mi · · hástam: this, the dextrarum iunctio, is the essential feature of the simplest wedding-ritual, see Haas, 277, 316; cf. hasta-grābhá (86[19]) and pāṇi-grāha (64[17]); the AV. modernizes, reading, gṛhṇāmi. With the concordant stanza of the AV. are grouped several others (48, 49, 51) of like import. — 'With me as husband' (343b). — yáthā‿ásas, 'ut sis.' — U.f. máhyam tvā‿adus (829). — gā́rh-, 'for (our) being heads of a household, i.e. that we may establish a family.'

7–8. ábadhnāt, 730. — See ṛtá2. — See loká 2b and cf. sukṛtá with sukṛ́t. This phrase is equiv. in *form* to the older one (84[11]), but refers here rather to the 'world of the pious' on earth.

> I loose thee from Varuṇa's bond,
> With which kindly Savitar bound thee. —
> At the altar, in the company of the good,
> I put thee unharmed with thy husband.

— The first half-stanza is an allegorical, and the second a literal address to the bride. In the allegory, the bond of Varuṇa is night (Hillebrandt). Savitar is the 'Impeller,' not only of the rising, but also of the setting sun (RV. i.35.3[a]). He brings rest (ii.38.3,4) by sending night, whose gentle bond he lays (Muir, v.235–7) upon his daughter, Sūryā, 'The Sun,' till she is released for her bridal with Soma, 'The Moon' (masc.), a union which is the prototype (cf. Haas, 328) of human marriages.

From the more literal point of view, the bond of Varuṇa, as the upholder of the established order of things, is (not night —

still less sickness — but) the tie by which a maid is bound to her father till a man come to loose and take her. — See the discussions of Haas, 319–20, 277–8, and of Hillebrandt, *Varuṇa*, p. 59.

9–10. prá · · muñcāmi: acct! 596, 597; similar cases at 74[1] and 92[16]; supply either imā́m, or (since a change of address to Indra is quite natural) tvā́m. — U.f. amútas (171[4]) karam (831[2]) | yáthā‿iyám · · ásati, 'ut haec sit.' — mīḍhvas, 462a.

— Sāyaṇa comments thus: itaḥ pitṛ-kulāt pra muñcāmi tvām; na‿amuto bhartṛ-gṛhāt pramuñcāmi. amuto bhartṛ-gṛhe subaddhāṁ karam.

11–12. Said to the bride as she gets into the wagon. Pūṣan is the best of guides for earthly travellers also — cf. p. 381–2. — See gṛhá, *pl.* — U.f. yáthā‿ásas. — See √vad+ā.

13–14. Said just as the wedding-train starts. — √2vid, 848. — AV. modernizes, reading sugéna. — áti‿itām, 617. — Pronounce ápa drāntu (617).

15–16. imā́m sam-ā́‿ita, páçyata 'come near to this one together, i.e. crowd around her, (and) take a look.' Cf. note to 100[15]. — dat-tvā́ya, 993, from the quasi-root dad (955c). — U.f. átha‿ástam ví párā‿itana (618).

17–18. priyám (priya 2b), subject of sám-ṛdhyatām. — enā́ (502[2], here = anéna) etc.: 'with this (man) as husband unite thyself.' — ádhā jívrī etc., said to both. 'Old,' i.e. until ye become so.

19. This stanza (43) has interesting variants in AV., and at MS. ii.13 end. — Pronounce sám-anaktu (689).

NOTES TO PAGE 90.

1. patilokám, 'husband's home:' not till later, 'husband's heaven.'

2–3. edhi, 636. — Pronounce vīrasúur · · sionā́. — AV. reads devṛ́-kāmā.

— Note that 44*a*, *b*, and *c* are of 11 syllables, while 44*d* (= 43*d*) is of 12. Although this discrepancy is not very rare, it yet helps to bring out the character of *d* as a *formula sollennis:*

— 'Be a blessing to our bipeds, a blessing to our quadrupeds.' It is most interesting to note that a similarly comprehensive formula occurs elsewhere: in the Avesta, Yasna xix.8(18–19), Vd. xv.19(59), see KZ. xxv. 195; and on the Iguvine Tables, VI b 10–11, see Bréal's ed., pages XL, 125.

4–5. U.f. dáça‿asyām putrā́n ā́ dhehi (668). There is no end of evidence (e.g. Zimmer, p. 319) to show that the desire for male children was very strong, and that the birth of daughters was unwelcome. A wife who bears only daughters may be put away — Manu ix.81. — kṛdhi, 839. — 'Put ten sons in her. Make her husband an eleventh.' The logical incongruity is paralleled by *Paradise Lost*, iv. 323–4, and by the Greek classics.

6–7. Pronounce çvaçruám: specimen of a very rare form of transition to the devī-declension, see 358. — Pronounce nánāndri: AV. reads nánāndus. — See ádhi.

— This throws an interesting light on ancient family-life. — Note that of the Ger. correspondents to çváçura and çvaçrū́, viz. *Schwäher* and *Schwieger*, the former has died out and given place to the term *Schwiegervater*. The mothers-in-law have thus made their mark in the language — see Kluge.

8–9. U.f. sám (sc. añjantu) ā́pas hṛ́dayāni (note neglect of dual) nāu (gen.). A real anointing of both took place. — In line 9, a dadhātu goes with each sám, and nāu is acc. — Dhātṛ́ is esp. the deity who 'puts' fruit in the womb — RV. x.184.1. — See u 1 end.

SELECTION LIX. **RV. x.137.** Exorcism for a sick person. — Tradition assigns each stanza to one of the Seven Rishis as author. Stanza 4 is spoken by the Wind, personified; the rest, by the exorcist. Respecting the general character of the hymn, see Kaegi, 85–86(115). See also the beautiful essay of Kuhn, KZ. xiii.49–74 and 113–157, who compares similar Vedic and Germanic spells. Nearchus says (Strabo, xv.45, p. 706) that the Hindus trust to wandering enchanters (ἐπῳδοί) for cures, and that this is about all their ἰατρική amounts to. The hymn is translated by Aufrecht, ZDMG. xxiv.203. It corresponds in general to AV. iv.13; but see note to stanza 6.

10–11. Note the accentless and accented vocatives. —See √nī+ud and 248c. —U.f. utá‿ā́gas cakrúṣam (=cakṛvā́ṅsam, 462c). The disease is a punishment for sin, cf. p. 374.

12–13. See 1 idám end. —Zimmer queries, p. 45, whether the two Monsoons are here meant. —ā́ síndhos, see ā́ 4. —'Away let the other blow what infirmity (there is,' 512b).

15. Pronounce tuám. —See √i.

16–17. ā́ · · agamam and ā́‿abhārṣam (882): note use of aorists (928)—'I have just come and brought,' says the Wind. —átho, 1122a[2], 138c. —√2su+parā.

18–19. Pāda *c*, bad metre. —ayám, the sick man.

20. U.f. íd vāí, see vāí.

Notes to Page 91.

1. 'The waters are healers (lit. healing) of everything.' On use of sárva, see 77[11]n. The AV.-concordants of this stanza are at AV. vi.91.3 and iii.7.5 and read viçvasya.

—Stanza 6. In place of this stanza the AV. has interpolated RV. x.60.12, evidently because it has to do with the laying on of hands—see the following.

2–3. That the laying on of hands has especial virtue is a wide-spread belief—cf. Acts viii.17f, and above, p. 369[a] top. The Greeks attributed to each of the Δάκτυλοι Ἰδαῖοι a name and a particular healing power. The finger next to the little finger (see note to 104[11]) is called, *digitus medicus* by Pliny, and *medicinalis*, in the laws of Henry I. of England; and it has a special and beneficent magic power.—W. Grimm, *Kleinere Schriften*, iii.440f, 442.

—'With hands, ten-fingered (the tongue is leader of the charm), healing,—thee with these thee we touch.' The parenthesis may mean that the tongue brings out a charm to precede the laying on of hands. Text probably corrupt; AV. variants interesting.

Selection LX. RV. x.154. To Yama.—Funeral-hymn.—Rubricated at 103[13], see p. 402. Recurs at AV. xviii.2.14–18, with interesting variants. Translated, Muir, v.310. To judge from the ritual, the subject of ápi gacchatāt in each stanza is the spirit of the departed. He is to go and join the Fathers—saints, warriors, poet-sages,—a description of whom makes up most of the hymn. In stanzas 4 and 5, gacchatāt (see 570) is a 3d sing., 'O Yama, let him go;' in the rest, it may be a 2d or a 3d.—Ludwig, ii.394, v.311, interprets otherwise, taking mádhu as subject of ápi gacchatāt (√gam+api).

4–5. 'Some · · others' (éke), i.e. of the Fathers, "who revel in bliss with Yama" (83[18]). —See √ās+upa. —'For whom mádhu flows:' Yama and the Fathers are the eager recipients of sweet drink-offerings—cf. AV. xviii.2.1–3, and RV. x.15 passim. —tā́ṅç cid='thóse:' tā́ṅç cid evá='jùst those.'

6–7. Pronounce súar. —'Who made tápas their glory.' —Heaven can be won only by the pious and (stanza 3) the brave: cf. MBh. iii.43.4=1759, and 42.35=1748f.

10–11. See cid2. —U.f. pū́rve ṛtasā́pas. —Cf. 85[4].

12–13. 'Who keep (=confine themselves to) the sun, i.e. who hover about the sun.' The righteous after death are transformed into rays of the sun or into stars (Muir, v. 319f; see 100[8]n.). Thus ÇB. i.9.3[10], ya eṣa tapati, tasya ye raçmayas, te sukṛtas. So MBh. iii.42.38=1751f:

> ete sukṛtinaḥ, Pārtha,
> yān dṛṣṭavān asi, Vibho,
> tārārūpāṇi bhūtale.

Selection LXI. RV. x.155.5. Burial-stanza.—Rubricated, 105[21]. The preceding four stanzas are a *deprecatio* addressed to Arāyī, a vile and murderous witch. This stanza, the last, dwells upon the safety of the godly.

14–15. pári · · aneṣata and pári · · a-hṛṣata, 882; akrata, 834a. Note the use of the aorists, 928—where all is translated. —ā́ dadharṣati, perf. subj., 810b.

Selection LXII. MS. ii.13.23. Hiraṇyagarbha.—The god Ka or Who (see notes to selection lxviii.).—The RV. version (x.121) of this famous hymn has been translated by Max Müller, ASL. 569, and *Chips*, i.29; by Ludwig, no. 948; and by Muir, with comments, iv[2].15–18.

—STRUCTURE of the hymn. The seven stanzas here given (or perhaps only 2–6) constitute the original stock of the hymn. To this is added, in the MS.-version, an eighth stanza, quite impertinent to the rest; and in the RV.-version, three stanzas (8, 9, 10), whose character is determinable by various and interesting criteria.

Pāda *d* of each stanza is a refrain, 'Whom as god shall we worship with oblation? i.e. Who is the god that we are to worship with oblation?' The later Vedic texts understand it, 'We will worship the god Who or Ka,' making of the interrogative pronoun a deity whom they identify with Prajāpati (selection lxviii.). The other pādas of stanzas 2–6 are relative clauses with yás, yásya, yéna, yásmin. These may refer

A. To deváya: 'Who (interrog.) is the god,—who (relative) became king, etc. etc.,—that we are to worship?' Ludwig: 'Ka, the god,—who is become king, etc. etc.,—we would wait upon with havis.'—Better, perhaps,

B. To hiraṇyagarbhás, although stanza 1 (and 7 as well) looks as if it might have been an afterthought. This leaves the connection of the refrain with the rest of each stanza very loose; but this is perhaps just what it ought to be.

—The hymn corresponds to RV. x.121. The comparative study of the differing versions of the same traditional material, as it appears in different Vedic texts, is interesting and instructive; and there is no better opportunity for it than this (see Preface, p. v, N.2).

The hymn occurs also at TS. iv.1.8; in the VS., with the stanzas scattered, at xiii.4, xxiii.3, xxv.13, xxv.12, xxxii.6,7, xxvii.25; and at AV. iv.2. The TS. version follows that of the RV. most nearly. Disregarding the order, the same is true of the VS. The AV. version looks like an unsuccessful attempt at writing down a half-remembered piece.

—ACCENT-MARKS, etc. The vertical stroke designates the acute accent; the horizontal hook, the circumflex. Details in L. von Schroeder's ed., book i., preface, p. XXIX. Phonetic peculiarities, ibidem, XXVIII. Final m before sibilants, y, r, and v, is marked by the 'dot in the crescent,' e.g. praçíṣam, line 4. See also Preface to this Reader, p. v, note 7.

16. Cf. 57[3]N.

NOTES TO PAGE 92.

1. dyā́m · · imā́m, see dív3.

2–3. pra‿aṇatás (192b), gen. s., pres. ppl. —íçe: form, 613, cf. 70[18]N.; acct, 628. — asyá, acct!, 74[9]N. —dvipádas etc., see 90[8]N. —RV.-reading better in this stanza.

4–5. 'On whose command all wait, on whose (command) the gods (wait)—.' — chāyā́ etc.: cf. Bhagavad Gītā, ix.19.

6–7. mahitvā́, as instr. sing., 280. Müller's rendering—'Whose greatness (as acc. n. pl.) the mountains and sea (neuter, as at vi.72.3) with the Rasā proclaim'—would require pra‿āhús. —devī́ṣ, as adj. (see devá 1), 'heavenly = of heaven,' not 'divine.'

—Pāda *c:* díç, q.v., is 'a point of the sky:' of these there are usually four; sometimes are mentioned 5, 6, 7, 8, and 10 (explained by BR. s.v. díç). When five are mentioned, we may understand them as N., E., S., W., and the zenith: cf. AB. vi.32, pañca vā imā diçaç: catasras tiraçcya, ekā‿ūrdhvā. Occurring *with* díças, the word pradíças may mean 'intermediate points,' and, with the zenith, count as five. But considering the (faulty) concordant of RV., TS., and VS.,

yásya imā́ḥ pradíço yásya bāhū́,

further, RV. ix.86.29[b], AV. i.30.4[c], and esp. iii.4.2[b],

tuā́m imā́ḥ pradíçaḥ páñca devī́ḥ,

I am inclined to deem the pāda before us a jingle of incoherent reminiscences.

Whose (are) all these mountains, by reason of (his) greatness;
Whose (possession) they call the ocean, with the Rasā;
The points, whose are the five fore-points of heaven; · · ·.

8–9. dṛḍhā́, spondee, 224a. —U.f. súar, see 178 and 173a, and 74[12]N. —The adjectives ugrā́ and dṛḍhā́ may be attributives, and stabhitā́ or stabhitā́s supplied as predicate for the substantives of line 8. — Pāda *c* = RV. ii.12.2[c]. —vi-mamé, √1 mā. Respecting the tripartite world, see under rájas, and Kaegi, 34(49) and notes 117–8. — antárikṣam: ÇB. i.2.1[16], antarikṣeṇa hi‿ime dyāvā-pṛthivī viṣṭabdhe; cf., at Od. i.54, the κίονας

μακρὰς, αἳ γαῖάν τε καὶ οὐρανὸν ἀμφὶς ἔχουσι.

10–11. Pronounce -pṛthvī́. — See ádhi and √tan+vi. — U.f. sū́ras éti: in the MS., final -as and -e if accentless, become -ā before an accented initial vowel. So 93[12].

12–13. U.f. yád mahatī́s víçvam ā́yan (620). See víçva 1c. — The RV., TS. [with nír for sám], and VS. read

táto devā́nāṁ sám avartata‿ásur ékaḥ.

The athetesis of the hypermetric ékaḥ, made by Bollensen, *Orient und Occident*, ii.485 (1864), and again by Grassmann, is here beautifully confirmed by the MS.

Selection LXIII. MS. i.5.12. Legend of Yama and Yamī. — The creation of night. — Respecting Yama and Yamī, see notes to 85[12]f.

— The prose of the Brāhmaṇas is not difficult. In reading it, the chief thing is some familiarity with the style, i.e. ability to divide up the discourse aright into the little clauses and choppy sentences with which it proceeds. As a help to this it is important to observe that the particle *átha* marks the beginning of a new clause, and that the postpositive *vāi* marks the foregoing word as the first of its clause. Analogous is the use of *nāma* to distinguish a proper name from an identical appellative. Cf. Pliny, *Epp.* vi.31, evocatus in consilium ad centum cellas (hoc loco nomen) · ·.

As my colleague, Professor A. P. Peabody, has observed in his translations of Cicero's *Offices* and *Tusculans*, there are certain connectives and illatives which are employed as mere catchwords for the eye. In manuscripts (Greek, Latin, Sanskrit) written with letters of one size, with no separation of words, and with very few stops, these particles serve the purpose effected now-a-days by capitals, by division or spacing, and by punctuation. In spoken language it is often wrong to render them otherwise than by inflection or by stress of voice.

14. U.f. vāí. — See √brū+apa.

14–15. U.f. tā́m yád ápṛchan (207), sā́ abravīt: "adyá amṛta" íti. té abruvan: "ná vāí iyám etc." — Difference between imperf. amriyata and aor. amṛta (834a) illustrated at 928[3]. — Accent of tè, Whitney 84d, 135.

15–16. Lit. 'Not (if things keep on) in this way (itthám) does she forget him.'

16. Note the fine distinction. The gods use the solemn old Vedic form rā́trīm; the narrator, the later and more colloquial rā́trim. Similar distinction at ÇB. xi.5.4[4]: cf. 98[20]n., 103[14]n. Not uncommon is the assumption that the gods have words or a dialect peculiar to themselves. Thus ná with the gods means the same as iva, AB. ii.2.14,15. Cf. Iliad i.403, ii.814, xiv.291, xx.74, Od. x.305; and A. F. Pott's *Antikaulen*, p. 71.

— sṛjāvahāi, faulty reading for -mahāi? — U.f. áhar vā́vá tárhi ā́sīt, ná rā́tris: verb-acct, cf. 89[9]n.

— 'Yama died. The gods sought to console Yamī for the loss of Yama. — When they asked her, she said, To-day hath he died. They said, In this way she will never forget him. Night let us create. Only day in those times existed — not night. The gods created night. Then came into being the morrow. Then she forgat him. Therefore they say, 'Tis days and nights make men forget sorrow.'

Selection LXIV. MS. i.10.13. Legend of the winged mountains. — The myth is often alluded to by the later poets: see Stenzler's note to Kumāra-sambhava, i.20, and Bollensen's to Vikramorvaçī, str. 44. BR. observe that it is often difficult to distinguish between the mgs 'mountain' and 'cloud' which belong to párvata. In letting loose the heavenly waters, Indra splits open the 'mountains' as well as the 'clouds.' The Maruts house on the 'heights' or in the 'clouds,' etc.

19. Explained under yá3.

Notes to Page 93.

1. U.f. parā-pā́tam (995) āsata, yátra-yatra (1260 — see yátra) ák-. — iyám, see 1 idám, middle: so imā́m, line 2.

2. téṣām = párvatānām. — achinat, 692. — tāís = párvatāis, used evidently in the manner of paper-weights. — adṛṅhat, √dṛh. The like achievement at RV. ii.12.2.

3. Explained under yá3.

4. U.f. yónis hí eṣām (accentless, 74[9]n.) eṣā́s, 'For thís is the'r place-of-origin.'

Selection LXV. MS. ii.1.12. The potency of the sacrifice. — A passage much resembling this occurs at TS. ii.4.13 = Muir, 1[2].21. Respecting the myths of Indra's birth and Aditi's motherhood, see Hillebrandt, *Aditi*, p. 43; Perry, JAOS. xi.127f, 148f; and *Litteratur-Blatt für Orient. Philol.*, ii.4.

5. 'The Āindrābārhaspatyan oblation he should offer (nír-vapet), who, as a sovereign, shouldn't exactly succeed in his attacks.' This is a typical Brāhmaṇa passage. It invents a legend showing the efficacy of some ritual observance in former times, to prove the usefulness of repeating the same rites in analogous circumstances. —Peculiar interest attaches to this occurrence of the √stigh — see Schroeder's ed. of MS., Introduction, p. XIV; also ZDMG. xxxiii.104f, where the substance of the passage is given.

6. U.f. odanám apacat. —úñçiṣṭam, see this: final t (= d) before ç becomes ñ in MS. —āçnāt, √2aç.

6-7. U.f. tám vāí índram antár evá · · sántam · · ápa‿āumbhat (√ubh; augment, 585): 'Indra, being (yet) an embryo, withín (her), she bound with an iron bond.' — ápa‿ubdhas, 160.

8. ayājayat, see √yaj, caus.

9-10. tásya = índrasya. —vyàpadyata = of course, ví-apadyata: cf. Whitney, 84a. —U.f. abhi-pary-ā́‿avartata, 1080, 1083.

10. U.f. yás · ·, tám eténa yājayet · ·, 'One should teach him to sacrifice with this Āindrābārhaspatyan (oblation), who *etc.*'

11. eṣás, same as yó and tám, line 10.

12-13. U.f. nir-upyáte, impers. 'it is offered:' combination, 92[11]N.; form, √vap, 769; accent!, 596. kriyate, √1 kṛ 12, 'it is sacrificed.' —'Offering is made to B., sacrifice is made to I.: (then) on áll sides (the god) releases him' (enam). 'Him,' i.e. the sin-bound king of lines 10-11, who is also the subject of abhi-pary-ā́-vartate.

SELECTION LXVI. TS. ii.6.6. Legend of Agni the oblation-bearer, and of the fish.— This is the Brāhmaṇa form of the myth which is the subject of RV. x.51, and is adverted to in x.52 = selection lvi. To their version of x.51, GKR. add on p. 106 a translation of the selection before us (lxvi.). It is also rendered by Muir, v.203, and by Eggeling, SBE. xii.452. Ludwig, v.504-5, gives other Brāhmaṇa forms of this myth: cf. esp. ÇB. i.2.3[1] = SBE. xii.47. For Epic forms of the same, see Ad. Holtzmann, *Agni nach den Vorstellungen des MBh.*, p. 11, and esp. MBh. iii.222.7 = 14214f.

14-15. tráyas, 482c. —√2mi+pra, 770a.

15-16. 'Agni feared, (thinking,) "In this way, surely, he (syás) will get into trouble, i.e. if things keep on in this way, I shall get into trouble."' He speaks of himself here (as also at x.51.6[a]) in the 3d person (syás). Note the common root of ā́‿artim and ā́‿ariṣyati.

16. nílāyata: in strictness, to be divided thus, níl-āyata, 'he went out, took himself off, hid.' This is for nír a-ayata, an imperf. mid. of √i (after the model of a-jayata from √ji) with the prefix nis or nir; for according to Pāṇini (viii.2.19), the r of a preposition with forms of the verb-stem aya is regularly changed to l — cf. 1087c.

In the Hindu mind, these forms of the verb-stem nil-aya were evidently confused with those of ni-laya, which yield a like mg — see BR. under √lī+ni. On this account, doubtless, the pada-pāṭha, which usually gives the division of compound verbs, refrains here. The confusion is further attested by the analogous passage of the ÇB., which has, in the Mādhyaṁdina text (i.2.3[1]), ni-lilye, and in the Kāṇva text, ni-layāṁ cakre — see SBE. xii.p.xlvi. The proper form from √lī in the passage before us would of course be ny-àlayata.

16-17. U.f. pra‿éṣam (see √2iṣ+pra2 and ref.) āicchan (√1 iṣ, 585). In the metaphor, Agni is implicitly likened to a hunted beast.

17-18. tám açapat etc., 'Him (the fish) he (Agni) cursed (as follows): "dhiyā́ · · pra‿ávocas."' See dhí 1. —vadhyāsus (form! 924) and ghnanti (637) have as subject 'people.' —The loose use of sás, tám, etc., is one of the chief stylistic faults of the Brāhmaṇas.

19. ánv-avindan: √2vid; subject, 'the gods.' —See √vṛt+upa‿ā.

NOTES TO PAGE 94.

1-2. U.f. gṛhitásya (sc. ghṛtásya) á-hutasya (see √hu) · · skándāt (736), tád me · · asat. —bhrā́tṛṇām: the TS. reg. has short ṛ in the gen. pl. of these words. —'He said: "Let me make a condition (√2vṛ): Just what of the (sc. ghee) (when) taken (into the sacrificial ladle, but) not (yet) poured into the fire (á-hutasya), may fall outside the enclosure, let that be the portion of my brothers."'

Selection LXVII. AB. iii.20. Legend of Indra and the Maruts, and Vṛtra.—Translated, Muir, v.93. In selection xlvii. = RV. viii.85.7f, the Maruts are praised because they stood by Indra when all the other gods forsook him. The passage before us is an expansion of that myth, a "reproduction plus ou moins amplifiée d'un cliché emprunté au livre des hymnes."

From other passages, it would appear that the Maruts also were faithless, cf. Muir, v. 92 and 82[1]N. Both views are involved in the explanation of the Mid-day Soma Feast, ÇB. iv.3.3[5]f, where the Maruts first withdraw from Indra and afterwards help him (SBE. xxvi.334f).

4–5. hanişyan, 948[2]. —U.f. "anu mā tiṣṭhadhvam; upa mā hvayadhvam" (√hū). Note the free position of the prefixes (1081). —tathā‿iti, '"Yes," said they.'

5–6. U.f. sas (Vṛtra) avet (see √1 vid3, and 620): "mām etc.; hanta! imān bhiṣayāi" (√bhī, caus., 1042f, 1043.2).

7. √çvas+abhi-pra: imperf., 631. —adravan: simple root dru, without prefix; note that the prefix ā with √dru exactly reverses its meaning; so with √√dā, hṛ, and muc.

8–9. U.f. m- ha enam na ajahus (√2hā, 661, 656): "prahara bhagavas! (454b) jahi! (637[2]) vīrayasva!" iti eva enam · · upa‿atiṣṭhanta. See vác.

9–10. tad etad (see etad) = 'this.' —See √vac+abhy-anu. —'The Rishi, seeing this (occurrence), described (it) in the Vedic words, "At Vṛtra's snorting, thee."' These words are a quotation of the beginning of RV. viii.85.7f, and illustrate the way in which the Vedic stanzas are cited in the secondary literature.

10–11. U.f. sas (Indra, this time) avet: "ime · ·; ime · ·; hanta! imān asmin ukthe ā bhajāi." See √bhaj+ā: the subjunctive has the force of a future.

Selection LXVIII. AB. iii 21. Legend of Indra and the god Ka or Who.—Compare selection lxii. and see Müller, ASL. 432f. The identification of Prajāpati with Ka is very common: see, e.g. ÇB. i.1.1[13], vii.4.1[19], xi.5.4[1].

13–14. U.f. · · vi-jitya, abravit prajāpatim: "aham etad asāni (636), yad tvam (sc. asi); aham mahān asāni."

15. U.f. "yad eva etad avocas." The etad, q.v., goes appositively with yad, marking the thing designated by yad as something preceding, and so may be rendered by 'just' or 'a moment ago.' P. asks, '"Who am I, then?" "Exactly what thou just saidst,"' replied Indra.

15–16. 'Then P. became Ka by name = got the name of Ka. (For) P. is Ka by name = has the name Ka.' Note that the predicate comes first.

16–17. See yad2. 'As for the fact that Indra became great, therein (lies) Great-Indra's Great-Indra-ness' (cf. ÇB. ii.5.4[9]). This is a specimen of the verbal and etymological explanations of the Brāhmaṇas: cf. 64[7]N.

Selection LXIX. ÇB. ii.2.2[6]. The two kinds of deities, the gods and the Brahmans. —A little oratio pro domo of an oft-recurring kind (see ISt. x.35). Translated by Muir, i[2].262 (he quotes TS. i.7.3[1] by way of illustration), and Eggeling, SBE. xii.309.

18. U.f. devās (predicate) aha eva devās (subject): 'The gods of course are gods.' So mártyā ha vấ ágre devấ āsuḥ, 'In the beginning, the gods were mortals' (not 'The mortals were gods').—Delbrück, *Altindische Wortfolge*, p. 26.

18f. 'Then (they) who are the Brahmans, the learned (√çru 1), the scholars (see √vac +anu, and 807),—they are the human gods.'

Notes to Page 95.

2–3. 'For (*lit.* of) the gods, (the sacrifice is) just the oblations; for the human-gods, the B., the learned, the scholars, (it is) the dakṣiṇā.' —prīṇāti, subject indefinite.

4. U.f. brāhmaṇān çuçruvuṣas, 203. —Note the fond repetition. —enam, same as subject of prīṇāti.

Selection LXX. ÇB. ii.2.2[19]f. Truth, untruth, and silence. — Translated by Delbrück, *Wortfolge*, 29,79; Eggeling, SBE. xii. 312,452.

6–8. abhi-ṣiñcet, 758. — 'Of this fire-consecration a (concomitant) duty is Truth. He who speaks the truth, — as (if) the enkindled fire, it with ghee he should besprinkle, so he makes it blaze up; of him greater and greater the dignity becomes; from day to day better he becomes.' — Note the childish verbal anticipations and repetitions, esp. of pronouns.

11–12. U.f. tad u ha api: Eggeling renders all four particles by a simple 'Now.' — '"Thou'rt old (enough). Establish thy two fires."' See √1 dhā+ā3. This ceremony was an essential preliminary to matrimony and to setting up in life as a householder. Described at ISt. v.285f, x.327f.

12–14. U.f. sas ha uvāca: "te mā etad brūtha: 'vācaṁyamas eva edhi.' na vāi · · vaditavyam; na vadan jātu, na anṛtam vadet. etc." 'He said: "What ye say to me, then, amounts to this: 'Just hold thy peace.' By no means by an āhitāgni may untruth be spoken. By not speaking at all, one would not speak untruth. (I.e. Only by silence can one wholly avoid untruth.) To such an extent (of silence, namely), is truth a duty."' — See ha end. — See ta2. Lit. 'Ye, those, to me this are saying.' — See tāvant2.

Selection LXXI. ÇB. x.4.3[1]f. How the gods got immortality and how Death got his share. — Translated, Muir, iv[2].57f; in part, v.316f. Cf. iv.54f and v.12f. Metrical paraphrase by Monier-Williams, *Indian Wisdom*, 34, = Hinduism, 35, = *Religious Thought and Life in India*, 24. On the symbolism of the Brāhmaṇas, see p. 357, § 92; Oldenberg's *Buddha*, 19(20)f; Schroeder, ILuC. p. 127f.

15–18. 'Death (subject) is this thing (eṣas, predicate, masc. to conform in gender with mṛtyus — cf. 78[20] and n.), what the Year is. For this one, by means of days and nights, exhausteth the life of mortals. So they die. Therefore 'tis this one that is called Death. The man who knoweth this Death to be the Year, not of him doth this one before old age by days and nights exhaust the life. To perfectly complete duration of life attaineth he.' — U.f. sarvam ha eva āyus: cf. 86[11]n.

19. U.f. āyuṣas antam gacchati, see √gam3.

Notes to Page 96.

3–5. U.f. antakāt · · bibhayām cakrus (1071d) yad (see 38[1]n.) etc. 'The gods were afraid of this Ender, Death, the Year, Prajāpati, [hoping] "May this one by days and nights not get at the end of our (no) life."' Similar construction (yad · · na and optative) after verb of fearing, ÇB. iv.3.3[11].

5. U.f. te · · yajñakratūn tenire (794e).

5f. The Sacrifices are described by Weber, ISt. x.321f. The Hindus did not class them according to their purpose, as thank-offerings, expiatory offerings, etc. They grouped them

A. according to the Material used, as: 1. oblations of milk, ghee, corn; 2. animal sacrifices; 3. libations of Soma. And again

B. according to the Time, as: 1. at the beginning (x.328) of each day and of each night (agnihotra); 2. at the beg. (x.329) of the lunar half-month; 3. at the beg. (x.337) of the three seasons, — spring, rains, autumn; 4. at the beg. (x.343) of the two harvests. The offering of first-fruits or nava-sasya‿iṣṭi; in the spring, of barley; in the autumn, of rice; 5. at the beg. (x.344) of the solar half-year, the paçu-bandha; 6. at the beg. (x.352) of the new year, the Soma-sacrifice.

With this last, often occurs the elaborate ceremony of building the fire-altar of bricks, ISt. xiii.217–292. This ceremony is called the 'Fire-piling,' agni-cayana (see √1 ci), or briefly agni.

Schröder gives in brief compass a sketch of a specimen-sacrifice, ILuC. p. 97–109.

7. U.f. na amṛtatvam ānaçire (788[4]). te ha api agnim (= agni-cayanam) cikyire (787). — That the gods were once mortal (94[18]n.) is doubtless a late notion. The path of Death is ítaro devayā́nāt, 86[4]: cf. also ZDMG. xxxii.300.

8–9. See √1dhā+upa. — U.f. yathā idam

(see 2idam) api etarhi eke upa-dadhati: "A polemical hit aimed by the author of the Brāhmaṇa at some contemporaries who followed a different ritual from himself." — Muir. Cf. Chāndogya Upaniṣad, i.12.4 = SBE. i.21. — See iti 1.

10–11. Ppls w. cerus, see √car2 and 1075b. — See √1 rudh+ava, *desid.*, 1027.

11–13. U.f. "na vāi · · · upa dhattha: ati vā eva · ·; na vā · ·; tasmāt na · ·."

13–14. See ha end. — See explan. under ta2. — See yathā6.

15–18. The protasis-clauses begin with ṣaṣṭim and ṣaṣṭim and atha lokampṛṇās: the apodosis-clauses, with atha me and atha amṛtās. The second protasis-clause has an appendix, adhi ṣaṭtriṅçatam, see adhi. — For impv. with conditional mg, cf. example under atha2, and 82[2]N. — For daça *etc.*, see 480.

— 'Put ye on 360 P's; 360 Y's, and 36 besides; then 10,800 L's. Then (if ye do) shall ye etc.' The days of the year number 360; and 360 × 30 = 10,800. But see also Weber, ISt. xiii.254–5. Note that $108 = 2^2 \times 3^3$.

18–19. The acquisition of immortality is otherwise related, ÇB. ii.2.2[8]f, Muir, ii[3].372.

21–23. U.f. "na atas · · asat (636[3]): yadā eva · · harāsāi (736), etc." See atas3. '"From this time on, not any other with his body shall be immortal: just when thou this (thy) allotted-portion shalt seize, then parting with his body he shall be immortal, who is to be immortal either by knowledge or by works."'

23f. See yad2 end. 'As for their saying thát, "Either by knowledge or by works," — this is that knowledge, (*lit.* which is agni =) namely agni; and these are those works, namely agni.' Here agni = agni-cayana. — Cf. 66[23].

Notes to Page 97.

1–2. U.f. te, ye evam etad vidus, ye vā etad karma kurvate, etc. Promises to them "who have this knowledge" recur times unnumbered in the Brāhmaṇas. As between 'knowledge' and 'works,' knowledge is the better: ÇB. xiv.4.3[24] = SBE. xv.96. On this passage, see Oldenberg, *Buddha*, 46 = 47.

4. U.f. te etasya (= mṛtyos) eva annam.

Selection LXXII. ÇB. xii.7.3[1]f. Legend of Indra and Namuci. — For the origin of this story, see 81[16]f and notes. Translated, Muir, v.94. Other forms of the story: Muir, iv[2].261; Ludwig, v.145. The MBh. has it at ix.43.33 = 2433f; see ZDMG. xxxii.311.

6–7. 'N. stole I's strength *etc.*, along with his surā.'

7–10. U.f. sas (Indra) · · upa‿adhāvat: "çepānas asmi (see √√çap, as) namucaye, 'na tvā · · · na ārdreṇa;' atha me idam ahārṣit. idam me ā jihīrṣatha?" iti. — Note the difference (929, 928) between aharat and ahārṣit. — Note reversal of mg (94[7]N.) effected by ā with jihīrṣatha (1028b): '"Are ye willing to fetch it back for me?"'

10. "astu nas atra api; atha ā harāma:" '"Let there be of us in this also (a share); in that case, we'll fetch (it) back."'

10–11. '"Together ours (is) that; so fetch it back." Thus said he.'

11. iti (the one before tāu açvināu) = 'on the strength of that agreement.'

12. asiñcan: see √sic3.

13. vy-uṣṭāyām (√1 vas) rātrāu, 303b. So an-udite āditye.

14. √3vas+ud — a queer verb to use for this mg. — U.f. ṛṣiṇā abhy-anu‿uktam "apām phenena" (81[16]) iti.

Selection LXXIII. Nirukta ii.16. Explanation of RV. i.32.10, selection xxxii., page 70[19.20]. — See Roth, *Erläuterungen*, 21f, and Muir, ii[3].174f.

15–16. The iti marks aniviçamānānām as a gloss to the quoted "átiṣṭhantīnām." So asthāvarāṇām is a gloss to the "aniveçanánām" of the sacred text; and in like manner, meghas to "çáriram."

16. Starting from the 3d pers. s. pres. ind. act. of a verb-root (e.g. çamnāti from √3çam), and treating it as a declinable noun-stem, like mati, the Hindu forms an ablative sing., e.g. çamnātes, to express "derivation from a root." Render: 'çarira is from the root çṛ *break*, or from the root çam *harm*.' So with drāghati and the following two.

19f. After the verbal explanations, comes the mythological discussion. 'Who then is Vṛtra? "A cloud" say the etymologists.

"An Asura descended from Tvaṣṭar" say the tellers of old legends.' There were, then, already schools of conflicting opinions. Cf. Muir, ii^{3}.170f.

NOTES TO PAGE 98.

1. The genitives limit miçrībhāva-, 1316.

2–3. -karmaṇas is abl. — 'In this process (tatra), · · battles, so to speak, take place.'

3. ahivat etc.: 'The m- and b- (sc. speak of V.) as a dragon.'

4. √1 vṛ+ni (1045): subject, Vṛtra.

5. U.f. tadabhivādinī eṣā ṛk bhavati.

SELECTION LXXIV. Wedding-customs and the wedding-service. Āçvalāyana Gṛhya-sūtra, book i., chap's 5, 7, 8. — Stenzler published the text in the *Abhandlungen für die Kunde des Morgenlandes*, vol. iii., 1864; and the translation, vol. iv., 1865. Cf. Weber, *Indische Streifen*, ii.296f. The text appeared with a Hindu comment in the *Bibliotheca Indica*, 1866–69. English translation by Oldenberg, SBE. xxix.159f.

—On the subject-matter of this selection, the following essays and books may be consulted. The most important is the essay of Haas, with additions by Weber, ISt. v.267–410; cf. esp. the synoptic index, 410–12. Haas gives the text and an annotated translation of our selection at pages 289f, 362f.

See also notes to selection lviii., p. 389. Further, Kaegi, 74(102), and notes; Zimmer, 309f; Kaegi in *Fleckeisen's Jahrbücher*, 1880, 456f; and Colebrooke's *Essays*, i.217–38.

—Birth, reproduction, and death are the three great facts of all organic life. It is therefore natural that the customs connected with marriage and burial should take so important a place in the traditions of primitive peoples. It can hardly be doubted that a considerable body of these customs have their root in Indo-European antiquity. For we find, as between the various members of this family, many and most striking coincidences of usage. The systematic exposition and criticism of these coincidences form one of the most interesting chapters of comparative philology. It is not feasible to point them out in detail here. In lieu of this may be cited —

For purposes of comparative study: Joachim Marquardt, *Privatleben der Römer*, i^{2}.28f; A. Rossbach, *Die Römische Ehe*, Stuttgart, 1853; G. F. Schömann, *Griechische Alterthümer*^{2}, ii.529–36; K. Weinhold, *Die Deutschen Frauen* (Wien, 1851), p.190–274, or *Altnordisches Leben* (Berlin, 1856), 238–59; Spiegel, *Erānische Alterthumskunde*, iii.676–81.

—SYNOPSIS of the subject-matter (with references to passages in vol. v. of the ISt., where Haas and Weber treat of the Hindu customs or cite analogous ones): —

CHAPTER v. Test of the bride by means of exorcised lumps of earth. See ISt. v.288f.

CHAP. vii. The marriage ceremony. Dextrarum iunctio (v.277,311). Bride led around the fire and water (v.318N.2, 396N.). Amo 'ham asmi (v.216). Mounting the stone (v.318N.1). Oblation (v.318N.3). Loosing braids (v.320). Seven steps (v.320f, 321N.).

CHAP. viii. Wedding journey (v.327f). Arrival at new home (v.329). Pellis lanata (Rossbach, 113f, 324; Marquardt, 50). Continence (v.325f, 331).

VEDIC CITATIONS. If the entire first pāda of a stanza is quoted, the entire stanza is meant. If only part of the first pāda of a hymn is quoted, the entire hymn is meant. If more than a complete pāda is quoted, then three stanzas are meant. — Stenzler, note to AGS. i.20.9.

SYNOPSIS of RV.-mantras

cited at		
98^{19}	gṛbhṇāmi te	$= 89^{5}$
99^{22}	pra tvā muñcāmi	$= 89^{7}$
99^{22}	'The following'	$= 89^{9}$
100^{10}	pūṣā tveto	$= 89^{11}$
100^{11}	açmanvati (½ *stanza*)	$= 89^{3}$
100^{12}	'The following' (½ *stanza*)	$= 89^{4}$
100^{12}	jīvaṁ rudanti	$= 88^{4}$
100^{14}	mā vidan	$= 89^{13}$
100^{15}	sumañgalīr	$= 89^{15}$
100^{15}	iha priyam	$= 89^{17}$
100^{18}	ā naḥ prajām (4 *stanzas*)	$= 89^{19}$
100^{19}	sam añjantu	$= 90^{8}$

6. 'The family (of the intended bride or groom) in the first place one should consider, according to the rule, "Who on the mother's and on the father's side, —" as aforesaid.'

The rule referred to is in Āçvalāyana's Çrāuta-sūtra, ix.3.20 (p. 714, *Bibl. Ind.*), and continues thus,

"— for ten generations back, are endowed with knowledge, austerity, and works of merit." See Weber's interesting discussion of ancestor-tests, ISt. x.84–8.

8–11. U.f. aṣṭāu piṇḍān kṛtvā (127[2]), · · · piṇḍān abhimantrya, kumārīm brūyāt, "eṣām ekam gṛhāṇa" (722). 'Making eight lumps (of earth), conjuring the lumps with the mantras "ṛtam · · · · dṛçyatām," he should say to the girl, "Take one of these."' —Germanic bride-tests cited, ISt. v.288N.

11–12. U.f. kṣetrāt ced ubhayataḥ-sasyāt gṛhṇīyāt, "annavatī asyās prajā bhaviṣyati," iti vidyāt. 'If she take (the lump made) from the field that bears two crops a year, "Rich in food will her children be," thát he may know.' —'Two crops:' cf. Megasthenes, as preserved by Diodorus (ii. 35,36) and Strabo (xv.20, p. 693).

12–15. Most of the remaining seven conditional periods are abbreviated to two words: thus goṣṭhāt answers to kṣetrāt and paçumatī to annavatī; and the rest is to be supplied from the first period. No's 4, 5, and 7 begin respectively with avidāsinas, ādevanāt, and iriṇāt. But patighnī is predicate to a supplied kumārī rather than to prajā.

14. dvi-pravrājinī: to be preferred, perhaps, is the reading vipravrājinī (√vraj + vi-pra), 'wandering hither and thither;' but the mg amounts to the same thing.

16. In order of extent stand deça, 'country,' janapada, 'district,' nagara, 'town,' grāma, 'village,' kula, 'family.' But at weddings and funerals, village-customs stand first in importance—PGS. i.8.11,13 or SBE. xxix.285. On conflicts, cf. Stenzler's note to AGS. i.7.2, and 59[18]N. —tān begins new clause. —prati‿iyāt, 616.

17–21. dṛṣadam açmānam, 'a millstone (which is) stone' (not, e.g. burnt clay). Apposition, cf. 101[12]. —See √rabh+sam-anv-ā: sc. kumāryām, loc. absol. —Note how the quoted sacred text has gṛbhṇāmi, while the later one has gṛhṇīyāt: cf. 92[16]N. —kāmayīta (1043.3), as if of the 1st gen'l conj., instead of kāmayeta. So vācayīta, 101[2], 106[4]; kalpayīran, 105[1]. —pumāṅsas etc.; δύνασθαι · · ποιεῖν καὶ ἀρρενογόνους καὶ θηλυγόνους etc., Megasthenes, in Strabo, xv.60, p. 713; also ÇB. xiv.9.4[14]f or SBE. xv.219f. —'To the west of the fire, a millstone setting, to the north-east, a water-jar, while she touches him, he, offering, standing facing west, of her, facing east, seated, with RV. x. 85.36, the thumb only should grasp, in case he should desire "pumāṅsas · · jāyeran."'

Notes to Page 99.

1. pari-ṇayam: we should read pari-ṇayañ or (BI.) -an, pres. ppl. —'Leading (her) thrice to the right around the fire and the water-jar.' The analogies are remarkable: cf. ἐπιδέξια, the Roman *dextratio*, the Gaelic "walking the deasil," etc. Consult SBE. xii.37, 45, 272, 442; Rossbach, 231, 314f: Marquardt, i[2].51 and N.1. Circumambulations followed the course of the sun on occasions of joy; and were reversed (104[21]) on occasions of sorrow.

2–3. Pronounce: sā tvam asi; amo aham. —These interesting formulae occur at AV. xiv.2.71; ÇB. xiv.9.4[19]; PGS. i.6.3; AB. viii.27; ÇGS. i.13.4. For pāda *d*, the first three have sāmāham asmi; ṛk tuam. —The sāman is conceived as male (ÇB. iv.6.7[11]), and as sprung from the ṛc (as it is), or as husband of it (ÇB. viii.1.3[5]). But to the Hindu mind this lugging in of sāma has a charming mystic significance, inasmuch as sā plus ama makes sāma (see AB. iii.23; and SBE. i.13). —The conception of heaven as male and of earth as female is common —see Preller, *Gr. Mythologie*[3], i.37f. —The Vedic formula has a general significance not unlike that of the ancient *quando* (or *ubi*) *tu Gaius ego Gaia* and the German *Wo ich Mann bin, da bist du Frau, und wo du Frau bist, da bin ich Mann.* For the Latin formula, see Rossbach, p. 351; ISt. v.216; Fleckeisen, 1880, p. 457; and esp. the discussion by Marquardt, i[2].49N.2. For the German, see ISt. v.216. Another use of the Vedic formula, ISt. x.160.

4–5. ehi, used just like ἄγε or φέρε; but cf. the variants noted ISt. v.332N. —If we could read priyāu, the metre would be in order (8+8+11+8); but cf. TS. iv.2.5[1].

6. Force of repetition—'With each leading-around' (1260). —She mounts the stone or puts her foot on it as a symbol of the way in which she is to put her foot on her enemies.

9. U.f. **vadhv-añjalāu** (134 end) **upastīrya** (see √**stṛ+upa**). The loc. is adjunct of **ā-vapati** as well as of the gerund.

9–11. The first pouring (**upastaraṇa**) of **ājya** and the two strewings of parched grain on the bride's hands, and the second sprinkling (**pratyabhighāraṇa**) of **ājya**, constitute the four portions "cut off" or separated from the **havis** or sacrificial food. The first is done by the groom; the rest by the brother. The descendants of Jamadagni used to "cut off" five such portions (ISt. v.366; x.95) and so had to strew grain three times. — Oldenberg's note. —**eṣas**, refers back.

—'(The groom) having poured the sacrificial butter on the bride's hollowed-and-joined-hands, her brother or brother's representative strews parched grain (on her hands) twice [Thrice (is the custom) of the Jamadagnians.], sprinkling again (sc. **ājya**) over the **havis** (= what he has left of the grain in the basket) and over the **avatta** (= what grain he has strewn on her hands). This (as just stated) is the cutting-off-usage.'

12–17. **ayakṣata**, 882. —**pra · · muñcātu** (cf. 89[9]), impv., w. lengthening (ISt. v.340n.): so **nudātu**, **svadātu**. —These stanzas are mere adaptations of blank forms, so to say. For examples of the changes (called **ūhās**) which circumstances demand, see AB. ii.6.6; cf. AGS. iii.8.7. The forms are filled out (see **nigama** in BR.) with a deity-name, which, as here, does not always fit the metre.

18. 'With the above mantras (uttered by the groom), she, not-parting (fem.) her joined-hands, should offer (the grain in them), as with a **sruc**.' The nose of the **sruc** is at the side. She is therefore to pour out the grain so, — not over her finger-tips.

—For the case of families who do not strew grain but twice, we must assume that the bride, when making her second oblation, does not offer all the grain in her joined-hands, but leaves some for her third oblation. Her fourth is from the basket.

18–19 (§ 14). 'Without (any) leading around (on the part of the groom), (the bride should offer grain) with the nose of the basket towards herself in silence the fourth time.' The "silence" refers of course to the groom. The bride does not say anything at any time (cf. SBE. xxix.37).

—As prescribed above, the rites are performed in the order following:

I. II. **First and second rounds:**
a. leading around, § 6;
b. mounting stone, § 7;
c. strewing grain, § 8;
d. oblation w. mantra 1 or 2, § 13.

III. **Third round:**
a. leading around;
b. mounting stone;
c. sprinkling ājya, § 10;
d. oblation w. mantra 3, § 13.

IV. **Fourth time:**
a, *b*, and *c* fall out;
d. oblation in silence.

19–20. U.f. **ā‿upya ā‿upya** (127 end) **ha** (see **ha**) **eke** etc. 'Some lead her around after each strewing (of) the grain. In this way (**tathā**) the last two oblations do not fall together.' That is, some do the rites in the order:

c. strewing or sprinkling;
d. oblation w. mantra;
a. leading around;
b. mounting stone.

In this way, the fourth oblation comes directly after the third mounting of the stone.

20–21. **asyāi**, 365.3. 'Then he loosens her two braids, if they are made; (i.e. if) two braids of wool at her two temples are tied.'

22. He loosens the right one with RV. x.85.24. —**uttarām** (sc. **çikhām**) **uttarayā** (sc. **ṛcā**): see **uttara** 3, 4.

23. The AB. at i.14.5f tells why the NE. is called **a-parājitā**. See also A. Kuhn, *Entwicklungs-stufen der mythenbildung*, *Abh. der Berliner Akad.*, 1873, p. 126f.

Notes to Page 100.

1–3. U.f. **iṣe ekapadī** (sc. **bhava**), etc., 'be taking one step for strength = take one step for strength; two for vigor;' and so on. —The body consists of *five* elements. At one period, the seasons are reckoned as *six:* **çiçira**, **vasantá**, **grīṣmá**, **varṣá**, **çarád**, **hemantá**.

4. See **saptapada** in vocab. Seven, as a sacred number, became the symbol for 'many' or 'all.' Doubtless the word always suggested both the literal and the transferred mgs. Orig., **sakhā saptapado bhava**,

'Be a constant friend,' was a mere general formula, used on sealing a friendship, e.g. between two men, who would take seven steps together hand in hand by way of ratifying their bond. **Sāptapadam māitram**, 'Friendship (if genuine) is constant,' became a common proverb.

— The application of the formula to the wedding-ceremony is prob. only a secondary and special use; although it came to be exceedingly important. Here **saptapadī** being taken with strict literalness, it became necessary to lead up to it by six other formulae — as in the text. The matter is explained at length and illustrated, by Haas and Weber, ISt. v.320–22: cf. BR. s.v. **saptapada**; and AV. v.11.10.

6. The two gerunds seem to go with the subject of **abhy-ut-krāmayati**, i.e. the groom.

8. **vaset**: subject, the bride. — **sapta ṛṣīn**, 127[2]. — See **iti** 3.

8–9. **dhruvam**, as symbol of fixity and constancy (see PGS. i.8.19 and ÇGS. i.17.3). For the legend of Dhruva's translation to the skies, see Viṣṇu Purāṇa, book i, chap. 12. — **arundhatīm**: cited, with many other examples of faithful and happy wifehood, at MBh. i.199.6 = 7352 and v.117.11 = 3970; cf. also ISt. v.195. There was a superstition that one whose life was near its close could not see these stars (ISt. v.325: *Indische Sprüche*, 2d ed., no. 2815). — **ṛṣīn**: here, as so often, the heavenly lights are the souls of pious sages and saints departed — see note to 91[12]. — The bride has nothing to say during the ceremony, and keeps silence after it until (cf. 103[20]) starlight.

10. U.f. **prayāṇe** (loc. 303b), the wedding-journey, from the bride's village to the groom's. See ISt. v.327f.

11–12. Rules 2 and 3 are for the case that they have to cross a stream.

12. **rudatyām**, 'if she weeps,' loc. abs.

13. So in Rome a boy went ahead with a nuptial torch. Cf. Rossbach, 362–3.

14–15. 'At every dwelling' — as the wedding-train passes it. The procession called out eager gazers then, as now. Indeed, to judge from AV. xiv.2.73, even the Manes were supposed to crowd about for a look at the bride (ISt. v.277). — U.f. · · **iti īkṣakān īkṣeta**.

17. U.f. **ānaḍuham carma ā-stirya**: compare the *pellis lanata* (Rossbach, 112, 324). — **tasminn** = **carmaṇi**. The two foll. words are loc's s. fem., supply **kumāryām** (303b).

18–19. **catasṛbhis**, sc. **ṛgbhis**.

19–20. **dadhnas** (431) etc.: 'Partaking of curds, he should offer (them) in turn (to her); or, with the rest of the **ājya**, he anoints (**anakti**, √**añj**) his and her heart.' **hṛdaye**: better as dual, on account of the **nāu** (dual, 90[8]) in the stanza which accompanies the action.

20–21. See **ūrdhvam**. — **brahma-cāriṇāu**: see ISt. v.325N.3, 331. — U.f. **alamkurvāṇāu**, 714.

22. Counting of time by nights: see Kaegi, N.68* and citations, and Zimmer, p. 360. — 'Or, "(They should be continent) a year," (say) some: a Rishi is born in this way (**iti**).' 'In this way' = 'on condition and as reward of such self-restraint.'

NOTES TO PAGE 101.

1. Marital intercourse is declared by Āpastamba to be a duty resting on the authority of Holy Writ (**brāhmaṇa-vacanāc ca saṁveçanam**, ii.1.19 = SBE. ii.101). The Scripture-passage, acc. to Bühler, is TS. ii.5.1[5], **kā́mam ā́ vī́janitoḥ sám bhavāma**, 'Let us have intercourse after our heart's desire till a child be begotten.' Explicit is Bāudhāyana, iv.1.17 = SBE. xiv.315; MBh. xii.21.12 = 626. Cf. Ludwig, v.549 (N. to RV. i.179.2), and iv. 315: also Exodus xxi.10f, and I Cor. vii.3.

2. See √**vac**, *caus.*: form, cf. 98[20]N.

SELECTION LXXV. The customs and ritual of cremation and burial. Āçvalāyana Gṛhya-sūtra, b'k iv., chap's 1–6. — Text and translations as at the beginning of introduction to selection lxxiv. Roth compares the ceremonies here described with those implied by the text of RV. x.18 in his essay, *die Todtenbestattung im indischen Alterthum*, ZDMG. viii.467–75, reprinted in part by Zimmer, p. 404f. The same subject is treated at length by Max Müller, ZDMG. ix.p.I–LXXXII. We may mention also Colebrooke's

Essays, i.172–95; the papers of Wilson and of Rājendralāla Mitra, cited above, p. 382f; and especially Monier-Williams, in *Religious Thought and Life in India*, chap. xi., *Death, Funeral Rites, and Ancestor-worship*, and in *Ind. Ant.* v.27. Cf. also in general the introduction to selection liii., p. 382f.

The ceremonies in question have three main parts: the cremation; the gathering and burial of the bones; and the expiation. —These are followed by the çrāddha, described at AGS. iv.7, SBE. xxix.250f, 106f.

SYNOPSIS of RV.-mantras

cited at		
102^{1}	apeta vīta	$= 83^{15}$
102^{7}	ud īrṣva nāri	$= 86^{18}$
102^{8}	dhanur hastād	$= 86^{20}$
102^{20}	agner varma	$= 84^{16}$
102^{21}	ati drava	$= 83^{17}$
103^{1}	imam agne	$= 84^{18}$
103^{12}	prehi prehi	$= 83^{11}$
	and 23 others, see note	
103^{17}	ime jīvā	$= 86^{8}$
104^{11}	çītike	$= 85^{10}$
104^{14}	upa sarpa	$= 87^{2}$
104^{15}	'The following'	$= 87^{4}$
104^{15}	'The following'	$= 87^{6}$
104^{16}	ut te stabhnāmi	$= 87^{8}$
104^{20}	kravyādam (½ *stanza*)	$= 84^{20}$
105^{5}	ihāivāyam (½ *stanza*)	$= 85^{1}$
105^{9}	tantuṁ tanvan	$= 89^{1}$
105^{11}	ā rohatāyur	$= 86^{14}$
105^{12}	imaṁ jīvebhyaḥ	$= 86^{10}$
105^{14}	param mṛtyo (4 *stanzas*)	$= 86^{4}$
105^{15}	yathāhāni	$= 86^{12}$
105^{17}	imā nārīr	$= 86^{16}$
105^{18}	açmanvatī	$= 89^{3}$
105^{21}	āpo hi ṣṭhā (3 *stanzas*)	$= 83^{1}$
105^{21}	parime gām	$= 91^{14}$
103^{3}	'Sun-hymns,' *see note*	
106^{3}	'Blessings,' *see note*	
106^{3}	apa naḥ (8 *stanzas*)	$= 72^{8}$

—For purposes of comparative study (cf. p. 398) we cite: Joachim Marquardt, *Privatleben der Römer*, i².340f; Schömann, *Griechische Alterthümer*², ii.539f; K. Weinhold, *Altnordisches Leben* (1856), 474–504; the same author's *Heidnische Todtenbestattung in Deutschland* (with illustrations), *Sitzungsberichte der Wiener Akad.*, 1858, 1859; Spiegel, *Erānische Alterthumskunde*, iii.701–6; Geiger, *Civilization of the Eastern Irānians*, i.84f; and finally the masterly essay of J. Grimm, *Ueber das Verbrennen der Leichen*, *Abh.* der *Berliner Akad.*, 1849, p. 191f = *Kleinere Schriften*, ii. 211f, who treats of the custom among almost all peoples of Indo-European stock. See p. 230 = 261f for the custom among our Anglo-Saxon forefathers, a remembrance of which lives in the modern English *Bale-fire*. Cremation is common throughout the MBh.—Holtzmann, *Agni*, p. 10.

3–4. Protasis, ·· ced upa-tapet; apodosis, ··· ud-ava-syet (√sā).

5. enam, the sick householder.

6. U.f. ·· paçunā iṣṭyā iṣṭvā (√yaj), ava-syet. See Stenzler's note to § 4. —See √sthā + sam.

7–8. The quarter and the slope are in general to the south, the region of the dead (cf. ÇB. i.2.5[17]).

9. ity eke, see iti 2c. —tāvad-āyāmam (sc. khātam syāt), 'the trench should be having so much length.'

10. vitasty-avāk, 'span-deep': or, for vitasti-mātram avāk. —'On all sides, the çm- should be an open space.'

11. '"But thorn-plants and milk-plants" as aforesaid' [viz. at AGS. ii.7.5, "he should dig out with their roots and remove them"]. Cf. 98[5]N.

12. çm- is both a burning-ground and a burial ground: here, the former, as is shown by ādahanasya. For a similar definitive apposition, cf. 98[17].

13. 'This has been stated above'—at Çrāuta-sūtra, vi.10.2, given in Stenzler's note.

14. Rule 17, sc. 'should be.'

16. etām diçam, 'to that quarter,' mentioned 101[7].

16–18. Rules 2–7: nayanti may be repeated w. the accusatives. Rule 2, cf. 104[9].

20. The cord is usually worn over the shoulder; cf. Stenzler's note to AGS. iv.2.9. —On returning (103[21].), the order of march is reversed.

21. evam, in the order named. —kartā, subject of pra‿ukṣati, next line. —prasavyam, cf. 99[1]N.

NOTES TO PAGE 102.

2–3. The oblation-fire, the householder's fire, and the southern fire are the three sacred fires which are to be started and maintained in every family. Here they are set respectively in the SE., NW., and SW. parts of the sacred place.

3–4. enam, 'for him,' i.e. the dead man (Oldenberg), or the conductor of the ceremony (see Stenzler). This second accusative with (idhmacitim) cinoti is strange.

4–6. The first tasmin, masc., refers to -citim, fem.!; the second, neuter, to -ajinam. 'On it they set the dead man, carrying (hṛtvā) him to the north of the g-, with his head towards the ā-.'

6. 'To the north (of the corpse) they set the wife; and a bow for a Kṣatriya.'

7–8. U.f. tām (= patnīm) ut-thāpayet · · · vā, "ud īrṣva nāri etc." See 86[18]N.

8. 'The conductor of the ceremony should repeat (the stanza) in case of a Çūdra (= in case a Ç. raises her up from the pile).'

9. dhanus, sc. apa-nayet. — Rule 21 = exactly 'Ditto in case of a Çūdra.'

9–10. 'Having strung it, without (= before) piling the pile (of things mentioned below), breaking (√1 çṛ) it, he should throw it on the fuel-pile.'

11 f. Müller gives pictures of these various implements, ZDMG. ix.p.VII f, LXXVIII f.

14. bhittvā ca ekam, 'and breaking (it in two pieces, in case there is only) one (sruva).'

18. āsec-, sc. pātrāṇi. — See √1 pṛ. — putras, the dead man's.

19. 'And the metallic ware (and) pottery.'

21–22. U.f. vṛkkāu (134 end) ud-dhṛtya (√1 hṛ). — dakṣiṇe (sc. pāṇāu) dakṣiṇam (sc. vṛkkam ā-dadhyāt), etc.

22–23. '"And two meal-cakes," (say) some [, he should put on the hands of the corpse]. "(Only) in the absence of the kidneys," (say) others.' — sarvām, sc. anustaraṇīm.

NOTES TO PAGE 103.

1–2. See √mantraya + anu: 'accompanies the fetching · · w. the stanza "imam etc."'

2–4. U.f. · · jānu ā‿acya, · · juhuyāt, "agnaye svāhā etc." — pañcamīm (sc. ājya‿āhutim juhuyāt) urasi pretasya —

4–5. U.f. "asmāt (accent, asmát, 74[9]N.) vāi (see vāi) · · · tvat adhi (see adhi) jāyatām," a metrical mantra, substantially identical with VS. xxxv.22. — asāu, voc., 'O so-and-so.'

6. See √2iṣ + pra3.

6–8. 'If the āh- should reach (the corpse) first, "In the heaven-world it has reached him" — this may one know. Happy will that one be in that world: so (will) this one, that is, the son, in this (world).' U.f. rātsyati (√rādh) asāu amutra: evam ayam asmin, iti putras. The last iti marks putras as an explanation of ayam.

8–11. Rules 3–4 are counterparts of 2.

11–12. Rule 5: loc. = 'in case of.' — ṛddhim vadanti, see √vad 3. — "The higher the smoke of the pyre rises, the more distinguished will the departed be in the other world." — Weinhold, *Altnord. Leben*, 480–1.

12. tam, like sas (line 13) and eṣas (16), refers to the departed.

12–13. · · · iti samānam, 'with the mantras "prehi prehi etc." in the same way' — as indicated, namely, in the Çrāuta-sūtra, at vi.10.19–20 (p. 505–6), i.e. with the 24 stanzas there enumerated. They are RV. x.14. 7,8,10,11; x.16.1–6; x.17.3–6; x.18.10–13; x.154.1–5; and x.14.12. The text of all these stanzas is given in the RV. order in the Reader, pages 83–91.

14. svargam lokam: note the fine distinction between this and the later svargalokam (as cpd). The old two-word form is used in lines 14 and 16, as virtual quotations from an older text; and above, at line 5, a quoted mantra; but the cpd is used in the Sūtra proper, line 7. Cf. 92[16]N.

15. U.f. avakām, çīpālam iti (marks çīas a gloss to avakām) ava-dhāpayet. tatas (= gartāt) ha (see ha) vāi etc.

17. With regard to the pertinence of the mantra, see Roth, ZDMG. viii.472, 468. — savyāvṛtas, cf. 99[1]N.

18–20. The end of each clause is marked by a gerund. — U.f. udakam a-vahat · · un-majjya, · · gṛhitvā, ut-tīrya, · · enāni (= vāsāṅsi, i.e. the ones they had on before changing) ā-piḍya, · · āsate. — See á4. — Similarly, the bride keeps silence till starlight, 100[8]N.

— See nāman2. — Each of the relatives, facing southward, performs the lustration, saying to the departed, "O thou of the family of the Kāçyapans, O Devadatta, this water is for thee" (kāçyapagotra, devadatta, etat te udakam). — Scholiast.

21. 'Or, while (a bit) of the sun is (still) seen, they may go home.' —Rule 12: cf. $101^{2)}$N.

22. U.f. **prāpya agāram, · · · a-kṣatān, tilān, apas** etc.

NOTES TO PAGE 104.

1. More fully, **krītena vā, utpannena vā** (sc. **annena**): see √**pad+ud**.

3f. Render the locatives by 'in case of,' i.e. here 'in case of the death of.' —**dāna‿adhyayane**, acc. dual n., 1253a.

8. See **ūrdhvam**. —'Tenth' (see **daçamī**) — counting from the day of death. — **kṛṣṇapakṣasya ayujāsu**, sc. **tithiṣu**. —See **eka-nakṣatra**. Of the 28 lunar mansions, six form three pairs, named 'former' and 'latter' Phalgunī (9–10), Aṣāḍhā (18–19), and Bhadrapadā (24–25). Accordingly, under these asterisms, or in the lunar months named after them, the gathering is forbidden.

See Whitney, OLSt. ii.351f, 360. But cf. Weber, *Abh. der Berliner Akad.*, 1861, p. 322.

9. 'In a plain male urn (they put) a man (i.e. his bones); in a plain female (urn — sc. **kumbhyām**), a woman.' If the urn has protuberances on it, like a woman's breasts, it is regarded as a female urn. Many such have been found by Schliemann — see his *Ilios*, numbers 986, 988–93. A male urn is one without these breasts.

9–10. § 3, cf. 101^{17}. —**prasavyam**, 99^{1}N.

11–12. U.f. **aṅguṣṭha‿upakaniṣṭhikābhyām** (cf. 105^{16}) **ekāikam asthi a-** etc. Even the Brāhmaṇas give evidence of a well-developed body of popular beliefs about the fingers: cf. ÇB. iii.1.3[25]; iii.3.2[2.13]f, and Eggeling's Index, SBE. xxvi.461, s.v. *fingers*. See the beautiful essay of W. Grimm, *Ueber die bedeutung der deutschen fingernamen, Kleinere Schriften*, iii.425–50.

But with the finger next the little one is associated — now something mysterious, now something uncanny (as here): this appears from the fact that it is the 'nameless' one not only in Sanskrit (**a-nāmikā**), but also with Tibetans, Chinese, Mongols, Lithuanians, Finns, and North American Indians. See Grimm, l.c. 441–47; and 91^{2}N.

13. The scholiast takes **pavana** as a 'winnowing-basket' used to sift out the small bones yet remaining among the ashes, and not picked up by hand. Is it not rather a 'fan to blow the ashes from the carefully gathered bones in the urn'?

13–14. U.f. **yatra · · na abhi-syanderan, anyās varṣābhyas, tatra** (sc. **kumbham**) **· · ava-dadhyus**. 'Whereunto from all sides no water other than rain would flow.'

15–16. Rule 8: **uttarayā** (sc. **ṛcā**) = RV. x.18.11 = 87^{4}. —**ava-kiret**, √**3kṛ**. —Rule 9: **uttarām** (= RV. x.18.12 = 87^{6}), sc. **japet**.

16–17. U.f. **kapālena** (sc. **kumbham**) **api-dhāya, atha an-avekṣam praty-ā-vrajya, apas** etc. —**asmāi**, the deceased.

18. See √**1mṛ+abhi**. For the force of the prefix, cf. what was said by a little newsboy, as reported by my colleague, Professor Lane, "My mother *died on me* and my father runned away." —See √**2kṣi+apa**.

19. U.f. **purā udayāt**.

20–22. **tam = agnim**. —**ny-upya**, √**2vap**. —See under **yatra**. —**prasavyam**: the left is associated with evil or sorrow (see 99^{1}N.); cf. Latin *laevum omen* or *numen*. —U.f. **savyān ūrūn ā-ghnānās** (637).

NOTES TO PAGE 105.

1. **upa-kalpayiran** (for **-yeran**, see 98^{20}N.), 'they should provide': the verb has 11 objects (lines 1 to 4).

2–3. U.f. **çamīmayyāu araṇī**. A legend explaining why the sacred fire is made with sticks of **çamī** (see this) is given at MBh. ix. 47.14 = 2741 f.

4–5. **agni-velāyām**, 'at the time of the (evening) agnihotra': cf. 96^{5}N.

6. U.f. **āsate** etc., similarly $103^{2)}$.

7. U.f. **itihāsa-purāṇāni iti** (see **iti3**) **ā-khyāpayamānās** (1042d). Story-telling followed the cremation in Germanic antiquity also — cf. Weinhold, *Altnord. Leben*, 482, and the very end of the Beōwulf.

7–10. 'When sounds are hushed (√**ram**),

or when (the others) have gone home or to bed, starting (pra-kramya) from the south side of the door, a continuous water-stream (the conductor of the ceremony) should offer, with the words "· · ·," (going round) to the north (side of the door—u.f. iti ā uttarasmāt).'

10-12. Rule 8: cf. 100^{16}f.

13-15. uttaratas, with agnes. —U.f. amātyān īkṣeta.

17. U.f. akṣiṇī (343f) ā‿ajya (√añj) parācyas (407^{3}) vi-sṛjeyus (sc. taruṇakāni).

18. añjānās (sc. yuvatīs) īkṣeta (subject, 'the conductor,' kartā).

19-22. 'Then, standing off (ava-sthāya) in the NE., while (the others) circumambulate (pari-krāmatsu) with fire, and bull's dung, and a continuous water-stream, with the tṛca "āpo hi ṣṭhā etc.," he should repeat "parīme gām etc."' —ud-ā-haranti, compare 101^{4}.

NOTES TO PAGE 106.

1. U.f. yatra abhi-raṅsyamānās (√ram, 939) bhavanti, 'where they are about (= intending) to tarry': not so well the vocab. —See ahata. Respecting the Hindu washerman, his work, and tools, see G. A. Grierson, *Bihār Peasant Life* (Trübner, 1885), p. 81f.

2. U.f. ā udayāt. udite etc.

3. The scholiast to AGS. ii.3 end, enumerates the "Sun-hymns" and the "Blessings." The "Sun-hymns" are RV. x.158; i.50.1-9; i.115; and x.37. The "Blessings" are RV. i.89; v.51.11-15; and x.63. Cf. SBE. xxix.114. Of all these, only the second is given in the Reader—see Preface, page v, note 4.

3-4. U.f. annam saṁskṛtya (1087d), "apa nas çoçucat‿agham" (= RV. i.97 = 72^{8}f) iti pr- hutvā. Cf. Preface, p. v, N.4.

4-5. vācayita (see √vac, *caus.*): we should expect -yeta—cf. 98^{20}N.

POSTSCRIPT.

Not without grave misgivings can a Vedic commentary be put forth. The hard places are very hard. Nevertheless, an unsatisfactory bit of exegesis may be a valuable approximation to the truth or may even suggest the correct solution of a difficulty.

Inasmuch as Professor Whitney has been so kind as to look over the manuscript of the Notes, it ought to be said that there are various things in the Vedic part of the work of which he does not approve.

The earliest English version of the Fables of Bidpai, *The Morall Philosophie of Doni*, by Sir Thomas North (see above, p. 313), has just been reprinted, with a valuable introduction by Joseph Jacobs, and published by David Nutt, London, 1888.

The second edition of Whitney's Grammar may soon be looked for. The section-numbers are substantially unchanged; but the subsections are marked with a, b, c, etc. The references in the Notes (see p. 289, above) are to the first edition of the Grammar. Users of the second edition will often have to seek, e.g., 844^{2} under 844a, 371^{12} under 371k, and the like.

In addition to the lexicons mentioned above, page xviii, there has recently appeared a *Sanskrit-Wörterbuch nach den Petersburger Wörterbüchern bearbeitet von* Carl Cappeller (Strassburg, Karl J. Trübner. 1887. Royal 8°, pages 541. Price 15 Mark). This is so excellent, cheap, and convenient as to deserve the warmest commendation. An English version is in progress.

C. R. L.

HOLLIS HALL, HARVARD COLLEGE,
CAMBRIDGE, MASSACHUSETTS,
August, 1888.

PART III.

SANSKRIT-ENGLISH VOCABULARY.

[*For Explanations and Abbreviations, see pages* 289–294.]

1 **a**, *pron. root, see* idam *and* 502.

2 **a**, *negative prefix, see* an.

áṅça, *m.* (that which one gets, *i.e.*) one's portion; *and so, generalized*, portion, part. [√1 aç, 'get.']

aṅçú, *m.* juicy internodium *or* shoot of the Soma-plant; *and so*, shooting ray (of light).

aṅçumánt, *a.* rich in beams, radiant; *as m.* the sun, 16[4]. [aṅçú, 1235b.]

áṅsa, *m.* shoulder. [perhaps, 'the strong' (part), √am, 1197a: cf. *ὦμ-ος*, Lat. *um-erus*, Goth. *amsa*, 'shoulder.']

a-kasmāt, *adv.* without any "wherefore"; without apparent cause; unexpectedly; accidentally.

akasmād-āgantu, *m.* an accidental arrival, a chance comer.

a-kāra, *m.* the sound *or* letter a. [Whitney, 18.]

a-kāraṇa, *n.* lack of cause; -am, *adv.* causelessly.

a-kīrti, *f.* non-fame, disgrace.

akīrti-kara, *a.* causing disgrace, disgraceful.

á-kṛta, *a.* not done; uncooked.

aktú, *m.* —1. ointment; —2. light, beam of light; —3. night. [for 2, cf. *ἀκτίς*, 'beam.']

a-kriyamāṇa, *a.* not being accomplished. [√1 kṛ, 'do,' 770c.]

a-krūra, *a.* not harsh.

1 **akṣá**, *n. for* akṣán *at end of cpds* [1315a].

2 **akṣá**, *m.* a die for playing. [named, perhaps, from its 'eyes' (1 akṣá) or 'spots.']

ákṣa, *m.* axle. [cf. *ἄξων*, Lat. *axis*, AS. *eax*, Eng. *axe* (i.e. 'axle'), and *axle.*]

á-kṣata, *a.* unhurt, uninjured; unbroken; *as m. pl.* unbroken *or* unhusked grains, *esp.* of barley.

akṣata-kesara, *a.* having an uninjured mane.

akṣata-deha, *a.* having an unhurt *or* perfect body.

akṣán [431], *n.* eye. [cf. *ὄπ-ωπ-α*, 'have seen,' *ὤψ*, 'eye'; *ὄσσε*, **ὀκ-jε*, 'eyes'; Lat. *oc-ulus*, 'eye'; the kinship of AS. *eáge*, Eng. *eye*, remains to be proved: cf. √īkṣ.]

akṣa-priya, *a.* beloved of the dice, *i.e.* lucky at gaming.

a-kṣama, *a.* not equal to a thing; unable, *w. inf.*

a-kṣaya, *a.* imperishable.

akṣayatva, *n.* imperishability. [akṣaya.]

a-kṣára, *a.* imperishable; *as n.* word; syllable; the sacred syllable, om, 60[14]; sound, letter, 61[4].

akṣara-nyāsa, *m.* the commitment to letters, the writing.

a-kṣāra, *a.* not pungent.

akṣārālavaṇa, *n.* that which is not pungent and not salt. [alavaṇa: 1253b.]

akṣārālavaṇāçin, *a.* eating that which is not pungent and not salt, abstaining from seasoned and salted food. [āçin.]

ákṣi [431], *n.* eye; *see* akṣán.

akṣāuhiṇī, *f.* a complete army.

akṣāuhiṇī-pati, *m.* master of an army; general.

a-khila, *a.* without a gap, entire; all.

a-gadá, *a.* not having disease, well, healthy, whole; wholesome; *as m.* medicine.

agāra, *m. n.* house.

agní, *m.* fire; *esp.* a sacred fire; the god of fire, Agni, mediator between men and gods, messenger who carries the sacrifice to them, protector from the terrors and spirits of darkness, and keeper of house and hearth. [perhaps, 'the quickly moving *or* agile one,' √aj, 1158: cf. Lat. *ignis*, 'fire,' *agilis*, 'agile'; akin, poss., is αἴγλη, 'flashing light.']

agni-kuṇḍa, *n.* round hole in the ground for the sacred fire.

agni-velā, *f.* fire-hour, time for kindling the sacred fire; afternoon.

agni-hotrá, *n.* fire-sacrifice (a burnt-offering of fresh milk).

agnihotra-hávaṇī, *f.* fire-sacrifice ladle.

agny-ādhéya, *n.* placing *or* setting up of the sacred fire. [acct, 1272.]

ágra, *n.* —1. front; agre, in front, before, in presence of, *w. gen.*; —2. beginning; agre, in the beginning, in the first place, first; —3. tip, end. [perhaps, 'that which goes before, leader,' √aj: cf. ἄγω, 'lead,' στρατ-ηγός, 'army-leader.']

agratás, *adv.* in front [1098c[3]]; before (one's self); *w.* kṛ, place in front, cause to lead. [agra, 1098b.]

agryá, *a.* foremost, best. [ágra, 1212c.]

aghá, *a.* distressful, harmful; *as n.* harm, trouble, evil; sin; sorrow. [like aṅhú, 'narrow,' and áṅhas, 'distress,' from √*aṅgh or aṅh, 'straiten': cf. ἄχος, 'distress'; ἄγχω, Lat. *ango*, 'strangle'; AS. *ange*, 'anxious,' Ger. *enge*, 'narrow,' *Angst*, 'distress': for connection of mgs, cf. Eng. *straiten*, 'to narrow' and 'to distress.']

√ **aghāya** (aghāyáti). harm; plan mischief. [agha, 1059b.]

á-ghoracakṣus, *a.* not evil-eyed.

á-ghnya, *m.* bull (the animal that is 'hard to overcome,' or more exactly, 'not to be slain').

ághnyā, *f.* cow. [formed as a pendant to aghnya.]

aṅká, *m.* —1. the bend at the groin made by taking a sitting position, lap; —2. the bend just above the hip (where babes, sitting astride, are carried by Hindu women —*see* āroha); —3. hook; —4. (*like Eng.* pot-hook) mark, sign. [√añc: for 1, cf. ἀγκών, 'bend in arm *or* wall *or* shore'; for 3, cf. ὄγκος, Lat. *uncus*, AS. *ongel*, 'hook'; cf. Eng. *angle*, not a borrowed word.]

√ **aṅkhaya** (aṅkháyati [1056, 1067]). hook on, grapple. [from aṅka, 'hook,' despite the aspiration.]

+**pari**, clasp, embrace.

√ **aṅg**. move, *in derivs.*

aṅgá, *asseverative particle.* yád aṅgá, just when; té aṅgá, they only.

áṅga, *n.* limb, member; *by synecdoche*, body, person, form. [√aṅg: for mg, cf. aṅgúli, aṅgúṣṭha.]

aṅgana, *n.* court. [orig., perhaps, 'gangway,' √aṅg.]

aṅganā́, *f.* a (fair) form, *i.e.* a woman. [áṅga.]

áṅgāra, *m.* coal.

áṅgiras, *m.* —1. *orig., probably,* messenger; *esp.* messenger between gods and men; *by eminence*, Agni; —2. *as pl.* Angirases, a name applied by the Hindus to a certain race among their forefathers (perhaps because their intercourse with the gods was conceived as very intimate), these forefathers being regarded as half divine; —3. *as s.* the (mythical) ancestor of the Angirases.

aṅgúli, *f.* finger. [√aṅg, 1191: for mg, cf. áṅga.]

aṅgúṣṭha, *m.* thumb. [for mg, cf. áṅga.]

√ **ac** *or* **añc** (ácati, áñcati; akná, añcitá; -ácya). bend. [cf. aṅka and vbl añc.]

+**ā**, bend.

a-cara, *a.* not moving; *as subst.* plant (as distinguished from animals).

a-cala, *a.* immovable; *as m.* mountain.

a-cit, *a.* not knowing; unwise; foolish.

á-citti, *f.* unwisdom; folly.

a-citvā, *grd.* without piling. [√1 ci.]

a-cintya, *a.* incomprehensible.

áccha, *vbl prefix.* to, unto; hither; *w.* √√ 2 naç, yā, vah, vṛt; *often* acchā, 248a.

√ **aj** (ájati, -te). drive. [orig. 'put in motion': cf. Lat. *ago*, 'lead, drive'; ἄγω, 'lead': cf. also agra, ajira, āji.]

+**ud**, drive out.

ajá, *m.* he-goat. [prob. 'the agile one,' √aj: cf. αἴξ, 'goat.']

a-jára, *a.* not aging; ageless.

ajarāmaravat, *adv.* as if ageless and immortal. [ajara-amara, 1107, 1257.]

á-jasra, *a.* not dying out; perpetual (of fire).

ajā́, *f.* she-goat. [see aja.]

á-jāta, *a.* unborn.

ajína, *m.* goat-skin; pelt. [aja: cf. *αἰγίς*, 'goat-skin, Aegis,' w. *αἴξ*, 'goat.']

ajirá, *a.* agile, swift. [√aj, 1188e: cf. Lat. *agilis*, 'agile.']

√ **ajirāya** (ajirāyate). be swift; press swiftly onward. [ajira, 1059b.]

a-jña, *a.* not knowing, ignorant; foolish; *as m.* fool.

á-jñāta, *a.* unknown. [√jñā: cf. *ἄ-γνωτος*, Lat. *i-gnotus*, Eng. *un-couth*, 'unknown.']

ajñāta-kulaçīla, *a.* whose family and character are unknown.

a-jñātvā, *grd.* without knowing.

a-jñāna, *n.* ignorance; -āt *and* -atas, out of ignorance.

√ **añc**, *see* √ac.

añc, *as vbl at end of cpds* [*see* 407–9], turning, directed; *e.g.* úd-añc, directed upward. [for mg, cf. Eng. *-ward* (in *to-ward*, etc.), which is akin w. √vṛt, 'turn.']

√ **añj** *or* aj (anákti, aṅkté; ānáñja, ānajé [788]; ā́ñjīt; aktá; aktvā́; -áñjya, -ájya). —1. smear; anoint; —2. adorn. [cf. aktu: cf. Lat. *ungo*, 'anoint.']

+**ā**, anoint.

+**vi**, —1. anoint; —2. adorn; *and so*, bring to notice; vyàkta: adorned, fair; manifest; —*caus.* make clear *or* manifest.

+**sam**, —1. anoint; —2. adorn; —3. unite by anointing, 89[19]; —4. *generalized*, unite with, take to one's self (*e.g.* food), 88[10].

añjalí, *m.* the two hollowed and open hands placed side by side; the hands so placed and raised to the forehead, *i.e.* a gesture of reverent salutation; a double handful (as measure).

áñjas, *adv.* quickly, suddenly. [prob. adv. acc. or instr. of an obsolete subst. áñjas, 'a slippery way *or* a gliding motion,' √añj.]

√ **aṭ** (áṭati, -te; aṭiṣyáti; aṭitá; aṭitvā́). wander about. [cf. √at.]

aṭanī, *f.* the notched end of a bow.

aṭavī, *f.* forest. [perhaps, 'roaming-place,' √aṭ.]

aṇḍa, *n.* egg.

aṇḍa-ja, *a.* egg-born; *as m.* bird.

√ **at** (átati, -te; atitá). wander about. [cf. √aṭ.]

a-tandrita, *a.* unwearied.

átas, *adv.* —1. (*as abl. of pron. root* a [1098], *and synonymous w.* asmāt) from it; *so* 22[9], *sc.* pañkāt; ato 'nya, other than it, 68[12]; —2. from this (place), 83[15]; —3. from this (time), 96[21]; *cf.* ūrdhvam; then, 40[16]; —4. from this (cause), 35[10]; therefore, 27[3], etc.; *w. correl.* yatas, 36[3]; hence; and so, 30[4], 42[21]; so then, 73[12]. [pron. root a, 502.]

áti, *adv.* across, beyond, past, over, *as vbl prefix; in cpds*, to excess, excessive, *see* 1289b; *as prep.* beyond, over. [cf. *ἔτι*, 'further, besides'; Lat. *et*, 'besides, and.']

atikrama, *m.* act of overstepping *or* overcoming. [√kram + ati.]

átithi, *m.* guest. ['wanderer,' √at.]

ati-durvṛtta, *a.* excessively wicked.

ati-dūra, *a.* very far *or* distant; *as n.* great distance.

ati-bhāra, *m.* excessive burden.

ati-lāulya, *n.* excessive greediness.

ati-vṛṣṭi, *f.* excessive rain.

á-tiṣṭhant, *a.* not standing; restless. [√sthā.]

ati-saṁcaya, *m.* excessive accumulation.

ati-saṁnidhāna, *n.* excessive nearness.

atīndriya, *a.* transcending the senses; *as n.* soul, spirit. [ati + indriya, 1310a.]

atīva, *adv.* exceedingly; very. [ati + iva.]

a-tyājya, *a.* not to be abandoned.

aty-ugra, *a.* extraordinary. ['excessively strong.']

atyugra-puṇyapāpa, *a.* extraordinarily good and bad; *as n. pl.* extraordinarily good and bad deeds.

átra (átrā, 248a), *adv.* —1. (*as loc. of pron. root* a [1099[4]], *and synonymous w.* asmin) *substantively:* in it, 97[10]; in this case, 31[5]; in that case, 18[17]; on this point, 29[2]; *adjectively: w.* antare: in this interim, meantime, 24[19], 45[2], 50[22], 55[4]; on this occasion, at this juncture, 19[11]; atra sarasi, in this pool; —2. in this *or* that (place); here, 25[16]; there, 33[5], 89[4]; in that world (*opp. to* 'in this world'), 87[1,7,9]; —3. in that (time), then, 56[12]. [pron. root a, 502.]

átri, *m.* Atri, name of a famous Rishi.

átha (áthā, 248a), *adv.* *expresses a sequence, temporal or resultant:* then; so; so then; accordingly; thereupon; —1. *temporal: e.g.* áti drava, áthā · · úpehi, run past, and then go unto · ·, 83^{18}; *in apodosis after* yadā́, 84^{5,6,7}, 96^{22}; —2. *resultant: e.g.* marúdbhiḥ sakhyám̐ te astu, átha jayāsi, make friends with the Maruts, and then (if thou dost) thou shalt conquer, 82^{2} N.; —3. *very frequent as a simple continuative:* now; so; then; *usually at beginning of sentence* (*e.g.* 20^{1}) *or çloka* (*e.g.* 2^{6}); *sometimes within the çloka* (*e.g.* 3^{14}); *exceptionally at the end,* 13^{9}; *at beginning of section or book,* now, 98^{16}; here beginneth (*cf.* íti), 1^{1}; *sometimes much attenuated in meaning; often almost equivalent to a capital letter, to mark the beginning of a new clause, e.g.* 94^{18}; *connecting parts of sentence,* 4^{11}; —4. *pleonastically w.* tatas, 13^{9}; *mere verse-filler,* 10^{19}; —5. átho, *i.e.* átha u, and also, 90^{16}; —6. *serving as a* point d'appui *for an enclitic, which may thus precede its word: e.g.* devo, 'tha vā yakṣas, a god or a Yaksha, *instead of* devo, yakṣo vā, 8^{18}; *so* 2^{12}; *in this use,* vā : atha vā : : que : atque; *cf.* 27^{21}; *cf.* vā; —7. atha vā, or rather, 26^{7} N. [pron. root a, 1101, 502; later form of ádhā (which is more common in the Veda): cf. Lat. *at,* 'then, further, but.']

√ ad (átti; atsyáti; áttum). eat; consume. [cf. ἔδω, Lat. *edo,* AS. *etan,* Eng. *eat:* cf. anna.]

ád, *vbl.* eating, consuming, *in cpds.*

ada, *a.* eating, *in cpds.* [√ad.]

a-dan̈ṣṭrin, *a.* without tusks *or* large teeth.

á-datta, *a.* not given.

a-dantajāta, *a.* not having teethed. ['not having grown teeth,' for a-jāta-danta.].

adás [501], *pron.* yon, yonder, that, that there, *in opposition to the one here or just mentioned: e.g.* asāu, 22^{7}, that one (the traveller—*last mentioned at* 20^{19}); *so* 31^{10}; asāv amutra, ayam asmin, that one in that world, this one in this, 103^{7}; that one (*correl.* ya), 7^{6}, 37^{11}; *as designation of persons not to be named,* so-and-so, N. or M.; asāv aham, I am so-and-so, 61^{14}; 60^{21}; 103^{6}; *follows at a distance the word to which it refers, thus emphasizing it,* 23^{1}. [see 501 and 503.]

áditi, *a.* without bond *or* limit; infinite; *as f.* infinity, the endless heaven, 79^{19}; infinity, *personified as a goddess,* Aditi, 75^{8}. [apparently a + *diti, acct, 1304a^{2}: diti, 'bond,' would be a reg. deriv. of √3dā, 'bind,' but does not occur as such, although there is a word díti, q.v., of quite different mg and origin.]

a-dīna, *a.* not depressed.

adīnātman, *a.* with cheerful spirit, undaunted. [ātman.]

á-durmañgala, *f.* -ī, *a.* bringing no bad luck. [for declension, cf. sumañgála, -galī́, and 355b.]

a-dṛ́ṣṭa, *a.* unseen, unnoticed. [√dṛç.]

adṛṣṭa-kāma, *m.* love for one not yet seen.

a-devá, *m.* non-god, who is no god. [1288a^{4}.]

adbhís, *see* 393.

ádbhuta, *a.* wonderful; *as n.* wonder. [despite anatidbhuta, prob. from at(i)-bhūta, 'transcending what has existed,' 1310a: cf. ambara.]

ádbhuta-rūpa, *a.* having wonderful beauty.

adyá, *adv.* to-day; adya niçi, in this night (just past), 51^{8}; now; adya yāvat, until now; adya‿ārabhya, from now on. [perhaps from *a-dyavi, 'on this day,' 1122f, see dyu: cf. Lat. *ho-die,* 'to-day.']

a-dravya, *n.* non-thing, unworthy object.

ádri, *m.* rock; stone; *esp.* Soma-stone (for bruising the Soma); missile stone.

adrivant, *a.* having *or* armed with the hurling-stone.

ádha (ádhā, 248a), *Vedic adv.* *expressing a sequence:* then, so, 79^{8}; so then, 89^{18}; adha yad, just then when, 76^{14}; (then, *i.e.* besides, *i.e.*) and, 77^{18}, 78^{6}. [1104^{8}: cf. átha.]

a-dhanya, *a.* not rich; poor.

adhamá [525], *a.* lowest; worst. [cf. adhas and 474: cf. Lat. *infimus,* 'lowest.']

ádhara [525], *a.* lower. [cf. adhas and 474: cf. Lat. *inferus,* 'lower'; Eng. *under.*]

á-dharma, *m.* unrighteousness.

adhaḥ-çāyin, *a.* lying low, *i.e.* sleeping on the ground.

adhás, *adv.* below; down.

adhástāt, *adv.* below; *as prep., w. gen.* [1130], under. [adhas, 1100b.]

ádhi, *adv.* over, besides, in addition, 96^{16}; *as prep.* above, over, on; *w. instr.* (*of* **snú** *only*), away over, 79^{11}; *w. abl.* from, out of, 103^{4}; *w. loc.:* over, 90^{7}; on, 70^{13}, 92^{11}.

adhika, *a.* (*like Eng.* over *in adj. uses*) additional; surpassing the usual measure, superior, extraordinary; *as n.* surplus. [ádhi, 1222a.]

adhika-rūpavant, *a.* surpassingly *or* most beautiful.

adhikānurāga, *m.* superior affection *or* most affection. [anurāga.]

adhikāra, *m.* authority; office; duties of office. [√1kṛ + adhi, 'put over *or* in office.']

ádhijya, *a.* having the bow-string up *or* on, *i.e.* strung. [2jyā́, 1305.]

adhi-pa, *m.* lord; ruler. ['over-keeper,' 1289a: cf. 354.]

ádhi-pati, *m.* over-lord; sovereign. [1289a.]

adhi-pā́ [352], *m.* lord. ['over-keeper,' 1289a.]

adhiṣṭhā́na, *n.* standing-place; (of the soul) a dwelling-place *or* manifestation. [√sthā + adhi.]

adhunā́, *adv.* now.

adho-nivīta, *a.* having the sacred cord (worn) low. [adhas.]

adhyayana, *n.* reading; study, *esp.* of the Veda. [√i + adhi, 1150. 1a.]

adhyāya, *m.* reading; study, *esp.* of the Veda; (*like Eng.* lesson), *lectio*, chapter, 56^{16}, 58^{15}, etc. [√i + adhi, 1148. 2.]

adhvará, *m.* religious *or* liturgical service; sacrifice, *esp.* Soma-sacrifice.

√ **adhvarya** (adhvaryáti). perform sacrifice. [adhvara, 1059d.]

adhvaryú, *m.* priest, who did the actual work of the sacrifice, and appears in the oldest period as companion of the hotṛ — *see* ṛtvij. [√adhvarya, 1178h.]

an, *before consonants* **a**, *negative prefix.* [1121a; acct, 1288a, 1304a: cf. ἀν-, ἀ-, Lat. *in-*, Eng. *un-*.]

√ **an** (ániti [631]; ána; ániṣus; aniṣyáti; anitá; ánitum; -ánya). breathe, blow; live. [cf. anila, ἄνεμος, Lat. *anima*, 'current of air'; Goth. *an-an*, 'breathe.']
 +**pra**, breathe.

aná, *pron. stem, see* **idam**.

an-agha, *a.* faultless.

anaḍváh [404], *m.* bull. ['cart-drawing,' ánas + váh.]

an-adhigata, *a.* un-studied.

an-anuṣṭhāna, *n.* non-observance, neglect.

an-antará, —**1.** *a.* having no interval; immediately adjoining; -am, *adv.* immediately afterwards, afterwards; thereupon; —**2.** *as n.* non-interval, *in* sam-.

an-amīvá, *a.* without sickness *or* trouble, well; *as n.* weal. [ámīvā, 1304a.]

an-arghya, *a.* not to be priced, priceless.

anarghyatva, *n.* pricelessness. [1239.]

an-artha, *m.* non-advantage; disadvantage.

anala, *m.* fire.

an-avadyá, *a.* not un-praiseworthy; blameless, faultless.

anavadyāñga, *f.* -ī, *a.* having a faultless body. [áñga.]

an-avekṣa, *a.* without any looking around; -am, *adv.* without looking around. [avekṣā.]

an-avekṣamāṇa, *a.* not looking around. [√īkṣ + ava.]

an-açrú, *a.* without tears. [áçru, 1304a.]

a-naṣṭa, *a.* not lost. [√1naç.]

ánaṣṭa-paçu, *a.* who loses nothing from his herd. [prop. 'having a not lost herd.']

ánas, *n.* cart for heavy burden. [cf. Lat. *onus*, 'burden.']

án-āgata, *a.* not arrived; not (yet) come, impending, future. [√gam + ā.]

anāgatavant, *a.* having to do with the future. [1233.]

anāgata-vidhātṛ, *m.* arranger for the future; Forethought, name of a fish.

án-āgas, *a.* without sin. [acct, 1304a[2]].

an-ādhṛṣyá, *a.* un-approachable. [acct, 1285.]

an-āmayá, *a.* without disease, healthy; *as n.* health.

an-āmayitnú, *a.* not sickening; healing

an-āyudhá, *a.* weaponless; defenceless. [áyudha, 1304a.]

an-āruhya, *grd.* without going into (danger). [√ruh + ā.]

anila, *m.* wind. [√an, 1189.]

á-niviçamāna, *a.* not going to rest. [acct, 1283.]

a-niveçaná, *a.* having no resting-place, unsettled. [nivéçana, 1304a.]

an-iṣṭa, *a.* undesired; disagreeable; unapproved, unlawful. [√1 iṣ.]

aniṣṭa-cintana, *n.* the thinking about something unlawful.

an-iṣṭvā, *grd.* without sacrificing. [√yaj.]

ánīka, *n.* —1. face; —2. *fig.* appearance; —3. of a hatchet (face, *i.e.*), sharp edge; —4. front, *and so, by synecdoche,* troop. [so Lat. *acies* has mgs 3 and 4.]

a-nītijña, *a.* not knowing discreet conduct.

ánu, *prep.* after, along, toward; *w. acc.* along *or* over; after, *i.e.* according to.

anugati, *f.* a going after. [√gam + anu.]

anucará, *a.* going after; *as m.* attendant; companion. [√car + anu.]

anu-jīvin, *a.* living upon, dependent; *as m.* a dependent. [√jīv + anu.]

ánu-tta, *ppl. see* √1 dā + anu.

á-nutta, *a.* un-moved, *i.e.* invincible. [√nud.]

anuttama, *a.* most highest; best, most excellent; supreme. [lit. 'most best,' formal superl. to anuttara, which is itself logically a superl.]

an-uttara, *a.* not having a superior, *i.e.* best. [for mg, cf. niḥçreyasa.]

án-udita, *a.* not arisen. [√i + ud.]

an-udyoga, *m.* non-exertion.

anunaya, *m.* conciliation. [√nī + anu.]

an-upakārin, *a.* not doing *or* unable to do a friendly service.

anu-pūrva, *a.* following the one preceding, one after another; *-ám, adv.* in regular order. [1310a.]

ánumati, *f.* approbation; favor (of gods to the pious); *personified*, Grace. [√man + anu.]

anumāna, *n.* the forming of a conception. [√1 mā + anu, 'conceive.']

anurāga, *m.* affection. [√raj + anu.]

anurodha, *m.* regard. [√1 rudh + anu.]

anurodhin, *a.* having (some) regard for. [√1 rudh + anu.]

an-ulbaṇá, *a.* not lumpy; smooth *or* perfect (of a weft). [1288a[4].]

anuvṛtti, *f.* sequence, *and so,* continuance. [√vṛt + anu.]

ánu-vrata, *a.* acting according to the will *or* command (of another), obedient; devoted to, *w. acc.* [272], 6[16], 100[4]. [1310a: cf. apavrata.]

anuçaya, *m.* repentance. [perhaps 'that which lies down after one *or* follows one to his bed': √çī + anu.]

anuṣṭhāna, *n.* devotion to, observance. [√sthā + anu.]

anuṣṭheya, *grdv.* to be accomplished. [see √sthā + anu, and 963a.]

anusaraṇa, *n.* a going after, a searching. [√sṛ + anu.]

anustaraṇa, *a.* strewing over, covering over; *—f.* anustáraṇī (*sc.* go), a cow, slaughtered at the funeral ceremony, and the pieces of which are used for covering over the corpse, limb by limb. [√stṛ + anu.]

anūcāná, *see* 807 *and* 784.

an-ṛta, *a.* untrue; ánṛta, *n.* untruth; wrong. [ṛtá, 1288a.]

an-eka, *a.* not one, *i.e.* more than one; many.

anekadhā, *adv.* many times. [1104.]

anekaças, *adv.* in large numbers. [1106.]

á-nedya, *a.* not to be blamed; blameless. [acct, 1285a.]

an-enás, *a.* free from guilt. [énas, 1304a.]

an-oṁkṛta, *a.* not having om uttered, *i.e.* unaccompanied by om. [see oṁkṛta.]

ánta, *m.* —1. vicinity, proximity; —2. border; limit; end. [see ánti: cf. Eng. *end.*]

antaḥ-pura, *n.* inner stronghold *or* citadel; inner apartment of the royal citadel, gynaeceum, harem, 2[21]. [antar, 1289a.]

ántaka, *m.* ender (death). [ánta, 1222a.]

anta-kara, *a.* end-making; *as m.* destroyer.

ántama, *a.* nearest, very near; *as m.* intimate, companion. [see ánta, mg 1, and 474: cf. Lat. *intumus*, 'inmost.']

antár, *adv.* inward, inwardly, within; *prep., w. loc.:* between, among, within; along with, 78^{12}; cf. √√i, gam, dhā. [cf. Lat. *inter*, 'between.']

1 **ántara**, *a.* very near, *only in V. and B.* [see ánta, mg 1, and 474.]

2 **ántara**, *a.* inner; *as n.* —1. the interior, middle; jala‿antare, in the middle of the water = in the water, 50^{7}; vana‿antara-saṁcārin, wandering in the forest, 49^{13}; —2. interval —*see* atra; —3. distance between two things; the difference, 29^{7}; —4. difference, *at end of cpds* [1302c 5]: · · -antara, that which has a difference of · ·, *i.e.* another · ·, 33^{1}, $38^{12, 23}$, 43^{6}; —5. occasion, juncture, 19^{11}. [antár: cf. ἔντερα, 'inwards, guts.']

antar-ātman, *m.* the in(-dwelling) soul; heart. [1289.]

antári-kṣa, *n.* the atmosphere, *see* 92^{9} N. ['lying *or* situate in the middle' between heaven and earth: antar + kṣa: for mg, cf. τὸ μεσηγύ, as used of the aerial space traversed by Iris.]

antarikṣa-ga, *a.* moving in the air; *as m.* bird. [for mg, cf. khaga.]

antarikṣa-loká, *m.* atmosphere-world [1280b]; the atmosphere, regarded as a separate world.

antar-gata, *a.* gone within, *i.e.* being within; hidden.

antardhāna, *n.* a hiding; disappearance; *w.* i, disappear. [√1 dhā + antar, q.v.]

antar-lajjā, *f.* inward shame. [1289.]

antar-vedi, *a.* situate within the sacrificial bed; -dí, *adv.* within the sacrificial spot. [1310a.]

ánti, *adv.* opposite, in front, before; near. [see ánta: cf. ἀντί, 'opposite,' ἄντα, 'face to face'; Lat. *ante*, 'before'; *antīcus*, 'former, ancient'; AS. *and-swaru*, Eng. *an-swer*.]

1 **antiká**, *n.* neighborhood *or* presence; *used like* samīpa, *q.v.* [ánti.]

2 **antika**, *for* anta *at end of cpds*, 1222, 1307; grahaṇa‿antika, having acquisition as its conclusion.

antimá, *a.* last. [ánti, 474: for mg ('endmost'?), cf. ánta 2, and antya.]

ante-vāsín, *m.* pupil. [lit. 'abiding in the vicinity,' 1250c.]

antya, *a.* being at the end, last; lowest; of lowest caste. [ánta.]

antya-jāti, *a.* having lowest birth.

antyajātitā, *f.* condition of having lowest birth. [1237.]

antya-strī, *f.* woman of lowest caste.

andhá, *a.* blind; blinding (of darkness).

ándhas, *n.* darkness. [cf. andhá.]

ánna, *n.* food; *esp.* rice, *usually* boiled, the chief food of the Hindus; grain. [√ad, 1177a: cf. εἶδαρ, Lat. *esca*, **ed-ca*, 'food'; *ador*, 'spelt'; AS. *āta*, Eng. *oat*.]

anna-prāçana, *n.* rice-feeding, the first feeding of an infant with rice.

anna-rasa, *n.* food and drink. [1253b.]

ánnavant, *a.* provided with food. [ánna.]

anyá [523], *pron. a.* another, other, else; anyac ca, and another thing, *i.e.* again, *see* ca 3; other than, different from, *w. abl.*, 3^{4}, 24^{19}, 68^{17}, 104^{14}; *otiose*, 2^{12}; yad anyat kiṁ cana, whatever else, 9^{16}; anya *or* eka · · anya, the one · · the other, 90^{13}, 29^{8}. [cf. ἔνιοι, 'some'; Goth. *an-þar*, 'other,' Eng. *other*.]

anyatama, *a.* one of several, some one. [anya, 525^{3}.]

anyátas, *adv.* from another direction [1098b], otherwise; elsewhere [$1098c^{3}$], to another place. [anya.]

anyáthā, *adv.* otherwise, 18^{9}; *w.* bhū, become otherwise, suffer change, 17^{5}; otherwise than it really is, falsely, 35^{20}; otherwise (*i.e.* if not), 48^{8}. [anya.]

anya-hrada, *m.* another pool.

anye-dyús, *adv.* on the next day. ['altero die': 1250c.]

anyonya, *pron. a.* one the other, *for* anyò 'nyá [175a], *the first part being a crystallized nom. s. m.* [1314c]; *w. value of gen.*, anyonyam prati hṛcchaya = anyasya‿anyam prati h., love of one towards the other, 2^{19}. [see paraspara.]

anváñc [409c], *a.* directed after, following after, being behind. [ánu + áñc.]

anvita, *see* √i + anu.

áp [393], *f. plurale tantum.* water; waters. [unrelated to Lat. *aqua*, 'water,' Goth. *ahva*, 'stream.']

ápa, *prep.* away, forth, off; *opp. of* úpa, *see* √√ i, kṛ. [cf. ἀπό, Lat. *ab*, 'from'; Eng. *off*, *of*.]

apakāra, *m.* injury. [√1 kṛ + apa.]

apakārin, *a.* injuring. [do.]

apacāra, *m.* going off; absence. [√car + apa.]

á-patighnī, *a. f.* not husband-slaying. [402: acct, 1288a.]

ápatya, *n.* offspring; child; young (of animals). [ápa, 'off,' 1245b.]

a-pád [391], *a.* footless. [cf. ἄποδ-ες, 'halt': 1304a.]

apabhraṣṭa, *a.* fallen off; deviating (from good grammar); provincial. [√bhraṅç + apa.]

ápara [525], *pron. a.* hinder, *opp. of* pūrva; following a former one (pūrva), 86[13]; later; westerly, *opp. to* pūrva — *cf.* prāñc; a following one, *i.e.* an other; aparaṁ ca, and another thing, and further, *see* ca 3; — aparī [*cf.* 355b], *f. pl.* the future (days), the future. [lit. 'remoter,' fr. ápa, 474.]

a-parāñmukha, *a.* not having an averted face, *i.e.* not turning the back, 5[19].

á-parājita, *a.* unconquered; *w.* diç, the northeast quarter, 99[23] N. [√ji.]

aparādha, *m.* sin. [√rādh + apa.]

a-parijāta, *a.* not completely grown (of an embryo), *i.e.* prematurely born, still-born. [see pari-jāta and ref.]

a-pariṇīya, *grd.* without any leading around. [√nī.]

á-parimita, *a.* unmeasured, unlimited. [√1 mā.]

ápa-vrata, *a.* disobedient; stubborn. ['away from command,' 1310a: cf. ánu-vrata.]

apás, *see* ap.

ápas, *n.* work. [perhaps from √*ap, 'reach, take hold of' — see √āp: cf. Lat. *opus*, 'work.']

apāya, *m.* a going away; what takes one from the mark (*cf.* upāya); danger; disadvantage; diminution. [√i + apa, 1148.1a: for mg, cf. Eng. *untoward*.]

a-pārá, *a.* boundless. [pārá: acct, 1304a.]

ápi, *indecl.* unto, close upon *or* on; — 1. *prep.* to, *w.* √gam; — 2. *adv.* (thereto, besides, *i.e.*) further, also; *connecting clauses* (63[23]) *or words* (65[11]); *connecting sentences*, api ca, and besides, 29[9], *see* ca 3; ·· api ·· api, both ·· and, 54[23]; ··, ·· ca‿api, and, 5[12], 26[5]; ·· ca, ·· cāpi, both ·· and also, 12[1]; ··, ·· cāiva, ·· cāpi, 65[15]; ·· cāpi, ·· ca, 3[21], 16[11]; ·· cāpi, ·· ca, ·· ca, 16[6], 60[10]; na ··, na‿api ··, neither ··, nor ··, 9[9]; na ··, na cāpi, 22[12]; na ··, na ··, ·· api ca, neither ··, nor ··, nor also ··, 2[12]; ··, ·· vā, ·· vā‿api, either ··, or ··, or even ··, 62[2]; — 3. also, too, *immediately following the emphasized word*, 6[12], 11[3], 21[18], 24[21]; mām api, me too, 41[20]; — 4. even, *immediately following the emphasized word, and often marking a circumstance under which a thing is true where this is not to be expected: e.g.* 2[13], 28[7, 18], 33[19]; tathā‿api, so even, *i.e.* nevertheless, 21[11]; *concessively*, although, 29[1], 21[14], 51[1, 5]; *w.* na, not even, 19[15]; *w. indefinites*, kadā cid api na, not ever at all, 31[14], 32[3]; — 5. but, *immediately following a new subject, after change of subject*, 6[15], 28[21], 32[22], 41[17, 20, 21]; — 6. at least, 28[9, 11]; — 7. *converts an interr. into an indef.* [507]; *so* ka, 17[11], etc.; katham, 51[1]. [cf. ἐπί, 'on, upon'; perhaps Lat. *op-*, *ob-*, 'unto, on.']

a-pīḍayant, *a.* non-oppressing. [√pīḍ.]

a-pūrvá, *a.* having no predecessor; unprecedented; incomparable. [pū́rva: acct, 1304a.]

apekṣā, *f.* regard; expectation. [√īkṣ + apa.]

á-praja, *a.* having no offspring, childless. [prajā, 367b.]

a-prajñāta, *a.* undistinguished *or* not clearly to be known. [√jñā.]

a-pratarkya, *a.* un-imaginable.

a-pratima, *a.* without match *or* equal; unequalled. [pratimā, 367b.]

á-pratīta, *a.* not gone against; not withstood; invincible. [√i + prati.]

a-pratta, *a.* not given (in marriage). [√1 dā + pra, 1087c.]

á-prayucchant, *a.* not heedless; watchful. [√2 yu + pra, q.v.]

á-priya, *a.* not dear; disliked; disagreeable.

apsarás, *f.* one of a class of semi-divine beings, wives of the Gandharvas; an Apsaras, 67[12] N. [1151. 2d.]

a-buddhimant, *a.* unwise; foolish.

ábda, *m.* *lit.* water-giving; (*then, perhaps,* rainy season, *and so*) year. [ap + da, but w. irreg. acct, 1269: for mg, see varṣa.]

a-bhakṣya, *a.* not to be eaten; *as n.* that which ought not to be eaten.

á-bhaya, *a.* dangerless; *as n.* safety; feeling of safety; *superl.* greatest safety. [bhayá: acct, 1304a[2].]

a-bhāva, *m.* non-existence; absence; lack.

a-bhāvin, *a.* not about to be, not destined to be.

abhí, *adv.* to, unto; against; *frequent as vbl prefix; as prep.* unto, *w. acc.* [cf. ἀμφί, 'around'; Lat. *ambi-*, *amb-*, 'on both sides, around'; AS. *ymbe*, Ger. *um*, 'around'; for mg, cf. abhitas.]

abhijña, *a.* knowing, acquainted with. [√jñā + abhi, 333.]

abhítas, *adv.* on both sides; on all sides, 101[10]; around; near. [abhí.]

abhidrohá, *m.* offense. [√druh + abhi.]

abhidhā́, *f.* name; *cf.* ākhyā. [√1 dhā + abhi, q.v.]

abhidhāna, *n.* name; designation. [do.]

abhidhyāna, *n.* the thinking upon. [√dhyā + abhi.]

abhiniveça, *m.* inclination towards. [√viç + abhi-ni.]

abhibhāṣin, *a.* addressing. [√bhāṣ + abhi, 1183[3].]

abhíbhūti, *f.* superiority; *as a.* [1157. 2], superior. [√bhū + abhi.]

abhíbhūty-ojas, *a.* having superior might.

abhímāti, *f.* hostile plot; *concrete,* plotter, foe. [√man + abhi, 1157. 1d: ā *irreg.*]

abhi-mukha, *a.* having the face towards; facing; turned towards. [1305.]

abhivāda, *m.* salutation; *at* 60[22], signification. [√vad + abhi.]

abhivādana, *n.* salutation. [do.]

abhivādin, *a.* signifying. [do.]

abhivādya, *grdv.* to be saluted. [do.]

abhi-çiras, *a.* having the head towards, *w. acc.* [1305.]

a-bhīta, *a.* fearless; -vat [1107], fearlessly.

abhīpsu, *d.* desirous of obtaining, *w. acc.* [√āp + abhi, 1178f, 1038.]

abhy-adhika, *a.* additional; more.

abhy-antara, *a.* situated in the inside [1310a]; *as n.* interior; interval.

abhy-ātma, *a.* directed towards one's self [1310a]; -ám, *adv.* towards one's self [1310d].

abhyāsa, *m.* study. [√2 as + abhi, q.v.]

abhrá, *n.* rain-cloud. [cf. ὄμβρος, 'rain'; Lat. *imber*, 'rain': cf. ámbhas and ambu, 'water.']

abhrāvakāçika, *a.* (having, *i.e.*) affording an opportunity for the rain, exposing one's self to the rain. [abhra + avakāça, 1307.]

√ am (ámīti [634]; āmé; āmáyati). press on violently; harm; *caus.* [1041[2]], harm; be sick. [cf. aṅsa.]

áma, *pron.* this; he. [503[4]: cf. amā́.]

a-mantú, *a.* without intention. [mántu: 1304a.]

a-mára, *a.* deathless; immortal; *as m.* an immortal, a god; -vat [1107], *adv.* like a god. [mará: 1304a[2] end.]

amarottama, *a.* chief of gods. [uttama.]

amaropama, *a.* like a god. [upamā, 367b.]

á-martya, *a.* immortal.

a-marṣa, *m.* non-endurance; impatience; anger.

a-mahātman, *a.* not high-minded.

amā́, *adv.* at home, chez soi; amā kṛ, keep by one. [áma, 1112a and e.]

amā́tya, *m.* inmate of the same house, relative. [amā́, 1245b.]

a-māyā, *f.* no guile; sincerity.

amā-vāsa, *m.* a dwelling (of the moon) at home (*i.e.* with the sun).

amāvāsyà, *a.* of amāvāsa; *f.* -ā, *w. or without* rātri, the night of amāvāsa, *i.e.* night of new moon. [1212d 4.]

a-mithuna, *a.* not forming pairs (of both sexes).

a-mīmāṅsya, *a.* not to be called in question.

ámīva, *n., but generally* -ā, *f.* plague, distress; *as m.* tormenting spirit. [√am.]
amīva-cā́tana, *f.* -ī, *a.* driving away disease. [1271.]
amīva-hán [402], *a.* slaying the tormenting spirits.
amú, *pron. root, see* adas. [503[2].]
amútas, *adv.* from there, *opp. of* itas; there. [amu.]
amútra, *adv.* there; in the other world, *opp. of* iha *or* asmin (loke). [amú.]
amuyā́, *adv.* so. [amú, 1112a, e end.]
a-mṛ́ta, *a.* immortal; *as subst.* an immortal; *as n.* immortality; the drink of immortality, ἀμβροσία. ['not dead,' mṛtá, 1284a: cf. ἄ-μβροτος, 'immortal.']
amṛtatvá, *n.* immortality. [amṛta.]
ámbara, *n.* garment; sky. [prob. 'covering, envelope,' √1 vṛ + anu, for an(u)-vara: cf. adbhuta.]
ambu, *n.* water. [see abhrá.]
ambu-ja, *a.* water-born; *as n.* lotus.
ámbhas, *n.* water. [see abhrá.]
áya, *a. subst.* going, a going. [√i, 1148. 1ab.]
áyana, *n.* a going; place of going, way; course; *esp.* course (of the sun from one solstice to the other), *i.e.* half-year. [√i, 1150. 1a.]
áyas, *n.* metal; iron. [cf. Old Lat. *ais*, gen. *ais-is*, Lat. *aes*, 'metal, bronze'; AS. *ār*, 'bronze,' Eng. *ore;* perhaps AS. *īsern*, *īren*, Eng. *iron*, 'ferrum, ferreus.']
ayasmáya, *a.* iron. [see maya.]
a-yúj, *a.* not paired; in uneven numbers. [cf. ἄ-ζυξ, 'unyoked.']
a-yujá, *a.* not paired, uneven. [cf. ἄ-ζυγος, 'unpaired'; also ζυγὰ ἢ ἄζυγα, the game 'even or odd.']
á-yuddha, *n.* no fight. [1288a.]
a-yoddhṛ́, *m.* non-fighter, coward. [1288a[4].]
ará, *m.* spoke. [√ṛ, caus. 'fit in.']
áraṇa, *a.* distant, strange.
aráṇi, *f.* piece of wood for kindling fire by attrition.
áraṇya, *n.* wilderness, forest. ['strange land,' fr. áraṇa.]
araṇya-rājya, *n.* forest-sovereignty.
araṇya-vāsin, *a.* dwelling in the forest.
araṇyānī́, *f.* wilderness. [araṇya, cf. 1223b.]
a-rapás, *a.* without infirmity; whole. [rápas, 1304a.]
áram, *adv.* so as to fit *or* suit, ready, at hand, enough; *w.* kṛ, make ready, serve, 79[2]; *w.* gam, attend upon. [adv. acc. of ara, √ṛ, 1111d: cf. alam.]
á-rāti, *f.* non-favor; malignity; *personified, pl.*, malign hags. [acct, 1288a.]
arí [343d], *a.* —1. eager, *esp.* in one's relations to the gods, *and so*, pious; —2. greedy; —3. hostile; *as m.* enemy. [√ṛ, 'go for': cf. árya.]
á-riṣṭa, *a.* unharmed. [√riṣ: acct, 1284.]
ariṣṭátāti, *f.* unharmedness, health. [áriṣṭa, 1238.]
aruṇá, *a.* ruddy; *as m.* Aruna, name of a teacher, 95[11]. [cf. aruṣá.]
a-rundhatī́, *f.* Arundhatī, name of the faint star Alkor in Ursa Major, conceived as consort of the Seven Rishis. [√rudh, 691: acct, 1283a.]
aruṣá, *f.* áruṣī, *a.* ruddy. [see 362b[2]: cf. aruṇá.]
are, *word of address.* Ah! [voc. of ari, 1135c: cf. re.]
a-roga, *a.* not having disease, diseaseless.
arká, *m.* the sun. [√ṛc, 216.1.]
arghá, *m.* worth, price. [√arh.]
arghya, *a.* of price *or* that may be priced. [argha, 1212.]
√ arc, see √ṛc.
arcís, *n.* flame. [√ṛc, 1153.]
√ arj, *see* √2 ṛj.
arjana, *n.* acquisition. [√2 ṛj, 'get.']
árjuna, *a.* silver-white. [√3 ṛj, q.v.]
ártha, *m.* —1. aim, object, purpose, errand, sake; artham *and* arthe [1302c 4], for the sake of, on account of, for, *esp. frequent at end of cpds;* —2. (object, *i.e.*) thing, matter, affair, cause, business; —3. (object, *i.e.*) advantage, profit (*w. instr.*), wealth, property; —4. aim, intent, meaning, 59[15]. ['that which one goes for,' √ṛ, 1163.]
artha-tattva, *n.* true state of the matter *or* case.
√ arthaya (artháyate, -ti). seek for an object. [artha, 1067.]
+**abhi**, ask, entreat.
+**pra**, desire, sue for.

arthārjana, *n.* acquisition of an object. [arjana.]

arthín, *a.* having an object, desiring, seeking; (begging, *i.e.*) needy. [artha.]

arthya, *a.* wealthy. [artha.]

ardhá, *a.* half; *as m.* the half.

ardharcá, *m.* half-stanza. [ardha + ṛca.]

árdhika, *a.* amounting to half. [ardha.]

árpaṇa, *n.* the sending, consignment, entrusting. [caus. of √ṛ.]

árbuda, *n.* a hundred millions.

arbuda-çikhara, *m.* Million-peaks, name of a mountain.

aryá, *a.* faithful; attached, kindly, 79[3]. ['going eagerly to,' √ṛ: cf. árya.]

aryamán [426a], *m.* bosom-friend, *esp.* a bridegroom's friend, παρανύμφιος; Aryaman, name of an Aditya (invoked at the wedding, and often with play upon the appellative mg of the word). [aryá.]

arvāk-kālika, *a.* belonging to hither *or* nearer time, posterior; -tā, *f.* posteriority. [arvāñc (1249a) + kāla, 1222c 2.]

arvā́ñc [409a], *a.* directed hitherwards; *w.* kṛ, bring hither; *w.* nud, thrust hither, *i.e.* downwards.

√ **arh** (árhati, -te; arháyati). deserve; have a right to; *w. inf.*, be able; *w. inf.*, *as a weak imperative*, 7[17]; *caus.* give a right to, present with.

arha, *a.* deserving; worthy; fit. [√arh.]

a-lakṣaṇá, *a.* without any characteristic mark; without special mark, *i.e.* plain, unornamented. [lakṣaṇá.]

á-lakṣita, *a.* unnoticed. [√lakṣaya.]

a-labhamāna, *a.* not catching.

álam, *adv.* enough; *sometimes equiv. to an adj.*, adequate, fitting, ready; —*w. instr.* enough with, have done with; —*w.* kṛ, make ready, adorn; sv-alaṁkṛta, well adorned; sam-alaṁkṛta, well (sam *intens.*, 1077b) adorned. [later form of áram.]

a-lavaṇa, *a.* not salt.

a-lasá, *a.* not lively; without energy; slothful; tired.

a-lobha, *m.* non-greed; absence of cupidity.

álpa, *a.* small.

alpa-dhī, *a.* small-minded, of small intelligence.

alpaçás, *adv.* to a small degree. [alpa.]

√ **av** (ávati; ā́va; ā́vīt; aviṣyáti; ūtá; -ávya). —1. set a-going; —2. further, favor, wish well; —3. refresh; —4. have pleasure in (*acc.*). [cf. Lat. *avēre*, 'have pleasure in,' *ave*, 'hail.']

+ pra, show forth favor; *then*, be attentive *or* heedful (*as, conversely, in Eng.* attention *has come to mean* 'act of kindness *or* courtesy').

áva, *vbl prefix.* down; off.

ávakā, *f.* grassy swamp-plant, Blyxa octandra Richard.

avakāçá, *m.* —1. open place; —2. (place, *and so*) opportunity. [√kāç + ava.]

avajñā, *f.* contempt. [√jñā + ava: for mg, cf. avamāna.]

avatāra, *m.* descent, *esp.* of supernatural beings to the earth; an epiphany; incarnation, *Anglo-Indian* avatár. [√tṛ + ava.]

ávatta, *see* 1087e.

avadā́na, *n.* cutting off. [√2 dā + ava.]

a-vadyá, *a.* un-praiseworthy; *as n.* imperfection. [1285.]

√ **avadhīraya** (avadhīrayati). despise; reject.

a-vadhyá, *a.* not to be harmed, inviolable. [vádhya, 1285.]

avadhya-bhāva, *m.* inviolability, 35[21].

avanata-kāya, *a.* with bent down body, 34[17]. [√nam.]

avamāna, *m.* contempt; self-contempt, 50[14]. [√man + ava: for mg, cf. avajñā.]

avalambitavya, *grdv.* to be held on to. [√lamb + ava.]

a-vaçá, *a.* not willing *or* submissive; uncontrolled. [váça: acct, 1288a[4].]

avaçyam, *adv.* necessarily, surely. [fr. an unused adj. a-vaçya, 'unyielding.']

ávas, *n.* furtherance; grace. [√av.]

avás, *adv.* downwards; *w. abl.* [1128], down from. [cf. áva.]

avasá, *n.* refreshment, nourishment. [√av, mg 3.]

avasara, *m.* occasion. [√sṛ + ava: for mg, cf. Lat. *cāsus*, 'occasion,' w. *cadere*, 'fall,' and Ger. *Fall*, 'case, instance,' w. *fallen*, 'fall.']

avasā́na, *n.* place of rest. [√sā + ava.]

avasthā́, *f.* state, condition. [√sthā + ava · for mg, cf. Lat. *status* w. *stāre.*]

a-vahant, *a.* not flowing, standing. [√vah, mg 4.]

a-vācya, *a.* not to be spoken to.

ávāñc [409a], *a.* directed downwards; *acc. s. n.* avāk, *adv.* downwards, in depth.

ávi, *m.* sheep; *as f.* ewe. [cf. ὄϊς, *ὄϝις, Lat. *ovis*, 'sheep'; Eng. *ewe.*]

a-vicchindant, *a.* not severing. [√chid.]

a-vicchinna, *a.* not severed, continuous. [do.]

a-vijñāya, *grd.* without discerning. [√jñā.]

a-vijñeya, *a.* unknowable. [do.]

a-vidāsin, *a.* not drying up, perennial. [√das.]

á-vidvāṅs, *a.* unwise; *as m.* fool. [acct, 1288a.]

a-vidhavā́, *f.* not widow. [vidhávā: acct, 1288a[4].]

a-vidhānatas, *adv.* not according to regulation.

a-vipluta, *a.* not dishonored; unsullied. [√plu + vi, q.v.]

a-viveka, *a.* without discrimination.

avivekatā, *f.* lack of judgment. [1237.]

a-viçaṅka, *a.* without hesitation, unhesitating. [viçaṅkā, 334[2], 1304a.]

a-viṣaya, *m.* a non-province; something out of one's line *or* that one has no business to do; unlawful thing.

a-vṛká, *a.* not harmful; -ám, *adv.* harmlessly, lovingly. [vṛ́ka: acct, 1288a[4].]

avekṣā, *f.* a looking around. [√īkṣ + ava, 1149[3].]

a-vyakta, *a.* not manifest; *as m.* The All-soul, 67[17]. [√añj.]

a-vyaya, *a.* imperishable; not subject to change; unbroken. [1288a.]

√ 1 aç, *orig.* aṅç (açnóti, açnuté; ānáṅça, ānaçé [788[4]]; ā́ṣṭa; aṣṭá; áçitum). reach; attain; obtain, get. [cf. ποδ-ηνεκ-ής, 'reaching to the feet'; ἤν-εγκ-α, 'carried': see also the closely related √2 naç.]
+upa, attain to.

√ 2 aç (açnā́ti; ā́ça; ā́çīt; açiṣyáti; açitá; áçitum; açitvā́; -ā́çya). partake of; taste; eat. [a specialization of √1 aç: cf. ἔκ-ολος, 'bit': for mg, cf. bhakṣ.]
+pra, partake of; *caus.* feed.

a-çaknuvant, *a.* not being able. [√çak.]

a-çakya, *a.* impossible.

a-çaṅka, *a.* without hesitation. [çaṅkā: cf. aviçaṅka.]

açaná, *n.* food. [√2 aç.]

a-çuci, *a.* impure.

á-çubha, *a.* disagreeable.

á-çeva, *a.* not dear; hostile. [çéva: acct, 1288a.]

a-çeṣa, *a.* without remainder, entire; -tas, *adv.* entirely, without exception.

áçman, *m.* —**1.** stone; —**2.** thunderbolt; —**3.** vault of heaven, 79[9]. [cf. ἄκμων, 'anvil, thunderbolt'; kinship w. Eng. *hammer* uncertain.]

áçmanvant, *a.* stony. [áçman.]

áçru, *n.* tear.

áçva, *m.* horse; áçvā, *f.* mare, steed. [cf. ἵππος, dialectic ἴκκος, Lat. *equus*, Old Saxon *ëhu*, AS. *eh*, *eoh*, 'horse.']

açva-kovida, *a.* well skilled in horses.

açva-medhá, *m.* horse-sacrifice.

açvín, *a.* horsed; *as dual m.* the Açvins, gods of the morning light, 85[15] N. [açva.]

áçvya, *a.* consisting of horses; of a horse. [açva: cf. ἵππιος, 'of a horse.']

aṣṭá [483[3]], *num.* eight. [cf. ὀκτώ, Lat. *octō*, AS. *eahta*, Eng. *eight.*]

aṣṭamá, *a.* eighth. [aṣṭá, 487[6].]

aṣṭa-vidha, *a.* of eight sorts; eight-fold. [vidhā, 1302c 5.]

aṣṭāṅga, *n.* eight members. [aṅga, 1312.]

aṣṭāṅga-pāta, *m.* a fall on eight members, *i.e.* on hands, knees, feet, breast, and face, *i.e.* a most profound obeisance.

áṣṭi, *f.* attainment. [√1 aç.]

√ 1 as (ásti [636]; ā́sa). —**1.** be, exist; be present *or* on hand; take place, happen; asti, āsīt, there is, there was, *very frequent at beg. of stories;* —**2.** be, *w. predicate possessive gen., i.e.* belong to; asti mama, I have; *observe that Skt. has no verb for* 'have'; —**3.** *most frequent as simple copula; further, w. ppls: e.g.* prāpto 'si, art thou come, didst thou come, 9[1]; hantavyo 'smi, *occidendus sum*, 3[2]; çepāno 'smi, I have sworn, 97[7]; *redundantly* [303b[4] end]: *e.g.* tathā‿anuṣṭhite sati, it being thus performed, 35[17]; *so* 37[13], 39[16,22]; prahṛṣṭaḥ san, being pleased, 48[12]; —4. *w. advs:* tūṣṇīm āsīt, kept silent; evam astu, so be it; *w.* prādus, *see s.v.;* —5. become, 96[19]. [w. ás-ti, s-ánti, 'is, are,' cf. ἔσ-τι, 'ís, exists,' εἰσί, Doric ἐντί, *ἄντι, 'are,' Lat. *es-t, s-unt,* AS. *is, *is-t, s-ind,* 'is, are,' Eng. *is;* cognate are *a-m, ar-t, are.*]

√ **2 as** (ásyati, -te; ā́sa; asiṣyáti; astá; ásitum; asitvā́; -ásya). throw, cast, shoot; throw aside. [cf. así, 'the brandished' sword; Lat. *ensis,* 'sword'; *ālea, *aslea,* 'die,' like Ger. *Würfel,* 'die,' fr. *werfen,* 'throw.']

+**vy-ati**, throw over, cross.

+**abhi**, throw (one's self) upon, direct (one's attention) to, study. [for mg, cf. προσέχειν without τὸν νοῦν.]

+**ni**, throw down; deposit; commit.

+**pari-ni**, throw down over, stretch over.

+**nis**, throw out; root out; destroy.

+**vi**, —1. cast asunder; cast *or* throw away; —2. break in pieces, 70[14].

+**sam**, cast *or* put together.

a-saṁhrādayant, *a.* not causing to rattle. [√hrād.]

a-satyasaṁdha, *a.* unfaithful, treacherous.

á-sant, *a.* non-existing; *as n.* non-existence.

a-sapiṇḍa, *a.* related more distantly than in the sixth generation, *see* sapiṇḍa.

a-samartha, *a.* unable.

a-sampatti, *f.* non-success.

a-sambaddha, *a.* un-connected, in-coherent, *w. same fig. mg as in Eng.* [√bandh.]

a-sambandha, *a.* not having relationship.

a-sambhāvya, *a.* unsupposable, impossible.

a-saha, *a.* impatient.

ásu, *m.* vital spirit; vigorous life. [√1 as.]

a-sutṛ́p, *a.* insatiable. [1288a[4].]

asu-tṛ́p, *a.* life-robbing. [vbl of √2 tṛp.]

ásu-nīti, *f.* the leading *or* continuing of life (in the other world); spirit-life; spirit-world. [acct, 1274.]

a-sunvá, *a.* not pressing (Soma), *i.e.* indifferent to the gods, godless. [see 1148. 3b and 716.]

ásura, —1. *a.* spiritual (used of the gods, and designating esp. the difference between celestial and mundane existence); —2. *as m.* a spirit of life, a god; ásura adevá, spirit that is no god, demon, 82[6]; —3. *later,* demon (45[6]), enemy of the gods, an Asura, a not-god (as if the word were a-sura — whence, by popular etymology, the pendant sura, 'god'). [asura, 1226 (cf. 1188f), and as-u fr. √1 as, 1178b.]

asuryà, *a.* godlike; *as n. pl.* godhead. [ásura, 1212d4.]

√ **asūya** (asūyáti). be impatient.

asūyā, *f.* impatience. [√asūya, 1149[6].]

ásṛj [432], *n.* blood, 24[22]. [cf. Cyprian ἔαρ, 'blood.']

asāú, *see* 501 *and* adas.

ásta, *n.* home; ástam, *w.* i, gam, yā, go home; *esp.* of the sun [*see* 1092b], set. [prob. √1 as: for mg, cf. bhavana.]

asta-māuna, *a.* having thrown aside *or* abandoned silence. [√2 as.]

asti, *f.* being. [√1 as.]

asthán [431], *n.* bone. [cf. ὀστέον, Lat. stem *ossi-, *osti-,* nom. *os,* 'bone.']

a-sthāvara, *a.* not standing.

ásthi, *see* asthán.

a-spṛçant, *a.* not touching. [√spṛç.]

asmá [494], *pron. stem.* we, us. [cf. ἡμεῖς, Lesbian ἄμμες, 'we.']

asmád, *as stem in cpds* [494], our; *as pl. majestaticus,* my.

asmā́ka, *a.* of us; our. [asma, 516[4].]

á-svapant, *a.* not sleeping. [√svap.]

a-svastha, *a.* not well, ill; not self-contained, not master of one's self.

a-sveda, *a.* free from sweat.

√ **ah** (ā́ttha, ā́ha, āháthus, -tus, āhús [801a]). say; call; āhus, they say. [cf. Lat. *aio,* 'say,' *ad-ag-ium,* 'saw, proverb,' *nego,* 'say no.']

+**pra**, declare to be.

1 **áha**, *assev. particle.* certainly, of course; namely. [pron. root a: cf. 1104[3] end.]

2 **áha**, *for* áhan *in cpds.* [1209a, 1315a.]

á-hata, *a.* —1. not beaten; —2. (since Hindu washermen wet the clothes and pound them with stones) unwashed, of a garment, *i.e.* new. [√han.]

áhan, **áhar**, **áhas** [430a], *n.* day (as opp. to night), *e.g.* 92[16]; day.
ahám [491], *pron.* I. [cf. ἐγώ, Lat. *ego*, AS. *ic*, Eng. *I*: see 491 and ma etc.]
áhar, *see* áhan.
ahar-niça, *n.* day and night, νυχθήμερον; -am, *adv.* constantly. [niçā: 1253b.]
ahalyā, *f.* Ahalyā, Gautama's wife.
áhas, *see* áhan.
a-hastá, *a.* handless. [hásta, 1304a.]
ahaha, *excl. of joy or sorrow.* [1135a.]
a-hārya, *a.* not liable to be stolen.
ahāryatva, *n.* non-liability to be stolen. [1239.]
áhi, *m.* serpent; *esp.* the dragon of the sky, *often identified w.* the demon Vritra. [see under agha: cf. ἔχις, Lat. *anguis*, 'serpent'; ἔγχελυς, Lat. *anguilla*, 'eel.']
á-hiṅsā, *f.* non-injuring (any creature).
áhi-gopā [352], *a.* having the dragon as their keeper. [1302[1].]
ahivat, *adv.* as a dragon. [1107.]
ahi-hátya, *n.* the slaying of the dragon; the (victorious) fight with the dragon. [acct, 1272a, 1213c.]
á-hṛṇāna, *a.* not being angry. [√2hṛ.]
aho, *excl. of astonishment, pleasant or unpleasant.* [1135a: euphony, 138f.]
aho-rātrá, *n.* day and night, νυχθήμερον. [áhas + rā́tri, 1253b: see rātra.]

ā́, *adv.* —1. hither, unto, *as prefix w. verbs of motion*; —2. *conjunctively*, thereto, besides; ca ·· ā, both ·· and, 85[5]; —3. *asseveratively*, (up to, *i.e.*) quite, entirely, 73[20]; —4. *as prep.*, *w. abl.*: hither from, all the way from; *and then* [293c], all the way to, until, 49[13], 64[14], 103[20], 105[6], 106[2]; as far as, 105[10]. [cf. Lat. *ā*, 'from,' which is not akin w. *ab*, 'from.']
ākará, *m.* —1. accumulation, abundance; —2. mine. [√3kṛ + ā, q.v.]
√ ākarṇaya (ākarṇayati; ākarṇita; ākarṇya). listen; give ear to; hear. [denom. fr. the possessive adj. *ākarṇa, 'having the ear to, *i.e.* listening.']
ākarṣaka, *a.* attractive; —*f.* -ikā [1222d], Pleasanton, as name of a town. [√kṛṣ + ā.]
ākarṣikākhya, *a.* having the name ākarṣikā. [ākhyā.]
ākāra, *m.* make; shape; appearance. [√1kṛ + ā: cf. ākṛti.]
ākāravant, *a. like the Eng.* shapely. [ākāra.]
ākāçá, *in Veda, m.*; *later, n.* free *or* open space; sky. [prop. 'outlook, clearness,' √kāç + ā.]
ākula, *a.* —1. bestrewn, covered, filled; —2. *fig.* confused; agitated. [√3kṛ + ā, q.v.]
√ ākulaya (ākulayati). confuse; ākulita, at one's wit's end. [ākula.]
ā́kūta, *n.* intention. [√kū + ā.]
ā́kṛti, *f.* make; shape; appearance. [√1kṛ + ā, 1157.1d: cf. ākāra.]
ākhú, *m.* mold-warp; mouse. ['burrower,' √khā + ā, 1178a end.]
ākhyā, *f.* name; *at end of cpds*, having ·· as name. [√khyā + ā.]
ākhyā́na, *n.* tale. [√khyā + ā, 1150.]
āgantavya, *grdv.* *see* √gam + ā.
āgantu, *m.* arrival; *and so, as in Eng.*, person arriving. [√gam + ā, 1161.]
āgamana, *n.* a coming hither; *w.* punar, a returning. [√gam + ā.]
ā́gas, *n.* sin. [orig., perhaps, 'a slip,' √añj: cf. ἄγος, 'guilt': different is ἅγος, see √yaj.]
ā́ghṛṇi, *a.* glowing, beaming. [√2ghṛ, 'glow,' + ā, 1158.]
āṅgirasá, *a.* descended from Angiras. [áṅgiras, 1208a.]
ācamana, *n.* the rinsing of the mouth. [√cam + ā.]
ācamanīya, *m.* dish for use in rinsing the mouth. [ācamana, 1215.]
ācāra, *m.* walk and conversation; conduct; usage; observance. [√car + ā.]
ācāryà, *m.* teacher, *esp.* of the Veda. [perhaps, 'the man of observances,' fr. ācāra, 1212d 4.]
ājarasám, *adv.* to old age. [from the phrase ā́ jarás-am.]
ājarasā́ya, *adv.* to old age. [dat. (1113) formed fr. the preceding, as if that were acc. of ājarasá.]
ājí, *m.* race; contest; battle. [√aj, 1155: cf. ἀγ-ών, 'contest.']

ā́jñā, *f.* order; command. [√jñā + ā.]

ā́jya, *n.* clarified butter (for anointing, etc.); *cf.* ghṛta. [√añj + ā, see 100[20]: for mg, cf. Eng. noun *smear*, 'ointment,' and verb *smear*.]

ājya-çeṣa, *m. n.* rest of the clarified butter.

ājyāhutí, *f.* oblation of clarified butter. [āhuti.]

ā́ñjana, *n.* ointment. [√añj + ā : cf. Lat. *unguen*, 'ointment.']

āḍhyá, *a.* wealthy; rich. [perhaps fr. arthya.]

ā́t, *adv.* thereupon; ā́d íd, then indeed. [lit. 'from that,' abl. of á, 1114a.]

ātithyá, *n.* hospitality. [átithi, 'guest,' 1211.]

ātma, *for* ātman *in cpds*, 1249a[2].

ātmaka, *for* ātman *in mg* 4 *at end of cpds* [1222, 1307]; *e.g.* māra‿ātmaka, murder-natured, murderous.

ātmán, *m.* —1. breath; —2. spirit; soul (*cf.* 84[8] N.), as principle of life and feeling; —3. self; *very often so used as a simple reflexive pron.* [514]; *e.g.*, myself, 36[16]; thyself, 26[15]; himself, 4[19]; *in genitive:* his, 17[16]; her, 46[5]; one's own, 21[18], 58[22]; —4. nature, character, peculiarity; *esp. at end of cpds, see* ātmaka; —5. the soul κατ' ἐξοχήν, the soul of the universe, 66[8]. [cf. ἀϋτμήν, 'breath'; ἀτμός, 'vapor'; AS. *æþm*, *æðm*, 'breath': for mg, cf. πνεῦμα and Lat. *anima*, 'breath, spirit.']

ātma-pakṣa, *m.* one's own party.

ātma-prabha, *a.* having his *or* their own splendor. [prabhā, 354.]

ātma-bhava, *m.* the coming into existence of one's self.

ātma-māṅsa, *n.* one's own flesh.

ātmavát, *adv.* as one's self. [ātma, *i.e.* ātman: 1107.]

ātma-çakti, *f.* one's own power.

ātma-çoṇita, *n.* one's own blood.

ātma-saṁdeha, *m.* danger of one's self, personal risk.

ātma-hita, *n.* one's own welfare.

ātmāupamya, *n.* likeness to one's self, *i.e.* a putting one's self in another's place. [āupamya.]

ādara, *m.* respect, notice, care. [√2 dṛ + ā, 'regard.']

ādáhana, *n.* burning-place, place of cremation. [√dah + ā.]

ādāna, *n.* receiving. [√1 dā + ā, 'take,' 1150.]

ādi, *m.* —1. in-ception, beginning, 60[8]; ādim ādatte, he makes a beginning; ādāv eva, just before, just now; —2. *esp. at end of adj. cpds* [*see* 1302c 1]: ·· -ādi, having ·· as the beginning, *i.e.* ·· and so forth; *or, the qualified noun being omitted, and the adj. cpd being used as subst.*, ·· and so forth. [undoubtedly fr. √1 dā + ā, 'take,' 'a taking hold of, *i.e.* beginning,' 1155.2e: for mg, cf. Lat. *in-cipere*, Ger. *an-fangen*, 'take hold of, begin.']

ādika, *equiv. to* ādi *in use* 2. [1222, 1307.]

ādityá, *m.* —1. son of Aditi, name applied to the gods of the heavenly light, Varuna, Mitra, Aryaman, etc.; —2. Aditya, name of the sun-god, son of Aditi; the sun. [áditi, 1211.]

ādin, *a.* eating, devouring. [√ad, 1183[3].]

ādevana, *n.* gambling-place, 98[13]. [√1 dīv, 'play,' + ā.]

ādya, *a.* first; *equiv. to* ādi *in use* 2. [ādi, 1211.]

ā́dhipatya, *n.* sovereignty. [ádhipati, 1211[2] end.]

ādhṛṣya, *grdv.* to be ventured against; approachable. [√dhṛṣ + ā, 963d.]

ādheya, *n.* a placing, *esp.* of the sacred fire. [√1 dhā + ā, 'put,' 1213c.]

ā́dhvaryava, *n.* service of sacrificing priest. [adhvaryú, 1208c.]

ā́naḍuha, *a.* of a bull, taurine. [anaḍúh, weak form of anaḍvah, 404; 1208a.]

ānana, *n.* mouth; face. [prop. 'the breather,' √an: cf. ἠνεσ-, 'face,' in προσ-ηνής and ἀπ-ηνής, 'with face turned towards,' 'with face averted': for mg, cf. nayana.]

√ āp (āpnóti; ā́pa; ā́pat; āpsyáti; āptá; ā́ptum; āptvā́; -ā́pya; āpyáte; ī́psati [1030]; āpáyati). reach; win; get; bring upon one's self; —āptá: —1. having reached; extending over; *and so*, adequate, suitable, fit; —2. having reached, *i.e.* being near *or* intimate, *and so, as m.*, a friend; —īpsitá, whom *or* what one desires to obtain, sought for, desired. [prob. for ā-ap, 108g, see ápas: cf. *ἤπιος*, 'approachable, friendly'; Lat. *ap-iscor*, 'reach,' *ap-ere*, 'seize, fasten'; *ἅπτω* (√ἀφ for ἀπ), 'fasten.']

+abhi, reach to a thing, attain; *desid.* strive to win; *caus.* cause to reach the mark, *i.e.* carry out fully, 96[12].

+ava, come upon, fall in with; obtain, acquire; take upon one's self; incur.

+pra, reach; arrive; come upon; catch; win, obtain, get; incur; —prāpta: reached, found, caught, obtained; reached, arrived, having come; —*caus.* cause to arrive at, bring to, 53[17]; prāpaṇīya, to be brought to, 53[15].

+vi, reach through, pervade, 66[9].

āpaṇa, *m.* market. [√paṇ + ā.]

āpad, *f.* misfortune. [lit. 'a getting into' (trouble), √pad + ā: for specialization of mg, cf. ārti, and Eng. *ac-cident*, lit. 'a happening' (of trouble).]

ā́pas, *see* áp.

āpí, *m.* friend. ['one who has reached *or* stands near another' (cf. āpta), √āp: cf. *ἤπιος*, s.v. āp.]

āpta-dakṣiṇa, *a.* having *or* accompanied by suitable presents. [dakṣiṇā, 334[2].]

ābdika, *a.* annual; · · -ābdika, · · -ennial, lasting · · years. [abda.]

ābharaṇa, *n.* ornament (jewels, etc.). ['what is worn,' √bhṛ + ā: for mg, cf. *φᾶρος*, 'garment,' w. *φέρω*, and Ger. *Tracht*, 'dress,' w. *tragen*, 'wear.']

āmá, *a.* raw. [cf. *ὠμός*, 'raw'; Lat. *amārus*, 'bitter.']

āmaya, *m.* injury; disease. [caus. of √am.]

āmayitnu, *a.* sickening. [caus. of √am, 1196b.]

āmiṣa, *n.* flesh. [cf. āmá and ā́mis.]

āmiṣāçin, *a.* flesh-eating. [āçin.]

ā́mis, *n.* raw flesh; flesh. [cf. āmá.]

āmóda, *a.* gladdening; *as m.* fragrance. [√mud + ā.]

āyátana, *n.* foot-hold; resting-place; *esp.* place of the sacred fire, fire-place. [√yat + ā.]

ā́yata-locana, *a.* having long eyes. [√yam + ā.]

āyasá, *a.* metallic, of iron; *as n.* metal, iron. [áyas, 1208a.]

āyāma, *m.* *like Eng.* extent, *i.e.* length. [√yam + ā, 'extend.']

āyú, *a.* active, lively. [√i, 1178a: prob. akin are *ἠΰς*, **ἠjύ-s*, *ἐΰς*, 'active, doughty, mighty,' *εὐ-*, 'strongly,' *εὖ*, generalized, 'well': for mg of āyú, cf. the phrase "full of *go*."]

ā́yudha, *n.* weapon. [√yudh + ā.]

ā́yuṣmant, *a.* having life *or* vitality; long-lived; old. [ā́yus, 1235a.]

ā́yus, *n.* (activity, liveliness, *and so*) life; vitality; *personified as a genius*, Ayus, 85[18]; period *or* duration of life; long life; (*like Eng.* life, *i.e.*) living creatures. [√i, 1154, cf. āy-ú: cf. *αἰ-ών*, Lat. *ae-vu-m*, AS. *ǣw*, *ǣ*, 'life-time, time'; AS. *āwa*, *ā*, Eng. *aye*, 'ever'; AS. *ǣf-re*, Eng. *ev-er*.]

āraṇyaka, *a.* pertaining to the wilderness; *as n.* forest-treatise (to be read in the solitude of the wilderness — *Whitney, p.* xvi.). [áraṇya, 1222e.]

ārādhana, *n.* the gratifying, propitiation, service. [√rādh + ā, caus.]

ārogya, *n.* *lit.* diseaseless-ness, *i.e.* health. [aroga.]

ārohá, *m.* the swelling hips *or* buttocks of a woman. [prop. 'the seat' on which a child is carried astride by its mother, √ruh + ā, 'get upon, take one's seat upon': see aṅka and cf. the words of an ogress, MBh., āruha mama çroṇīṁ, neṣyāmi tvāṁ vihāyasā, 'get upon my hip, I will carry thee through the air.']

ā́rta, *a.* visited, *esp.* by trouble; afflicted; stricken; distressed. [√ṛ + ā, q.v.: for mg, cf. American slang phrase *gone for*.]

ā́rti, *f.* a visitation (of evil), *i.e.* trouble, misfortune, *see* 93[15] N. [√ṛ + ā: for mg, cf. ārta and āpad.]

ārdrá, *a.* wet.

ārdrá-vāsas, *a.* having wet garments.

ā́rya, *a.* belonging to the faithful, *i.e.*, *as m.*, man of one's own tribe, an Aryan, as designation of a man of the Vedic Indian tribes; *as adj.* Aryan; noble; reverend (used in respectful address). [aryá, 1208f: cf. Avestan *airya*, 'Aryan'; New Persian, *īrān*, 'Persia'; Hdt. vii. 62, *οἱ Μῆδοι ἐκα-*

λέοντο πάλαι Ἄριοι; Keltic nom. *eriu*, acc. *erinn*, name of Ireland; Eng. *Ir-ish*: cf. arí, aryá.]

ālasya, *n.* sloth. [alasa.]

ālasya-vacana, *n.* sloth-dictum, as designation for the ignava ratio *or* fatalist's argument.

ālāpá, *m.* talk; conversation. [√lap + ā.]

ālokana, *n.* the beholding. [√lok + ā.]

āvá, *pron. stem*, 491.

āvís, *adv.* forth to sight, in view; *w.* kṛ, make visible. [1078.]

āvṛ́t, *f.* a turning. [√vṛt + ā.]

āça, *m.* food. [√2 aç, 'eat.']

āçayá, *m.* lying-place; abode. [√çī + ā.]

āçás, *f.* wish, hope. [çaṅs + ā.]

āçā́, *f.* hope. [younger form of āçás.]

ā́çā, *f.* region; quarter of the sky). [specialized from 'place, objective point, that which one reaches,' √1 aç, 'reach.']

āçāvant, *a.* hopeful. [āçā́.]

āçín, *a.* eating, *in cpds.* [√2 aç, 1183[3].]

āçís [392], *f.* wish *or* prayer, *esp.* for good. [√çās + ā, 639, 225[2]: cf. praçís.]

āçīr-vāda, *m.* expression of a (good) wish, *i.e.* a benediction. [āçís, cf. 392.]

āçīrvādābhidhānavant, *a.* containing a designation of a benediction. [āçīr-vāda + abhidhāna, 1233.]

āçú, *a.* swift. [cf. ὠκύ-ς, 'swift'; Lat. *ōc-ior*, 'swifter.']

āçcarya, *n.* wonder; prodigy.

āçrama, *m.* —1. (place of self-castigation, *i.e.*) hermitage; —2. stadium in a Brahman's religious life (of which there are four: that of the student *or* brahmacārin, that of the householder *or* gṛhastha, that of the hermit *or* vānaprastha, and that of the beggar *or* bhikṣu), *see* 65[3] N. [√çram + ā.]

āçraya, *m.* that on which anything leans *or* rests; support; refuge; protection; authority. [√çri + ā.]

āçraya-bhūta, *a.* having become a protection, *i.e.*, *as m.*, protector. [1273c.]

ās, *excl. of joy or of displeasure.* ah!

√ **ās** (ā́ste [628], ā́sīna [619[3]]; āsā́ṁ cakre; ā́siṣṭa; āsiṣyáte; āsitá; ā́situm; āsitvā́; -ā́sya). —1. sit; seat one's self; settle down, 93[1]; —2. abide; dwell, 85[19]; stay; remain; continue, 64[14]; —3. *w. ppl.* [1075c], continue (doing anything), keep on, 32[14,18]. [cf. ἧσ-ται, 'sits'; Lat. *ānus*, **ās-nu-s*, 'seat, buttocks'; Old Lat. *āsa*, Lat. *āra*, 'family-seat, hearth, altar.']

+ adhi, take one's place in, *i.e.* visit, 49[16]; get into (shoes), *i.e.* put on, 45[17].

+ upa, sit by (in sign of readiness to serve), wait upon (a command), 92[4]; sit by (expectantly), sit waiting for, 91[4].

+ pary-upa, sit around, surround, 2[7].

āsana, *n.* sitting, 4[12]; seat. [√ās.]

āsāra, *m.* (*like Eng. colloq.* a pour, *i.e.*) pouring rain. [√sṛ + ā, 'run.']

āsurá, *a.* demonic; *as m.* demon. [ásura, 1208f.]

āsécana, *n.* cavity (into which one pours). [√sic + ā.]

āsecanavant, *a.* having a cavity, hollow. [āsecana.]

āhati, *f.* blow. [√han + ā, 1157[1] and 1d.]

āhanás, *a.* swelling, fermenting, foaming.

āhávana, *n.* oblation. [√hu + ā.]

āhavanī́ya, *a.* of *or* for the oblation; *w.* agni, oblation-fire; *as m.*, *without* agni, oblation-fire (the one that receives the oblation), *see* 102[2] N. [āhavana, 1215.]

āhāra, *m.* the taking to one's self (of food), eating; what one takes, *i.e.* food. [√hṛ + ā.]

āhāra-dāna, *n.* giving of food.

āhāra-parityāga, *m.* relinquishment of food.

āhārādi, *n.* food and so forth. [ādi, 1302c 1.]

āhārārthin, *a.* seeking food. [arthin.]

ā́hitāgni, *a.* having a set *or* established fire; *as m.* one who is keeping alive a sacred fire. [āhita, √1 dhā + ā, 'set': 1299a.]

ā́huti, *f.* oblation, offering (used both of the act and of the thing offered); *cf. the later word* homa. [√hu + ā: w. -huti, cf. χύ-σι-ς, 'a pouring.']

āhvāna, *n.* call; invitation. [√hū or hvā + ā.]

i, *pron. root, see* idam *and* 502[3].

√ **i** (éti [612]; iyā́ya, īyús [783b[2]]; eṣyáti; itá; étum; itvā́; -ítya). —1. go; go to *or* towards; come; enter; —2. move on, 88[12]; pass; —3. go to, *i.e.* attain (a thing *or* condition); —íyase [1021[2]], goest hither and thither, 90[15]; —īmahe [1021[2]], (*like Ger.* an-gehen) we approach with prayers, beseech. [w. i-más, cf. ἴ-μεν, Lat. *i-mus*, 'we go'; Goth. *i-ddja*, AS. *eode*, 'went'; radically akin, perhaps, is AS. *gān* (stem *gā* for **ga-i*, *ga-* being the inseparable prefix), Eng. *go*, Ger. *gehen*: see also āyú, ā́yus.]

+ati, go beyond *or* past *or* over; overwhelm; transcend; leave behind, get rid of, 68[9]; escape.

+adhi, come upon, notice; take notice, 87[18]; —*middle* adhīté [612 note], go over for one's self, repeat, learn, read; *ppl.* adhīta: *w. act. mg*, learn-ed, 18[6]; *w. pass. mg*, learnt, 21[15]; —*caus.* adhyāpáyati [1042e], cause to learn, teach.

+upa‿adhi, *in* upādhyāya.

+anu, go along *or* after; accompany; *ppl.* anvita, accompanied by, endowed *or* filled *or* connected with.

+sam-anu, *the same.*

+antar, go within; retire, withdraw.

+apa, go off; slink away.

+abhi, go unto; become embodied in.

+ava, approach.

+ā, come near *or* unto *or* hither; *w. the adv.* punar, go back.

+abhy-ā, approach, go near.

+upa‿ā, come unto.

+sam-ā, come near to together; assemble.

+ud, go up, rise (of the sun).

+upa, go unto; fall to the lot of; *ppl.* upeta, gone unto, attended by, provided with.

+sam-upa, come hither.

+ni, go into *or* in; *cf.* nyāya.

+parā, go away *or* forth; depart.

+anu-parā, go forth along (a path).

+vi-parā, go away separately.

+pari, circumambulate; walk round (the fire).

+pra, —1. go forward *or* onward, 83[11]; *esp.* go forth out of this world, *and so* (*like Eng.* depart), die; pretya, after dying, *i.e.* in the other world (*opp. of* iha); preta, dead; —2. come out, stick out, be prominent.

+prati, go against, withstand; go back to; recognize, 98[16]; pratīta, recognized, approved.

+vi, go asunder; separate; disperse, 83[15]; spread one's self over, *i.e.* pervade, 72[2]; vīta, *at beg. of cpds*, having departed ··, *i.e.* free from ··.

+sam, come together; assemble.

icchā, *f.* wish; desire; inclination. [√1 iṣ, 'seek': cf. AS. *ǣsce*, 'an asking.']

íj, *vbl.* sacrificing, *in* ṛtv-íj. [√yaj, 252.]

ijyā, *f.* sacrifice. [√yaj, 252.]

ítara [523], *pron. a.* other; the other; another; other than, *i.e.* different from, *w. abl.* [pron. root i, 502[3]: cf. Lat. *iterum*, 'another time.']

itás, *adv.* —1. *used like the abl. of a pron.* [1098c[2]], 24[18]; —2. from this (place), from here; here; from this (world), 5[8]; itas tatas, here and there; —3. from this (time), now, 41[8]. [pron. root i, 502[3].]

íti, *adv. see* 1102a. —1. in this way, thus; so; iti devā akurvan, thus the gods did, 96[9]; —2. *used w. all kinds of quotations made* verbis ipsissimis: tathā‿ity uktvā, upon saying "Yes," 4[2]; sa pṛṣṭavān kāu yuvām iti, he asked, "Who are ye," 45[5]; evam astu iti tāu dhāvitāu, with the words, "So be it," the two ran off, 45[16]; *so* RV., 85[12]; *so* MS., 92[15]; ity ākarṇya, on hearing (so, *i.e.*) the preceding çlokas, 17[16]; *cf.* 18[10]; —2a. *designating something as that which was, or under the circumstances might have been said or thought or intended or known, sometimes* (46[16]) *preceding it, but usually following it*: martavyam iti, at the thought, "I must die," 29[9]; gardabho 'yam iti jñātvā, recognizing (the fact), "This is an ass," 34[20]; —2b. *interr. in place of the exact quotation:* kim iti, alleging *or* intending what, under what pretext, with what intention, 30[4], 41[5]; —2c. *used in giving an authority:* iti dhāraṇā, so (is) the rule, 62[17]; ity eke, so some folks (say), 101[9]; —2d. *used in citing a Vedic verse by its first word* (60[13]) *or words* (98[20], etc.); —2e. *at the end of a section or book* (*cf.* atha), here endeth, 4[4]; —2f. *w. verbs* *of naming, considering, etc., the predicate, marked by* iti, *is nom., sometimes acc.* — *both constructions at* 61^{22}; damayantī iti viçrutā, known as *or* named "D.," 6^{3}; —3. *used to include under one head or as in a list several separate objects*, 21^{7}, 100^{8}, 105^{7}; —4. evam *superfluously added*, 61^{12}; iti *doubled*, 60^{11}; —5. iti ha = iti, 12^{8}, 61^{18}. [pron. root i, 1102a: cf. Lat. *itidem*, 'just so.']

itihāsá, *m.* story, legend. [agglomeration of iti ha āsa, 'thus, indeed, it was': 1314b.]

itthā́ (*V. only*) *and* itthám, *adv.* in this way; so; kíṁ ta itthā́, how does this happen thee? 73^{8}. [adverbs made from the acc. sing. neut., i-d, of the pron. root i, see 1101: cf. Lat. *itā* and *item*, 'so.']

ity-ādi, *at end of possessive adj. cpds used substantively*, that which has "· · ·" as its beginning, *i.e.* "· · ·" and so forth. [see 1302c 1 end.]

íd, *V. pcl.* just; exactly; even; *emphasizing the preceding word and to be rendered by laying emphasis on that word.* [acc. of pron. root i, 1111a: cf. Lat. *i-d*, 'it.']

1 **idám** [501-2 — *forms made from four stems*, á *and* aná, í *and* imá, *those from* á *being often unaccented, see* 74^{9} N.], *pron.* this, this here, τόδε, *e.g.* 20^{9}, 86^{10}, 87^{8}; *contrasted w.* asāu, 'that one,' 103^{7}; asmin loke, in this world, 66^{12}; *without* loke *and contrasted w.* amutra, 103^{8}; idaṁ viçvam bhuvanam, this whole world, 85^{12}; idam sarvam, this entire (world), 63^{21}; *so* 66^{19}; *so* idam, τὸ πᾶν, $56^{15,17}$; iyam pṛthivī, this earth, 10^{10}; iyam *alone*, this earth, $93^{1,2}$; —*refers very often, like* τάδε, *to something following* (*just as* etad *and* ταῦτα *to something preceding*), *e.g.* 13^{22}, 26^{7}, 45^{14}, 51^{6}; *occasionally refers to something immediately preceding, e.g.* 10^{17}, 24^{9}, 74^{12}, 79^{4}; —*joined w. pronouns:* ko 'yam āyāti, who comes here? 27^{12}; yo 'yaṁ dṛçyate, which is seen here, 46^{17}; mām imam, me here, 76^{16}; *nom. to be rendered* here is *or* are, 56^{1}, 4^{21}; imāu vātas, blow hither, 90^{12}. [cf. Lat. *i-d*, Goth. *i-ta*, Ger. *es*, 'it.']

2 **idám**, *adv.* now, 86^{19}; here, 80^{9}, 96^{9}. [1111a: cf. 502.]

idā́nīm, *adv.* now. [pron. root i, 1103b.]

√ **idh** *or* indh (inddhé [694]; īdhé [783b]; āíndhiṣṭa; indhiṣyáti; iddhá; -ídhya). kindle. [cf. αἴθ-ω, 'burn'; Lat. *aed-e-s*, 'fire-place, hearth, dwelling' (cf. *stove* and Ger. *Stube*, 'room'); *aestus*, **aid-tu-s*, 'heat'; AS. *ād*, 'funeral pile'; *āst*, Eng. *oast*, 'kiln for drying hops *or* malt.']
+ **sam**, kindle, *trans. and intrans.*

idhmá, *m.* fuel. [√idh, 1166: for mg, cf. Eng. *kindlings.*]

idhma-citi, *f.* fuel-pile.

√ **in** (in-ó-ti, *prop.* i-nó-ti [713]). drive; force; *in* enas. [cf. √inv.]

índra, *m.* Indra, name of a Vedic god; *in the later language*, the best of its kind, chief, prince. [none of the numerous proposed derivations is satisfactory.]

índra-purogama, *a.* having Indra as leader, preceded by Indra. [1302c 2.]

indra-loká, *m.* Indra's world, heaven.

índra-çatru, *a.* having Indra as his conqueror. [1302.]

indra-senā́, *f.* Indra's missile weapon; personified as his bride, RV. x. 102.2; *hence*, name of a woman, *see* 16^{11} N.; —*m.* -a, name of a man, *formed as a mere pendant to the fem.* [índra + 1 sénā.]

indrāgní, *m.* Indra and Agni. [índra + agní: acct, 1255b.]

índrā-bṛ́haspáti, *m.* Indra and Brihaspati. [acct, 1255a.]

indrāyudha, *n.* Indra's weapon, the rainbow. [āyudha.]

indriyá, *a.* belonging to Indra; *as n.* —1. the quality pertaining especially to Indra, *i.e.* great might, power, 73^{18}, 97^{6}; —2. *in general*, one of a man's powers, *i.e.* a sense *or* organ of sense. [índra, 1214b.]

√ **indh**, *see* idh.

√ **inv** (ínvati). drive; send. [secondary root from i, 749b, 716: cf. in.]

imá, *pron. stem, see* idam.

iyacciram, *adv.* so long. [iyant (1249a) + ciram.]

íyant [451], *a.* so great; so much: [fr. pron. root i, 502.]

iras, *n.* ill-will; anger; *assumed as basis of the following denom.* [√ṛ, 'go for' in hostile sense: cf. Lat. *īra*, 'anger.']

√ **irasya** (irasyáti). be evil disposed. [iras, 1058.]

irasyā́, *f.* ill-will; wrath. [√irasya, 1149[6]: cf. īrṣyā.]

íriṇa, *n.* a run *or* runlet; gulch; gullied *and so* desert land. [√ṛ, 1177b: for mg, cf. Provincial Eng. *run*, 'brook.']

iva, *encl. pcl.* —1. as; like; —2. *used to modify a strong expression*, in a manner; so to speak, 56[16]; as it were, 1[10]; perhaps; almost, 34[13]; —3. *sometimes* (*like* eva), just, quite; **nacirād iva**, right soon. [pron. root i, 1102b.]

√ **1 iṣ** (iccháti [753]; iyéṣa, īṣús [783b]; āíṣīt; eṣiṣyáti; iṣṭá; éṣṭum; -íṣya). seek; desire; *esp. w. inf.* [981[3]]; *pass.* be desired; be approved *or* recognized, *and so* pass for, 59[18]; iṣṭá, desired, *i.e.* desirable, 1[4]. [radical mg, 'go, go for,' √2 iṣ being merely a causative of √1 iṣ: cf. ἵμερος, *ἴσμερος, 'desire'; w. icchā, 'desire,' cf. AS. *āsce, 'petition,' whence *āscian*, Ger. (*h*)*eischen*, Eng. *ask*: icchati for *isskati, cf. √vāñch.]

+**anu**, seek after.

+**abhi**, seek for; *ppl.* abhīṣṭa, desired, dear, 21[18].

√ **2 iṣ** (iṣáyati [1042a[2]]; *also* íṣyati [761c]; iyéṣa, īṣús [783b]; iṣitá; íṣayitum; -íṣya). send; set in swift motion; impel, 74[19]. [caus. of √1 iṣ, q.v.]

+**pra**, —1. preṣáyati: send forth; send, *e.g.* 9[10]; —2. préṣyati: drive forth, impel; start up (*e.g.* game); prāiṣam [970a] āicchan, sought to start up, 93[16]; *and so* —3. préṣyati: call upon *or* summon (*technical term used of the chief priest's calling upon another to begin a text or action*), 103[6].

íṣ, *f.* refreshment; strength; vigor; *w.* ūrj, drink and food, *like Ger.* Kraft und Saft.

iṣá, —1. *m.* = íṣ [399]; —2. *as a.* vigorous, fruitful.

íṣu, *m. f.* arrow. [√2 iṣ, 'send': cf. ἰός, *ἰσός, 'arrow.']

1 iṣṭá, *see* √1 iṣ, 'desire.'

2 iṣṭá, —1. offered; —2. *as n.* offering, sacrifice, holy work. [√yaj, 252.]

íṣṭakā, *f.* brick used in the sacred firepile. [2 iṣṭá.]

iṣṭa-lābha, *m.* acquisition of a desirable object. [1 iṣṭá.]

iṣṭā-pūrtá, *n.* what is offered (to the gods) and bestowed (upon them), *i.e.* what a man offers to the gods for his benefit after death, *and so, by metonymy*, such fruit of these offerings as can come to him, 83[13] N. [2 iṣṭá, 247, 1253b.]

íṣṭi, *f.* sacrifice (simple offering of butter, fruit, etc.), 101[6]. [√yaj, 252, 1157. 1a.]

ihá, *adv.* here, *opp. of* atra (87[1]) *and* amutra (64[6]); hither, 9[2]; here on earth, *ici bas*, 27[2]; *opp. of* pretya (√i), 59[2], 58[17]; in this book, 17[6]; *w. loc.* [*cf.* 1099[4]], **iha samaye**, in this case, 41[10], 42[15]. [pron. root i, 1100a.]

√ **īkṣ** (íkṣate; īkṣā́ṁ cakre; āíkṣiṣṭa; īkṣiṣyáte; īkṣitá; íkṣitum; īkṣitvā́; -íkṣya; īkṣyáte). look; look at; see; behold. [desid. of √*aç, 'see,' contained in ak-ṣán, 'eye,' etc., 108g: see akṣán.]

+**apa**, look off to (*like Ger.* es absehen auf); regard; expect.

+**ava**, look after; look after one's self, *i.e.* look behind *or* around.

+**upa**, *w. two mgs, like Eng.* overlook: —1. look over, *i.e.* inspect; *and* —2. (*more commonly*) look beyond, *i.e.* neglect.

+**nis**, look out *or* after; contemplate.

+**pari**, look about one; investigate; consider.

+**vi**, look; look on; vīkṣita, beheld.

+**sam**, look upon; behold; perceive.

íkṣaka, *m.* beholder; spectator. [√īkṣ, 1181.]

īkṣaṇa, *n.* a look; glance. [√īkṣ.]

√ **īñkh** (íñkhati, -te; īñkháyati, -te [1041[2]]). move unsteadily.

+**pra**, rock *or* pitch onward.

√ **īḍ** (íḷe, íḷiṣe, íṭṭe [628, 630]; *perf.* īḷé; īḷitá). supplicate; call upon; praise. [Whitney, 54.]

íḍya, *grdv.* to be praised. [√īḍ, 963[2] and d: pronounced íḷia, Whitney, 54.]

īdṛ́ça, *a.* of this sort; such. [502 end, and 518.]

īpsitá, *a.* desired to be obtained; desired. [desid. of √āp, 1030.]

īm, *encl.* —1. *as acc. s. of pron. root* i, him, her, it; him, 79[7]; —2. *indef.*, yá īm, *quicunque*, RV. x. 125.4; —3. ká īm, who pray? 77[18]; —4. *to avoid hiatus: between* átha *and* enam, 84[5,6]. [see 1111a and 502 end.]

√ **īr** (írte [628]; īrṇá; īráyati, -te; īritá). set one's self in motion; —*caus.* set in motion; cause to go forth, *i.e.*: —1. bring into existence; —2. utter (a sound), 14[23]. [near akin w. √ṛ.]

+**ud**, rise up; *caus.* rouse; send out; utter; announce, 53[16].

+**sam-ud**, *caus.* utter, declare.

+**pra**, *caus.* drive *or* steer onward (ship).

+**sam**, *caus.* bring together, *i.e.* into shape *or* being; create, 75[6]; sameriré, established (as an ordinance), *instituerunt*, 88[5] N.

īrṣyā́, *f.* ill-will; envy; jealousy. [contracted fr. irasyā́, q.v.: cf. çīrṣ-an and çiras.]

√ **īç** (íçe [628]; īçiṣyáti). own, be master of, *w. gen.* [cf. AS. *āg-an*, 'possess,' Eng. *owe*, 'possess' (so Shakespere often), 'possess another's property, be in debt'; thence the participial adj. *āgen*, Eng. adj. *own*, 'proprius'; thence the denom. *āgnian*, Eng. verb *own*; further, to *āh*, preterito-present of *āgan*, is formed a secondary past tense, *āhte*, 'possessed,' Eng. *ought*, 'possessed' (so Spenser), 'was under obligation.']

īçá, *m.* master; lord. [√īç.]

īçvará, *m.* master; lord; prince; rich man, 22[2]. [√īç, 1171a.]

√**īṣ** (íṣate; īṣé; īṣitá). hasten from, flee before, *w. abl.* [if not desid. of √i (108g[1] end), perhaps akin w. √1 iṣ, orig. 'go.']

---

u, *Vedic encl. copula.* —1. and; also; further; *used in one* (*oftenest the latter*) *of two clauses or sentences containing things alike or slightly contrasted* (*e.g.* 78[14], 79[9]), *esp. in anaphora* (*e.g.* 79[5], 90[9]); —2. now, straightway, *w. verbs present and past and w. imperatives or imperative subjunctives*, 71[10], 85[15], 85[5], 87[8]; *often followed by* sú, right soon; —pragṛhya [*see* 1122a[2], 138c] *when combined with* átha (90[16]), úpa (78[14]), mā́ (87[8]); *for* 83[9] *and* 84[11], *see notes*; —3. *in classical Skt. only w.* (atha, kim, *and*) na, and not, 21[14], 27[17].

u-kāra, *m.* the sound u. [Whitney, 18.]

uktá, *see* √vac.

ukti, *f.* expression; declaration, 53[16]. [√vac, 1157.1a.]

ukthá, *n.* utterance, *esp.* of devotion; praise; hymn of praise; invocation. [√vac, 1163a.]

uktha-várdhana, *a.* strengthening, *i.e.* refreshing *or* delighting one's self with hymns of praise. [acct, 1271.]

√ **ukṣ** [252] *or* vakṣ (ukṣáti, -te; áukṣīt; ukṣiṣyáti; ukṣitá; -úkṣya). sprinkle; besprinkle; drop, *intrans.*, 75[7]. [secondary form (108g end) of √*uj or ug: cf. ὑγ-ρός, 'wet'; Lat. *ūvens* (*ugvens) *caelum*, 'the dropping sky'; w. ukṣán, 'besprinkler, impregnator, bull,' cf. Goth. *auhsa*, 'bull,' Eng. *ox*, and for mg, √vṛṣ.]

+**pra**, sprinkle before one by way of consecration.

ugrá, *a.* mighty; exceedingly strong; terrible. [√vaj, 252, 1188; see ójas.]

ugrá-çāsana, *a.* having a terrible way of ruling; *as m.* a strict ruler. [1298a.]

√ **uc** (úcyati [*only w. preps*]; uvóca [783b], ūciváṅs [803]; ucitá). be pleased; be wonted; ucitá: —1. with which one is pleased; proper; suitable; —2. accustomed.

uccá, *a.* lofty; uccāís, *adv.* [1112c], high; *of sound*, loud. [fr. uccā́, adv. instr. (1112e) of údañc.]

uccaya, *m.* heap, pile, collection. [√1 ci + ud, 'heap up.']

uccārá, *m.* evacuation; excrement. [√car + ud.]

uccāvacá, *a.* high and low; various; diverse. [ud + ca w. ava + ca, 1314b.]

ú cchiṣṭa, *ppl.* left; *as n.* leavings, *esp.* of a sacrifice *or* of food. [√çiṣ + ud.]

ucchedin, *a.* destroying. [√chid + ud.]

ujjayinī, *f.* Oujein, name of a city, Ptolemy's Ὀζήνη. [fem. of ujjayin, 'victorious,' √ji + ud, 1183[3]: of like mg are Νικό-πολις and *Cairo*.]

9*

√ uñch (úñchati, uñcháti; úñchitum). sweep together, glean. [for *unsk, *vansk, orig. 'wipe, *or* whisk, *i.e.* sweep': cf. AS. *wascan*, 'wash,' Eng. *wash* and *whisk*.]

+**pra**, wash away; wipe out, 23[2].

úñçiṣṭa, *same as* ucchiṣṭa.

utá, *conj.* and; also; even; *connecting words, clauses, and sentences; repeated:* uta ·· uta ·· (uta), both ·· and ·· (and); *at beg. of verse*, 78[12]; —uta vā: or even, 87[20]; or, 84[14] (*cf.* atha, 6); apy uta, also.

utkarṣa, *m.* elevation. [√kṛṣ + ud.]

uttamá, *a.* —1. up-most; highest; best, *esp. at end of cpds;* excellent; chief; —2. (out-most, *i.e.*) ut-most; extreme; last (*see* 67[6] N.), 99[20]. [úd, 'up, out,' 473.]

uttamagandhāḍhya, *a.* rich in excellent odors, 15[19]. [uttama-gandha + āḍhya.]

uttamādhamamadhyama, *a.* highest and lowest and midmost; best and worst and middling. [uttama + adhama + madhyama, 1257.]

úttara [525[2]], *a.* upper; higher; —1. being above, (*opp.* adhara) 70[18]; having the upper hand, victorious, 81[21]; —2. northern (on account of the Himālayas, *cf.* udañc); ā‿uttarasmāt, as far as the north (side), 105[10]; —3. the left (because in prayer the face is turned eastward: *cf.* dakṣiṇa), 99[22]; —4. (*like* ὕστερος) the latter (*opp.* pūrva); later; following, 99[22]; -am, *as adv.* finally, last, 104[12]; —5. *as neuter subst.* the final element of a phrase of salutation, 60[8]; —6. answer, retort. [úd, 473: cf. ὕστερος, 'latter'; Eng. comp. *ut-ter*, 'outer.']

uttaratás, *adv.* northward; to the north of; *w. gen.* [1130], 105[13]. [uttara.]

uttara-dāyaka, *a.* giving answer; contradicting.

uttara-paçcima, *a.* north-westerly.

uttara-purastāt, *adv.* north-east of; *w. gen.*, 1130.

úttara-loman, *a.* having the hair above, with the hairy side up.

uttarā́, *adv.* northerly. [úttara, 1112e, 330[4].]

uttarā-patha, *n.* the northerly way; the north country.

úttareṇa, *adv.* northerly; north of, *w. acc.* [1129], 102[5]. [uttara, 1112c.]

uttarottara, —1. *a.* higher and higher [1260]; -am, *as adv.* more and more, 24[3]; —2. *as n.* answer to an answer [1264]; wordy talk, 24[9]. [uttara + uttara.]

utthā, *see* 233a.

utpala, *n.* a Nymphaea, *i.e.* water-lily *or* lotus. [√paṭ + ud.]

utpādana, *n.* procreation. [caus. of √pad + ud.]

utphulla, *a.* wide open. [√phal + ud, 958.]

utsavá, *m.* —1. an undertaking, beginning; —2. feast-day, festival, 25[4], 49[10]. [√2 su + ud, 'set a-going'; but the development of 2 from 1 is not clear.]

úd, *prefix. never used alone;* up, up forth, out. [cf. AS. *ūt*, Eng. *out:* see uttara, uttama.]

√ ud *or* **und** (unátti; unná, uttá; -údya). —1. spring; boil *or* bubble up; flow; —2. wet, bathe. [cf. Lat. *und-a*, 'wave'; w. ud-an, 'water,' cf. ὕδ-ωρ, Eng. *wat-er;* w. ud-ra, 'otter,' cf. ὕδ-ρα, 'water-snake,' Eng. *otter*.]

+**sam**, flow together; wet.

uda, *n.* water. [√ud.]

udaká [432], *n.* water. [√ud.]

uda-kumbhá, *m.* water-jar; jar with water.

udag-ayaná, *n.* north-course (of the sun), *or* the half-year from the winter to the summer solstice. [udañc.]

údagdaça, *a.* having the seams upward. [udañc + daçā, 'fringe, border, seam.']

udañ-mukha, *a.* having the face to the north. [udañc, 1249a, 161.]

údañc [409b], *a.* directed upward; directed northward (on account of the Himālayas), *cf.* uttara), northerly; *in cpds*, udak, 1249a. [ud + añc, 407.]

udayá, *m.* a going up; rising (of the sun). [√i (1148. 1a) + ud.]

udára, *n.* belly. [orig., perhaps, 'rising, swelling,' √ṛ + ud: for mg, cf. the relation of *belly* to AS. *belgan*, 'swell.']

udārá, *a.* (*like Eng.* exalted, *i.e.*) noble, excellent. [√ṛ + ud, 'rise.']

udāra-carita, *a.* of noble behavior.

uditá, *see* √vad; **úd-ita**, *see* √i.
údīcī, *see* 407[3], 409b.
udumbalá, *a.* brown.
uddiçya, at, towards, *see* √diç.
uddhata, *see* 163 *and* √han.
údbāhuka, *a.* having the arms out *or* extended. [ud + bāhu, 1305, 1307.]
udya, *grdv.* to be spoken *or* pronounced. [√vad, 1213c end, cf. 963c.]
udyama, *m.* raising (of the hands to work); exertion. [√yam + ud.]
udyā́na, *n.* —1. a walking out; —2. (place for walking out, *i.e.*) garden, park. [√yā + ud, 1150.]
udyoga, *m.* undertaking; exertion. [√yuj + ud, 216. 1.]
udyogin, *a.* active; energetic. [udyoga.]
udvigna-manas, *a.* having a terrified mind, distressed. [√vij.]
unmatta-darçana, *a.* having a frantic look. [√mad + ud.]
unmārga, *m.* by-way, evil way. [ud + mārga.]
unmārga-gāmin, *a.* going in evil ways.
úpa, —1. *vbl prefix.* to, unto, toward; *opp. of* ápa; —2. *prep., w. acc.,* unto, 81[15]; *w. loc.,* in, 77[5]; —3. *in noun cpds* [1289b], *denoting something near, accessory, or subordinate.* [cf. ὑπό, Lat. *s-ub,* 'under.']
upakaniṣṭhikā (*sc.* aṅguli), *a. f.* next to the little, *i.e.* the third (finger). [upa (mg 3) + kaniṣṭhaka, 1222d.]
upakartṛ, *m.* one who does kindness; benefactor. [√1 kṛ + upa, q.v.]
upakāra, *m.* friendly service; kindness. [√1 kṛ + upa, q.v.]
upakāraka, *a.* doing friendly service. [upakāra.]
upakārin, *a. the same; as m.* benefactor. [√1 kṛ + upa, q.v.]
upacārá, *m.* a coming to *or* waiting upon; *pregnantly,* (polite) attention; (correct) procedure, *i.e.* duty. [√car + upa.]
upatya, *a.* lying under. [upa, 1245b: cf. ὕπ-τιο-ς, 'lying under, supine.']
upatyakā, *f.* land lying at the foot (of a mountain). [upatya.]
upadeça, *m.* a pointing out to, a direction; instruction; advice. [√diç + upa.]
upadeçin, *a.* giving (good) instruction. [√diç + upa.]
upadeṣṭavya, *grdv.* to be taught. [do.]
upanāyana, *n.* investiture. [technical term, see √nī + upa.]
upapṛ́c, *a.* clinging close to, *w. gen.* [√pṛc + upa.]
upabhṛ́t, *f.* wooden cup (used in sacrifices), *see* srúc. ['tó-bringer,' √bhṛ (383b) + upa.]
upabhoga, *m.* enjoyment; eating. [√2 bhuj + upa, q.v.]
upamá, *a.* highest. [úpa, 474.]
upamá-çravas, *a.* having highest glory; *as m.* Upamaçravas, *a name like* Μεγιστο-κλῆς *or* Ὑψι-κλῆς.
upamā́, *f.* comparison, image; *and so* likeness, resemblance; *at end of cpds,* having likeness with · ·, like · ·. [√1 mā + upa, 'compare.']
upamārtha, *m.* purpose of an image; -ena, figuratively. [artha.]
upayoga, *m.* ap-plication; use; utility. [√yuj + upa.]
upári, *adv.* above; *as prep., w. gen.* [1130], above; *at end of cpd* [1314f], upon, 39[16]. [cf. ὑπείρ, *ὑπέρι, Lat. *s-uper,* 'over.']
úpalā, *f.* upper mill-stone; *cf.* dṛṣad.
upavañcana, *n.* a tottering unto, a faltering approach. [√vañc + upa.]
upavana, *n.* small forest, *i.e.* grove. [upa (mg 3) + vana.]
úpavīta, *ppl.* wound about, *esp.* with the sacred cord; *as n.* [1176a], the being surrounded with the sacred cord; the cord itself. [√vyā + upa, 954c.]
upaveçá, *m.* a sitting down. [√viç + upa.]
úpaveçi, *m.* Upaveçi, name of a man.
upaçama, *m.* stopping; cessation. [√2 çam + upa, 'stop.']
upasaṁgrahaṇa, *n.* the clasping and taking to one's self (the feet of another), *as sign of great respect.* [√grah + upa-sam.]
upasevā, *f.* a serving; a being devoted to. [√sev + upa.]
upasevin, *a.* serving; revering. [√sev + upa.]
upastha, *m.* lap, groin

upākhyāna, *n.* subordinate tale; episode, 1[1]. [upa (mg 3) + ākhyāna.]

upādāna, *n.* the taking to one's self; appropriation. [√1 dā + upa‿ā, 'take.']

upādhyāya, *m.* teacher. [√i + upa‿adhi.]

upānáh, *f.* sandal; shoe. ['under-bond,' √nah + upa (247): for mg, cf. ὑπό-δημα, 'sandal.']

upāntá, *n.* proximity to the end; edge; immediate neighborhood. [upa (mg 3) + anta.]

upāya, *m.* approach; that by which one reaches an aim; means; expedient, 39[2]; stratagem; advantage, 39[6]. [√i + upa, 1148. 1a: for mg, cf. Eng. *to-ward*, as an adj.]

upā́yana, *n.* approach. [√i + upa, 1150. 1a.]

upārá, *m.* transgression. [√r̥ + upa.]

upekṣā, *f.* overlooking; neglect. [√īkṣ + upa.]

upoṣita, *ppl.* having abstained (*i.e.* from food), having fasted; *as n.* [1176a], fasting. [√3 vas + upa, q.v.]

√ **ubh** (ubhnā́ti, umbháti [758]; ubdhá; -úbhya). unite; couple. [cf. ubhá.]
  + **apa**, bind, fetter.

ubhá, *a.* both. [cf. ἄμφω, Lat. *ambō*, AS. nom. fem. neut. *bā*, Goth. nom. neut. *ba*, nom. masc. *bai*, w. dental extension, *bajoþs*, all meaning 'both,' Eng. *bo-th*: orig., perhaps, 'couple,' and akin w. √ubh.]

ubháya [525[4]], *a.* of both sorts; both. [ubhá.]

ubháya-kāma, *a.* desirous of both.

ubhayátas, *adv.* from both sides; in both cases. [ubháya, acct!]

ubhayataḥ-sasya, *n.* having a crop at both times, *i.e.* bearing two crops a year.

urá-ga, *m.* serpent. ['breast-going,' ura for uras: for mg, cf. khaga.]

úras, *n.* breast. [perhaps, 'a cover,' from √1 vr̥, 'cover,' 1151. 1b, w. a specialization like that in Eng. *chest*, 'thorax.']

urú, *f.* urvī́, *a.* (*prop.* encompassing, *and so, like Eng.* capacious) extensive, wide, great; *as n.* (*like Ger.* das Weite) the distance. [√1 vr̥, 'encompass,' 1178a: cf. εὐρύ-s, 'wide.']

uru-vyácas, *a.* having wide embrace, wide extending. [acct, 1298b.]

√ **uruṣya** (uruṣyáti). to distance, *i.e.* escape; put another in the distance, *i.e.* save. [urú, 'the distance,' 1061[2].]

urū-ṇasá, *a.* having broad snouts. [urú (247) + nás, 193, 1315c: acct, 1298b.]

ulū́khala, *n.* a mortar.

úlba *and* úlva, *n.* enveloping membrane of an embryo. [for *ur-vá, √1 vr̥, 'enclose,' 1190: cf. Lat. *vol-va*, 'covering, womb.']

ulbaṇá, *a.* lumpy, knotty, thick, massy. [ulba, for *urva, hence ṇ, 189.]

√ **uṣ** (óṣati; uvóṣa; āúṣīt; uṣṭá). burn. [for cognates, see the collateral form √1 vas, 'light up,' also uṣás, usrá, etc.: cf. εὕω, 'singe'; αὔω, 'kindle'; Lat. *ūr-o*, 'burn,' and *ustus* = uṣṭá-s; AS. *ys-le*, 'glowing ashes.']

uṣás [415b], *f.* morning-red; dawn; *personified*, Dawn. [√1 vas, 'light up, dawn,' 252: cf. ἠώς, Aeolic αὔως, Lat. *aurōra*, **ausōs-a*, 'dawn'; radically cognate also is Eng. *eas-t*, 'the point where day breaks': see uṣ and usra.]

úṣṭra, *m.* camel.

uṣṇá, *a.* hot. [√uṣ, 1177a.]

usrá, *a.* bright; of *or* pertaining to the dawn; *as f.*, usrā́, dawn. [√1 vas, 'light up,' 252, 1188, 181a: w. us-rá, cf. Old Germanic *Aus-t-rō*, a goddess of the (year-dawn, i.e.) spring-light, and AS. *Eos-t-ra*, the name of whose festival, *easter*, 'Easter-day,' occurring in April, was transferred to the Christian festival that replaced it; for *t* between *s* and *r*, see under svasr̥: see uṣ and uṣas.]

ūtí, *f.* furtherance, help, blessing; refreshment, food. [√av, 1157.]

ū́dhan, ū́dhar, ū́dhas [430b], *n.* udder. [cf. οὖθαρ, Lat. *ūber*, AS. *ūder*, Eng. *udder.*]

ūná, *a.* lacking. [cf. εὖνις, 'bereft'; AS. *wan*, 'lacking,' *wanian*, 'decrease,' Eng. *wane.*]

ūrú, *m.* thigh. [prob. 'the thick' of the leg, from urú.]

ū́rj, *f.* sap; strength; vigor; nourishment. [√*varj, 'swell with, be full of': cf. ὀργάω, 'swell with, abound'; Lat. *virga*, 'swelling twig.']

ūrṇa, *n., and* **ū́rṇā**, *f.* wool. ['cover,' √1vṛ, 'cover' (cf. 712): cf. εἶρος, *ἔ-Ϝρ-ος, Lat. *vellus*, Goth. *vulla*, Eng. *wool.*]

ū́rṇa-mradas, *a.* having the softness of wool, soft as wool.

ūrṇā-stukā, *f.* braid *or* plait of wool.

√ ūrṇu, *see* 712, *and* √1vṛ.

ūrdhvá, *a.* tending upwards; upright; elevated; -am, *as adv.*, upwards; over; beyond; after, *w. abl.* [1128]; ata ūrdhvam, from now on. [cf. Lat. *arduus*, 'lofty.']

ūrdhva-dṛṣṭi, *a.* having an upward gaze. [1298.]

ūrmí, *m.* wave. [lit. 'roller, rolling billow,' √*vṛ, 'roll, turn hither and thither': cf. ἴλλω, *Ϝι-Ϝλ-ω, Lat. *volvo*, 'roll'; Ger. *Welle*, 'wave.']

√ 1ūh (ū́hati; áúhīt; ūḍhá, ūhitá; ū́hitum; -ū́hya). remove.

√ 2ūh (óhate [745a]; ūhé; áúhīt, áúhiṣṭa; ū́hitum; -ū́hya). notice.
+**api**, grasp; understand, 88[10].

√ ṛ (íyarti [643c]; ṛṇóti; ṛccháti [753 end, 608]; ā́ra [783a[2]]; ā́rat; ariṣyáti; ṛtá; ṛtvā́; -ṛ́tya; arpáyati [1042d]). move, *as trans. and as intrans.*; —1. rise, 73[10]; come upon *or* unto, reach, attain; —2. raise (*e.g.* dust); —*caus.* send; put; fasten; fit in. [w. ṛ-ṇó-ti, cf. ὄρ-νυσι, 'rouses'; cf. Lat. *or-ior*, 'rise,' *or-tus*, 'risen'; ὦρ-το, 'rose,' = ā́r-ta, 3d sing. aor. mid.; w. ṛ-cchá-ti, cf. ἔρ-χε-ται, 'goes,' also ἐλ-θεῖν, 'go'; w. caus., cf. ἀρ-αρίσκω, 'fit,' Lat. *ar-tu-s*, 'well-fitted, close, narrow'; see also ṛtá.]
+**ā**, —1. get into (trouble), 93[15] N.; —2. (*like the American* go for, 'treat harshly by word *or* deed') visit with trouble; *ppl.* ā́rta, visited by trouble, distressed.
+**ud**, rise; raise.
+**upa**, go against, transgress. [for mg, cf. ṛṇá.]
+**nis**, (go forth, *i.e.*) dissolve connection with.
+**sam**, come together, meet; go along with, 73[9]; —*caus.* send; deliver to; consign, entrust.

ṛkti, *f.* praise, *in* su-v-ṛktí. [√ṛc.]

ṛg-vedá, *m.* the Rigveda (each stanza of which is called an ṛc in distinction from a yajus and a sāman).

√ ṛc (árcati; ānárca, ānṛcé [788]; arciṣyáti; arcitá; árcitum; arcitvā́; -árcya; arcáyati). —1. beam; —2. praise; sing (praise); sing (of the winds); honor; —*caus.* [1041[2]], salute. [cf. arka.]

ṛ́c, *f.* —1. hymn of praise; *esp.* a stanza that is spoken, as distinguished from one that is sung (sāman) or from a sacrificial formula (yajus); —2. stanza *or* text to which a certain rite or explanation has reference, 98[5]; —3. the collection of ṛc's, the Rigveda, 57[14], 63[3]. [√ṛc.]

ṛca, *for* ṛc, *at end of cpds* [1209a, 1315c].

√ 1ṛj *or* **ṛñj** (ṛñjáti, -te; ṛ́jyati, -te). reach out, *esp.* in a straight direction (*and so, the opp. of* √vṛj, 'bend, turn,' *q.v. and see* ṛjú), stretch out, *intrans.*; press on; *with this root, compare the root* rāj, *mg* 1. [cf. ὀρέγ-ω, 'reach out'; Lat. *reg-ere*, 'direct'; Eng. *right*, 'straight, not wrong.']

√ 2ṛj (árjati; arjáyati [1041[2]]; arjitá). reach, *and so*, get *or* obtain. [the same as √1ṛj, but w. another conjugation and w. trans. mg: for mg, cf. Eng. *reach*, intrans., w. *reach*, trans., and Ger. *langen* and *erlangen.*]

√3ṛj, *in* ṛj-rá, 'ruddy,' árj-una, 'silver-white'; *see also the root* raj *and root* rāj, *mg* 2. [cf. ἀργ-ός, 'bright'; Lat. *arguo*, 'make clear'; w. rajatá, 'silver,' cf. ἄργυρος, Lat. *argentum*, 'silver.']

ṛjīṣá, *a.* on-rushing. [√1ṛj, 1197b.]

ṛjīṣín, *a.* on-rushing. [ṛjīṣá, 1230a.]

ṛjú, *a.* straight, right, *opp. of* vṛjiná, 'crooked, wrong.' [√1ṛj, 1178a.]

√ ṛñj, *see* √1ṛj.

ṛṇá, *a.* (having gone against *or* transgressed, *and so*) guilty; *as n.* [1176a *and* 1177], guilt; debt, 25[2]. [√ṛ: cf. Lat. *reus*, 'guilty': for mg, cf. upārá.]

ṛtá, *a.* fit, right; true; *as n.* [1176a], —1. established order; *esp.* eternal *or* divine order; —2. order in sacred things, sacred custom, pious work, 69[15], 74[9]; ṛtasya yoni *or* sadana, central place of sacred work *or* belief: *in this world*, the altar, 89[8]; *in the other world*, the holy of holies, 75[7]; —3. truth, 98[8,9]; —ṛtena, rightly. [prop. 'fitted, made firm,' √ṛ: for form and mg, cf. Lat. *ra-tu-s*, 'settled.']

ṛta-sáp [387a], *a.* following after right, righteous.

ṛtā́van, *f.* -varī, *a.* true to established order (of regularly recurring natural phenomena, *e.g.* dawn), 75[17]; true to sacred law, pious (Manes), 91[10]; holy, sacred (god), 75[8]. [ṛta, 247: for fem., 435, 1171[2].]

ṛtā-vṛ́dh, *a.* rejoicing in right, holy (Manes). [ṛta, 247.]

ṛtú, *m.* —1. a fixed and settled time; *esp.* time for sacrificing; —2. time of year, *i.e.* season; —3. the menses. [√ṛ, 1161a: cf. ἀρτύ-ω, 'fit together, prepare'; Lat. *artu-s*, 'joint.']

ṛté, *prep.* without; except. [1128 end, 1129 end.]

ṛtv-íj, *a.* offering at the appointed time; *as m.* priest; *in the ritual, pl.*, priests, of whom there are four, hótṛ, adhvaryú, brahmán, and udgātṛ́. [ṛtú + íj.]

ṛ́ddhi, *f.* welfare; blessedness. [√ṛdh, 1157.]

√ ṛdh (ṛdhnóti; ānárdha, ānṛdhé [788]; ardhiṣyáte; ṛddhá; ṛdhyáte). thrive; succeed; prosper, *both as intrans. and as trans.* [cf. √vṛdh, rādh: cf. ἄλθομαι, 'get well.']

+ **sam**, *pass.* be prospered, *i.e.* fulfilled.

√ 1ṛṣ (árṣati; ānárṣa [788]). flow; glide. [cf. ἄψ-ορρος, 'flowing back,' παλίν-ορσος, 'darting back.']

√ 2ṛṣ (ṛṣáti; ṛṣṭá). push; thrust.

ṛ́ṣi, *m.* —1. singer of sacred songs, poet; priestly singer; *regarded by later generations as* a patriarchal saint *or* sage of the olden time *and as occupying a position given in other lands to the heroes and patriarchs;* one of those inspired poets who "saw" the Vedas, which were "revealed" to them; —2. sapta‿ṛṣayas: the many Rishis; *later*, the seven stars of the Great Bear; —3. a Rishi, *i.e.* a person renowned for piety and wisdom, 100[22]; — *see note to* 1[14].

ṛṣṭí, *f.* spear. [√2ṛṣ.]

ṛṣvá, *a.* lofty.

---

e, *pron. root in* éka, etá, ena, evá, evám.

éka [482a], *num.* —1. one; only; alone (by one's self); alone (excluding every one else); sole; single; solitary; *advly in cpds*, solely; —2. one (of two *or* more); the one, *followed by* anya, dvitīya, para; eke ·· eke, some ·· others; eke, some folks, some; —3. *later*, a certain, *quidam; or almost as an indef. article* [482a[3]], a *or* an, 20[8]. [pron. root e.]

eka-tatpara, *a.* solely intent on, 45[4].

ekatra, *adv.* in one place. [eka, 1099.]

ekadā, *adv.* at one time, simultaneously, *at* 37[9]; *elsewhere*, at a certain time, *i.e.* once upon a time. [eka, 1103.]

eka-deça, *m.* a certain place, *and so*, a place *or* spot *or* part.

eka-nakṣatrá, *n.* lunar mansion consisting of a single star *or* one whose name occurs but once, *see* 104[8] N. [nákṣatra, 1312.]

éka-patnī, *f.* wife of only one man, faithful wife. [acct, 1267a.]

eka-pada, *f.* -ī, *a.* having (*i.e.* taking) one step.

eka-bhakṣa, *m.* sole food; *at end of cpds* [1298], having ·· as sole food, eating ·· alone.

eka-mati, *a.* having one mind, unanimous.

eka-varṇa, *a.* having one color, not brindled.

ekākín, *a.* solitary. [eka.]

ekāñjali, *m.* one handful. [añjali.]

ékādaça, *num.* eleven. [éka + dáça, 476[2].]

ekādaçá, *a.* eleventh. [ékādaça, 487[7].]

ekānta, *m.* an end; a retired *or* secret spot. [anta.]

ekāpāya, *m.* diminution by one. [apāya.]

ekārtha, *m.* one purpose, *i.e.* one and the same purpose. [artha.]

ekāhá, *m.* one day. [2áha.]

ékāika, *a.* one by itself; one singly; each one singly; every single one. [eka + eka.]

ekāikaças, *adv.* one by one; severally. [ekāika, 1106.]

ekona, *a.* lacking one. [ūna, 477a.]

etá, *see* etád *and cf.* 499b *with* 497.

éta, *a.* rushing; darting; *as m.* deer. [√i, 1176c.]

etat-sama, *a.* equal to this. [1265.]

etat-samīpa, *n.* presence of this one. [1264.]

etád [499b], *pron.* this here, *prop. referring to something near the speaker* (*e.g.* 18[8], 19[12], 51[19]); this; *refers almost always to what precedes* (*e.g.* 6[9], 19[3], 51[18], 68[5]), *has just happened* (*e.g.* 20[11], 25[12, 13]), *or has just been mentioned* (*e.g.* 7[5], 25[18], 28[11]), *as being nearer the speaker; very seldom*—28[6], 92[19], 96[5]—*to what follows; joined with other pronouns: w.* yad, 94[15]; *w.* tad, 45[9], 95[6]; *w.* aham *to be supplied*, 52[9]. [pron. root e, 499b: in usage, etád : idám : : ταῦτα : τάδε.]

etad-artham, *adv.* for this purpose; therefore. [499b[2], 1302c[4].]

etárhi, *adv.* nowadays. [etá, 1103c.]

etā-dṛç, *a.* such; etādṛk, *acc. s. n.*, such as I have, 82[14]. [518.]

etā-dṛça, *a.* such; et. · · yat, such · · that. [518.]

etā́vant, *a.* thus much, 12[9]; etāvān · · yena, so great · · that, 21[10]. [etá, 517.]

√ edh (édhate; edhā́ṁ cakre; āídhiṣṭa; edhitá; édhitum). thrive; prosper. [ident. w. √ṛdh, q.v.: cf. geha w. gṛha.]

ena [500], *encl. pron. used only substantively: unemphatic* him, her, it, them. [pron. root e.]

énas, *n.* sin. [perhaps, 'deed of violence,' √in.]

énasvant, *a.* sinful. [énas.]

enā́, *adv.* in this way; here; pará enā́: beyond here; beyond, *w. instr.*, RV. x. 125. 8; there; yátra · · enā́, whither · · thither. [pron. root a, see idám, and cf. 502[2] and 1112a.]

eraṇḍa, *m.* Ricinus communis, *i.e.* castor-oil plant *or* Palma Christi.

evá, *adv.* —1. in this way; so; *in this signification Vedic only, its place being supplied in post-Vedic by* evám; yáthā · · evá, as · · so, 86[13]; evá‿íd, in very truth, 74[6]; —2. just, exactly, *etc., emphasizing the preceding word; in this sense Vedic* (69[5], 85[1], 87[1], 91[5]) *and post-Vedic; requires the most various translations — sometimes mere stress of voice:* precisely; no more nor less than; nothing short of; no other than; merely; quite; without exception; andha eva, blind outright; vasudhā‿eva, the whole earth; mṛtyur eva, sure death; mūṣika eva kṛtas, was changed back to a simple mouse; cintayann eva, just while he was thinking; uktam eva mayā, just what I told thee; lokāiḥ kiṁcid vaktavyam eva, folks will be sure to say something; eka eva, entirely alone; pumāṅsa eva, only males; —*in connection w. pronouns and adverbs:* etad eva, this very; tathā‿eva, all so, *i.e.* also; na‿eva, by no means; *w. very attenuated mg in* ca‿eva, and also, *and* eva ca, and also, *the latter at end of a çloka*, 58[15]. [pron. root e, 1102b: sometimes evā́, 248a.]

evaṁ-víd, *a.* knowing so *or* such, *i.e.* well instructed, knowing what's what.

evaṁvidha, *a.* of such sort, such. [evam (1306) + vidhā, 1302c 5.]

evám, *adv.* in this way; so; *post-Vedic, and supplying the place of* evá *in mg* 1; *used first w.* √vid: yá eváṁ vidús, who know thus, have this knowledge, 97[1, 3]; yathā · · evam, as · · so; *very frequent w.* uktvā *or* çrutvā, upon saying *or* hearing this; evam ukta, thus addressed; *w. impers. used ppl.*, 7[8], 39[22]; evam astu, so be it; mā‿evam, not so! yady evam, if that's the case, 48[11]; evam, in that case, 11[4]; evam, likewise, 103[7]; *refers back* (*e.g.* 28[21], 52[8]), *or forward* (*e.g.* 31[5], 37[8], 50[6]); *used superfluously w.* iti, 61[12]; *as equiv. to* evaṁvidha, 15[4]. [pron. root e, 1102b.]

evam-bhūta, *a.* such. [see 1273c.]

eso, *a Prakrit form for* eṣas, 49[8]

āikamatya, *n.* unanimity. [ekamati, 1211.]

āitihāsika, *m.* teller of old legends. [itihāsa, 1222e 2.]

āindrābārhaspatyá, *a.* belonging to Indra and Brihaspati. [índrābṛ́haspáti, 1204c.]

ókas, *n.* wonted place; home. [√uc.]

oṁ-kṛta, *a.* having an uttered om, accompanied by om. [the natural order would require kṛtāum: order inverted to avoid such an undeclinable stem.]

ójas, *n.* strength; power. [√vaj or uj, 252, cf. ug-rám ój-as, 78[6]: cf. Lat. *augus-tus*, 'mighty, *i.e.* august.']

ojo-dā́ [352], *a.* strength-giving.

odaná, *m. n.* grain boiled with milk; porridge. [√ud: for mg, cf. Eng. *broth* and *brew.*]

opaçá, *m.* top-knot; plume. [perhaps for *ava-paça, √2 paç.]

óm, *a word of solemn asseveration and reverent acknowledgment, somewhat like ἀμήν; a sacred mystic syllable, uttered at the beg. and end of Veda-reading; cf.* praṇava. [origin uncertain.]

óṣadhī, *later* **óṣadhi**, *f.* herb; plant; a 'simple.

āupamya, *n.* similitude; likeness. [upamā́, 1211.]

āúpaveçi, *m. patronymic of Aruna.* [úpaveçi (or upaveçá?): cf. 1221.]

āuṣadhá, *a.* consisting of herbs; *as n.* herbs *collectively*; simples; medicine. [óṣadhi, 1208d.]

---

1 ká [504], *pron.* —**1.** *interrogative.* who, what; *used as subst.* (7[6, 7]) *or as adj.* (18[17]); kim *w. instr.: e.g.* kiṁ yuddhena, what (is there) with fighting, what's the use of fighting, 45[14]; *so* 17[19], 24[9]; *so* ko 'rthas, 17[18]; kim *w. instr. and gen.: e.g.* nīrujaḥ kim āuṣadhāis, what has a well man (to do) with medicines, 22[8]; *so* 32[21], 51[20]; ka *w. particles:* ko nāma, who indeed; ko nu, who pray; ko vā, who possibly, 18[1];

—**2.** *indefinite, both adj. and subst., chiefly in negative clauses and w. the particles* [*see* 507] ca, caná, cid, ápi; —**2a.** *w.* mā́: mā́ kásmāi dhātam abhy àmitríṇe nas, deliver us not over to any foe; —**2b.** ka ca, some, any, *adj. or subst.*; kiṁ ca, anything; *w. relative,* yāç (ca) kāç ca, (and) what soever, 68[10]; —**2c.** *w.* ca na *and* cana: ka ca na, also *or* even not any; *esp. after a negative:* na taṁ çaknuvanti vyāhartum api, kiṁ ca na, can not even speak to him, not even anything, *i.e.* can not even speak anything to him, 8[19]; *so* 96[21]; *and so* (*the feeling for the negation in* cana *in such collocations becoming lost*), ka cana *means* any, anything, *cf.* cana; *w. relative,* soever; yat kiṁcana, whatsoever, 9[16]; —**2d.** *very often* ka cid: any body *or* thing; certain, 18[11]; *often w. negative: e.g.* 9[9]; 24[11] (*twice with, twice without*); kiṁcit kiṁcid, each a little, 27[9]; *w. relative,* ya ka cid, whosoever, whatsoever, any soever, 21[11]; kāni kāni cid, any soever, 82[15]; —**2e.** ka api, something, somebody, 17[11]; some, a *or* an, a certain, 21[2]; na ka api: nothing, 39[21]; no, no one, 20[10];

—**3.** *derivs of* ka, *see* 505; —**4.** *exclamatory, at beg. of cpds: cf., e.g.,* kā-puruṣa, kim-prabhu, ku-dṛṣṭi, ko-vida, *and see* 506, 1121e; —**5.** *for* kim *as adv., see* kim. [for the stem-forms ka, ki, ku, see 505: cf. Ionic κο-, Attic πο-, in κό-θεν, κῶς, etc., 'whence, how'; τί-ς, τί, Lat. *qui-s, qui-d,* AS. *hwā, hwæ-t,* Eng. *who, wha-t*; w. katará, 'which of twain,' cf. κό-τερο-ς, Lat. *uter,* AS. *hwæ-ðer,* Eng. *whe-ther,* 'which of twain'; w. ka as indef., cf. τι-ς, 'any one.']

2 ka, *m.* Who, as name of a god, 94[15, 16] N.

kaṅsá, *m.* metallic vessel; *as collective,* metallic implements.

kakṣā, *f.* —**1.** region of the girth; —**2.** girdle, cincture; —**3.** (*like French* ceinture) circular wall; *and so* the enclosed court. [cf. kañkaṇa: cf. Lat. *cinc-tus,* 'girded'; for 1, cf. *coxa,* 'hip'; for 3, cf. *canc-er,* 'fence.']

kañkaṇa, *n.* ring-shaped ornament, bracelet. [cf. kakṣā.]

kañkāla, *m. n.* skeleton.

kaccid, *see* **kad.**

kaccha, *m.* border; shore; marsh-land; the district Cutch.

kaccha-pa, *m.* tortoise. ['keeping, *i.e.* inhabiting the marsh,' vbl 2 pa.]
kaṭaka, *m. n.* dale.
káṇa, *m.* a small grain (as of dust or rice). [cf. kaniṣṭha.]
káṇṭaka, *m.* thorn.
kaṇṭaki-kṣīrin, *m. pl.* thorn-plants and milk-plants.
kaṇṭakin, *a.* thorny; *as m.* thorn-plant. [kaṇṭaka.]
katham, *Vedic* **kathā́**, *interr. adv.* how? in what way? **katham etat**, how's that? **kathaṁ nu**, how indeed? **kathaṁ cana**, in any wise soever (*emphasizing a preceding negation*); **katham api**, somehow. [ka, 1101.]
√ **kathaya** (**kathayati**). tell; talk about; *pass.* be called, pass for. [lit. 'tell the how,' 'τὸ ὅπως λέγειν': denom. fr. katham, 1058.]
1 **kathā́**, *see* **kathám**.
2 **kathā**, *f.* —1. story, tale, fable; discussion; —2. *personified*, Story, 56[9]. [prop. 'the how, τὸ ὅπως,' 1 kathā́.]
kathā-chala, *n.* cover *or* guise of a fable.
kathā-pīṭha, *n.* pedestal of Kathā, name of the first book of the Kathā-sarit-sāgara. [2 kathā, mg 2.]
kathāvatāra, *m.* incarnation of Kathā. [2 kathā (mg 2) + avatāra.]
kathā-sarit-sāgara, *m.* Story-stream-ocean, title of Soma-deva's collection.
kád, *interr. pcl.* nonne, num; *w.* cid, nonne, num; **kaccid dṛṣṭā**, was she seen? [crystallized acc. s. n. of ka, 1111a.]
kadā́, *adv.* when? **na kadā cana**, not at any time soever, never; **kadā cid**, once on a time, one day; **kadā cid api na**, never. [ka, 1103.]
kádru, *a.* brown; **kadrū́** [355c], *f.* brown Soma-vessel.
√ **kan** *or* **kā** (**caké**; **ákānīt**). be glad. [cf. √kam and √can.]
kánaka, *n.* gold.
kanaka-sūtra, *n.* gold cord *or* chain.
kanaka-stambha-rucira, *a.* shining with gold columns.
kaniṣṭha, *a.* smallest; youngest. [cf. the following words and kaṇa and kanyā.]
kaniṣṭhaka, *a.* smallest; *f.* -ikā [1222d], *sc.* aṅguli, the little finger. [kaniṣṭha.]
kaniṣṭha-prathama, *a.* having the youngest as the first.
kánīyāṅs, *a.* smaller; younger. [cf. kaniṣṭha and 467[2].]
kandara, *n.* cave. [perhaps 'great cleft,' kam (see ka 4) + dara.]
kandarpa, *m.* the god of love. [perhaps 'of great wantonness,' kam (see ka 4) + darpa.]
kanyakā, *f.* girl. [kanyā, 1222b.]
kanyā̀, *f.* girl; maiden; daughter. [cf. kaniṣṭha.]
kanyā-ratna, *n.* girl-jewel, excellent maiden.
kapaṭa, *m. n.* fraud.
kapaṭa-prabandha, *m.* continued series of frauds; machination, plot.
kaparda, *m.* small shell used as a coin, 80 = 1 paṇa; **-aka**, *m. the same.*
kapā́la, *n.* —1. cup *or* dish, 102[13]; —2. cover *or* lid, 104[16]; —3. cranium. [for mg, cf. Lat. *testa*, 'earthen pot,' w. French *tête*, 'head.']
kapóta, *m.* dove.
kám, *pcl.* —1. *emphasizing the preceding word*, 79[11]; —2. *interr. pcl.*, 88[10]. [ka, 1111a: cf. kád, kím.]
√ **kam** (**cakamé**; **kamiṣyáte**; **kāntá** [955a]; **kāmáyate**, **-ti** [1041[2]]). wish; will; desire; love. [cf. √kan and √can.]
kamaṇḍalu, *m.* water-jar.
√ **kamp** (**kámpate**; **cakampé**; **kampitá**; **kámpitum**; **-kámpya**). tremble *or* shake.
kambalá, *m.* woolen cloth.
kambu, *m.* shell.
kambu-grīva, *m.* Shell-neck (*i.e.* having folds in the neck like a spiral shell), name of a tortoise. [grīvā́.]
1 **kará**, —1. *a.* doing; making *or* causing *or* producing, *at end of many cpds*; —2. *as m.* the hand (*lit.* the busy one); —3. *as m. nomen actionis*, the doing, performance, *in* duṣkara, sukara. [√1 kṛ: cf. Lat. *cerus*, 'creator.']
2 **kara**, *m.* ray, beam. [prob. same as 1 kara 2: the rays of the heavenly bodies are conceived as their hands and feet, cf. pāda 4.]

kara-vāri, *n.* water from the hand.

karuṇa, *a.* mournful, pitiable; -ā, *f.* pity.

karuṇā-para, *a.* compassionate. [1302b.]

karkaṭa, *m.* crab; **-aka**, *the same.*

kárṇa, *m.* ear.

kartá, *m.* (earth-) cut, ditch. [√kṛt: see garta.]

kartṛ́, *m.* doer; accomplisher; officiating priest, 101²¹. [√1kṛ.]

kartavya, *grdv.* to be done *or* made, *w. the various mgs of* √1kṛ. [√1kṛ.]

kartavyatā, *f.* the to-be-done-ness; -tām brūhi, tell me what I must do. [1237.]

karpūra, *m. n.* camphor.

karpūra-paṭa, *m.* Camphor-cloth, name of a certain washerman.

karpūra-vilāsa, *m.* Camphor-joy (*lit.* having pleasure in camphor), name of a washerman.

karma, *for* karman *in cpds,* 1249a².

karma-ceṣṭā, *f.* deed-performance; action.

karma-ja, *a.* deed-born, resulting from the actions of a life.

karma-doṣa, *m.* deed-sin, sinful deed.

kárman, *n.* deed, work, action; sacred work (as sacrifice, ablution); rite, 59¹. [√1kṛ.]

kárhi, *adv.* when? karhi cid, at any time. [ka, 1103c.]

√ **kal** (kāláyati). drive. [cf. κέλεται, 'urges on'; βου-κόλος, 'cattle driver'; Lat. *celer,* (like colloq. *driving,* i.e. 'hurrying') 'swift.'] **+anu-sam**, lead along after.

kala, *a.* dumb; indistinct; -am, *adv.* gently, *and so* pleasantly (of humming).

kalaha, *m.* strife, contention.

kalā́, *f.* a small part, *esp.* a sixteenth.

kálpa, *m.* ordinance, precept; manner, way; etena kalpena, in this way.

kalmaṣa, *n.* spot, stain; *fig., as in Eng.,* sin.

kalmaṣa-dhvaṅsa-kārin, *a.* sin-destruction-causing, preventing the commission of crime.

kalya, *a.* well, healthy. [cf. καλός, 'fair': prob. not akin are AS. *hāl,* Eng. *hale, whole.*]

kalyā́ṇa, *f.* -ā́ṇī [355b], *a.* fair, lovely. [kalya.]

kalyāṇa-kaṭaka, *m. n.* Fair-dale, name of a place.

kaví, *a.* wise, possessed of insight (of gods, *esp.* Agni); *as m.* wise man, seer, sage; poet; *pl.* wise men of eld (whose spirits hover about the sun), 91¹². [prop. 'seer,' √kū, 'see,' for *skū: cf. θυοσκόος, *-σκοϝο-ς, 'inspecting the sacrifice'; Lat. *cav-ēre,* 'look out, be cautious'; Ger. *schauen,* AS. *sceāwian,* 'look,' Eng. *show,* 'cause to look at.']

kaví-kratu, *a.* having the power *or* insight (krátu) of a wise one; intelligent. [1296.]

√ **kas** (kásati; kastá; kāsáyati). move. **+vi**, move asunder; open; bloom; *caus. pass.* be made to bloom.

kásmāt, *adv.* why? wherefore? [ka, 1114a.]

kāṅsya, *a.* brazen; *as n.* brass. [kaṅsá.]

kāka, *m.* crow; —*f.* kākī, crow-hen; *cf.* vāyasa, 'crow.'

√ **kāṅkṣ** (kā́ṅkṣati, -te; cakā́ṅkṣa; kāṅkṣitá). desire, long for. [desid. of √kam, but reduplicated somewhat like an intens. (1002), *kām-ka(m)-s.]

kācá, *m.* glass.

kāca-maṇi, *m.* rock-crystal, quartz. [lit. 'glass-jewel.']

kāñcana, *n.* gold.

kāṇá, *a.* one-eyed; perforated (of the eye), blind.

kāṇa-bhūti, *m.* Kānabhūti, name of a Yaksha, *see* 53³ N. [lit. 'Blind-luck.']

kā́ṇḍa, *m. n.* section; joint of a stalk from one knot to another; arrow.

kāntāra, *m. n.* great *or* primeval forest.

kānti, *f.* loveliness. [√kam, 1157, cf. 955a.]

kā-puruṣa, *m.* miserable man, coward. [see 1ká 4, and 506.]

kā́ma, *m.* wish, desire, longing; love; *at end of possessive cpds* [1296], having desire for ··, desirous of ··; kāmam, *see s.v.* [√kam.]

kāma-dúh (-dhuk, -duham, -dhugbhis, etc. [155]), —**1.** *a.* yielding wishes, granting every wish; —**2.** *as f., sc.* dhenu, the fabulous Wonder-cow. [for 2, cf. the horn of Amalthea.]

kā́mam, *adv.* at will; if you please; kāmaṁ tu · · na tu, if she please, · ·, but by no means · ·, 64[12]. [kāma, 1111b.]

kāmín, *a. subst.* affectionate (spouse). [kāma.]

kāminī-sakha, *a.* in the company of his wives. [see sakha.]

kāya, *m.* body. [√1ci, 'build,' Whitney 43: for mg, cf. δέμας, 'body, form,' and δέμω, 'build,' and Eng. noun *build*, as used of 'a man's figure.']

kāyika, *a.* corporeal; performed by the body. [kāya.]

kāra, *a.* making; *as m.* maker; deed, action; sound. [√1kṛ.]

kāraṇa, *n.* that which makes *or* occasions; cause, 57[7]; occasion; reason; sake, 10[1]; ground for a judgment, 22[11]. [√1kṛ.]

kārin, *a.* causing. [do.]

kārú, *m.* praiser, poet, singer. [√2kṛ, 'mention with praise.']

kārttikeya, *m. metronymic of* Skanda, god of war (so called because he was nourished by the Pleiads, kṛttikās): *cf.* kumāra *and* svāmikumāra. [kṛttikā, 1216.]

kāryà, *grdv.* to be done, faciendus, *w. the various shades of mg belonging to* √1kṛ; requiring to be instituted, 4[19]; requiring to be shown; *—as n.* what is to be done; business; work; matter, 4[17]; affair; duty; emergency. [√1kṛ, 963b.]

kārya-kāla, *m.* time for action.

kārya-hantṛ, *m.* business-destroyer, mar-plot.

kāryākṣama, *a.* unequal to *or* unfit for work. [akṣama.]

kālá, *m.* —1. the right *or* proper *or* appointed time; —2. time *in general;* —3. Time, as the destroyer, *i.e.* Death.

kāla-pāça, *m.* snare of Death.

kāvya, *n.* poetry; poem. [kaví.]

kāvyaçāstra-vinoda, *m.* entertainment with poetry and science. [kāvya-çāstra, 1252.]

√ kāç (kā́çate; cakāçé; kāçitá; -kā́çyā). be visible; shine.

+**ava**, be visible, lie open.

+**ā**, look on.

+**pra**, shine out; become clear.

kā́ça, *m.* visibility, *in* sakāça. [√kāç.]

kāṣṭhá, *n.* stick of wood; log.

kāṣṭha-ccheda, *m.* dearth of wood. [227.]

kāṣṭha-bhārika, *m.* wood-carrier.

kā́ṣṭhā, *f.* race-course; course; track of the winds and clouds in the sky.

kāṣṭhika, *m.* woodman. [kāṣṭha.]

ki, *cf.* 1ká4, *and* 504.

kiṁ-suhṛd, *m.* a bad friend. [see 1ká4, and 506.]

kitavá, *m.* gambler; *f.* -vī, *as a.*, addicted to gaming. [poss. kim + tava, 'what of thee?' 'what is thy stake?']

kím, —1. *as nom.acc.s.n. to* ká, *see* 1ká; —2. *as interr. adv.* [1111a], how? 73[8]. why? 18[10]; —3. *as interr. pcl.:* num; kim aham ajñas, am I a fool? 39[21]; an, 78[13]; —4. *in connection w. other pcls:* kiṁ ca, moreover, *see* ca3; kiṁ tu, however, 20[12]; kiṁ cana, somewhat, 46[9]; kim punar, how much more (*or* less)? 17[15]. [see under 1ká.]

kim-artha, *a.* having what as object; kimártham, *as adv.* why? [1302c4.]

kim-prabhu, *m.* a bad master. [see 1ká4, and 506.]

kim-bhṛtya, *m.* a bad servant. [do.]

kiyad-dūra, *n.* small distance; -re, *as adv.* [1116], a little way. [kiyant.]

kíyant [451], *pron. a.* —1. how great? how much? what sort of a? 45[10]; —2. (how great, *in a derogatory sense, i.e.*) not great; small, 46[1]. [1ká or ki, 505, 1172[2].]

kiyā́mbu, *n.* water-lily, *perhaps.* [cf. ambu.]

kíla, kílā [248a], *adv.* indeed, *emphasizing the foregoing word.*

kís, *interr. pcl. so at* 88[10]. [1ká, 504[2]: see 1117: cf. nákis.]

kīṭa, *m.* worm; caterpillar.

kīdṛg-vyāpāra, *m.* what business. [kīdṛç, 145.]

kīdṛgvyāpāravant, *a.* having what business. [1233.]

kīdṛ́ç, *a.* of what sort? [see 518.]

kīrí, *m.* praiser. [√2kṛ.]

√ kīrtaya (kīrtáyati [1056, 1067]; *pass.* kīrtyáte). —1. make mention of; tell; —2. repeat; call. [kīrtí, 1061[2].]

+**pari**, tell around, announce.

+**sam**, announce.

kīrtí, *f.* mention; *esp.* good report, fame. [√2kṛ.]

ku, *see* 1ká4, *and* 504.

kukkura, *m.* dog. [younger form of the onomatopoetic kurkurá.]

kuṭumba, *n.* household; family; -aka, *the same.*

kuṭṭanī, *f.* bawd.

kuṇḍa, *n.* round vessel; round hole in the ground (for water or sacred fire).

kuṇḍala, *n.* ring, *esp.* ear-ring. [cf. kuṇḍa and 1227.]

kútas, *adv.* from what place? whence? wherefore? why? how? 19[17]. [1ká or ku, 505.]

kutūhala, *n.* —1. interest felt in something extraordinary; eagerness; -āt, *as adv.* [1114b], eagerly; —2. interest caused by something remarkable, 56[11].

kútra, *adv.* where? whither? [1ka or ku, 505.]

ku-dṛṣṭi, *f.* a bad *or* false view; heterodox philosophy. [see 1ká4, and 506.]

kuntī, *f.* Kuntī, one of the two wives of Pāndu.

√ **kup** (kúpyati; cukópa; kupitá). —1. become moved *or* agitated; boil; *and so* —2. *fig., as in Eng.,* be angry; boil with rage.

+**pra**, *the same.*

kumārá, *m.* —1. new-born child; boy; youth, 51[10]; —2. The Youth, epithet of Skanda, the eternally youthful god of war—*see* kārttikeya; —*f.* -rī́, girl. [cf. sukumāra.]

kumāra-datta, *m.* name of a man. ['given by the god Kumāra.']

kumbhá, *m.* jar; pot; urn. [cf. κύμβη, 'vessel.']

kumbha-kāra, *m.* pot-maker, potter.

kumbhikā, *f.* pitcher. [kumbha.]

kúru, *m. as pl.* the Kurus, a people of India; *as sing.* Kuru, the ancestor of that people.

kuru-çrávaṇa, *m.* name of a prince. [lit. 'glory of the Kurus,' like Πυθο-κλῆς: acct, 1271.]

kúla, *n.* —1. herd *or* large number *or* swarm (of quadrupeds, birds, insects); —2. race; family; *and so, as in Eng.,* good family, noble stock. [√3kṛ, q.v.: cf. ākula.]

kula-çīla, *n.* family and character. [1253b.]

kúlāla, *m.* potter.

kú-liça, *m.* axe. [perhaps 'cutting well,' see 1ká4, and 506.]

kulīna, *a.* of good family. [kula, 1223d.]

kulīra, *m.* crab.

kuçá, *m.* grass; *esp.* the sacred grass, Poa cynosuroides, with long stalks and numerous pointed leaves.

kuça-piñjūla, *n.* tuft *or* bunch of Kuça.

kúçala, —1. *a.* in good condition; equal to *or* fit for a task; able; clever, 46[18]; —2. *as n.* welfare, well-being; kuçalaṁ te, hail to thee.

kuçalin, *a.* well; prosperous. [kuçala 2.]

kuça-hasta, *a.* having Kuça in the hand. [1303.]

√ **kū** (kuváte). *found only w.* ā, *and perhaps meaning* see, look. [prob. for *skū, see under kavi.]

+**ā**, look forward to, *i.e.* intend. [see ākūta.]

kū́ṭa, —1. *n.* horn; —2. *m. n.* peak. [for mg 2, cf. the Swiss peak-names, *Schreckhorn, Wetter-horn,* etc.]

kū́pa, *m.* cave, hole; well. [cf. κύπη, 'cave, hut,' Lat. *cūpa,* 'vat,' 'niche for the dead,' borrowed Eng. *coop,* 'vat,' whence *cooper.*]

kūrmá, *m.* tortoise.

√ **1kṛ** (*Vedic,* kṛṇóti, kṛṇuté [715]; *later,* karóti, kuruté [714]; cakā́ra, cakré; *V.* ákar, ákṛta [831, 834a]; *later,* ákārṣīt; kariṣyáti; kṛtá; kártum; kṛtvā́; -kṛ́tya; kriyáte; cíkīrṣati; kāráyati, -te). do, make, *in the various meanings and uses of these words; thus,*

—1. perform, 59[21]; accomplish; cause; effect; prepare, 83[15]; undertake, 52[2]; commit, 29[12]; show: *e.g.* honor, 5[6]; familiarity, 9[17]; compassion, 21[19]; love, 42[18]; favor, 52[21]; contempt, 54[16]; attend to: an affair, 11[4]; engage in: trade, 46[11]; a quarrel, 42[19]; —2. do something (good *or* bad) for a person (*gen.*), 3[2], 9[15]; —3. make *or* procure for another, 82[4]; grant; —*middle:* get for one's self; assume: human voice, 3[14]; take on: form *or* shape, 48[3], 49[6]; —4. execute; follow: advice, 40[7]; —5. work over, prepare: food, 68[3]; —6. accomplish; be good for, 18[5]; —7. make: a sound, 26[17]; utter: the syllable om, 60[8,9];

—8. (*like Eng.* do *in* don, doff) put in *or* on; *w. loc.*, 81[1], 43[6]; set, 105[14]; *w. adverbs: see* **agratas, amā, āvis, tiras, puras, bahis**; —9. make a person (*acc.*) to be something (*acc.*), 79[12]; transform into, 40[13] ff.; render, *w. factitive predicate acc.*, 18[8]; *w. the predicate in composition* [1094]: *e.g.* **sajjī-kṛ**, make ready, 34[17]; —10. *w. adv. in* -**dhā**, divide in parts, 57[10]; —11. do, go to work, proceed, 37[8]; *pass. impers.*, 30[16]; —12. do, *esp.* sacred work; *with* **karma**, 97[2]; *without* karma (*like* ῥέζειν θεῷ *and* facere), to sacrifice, 93[12]; —*see also* **kṛta**.

—*desid.* desire to perform; *ppl.* [1037], **cikīrṣita**, that which is sought to be done, intention.

—*caus.* cause to do *or* make *or* be done *or* made; see to it that a thing takes place, 16[1]; *pass.* **tena sa praṇāmaṁ kāritas**, by him he was caused to make obeisance, 36[7]; *caus. equiv. to simple verb*, 26[5].

[cf. *αὐτο-κρά-τωρ*, 'self-actor, independent'; *Κρό-νος*, an old harvest-god, 'Perficus, the Completer, Ripener'; Lat. *cer-us*, 'creator'; *κραίνω*, 'accomplish'; Lat. *creāre*, 'create': *see* **kratu**: orig. root-form, perhaps **skṛ**, 1087d.]

+**adhi**, put over; put in office.

+**apa**, put off; injure, *opp. of* **upakṛ**.

+**aram** *or* **alam**, *see these words.*

+**ā**, bring hither, 74[10]; prepare, fashion, make.

+**vy-ā**, separate, analyse.

+**upa**, bring something to some one; do a service, act as an auxiliary, *opp. of* **apakṛ**. [w. the use of upa, cf. that of *sub* in *subvenire*, 'aid.']

+**pari**, (*poss.* surround, deck, *and so*) make ready; adorn.

+**pra**, —1. carry forward, accomplish; effectuate, cause; —2. *mid.* set before; put before one, *i.e.* make the subject of discussion *or* treatment; *w.* **buddhim**, put a plan before one's self, *i.e.* decide.

+**prati**, work against, counteract.

+**sam**, —1. put together; conficere, prepare; —2. treat according to the sacred usages, administer a sacrament to, *see* **saṁskāra**; consecrate, 106[3]; —3. adorn.

√ **2 kṛ** (**ákārīt**; *intens.* **cárkarti**). mention with praise.

√ **3 kṛ** (**kiráti** [242]; **cakā́ra, cakré; ákārīt; kariṣyáti; kīrṇá** [957b]; **-kī́rya**). pour out *or* scatter abundantly (*e.g.* hail-stones); cast forth (missiles); strew; cover *or* fill with. [cf. **kula**, 'swarm.']

+**vy-ati**, *pass.* be scattered in various directions; be brought to confusion. [cf. **vyatikara**, 'disaster.']

+**ava**, strew (loose earth); throw in.

+**ā**, scatter abundantly; cover over, fill; **ākīrṇa**, bestrown, covered. [cf. **ākara**, 'abundance, mine,' **ākula**, 'full.']

+**sam-ā**, bestrew; cover.

kṛcchrá, *a.* distressful; troublesome; *as n.* trouble.

kṛcchra-karman, *n.* hard work; drudgery.

√ **kṛt** (**kṛntáti, -te** [758]; **cakárta; ákṛtat; kartiṣyáti, kartsyáti; kṛttá; -kṛ́tya; kṛtyáte**). cut; cut off. [cf. **kaṭa** (for **karta**, 'cut, depression in the head,' *i.e.*), 'temple,' and *κρότ-αφος*, 'temple'; Lat. *curt-us*, 'docked, short.']

+**ud**, cut out *or* off; cut up, butcher.

1 **kṛt**, *vbl in cpds.* making; doing; causing; *as m.* maker. [√1 **kṛ**, 1147c.]

2 **kṛt**, a time, *in* **sa-kṛt**. [perhaps fr. √1 **kṛ**, 'a doing, a time': cf. **kṛ́tu**, 'a time.']

kṛtá, *a.* —1. made; done; —2. prepared; —3. attained; —4. well done, *and so*, good; —5. *as n.* deed; —6. (*perhaps* made, *i.e.* won) *and so*, the side of the die marked with four spots, the lucky *or* winning one; —7. the golden age, name of the first **yuga**, *see* 58[2] N. [√1 **kṛ**.]

kṛta-kṛtya, *a.* having one's duty done *or* end attained.

kṛtakṛtyatā, *f.* condition of having performed one's duty. [1237.]

kṛta-buddhi, *a.* having a made-up mind, of resolute character.

kṛta-māuna, *a.* having a kept silence, silent.

kṛta-saṁketa, *a.* having an agreement made, agreed upon as a rendezvous.

kṛtāñjali, *a.* having a made gesture of reverence, with reverent gesture. [**añjali.**]

kṛtānná, *n.* prepared *or* cooked food. [**anna.**]

kṛtāvajña, *a.* having contempt (done, *i.e.*) shown to one, disdained. [**avajñā.**]

kṛ́ti, *f.* —1. the doing, the production; —2. a production, literary work. [√1**kṛ.**]

kṛ́tu, a doing, a time; *only in acc. pl.* **-kṛtvas**, *and that at the end of cpds.* [√1**kṛ**, 1105[2].]

kṛte, *as prep.* on account of, for the sake of, for, *w. gen.* [1130] *or in composition.* [loc. of **kṛta**, lit. 'in the matter of' (cf. mg 5), 1116.]

kṛ́tti, *f.* pelt, hide. [√**kṛt**: for mg, cf. δέρμα, 'hide,' and δείρω, 'flay.']

kṛ́ttikā, *f. pl.* the Pleiads. [cf. **kṛtti**: perhaps the constellation was conceived as having the shape of a pelt.]

kṛtya, *grdv.* to be done; *as n.* that which ought to be done *or* is to be done, *and so*, duty, purpose, end; —*f.* **-ā́**, action, deed. [√1**kṛ**, 963b end.]

kṛ́tvas, *adv.* times; *see* **kṛtu.**

kṛtsná, *a.* whole; entire.

√ **kṛp** (**kṛ́pate** [745b]). mourn, lament.

kṛpā, *f.* pity, compassion. [√**kṛp.**]

kṛ́mi, *m.* worm.

√ **kṛç** (**kṛ́çyati** [761a]; **cakárça**; **kṛçitá**). grow lean. [cf. κολοκ-άνος, 'long lank person,' κολοσσός, *κολοκ-jos, 'colossus'; Old Lat. *crac-entes*, Lat. *grac-iles*, 'lean, slender.']

kṛçá, *a.* lean, haggard. [√**kṛç**, 958.]

√ **kṛṣ** (**kárṣati**; **kṛṣáti**; **cakárṣa**; **ákṛkṣat**; **karṣiṣyáti**; **krakṣyáti, -te**; **kṛṣṭá**; **kráṣṭum**; **kṛṣṭvā́**; **-kṛ́ṣya**). —1. **kárṣati**: tug, draw, pull; —2. **kṛṣáti**: draw furrows; plough.

+**ā**, draw on, attract; draw from (a source).

+**ud**, pull up, elevate.

+**pra**, draw forward, place in front.

kṛṣṭí, *f. pl.* people, folk. [√**kṛṣ**, mg 2: orig. 'tillages, tilled lands,' then 'settlement, community.']

kṛṣṇá, *a.* black, dark; *w.* **pakṣa**, the dark half of the lunar month, from full to new moon; *as m.*, *sc.* **pakṣa**, the dark lunar fortnight.

kṛ́ṣṇa, *m.* the black antelope.

kṛṣṇa-pakṣa, *m.* the dark lunar fortnight.

kṛṣṇa-sarpa, *m.* a very poisonous black Cobra, Colŭber Naga.

kṛṣṇājiná, *n.* skin of the black antelope. [**ajína.**]

√ **kṛṣṇāya** (**kṛṣṇāyáte**). blacken. [**kṛṣṇá**, 1059b.]

√ **kḷp** (**kálpate**; **cākḷpé** [786]; **kalpsyáte**; **kḷptá**; **kalpáyati, -te**). be in order; be suitable *or* serviceable to; help; **kḷptá**, in order, fixed, settled; —*caus.* put in order; ordain; arrange; dispose; fix (*in the manifold applications of this word as used colloquially*). [prob. not akin are Goth. *hilpan*, Eng. *help.*]

+**upa**, *caus.* prepare; furnish; provide.

+**sam**, *caus.* arrange together; determine; will; purpose.

kḷpta-keçanakhaçmaçru, *a.* having hair and nails and beard in order, *i.e.* trimmed. [**keça-nakha-çmaçru**, 1252.]

kḷptānta, having its end prescribed; limited. [**anta.**]

kéta, *m.* intention; desire; will. [√**cit**, 'look, be intent upon.']

ketú, *m.* brightness; *pl.* beams. [√**cit**, 'look, appear, shine': cf. Goth. *haidu-s*, ('appearance, manner,' i.e.) 'way,' AS. *hād*, 'way, manner, condition,' Eng. *-hood*, *-head* (as in *maidenhood*, *godhead*), Ger. *-heit*: cf. under **maya.**]

kévala, *a.* exclusive; excluding all else; alone; **-am**, *adv.* only.

kéça, *m.* hair (of the head); mane. [see **kesara.**]

keça-pakṣa, *m. du.* the two sides of the hair of the head; the temples.

keça-çmaçru-loma-nakha, *n. pl.* hair of the head, beard, hair of the body, and nails. [1253a.]

keçānta, *m.* hair-end; long hair hanging down; locks.

keçín, *a.* maned, with flowing mane. [keça.]

késara, *m.* hair; mane. [written also keçara, cf. keça: cf. Lat. *caesaries*, 'hair, mane,' but not Eng. *hair.*]

kesarāgra, *n.* ends of a mane. [agra.]

kāivarta, *m.* fisher.

koṭara, *n.* hollow of a tree.

koṭṭa, *m.* fort.

ko-daṇḍa, *m.* bow (of an archer). ['good-stick,' see 1 ká 4, and 506.]

kodaṇḍāṭanī, *f.* the notched end of a bow. [aṭanī.]

kopa, *m.* anger; -āt, *adv.* [1114b], angrily. [√kup.]

kopākula, *a.* full of anger. [ākula.]

kolāhala, *m. n.* uproar, confused cry. [onomatopoetic.]

ko-vida, *a.* well knowing *or* skilled. [see 1 ká 4, and 506.]

kāutuka, *n.* curiosity, eagerness; -āt, *adv.* [1114b], eagerly.

kāunteya, *m.* son of Kuntī, *i.e.* king Yudhishthira. [metronymic, 1216.]

kāuravya, *m.* descendant of Kuru, *i.e.* Yudhishthira. [patronymic, 1211: cf. 1208c.]

kāulālá, *n.* pottery. [kúlāla.]

kāuçala, *n.* cleverness; ability. [kúçala.]

krátu, *m.* power, *whether* of body *or* of mind *or* of both: —1. might, 73[17]; —2. will, 75[2]; understanding, 80[5]—*cf.* dakṣa; inspiration, insight, *esp.* for sacred songs and acts; —3. sacred deed, sacrifice, 16[7]; ceremony, *cf.* yajñakratu. [√1 kṛ, 'do, effect,' 1161: orig. sense of word in mgs 1 and 2 was prob. 'an effecting, a power to do *or* carry out': for mg 3, see √1 kṛ 12: cf. κρατύς, 'mighty,' AS. *heard*, 'strong, hard,' Eng. *hard.*]

√ **kram** (krā́mati [745d], krámate; cakrā́ma, cakramé; ákramīt; kramiṣyáti, -te, krańsyáte; krāntá [955a]; krámitum, krā́ntum; kramitvā́, krāntvā́; -krámya; kramyáte; kramáyati, krāmáyati [1042c[2] mid.]). step; go; go towards.

+**ati**, step beyond; excel; overcome.

+**sam-ati**, excel. [sam intens., 1077b end.]

+**ā**, step near to; come upon; attack; overpower.

+**ud**, go out; depart (of the vital spirit); *caus.* cause to disembark.

+**abhy-ud**, *caus.* cause to step out.

+**upa**, step unto; approach, 3[10].

+**nis**, go out.

+**parā**, step forth; advance boldly; *and so,* show one's strength *or* courage. [hence parākrama, 'valor': cf. kram + vi.]

+**pari**, go around, circumambulate.

+**pra**, step forward; set out; start from.

+**vi**, move away *or* on; proceed; attack boldly; *and so,* show one's courage. [hence vikrama, 'valor': cf. kram + parā.]

+**sam**, come together; approach; enter (a zodiacal sign, said of the sun).

kráma, *m.* —1. step; regular progress *or* order; -eṇa, -āt, gradātim, *cf.* yathākramam; —2. procedure; method; way, 36[21]. [√kram.]

kramaças, *adv.* step by step; gradually; in order. [1106.]

kravyá, *n.* raw flesh; corpse; carrion. [√*kru, which perhaps means 'coagulate, become stiff': w. kravís, 'raw flesh,' cf. κρέας, *κρέϝας, 'flesh'; w. krū-rá, 'bloody, raw,' cf. Lat. *crū-dus*, 'bloody, raw,' *cruor*, 'blood'; cf. AS. *hrāw*, 'corpse'; Eng. *raw*, Ger. *roh*, 'raw.']

kravya-vā́hana, *a.* carrying off the corpses.

kravyád, *a.* consuming corpses. [ád.]

kravyāda, *a. the same.* [ada.]

kriyā, *f.* action; performance; doings; labor, pains. [√1 kṛ, 1213d.]

√ **krī** (krīṇā́ti, krīṇīté; kreṣyáti; krītá; krétum; krītvā́; -krī́ya). buy, *w. instr.* [281b] *of price.* [perhaps akin w. √1 kṛ, and so meaning 'do business, trade.']

+**upa**, buy.

+**vi**, sell; sell for (*instr.*).

√ **krīḍ** (krī́ḍati, -te; cikrī́ḍa, cikrīḍé; krīḍiṣyáti; krīḍitá; krī́ḍitum; -krī́ḍya). play, sport.

krīḍā́, *f.* play, sport. [√krīḍ.]

krītotpanna, *a.* bought or on hand (of food). [utpanna, √pad.]

√ **krudh** (krúdhyati, -te [761]; cukródha; ákrudhat; kruddhá; króddhum; kruddhvā́). be angry.

krudh, *f.* anger.

krúdhmi *or* krúdhmin, *a.* wrathful. [√krudh: cf. 1167 and 1231: paroxytone.]

√ **kruç** (króçati; cukróça; ákrukṣat; kruṣṭá; króṣṭum; -krúçya). cry out; call; howl. [cf. κραυγή, 'cry,' for *κραυκ-η: for γ in place of κ, cf. τήγανον, 'crucible,' w. τήκω, 'melt.']

krūrá, *a.* bloody; raw; *fig.* harsh. [see under kravya.]

kroḍá, *m.* —1. breast, bosom; —2. interior. [for mg 2, cf. garbha 2.]

królha, *m.* anger. [√krudh.]

króça, *m.* call; calling distance; *Anglo-Indian* a Kos. [√kruç.]

kroçamātrāvasthita, *a.* stationed at the distance of a Kos. [kroça-mātra + avasthita.]

√ **kliç** (klíçyate, -ti; cikléça; kliṣṭá; kléṣṭum; -klíçya). be distressed.

kleça, *m.* pain; trouble. [√kliç.]

kvà, *V.* kúa, *adv.* —1. where? whither? kúa babhūvus, what has become of? —2. kva cid: anywhere; in any case, ever, 27[20]; *w.* na, never. [1 ká, 505.]

kṣa, *as collateral form of* √1 kṣi *in* kṣa-tra, *and as vbl of the same, w. the mg* 'abiding, situate,' *in* antari-kṣa.

kṣaṇa, *m.* instant; moment; -eṇa, -āt, *as advs* [1112b, 1114b], instantly. [prob. 'the time of a glance,' a shortened form of īkṣ-aṇa, 'glance': for mg, cf. Eng. "in the *twinkling of an eye*," and Ger. *Augen-blick*, 'glance of an eye, *i.e.* moment.']

kṣaṇika, *f.* -ī, *a.* momentary. [kṣaṇa.]

kṣatá, *ppl. of* √kṣan.

kṣatrá, *n.* —1. rule, dominion, power, 86[20]; —2. *later,* the temporal power, imperium (as distinguished from the spiritual power, bráhman, 'sacerdotium'); the second *or* princely caste or a member of it. [from kṣa = √1 kṣi 2: cf. kṣatra-pa, 'governor of a dominion, satrap,' and the borrowed σατρά-πης.]

kṣatra-bandhu, *m.* one who belongs to the kṣatra *or* second caste.

kṣatríya, *m.* —1. ruler, 75[1]; —2. one who belongs to the kṣatra *or* princely caste, a Kshatriya, 57[16]N. [kṣatra, 1214a.]

√ **kṣan** (kṣaṇóti, kṣaṇuté; ákṣaṇiṣṭa; kṣatá). harm; hurt; break. [closely akin w. √2 kṣi, q.v.]

kṣantavya, *grdv.* to be put up with *or* pardoned. [√kṣam, 212.]

kṣapā́, *f.* night. [cf. σκέπω, 'cover,' ψέφας, 'darkness': for ψ, cf. √kṣar.]

kṣapāha, *n.* a night and day, νυχθήμερον. [2 aha, 1253b.]

√ **kṣam** (kṣámate, -ti; cakṣamé; kṣamiṣyáte, kṣaṅsyáte; kṣāntá [955a]; kṣántum; kṣamyáte). —1. be patient; endure; put up with; kṣānta, patient; —2. forgive; pardon.

kṣamá, *a.* patient; bearing *or* enduring; *and so,* equal to a thing, able. [√kṣam.]

kṣamā, *f.* patience; long-suffering. [do.]

1 **kṣáya**, *m.* dwelling-place. [√1 kṣi.]

2 **kṣaya**, *m.* destruction; decay. [√2 kṣi.]

√ **kṣar** (kṣárati, -te; cakṣára; ákṣār [890]; kṣaritá). —1. flow; —2. liquefy; melt away; *and so,* perish. [for *skar: cf. ψείρω (*σπείρω) = φθείρω, 'destroy,' ἐ-φθάρ-η, 'perished': for ψ, cf. kṣapā, kṣíti: for φθ, cf. 2 kṣi.]

kṣara, *a.* perishable. [√kṣar.]

√ **kṣā** (kṣā́yati [761d 1]; kṣāṇá). burn.

kṣāra, *a.* pungent; saline. [√kṣā: cf. ξηρό-ς, 'dry': for mg, cf. Eng. *caustic,* lit. 'burning,' fig. 'pungent.']

√ **1 kṣi**, *with two meanings,* 'dwell,' *and* 'rule,' *attaching themselves to the stems* kṣi *and* kṣáya *respectively; thus,*

—1. kṣé-ti, *3d pl.* kṣi-y-ánti: abide *or* while *or* dwell, *esp.* in quiet and safety, 79[18]; inhabit. [cf. kṣití, 1 kṣáya, kṣétra, kṣéma 1, 'dwelling-place'; ἀμφι-κτί-ονες, 'dwelling around,' κτί-σι-ς, 'settlement.']

+ **upa**, rest on, be dependent on.

—2. kṣáya-ti: pos-sess, be-sitzen; be master of; rule, 71[9]. [cf. kṣéma 2, 'pos-

session'; κέ-κτη-μαι, 'am master of,' κτά-ομαι, 'get.']
[cf. the collateral form kṣa: for connection of 1 and 2, cf. the relation of Lat. *sedēre*, 'sit,' and *pos-sidēre*, 'be master of,' and of Ger. *sitzen*, 'sit,' and *be-sitzen*, 'be master of.']

√ **2kṣi** (kṣiṇā́ti, *later* kṣiṇóti; ákṣeṣṭa; kṣitá, kṣiṇá; -kṣíya; kṣīyáte; kṣapáyati [1042e]). destroy; make an end of; exhaust; —*pass.* wane; kṣīṇa, ruined, lost; —*caus.* weaken. [cf. φθίνω, *φθινϝω, 'perish, wane,' φθί-μενος, 'dead': for φθ, cf. kṣar: w. the secondary kṣa-n, cf. κτά-μενος, 'slain,' κτείνω, *κτεν-jω, 'slay.']
+**apa**, *pass.* be afflicted, suffer loss.

kṣit, *vbl.* inhabiter *or* ruler, *at end of cpds.* [√1kṣi 1 and 2: see 1147c.]

kṣití, *f.* dwelling, abode, 79[18]; piece of ground *or* land; the earth, the ground. [√1kṣi 1: cf. κτί-σι-s, 'settlement.']

kṣíti, *f.* destruction. [√2kṣi: cf. ψί-σι-s = φθίσις, 'decay': for ψ, cf. kṣar.]

√ **kṣip** (kṣipáti, -te; cikṣépa, cikṣipé; kṣepsyáti, -te; kṣiptá; kṣéptum; kṣiptvā́; -kṣípya; kṣepáyati). dart; cast; throw; *caus.* cause to fly *or* burst, 84[4].
+**ā**, —1. throw at; —2. *fig.* (*like Eng.* fling, make flings at), deride, put to shame, 8[10]; —3. draw towards one's self, call out (a person to vindicate himself), 55[6].
+**ni**, throw down (one's self, one's body).
+**vi-ni**, lay down separately *or* orderly.
+**sam**, dash together in a heap; destroy.

kṣipta-laguḍa, *a.* having the cudgel thrown.

kṣiprá, *a.* darting; quick; -am, *adv.* quickly. [√kṣip.]

kṣīrá, *n.* milk. [prob. √kṣar.]

kṣīrín, *a.* milky; *as m.* milk-plant. [kṣīra.]

kṣīrodaka, *n.* milk and water. [udaka: 1253b.]

√ **kṣud** (kṣódati, -te; cukṣóda; kṣuṇṇá; -kṣúdya). shatter; stamp upon; grind small.

kṣudrá, *a.* small. [√kṣud.]

kṣudra-buddhi, *m.* Small-wit, name of a jackal. [1298.]

kṣud-vyādhi, *m.* hunger and disease. [kṣudh: 1253a.]

√ **kṣudh** (kṣúdhyati; kṣudhitá). be hungry; kṣudhitá, hungry.

kṣúdh, *f.* hunger. [√kṣudh, 383a.]

kṣudhā, *f.* hunger. [√kṣudh.]

kṣudhārta, *a.* distressed with hunger. [kṣudhā + ārta.]

kṣétra, *n.* dwelling-place, 87[17]; piece of ground; field. [√1kṣi 1.]

kṣetra-pati, *m.* master of a field; farmer.

kṣéma, *m.* —1. abode; place of rest; security; well-being, 61[8]; —2. possession; kṣeme · · yoge, in possession · · in acquisition, *i.e.* in the enjoyment of what we have got and in the getting of more. [√1kṣi 1 and 2: for *ske-ma, 1166: cf. Goth. *haim-s*, 'village'; A.S. *hām*, Eng. *home*, and *-ham* in place-names; perhaps also κώμη (if for κϝώμη?), 'village.']

---

khá, *n.* —1. hole; hollow; —2. opening; —3. hole in the hub of a wheel; —4. void space; the sky. [√khan, cf. 333.]

kha-ga, —1. *a.* moving in the sky, flying; —2. *as m.* bird. [for mg 2, cf. antarikṣa-ga and kha-gama, 'bird,' ura-ga and bhujaṁ-gama, 'snake,' and turaṁ-ga, 'horse.']

kha-gama, *the same.*

khaṇḍa, *a.* broken; *as m.* a break, section, piece; khaṇḍaka, *m.* lump-sugar. [hence, prob., through the Persian, Arabic, Italian, and French, the Eng. *candy*.]

√ **khaṇḍaya** (khaṇḍayati). break; khaṇḍita, broken (of a command). [khaṇḍa, 1055.]

√ **khan** *or* khā (khánati, -te; cakhā́na, cakhnús; ákhān [890]; khaniṣyáti; khātá; khánitum; khanitvā́, khātvā́; -khā́ya; khanyáte, khāyáte; khānáyati). dig; *caus.* cause to be dug. [if for *skan, cf. Lat. *can-ālis*, 'ditch, canal.']
+**ā**, dig, burrow, *in* ākhu.

khára, *a.* harsh; *as m.* ass (so called from his harsh bray), 67[19].

khála, *m.* —1. threshing-floor; —2. a mean, low-lived fellow. [the tertium comparationis for 1 and 2 is perhaps 'dirt.']

khálu, *pcl.* —1. now (*continuative*); atha khalu, now; —2. indeed (*emphasizing the preceding word*), 55^{3}; —3. to be sure (*concessive*), 98^{3}.

√ **khā**, *see* khan.

√ **khād** (khā́dati; cakhā́da; khādiṣyáte; khāditá; khā́ditum; khāditvā́; khādyáte; khādáyati). chew; bite; eat, *esp.* of animals; feed on, 24^{16}; devour, 21^{11}; khāditá, eaten, 23^{5}, etc. [if for *skand or sknd, cf. κνίζω, √κνιδ, 'bite, sting,' κνίδη, 'nettle,' but not Eng. *nettle.*]

khāditavya, *grdv.* edendus. [√khād.]

√ **khid** (khidáti; khinná; -khídya). depress, *but only fig.*

+**ud**, pull out.

khilá, —1. *m.* piece of waste land between cultivated fields; a bare spot; —2. a gap.

khu, *a Prakrit form for* khalu.

khe-cara, *a.* moving in the sky. [kha, 1250c.]

khecaratva, *n.* power of flying (by magic). [1239.]

kheda, *m.* depression, sorrow. [√khid.]

kheda-vaça, *a.* having depression as one's controlling influence, under the dominion of sorrow.

√ **khyā** (khyā́ti; cakhyāú; ákhyat [847]; khyāsyáti; khyātá; khyā́tum; -khyā́ya; khyāyáte; khyāpáyati, -te [1042d]). *simple verb only in pass. and caus.* —*pass.* be well known; be talked of; —*caus.* make known. [orig. mg, perhaps, 'shine, appear *or* look (intrans.), see (trans.)'.]

+**abhi**, look at; behold, 78^{13}.

+**ā**, —1. show, tell; narrate, 55^{19}; —2. designate, name; —*caus.: act.* tell; *mid.* have told to one's self, 105^{7}.

+**praty-ā**, (*lit.* show back, *i.e.*) turn away, repulse, reject, 9^{20}; refuse. [the Ger. *zurück-weisen* has just the same mgs.]

+**vy-ā**, show to discriminately, *i.e.* explain.

+**sam**, tell together, *i.e.* reckon up.

+**pari-sam**, reckon up completely, 58^{6}.

khyāti, *f.* the being well known; fame; khyātiṁ gam, become famous. [√khyā.]

---

ga, *vbl.* going, *in many cpds;* situate, *e.g. in* madhyaga; *as m. nomen actionis,* the going, *in* durga, suga. [√gam, cf. 333.]

gagana, *n.* sky.

gáṅgā, *f.* the Ganges. [fr. √gam = gā, w. intens. reduplication, 1002b.]

gaja, *m.* elephant.

gaja-yūtha, *m.* herd of elephants.

gajendra, *m.* a great elephant. [see indra.]

gaṇá, *m.* —1. troop, (of Maruts) 90^{18}; crowd, (of friends) 3^{9}; host (of stars); flock, (of birds) 3^{8}; —2. *pl.* troop-deities, inferior deities which regularly appear not singly, but in troops, 67^{13}; *esp.* those that compose the retinue of Çiva; *then, as sing.,* a single one of Çiva's attendants, a Gana, 55^{20}; —3. a number.

gaṇanā, *f.* a numbering, calculation, taking into account. [√gaṇaya.]

√ **gaṇaya** (gaṇayati). number, calculate. [gaṇa, 1055.]

gaṇita, *ppl.* calculated; *as n.* [1176a], calculation, arithmetic. [√gaṇaya.]

gatá, *ppl.* —1. gone, 2^{21}; departed; *w. inf.* snātuṁ gata, gone to bathe, 44^{2}; *so* 41^{2}; —2. *often at beg. of cpds, see these;* —3. gone to: *w. acc.* 5^{8}, 15^{20}; *w.* prati *and acc.*, 23^{15}; —4. (having arrived at, *i.e.*) situated in: *w. acc.*, 62^{15}; *w. loc.*, 5^{14}; *in cpd, e.g.* svahasta-gata, situated on my own hand; —5. gone to a condition, *see* √gam 4; attained to, (fame) 56^{12}; -conditioned, *in* durgata, sugata. [√gam, 954d.]

gata-prāṇa, *a.* whose breath is gone, dead.

gata-saṁkalpa, *a.* whose purpose *or* will for the moment is gone, purposeless. [1299.]

gatānugati, *f.* the going after him who has gone (before), the following in the old ruts. [anugati.]

gatānugatika, *a.* addicted to following in the old ruts. [gatānugati, 1222a.]

gatásu, *a.* whose life is gone. [asu.]

gáti, *f.* —1. a going, way of going, ability to go; —2. progress, 18[18]; eventus, issue, 20[13]; —3. way of escape, refuge, 52[15]; —4. the way *or* course *esp.* of the soul through different bodies, metempsychosis; *and so*, a condition of the soul during these transmigrations, a man's lot *or* fate, 53[12], 65[10], 66[6], 66[21] ff. [√gam, 1157: cf. *βά-σι-ς*, 'going, power to go.']

√ **gad** (gádati; jagā́da; gadiṣyáte; gaditá; gáditum; -gádya). speak.
  + **ni**, say.

gada, *m.* disease.

gantavya, *grdv.* eundum, *used impers.* [√gam.]

gandhá, *m.* smell; *pl.*, *w.* çubha, perfumes.

gandharvá, *m.* —1. *orig.*, *perhaps*, the deity of the moon, the Gandharva; —2. *in Epos*, *pl.* Gandharvas, heavenly singers belonging to Indra's court; *as sing.* one of these, a Gandharva.

gabhīrá (*V.*, *later*) gambhīrá, *a.* deep.

√ **gam** (gácchati, -te [747, 608]; jagā́ma, jagmé; *V.* ágan [833], *later* ágamat; gamiṣyáti, -te; gatá; gántum; gatvā́; -gátya, -gámya; gamyáte; jígamiṣati; gamáyati, -te). —1. go, move; go to, 3[6]; go towards; go away, 28[17], 36[6]; come; *w.* pratīpam, go wrong; —2. go by, pass (*intrans.*): of time, 20[3]; of days, 29[13]; —3. come unto, *i.e.* arrive at, *w. acc.*, 3[7], 84[7]; reach, *w. loc.*, 69[8]; come into, *w. loc.*, 71[6]; get at, 95[19]; —4. go to a state *or* condition: *w.* pañcatvam, go to dissolution, *i.e.* die, 32[21], etc.; *so* to destruction, 29[6]; despondency, 44[18]; *w.* nijām gatim, (went) to his own proper condition, *i.e.* became a Yaksha once more, 53[12]; —5. manasā gam, (go with the mind, *i.e.*) perceive, 15[10].

[cf. *βαίνω* (**βανjω*, **γϝεμjω*), 'go'; Lat. *věnio*, **gvěmio*, 'come'; AS. *cum-an*, Eng. *come*; for the *kw* which is to be expected in Germanic as answering to the old *gv*, cf. Ger. *be-quem*, Old Eng. *cwēme*, 'convenient, fit, pleasant': cf. gáccha and *βάσκε*, 'go thou'; gatá-s, 'gone,' and *βατό-ς*, '(gone over, *i.e.*) passable'; gáti-s and *βάσι-ς*, 'a going': see also √gā.]

+ **adhi**, —1. go to; attain; —2. get at, learn, study, read—*cf.* √i + adhi.
+ **anu**, go after, follow.
+ **antar**, go within, enter.
+ **api**, go unto, join, 91[5] ff.
+ **abhi**, go unto, 1[14]; go.
+ **aram**, *see s.v.*
+ **ava**, come down.
+ **ā**, —1. go to, 6[10]; come to; come hither, 5[22], 10[23]; —2. return (52[22]), *usually w.* punar, 4[3], etc.; —ā́gata: —1. arrived, come, 7[9]; *w. inf.* çrotum āgata, come to hear, 28[5]; *so* 27[10]; arrived (as guest), 28[7]; —2. returned, 24[17]; —3. having gone to a condition, *e.g.* death, 46[3]; —āgantavyam, *grdv.*, *as impers. pass. w.* anena, this one will come hither; —*desid.* desire to return, 101[5].
+ **abhy-ā**, come unto, visit; abhyāgata, *as subst.* guest.
+ **upa‿ā**, approach.
+ **sam-upa‿ā**, go to together.
+ **sam-ā**, assemble; meet, 61[8].
+ **ud**, go out, proceed from.
+ **upa**, go unto, approach.
+ **nis**, proceed from (*abl.*), 51[11]; nirgata, departed.
+ **prati**, come back, return.
+ **vi**, go asunder; vigata, gone, vanished.
+ **sam**, *mid.* come together, meet; unite one's self with; *and so*, come to enjoy; —*caus.* assemble, *as trans.*

gama, *a.* going, *at end of cpds.* [√gam.]

gambhīrá, *a.* deep; *cf.* gabhīrá.

garut, *n.* wing.

garútmant, *a.* winged; *as m.* bird. [for mg, cf. pakṣin.]

√ **garj** (gárjati; jagárja; garjitá; garjitvā́; -gárjya). roar.

garjana, *n.* roar.

gárta, *m.* (earth-)cut, ditch. [younger form of kartá, q.v.]

gardabhá, *m.* ass; -ī́, *f.* she-ass. [1199.]

gárbha, *m.* —1. uterus concipiens, the conceiving womb; abde garbhād ekādaçe, in the eleventh year from (the womb, *i.e.*) conception; —2. (*as in Milton's* Earth's inmost womb) the interior, inside, 34[5], 43[2], *cf.* kroḍa; *at end of cpds*, having · · in the interior, containing · ·, *cf.*

padmagarbha; —3. conceptum, fruit of the womb; garbhaṁ dadhānās, conceiving fruit, 92[12]; embryo, 46[5], 93[7]; scion; *and so* —4. a new-born child. [√grabh, 'concipere': with garbha in mg 1, cf. δελφύς and δολφός, 'womb,' ἀ-δελφός and ἀ-δελφε-ιό-ς (= sá-garbh-ya-s), 'of the same womb, *i.e.* brother'; in mg 3, cf. βρέφος, 'embryo,' and Eng. *calf* in *mooncalf:* in mg 4, cf. Goth. *kalbo*, Eng. *calf*.]

garbhavant, *a.*, *in fem. only*, pregnant. [garbha 3: see 1233.]

garbha-stha, *a.* being in the womb, unborn.

√ **garh** (gárhate; jagarhé; garhitá; gárhitum; -gárhya). blame, reproach; garhita, despised.

√ **gal** (gálati; galitá). —1. drip; —2. fall; galita, fallen out, gone (claws, teeth, eyes). [hence jala, 'water': cf. √βαλ in intrans. mg, e.g. ποταμὸς εἰς ἅλα βάλλων, 'river flowing into the sea'; Ger. *quellen*, 'flow, spring,' *Quelle*, 'fountain.']

gava, *equiv. of* go, 'bull, cow, beeve,' *in cpds.* [see 1209a.]

gávyūti, *f.* pasture-land; *generalized*, territory, abiding-place. [lit. 'having food for cattle,' gó + ūtí, see go 4: the y is euphonic, cf. 258.]

√ **gā** (jígāti; ágāt). go; come. [collateral form of gam, q.v.: w. jígāti, cf. Laconic βίβāτι, 'strides'; w. ágāt, cf. ἔβη, 'went.']

+**abhi**, go unto; *w.* çramam, become weary.

gātú, *m.* —1. motion, movement, course; —2. progress; *equiv. to the Eng.* -fare *in* wel-fare (*for mg, cf. verb* fare, 'get on, go') — *see* sugātuyā; —3. (place of recourse, *i.e.*) refuge, abiding-place, 83[9]. [√gā, 'go,' 1161.]

gā́tra, *n.* —1. (means of moving, *i.e.*) a limb of the body; —2. *by synecdoche*, the body. [√gā, 'move,' 1185a.]

gāmin, *a.* going, going upon, going to. [√gam, 1183[3].]

gārbha, *a.* relating to the embryo *or* to pregnancy (of sacrifices). [garbha, 1208f.]

gārbhika, *a.* relating to the womb, prenatal. [garbha, 1222c 2.]

gā́rhapatya, —1. *a.* pertaining to the householder; *as m.*, *sc.* agni, the householder's fire, 102[2] N.; —2. *as n.* the being head of the house, 89[6]; the housekeeping, 89[11]. [gṛhápati, 1211.]

gír [392], *f.* —1. invocation, praise, 74[12]; —2. *sing. and pl.* speech, words, 87[16], 49[9]; —3. voice, 3[14]. [√1 gṛ, 242[1,3].]

girí, *m.* mountain, 55[8].

√ **gu** (*intens.* jóguve [1007[3]]). cause to sound, proclaim. [cf. γόος, βοή, 'cry'; Lat. *bovāre*, 'howl.']

guṇá, *m.* —1. a single thread of a cord; a string; *esp.* bow-string; —2. quality; adscititious quality, as distinguished from the real nature (svabhāva, 'ingenium'), 22[20]; —3. *as philosophical technical term*, one of the three pervading qualities of all nature, *to wit*, sattva, 'goodness,' rajas, 'passion,' and tamas, 'darkness,' 66[8] ff.; —4. *as specialization of mg* 2, a good quality, virtue, 1[4, 12], etc.; excellence. [for play on mgs 1 and 4, see nirguṇa and 18[5].]

guṇa-deva, *m.* Gunadeva, a pupil of Gunāḍhya. [lit. 'having virtue as his god,' 1302.]

guṇavant, *a.* virtuous, 18[4]; excellent, 3[22]. [1233.]

guṇaçālin, *a.* possessing virtues, excellent. [see çālin.]

guṇāḍhya, *m.* Gunādhya, *see* 53[3] N. [lit. 'rich in virtue,' āḍhya.]

guṇānvita, *a.* endowed with excellence; (of an asterism) lucky. [anvita, √i.]

guṇin, *a.* virtuous, excellent. [guṇa.]

√ **gup** (jugópa; gopsyáti; gupitá, guptá; gópitum, góptum; gupyáte; júgupsate, -ti). keep; guard; *desid.* seek to keep one's self from, *i.e.* shun, detest; *ppl.* jugupsita, detested, inspiring aversion, 59[12]. [prob. a secondary root, originating in the denom. verb-stem gopaya: see this and go-pa.]

gurú, *a.* —1. heavy; *and so* —2. *fig.* (*like Eng.* weighty), important; —3. worthy of honor, 28[13]; —4. *as m.* the one to be honored κατ' ἐξοχήν, the teacher *or* Guru, 60[4] ff.; *loc.* gurāu: in the house of the Guru, 61[23]; in case of a Guru, 104[4]. [cf.

the comp. gárīyāṅs: cf. βαρύς, Lat. gravis, *garu-i-s, Goth. kaurus, 'heavy.']

√ **guh** (gū́hati [745c]; jugū́ha [793f], juguhé; ághukṣat [916, 155]; gūḍhá [222[3]]; gū́hitum; -gúhya). hide; gūl̤há, hidden, 76[15].

+**apa**, hide (*trans.*) away from, *w. abl.*, 85[14]; put away, get rid of, 77[1].

gúh, *f.* hiding-place; *instr.* guhā́: *used as adv.* gúhā [1112e], in secret. [√guh.]

gúhā, *f.* hiding-place; cavern. [do.]

gúhya, *grdv.* cēlandus; secret, hidden. [do.]

guhyaka, *m.* one of a class of demigods, who, like the Yakshas, wait on Kubera, god of wealth, and, dwelling in mountain caverns (guhā), keep his treasures. [so named from their living in caverns or hidden places: 1222.]

√ **1gṛ** (gṛṇā́ti, gṛṇīté; jagā́ra; gariṣyáti; gīrṇá [957b]; -gírya). —1. invoke, call; —2. salute, praise; —3. speak out, say. [cf. gír, 'speech, voice'; γῆρυς, 'speech, voice'; Doric γαρύεν, 'speak'; Lat. garrio, 'talk'; Eng. *call*.]

+**sam**, chime in with, agree.

√ **2gṛ** (giráti; jagā́ra; ágārīt; gīrṇá [957b]; -gírya). swallow. [cf. βορά, 'food,' βι-βρώ-σκω, 'eat,' δημο-βόρ-ο-ς, 'folk-devouring'; Lat. *carni-vŏr-us*, 'flesh-eating,' *de-vorāre*, 'swallow down, devour.']

+**ni**, swallow down; devour (the sun in an eclipse), 76[16]—*see* √gras.

√ **3gṛ** (*aor.* ájīgar [867]; *intens.* jā́garti [1006]; *caus.* jāgaráyati). —1. *intens.* be awake; wake, *intrans.*; jāgṛhi [1011], be thou watchful, have a care for, *w. dat.*, 89[17]; wake up, *intrans.*, 30[16]; —2. *caus.* wake, *trans.*, 30[5]. [for the history of the word, see 1020: for 1, cf. ἐ-γρή-γορ-α, 'am awake,' ἔ-γρ-ετο, 'awoke' (intrans.); for 2, cf. ἐγείρω, 'wake' (trans.).]

gṛ́tsa, *a.* clever; wise.

√ **gṛdh** (gṛ́dhyati; jagárdha; ágṛdhat; gardhiṣyáti; gṛddhá; gṛddhvā́). —1. take long strides; —2. be eager *or* greedy for. [for *ghṛdh: cf. Eng. *greedy*.]

gṛ́dhra, —1. *a.* greedy; —2. *m.* vulture. [√gṛdh, 1188a: the Ger. offers an exact parallel: *Geier*, 'vulture,' is prop. 'the greedy (bird),' from *Gier*, 'greediness.']

gṛdhra-kūṭa, *m.* Vulture-peak, a mountain in Magadha.

gṛhá, *in V., m.; later, m. in pl.; otherwise, n.* house, 28[7], 79[15]; *w.* mṛnmaya, house of earth, the grave; gṛhaṁ gam, go home, 52[10]; *so* 40[3], 68[17]; *as pl.* the house as consisting of various rooms and buildings, 89[12]; mansions, 87[7]. ['that which receives one,' √grah: cf. geha.]

gṛhá-pati, *m.* master of the house. [acct, 1267a.]

gṛhá-patnī, *f.* mistress of the house. [do.]

gṛha-stha, *a.* abiding in a house; *as m.* householder *or* Brahman in the second stage of his religious life, *see* āçrama.

gṛhāçrama, *m.* house-stage, second stage in a Brahman's life, *see* āçrama.

gehá, *n.* house. [ident. w. gṛhá: cf. the ident. √√ṛdh and edh.]

gó [361c], *m.f.* —1. a beef *in its old sense of* bull *or* cow; *pl.* beeves, kine, cattle; the Vedic type or symbol of all welfare and blessing and riches (*e.g.* 80[16]), like "milk and honey" with the Hebrews; —2. beef *in the derived and now usual sense of* flesh; *pl.* pieces of flesh, 84[16]; —3. (the milch cow of kings, *i.e.*) the earth, 63[7]; —4. *observe that* gavyūti, gotra, gopa, gopati, gomaya, *and many other cpds of* go *lose their special reference to cattle and take a more general mg.* [cf. βοῦς, stem βοϝ, 'a beef, ox, cow'; Lat. *bos*, stem *bov*, 'ox, cow'; AS. *cū*, Eng. *cow*.]

go-ghná, *a.* kine-killing; *as m.* cow-slayer.

gótama, *m.* Gotama, a Vedic seer of the tribe of Angiras.

gotrá, *n.* —1. cow-stall, cattle-pen; —2. *perhaps*, pen of cattle, *and so* —3. group *in general* (*see* go 4); —4. *esp.* family, 19[16]; —5. family name, 103[19], *see* nāman 2. [from go: mgs 2 and 3 are not authenticated by the literature.]

gotra-ja, *a.* born in the family; *as m.* a relative.

go-pá, *m.* —1. cow-keeper, cow-herd; —2. keeper *in general* (*see* go 4). [2pa.]

gó-pati, *m.* —1. lord of kine; —2. lord *in general* (*see* go 4). [acct, 1267a.]

√ **gopaya** (gopayati, -te). be keeper, keep. [gopa, 1055.]

go-pā́ [351], *m.* —1. cow-keeper; —2. keeper *in general* (*see* go 4), 85[16]; protector, 69[15]. [2 pā.]

√ **gopāya** (gopāyáti, -te). be keeper; keep, 91[12]. [gopā, 1055.]

gomáya, —1. *a.* bovine; *as n.* —2. cow-dung, 103[22]; —3. dung *in general* (*see* go 4); *w.* ānaḍuha, dung of a steer, 105[3, 20]. [see maya.]

go-yukta, *a.* yoked with cattle; *w.* cakra, wagon drawn by cattle. [√yuj.]

go-rakṣaka, *m.* cattle-keeper, cow-herd.

gó-ṣakhi [343a], *a.* having cattle as companions, rich in cattle. [sákhi, 186.]

go-ṣṭhá, *m.* cow-stall, byre. [stha, 186.]

gāuṇika, *f.* -ī, *a.* standing in relation to the three guṇa's, *see* guṇa 3. [guṇa, 1222e 2.]

gāutamá, *m. patronymic from Gotama;* Gautama, name of various men. [gótama, 1208f.]

√ **grath** *or* granth (grathnā́ti; granthiṣyáti; grathitá; -gráthya). —1. string together, connect; —2. put together, *i.e.* com-pose (a literary work). [for mgs, cf. Lat. *com-pōnere*, 'put together, compose'; also *serere*, 'connect, entwine,' w. *sermo*, 'discourse.']

grantha, *m.* —1. (a string of words, *i.e.*) verse *or* couplet, 53[6], etc; —2. a composition, book, work, 17[8]. [√granth: for mgs, see under grath, and for 1, cf. Lat. *serere* w. *series*, 'row, string.']

granthín, *a. subst.* having books, bookish, book-reader. [grantha.]

√ **grabh**, *in Rigveda; later*, grah.

—*from* grabh: gṛbhnā́ti, gṛbhṇīté; jagrā́bha, jagṛbhé; ágrabhīt, ágrabhīṣṭa [900]; gṛbhītá; gṛbhītvā́; -gṛ́bhya.

—*from* grah: gṛhṇā́ti; jagrā́ha, jagṛhé; ágrahīt, ágrahīṣṭa [900]; grahīṣyáti, -te; gṛhītá; gráhītum; gṛhītvā́; -gṛ́hya; gṛhyáte; grāháyati, -te.

—1. grasp; seize with the hand; hold; take; *w.* hástam *or* pāṇím, take the hand (of the bride at the wedding), 89[5]; take hold on (*loc.*), 14[18]; gṛhīta keçeṣu, seized by the hair; *used* of a rabbit taking, *i.e.* leading with him a lion, 33[4]; —2. take possession of, take, 46[22]; get, 44[5]; —3. receive, accept, 20[10], 56[1]; —4. of fluids, take in the ladle, 94[1]; —5. of names, take upon the lips, mention, 64[13], 103[19]; —6. *fig.*, *as in Eng.*, grasp, *i.e.* perceive, know; —7. get, learn; —*caus.* cause to learn. [see under garbha: connection w. Eng. *gripe*, Ger. *greifen*, exceedingly doubtful.]

+**pari**, —1. hold on both sides; *and so* —2. become master of; master, overcome, surpass.

+**prati**, take hold of, 59[23]; accept.

+**vi**, —1. hold asunder; separate; make a division; *and so* —2. quarrel; fight.

+**sam**, hold together, clasp.

+**upa-sam**, clasp with the hands.

√ **gras** (grásate; jagrasé; ágrasīt; grasiṣyáte; grastá; grasitvā́; grasyáte; grāsáyati). —1. swallow; devour, 10[10]; —2. of the demon Rāhu, who swallows, *i.e.* eclipses sun and moon, 23[1]. [perhaps akin w. √2 gṛ, 'swallow.']

√ **grah**, *see* grabh.

gráha, *m.* seizure (with a claw, *i.e.*), bite. [√grah.]

gráhaṇa, *n.* the grasping, *i.e.* acquisition. [√grah 6, 7.]

grābhá, *a. subst.* grasping, grasper. [√grabh.]

grā́ma, *m.* —1. inhabited place, hamlet, village, *see* 98[16] N.; —2. the inhabitants, community.

grā́ma-kāma, *a.* having desire for the village, fond of abiding in the village.

grā́van, *m.* stone; *esp.* stone for pressing the Soma.

grāhá, *a. subst.* grasping, grasper, *in cpds.* [√grah.]

grāhyà, *grdv.* to be grasped; perceivable. [do.]

grīvā́, *f.* nape of the neck; neck. [for *gaᵉrvā́: cf. Aeolic δέρρα, *δερϝα, Epic δειρή, 'throat, neck.']

grīṣmá, *m.* summer.

---

gha, *form of* ghan, *i.e.* han, *in cpds.* [1143c, 333.]

ghaṭa, *m.* a jar.

ghaná, *m.* —1. slayer; —2. slaughter; —3. a compacted mass, lump; —4. cloud. [√ghan, *i.e.* han: cf. φόνο-s, 'slaughter.']

gharmá, *m.* warmth, heat. [√2 ghṛ: cf. θερμό-s, for *φορμός, Lat. *formus*, 'warm.']

√ **ghuṣ** (ghóṣati, -te; jughóṣa; ghuṣṭá; -ghúṣya; ghoṣáyati). sound; make a noise.

√ **1 ghṛ** (jígharti; ghṛtá; ghāráyati). besprinkle; be-drop; drip (*trans.*); ghṛtá, *see s.v.*

+praty-abhi, *caus.* sprinkle over repeatedly.

+vy-ā, sprinkle here and there.

√ **2 ghṛ**, glow, be warm, *in* ā́-ghṛṇi, 'glowing,' *and* gharma, *q.v.*

ghṛtá, *n.* —1. butter, clarified and then hardened, *Anglo-Indian* ghee, much used for culinary (*cf.* 68^{1}) and religious (*cf.* 88^{17}) purposes: *cf.* ā́jya, 'butter in a melted state'; —2. butter *or* fat *in general*, also as symbol of fruitfulness and abundance. [√1 ghṛ, 'drip,' 1176a: for mg, cf. Eng. *dripping*, 'fat which falls in drops from meat in roasting.']

ghṛta-paçu, *m.* sacrificial beast made of ghee.

ghṛta-çcút, *a.* dripping with (ghee, *i.e.*) fatness.

ghorá, *a.* awful; dreadful; horrid.

ghora-cakṣus, *a.* having an evil eye.

ghorākṛti, *a.* having an awful form. [ākṛti.]

ghóṣa, *m.* noise. [√ghuṣ.]

ghna, *a.* killing; destroying; removing. [√ghan, *i.e.* han: see 216.9.]

ghnya, *grdv.* to be slain, *in* aghnya. [do.]

√ **ghrā** (jíghrati [749a]; jaghrāú; ghrātá; -ghrā́ya; ghrāyáte; ghrāpáyati [1042d]). smell; snuff at.

---

ca, *encl. conj.* and, also, τε, que; —**1a.** *is found, esp. in the older literature, with both parts to be connected* (*e.g.* $71^{5,7}$, $97^{7,11}$; *so* 13^{5}, 16^{12}, 17^{3}, 19^{10}, 38^{7}, 9^{2}); *or only with the latter, as is oftenest the case in the later language* (*e.g.* $2^{1,7}$, 3^{8}, 8^{8}; 82^{8}, 84^{16}; 98^{16}); —**1b.** *in case of three or more parts to be connected*, ca *occurs: with the last only* (*e.g. three parts*, 13^{2}, 17^{2}, 31^{14}, 44^{6}; 71^{8}, 72^{10}, 83^{15}; 106^{5}; *four parts*, 2^{2}, 17^{7}, 28^{10}; *five parts*, 2^{5}, 21^{5}, 25^{3}); *with the last two* ($7^{6,7}$, 22^{5}, 37^{15}, 45^{7}; 77^{12}); *sometimes after each*, ($29^{3,4}$); *very rarely after the first of a series* (26^{6}; 21^{22}); *various irregular combinations on page* 67 *passim*; *see also* 21^{20} N.;

—**2.** *variously combined: w.* eva (*e.g.* 13^{21}; 9^{16}, 11^{9}, 14^{15}; 5^{9}, 12^{5}, $14^{2,8,20}$, 15^{16}, 25^{4}; 30^{14}), *and w.* api (*see examples under* api); ·· ca, ·· tathā, ·· ca, both ··, likewise ··, and, $10^{8,9}$; ·· ca, ·· ā, both ··, and ··, 85^{5}; sa ca, *often at beg. of clause* (*e.g.* 24^{23}; *so* 34^{18}; 41^{7}); —**3.** anyac ca, api ca, kiṁ ca, tathā ca, *joining two proverbs of like drift*, moreover, further, likewise;

—**4.** *otiose*, 6^{9}; —**5.** *connecting things contrasted:* but, 8^{16}, 17^{20}, $18^{2,3}$, 19^{2}; and yet, 1^{12}, 3^{20}; —**6.** (even, *concessively, i.e.*) though, 26^{12}; —**7.** (*like Eng.* and *or* an, *and Icelandic* enda, 'moreover,' 'if') if — *see* ced; —**8.** *w. interrogatives, rendering them indef., see* ka, kim.

[cf. τε, 'and'; Lat. *que*, 'and'; Goth. *-h* and Ger. *-ch* in *ni-h* and *no-ch*, the exact equivalents of Lat. *ne-que*, 'and not, nor': for ca 8, cf. -τε and -κα in πο-τε and Doric πο-κα, 'at any time'; Lat. *quis-que*, 'any, each.']

cakrá, *n.* —1. wheel; chariot-wheel, wagon-wheel; —2. *by synecdoche*, wagon, *in* pīṭha-cakra. [prob. reduplicated form, ca-kra, fr. √*kṛ or *kḷ, 'roll,' cf. κυλίω, 'roll': w. ca-krá, cf. κύ-κλος, *κϝε-κλος, AS. *hweohl*, *hweōl*, Eng. *wheel*.]

√ **cakṣ** (cáṣṭe [628]; cacakṣé; cáṣṭum; -cákṣya). —1. appear; —2. look upon, behold; —3. (cause to appear, *i.e.*) announce, tell. [reduplicated form of √kāç, see 675 and 108g¹ end.]

+ā, —1. look on; —2. show, tell, 63^{1}.

+vi, appear far and wide, shine.

+sam, look upon, consider.

cákṣas, —1. *perhaps adj.* beholding, *see* 1296^{3} end; —2. *n.* look; eye. [√cakṣ.]

cakṣuḥ-pīḍā, *f.* eye-ache.

cákṣuṣmant, *a.* possessing eyes. [1235.]

cákṣus, *n.* eye. [√cakṣ, 1154.]

cañcala, *a.* moving to and fro; trembling. [√cal, 1148.4, w. intens. reduplication, cf. 1002b: cf. κίγ-καλ-ος, 'wag-tail'; Lat. *quer-quer-us*, 'shaking with fever chills.']

cañcu, *f.* beak, bill.

caṇaka, *m.* chick-pea.

cáṇḍa, *a.* impetuous; wrathful.

caṇḍāla, *m.* a Chandāla *or* man of the most despised class of society (born of Çūdra father and Brahman mother). [cf. caṇḍa.]

√ **cat** (cátant; cattá; *caus.* cātáyati). get off; hide; *caus.* drive away.

catasṛ, *fem. to* catúr.

catúr [482d], *num.* four. [w. catvā́ras, cf. τέτταρες, Lat. *quattuor*, Goth. *fidvor*, AS. *feōwer*, Eng. *four*.]

catur-akṣá, *a.* four-eyed. [see 1300b.]

caturthá, *f.* -ī́, *a.* fourth; -am, *adv.* the fourth time. [catúr, 487[5].]

catur-yuga, *n.* the four ages. [1312.]

catur-varga, *m.* group of four.

cátur-vidha, *a.* of four kinds; four-fold. [vidhā, 1302c 5.]

cátuṣṭaya, *a.* of four; *as n.* a collection of four, a quaternion. [catúr, 178: 1245a.]

catuṣ-pathá, *m. n.* place where four ways meet, quadrivium. [catúr, 178, 187: 1312.]

cátuṣ-pad, *a.* quadruped; *as n. s. collectively*, the four-footed beasts. [catúr, 178: 1300.]

catuṣ-pada, *f.* -ī, *a.* having (taken) four steps.

catvara, *m. n.* quadrivium. [catúr.]

catvār, *strong form of* catur, *q.v.*

√ **can** (ácanīt). be glad in; gladden. [collateral form of √kan: cf. √kan, kāma, cāru.]

caná, *adv.*, *immediately following the emphasized word.* —**1.** not even; svápnaç caná, not even sleep, 79[1]; —**2.** *w. preceding negation,* even; ná devā́nām áti vratám, çatā́tmā caná, jīvati, not beyond the decree of the gods, (not) even if hundred-lived, does one live, 88[2]; *hence, the feeling for the negation in* cana *in such collocations becoming faint,* —**3.** even, at all, *w. interrogatives, emphasizing their indefinite sense;* na kiṁ cana, not any thing even *or* at all, 8[19]; *see esp.* 1 ká 2c, *also* katham, kadā, *and* kim. [cf. Lat. *-quam* and *-cun-* in *quisquam, quicunque*, 'any one'; Goth. *-hun* in *ni hvas-hun*, 'not any one.']

candrá, *a.* shining, shimmering; *as m.* the moon; the moon-god. [for çcandrá, q.v.]

candrámas, *m.* the moon; the moon-god. [orig. a descriptive cpd, stem candra-mās (383d6), nom. candra-mās, and so with long ā throughout, but transferred to the ăs-declension (cf. 418).]

candrá-varṇa, *a.* of shining hue.

√ **cam**, sip, *only with* ā.

+ **ā** (ā́cāmati [745d]; ā́cacāma; ā́cānta [955a]; ācámya; ā́cāmayati). sip (water), *i.e.* rinse the mouth.

camasá, *m.* beaker; cup, made of wood, square, and with handle. [√cam, cf 1197.]

campaka, *m.* Michelia Champaka, a tree with strong-smelling yellow blossom.

campakavant, *a.* abounding in Champaka trees; *as f.* Champakavatī, name of a forest. [1233.]

√ **car** (cárati, -te; cacā́ra, cerús, ceré; ácārīt, ácariṣṭa; cariṣyáti; caritá; cáritum; caritvā́; -cárya; caryáte; cārá-yati, -te). —**1.** move, 77[12]; go; wander; wander about; *used* of men, beasts, waters, heavenly bodies; —**2.** (*like Eng.* proceed —*cf. Lat.* prō-cēdere, 'go on') act; *w. ppl.* [1075b], go on, *i.e.* keep on (doing a thing), 96[11]; —**3.** (*like Eng.* go about, *i.e.*) undertake, set about; bhāikṣaṁ car, go begging, beg; undergo (troubles), 88[12]; perform (a vow, duty); observe (silence); commit (offense *or* injustice), 80[9], 63[7]; sasyaṁ car, feed on corn, 34[16]; carita, *see s.v.* [cf. περι-τελ-λομένων ἐνιαυτῶν, 'as years go round,' and περι-πλ-ομένων ἐνιαυτῶν, 'as years went round,' with τ before a palatal and π before a non-palatal; also πόλ-ος, Milton's 'turning sphere': see also car + ud, and the younger collateral form cal, and under cañcala: akin is also √kal.]

+ **anu**, move along after, follow.

+ **apa**, go off, be absent.

+ **abhi**, go against, trespass against; *esp.* be unfaithful (of a wife).

+ā, —1. move unto, approach, 86[3]; —2. go to (an undertaking), set about; *and so*, do, 10[6], 64[11], 66[14]; practice (virtue); perform (vow); follow (rule); —3. proceed, conduct one's self, *cf.* ācāra, 'conduct.'

+ud-ā, rise up out of (*abl.*), 77[14], of the moon.

+sam-ā, proceed; do; perpetrate.

+ud, go up, rise, of the sun; *caus.* cause to go out, evacuate, *cf.* uccāra, 'evacuation.' [cf. sūryam uc-cárantam w. ἥλιον ἀνα-τέλλοντα, 'the rising sun.']

+upa, —1. come to; —2. come to, *esp.* in order to serve, *and so*, attend, wait upon politely; —3. proceed with, undertake.

+parā, move away from, 86[3].

+vi, move in different directions, spread over; of waters, overwhelm; wander about; *caus.* cause to go hither and thither in thought, balance, ponder.

+sam, go, walk, wander.

cara, *a.* moving; *as subst.* animal (as distinguished from plant). [√car.]

cárana, —1. *m. n.* foot; —2. *as n.* a wandering. [√car: for 1, cf. nayana.]

caritá, —1. *ppl.* done; —2. *as n. sing.* [1176a], (*like Ger.* Wandel *and Eng.* walk) behavior; proceedings; deeds. [√car.]

carita-vrata, *a.* having his (marital) duty performed.

carcā, *f.* a going over, repetition (of a word in a school-boy's Veda-recitation); a troubling one's self about. [perhaps fr. √car.]

cárman, *n.* skin; pelt.

carya, *grdv.* to be accomplished; —*f.* -ā, (*like Eng.* walk) way of life; a performing, busying one's self with. [√car.]

√ **carv** (carvitá, cūrṇá; cárvitum). chew, crush with the teeth.

carṣaṇí, *a.* active, busy; *as f. pl.* busy mortals, men, folk. [√car, 1159b end.]

√ **cal** (cálati; cacā́la, celús; caliṣyáti; calitá; cálitum). move; start off. [younger form of √car, q.v.: cf. κέλ-ευθος, Lat. *cal-lis*, 'path.']

cala, *a.* moving. [√cal.]

cāṇḍālá, *m.* a Chandāla. [see caṇḍāla and 1208f.]

cātana, *a.* driving away. [√cat, caus.]

cāturmāsyá, *n.* a sacrifice to be made every four months, *i.e.* at the beginning of each of the three seasons. [catur + māsa, 1211.]

cāndrāyaṇa, *n.* *with or without* vrata, the Chāndrāyana observance *or* lunar penance, 65[6] N. [lit. 'connected *or* according with the moon's course,' candra + ayana.]

cāraṇa, *m.* wanderer; *esp.* wandering player *or* singer. [caraṇa.]

cārin, *a.* moving; observing; busying one's self with. [√car.]

cā́ru, *a.* gladsome; dear; pleasant; fair. [√can, q.v., 1192: cf. Lat. *cā-rus*, 'dear.']

cāru-hāsin, *a.* sweetly laughing.

√ **1ci** (cinóti, cinuté; cikyé [787]; ácet; ceṣyáti, -te; citá; cétum; citvá; -cítya; cīyáte). —1. arrange in order; pile up; build; construct, *esp.* the sacrificial altar; *active, if the priest builds for others; middle, if the sacrificer builds for himself*; —2. gather together, collect; get possession of.

+ud, heap up, collect.

+sam, gather together, collect; accumulate.

√ **2ci** (cáyati, -te). —1. hate; —2. avenge, take vengeance on, punish. [cf. Arcadian ἀπυ-τείω, Attic ἀπο-τίνω, 'pay off,' ἀποτίνομαι, 'get paid to myself, take vengeance, punish,' ποινή, 'penalty.']

√ **3ci** (cikéti; cikā́ya, cikyús [787]; ácet; ceṣyáti; cétum; -cítya; cīyáte). —1 notice, observe; —2. look, investigate. [cf. √cit.]

+nis, (search out, *i.e.*) ascertain; determine; consider as certain *or* settled.

+vi-nis, (look out this way and that, *i.e.*) ponder, consider, 13[13].

+pari, investigate thoroughly, find out.

cikitú, *prob. f.* understanding. [√cit, 1178c.]

cikitvít, *adv.* with understanding. [cikitú, 1109.]

√ **cit** (cétati, -te; cikéta, cikité; ácāit; cittá; cetáyati, -te). —1. look at, notice; observe; consider; —2. be intent upon, intend; —3. understand, know; *perfect*, cikéta, has understood, knows; cikitvā́ṅs, wise; — *caus.* make to know, instruct. [extension of √3ci: the √cit shows an intrans. aspect, 'be noticeable *or* bright,' in ketu: cf. √cint.]

+**pra**, know.

cít, *vbl.* knowing. [√cit, 383a.]

cíti, *f.* pile. [√1ci.]

cittá, *n.* notice; thought; mind. [lit. 'noticed,' √cit, see 1176a.]

citta-pramāthin, *a.* disturbing the mind.

citti, *f.* understanding; wisdom. [√cit.]

citrá, *a.* —1. noticeable, excellent; —2. clear; bright; bright-colored; of sounds, clear, *i.e.* loud; —3. variegated, 10[8]; varied; —4. *as n.* a bright-colored thing, a picture. [√cit, 1188.]

citrá-çravas, *a.* whose praise is loud *or* whose fame is excellent.

citra-stha, *a.* being in a picture; painted.

citrāñga, *m.* Dapple-coat, name of a deer. ['having a variegated *or* mottled body': áñga.]

cid, *encl. pcl.* —1. *emphasizes, sometimes very gently, the preceding word:* even, 78[10,15]; just, 74[2], 79[4]; yāç cid, what very ones, 70[16]; at least, 79[14]; —2. *generalizes a pron.:* yé cid · · táñç cid, whatsoever · ·, unto all those, 91[10]; *so far Vedic;* —3. *in classical Skt., very common w. an interr., rendering it indef.:* kaç cid, a certain; na kā cid, not any; *see* ka, kad, kadā, karhi, kva. [acc. s. n. of pron. root ka, ki (505), w. palatalization: 1111a.]

√ **cint** (cintáyati, -te; cintayā́m āsa; cintayiṣyáti; cintitá; cintayitvá; -cíntya). —1. think, reflect, have a certain thought; —2. set one's thoughts upon, think upon *or* of, consider, turn one's attention to; —3. call attention to; make an observation, 35[9]. [younger form of √cit: cf. 255 and 240.]

+**vi**, reflect.

+**sam**, think to one's self.

cintana, *n.* a thinking upon. [√cint.]

cintā, *f.* —1. thought; —2. *esp.* (*like* μέριμνα), anxious *or* sad thought; sorrow; —3. plans, 43[3]. [√cint.]

cintā-para, *a.* having sad thought as one's chief thing, sunk in sad thought. [1302b.]

cintāviṣa-ghna, *a.* destroying the poison of sorrow.

cintitopasthita, *a.* which approached as soon as thought of. [lit. 'thought of and (immediately) at hand,' cintita + upasthita, 1257.]

cintya, *grdv.* to be thought of, comprehensible. [√cint.]

cirá, *a.* long, of time; -am, -āt, *as adverbs* [1111c, 1114c], long, for a long time.

cira-mitra, *n.* an old friend.

cīt-kāra, *m.* the sound cīt, *i.e.* the braying of an ass. [cīt, onomatopoetic.]

círa, *n.* strip of bark *or* cloth; rag.

√ **cud** (códati, -te; ácodīt; codáyati, -te). drive on; speed; excite; *caus. the same.*

+**pra**, *caus.* drive on; further; inspire.

√ **cur** (coráyati). steal.

curā, *f.* theft. [√cur.]

cūḍā, *f.* tuft of hair left on the crown of a child's head after the ceremony of tonsure.

cūḍā-karman, *n.* ceremony of tonsure, 59[19].

cūrṇa, *m. n.* meal, powder. [√carv: for mg, cf. piṣṭa.]

√ **cūrṇaya** (cūrṇayati). powder, crush fine; crush; smash. [cūrṇa, 1055.]

√ **cṛt** (cṛtáti; cacárta; cṛttá; -cṛ́tya). fasten together.

+**pra**, loosen, untie.

cétana, *a.* noticing; cetanā, *f.* consciousness; mind. [√cit.]

cétas, *n.* consciousness; mind; heart. [√cit.]

céd, *adv. never at beg. of sentence, clause, or half-verse.* if; *apodosis, if it follows, marked by* tad (37[4]), tatas (52[5]), *or not marked* (32[21], etc.), *or marked by* na, *if negative* (18[9]); na ced, if not, 52[8]; no ced, *forms a shortened but complete clause,* and if not, 27[17]. [ca + íd, 1133[5]: see ca 7.]

√ **ceṣṭ** (céṣṭati, -te; cicéṣṭa; ceṣṭitá; céṣṭitum; ceṣṭitvá). move the limbs; bestir one's self; be active; act.

ceṣṭā, *f.* activity; performance. [√ceṣṭ.]

ceṣṭita, *ppl.* performed; *as n. s.* [1176a], deeds. [√ceṣṭ.]

códana, *n.* an impelling; order; precept. [√cud.]

cāuḍa, *n.* ceremony of tonsure. [cūḍā.]

cāura, *m.* thief. [curā.]

√ **cyu** (cyávati, -te; cucyuvé; ácyoṣṭa; cyoṣyáte; cyutá; cyávitum; cyāváyati). —1. move, bestir one's self; —2. go off, disappear; —3. come to nought, 68[12]; —4. fall (from, *abl.*), 51[9]; —5. set agoing, undertake, mūlīri, 74[8]. [akin, perhaps, are *ἔ-σσευα*, 'impelled,' and *δορυ-σσόος*, 'lance-brandishing.']

+**pra**, *caus.* move *or* lead onward.

√ **1chad** (channá; chādáyati; chādayā́ṁ cakre; chāditá; chādayitvā́; -chā́dya). cover; cover over.

+**ā**, cover over; conceal, 25[10].

+**pari**, envelope, cover over.

+**pra**, cover; clothe one's self with (*instr.*).

√ **2chad** *or* chand (chántti; cacchánda; ácchān [890[2]]; chadáyati [mgs 1, 2]; chandáyati [mg 3]; chandayā́m āsa; chanditá). —1. appear, seem; —2. seem good to, please; —3. (please a person, *acc.*, with a thing, *instr.*, *i.e.*) offer a person, *acc.*, a thing, *instr.* [prob. ident. w. √çcand.]

chanda, *m.* pleasure; will. [√2chad.]

chala, *m. n.* (*perhaps* cover, *i.e.*) guise, disguise; pretence, deceit. [perhaps fr. √1chad.]

chāga, *m.* goat. [for *skāga: cf. Germanic *skēpo-*, for *skēqo-, Ger. *Schaf*, AS. *sceāp*, Eng. *sheep.*]

chāyā́, *f.* shade; shadow; image. [cf. *σκιά*, 'shadow.']

chāyā-dvitīya, *a.* having one's shadow as second, accompanied by one's shadow. [1302b.]

√ **chid** (chinátti; cicchéda; ácchāitsīt; chetsyáti; chinná; chéttum; chittvā́; -chídya; chidyáte). —1. cut off; hew down; sever; cut in two; nibble; —2. divide. [cf. *σχίζω*, √*σχιδ*, 'split'; Lat. *scindo, scidi*, 'cut'; AS. *sceādan*, 'divide,' Eng. water-*shed*, 'the divide between two valleys.']

+**ud**, —1. cut out; —2. destroy; —*pass.* be cut off, fail, be lacking.

+**vi**, cut asunder; sever.

chidrá, *n.* hole; defect; weak spot. [√chid.]

chucchundari, *m.* musk-rat.

cheda, *m.* cut; cutting off; failure, dearth. [√chid.]

---

já, *vbl.* born; born from; occasioned *or* produced by; *only in cpds.* [√jan, 333: cf. jā, the older form, 354.]

jágat [450d], *a.* movable; *as n.* all that moves, men and beasts. [√gam: cf. 383b[3] end.]

jaghána, *m. n.* the hinder parts, the buttocks.

jaghanyà, *a.* hindermost; last; lowest *or* worst. [jaghana, 1212d 4.]

jañgama, *a.* movable; *as subst.* all that moves, *equiv. to the ancient* jágat. [√gam, 1148.4, cf. 1002b.]

jáñghā, *f.* lower half of the leg, from knee to ankle; shin. [prob. fr. √1hā, 'move,' 1148.4, cf. 1002b.]

jaṭā, *f.* matted hair; tangled locks.

jaṭhára, *n.* belly; womb. [akin are Goth. *kilþei*, 'womb,' AS. *cild*, Eng. *child.*]

√ **jan** (jáyate [772]; jajā́na, jajñé [794d]; ájaniṣṭa; janiṣyáti, -te; jātá; janáyati, -te; ájījanat). *see* 761b end, *and* 772. —1. *transitive*, janáyati *and active forms:* beget; bring forth; generate *or* produce; —2. *intransitive*, jā́yate *and middle forms:* be born; be produced; come into being; be born again, 18[1]; be, 86[2]; jajñe, natus est, ortus est; jajñānās, children; *for* jāta, *see s.v.* [cf. *γε-γον-ώς*, 'born,' *ἐ-γέν-ετο*, 'became'; Lat. *genui*, 'begat'; AS. *cennan*, 'beget, bring forth'; AS. *cynn*, Eng. *kin*, 'race, family'; AS. *cyn-ing*, Eng. *king*, 'the man of (noble) kin'—for mg, cf. kulīna w. kula2: cf. also jana and jani.]

+**abhi**, *pass.* be born unto, be destined unto from birth.

+ā, *caus.* cause to be born for some one, *w. dat.*

+upa, *mid.* be born, arise.

+pra, *mid.* be born; *caus.* procreate.

+sam, *mid.* be produced; saṁjāta, having arisen.

jána, *m.* creature; man; person; *in pl.* (*e.g.* 40[16]), *and collectively in sing.* (*e.g.* 77[11]), folks; a people *or* race *or* tribe; dāívya jána, heavenly race, the gods. [√jan: cf. γένος, Lat. *genus*, Eng. *kin*, 'race.']

jana-padá, *m.* (tribe-place, *i.e.*) district; community.

jáni [343c], *f.* woman; wife. [√jan: cf. γυνή, Eng. *quean*, 'woman': for mg, cf. jāyā.]

janítra, *n.* origin. [√jan, 1185d.]

janitvá, *n.* wifehood. [jani.]

jániman, *n.* production, creation. [√jan, 1168.2a.]

jánī, *f. same as* jani.

janús, *n.* origin; ingenium, nature; creation. [√jan, 1154[2].]

jantú, *m.* creature; man. [√jan.]

jánman, *n.* birth; production; creature, 72[3]. [√jan.]

√ **jap** (jápati; jajápa; ájapīt; japiṣyáti; japitá, japtá; jápitum; japitvā́, japtvā́). say in under-tone; mutter.

jamád-agni, *m.* Jamadagni, a Rishi, friend of Viçvamitra, and foe of Vasishtha. [jamant, unclear: see 1309[4].]

jambuka, *m.* jackal.

jara, *a.* growing old, aging. [√jṛ.]

jarád-aṣṭi, *a.* long-lived. [jarant, see 1299b end.]

jarad-gava, *m.* Old-bull, name of a vulture. [jarant.]

jarad-dāsa, *m.* old slave *or* servant. [jarant.]

járant, *ppl.* aging; old. [√jṛ: cf. γέροντ-α, 'old man.']

jarás, *f.* the growing old; old age. [√jṛ: cf. γῆρας, 'old age.']

jaritṛ́, *m.* invoker; singer.

jalá, *n.* water. [see √gal.]

jala-dhara, *m.* rain-cloud. [lit. 'water-holder.']

jalāçaya, *m.* water-abode; lake. [āçaya.]

√ **jas** (jásyati; jajā́sa; jāsáyati). be exhausted *or* tired to death; *caus.* exhaust; quench.

jasra, *a.* dying out. [√jas.]

jā́ [352], *vbl.* born, *at end of cpds.* [√jan *or* jā: cf. já, later form of jā́.]

√ **jāgṛ**, *same as* √3 gṛ, *see* 1020.

jātá, *ppl.* born; grown; come into being, present; *at beg. of cpds:* arisen, existing, manifest; produced, aroused; *as n.* a living being; birth. [√jan, 955b.]

jāta-karman, *n.* birth-ceremony.

jāta-rūpa, *a.* having native beauty; splendid; -pá, *n.* gold.

jāta-viçvāsa, *a.* having arisen confidence, inspired with confidence.

jātá-vedas, *m.* Jātavedas, epithet of Agni. [perhaps, 'having knowledge of all beings, *i.e.* of gods and men,' or, better, 'having all beings *or* things as his possession.']

jāta-saṁkalpa, *a.* having a purpose *or* desire arisen, feeling a passion for another.

jātāmarṣa, *a.* having anger aroused, vexed. [amarṣa.]

jātāvamāna, *a.* having arisen contempt, filled with self-contempt. [avamāna.]

jāti, *f.* birth; position *or* rank. [√jan, 1157[1].]

jāti-mātra, *n.* mere rank. [see mātrā 2, and 1302c 3.]

jā́tu, *adv.* at all, ever; na jātu, not at all. [√jan, 1111d: development of mg unclear.]

jāterṣya, *a.* having jealousy aroused, jealous. [īrṣyā.]

jā́nu, *n.* knee. [cf. γόνυ, Lat. *genu*, Eng. *knee*, whence *kneel*.]

jāmadagnya, *a.* of Jamadagni; *as subst.* descendant of J. [jamádagni, 1211.]

jāyá, *f.* wife. [√jan: for mg, cf. jani.]

jārá, *m.* paramour.

jāla, *n.* net.

√ **1ji** (jáyati, -te; jigā́ya, jigyé [787]; ájāiṣīt, ájeṣṭa; jayiṣyáti, -te; jeṣyáti, -te; jitá; jétum; jitvā́; -jítya). overpower; conquer; win (battles); win by conquest. [cf. βία, 'force,' βιάω, 'to force'; Lat. *vis*, **gvis*, 'force': cf. √jyā.]

+ud, conquer; be victorious.

+parā, *pass.* be conquered.

+vi, *mid.* be victor; conquer (conquests); subdue.

√2ji (jinóti). enliven; quicken; *hence* [716], √jinv. [for *gvi: cf. βίος, 'life': see also √jīv.]

jijñāsā, *f.* investigation. ['effort to find out,' fr. desid. of √jñā, 1149[4].]

jitāpsaras, *a.* having the Apsarases conquered, surpassing the Apsarases. [apsaras.]

jitendriya, *a.* having the senses conquered, having the passions subdued. [indriya.]

√jinv (jínvati; jijínva; jinviṣyáti; jinvitá). be lively, hasten; *trans.* quicken; speed onward. [secondary root fr. √2ji, see 716.]

jívri, *a.* old. [for jírvi, √jṛ, 1193[2].]

jihvā́, *f.* tongue.

jihvāgra, *n.* tip of the tongue. [agra.]

jīmū́ta, *m.* thunder-cloud.

jīrá, *a.* quick. [√2ji, 1188: cf. √jyā.]

jīrá-dānu, *a.* having swift drops, swift dripping, *i.e.* well watered.

√jīv (jívati, -te; jijíva, jijīvé; ájīvīt; jīviṣyáti, -te; jīvitá; jívitum; jīvitvā́; -jívya; jīváyati). live; be alive; *caus.* make alive. [see √2ji: cf. Lat. *vīv-ere*, 'live'; AS. *cwicu*, 'alive,' Eng. *quick*, 'alive, lively.']

+anu, live after, be dependent on, live upon.

jīvá, *a.* living; *as m.* the principle of life, the individual soul, 66[4]. [√jīv: cf. Lat. *vīvus*, 'alive.']

jívana, *n.* existence. [√jīv.]

jīvana-hetu, *m.* cause of existence, *i.e.* means of subsistence.

jīva-pati *or* -patnī, *a. f.* having one's husband yet alive.

jīva-praja, *a.* having one's children yet alive. [prajā.]

jīva-loká, *m.* the world of the living (as distinguished from that of the Manes), 86[13], 23[12].

jīvitá, *ppl.* alive; *as n.* [1176a], life. [√jīv.]

jīvitavya, *grdv.* vivendum; *as n. impers.*, *see* 999. [√jīv.]

jīvitāçā, *f.* the wish for life, hope to save one's life. [āçā.]

jīvin, *a.* living. [√jīv.]

√juṣ (juṣáte, -ti; jujóṣa, jujuṣé; ájoṣiṣṭa; juṣṭá). taste, *esp.* with pleasure; relish; take pleasure in *or* accept graciously. [cf. γεύομαι, 'taste'; Lat. *gus-tus*, 'taste'; AS. *ceōsan*, Eng. *choose*.]

júṣṭa, *a.* acceptable. [ppl. of √juṣ, w. accent altered as in dhū́rta.]

juhū́ [356], *f.* sacrificial ladle for pouring the melted butter into the fire, *cf.* srúc. [√hu, 1147b[2].]

√jū (junā́ti [728]; jūjā́va [786[4]]; jūtá). speed, *intrans. and trans.*; incite, inspire; further, assist to. [cf. √2ji.]

√jṛ (*V.* járati; *later*, jíryati, -te; jajā́ra; ájārīt; jīrṇá [957b]). decay; grow frail *or* worn out *or* old. [cf. járant, 'old,' and γέροντ-α, 'old man'; jarás and γῆρας, 'old age.']

jógū [352], *a.* loudly singing; praising. [fr. intens. of √gu, 1147b[2], 1002a.]

jóṣas, *n.* pleasure. [√juṣ.]

jña, *vbl.* knowing, *at end of cpds.* [√jñā, 333.]

√jñā (jānā́ti, jānīté [730]; jajñáu, jajñé; ájñāsīt [911], ájñāsta; jñāsyáti, -te; jñātá; jñā́tum; jñātvā́; -jñā́ya; jñāyáte; jñāpáyati, -te, jñapáyati, -te [1042d[2]]; jñaptá). know; have knowledge of a person *or* thing; recognize; become aware of; learn; notice. [cf. ἔ-γνω, Lat. *co-gnōvit*, 'knew'; AS. *cann*, 'have learned, *i.e.* know, am able,' Eng. *can*; AS. *ge-cnāwan*, Eng. *know*.]

+sam-anu, wholly acquiesce in; approve; give leave; dismiss.

+abhi, recognize; know.

+praty-abhi, recognize.

+ava, look down upon; despise.

+ā, attend to, notice; *caus.* command.

+pari, carefully observe; find out.

+pra, know; *esp.* know one's way *or* bearings *or* how to go to work; prajñāta, clearly to be known, well known.

+prati, recognize, allow; promise; affirm.

+vi, distinguish; understand; know; recognize; consider as; observe; find out; —*pass.* vijñāyate, *in stating a dogma*, is well known *or* recognized (by good authorities); —*caus.* make any one know *or* understand; make a representation to, with a request *or* question *or* proposal; memorialize; interrogate.

jñātí, *m.* kinsman; relative. [√jan: cf. κασί-γνητος, 'brother-born.']

jñāna, *n.* knowledge; wisdom; *esp.* knowledge of the higher truths of religion and philosophy. [√jñā, 1150.]

jñānin, *a.* wise; possessing jñāna; understanding (what one reads), 68[15]. [jñāna.]

jñeya, *grdv.* to be known *or* considered as. [jñā.]

√**jyā** *or* ji *or* jī (jināti; jijyāú [785]; ájyāsīt; jyāsyáti; jītá). βιάω; overpower. [cf. 1 jyā́, 'power,' and √1 ji, 'overpower.']

1 **jyā́**, *f.* superior power; βία; force. [√jyā: cf. βία, 'force.']

2 **jyā́**, *f.* bow-string. [cf. βιός, 'bow.']

jyā́yāṅs, *a.* stronger *or* superior; older. [comp. of jyā, 'being strong *or* superior,' the vbl of √jyā, 470[2,3].]

√**jyut** (jyótati; -jyótya). light. [fr. √dyut.]

jyéṣṭha, *later* jyeṣṭhá, *a.* best; principal; first; oldest. [superl. of jyā, the vbl of √jyā, 470[3]: see jyā́yāṅs.]

jyeṣṭha-prathama, *a.* having the oldest as the first.

jyotiṣ-kṛ́t, *a.* light-making. [jyotis: 187.]

jyótiṣmant, *a.* full of light; light. [jyotis: 184b.]

jyótis, *n.* light (of sun, dawn, etc.); *as pl.* the heavenly bodies; stars. [√jyut.]

jyótsnā, *f.* moonlight. [jyotis: cf. 1195.]

jráyas, *n.* stretch; expanse. [√jri.]

√**jri** (jráyati). *perhaps*, go, stride; *used only w.* upa, stretch out to.

√**jval** (jválati, -te; jajvála; ájvālīt; jvaliṣyáti; jvalitá; -jválya; jvāláyati, jvaláyati, -te). burn bright; flame; *caus.* kindle, make to flame.

+**pra**, *caus.* kindle.

---

jhaṭ-iti, *adv.* with a jhaṭ, as quick as one could say "boo." [jhaṭ, onomatopoetic: see 1102a[2] mid.]

jhalla, *m.* a cudgel-fighting athlete (descended from outcast Kshatriyas).

ṭhio, *a Prakrit form for* sthito.

√**ḍhāuk** (ḍhāúkate; ḍuḍhāuké; ḍhāukitá; ḍhāukáyati). approach; *caus.* bring near.

+**upa**, bring to; provide.

---

tá [495], *pron.* he, she, it, they; that, those; *both subst. and adj.*, 1[15], 3[8,9]; —**1.** *correl. of* ya, *which usually precedes* [512], 3[14], 9[18], 10[5], 22[5], 29[15], 32[10], 70[16], 77[13]; *but* sa ·· ya, 17[22], 33[16], 73[9]; *otiose*, 18[20], 20[14]; —**2.** *in connection w. a pron. of the* 1st *or* 2d *pers.: e.g.* táṁ tvā ·· īmahe, thee, who art such a one (as aforesaid), we beseech, *i.e.* therefore we beseech thee, 76[13]; *cf.* 82[9]; tébhyo nas ·· brūhi, to us, who are these (unsuccessful ones—*just described*), tell thou, *i.e.* do thou tell us then, 96[13]; *similarly, w. a verb in the* 1st *or* 2d *pers., whose subject is not expressed*, 69[17], 73[2], 76[12,17], 83[1], 95[13], 99[4], 100[4]; —**3.** *w. other pronouns:* tasya ·· etasya, of this, 95[6]; yat tad ·· tad, what (was) that ··, that, 57[7]; ya ta, whoever, anybody, 18[4]; ya ya ·· ta ta, whoever ·· that, 13[12]; *cf.* 45[13]; —**4.** *attenuated in mg* (*like the Greek* ὁ) *to a simple article:* te devās, the gods, 92[14]; sa bhīmas, Bhīma, 1[15]. [w. sa, sā, tad, cf. ὁ, ἡ, τό, Goth. *sa, so, þata*, AS. *se, seō, ðæt*, 'he, she, it,' Eng. *that;* cf. also Lat. *is-tud*, 'that.']

√**takṣ** (tákṣati; tatákṣa, tatakṣé; átakṣīt; taṣṭá; -tákṣya). hew; work (wood); make (of wood or other material); fashion. [cf. tákṣ-an and τέκτ-ων, 'carpenter'; ἔ-τεκ-ον, 'produced'; Lat. *tignum*, 'log': cf. √tvakṣ and toka.]

taj-jīvana, *n.* his subsistence. [tad.]

√**taḍ** (tāḍáyati; tāḍayā́m āsa; tāḍitá; -tā́ḍya). beat.

+**pari**, strike; pelt.

tatá, *m.* father. [cf. τέττα, Lat. *tata*, 'papa': Eng. *dad*, though of similar make, has of course no direct connection.]

tátas, *adv.* —1. (*as abl. of pron. root* ta [1098], *and synonymous w.* tasmāt) out of it, 36[13]; —2. from that (place), from there, 103[15]; thence; there; itas tatas, here and there, hither and thither, 25[11], 29[15, 17]; —3. from that (time), thereupon, 2[22]; then, *very often, e.g.* 11[11], 20[11], 56[17]; *correl. w.* yad, 92[13]; *w.* yadā, 37[9]; *w.* ced, 52[5]; tataḥ prabhṛti, from then on, 4[7], 32[17]; —4. therefore; —5. *otiose*, 47[11]; 5[2, 11], 11[16]; then, *w. otiose* tadā, 3[1], 4[8]. [pron. root ta, 497, 1098.]

tat-kṣaṇa, *m.* that moment; -am, *adv.* in that moment, straightway. [tad.]

tat-tīra, *n.* its bank. [tad.]

tattva, *n.* (that-ness, *i.e.*) essence, real condition *or* state of a thing. [tad.]

tattva-jña, *a.* knowing the essence *or* the truth *or* what's what.

tat-para, *a.* having that as highest object; given over to, intent upon. [tad.]

tat-pārçva, *n.* his side. [tad.]

tat-prahṛṣṭa, *a.* pleased with that. [tad.]

tátra, *adv.* —1. (*as synonymous w. loc. of* tad *in all numbers and genders*) in *or* among *or* on this *or* these *or* them, 13[7], 21[8], 38[11], 57[22]; in this matter, 37[8]; herein, 98[2]; —2. there, *often, e.g.* 2[8], 5[6]; thither, 6[6], 11[14], etc.; *correl. w.* yatra, 24[4]; —3. on that occasion, in that case, then, 4[1], 14[22], 40[1]. [pron. root ta, 497, 1099.]

tatra-stha, *a.* abiding there.

tat-saṁnidhāna, *n.* his presence. [tad.]

tat-sapatnī, *f.* her co-wife. [tad.]

tat-samīpe, *adv.* near him. [tad: see samīpa.]

tat-sahacārin, *a.* accompanying him. [tad.]

táthā, *adv.* —1. so, thus, 11[4], 24[16]; in this way, 99[20]; *w.* yathā, yathā *regularly preceding:* yathā · · tathā: as · · so, 21[16], 61[6], 77[13]; in order that · · thus, 30[16], 37[7]; *but* tathā · · yathā, so · · as, 22[13], 43[20]; yathā yathā · · tathā tathā, to what degree · · to that degree, the more · · the more, 48[14]; yathā tathā, in one way or another, 62[9]; —2. *particle of assent*, so be it, yes, 4[2], 8[6], 48[12], 94[5]; that is so, 52[16]; —3. so, in like manner, 19[8]; *or, simply conjunctive*, also, likewise, 10[8], 12[13], etc.; tathā‿eva, just so (*cf. Middle Eng.* al so, *i.e.*), likewise, also, 1[11], 7[10]; tathā ca, 18[20], *see* ca 3; —4. tathā‿api, so even, even under those circumstances, nevertheless, 21[11]. [pron. root ta, 497, 1101.]

táthā-vidha, *a.* of such sort, in such condition. [tathā (1306) + vidhā, 1302c 5.]

tád, —1. *as nom. acc. s. n. to* ta, *see* ta; *used also in cpds and derivatives, see* 497; —2. *as adv.* there; yatra · · tad, where · · there, 103[18]; —3. then, in that case, 27[17], 36[5]; ced · · tad, if · · then, 37[5]; *so* yadi · · tad, 37[12]; tad · · yad, then · · when, 71[2]; *simply continuative:* tat ko vṛtras, who then is V., 97[19]; *so* 24[2]; —4. in this way, *i.e.* therefore, accordingly, 18[8], 19[13, 22], 27[14], etc.; yad · · tad, since · · therefore, 17[6]; *so* yatas · · tad, 37[7]. [cf. 495.]

tad-aṅga, *n.* his person.

tad-anantara, *a.* immediately adjoining that; -am, *adv.* [1311], immediately after that; thereupon.

tad-abhimukha, *a.* turned towards him; -am, *adv.* [1311], towards him.

tad-abhivādin, *a.* signifying that.

tad-ardhika, *a.* amounting to *or* lasting half of that.

tadā́, *adv.* at that time; then, 2[20]; in that case; *often otiose in Epos,* 3[7]; *so after* tatas, 3[1], 4[9]; yadā · · tadā, when · · then, 26[17]; yadā yadā · · tadā tadā, whensoever · · then, 31[11]; yadi · · tadā, if · · then, 25[9]. [pron. root ta, 497, 1103.]

tad-ākṛti, *a.* having the appearance of them (*i.e.* of Piçāchas).

tad-ājñā, *f.* his (the moon-god's) command.

tadāhāra-vartman, *n.* the way of that food. [tad-āhāra.]

tad-īpsita, *a.* desired by those two.

tadīya, *a.* pertaining to him, her, it, *or* them; such. [tad, 497.]

tad-upadeça, *m.* his advice.

tad-gṛha, *n.* his house.

tad-bhaya, *m.* fear of it *or* them.

tad-bhāṣā, *f.* that language.

tad-rasa, *m.* the essence of it.

tad-vacana, *n.* his words.

tad-vat, *adv.* in this way, so; likewise. [tad: 1107.]

tad-víd, *a.* knowing that; *as m.* connoisseur *or* judge.

tad-vṛkṣa, *m.* that tree.

tad-vṛddhi, *f.* the interest of them.

√ **1tan** (tanóti, tanuté; tatā́na, tené [794c]; átānīt; taṅsyáte; tatá; tántum; tatvā́; -tátya; tāyáte [772]). —1. stretch, *trans. and intrans.;* extend, reach; spread over; —2. continue, endure, 79[13]; —3. stretch (a weft *or* a line); continue (the line of a family); —4. *metaphorically,* of sacrifice and supplication (which are compared with a weft), perform, make. [cf. *τάννμαι,* 'stretch'; Lat. *tenēre,* 'hold,' *tendere,* 'stretch'; AS. *þenian,* Ger. *dehnen,* 'stretch': see also tanu.]

+**ā**, spread over; overspread (*esp.* with light), beshine; stretch (a bow).

+**pari**, stretch around; surround; envelope.

+**vi**, stretch out; spread out, cover; vitata, stretched, hung, dependent, 92[11].

+**sam**, hold together, *intrans.;* bind together; make continuous; saṁtata, (*just like Lat.* con-tinens) uninterrupted.

√ **2tan** (tányati). resound. [cf. *τόνος,* 'tone'; Lat. *tonare,* 'thunder'; AS. noun *þunor,* 'thunder,' whence denom. verb *þunrian,* Eng. *thunder;* AS. *þunres dæg,* Eng. *Thurs-day,* 'day sacred to the Old Germanic god of the thunder-storm, *þonar or* Thor': see tanyatú, 'thunder.']

tanú, *f.* [344[2]] tanu, tanū́, tanvī, *a.* thin, tenuis, slender; —tanu *or* tanū́ [decl. 356], *as subst. f.* body, 56[3], 89[18]; person; one's own person, self, *used like* ātman [514] *as reflexive pron.,* 73[12], 78[12]; outward form *or* manifestation, 84[11]. [prop. 'stretched out, thin,' √1tan: cf. *τανυ-,* 'extended, long,' in cpds; Lat. *tenuis,* Eng. *thin,* Ger. *dünn,* 'thin.']

tanu-trāṇa, *n.* body-cover, 34[17].

tanu-madhya, *a.* having a slender middle, *i.e.* slender-waisted.

tanū-tyáj, *a.* abandoning the body, risking life, brave.

tantí, *f.* cord; *esp.* a long line to which calves are tethered by means of short ropes; tantī, *the same.* [√1tan.]

tántu, *m.* thread, 89[1]; *metaphorically,* of the thread, *i.e.* course, of a sacrifice. [√1tan.]

tántra, *n.* thread; warp of a web; *fig.* fundamental doctrine; division of a work. [√1tan.]

√ **tand** (tándate). relax, grow weary.

tandrā, *f.* fatigue. [√tand, 1188c.]

tandrita, *a.* wearied, *only w.* a-. [tandrā, 1176b.]

tannimittam, -ena, *see* **nimitta**. [tad.]

tanyatú, *m.* thunder. [√2tan.]

√ **tap** (tápati, -te; tatā́pa, tepé [794e]; átāpsīt; tapsyáti; taptá; táptum; taptvā́; -tápya; tapyáte, tápyate [761b]). —1. be warm; burn, *intrans.;* —2. heat; make glowing; burn, *trans.;* —3. *fig.* (*like* √çuc), distress, pain; —4. *pass.* suffer; suffer voluntarily, castigate one's self, do penance. [cf. Lat. *tepēre,* AS. *þefian,* 'be warm.']

+**upa**, heat; become sick; sicken, *used impers., w. acc. of the person,* 101[3].

+**sam**, heat; pain.

tapaḥ-prabhāva, *m.* efficacy of devotion.

tápas, *n.* —1. heat, fire; —2. voluntary suffering (*see* tap 3, 4), self-castigation, self-torture (64[21]), mortification, asceticism, devotion. [√tap.]

tápasvant, *a.* full of devotion; pious. [1233a.]

tapasvín, *a. the same.* [1232.]

tapo-já, *a.* asceticism-born, whose element is asceticism. [tapas.]

√ **tam** (tā́myati, -te [763]; tatā́ma; átamat; tāntá [955a]). become darkened, of the eye; become powerless, deadened, stupefied, numb, *or* inactive. [orig. mg, prob., 'be dark,' see tamas: cf. támisrā, 'darkness,' Lat. *tenebrae,* **temsrae,* 'darkness,' Old High Ger. *dinstar,* 'dark'; Old High Ger. *dĕmar,* 'dusk,' Ger. *dämmern,* 'become twilight,' but not Eng. *dim.*]

támas, *n.* —1. darkness; —2. spiritual darkness, infatuation; —3. darkness *as* one of the three pervading qualities of all existence, *see* guṇa 3. [√tam.]

tamo-niṣṭha, *a.* resting *or* founded on darkness.

tamo-nuda, *a.* darkness-dispelling.

tamo-bhūta, *a.* dark, enveloped in darkness. [lit. 'become darkness,' tamas: 1273c.]

tára, *m.* crossing, passage. [√tṛ.]

taraṁ-ga, *m.* wave; wave *as* subdivision of a work entitled "ocean," 56[13], *cf.* 45[1] N. [lit. 'which goes crossing the water': taram, grd of √tṛ, 995, cf. 1250a.]

taráṇi, *a.* pressing onward. [√tṛ, 1159b.]

taru, *m.* tree. [prob. a modern form of dā́ru, q.v.]

taru-koṭara, *n.* tree-hollow.

táruṇa, *a.* young; tender; -ka, *n.* sprout. [cf. *τέρην*, 'tender, fine.']

taru-tale, under the tree, *see* tala.

√ **tark** (tarkáyati [1041[2]]; tarkayā́m āsa; tarkayiṣyáti; tarkitá; tarkáyitum; tarkayitvā́; -tárkya). —1. think over, 13[16]; reflect, 13[13]; —2. form an idea of. [orig. mg, 'turn,' and so (like Lat. *volvere animo*), 'turn over *or* revolve in one's mind': cf. tarku, 'spindle'; *τρέπ-ω*, Lat. *torqueo*, 'turn'; Old High Ger. *drāhsil*, 'turner,' Ger. *drechseln*, 'turn.']

+**pra**, form a conception of.

tárhi, *adv.* at that time; then; yadi ·· tarhi, if ·· then. [pron. root ta, 497, 1103c.]

tala, *m. n.* —1. surface; -tale, *at end of cpd, equiv. simply to* on, 6[17], 46[17]; —2. the surface *or* place under an object, *e.g.* a tree; -tale, *at end of cpd, equiv. simply to* under, 34[1], 43[8]; —3. *sometimes otiose in cpds, e.g.* nabhas-tala, sky-surface, *i.e.* sky.

tálpa, *m.* couch; bed. [for *star-pa, √stṛ, 1201[2] end: for mg, see under stṛ.]

talpa-çī́van, *f.* -varī, *a.* lying on beds. [1169. 2[2].]

taviṣá, *a.* powerful. [√tu, 1197b.]

táskara, *m.* robber.

tásmāt, *adv.* from this (cause), hence; therefore; yad ·· tasmāt, since ·· therefore. [pron. root ta, 1114a.]

tāta, *m. used in voc. s., to a father, but generally to a junior or an inferior,* my dear. [cf. tata.]

tādī́tnā, *adv.* then. [perhaps instr. (1112d) of *tādītna, and this fr. *tadi-tna, 'of that time,' and this fr. *tadi (1245e), correl. of yadi.]

tādṛ́ç, *a.* such. [see 518: for declension, see dṛ́ç.]

tādṛ́ça, *a.* such. [see 518.]

tāpasá, *m.* ascetic. [tápas.]

tāmasa, *a.* dark; pertaining to darkness *or* the guṇa called tamas. [támas.]

tāyú, *m.* thief. [cf. stāyú.]

tārā, *f.* star. [form of transition to the a-declension (399) from tṛ́, see under stṛ́.]

tāvac-chata, *f.* -ī, *a.* having *or* embracing so many hundreds. [tāvant (1249a) + çata.]

tāvat-kṛtvas, *adv.* so many times. [tāvant, 1249a.]

tā́vant [457], —1. *adj.* so great; so much; so many, 105[4]; extending so far, 101[9]; lasting so long, 58[9]; *correl. w.* yāvant, 101[9], 105[4]; —2. tāvat, *as adv.* so much; so far; to such an extent, 95[14]; so long; for a while, 19[1]; yāvat ·· tāvat: as long as ·· so long, 15[6], 32[3], 40[18]; when ·· then, 44[15]; just as ·· then, 22[7]; tāvat ·· yāvat, so long ·· as, 19[2], 42[3]; —3. at once; now, 24[20], 34[6], 53[17]; —3a. *w. 1st pers. pres. ind.*, first, before doing any thing else, at once, 20[18], 23[8], 38[11]; —3b. *w. imperative:* at once, 24[23]; tāvat ·· tatas *or* paçcāt, first ·· then *or* afterwards, 27[18], 38[4]; —4. *concessively*, iha samaye, tāvat, in this case, one must admit, 41[10]; —5. *emphasizing, like* eva, *what precedes*, 30[4], 25[7]. [pron. root ta, 517.]

tigmá, *a.* sharp. [√tij, 216. 5.]

√ **tij** (tejáyati; tejayā́m āsa; tejitá). be sharp. [orig. *stig: cf. *στίζω*, 'prick,' *στίγ-μα*, 'prick'; Lat. *in-stīgāre*, 'prick on'; Eng. *stick*, 'to pierce.']

títhi, *m. f.* a lunar day (of which there are 15 in a half-lunation).

tirás, —1. *prep.* through; across; —2. *as adv.* crossways, sideways; aside; *w.* kṛ [171[3], 1078[4]], put aside, treat disrespectfully, scold. [√tṛ, 'cross': cf. Lat. *trans*, 'across.']

tiras-kāra, *m.* a scolding. [√kṛ + tiras: 171[3].]

tiryaktva, *n.* condition of a beast. [tiryak, middle stem of tiryañc, 1249a: 1239.]

tiryáñc [409d], —1. *a.* directed across; horizontal; —2. *as subst. m.n.* beast (going horizontally, as opposed to man, who walks upright — ūrdhva); —3. *acc. s. n.* tiryak, *as adv.* across. [tiras or tir, w. añc, 409d: tir, like tiras, is akin w. √tṛ.]

tilá, *m.* —1. the sesame plant, Sesamum indicum; —2. its seed, which is eaten, and furnishes good oil.

tisṛ, *fem. to* tri, *see* 482c.

tīra, *n.* shore *or* bank. [prop. 'place of crossing *or* going into the water,' √tṛ.]

√ **tu** (táviti [633]; tūtā́va [786[4]]). have power; be strong. [orig. 'swell, grow': cf. *τύ-λη*, 'swelling, lump,' Corcyraean *τῦ-μο-ς*, 'mound'; AS. *þūma*, 'the big (finger),' Eng. *thumb;* further, túm-ra, 'fat, strong'; Lat. *tum-ulus*, 'mound,' *tum-or*, 'swelling.']

tú, *pcl.* *never at beg. of sentence.* —1. *w. imperative*, pray; —2. in sooth, 78[10]; —3. but, 8[12], 26[13], 34[10], etc.; on the other hand, 20[4]; tu · · tu, on the one hand · · on the other, 2[16, 17]; *so* · ·, · · tu, · · tu, 60[3]; na tv eva tu, but by no means, 63[10], 64[3]; kāmaṁ tu · · na tu, *see* kāmam; kiṁ tu, nevertheless, 39[5]; —4. *used loosely: as equiv. to* ca, 58[1]; *often as a mere expletive* [1122a[4]], *e.g.* 4[9], 64[13b].

tu, *pron. root of 2nd pers*, *see* tvad.

túc, *f.* progeny. [cf. toka.]

√ **tud** (tudáti; tutóda; tunná). strike; push. [cf. Τυδεύς, 'The Hammer, Martel'; Lat. *tundo, tu-tud-i*, 'strike, struck'; Goth. *stautan*, Ger. *stossen*, 'strike.']

+ **ā**, strike at, pick at.

√ **tur** (turáti, -te). press onward swiftly. [subsidiary form of √tṛ (242) and allied w. √tvar.]

1 **turá**, *a.* —1. swift, *esp.* of horses; -am, *as adv.* swiftly, *in* turaṁga; —2. quick, ready, willing, 78[17]. [√tur.]

2 **turá**, *a.* strong, mighty, 78[9]. [√tu, 1188.]

turaṁga, *m.* horse. ['swiftly going,' turam + ga, see 1 tura: for mg, cf. khaga.]

turī́ya, *a.* fourth. [for *ktur-ía: catúr, 487[5], 1215.]

√ **tul** (toláyati; tolayā́m āsa; tolayiṣyáti; tolitá; -tólya). —1. raise up; —2. *esp.* raise up a thing so as to find its weight; weigh; —3. counterpoise; —4. equal. [orig. mg, 'bear, *i.e.* hold up': in the cognates, the mg 'bear, *i.e.* endure' appears: cf. Lat. *tul-i*, 'endured'; Goth. *þul-an*, Eng. *thole*, 'endure'; Ger. *Ge-dul-d*, 'endurance'; also *ἔ-τλη-ν*, 'bore,' *πολύ-τλᾱ-ς*, 'much enduring'; Lat. *lātus*, **tlā-tus*, 'borne.']

tulā́, *f.* balance; weight; equality. [√tul: cf. Anglo-Indian *tola*, about 180 grains troy: cf. *τάλαντον*, 'balance, weight.']

tulya, *a.* keeping the balance with; equal to; like. [tulā, 1212d 4 end.]

tulyākṛti, *a.* having like appearance; alike. [ākṛti.]

tuvi, *a.* *in cpds.* mighty; much; many. [√tu, 1155.]

tuvi-bādhá, *a.* distressing many (enemies) *or* besetting (them) sore.

túviṣmant, *a.* mighty. [tuvis.]

tuvis, *n.* *in derivs.* might. [√tu, 1153.]

√ **tuṣ** (túṣyati, -te; tutóṣa; tuṣṭá; tóṣṭum; -túṣya; toṣáyati). become quiet; be satisfied *or* pleased; *caus.* satisfy; gratify.

+ **sam**, *caus.* satisfy.

tuṣṭi, *f.* satisfaction. [√tuṣ.]

tūṣṇī́m, *adv.* silently, in silence. [prob. fr. an obsolete *tūṣṇa, 'silent,' √tuṣ, 1111d.]

√ **tṛ** (tárati, -te; tiráti, -te; tatā́ra, terús [794e]; átārīt; tariṣyáti, -te; tīrṇá; tártum; tīrtvā́; -tī́rya; tāráyati). —1. cross over (a water, the sky); —2. get across *or* to the end; get through, escape; survive. [cf. *τέρμων*, Lat. *terminus*, 'boundary': see √trā and tiras: for treatment of root-vowel, see 242.]

+ **ava**, descend, *esp.* from heaven to earth; come down, *esp.* of divine beings who become incarnate as men; alight; betake one's self to; *caus.* take down *or* off.

+ **ud**, come up out of the water.

+ **abhy-ud**, come out of the water unto, cross the water unto, 89[4].

+ **pra**, take to the water; start on.

+ **vi**, cross through; traverse.

tṝ, *m.* star, *see* stṛ́.

tṛcá, *m. n.* strophe of three stanzas. [tri + ṛc, 243, 1315c.]

tṛ́ṇa, *n.* grass. [cf. (θρόνα =) τρόνα, 'flowers, herbs'; Eng. *thorn;* Ger. *Dorn,* 'thorn.']

tṛtī́ya, *a.* third. [fr. tri, through trita, 243, 487[4]: cf. τρί-τος, Lat. *ter-tius,* Eng. *thir-d,* Ger. *dri-tte,* 'third.']

√ **tṛd** (tṛṇátti, tṛntté; tatárda, tatṛdé; tṛṇṇá; -tṛ́dya). split; bore; open.
+ **anu**, bore after (waters), release, make flow.

√ **1 tṛp** (tṛ́pyati, -te [761a]; tatárpa; átṛpat; trapsyáti; tṛptá; -tṛ́pya; tarpáyati). be satisfied; become content; —*caus.* satisfy, please; nourish. [cf. τέρπω, 'satisfy, please,' τρέφω, 'nourish.']
+ **ā**, become content *or* glad.

√ **2 tṛp**, steal, *not actually occurring in vbl forms, but rendered probable by the deriv.* tṛpu, 'thief,' *the cpds* asu- *and* paçu-tṛp, *and by the Avestan* √tṛf, 'steal.'

√ **tṛṣ** (tṛ́ṣyati; tatárṣa; átṛṣat; tṛṣitá; tarṣáyati). be thirsty. [cf. τέρσ-ομαι, 'become dry'; Lat. *torret,* **tors-et,* 'grows dry, scorches'; Eng. noun *thirs-t;* Ger. *dorr-et,* 'grows dry'; also Lat. *terra,* **ters-a,* 'the dry (land).']

tṛṣā, *f.* thirst. [√tṛṣ.]

tṛ́ṣṇā, *f.* thirst. [√tṛṣ, 1177a.]

téjas, *n.* —1. sharpness, edge; —2. tip of flame *or* ray; gleaming splendor, 1[6]; fire; —3. (splendor, *i.e.*) beauty of person, 8[10]ff.; —4. (*like Eng.* fire, *i.e.*) energy, vigor, power; —5. moral *or* magic power, 11[23]; influence, dignity, 95[8]; majesty, 1[6], 2[4]. [√tij: observe that ἀκμή has mgs 1 and 4.]

téna, *adv.* in that way, 47[17]; so; therefore, 18[7], etc.; yatas *or* yad *or* yena · · tena, for the reason that · ·, therefore, 30[8], 57[6], 64[9]. [pron. root ta, 1112a: of like derivation and mg is τῷ.]

tāilá, *n.* sesame oil. [tilá, 1208f[1] end.]

toká, *n.* creation, progeny. [cf. √takṣ and √tvakṣ, and túc.]

toraṇa, *n.* arched portal; arch. ['passage,' √tur, subsidiary form of √tṛ, 'cross, pass.']

tyá [499a], *pron.* that; that well-known (*like Lat.* ille).

tyakta-jīvita, *a.* having life set aside, risking one's life, brave.

tyaktajīvita-yodhin, *a.* bravely fighting. [1279.]

√ **tyaj** (tyájati, -te; tatyā́ja, tatyajé; átyākṣīt; tyakṣyáti, -te; tyaktá; tyáktum; tyaktvā́; -tyájya; tyajyáte; tyājáyati). —1. withdraw from; leave in the lurch; abandon (dove, goat, tree); —2. renounce (passions, use of a language); relinquish (exertion); lay aside (a certain form, an earthly body); set aside, *i.e.* risk (life). [cf. σέβομαι, 'shrink back from in awe, revere.']
+ **pari**, leave to one's fate (a jackal); abandon; leave (one's party); relinquish *or* give up (play, food, affairs); parityakta, (abandoned by, *i.e.*) separated from, 66[3].

tyáj, *vbl.* abandoning, *w.* tanū-. [√tyaj.]

tyājya, *grdv.* to be abandoned. [√tyaj, 963c.]

trayá, *a.* triple, threefold, 57[13]; *as n.* triad, triplet, τριάς. [tri, 489[4].]

√ **tras** (trásati; tatrása, tatrasús, tresús [794e[2]]; átrāsīt; trasiṣyáti; trastá). tremble; fear. [cf. τρέω, τρέσ-σε, 'tremble, trembled'; Lat. *terreo,* 'affright'; a-trastas and ἄ-τρεστος, 'unterrified.']

trasádasyu, *m.* Trasadasyu, a generous prince, the favorite of the gods, and descended from Purukutsa. [perhaps for trasád-dasyu, 'affrighting the evil beings,' see 1309[4]. √tras.]

√ **trā** (trā́ti, trā́te [628]; trā́yate [761c]; tatré; átrāsta; trāsyáte; trātá; trā́tum; trātvā́). protect; rescue; rescue from, *w. abl.* [collateral form of √tṛ ('get through *or* across'), w. a caus. mg, 'bring through *or* across (trouble).']

trātṛ́, *m.* protector, saviour. [√trā.]

trāsa, *m.* terror. [√tras.]

trā́sadasyava, *m.* descendant of Trasadasyu, 87[12]. [trasádasyu, 1208c.]

trí [482c], *num.* three. [cf. τρεῖς, τρία, Lat. *trēs, tria,* Eng. *three,* Ger. *drei,* 'three.']

triñçát [485], *f.* thirty. [cf. tri.]

tríkadruka, *m. pl. perhaps designation of certain* Soma-vessels, three in number. [cf. trí and kadrū́.]

tri-kāla, *n.* the three times, present, past, and future. [kāla, masc.: 1312.]

trikāla-jña, *a.* knowing present, past, and future; omniscient.

tri-daçá [*declined like* **kāma**, 330], *m. pl.* the three times ten, the thirty, a name in round numbers for the 33 deities (12 Adityas, 8 Vasus, 11 Rudras, 2 Açvins), *i.e.* the gods. [**tri + daça**, 477c: cf. **triṅçat**.]

tridaçeçvara, *m. pl.* lords of the gods, *i.e.* the four chief gods, Indra, Agni, Varuna, and Yama. [**īçvara**.]

tri-divá, *n.* the triple *or* third *i.e.* highest heaven. [**dív**, 1315c: 1312[3].]

tri-dhā́tu, *a.* having three parts, tri-partite, threefold. [acct, 1300c.]

tri-pada, *f.* **-ī**, *a.* having (taken) three steps.

tri-rātrá, *n.* space of three nights, trinoctium. [**rā́tri**, 1315b, 1312[3, 4]: cf. the Eng. usage in *sen-night, fort-night.*]

tri-vidyā, *f.* the three sciences, *i.e.* Vedas. [1312[3].]

trí-vidha, *a.* of three sorts, threefold. [**vidhā**, 1302c 5: acct, 1300c.]

tri-vṛ́t, *a.* threefold, tri-partite. ['turning thrice, with three turns.']

tri-veda, *in cpds and derivs.* the three Vedas. [1312[3].]

tri-ṣavaṇa, *a.* pertaining to the three Soma-pressings; **-am**, *adv.* at morning, noon, and evening. [**savana**.]

trís, *adv.* thrice. [see **tri**: cf. τρίς, Lat. *ter*, **ters*, 'thrice': Eng. *thrice* is a gen. form, cognate in root only.]

trāividya, *n.* study of the three Vedas. [**trividyā**.]

trāivedika, *a.* relating to the three Vedas. [**triveda**, 1222e 2.]

try-adhiṣṭhāna, *a.* having three manifestations.

tvá, *pron. stem of* 2*d pers., see* **tvad**.

√ **tvakṣ**, work, *principally in derivs., and ident. w.* **takṣ**.

tvác, *f.* skin.

tvaj-jāra, *m.* thy paramour. [**tvad**, 494.]

tvát, *abl. of* **tva**, *and used in place of* **tva** *in cpds : by Hindus written* **tvad**, *q.v.* [494.]

tvat-kṛte, for the sake of thee. [1314f, 1130: **tvat** represents the stem **tva**, and in gen. relation.]

tvad [491], *so-called stem* [494] *of* 2*d pers. pron.* thou; *see* **tvat**. [w. the real root **tu**, cf. Doric τύ, Lat. *tū*, AS. *ðū*, Eng. *thou*, Ger. *du*, 'thou.']

√ **tvar** (**tvárate**; **tatvaré**; **tūrṇá** [*cf.* 957b], **tvaritá**; **tvaráyati**). hasten; **tvarita**, having hastened, in haste. [see √√**tur**, **tṛ**.]

tvarā, *f.* haste. [√**tvar**.]

tváṣṭṛ, *m.* **—1.** wright, workman, 75[6]; **—2.** Twashtar, the artificer of the gods (70[3]), former of fruit of the womb, giver of growth and long life (86[15]), father of Saranyū (85[12]). [√**tvakṣ**, 221.]

tvā́vant, *a.* like thee. [**tva**, 517.]

tvāṣṭrá, *m.* descendant of Twashtar. [**tvaṣṭṛ**.]

---

dá, *vbl.* giving, *in cpds.* [√1 **dā**, 333, 354.]

√ **daṅç** *or* **daç** (**dáçati** [746]; **dadáṅça**; **daçiṣyáti**; **daṣṭá**; **daṅṣṭvā́**; **-dáçya**). bite. [cf. δάκνω, 'bite'; Goth. *tahjan*, 'rend, tear.']

daṅça, *m.* gad-fly. [√**daṅç**.]

dáṅṣṭra, *m.* large tooth; tusk; fang. [√**daṅç**, 1185b.]

daṅṣṭrin, *a.* having tusks *or* large teeth. [**daṅṣṭra**.]

√ **dakṣ** (**dákṣati**, **-te**; **dadakṣé**; **dakṣiṣyáte**). *act.* suit; *mid.* be able *or* dexterous *or* strong. [cf. **dakṣa** and **dakṣiṇa**.]

dákṣa, *a.* able, dexterous, strong; *as m.* ability, faculty, strength, power; *esp.* spiritual power, will; **dakṣa** *and* **kratu**, will *and* understanding (as faculties of the **manas**, 'soul'). [√**dakṣ**: cf. δεξιός, 'clever, right,' and **dakṣiṇa**.]

dákṣiṇa, *a.* **—1.** clever, able; *and so* **—2.** (*as opp. to* awkward, gauche), right, of the hand, **hasta**, *e.g.* 102[11]; *so* **pāṇi**, 60[5]; foot, **pāda**, 60[5]; side, **pārçva**, 102[12]; **—3.** southern (because in prayer the face is turned eastward: *cf.* **uttara** 3), 105[8]; *sc.* **agni**, southern fire, 102[3] N.; **—4.** *as f.*, **dakṣiṇā**, *sc.* **go**, the able, *i.e.* fruitful cow, milch cow; milch cow as the customary reward for conducting a sacrifice; *then*, **—5.** *in general*, any reward *or* present for the sacrificing priest, *see* 106[5]; *so* 95[2, 3]; — *see also adv.* **dakṣiṇā**. [√**dakṣ**: cf. δεξιός, Lat. *dexter*, 'clever, right'; Goth.

taihsva, 'right hand': from dakṣiṇa in mg 3, comes *Deccan*, name of the country south of Hindustan, lit. 'the South.']

dakṣiṇa-paçcima, *a.* southwesterly.

dakṣiṇa-pūrva [525⁴], *a.* southeasterly.

dakṣiṇā́, *adv.* southerly; toward the south. [dákṣiṇa: acct, 1112e.]

dakṣiṇāgní, *m.* the southern fire, 103², *cf.* 102² N.

dakṣiṇāpara [525²], *a.* southwesterly. [dakṣiṇa + apara.]

dakṣiṇā́-pravaṇa, *a.* sloping to the south. [dakṣiṇā, adv.]

dakṣiṇābhimukha, *a.* facing southerly. [dakṣiṇā (adv.) + abhimukha.]

dakṣiṇāyana, *n.* south-course (of the sun), *or* the half-year from the summer to the winter solstice. [dakṣiṇa + ayana.]

dakṣiṇāraṇ'ya, *n.* the southern forest (a forest in the Deccan). [dakṣiṇa + araṇya.]

dákṣiṇāvant, *a.* abounding in gifts to the priests, *i.e.* (from the point of view of the priests) pious. [dákṣiṇā: see dakṣiṇa 5.]

dagdhá, *a.* —1. burned; —2. pained, tortured; —3. wretched, good-for-nothing, cursed, damned. [ppl. of √dah: for mg 2, cf. √çuc.]

dagdhodara, *n.* one's cursed belly. [dagdha + udara.]

daṇḍá, *m.* stick; staff (of Brahman), 59²³; mace, 97⁸; rod as symbol of dominion and punishment. [cf. δένδρον, 'tree.']

daṇḍa-bhaya, *m.* fear of the rod.

daṇḍín, *a.* bearing a staff; *as m.* warder. [daṇḍa.]

dattá, *a.* given; *as m.* (a son) given (by his parents to others for adoption); *common at end of proper names, esp. of Vaiçyas.* [ppl. of √1 dā, 955c.]

dadṛh', *a.* firm; dadhṛ́k, *acc. s. n., as adv.* firmly. [√dṛh.]

dadhán [431], *n.* sour milk; curds. [orig., perhaps, 'milk,' fr. √2 dhā.]

dádhi, *supplementary stem to* dadhan.

dadhi-karṇa, *m.* Curd-ear, name of a cat. ['having curd-ears, *i.e.* ears as white as curds.']

dadhṛ́k, *see* dadṛh.

dánt [396], *m.* tooth. [cf. ὀδόντα, Lat. *dentem*, Goth. *tunþus*, AS. *tōð*, Eng. *tooth*, Old High Ger. *zand*, Ger. *Zahn*, 'tooth.']

dánta, *m.* tooth. [dant, 399.]

√ dabh *or* dambh (dábhati; dadā́bha, dadámbha, debhús; ádabhat; dabdhá; dábdhum). harm with guile; hurt; deceive.

dábha, *m.* deception. [√dabh.]

√ dam (dā́myati [763]; dāntá [955a]; damitvā́; -dámya; damáyati). —1. be tame; —2. tame; conquer; become master; control. [cf. δαμάω, Lat. *domāre*, 'tame'; Eng. *tame*, Ger. *zahm*, 'tame.']

dám, *n.* house. [cf. δῶ, 'house': see under dáma.]

dáma, *m. n.* house, home. [cf. δόμος, Lat. *domus*, 'house, home': it is not certain whether dáma comes from √dam and so means lit. 'the place where one is master, one's *Gebiet*,' or whether it is to be connected w. δέμω, 'build': in the latter case, it would mean lit., like Ger. *Bau*, 'a building,' and should be connected w. AS. *timber*, **tem-ra*, 'building-material, a building,' Eng. *timber*, 'building-material,' Ger. *Zimmer*, 'building-material, a building, a room.']

damá, —1. *a.* conquering, *at end of cpds; as m.* —2. Dama, *i.e.* Victor, name of a son of Bhīma; —3. self-control. [√dam: cf. Ἱππό-δαμος, 'Horse-tamer,' etc.]

damana, —1. *a.* conquering, *at end of cpds;* —2. *as m.* Damana, *i.e.* Vincent, name of a priestly sage, and of a son of Bhīma. [√dam: cf. Lat. *dominus*, 'master.']

damayantī, *f.* Damayantī, *i.e.* Victoria, name of Bhīma's daughter. ['conquering (men),' fr. √dam, 1043.5.]

dám-pati, *m.* master of the house; *as dual*, master and mistress, man and wife; pair. [acct, 1267a.]

dambha, *m.* deception. [√dabh.]

√ day (dáyate; dayā́m āsa; dayitá). —1. part; allot; —2. take part in; sympathize with; have tender feeling for; love; —dayita, loved, dear; *as f.*, -tā, wife. [for 1, cf. κρέα δαίετο, 'parted, carved the meat'; for 2, cf. δαίεται ἦτορ, 'heart is divided *or* takes part in (?), *i.e.* sympathizes.']

dayā́, *f.* sympathy; compassion. [√day.].

dayālú, *a.* compassionate. [dayā, 1227[3].]

dayāvant, *a.* compassionate. [dayā.]

dayita, *see* √day.

dara, *m.* cleft, hole. [√1 dṛ.]

daridra, *a.* wandering about; mendicant; poor; *as m.* poor man. [fr. intens. of √1 drā, 'run about,' 1147b[2]: for mg, cf. Eng. *tramp*, in its American sense of 'vagrant beggar.']

darpa, *m.* wildness; wantonness; impudence; pride. [√dṛp.]

darbhá, *m.* grass-tuft; grass used at sacrificial ceremonies, *esp.* Kuça-grass, Poa cynosuroides. [√dṛbh.]

darça, *m.* sight; the moon when just becoming visible; the new moon; the day *or* festival of new moon. [√dṛç.]

darçaka, *a.* —1. seeing; —2. (*fr. caus.*) showing, making clear. [dṛç.]

darçatá, *a.* to be seen; visible. [√dṛç, 1176e.]

dárçana, *a.* seeing; *as n.* the beholding, sight; the becoming visible, 103[20]; appearance, 4[10]. [√dṛç.]

darça-pūrṇa-māsá, *dual m.* new and full moon; the days and the festivals of new and full moon.

dáça [483[4]], *num.* ten. [cf. δέκα, Lat. *decem*, Goth. *taihun*, Eng. *ten*, Ger. *zehn*, 'ten'; Eng. *-teen* in *six-teen*, etc.]

daçamá, *f.* -ī́, *a.* tenth; daçamī́, *sc.* tithi, tenth day of a lunar half-month. [daça, 487[6].]

daça-çata, *n.* ten hundred; a thousand.

dáçaçākha, *a.* having ten branches, *i.e.* fingers. [dáça + çā́khā: acct, 1300a.]

daçā, *f.* the threads projecting at the end of a weft, fringe; lamp-wick; *fig.* wick of life, course of life; time of life.

daçāhá, *m.* space of ten days. [dáça + 2 áha, 1312[4].]

√ **das** (dásyati; dadā́sa; ádasat; dastá; dāsáyati). suffer lack. [cf. √dās, dasyu: also δεύω, 'lack.']

+**vi**, become exhausted.

dásyu, *m.* demon, foe of gods and men. [cf. √das, dāsá.]

√ **dah** (dáhati, -te; dadáha, dehé; ádhākṣīt; dhakṣyáti; dagdhá; dágdhum; dagdhvā́; -dáhya; dahyáte). —1. burn with fire; burn; —2. *pass.:* be burned; be pained *or* tortured; —3. dagdha, *see s.v.* [for *dhagh: cf. Goth. *dags*, AS. *dæg*, Eng. *day*, Old High Ger. *tak*, 'day.']

+**ā**, *in* ādahana.

+**vi**, injure by burning, 84[17].

+**sam**, consume.

√ **1 dā** (dádāti, dádati [668]; dadāú, dadé; ádāt, ádita [884]; dāsyáti, -te; dattá [955c], -tta [1087e]; dā́tum; dattvā́; -dā́ya; dīyáte [770b]; dítsati [1030]; dāpáyati). give; bestow; grant; impart; *w. acc. of thing and dat. or gen., later also loc., of person*, 1[17], 23[20], 21[17]; varaṁ dā, grant a wish; çāpaṁ dā, (give, *i.e.*) pronounce a curse; sāubhāgyaṁ dā, (give, *i.e.*) wish conjugal felicity; dā, (give, *i.e.*) sell, *w. instr. of price*, 47[4]; uttaraṁ dā, make answer; çrāddhaṁ dā, perform a çrāddha, 44[3], 104[17]; punar dā, give back; —*desid.* desire *or* be ready to give. [cf. δίδωμι, Lat. *dă-re*, 'give.']

+**anu**, (*like Ger.* nach-geben, 'yield,' *and so*) grant, admit; *ppl.* ánutta [1087e], admitted.

+**ā**, take (*opp. of* give), 28[17]; grasp, 70[6]; ādāya, having taken, *equiv. to* with.

+**upa͜ā**, receive, appropriate.

+**pari**, deliver over; commit; entrust.

+**pra**, give; grant; impart (sciences); *ppl. f.* práttā [1087e], given in marriage, married.

√ **2 dā** (dyáti [761d 3]; dadé; ádāt, ádita [884]; diná [957a], -tta [1087e]; -dā́ya; dīyáte). cut. [cf. √day, dāya.]

+**ava**, cut off, *esp.* a part of the sacrificial cake; *ppl.* avatta [1087e], *as subst.* that which is cut off.

+**sam-ava**, cut in pieces and collect them; *ppl.* samávatta, *as subst.* gathered pieces.

√ **3 dā** (dyáti [761d 3]; ditá [954c]; -dā́ya; dīyáte). bind. [cf. δέω, δίδημι, 'bind.']

dā́, *vbl.* giving, *in cpds.* [√1 dā.]

dātavya, *grdv.* dandus. [√1 dā.]

dātṛ, *m.* giver; *as a.* [375[3]], generous, 21[4], 48[2]. [√1 dā.]

dā́na, *n.* giving, imparting; gift. [√1 dā, 1150: cf. Lat. *dōnum*, 'gift.']

dāna-dharma, *m.* the virtuous practice of alms-giving.

dānavá, *m.* child of Dānu, a Dānava, one of a class of demons, foes of the gods; Titan. [1 dā́nu, 1208c.]

1 **dā́nu**, *f.* Dānu, name of a demon, 70[18].

2 **dā́nu**, *n.* dripping fluid, drop, dew.

dānta, *a.* tamed, mild; subdued (as to one's passions); *as subst.* Dānta, name of a son of Bhīma. [ppl. of √dam, 955a.]

1 **dā́man**, *n.* a giving, gift. [√1 dā, 1168.]

2 **dā́man**, *n.* bond. [√3 dā, 1168.]

dāmbhika, *a. subst.* deceitful, deceiver. [dambha.]

1 **dāya**, *a.* giving. [√1 dā.]

2 **dāyá**, *m.* portion, inheritance. [√2 dā: cf. δαίς, 'portion, meal.']

dāyaka, *a.* giving. [1 dāya.]

dāra [264[2]], *m. pl.* wife.

dāridrya, *n.* poverty. [daridra.]

dā́ru, *n.* wood; log *or* billet of wood; stick. [see the equiv. drú and taru: cf. δόρυ, 'wood, beam, shaft'; δρῦς, 'tree, oak'; Goth. *triu*, 'wood, tree'; Eng. *tree*, 'wood' (so Wyclif), 'a large woody plant' (usual mg), 'a wooden bar' (in whiffle-*tree*).]

dāruṇa, *a.* hard; dreadful.

√ **dāç** (dā́çati; dadā́ça, dāçvā́ṅs [790b]). grant, offer; *esp.* serve *or* honor a god with offerings; dāçvā́ṅs, *as subst.* a pious servant of a god, 69[11]. [w. dadā́ça, cf. δέδωκα, 'granted, gave'; ἔ-δωκ-α is an imperfect indicative without thematic vowel, corresponding to *á-dāç-am; but both Greek forms became connected in the popular mind with δίδωμι, 'give.']

√ **dās** (*only with* abhi, abhidā́sati). bear ill-will to; try to harm. [cf. √das, dasyu, dāsa.]

dāsá, *m.* –1. foe; *esp.* supernatural foe, evil demon; –2. (*in opp. to* ārya) foe of the gods, infidel; *used like* Caffre *and* Giaour; –3. (subdued foe, *i.e.*) servant, slave, 79[2]; –dāsī́, *f.* female slave. [√dās: cf. √das, dasyu.]

dāsá-patnī, *a.f.* having the demon for their master. [acct, 1251b, 1295.]

díti, *f.* Diti, name of a deity without definite character, a mere pendant to aditi as sura to asura, and formed by popular etymology as sura from asura. [see aditi and dāitya.]

didṛ́kṣu, *a.* desirous to see. [fr. desid. of √dṛç, 1178f: acct!]

didyú, *m.* missile. [see √1 dīv or dyū, and 1147b[2].]

didhiṣú, *a.* desirous to win; *as m.* suitor; husband; *esp.* second husband. [fr. desid. of √1 dhā, 1178f, 1028d.]

dína, –1. *perhaps adj.* clear, *in* su-dína; –2. *as n.* day. [perhaps ppl. of √dī or di, 'shine,' w. shifted acct.]

dina-traya, *n.* day-triad, trīduum, space of three days.

√ **div**: *there is no verbal root* div *in Sanskrit: cf. noun* dív *and* √√1 *and* 2 dīv *or* dīū.

dív [361d], *m.* –1. sky, heaven, *e.g.* 72[2]; –1a. Heaven, *personified as* Father, *e.g.* RV. vi. 51. 5; –1b. duhitā́ divás, of the Dawn, daughter of the sky *or* of Heaven, 75[16]; –2. day, *e.g.* 70[8], 79[13]; –3. *observe that* dív *is sometimes fem. in Veda, so* 92[1, 8], RV. x. 125. 7.

[w. gen. div-ás, cf. the genitives Διός, *ΔιϜ-ός, Lat. *Jŏv-is*, and AS. *Tiw-es* in *Tiwes dæg*, Eng. *Tues-day*: (*Tiw* corresponds to the old Germanic *Tiu*, no longer a god of the sky or bright day, but rather a god of battle or fighting, the chief occupation of our early forefathers:) w. nom. dyāúṣ, cf. Ζεύς, *Δjηύς: w. voc. dyā̀uṣ pítar, cf. Ζεῦ πάτερ, Lat *Jū-piter*, 'Heaven Father': w. dúhitar divas, cf. θύγατερ Διός, ἄμβροτ' Ἀθάνα, Oedipus Rex 159: cf. also δῖος, 'heavenly'; Lat. nom. *Diovi-s*, 'god of heaven,' *Jŏv-em*, 'Jove'; *sub dio*, 'under the sky'; Eng. *Tewes-ley*, 'Tiw's lea,' a place in Surrey.]

divá, *n.* heaven; day, *in* divé-dive, day by day. [dív, 1209a.]

dívā, *adv.* by day. [fr. the instr. div-ā́, w. shifted acct, 1112e.]

divāukas, *m.* caelicola, god. ['having heaven as a dwelling': diva + okas.]

divyá, *a.* heavenly; divine. [dív.]

√ **diç** (diçáti; didéça; ádikṣat, ádiṣṭa [883]; dekṣyáti; diṣṭá; déṣṭum; -díçya; diçyáte; deçáyati). point; direct; show. [cf. δείκνυμι, 'show'; Lat. *dico*, 'show, tell'; AS. *tāh*, Ger. *zieh*, 'pointed out (as guilty), accused'; Ger. *zeigen*, 'show'; also AS. *tāh-te*, *tǣh-te*, Eng. *taught*, 'showed, instructed'; AS. *tācn*, Eng. *token*.]

+**apa**, show; make a false show of.

+**vy-apa**, make a false show of.

+**ā**, point out to, give a direction to, direct.

+**sam-ā**, point out to, direct; command.

+**ud**, point out; aim towards; uddiçya, *w. acc.*, with an aiming towards, *equiv. to the prep.* at, 26[22].

+**upa**, show to, teach, instruct; give advice to, advise.

+**pra**, point out, designate; direct.

díç, *f. just like Eng.* point, *i.e.* cardinal point, quarter of the heaven (N., E., S., W.); aṣṭāu diças, eight regions (N., E., S., W., and NE., SE., SW., NW.), 57[12]. [√diç, 'to point.']

√ **dih** (dégdhi; didihé; digdhá; -díhya). —1. stroke, touch lightly; —2. smear; —3. besmear, pollute. [for *dhigh: cf. ἔθιγον, 'touched'; Lat. *fingo*, 'form, fashion, *esp.* with the hand in soft material'; Goth. *daigs*, 'moulded mass of clay *or* bread-paste'; Old Eng. *dāg*, Eng. *dough*.]

+**sam**, *pass.* (be plastered together, be indistinct, *and so*) be uncertain, doubtful.

√ **dī** (dídeti [676]; dīdáya [786[3]], dīdiváṅs). shine, glance, gleam.

√ **dīkṣ** (díkṣate; didíkṣa, didīkṣé; ádīkṣiṣṭa; dīkṣiṣyáte; dīkṣitá; dīkṣitvá; -díkṣya). consecrate one's self, *esp.* for performing the Soma-sacrifice. [perhaps desid. of √dakṣ, 'make one's self suitable *or* ready': 108g.]

dīti, *f.* glance, flame, *actually occurring only in* su-dītí. [√dī, 1157. 1a.]

dídivi, *a.* shining. [√dī, 1193.]

dīná, *a.* scanty; cast down, sad; wretched.

dīnátā, *f.* scantiness; smallness. [dīna.]

dīnāra, *m.* denarius, name of a certain gold coin. [borrowed fr. Lat. *dēnārius*, a silver coin worth ten *asses*.]

√ **dīp** (dípyate; didīpé; dīptá; -dípya; dédīpti; dīpáyati, -te). blaze; flame; *caus.* kindle; *intens.* blaze brightly; *fig.* be radiant. [cf. √dī.]

+**ud**, blaze up; *caus.* cause to blaze up.

dīrghá, *a.* long, in space *and* in time; -am, *as adv.*; —*comp.* drághīyāṅs, *superl.* drághiṣṭha. [√drāgh: cf. δολιχός, 'long.']

dīrgha-karṇa, *m.* Long-ear, name of a cat.

dīrgha-rāva, *m.* Long-yell *or* Far-howl, name of a jackal. (Their howling is both long-continued and far-reaching.)

dīrgha-varṇa, *m.* a long vowel.

dīrghavarṇānta, *a.* having a long vowel as final. [anta.]

√ **1dīv** (dívyati; didéva [240[3]]; ádevīt; deviṣyáti; dyūtá; dévitum; -dívya). dice; play. [prop. dīū, see 765[1] and [2]: orig., perhaps, 'throw,' cf. didyu.]

+**ā**, *in* ādevana.

√ **2dīv** (dévati [240[3]]; dyūná [957a]; dévitum; deváyati, -te). lament. [prop. dīū, see 765[1] and [2].]

+**pari**, moan, bemoan; *caus. the same.*

duḥkhá, *a.* miserable; *as n.* misery, pain, sorrow. [cf. sukha.]

duḥkhita, *a.* pained. [duḥkha, 1176b.]

ducchúnā, *f.* calamity; harm. [dus + çuna, 'mis-fortune, ill-luck,' 168[3].]

√ **ducchunāya** (ducchunāyáte). seek to harm. [ducchunā, 1058.]

dur-, *the form taken by* dus *before sonants.*

dur-atikrama, *a.* hard to overcome. ['having a hard conquest,' cf. 1304b.]

dur-ātman, *a.* evil-minded; bad.

dur-gá, *a.* whose going is hard, hard to go through *or* to, impassable; *as n.* difficult place; danger.

dur-gata, *a.* ill-conditioned; unfortunate.

dur-jana, *m.* evil person; scoundrel.

dur-dānta, *a.* overcome with difficulty; *as m.* Hard-to-tame (Δυσνίκητος), name of a lion.

dur-nivāra, *a.* whose warding-off is hard; hard to get rid of.

dur-bala, *a.* of (poor, *i.e.*) little strength; feeble.

durbuddhi, *a.* of (bad, *i.e.*) small wit; foolish.

dur-bhága, *a.* ill-portioned, ill-favored; -ā, *f.* ugly woman. [acct, 1304b.]

dur-bhikṣa, *a.* (time) having its alms-getting hard, *i.e.* in which alms-getting is hard; *as n.* famine. [bhikṣā.]

dur-mañgala, *a.* of bad luck, bringing bad luck.

dur-matí, *f.* ill-will.

dur-máda, *a.* badly intoxicated; drunken. [acct, 1304b.]

dur-vijñeya, *a.* hard to distinguish.

dur-vipāka, *m.* evil issue (of one's destiny).

dur-vṛtta, *a.* of evil life, wicked.

√ **dul** (doláyati; dolitá). heave upwards; swing. [cf. √tul.]

dúvas, *n.* gift; oblation; worship. [√1dū.]

duvás, *n.* *perhaps same as* dúvas, *but see* 74[10] N.

√ **duvasya** (duvasyáti). reward with a gift; honor *or* worship (a god) with an offering. [dúvas.]

+**ā**, *perhaps* bring *or* entice hither by worship, *but see* 74[10] N.

√ **duṣ** (dúṣyati; ádoṣīt; duṣṭá; dūṣáyati [1042a[2]]). spoil. [see dus.]

duṣ-kara, *a.* whose performance is hard, hard to be performed. [dus.]

duṣ-kṛtá, *n.* evil deed; sin. [dus.]

duṣṭa, *a.* spoiled; bad, *morally;* cross. [ppl. of √duṣ.]

dus, *inseparable prefix, characterizing a thing as* evil, bad, hard; *forming w. action-nouns cpds w. the same mg as if compounded w. a future pass. ppl., e.g.* duṣ-kara, 'having its doing hard, *i.e.* difficult to be done.' [cf. √duṣ: also δυσ-, 'mis-'. see 225[2].]

dus-tara, *a.* having its crossing hard, hard to cross.

√ **duh** (dógdhi, dugdhé; dudóha, duduhé; ádhukṣat, -ata [918]; dhokṣyáte; dugdhá; dógdhum; dugdhvā́; doháyati). —1. milk; *then, generalized* —2. get the good out of a thing; —3. extract; —4. give milk; —5. *in general,* give *or* yield any good thing, 80[16]; —*çaus., like simple,* milk, extract. [for mg 2, cf. ἀμέλγεσθαί τινα, 'milk a person dry.']

+**nir**, milk out of; extract from.

dúh, *vbl.* yielding, *in* kāma-duh. [√duh.]

duhitṛ́ [373[3]], *f.* daughter. [derivation uncertain, 1182d: cf. θυγάτηρ, Goth. *dauhtar,* Eng. *daughter,* Ger. *Tochter,* 'daughter.']

√ **1dū**, *subsidiary form of* √1dā, *in* dúvas, duvasya. [cf. √√sthā and gā w. their equiv. collateral forms sthū and gū.]

√ **2dū**, go to a distance, *in* dūtá *and* dūrá. [cf. δεύομαι, 'am at a distance from something, fall short of.']

dūḍábha, *a.* hard to deceive. ['whose deceiving is hard': for duzdabha, i.e. dus + dabha, 199b[3].]

dūtá, *m.* messenger; ambassador, envoy. [√2dū, 1176a.]

dūrá, *a.* far; *as n.* the distance; —*case-forms as adverbs:* -am, to a distance, far away; -e, in the distance, afar; at *or* from a distance; -āt, from afar. [√2dū, 1188.]

dūrī-kṛ (dūrīkaroti). put far away; send off. [dūra, 1094.]

dū́rvā, *f.* millet-grass, Panicum Dactylon.

dūḷábha, *same as* dūḍábha, Whitney 54.

√ **1dṛ** (dṛṇā́ti; dadā́ra, dadré; ádārṣīt; dīrṇá; -dī́rya; dīryáte; dárdarti [1002b]; daráyati, dāráyati). burst, *trans. and intrans.;* —*caus. and intens.:* split; tear, *w. gen.* [cf. δέρω, δείρω, 'flay'; AS. *teran,* Eng. *tear,* Ger. *zerren,* 'tear, rend.']

√ **2dṛ** (driyáte; ádṛta; dṛtá; -dṛ́tya). *used only w.* ā, *see* 773. [cf. √δελ in δενδίλλω, 'glance at'; AS. *tilian,* 'be intent upon, attend to, *esp.* the earth, *i.e.* till (the soil),' Eng. *till;* Ger. *zielen,* 'aim at'; AS. *eorð-tilia,* 'earth-tiller.']

+**ā**, (look at, *i.e.*) regard; *pass.* be regarded, *i.e.* respected.

dṛḍhá, *see* √dṛh *and* 224a.

dṛ́ti, *m.* bag of leather; bellows. [√1dṛ: for mg, cf. δέρμα, 'skin bag *or* bottle.']

√ **dṛp** (dṛ́pyati; ádṛpat; darpiṣyáti, drapsyáti; dṛptá; darpáyati). be crazed, wild, proud, insolent, *or* arrogant.

√ **dṛbh** (dṛbháti; dṛbdhá). make into tufts.

√ **dṛç** (dadárça, dadṛçé; ádrākṣīt, ádṛṣṭa; drakṣyáti, -te; dṛṣṭá; drá́ṣṭum; dṛṣṭvā́; -dṛ́çya; dṛçyáte; dídṛkṣate; darçáyati). see; behold; —*pass.* be seen; be *or* become visible; appear; —*caus.* cause (a person, *acc.,* 33[3]) to see (a thing, *acc.,* 33[6], 35[7], 36[7]); show (*w. gen.* 63[2]); *w.* ātmānam, show one's self, appear, pretend to be (*e.g.* frightened, 41[4]). [present forms supplied by √1paç, q.v.: w. dadárça, cf. δέδορκε, 'saw': cf. Goth. *ga-tarh-jan*, 'make a show of.']

+**prati**, *pass.* appear over against one *or* before one's eyes.

+**vi**, *pass.* be seen far and wide.

+**sam**, behold; *caus.* show; *w.* ātmānam, show one's self, appear, pretend to be (*e.g.* dead).

dṛ́ç [218^{3}, dṛk, dṛçam, dṛgbhyām], —1. *vbl.* seeing, looking; —2. *as f.* the seeing; dṛçé, *as inf.* [970a], for beholding; —3. *in cpds* [518], look, appearance. [√dṛç.]

dṛça, *m.* the seeing; *in cpds* [518], look, appearance. [do.]

dṛçí, *f.* the seeing; dṛçáye, *as inf.* [970f], for beholding. [do.]

dṛ́çya, *grdv.* to be seen; worthy to be seen, splendid. [√dṛç, 963d.]

dṛṣád, *f.* stone; *esp.* nether mill-stone.

dṛṣad-upalā́, *dual f.* the nether and the upper mill-stone. [1253a, 1258.]

dṛṣṭá, *ppl. of* √dṛç, *q.v.*

dṛṣṭa-pūrva, *a.* seen previously. [equiv. to pūrvaṁ dṛṣṭa, see 1291.]

dṛ́ṣṭi, *f.* —1. seeing; —2. sense of sight; —3. glance, look; —4. view. [√dṛç: cf. δέρξις, 'sense of sight.']

√dṛh (dṛ́ṅhati, -te [mg 1, *cf.* 758]; dṛ́hyati, -te [mg 2, *see* 767]; ádṛṅhīt; dṛḍhá [224a]; dṛṅháyati). —1. *act.* make firm *or* steady *or* enduring; establish; *mid.* be firm; dṛḍhá [1176a], firm; —2. be firm; —3. *caus.* make stable. [cf. Old Lat. *forc-tis*, Lat. *fortis*, 'strong.']

dṛḷhá, *same as* dṛḍhá, √dṛh, Whitney 54.

déya, *grdv.* to be given *or* granted. [√dā, 963a.]

devá, *f.* deví, —1. *a.* heavenly, $74^{14, 16, 18}$, 92^{7}; *as subst.* —2. god, goddess; —2a. *pl.* the gods (in later times reckoned as 33, *cf.* tridaça); —2b. víçve devás, all the gods; *also* all-gods (a term comprehending into a class all the separate gods, *cf.* All-saints, *and see* viçvádeva); —2c. deví, The Goddess, *i.e.* Çiva's wife, Durgā; —2d. -deva, *at end of Brahman-names*, having ·· as god, *so, e.g.*, guṇadeva; —3. *m.* manuṣya-deva, god among men, *i.e.* a Brahman, *see* 95^{1}; *similarly*, —4. *m.* king, 19^{12}, 50^{4}, $51^{4, 7, 14}$; *so used* of a lion (32^{15}) *or even* of a jackal (36^{21}); *f.* queen. [perhaps fr. the noun dív (1209i): cf. Lat. *deus*, 'god': the alleged root div, 'shine,' has no existence.]

devá-kāma, *a.* having love for the gods. [acct, 1293^{2}, 1295.]

devátā, *f.* godhead *or* divinity, *both as abstract and as concrete;* devátā, *instr.*, with divinity (*collective*), *i.e.* among deities, 73^{20} [1237.]

devatvá, *n.* divinity, *abstract only.* [1239.]

deva-dūtá, *m.* messenger of the gods.

deva-dāivatya, *a.* having the gods as divinity, (of hymns) addressed to the gods.

deva-pati, *m.* lord of the gods, *i.e.* Indra.

deva-pā́na, *a.* serving the gods for drinking. [lit. 'god-drenching, *i.e.* gotttränkend': acct, 1271, 1251c.]

deva-yā́na, *n.* path of the gods, on which the intercourse between gods and men takes place. [acct, 1271, 1251c.]

devara, *m.* husband's brother. [devṛ́, 1209a.]

deva-rājá, *m.* king of the gods, *i.e.* Indra. [rājan, 1315a.]

deva-liñga, *n.* god-characteristic, mark by which a god may be distinguished from a man.

deva-çarman, *m.* Devaçarman *or* God's-joy, name of a certain Brahman. [of like mg is Θεό-χαρις.]

deva-saṁnidhi, *m.* presence of the gods.

devá-hūti, *f.* invocation of the gods. [acct, 1274.]

deví, *see* devá.

devī-kṛta, *a.* made by Durgā.

devī-koṭṭa, *m.* Goddess-fort, name of a town.

devī-vinirmita, *a.* laid out by Durgā. [√1mā.]

devṛ́ [369^{2}], *m.* husband's brother. [cf. δαήρ, Lat. *lēvir*, 'husband's brother.']

deçá, *m.* —1. (point, *i.e.*) place, 41^{18}; —2. country, 24^{5}, *see* 98^{16} N.; —3. place, *pregnantly, as in Eng., i.e.* proper place, 22^{5}; —4. *as in Eng.*, place *or* region of the body, *see* muṣka-, skandha-. [√diç, 'point.']

deça-bhāṣā, *f.* dialect of the country.

deṣṭṛ, *m.* pointer, guide, instructor; *f.* déṣṭrī, Instructress, as a deity, 90[9]. [√diç, 1182: cf. *δεικτηρ in δεικτήριος, 'pertaining to one who shows.']

deha, *m. n.* body; *mentioned w.* manas *and* vāc, 65[9]. [√dih, 'stroke lightly so as to mould *or* form,' and so, prob. 'the figure, form, shape,' like the Lat. *figūra*, 'shape, form,' from the cognate √*fig*, *fingo*: see √dih.]

dehin, *a.* connected with the body, 65[11]; *as m.* a living being, man. [deha, 1230.]

dāitya, *m.* descendant of Diti, *q.v.*; a Dāitya *or* demon. [díti, 1211.]

dāitya-dānava-mardana, *m.* Daitya-and-Dānava-crusher, epithet of Indra.

dāiva, *a.* of the gods, 57[21]; coming from the gods; divine; *as n.* divine appointment, *i.e.* fate, 18[12], etc. [devá, 1208f.]

dāivata, *a.* pertaining to a divinity; *as n.* —1. a divinity *or, collectively,* the divinities, *esp.* that *or* those celebrated in any Vedic hymn; —2. idol, 62[18]. [devatā, 1208e.]

dāivatya, *at end of cpds,* having ·· as divinity, addressed to ··, 63[5]. [devatā, 1211.]

dāivika, *a.* of the gods; divine. [deva, 1222e.]

dāívya, *a.* of the gods; divine. [devá, 1211.]

dola, *m.* a swinging; *f.* dolā, a dooly (*Anglo-Indian term*), a little bamboo chair slung on four men's shoulders. [√dul.]

√ **dolāya** (dolāyate). swing like a dooly; waver. [dolā.]

dolāyamāna-mati, *a.* having a wavering mind. [√dolāya.]

1 **doṣa**, *m.* —1. fault, defect; bad condition, 55[5]; —2. sin, transgression, fault, 11[8], 18[17], 65[21]; doṣam avāp, incur a transgression, 68[4]; —3. harm; evil consequence; doṣeṇa, doṣāt, by *or* as a bad consequence of, by, faute de, 23[21], 35[2]. [√duṣ.]

2 **doṣa**, *m.* evening, dark; *f.* doṣā́, evening, dark.

doṣā-vastṛ, *m.* illuminer of the darkness; *or, as adj.* [*cf.* 375[3]], lighting up in the dark.

dāutya, *n.* message. [dūtá, 1211.]

dyā́vā-pṛthiví, *dual f.* heaven and earth. [dív + pṛthivī́, 1255 and a[2].]

dyú, *same as* dív, 361d.

√ **dyut** (dyótate; didyuté; ádyutat; dyotiṣyáti; dyuttá; -dyútya). gleam; lighten; shine. [akin w. noun dív, q.v.: cf. also √jyut.]

+**vi**, lighten.

dyuti, *f.* sheen, 19[7]; lustre; dignity. [√dyut.]

dyumánt, *a.* heavenly, bright, splendid. [dyú.]

dyūtá, *n.* gambling. [√1 dīv, 1176a.]

dyó, *same as* dív, 361d.

dráviṇa, *n.* movable property (*as opp. to* house and field), wealth. [√dru, 1177b.]

dravya, *n.* —1. property; —2. *in general,* thing, object; —3. *esp.* worthy object. [√dru: see draviṇa.]

draṣṭavyà, *grdv.* to be seen. [√dṛç.]

√ 1 **drā** (drā́ti; dadrāú; ádrāsīt; *intens.* [1002c, 1024[2]] daridrāti). run; *intens.* run about, run hither and thither. [cf. δι-δρά-σκω, 'run': see √dru.]

+**apa**, run off. [cf. ἀπο-δρᾶναι, 'run off.']

√ 2 **drā** (drā́ti; drā́yate; dadrāú; ádrāsīt; drāsyáti; drāṇá). sleep. [cf. ἔδραθον, 'slept'; Lat. *dormīre*, 'sleep.']

+**ni**, go to sleep; sleep.

√ **drāgh**, *only in derivs.* drag, draw; draw out; extend; lengthen. [poss. for *dhragh (cf. √dhraj), and akin w. Eng. *drag*: but see dīrghá.]

drā́ghīyāṅs, *a.* longer, *as comp. to* dīrghá. [√drāgh, 467.]

√ **dru** (drávati, -te; dudrā́va, dudruvé; ádudruvat [868]; droṣyáti; drutá; drótum; drutvā́; -drútya). hasten; run; run away, flee, 94[7]. [ident. w. √dram, 'run,' and w. √1 drā, q.v.: cf. ἔδρᾰμε and ἔδρā, 'ran.']

+**ati**, run past *or* by; escape.

+**ā**, run unto, make an attack, charge, 94[5, 6].

+**upa**, run unto.

+**sam-upa**, run unto, rush at, 3[12].

drú, *m. n.* wood. [see dā́ru.]

drugdhá, *see* √druh.

druta, *ppl.* having hastened [952²]; -am, *as adv.* hastily, rapidly; quickly; immediately. [√dru.]

druma, *m.* tree. [drú: cf. δρυμός, 'a wood.']

√ **drumāya** (drumāyate). pass for a tree. [druma, 1058, 1059b.]

√ **druh** (drúhyati; dudróha; ádruhat; dhrokṣyáti; drugdhá; drógdhum; -drúhya). hurt (by deceit, wile, magic); strive to harm; *ppl.* drugdhá: *as m.* one who has striven to harm, hurtful foe; *as n.* misdeed. [if for *dhrugh, cf. Old High Ger. *triukan*, Ger. *be-trügen*, 'deceive so as to harm.']

+**abhi**, offend against.

dvá [482b], *num.* two. [cf. δύο, Lat. *duo*, Eng. *two*.]

dvaṁdvá, *n.* pair; quarrel. [dvaṁ-dvam is the repeated nom. s. n. of dva: cf. 1252².]

dvayá, *a.* twofold; of two sorts; *as n.* couple, pair. [dvá: cf. δοιός, 'double.']

dvā́daça [483⁴], *cardinal.* twelve. [dvá + dáça, 476³: cf. δυώδεκα, Lat. *duōdecim*, 'twelve.']

dvādaçá, *f.* -ī́, *ordinal.* twelfth; dvādaçī́ (*sc.* tithi), twelfth day of a lunar half month, 59⁹. [dvā́daça, 487⁷.]

dvādaça-rātra, *n.* space of twelve nights. [dvā́daça + rātri, 1315b, 1312³˒⁴.]

dvādaça-sahasra, *cardinal, n.* twelve thousand. [481.]

dvādaçasāhasra, *a.* consisting of twelve thousand. [dvādaça-sahasra, 1204c.]

dvā́r [388c], *f.* door. [perhaps 'the closure,' fr. √dvṛ, 'close,' for *dhvṛ: cf. θύρα, 'door'; Lat. *foris*, nom. s., 'door'; Eng. *door*.]

dvā́ra, *n.* door. [dvā́r, q.v.: 399.]

dvāra-pakṣa, *m.* side of the door.

dvi, *form of* dva *in composition and derivation.* [475⁶.]

dvi-já, *a.* twice-born; *as m.* member of one of the three upper castes, re-born by virtue of investiture (*see* √nī + upa), 60², 58²⁰, 59⁴, 62⁷; *in a narrower sense*, a Brahman, 21¹⁴, 43⁴, 55⁹, 64¹⁶.

dvi-jánman, *a.* having double birth; *as m. same as* dvija; man of one of the three upper castes, 59¹. [acct, 1300c.]

dvi-jāti, *a. and as m. same as* dvijanman; man of one of the three upper castes, 59¹⁹.

dvijottama, *m.* the highest of the twice-born, *i.e.* a Brahman. [dvija + uttama.]

dvitá, *a.* second. [dvi.]

dvitā́, *adv.* just so; so also; equally.

dvitī́ya, *a.* second. [dvitá, 487⁴, 1215d.]

dvídhā, *adv.* in two parts, in twain. [1104.]

dvi-pád [391], *a.* having two feet; *as m.* the two-footed one, man, 16²; *as n. sing.* that which is two-footed, *collectively*, men, 90¹˒³, 92³. [cf. δίποδα, Lat. *bipedem*, 'biped.']

dvi-pada, *f.* -ī, *a.* having (taken) two steps.

dvi-pravrājin, *f.* -nī, *a. in f.* going after two (men), unchaste, 98¹⁴.

√ **dviṣ** (dvéṣṭi, dviṣṭé; didvéṣa; ádvikṣat, -ata; dviṣṭá; dvéṣṭum). hate; show hatred; be hostile. [cf. ὀ-δύσ-αντο, 'became wroth,' w. prothetic ο.]

dvíṣ, *vbl.* hating, *in cpds*; *as f.* hate; as *m. concrete*, hater, foe. [√dviṣ.]

dvís, *adv.* twice. [see dvi, dva: cf. δίς, Lat. *bis*, *dvis, 'twice': the radically cognate Eng. *twice* is a gen. form.]

dvīpá, *m.* island.

dvīpi-carman, *n.* tiger-skin. [dvīpin.]

dvīpín, *a.* having islands *or* island-like spots; *as m.* leopard; tiger. [dvīpa.]

√ **dvṛ**, cover, close, *in derivs.* [see dvā́r.]

dvedhā́, *adv.* in two, in two kinds. [for *dvayadhā, fr. dvaya, 1104².]

dvéṣa, *m.* hatred. [√dviṣ.]

dvéṣas, *n.* hatred; *concrete*, hater, foe. [√dviṣ.]

---

dha, *vbl.* bestowing, granting, *in* vasu-dha. [√1 dhā, 333.]

√ **dhan** (dadhánti). set in motion. [cf. √dhanv.]

dhána, *n.* –1. the prize of the contest; *not only the* reward put up for the victor, *but also the* booty taken from the foe — *Vedic; so w.* √ji, win booty by conquest, 81²; *then*, –2. *in general*, wealth, riches, property, money. [√dhā, 'put': cf. θέμα, 'thing put up as a prize,' and for the mg also Ger. *Ein-satz*, 'stakes.']

dhanu, *m.* bow. [fr. dhanus, a transfer to the u-declension.]

dhanuṣ-kāṇḍa, *n.* bow and arrow. [dhanuś: see 1253b.]

dhánus, *n.* bow. [√dhan, 1154.]

dhánya, *a.* wealthy; fortunate. [dhana.]

√dhanv (dhánvati; dadhanvé; ádhanvīt). set in motion; run. [secondary form of √dhan.]

dhánvan, *n.* bow. [√dhan, 1169.1a.]

dhanvin, *a. subst.* having a bow, bowman. [dhanvan, 1230b.]

√dham or **dhmā** (dhámati [750]; dadhmāú; ádhmāsīt; dhamiṣyáti; dhamitá, dhmātá; -dhmā́ya). blow, breathe out; blow (pipe, shell, bag-pipe, bellows). [see 108g and 750.]

+ā, blow up; ādhmāta, *fig.* puffed up.

dhara, *a.* holding; bearing; keeping; wearing. [√dhṛ.]

dhárma, *m.* –1. custom, 98[16]; usage, 99[11]; right; duty, 28[6]; virtue, 21[7], 10[13], 15[17], 29[1]; (virtue, *i.e.*) good works, 29[5], 63[11]; correct course of conduct, 11[3]; dharme, in a question of right, 21[14]; –1a. dharmeṇa, *adv.*: as was right, 14[17]; dutifully, 16[5]; –2. law; prescription, rule; the law (as a system), 28[5], 58[16, 19]; –3. *personified*, Virtue, 67[17], 48[4].

[a post-Vedic word, taking the place of V. dhárman: dharma is fr. √dhṛ (1166b), perhaps in mg 6, and thus designating ancient custom or right as 'that which holds its own, which persists *or* endures'; but it may come fr. √dhṛ in mg 1, so that dharma is 'that which is established *or* settled'; in the latter case, cf., for the mg, *θέμις*, 'that which is established as custom or law,' w. *τίθημι*, 'set, establish,' and Ger. *Ge-setz*, 'law,' w. *setzen*, 'set.']

dharma-jña, *a.* knowing the law *or* one's duty *or* what is right.

dharma-jñāna, *n.* knowledge of the law.

dharmatas, *adv.* in a way which starts from dharma, *i.e.* in accordance with good usage, 59[19]; by rights, 61[16]. [dharma, 1098c[3].]

dhárman, *n.* established ordinance; steadfast decree (*e.g.* of a god), 80[10]; dhármaṇā, according to the established order of things, in a way that accords with nature, 84[8]. [√dhṛ, 1168.1c: see under dharma.]

dharma-mūla, *n.* the root *or* foundation of the law.

dharma-víd [391], *a.* knowing the law *or* one's duty, 1[15]; acquainted with good usage, 61[10].

dharma-çāstra, *n.* authoritative *or* canonical compend of dharma, 58[18]; law-book; law-shaster.

dharmātman, *a.* having virtue *or* right as one's nature; just. [ātman.]

√dhav (dhávate). run. [see under √dhū, and cf. *θέω*, √*θεϝ*, 'run.']

dhavala, *a.* dazzlingly white. [√2dhāv, 'rinse,' 1189, 1188.]

√1dhā (dádhāti, dhatté [668]; dadhāú, dadhé; ádhāt, ádhita [884]; dhāsyáti, -te; *V.* -dhita, *later* hitá [954c]; dhā́tum; dhitvā́; -dhā́ya; dhīyáte; dídhiṣati, dhítsati; dhāpáyati [1042d]).

–1. put, 86[10]; set; lay, 39[14]; –2. put in a place, bring to, *w.* tatra, 85[19]; *w. loc.*, 89[8], 95[5]; *w. dat.*, 83[1]; –3. put upon, direct towards; dharme dhā manas, set the heart on virtue, 66[7]; –4. put something for a person (*dat.*), *i.e.* bestow upon him, grant him, 84[1], RV. x. 125. 2; –5. put in a position, *i.e.* appoint, constitute, *w. double acc.*, 88[12]; –6. make, cause, produce; –7. hold, keep, 86[6, 9]; –8. *mid.* take to one's self, receive, obtain, win; *esp.* garbhaṁ dhā, conceive fruit in the womb, 92[12]; –9. *mid.* assume, 19[7]; maintain; –10. hita, *see s.v.*; –11. *desid. act.* desire to grant; *mid.* desire to win.

[The original meaning of the root is 'put'; but, from the proethnic period, a secondary development in the line ('set,' 'establish,' and so) 'make,' 'do,' is clear. The secondary mg has even won the more prominent place in Germanic and Slavic.

For the primary mg, cf. *τίθημι*, 'put' (the parallelism of its mgs is remarkable — *θέσαν λίθον*, 'they set a stone'; *θέσθαι υἱόν*, 'conceive a son,' etc., etc.); Lat. *ab-de-re*, 'put off *or* away,' and *con-de-re*, 'put together, construct, establish'; Eng. do, 'put,' in the contract forms *doff, don, dup;* Ger. *weg-thun*, 'do away *or* put away.'

For the secondary mg, cf. θεῖναί τινα βασιλέα, 'make one a king'; AS. *dōn hine tō cyninge*, 'make him a king'; Lat. *fīo*, 'am made'; Eng. *do, deed;* Ger. *thun*, 'do'; Slavic *dě-lo*, 'deed': observe that *fī-eri*, 'become,' is to *fă-c-ere*, 'make,' as *ī-re* (√*ja*), 'go,' is to *jă-c-ere*, 'make to go, throw.']

+antar, –1. put into the interior of a thing; *and so* –2. hide, conceal.

+api, put close upon; cover (a jar with its lid); ápihita, closed up. [cf. ἐπιτίθημι, 'put upon.']

+abhi, put on; put a name upon, designate; address; speak to, 43[10]; say, 42[20]; abhihitam, (it was) said, 38[13].

+ava, put down in; *esp.* duck (*trans.*) into the water; ávahita, fallen into the water; *caus.* cause to be laid in.

+ā, –1. put *or* lay *or* set in *or* on, *w. loc.*, 77[1], 79[12], 88[15], 90[5], 102[21]; –2. put on (wood on the fire), 82[15]; –3. *mid.* set for one's self on (the hearth a sacred fire), 95[12]; –4. *mid.* put on one's self, take on, 74[6]; –5. take, *i.e.* take away, 87[10].

+vy-ā, *pass.* be separated; be uncomfortable *or* sick.

+sam-ā, put upon; *w.* manas, concentrate the mind upon one thing; samāhita, intent, eager, 1[13].

+upa-sam-ā, set together (wood) unto (an already burning fire), put (fuel) on, 100[16], 105[10].

+upa, put on (*esp.* a brick *or* stone on the sacred fire-altar *or* enclosure), 96[8] ff.

+ni, lay down, 87[8]; set down (sacred fire), 85[6]; *w.* kriyām, put labor upon (*loc.*), take pains with, 19[14]; nihita, put down, lying low, 70[19].

+saṁ-ni, lay down together; put together; *pass.* be near together; saṁnihita, near, impending, 25[15].

+pari, put around; *esp.* put (part of a sacrificial fence) around (an altar), 105[13]; put around one's self, put on, (garments) 103[19], (shoes) 45[11]; clothe.

+puras, *see s.v.*

+pra, set forward. [cf. pradhana, pradhāna.]

+vi, –1. part, mete out, distribute; –2. spread abroad, RV. x. 125. 3; –3. (*like Lat.* dis-pōnere) arrange, determine; prescribe, 59[7]; vihita, ordained, 14[4]; –4. lay out, make, build; prepare, 54[18]; –5. accomplish, 56[12]; make, do (*in a great variety of applications*); vadhaṁ vidhā, do slaughter, slay, 32[14]; pūjāṁ vidhā, do *or* show honor, 28[13]; pravṛttiṁ vidhā, make an advance into, *w. loc.*, expose one's self to, 20[12]; upāyaṁ vidhā, employ an expedient, 39[2]; kiṁ vidheyam, what's to be done, 31[5]; tathā vidhīyatām, so let it be done, 11[4]; yathā · ·, tan mayā vidheyam, I must take such a course, that · ·, 37[6]; *cf.* 38[22].

+çrad, *see* çrad.

+sam, put together, unite; embroil in, *w. loc.*, 73[14].

√ **2dhā** (dháyati [761d2]; dadhāú; ádhāt; dhāsyáti; dhītá; dhā́tum; -dhíya; dhītvā́). suck; drink, 63[1]. [cf. dadhi, dhenu: also θήσατο, 'sucked'; γαλα-θηνός, 'milk-sucking'; θη-λή, 'breast'; Lat. *fē-lare*, 'suck'; Goth. *dadd-jan*, 'give suck.']

1 **dhā́**, *in cpds. as vbl.* bestowing, granting; *as subst.* place. [√1dhā, 'place, grant.']

2 **dhā́**, *in cpds. as subst.* drink. [√2dhā, 'drink.']

dhātu, *m.* layer, *as* part of a composite whole. [√1dhā, 'put, lay.']

dhātṛ́, *m.* establisher; creator; Dhātar, *as* name of a deity, 90[9] N. [√1dhā.]

dhāna, *a.* holding, containing. [√1dhā, 1150.]

dhānā́, *f. pl.* corns, *i.e.* grain.

dhānyà, *a.* cereal (*adj.*); *as n.* cereal (*noun*), grain. [dhānā́.]

dhāraṇa, *a.* holding; *as n.* a holding, keeping; wearing, 14[11]; -ā, *f.* established ordinance; rule, 62[17]. [√dhṛ.]

dhārā, *f.* stream, jet. [√1dhāv, 'run, pour.']

dhārāsāra, *m. pl.* stream-pourings, violent pourings. [āsāra.]

dhārin, *a.* holding; possessing, 22[23]; retaining, 68[14]. [√dhṛ.]

dhārmika, *a.* righteous; virtuous. [dharma.]

√ 1dhāv (dhā́vati, -te; ádhāvīt; dhāviṣyáti; dhāvitá; dhāvitvā́; -dhā́vya). run (of fluids), stream, pour; run (of animate beings). [see under √dhū.]

+**anu,** run after.

+**upa,** run unto.

+**sam-upa,** run on unto, 3^{13}.

+**pra,** run forth, flow; run.

√ 2dhāv (dhā́vati, -te; dadhāvé; ádhāviṣṭa; dhāutá; dhāutvā́; -dhā́vya). rinse.

dhi, *vbl.* containing, granting, *in cpds.* [√1dhā, 1155.2e.]

dhik, *excl.* fie! *w. acc.*

√ dhī (dī́dheti [676]; dīdhā́ya [786^{3}]; dhītá). think. [see √dhyā.]

+**anu,** think over.

dhī́ [351], *f.* —**1.** thought; dhiyā́-dhiyā, with each thought, every time it occurs to one; —**2.** (*like Ger.* An-dacht, *lit.* 'thinking upon,' *and then* 'devotion') religious thought, devotion, 69^{13}, 74^{19}, 82^{17}; *observe that* matí, mánas, manīṣā́, mántra, *and* mánman *show this same specialization of mg;* prayer, 74^{15}; —**3.** intelligence, insight, mind, 89^{1}; understanding, skill. [√dhī.]

1 dhītí, *f. perhaps* draught, *see* 82^{7} N. [√2dhā, 'drink,' 1157.1a.]

2 dhītí, *f.* —**1.** thought; —**2.** devotion; —**3.** skill. [√dhī: for 2, cf. dhī́ 2.]

dhīmant, *a.* gifted with understanding, wise. [dhī́.]

1 dhīra, *a.* wise, $78^{8,10}$. [√dhī, 1188a.]

2 dhīra, *a.* firm; resolute, 48^{2}. [√dhṛ: cf. Lat. *fir-mus,* 'firm.']

dhīvara, *m.* —**1.** a very clever *or* skilful man; —**2.** a fisher. [dhī́, 1171.]

dhúni, *a.* shaking, stormily moved, boisterous, wild. [fr. quasi-root dhun of dhunóti, √dhū.]

√ dhū (dhūnóti, -nuté; *later,* dhunóti, -nuté [*see* 711]; dudhā́va, dudhuvé; ádhūṣṭa [887a]; dhaviṣyáti; dhūtá, *later* dhutá; dhūtvā́; -dhū́ya). —**1.** move quickly hither and thither; shake; —**2.** fan (a fire); —**3.** shake off.

[orig. 'move violently, agitate': cf. θύω, θύνω, 'rush on'; θῡμός, 'agitation, anger, passion, spirit': θύω, 'sacrifice,' is poss. akin w. √dhū as a generalization of mg 2: closely akin w. √dhū is √1dhāv, 'run,' and also √dhav, 'run' (cf. θέω, √θεϝ, 'run'): see also under dhūma.]

+**ava,** shake down; *mid.* shake off from one's self.

dhūmá, *m.* smoke; vapor. [cf. Lat. *fūmus,* 'smoke': smoke has no such "swift eddying motion" as to make it easy to connect these names for it w. √dhū, q.v.; but on this connection their identification w. θῡμός should seem to depend: more prob. is the explanation of dhūmá as 'the enveloping *or* blackening,' fr. √1dhvan, as vāma fr. √van.]

dhūmaka, *m.* smoke, *at end of cpds* [1307] *for* dhūma; *f.* -ikā [1222d], *the same.*

dhūrta, *a. subst.* shrewd, sly, cunning; rogue. [ppl. of √dhvṛ, 'harm by deceit' (cf. 957b²): according to the grammarians, dhū́rta, w. acct altered as in júṣṭa: for a somewhat analogous development of mg, cf. Middle Eng. *schrewen,* 'curse,' whence *schrew-ed,* 'cursed, bad,' Eng. *shrewd,* 'bad, artful.']

dhūrta-traya, *n.* rogue-triad, trio of swindlers.

dhūsara, *a.* dusted over, dusty, dust-colored, gray. [√dhvaṅs, dhvas, 1188d: cf. 181a.]

√ dhṛ (dādhā́ra [786], dadhré; ádhṛta; dhariṣyáti, -te; dhṛtá; dhártum; dhṛtvā́; -dhṛ́tya; dhāráyati; ádīdharat). *mgs of caus. forms ident.* [1041^{2}] *w. those of simple forms;* hold, *in its various mgs, trans. and intrans.;*

trans. —**1.** hold, bear, support, 33^{11}, 39^{3}, $75^{6,7}$, 87^{9}, 92^{1}; make firm, 92^{10}; carry, 62^{12}; wear; —**2.** hold fast, 22^{10}, 33^{1}; hold in check, bear, withstand, 2^{20}, 8^{12}; —**3.** keep (a cat), 31^{9}; —**4.** set *or* lay *or* place in *or* on, *w. loc.,* 33^{12}, 41^{21}; —**5.** hold *or* make sure *or* ordain for some one (*dat.*); *mid.* be ordained for some one (*dat.*), belong of right to, 75^{3};

intrans. —**6.** *mid.* hold, *i.e.* remain, continue; *w. this mg, even in the active,* 15^{5}.

[cf. θρό-νος, 'support, seat,' θρᾶ-νος, 'bench,' θρῆ-σασθαι, 'sit'; Lat. *frē-tus,* 'held *or* supported by (*hence w. abl.*), relying on,' *frē-num*, 'holder, bridle.']

+ava, *caus.* —1. set down, fix; —2. (*like Eng.* hold) assume as certain, 44[14].

√ **dhṛṣ** (dhṛṣṇóti; dadhárṣa; ádhṛṣat; dhṛṣitá, dhṛṣṭá; -dhṛ́ṣya; dharṣáyati). be bold *or* courageous; dare; venture, 74[2]; —*caus.* venture on some one *or* something; offend; overpower; dharṣitá, overcome. [cf. θρασ-ύς, 'bold'; Lat. *fastus*, 'pride'; Goth. *ga-dars*, AS. *dearr*, Eng. *he dare* (all 3d persons sing. of a preterito-present); AS. *dors-te*, Eng. *durs-t*.]

+ā, venture against.

+prati, hold out against, withstand, 82[5].

dhṛṣṇú, *a.* daring; courageous, doughty, 78[7]; bold, 84[17]. [√dhṛṣ, 1162.]

dhenú, *f.* milch cow; cow. [√2dhā, 'suck,' 1162.]

dheya, *n.* the giving. [√1dhā, mg 4, 'bestow, give': 1213c.]

dhāirya, *n.* firmness; earnest *or* resolute bearing. [2dhīra, 1211.]

√ **dhmā**, *see* √dham.

√ **dhyā** (dhyáti, dhyā́yati [761d1]; dadhyāú; ádhyāsīt [911]; dhyāsyáti; dhyātá; dhyātvā́; -dhyā́ya). think upon; meditate. [see √dhī and 108g.]

+abhi, set the mind on something; sink one's self in thought, 57[1].

dhyāna, *n.* meditation. [√dhyā, 1150.]

dhyāna-para, *a.* having meditation as highest object, absorbed in contemplation. [1302b.]

√ **dhraj** (dhrájati; ádhrājīt). draw onward, advance, *intrans.* [see √drāgh, of which this is poss. a collateral form.]

√ **dhru**, *collateral form of* √dhvṛ.

dhrúti, *f.* a deceiving; infatuation. [√dhru.]

dhruvá, *a.* —1. holding *or* continuing, *i.e.* remaining fixed in place; *as m.* the pole-star, 100[8]; —2. of abodes certain, safe, 79[18]. [√dhṛ in mg 6: see 1190.]

dhruvā́, *f.* sacrificial ladle, 102[13], *see* srúc. [lit. 'holder,' √dhṛ in mg 1: see 1190.]

√ **dhvaṅs** *or* dhvas (dhváṅsati, -te; dadhváṅsa, dadhvasé; ádhvasat; dhvastá; -dhvásya). —1. fall to dust, perish; dhvasta, exhausted, hurt, impaired; —2. vanish, be off; —3. *only in ppl.* dhvasta, bestrewn, covered over, *esp.* with dust. [cf. Eng. *dus-t*; prob. also AS. *dwǣs* and *dysig*, 'foolish,' Eng. *dizzy*, Old High Ger. *tusic*, 'foolish.']

dhvaṅsá, *m.* the perishing; destruction. [√dhvaṅs.]

√ **1dhvan** (ádhvanīt; dhvāntá; dhvanáyati). —1. cover one's self; dhvānta, dark; —2. become extinguished; —*caus.* —1. envelope, cover over; —2. blacken. [perhaps akin w. √dhvaṅs: see dhūma: cf. AS. *dunn*, Eng. *dun*, 'dark, brownish-black.']

√ **2dhvan** (dhvánati; dadhvā́na; dhvāntá [955a]). sound, resound. [cf. Old Eng. *dune*, Eng. *din*.]

dhvaní, *m.* sound. [√2dhvan.]

√ **dhvṛ** (dhvárati). bend *or* make crooked; cause to fall; harm by deceit. [see dhūrta and dhruti: cf. AS. *dwellan*, 'lead astray, cause to delay,' Eng. *dwell*, intrans., 'delay, linger, abide'; Eng. *dwaul*, 'wander, rave,' *dwale*, 'stupefying potion'; Dutch *dwaal-licht*, 'ignis fatuus'; Goth. *dvals*, 'foolish'; Eng. *dull*, *dol-t*; Ger. *toll*, 'mad.']

---

na [491], *encl. pron. root of* 1*st person, see* ahám. [w. nas, 'us,' cf. νώ, 'we two,' Lat. *nōs*, 'us.']

ná, *adv.* —1. not [1122b], 3[2]; —1a. *in connected sentences or clauses: repeated simply:* 97[8], *octies;* 62[14, 15], *quinquies;* 63[13, 14], 71[4], *ter;* 4[13], 17[18], 74[1], 80[17], *bis; with* ca: na ··, na ·· ca, na ca ··, 62[16]; na ··, na ca ··, na ··, 63[1]; *with* api: *see* api 2; *with* u, 21[14]; —1b. *not repeated, but replaced by* api ca *or* vā‿api (*see these*), 2[12], 63[4]; —1c. *combinations:* na ca, 8[16]; na ·· ca, 13[7], 62[16]; nāiva, 22[19], 23[19], 96[10]; na vāi, 92[15]; na vā, 96[12]; na tu, 64[13]; na tv eva tu, *see* tu; na ha, 95[17]; na‿iva, not exactly, 93[5]; —1d. *tantamount to* a- *in negative cpds* [1122b[4]], *as* nacira, nātidūra, nādhīta, etc.; —1e. *at beg. of adversative clause: with adversative conj.*, 34[10]; *without*, 22[20], 41[13], 92[16]; —1f. *in emphatic litotes*, 21[9]; —1g. *substantive verb to be supplied*, 32[5] (asti); —1h. na *precedes* ced, *if it belongs to the protasis*, 63[9]; *if it immediately follows* ced, *it must be joined to the apodosis*, 18[9]; —1i. *for prohibitive negative, see* mā́; —1j. ná, 'not,' *coalesces metrically in Veda w. following initial vowel, e.g.* 70[12], 71[4], 83[9];

—2. like [*see* 1122d and d[2]], *in this sense Vedic only*, 70[15,18], 71[7,9], etc.; ná, 'like,' *does not coalesce metrically in Veda w. following initial vowel.*

[cf. *νη-*, Lat. *nĕ-*, negative prefix in *νη-κερδής*, 'gain-less,' *nĕ-fas*, 'not right, wrong'; AS. and Old Eng. *ne*, 'not'; AS. *nā* (*ne* + *ā*), 'not ever, never, no,' Eng. *no*; Eng. *na-* in *nathless*, AS. *nā þē læs*, 'not the less'; Eng. *n-* in *n-ever, n-aught*, etc.]

nákis, *indecl. subst. pron.* —1. no one, 78[1], 73[20]?; —2. nothing, 73[20]?; —3. *even as adv.* [*see* 1117], never, 75[11]. [ná + kís, see 504[2] end.]

nakulá, *m.* Viverra ichneumon, an animal like the polecat, often domesticated, and a bitter foe of serpents and mice.

nákta, *n.* night; -am [1111b], by night. [cf. *νύξ*, stem *νυκτ*, Lat. *nox*, stem *nocti*, Eng. *night.*]

√ **nakṣ** (nákṣati, -te; nanákṣa, nanakṣé). attain unto; *w.* dyām, mount up to heaven. [collateral form of √2 naç, 'attain.']

nákṣatra, *n.* —1. sīdus, heavenly body, *in Veda*, of sun as well as of stars; star, 13[3], 71[12]; *sing. collectively*, 78[11]; constellation; —2. asterism of the lunar zodiac, 59[10]. [perhaps the stars are they that 'mount up' to heaven, cf. √nakṣ w. dyām.]

nakhá, *m. n.* nail (on fingers or toes); claw; talon. [cf. *ὄνυξ*, stem *ὀ-νυχ*, Lat. *unguis*, 'nail, claw'; AS. *nægel*, Eng. *nail.*]

nakhín, *a.* having claws; *as m.* beast with claws. [nakha.]

nágara, *n., and* -rī, *f.* town, city.

nagaropānta, *n.* neighborhood of the town. [upānta.]

na-cira, *a.* not long; -āt, *adv.* [1114c], soon. [1122b[4].]

naṭa, *m.* dancer, mime, actor (these form a very despised caste). [√nṛt.]

naḍá *or* naḷá, *m.* reed. [Whitney 54: cf. 2 nadá and nala.]

√ **nad** (nádati; nanā́da, nedé; naditá; -nádya). sound; roar; bellow. [see 1 nadá and nadī́.]

1 **nadá**, *m.* the bellower, *i.e.* bull. [√nad.]

2 **nadá**, *m.* reed, rush. [cf. naḍá.]

nadī́, *f.* roaring stream; river. [√nad: cf. *Νέδα*, *Νέδων*, names of streams.]

nánāndṛ [369[2]], *f.* husband's sister.

√ **nand** (nándati, -te; nanánda; nandiṣyáte; nanditá; -nándya). be glad.

+ **abhi**, be glad in; greet joyfully.

nandana, *a.* gladdening; causing joy; *as m.* son, 21[17]; *as n.* Nandana, *or* Elysium, the pleasure ground of the gods, *esp.* of Indra, 49[18]. [caus. of √nand.]

nandi, *m.* The Gladsome One, euphemistic epithet of the dreadful god, Çiva-Rudra. [√nand: cf. çiva.]

nandi-deva, *m.* Nandideva, name of a Brahman. ['having Çiva as his god.']

nápāt, náptṛ [370], *m.* —1. *in Veda*, descendant *in general*; son; grandson, 87[18]; —2. *in Skt.*, grandson, 63[9]. [declension: in Veda, nápāt, nápātam, náptrā, náptṛbhis, etc.; in Skt., náptā, náptāram, náptrā, náptṛbhis, etc.: see 1182d: cf. *νέποδες*, 'young ones'; Lat. *nepōtem*, 'grandson'; AS. *nefa*, 'son's son *or* brother's son'—supplanted by Old French *neveu* (Eng. *nephew*), which in Old Eng. meant 'son's son' as well as 'brother's son.']

naptī́ [356], *f.* daughter, 72[6]; granddaughter. [*f.* to nápāt: acct, 355b.]

√ **nabh** (nábhate). burst; tear.

nábhas, *n.* —1. mist, clouds; —2. atmosphere, sky. [cf. *νέφος*, *νεφέλη*, 'cloud, mist'; Lat. *nūbes*, 'cloud,' *nebula*, 'mist'; AS. *nifol*, 'misty, gloomy'; Ger. *Nebel*, 'mist': for mg 2, cf. Ger. *Wolken* and AS. *wolcnu*, 'clouds,' w. Eng. *welkin*, 'sky.']

nabhas-tala, *n.* sky-surface, *i.e.* sky, *see* tala.

√ **nam** (námati, -te; nanā́ma, nemé [794e]; ánaṅsīt; naṅsyáti; natá [954d]; nāmitum, nántum; natvā́; -námya; namáyati). bow (*intrans.*), bend one's self; aim at a person (*gen.*) with (*instr.*), 73[15]; nata, bowed down, bending over, 68[19] N.; —*caus.* cause to bow, subdue; namyate, is subdued, 31[6].

+**ava**, bow down, 34[17].

+**ā**, bow down to.

+**ud**, raise one's self up, arise.

+**sam-ud**, rise.

+**nis**, bend out; contort one's self.

+**pra**, make obeisance before (*acc.*).

námas, *n.* bow, obeisance; adoration (by gesture or word); reverence; *used also like the Lat.* gloria *in the* Gloria patri. [√nam.]

namas-kārá, *m.* a making of namas; adoration. [171[3].]

namas-kṛ (*see* √1kṛ). do homage, 9[14]. [171[3], 1092a.]

√ **namasya** (namasyáti). pay reverence. [namas, 1063, 1058.]

námuci, *m.* Namuchi, name of a demon, foe of Indra, 81[16], 97[6].

nayana, *n.* eye. ['leader, organ of sense that leads,' √nī, 1150. 1a: for mg, cf. ānana, gātra, caraṇa, netra.]

nára, *m.* man, 3[21], etc.; *at* 57[5], the primal man *or* spirit. [transition-stem fr. nṛ, 1209a.]

nara-nārī, *f.* man and woman. [1253a.]

nara-pati, *m.* lord of men; king.

nara-vāhana, *a. subst.* having men as his team, drawn by men; epithet and name of Kuvera, god of wealth; name of a king, successor of Çālivāhana.

naravāhana-datta, *m.* Naravāhanadatta, name of a son of king Udayana.

naravāhanadatta-carita, *n.* adventures of N.

naravāhanadattacaritamaya, *f.* -ī, *a.* containing the adventures of N. [1225: see maya.]

nara-vyāghra, *m.* man-tiger, *i.e.* brave and noble man. [cf. naraçārdūla: 1280b.]

nara-çārdūla, *m.* man-tiger, *i.e.* best among men. [cf. naravyāghra: 1280b.]

nara-çreṣṭha, *a. subst.* best of men.

nara-sūnu, *f.* daughter of the primal man *or* spirit.

narādhipa, *m.* lord of men, *i.e.* king, prince. [adhipa.]

nareçvara, *m.* lord of men, *i.e.* king, prince. [īçvara.]

narottama, *a. subst.* best of men. [uttama.]

narmada, *a.* granting *or* causing fun; making gladness; *f.* -dā, Narmadā (called also Revā), the modern Nerbudda river. [narman + da.]

narman, *n.* fun.

nala, *m.* reed; Nala, name of a prince of Nishadha. [cf. naḍá, Vedic naḷá.]

nalopākhyāna, *n.* Nala-episode, 1[1]. [upākhyāna.]

1 **náva**, *a.* new; of an earthen dish, (fresh, *i.e.*) unburned. [prob. fr. nú, 'now,' q.v.: cf. νέος, Lat. *novus*, Ger. *neu*, Eng. *new.*]

2 **náva** [483[4]], *num.* nine. [cf. ἐννέα, Lat. *novem*, Ger. *neun*, Eng. *nine.*]

navatí [485], *f.* ninety. [2náva.]

náva-nīta, *n.* fresh butter. [perhaps 'fresh-brought,' as we say 'bring the butter, *i.e.* make it come,' in churning.]

návedas, *a. perhaps* well-knowing, cognizant of (*gen.*). [apparently fr. an affirmative particle na-, and vedas: see 1296[3] end.]

√ **1naç** (náçyati; nanáça, neçús; ánaçat; naṅkṣyáti [936]; naṣṭá; nāçáyati). be missing; get lost; vanish; perish, be ruined. [cf. νεκ-ρός, 'dead'; Lat. *nex*, 'death'; *nocēre*, 'harm.']

+**vi**, get lost; perish; *caus.* cause to disappear; bring to nought, 81[20].

√ **2naç** (náçati, -te; nanáça; ā́naṭ [833]). attain; reach, come up to, 74[1]; *w.* acchā, draw hither, 76[11]. [see √1aç, 'reach': cf. Lat. *nac-tus sum*, 'am having reached'; AS. *neāh*, comp. *neār*, superl. *neāhst*, Eng. *nigh*, *near* (as comp., Macbeth ii. 3. 146), *next*; AS. *ge-neah*, 'it reaches, es reicht, it suffices'; *ge-nōh*, Eng. *e-nough.*]

+**pra**, reach to, hit; fall upon, 78[8].

nás [397], *f.* nose. [nom. dual, nā́sā: cf. Lat. *nas-turcium*, 'nose-teaser, nasturtium'; *nār-es*, 'nostrils'; AS. *nosu*, Eng. *nose*; *nos-tril*, 'nose-thrill, nose-hole.']

nas [491], *encl. pron. form of* 1*st pers.* [cf. νώ, 'we two'; Lat. *nōs*, 'us.']

nasa, *for* **nás** *in cpds* [1315c].

√ **nah** (**náhyati** [761c]; **naddhá** [223[3]]; **-náhya**). bind; join. [despite **naddha** (a poss. false formation), and Avestan **nazda** (Morphologische Untersuchungen, iii. 144), probably for ***nagh**: cf. Lat. *nec-t-ere*, 'bind.']

+**upa**, tie on, lace.

nahí, *adv.* not, to be sure; **nahí me ásti**, to be sure, I have no · ·. [**ná** + **hí**, 1122a and b[4]: acct of verb, 595d.]

náhuṣa, *m.* Nahusha, name of an ancient king. [perhaps 'neighbor,' from **náhus**, and in that case a transfer-form (1209b).]

náhus, *m.* neighbor. [√**nah**.]

nā́ka, *m.* vault of heaven, firmament.

nātidūra, *a.* not very far. [**na** + **ati-dūra**, 1122b[4].]

√ **nāth** (**nā́thate**; **nāthitá**; **nā́thitum**; **-nā́thya**). turn with supplication to.

nāthá, *n.* a refuge; *as m.* protector; lord. [√**nāth**.]

nādhīta, *a.* un-learnéd. [**na** + **adhīta**, √**i**: 1122b[4].]

nā́bhi, *f.* –1. navel; –2. nave *or* hub. [cf. *ὀμφ-αλός*, Lat. *umb-ilicus*, AS. *naf-ela*, Eng. *navel*; also AS. *naf-u*, Eng. *nave*.]

nābhi-vardhana, *n.* the cutting of the navel(-string).

nāma-dhéya, *n.* the name-giving, naming, 59[9]; name, 17[9], 60[22]. [**nāman**.]

nā́man, *n.* –1. distinguishing characteristic; form; –2. name, 13[8], 60[21b], 78[9], 61[9]; **nāma grah**, (take *i.e.*) mention the name, 64[13]; personal name (*e.g.* **devadatta**), as distinguished from the gotra *or* 'family name' (*e.g.* **kāçyapa**, 'descendant of Kaçyapa'), 103[19] N.; *at end of cpds*, having · · as name, named · ·, *so* 11 *times*, *e.g.* 19[11]; –3. **nāma**, *adv.* [1111b], by name, *so* 19 *times*, *e.g.* 1[3], 60[21a], 94[16]; *also* **nāmnā**, 56[5]; *w. interrogatives*, pray, 54[16]. [origin unknown: cf. *ὄ-νομα*, Lat. *nōmen*, Eng. *name*.]

nārá, –1. *a.* human; –2. *as m.* man; –**nārī**, *f.* woman, 1[9], 86[18], etc.; wife. [**nṛ**, 1208b: for mg 2, cf. **mānava**.]

nārada, *m.* Nārada, name of an ancient devarṣi (*see note to* 1[14]), who often appears on the earth to bring news from the gods, and returns to heaven with reports from men.

nārāyaṇá, *m.* Nārāyana, son of the primal man. [simply a patronymic of **nara**, see 1219.]

nāvā́, *f.* ship. [transfer-form (1209, 399) fr. **nāu**, **nāv**.]

nāça, *m.* loss; destruction. [√**naç**, 'be missing.']

nā́sā, *dual f.* the two nostrils, the nose. [transfer-form (399) fr. **nás**, strong **nā́s**.]

nā́sikā, *f.* nostril; *dual*, the two nostrils; the nose. [**nā́sā**, 1222c 1.]

nāstika, *a. subst.* atheist, infidel, not believing the Vedas and Purānas. [fr. **na** + **asti**, 'there is not,' 1314b.]

nāhuṣa, *m.* descendant of Nahusha, patronymic of Yayāti. [**náhuṣa**, 1208 and f.]

ní, *prep.* down; in, into. [cf. *ἐνί*, 'in'; Eng. *ne-ther*, *be-nea-th*.]

nikaṭa, *a.* near; *as n.* neighborhood; presence. [1245g.]

nikhila, *a.* entire; all. [perhaps for **niḥ-khila**, 'without a gap,' **nis** + **khila**: 1305[2] end.]

nijá, *a.* own; belonging to our party, 24[6]; **nijo ripus**, foe in one's own camp, 37[15]; *often used as reflexive possessive pron.*, my own, his own, our own, etc.,—*or rather*, my (47[17]), his (50[14], 53[12], 56[4, 6]), etc. [perhaps 'in-born,' fr. **ni** + **ja**.]

niṇyá, *a.* inner; hidden, 70[20]; *as n.* secret, 78[3]. [**ni**.]

nítya, *a.* –1. own (*Vedic*), 79[16]; –2. constant; eternal, 57[7]; **-am**, *adv.* constantly, always, 17[16], 64[19]. [in mg 1, fr. **ni**, 'in,' 1245b, and so signifying 'inward, not alien.']

nitya-kāla, *m.* uninterrupted time; **-am**, *adv.* always, under all circumstances, 60[6].

nitya-snāyin, *a.* constantly making sacred ablutions. [1279.]

√ **nid** *or* **nind** (**níndati**; **ninínda**; **ánindīt**; **ninditá**; **-níndya**). blame; reproach. [cf. *ὄνειδος*, 'reproach.']

nidrā́, *f.* sleep. [√2 **drā**, 'sleep,' + **ni**.]

nidhána, *m. n.* end; death, 5[19]. [perhaps fr. √**dhā** + **ni**, 'put down *or* out of the way,' 'make an end of.']

√ **nind**, *see* **nid**.

nindaka, *a. subst.* scoffer. [√nid, nind.]

nibandhana, *n.* a binding, ligation, 59[3]; that on which a thing is fastened *or* rests *or* depends, condition, means, 46[7]. [√bandh + ni.]

nibhṛta, *a.* (borne down, lowered, *i.e.*) hidden; -am, *adv.* secretly. [√bhṛ + ni.]

nimajjana, *n.* bathing. [√majj + ni.]

nimitta, *n.* mark (for shooting at); sign, token; occasion *or* cause; -am, -ena, *adverbially*, because of; tannimittam, -ena, because of this, on account of this.

nimeṣá, *m.* closing *or* winking of the eyes. [√miṣ + ni.]

niyoga, *m.* a fastening on; injunction, *and so*, commission; business, 30[6]. [√yuj + ni: for mg, cf. *alicui injungere laborem*, 'fasten *or* impose a task on a person.']

nir, *for* nis *before sonants* [174]; *see* nis.

nir-antara, *a.* without interval *or* free space; completely filled, 53[10]; continuous; uninterrupted, 56[12].

nir-apāya, *a.* without failure *or* danger; infallible *or* safe.

nir-apekṣa, *a.* without regard *or* expectation; regardless, 52[20]; not expecting anything from another, independent, 31[17]. [apekṣā, 334[2].]

nir-āmiṣāçin, *a.* not meat-eating. [see nis 3.]

nir-āhāra, *a.* without food, abstaining from food.

nír-ukta, *a.* spoken out; loud; clear; *as n.* explanation; etymological interpretation of a word; *esp.* Nirukta, title of a commentary to the nighaṇṭavas *or* Vedic Glossary. [√vac + nis.]

nír-ṛti, *f.* dissolution; destruction. [√ṛ + nis, 1157. 1d.]

nir-guṇa, *a.* without a string, 18[5]; void of good qualities, 18[5]; worthless, bad.

nir-ṇāmá, *m.* contortion, sinuosity. [√nam + nis.]

nir-dhana, *a.* without money.

nir-buddhi, *a.* without wit, stupid.

nir-bhara, *a.* —1. without measure, much; -am, *adv.* very; -am prasupta, fast asleep; —2. full of.

nir-mala, *a.* without impurity; pure; clear.

nir-lakṣya, *a.* not to be perceived, avoiding notice. [see nis 3.]

nir-vañça, *a.* without family; alone in the world.

nir-vāta, *a.* windless; sheltered.

nir-viçeṣa, *a.* without distinction; undistinguished; alike; like.

nirviçeṣākṛti, *a.* having like appearance, looking just alike. [ākṛti.]

nivāra, *m.* the warding off. [√1 vṛ, 'cover,' + ni.]

nívīta, *ppl.* hung, *i.e.* draped, with hangings, *esp.* with the sacred cord; *as n.* [1176a], the wearing the sacred cord about the neck; the sacred cord itself. [√vyā + ni.]

nivṛtta, *ppl.* —1. turned away; *esp.* of an action which is turned away, *i.e.* not directed (to any ulterior purpose *or* object), free from hope of reward in this world or the next, disinterested, *opp. of* pravṛtta, *q.v.*; —2. having turned away from, *and so* abstaining from, 29[8]. [√vṛt + ni.]

nivéçana, *n.* a going in and settling down to rest; resting-place; sleeping-place, bed, 105[8]; dwelling, 8[6]. [√viç + ni: for mg, cf. bhavana.]

níç [397], *f.* night. [cf. nákta.]

niçā, *f.* night. [cf. níç, nákta.]

niçcaya, *m.* (ascertainment, determination, *i.e.*) a fixed opinion *or* a firm resolve. [poss. fr. √3 ci, 'notice, look,' + nis; but better, perhaps, fr. √1 ci + nis, and so, 'an un-piling, *i.e.* discrimination, determination.']

niçcala, *a.* not moving. [nis + cala: see nis 3.]

niçcita, *ppl.* determined, decided; -am, *adv.* decidedly, surely. [see under niçcaya.]

niḥçreyasa, *a.* without a superior, *i.e.* best; *as n.* final beatitude. [nis + çreyasa: acct, 1305[3].]

niḥçvasa, *m.* breathing out, expiration; sigh. [√çvas + nis.]

niḥçvāsa-parama, *a.* having sighs as chief thing, much addicted to sighing. [1302b.]

niṣadha, *m. pl.* the Nishadhans, name of

a people; Nishadha, name of a country, 1⁷ N., 4³.

niṣadhādhipa, *m.* ruler *or* king of the Nishadhans. [adhipa.]

niṣūdana, *m.* finisher (*in its colloquial sense*), one who makes an end of, destroyer. [√sūd + ni.]

niṣeka, *m.* an injecting, *esp.* of semen, impregnation; the ceremony performed upon impregnation. [√sic + ni.]

niṣevin, *a.* devoting one's self to; cohabiting with, 67[22]. [√sev + ni.]

niṣkramaṇa, *n.* the stepping out; *esp.* the first going out with a child. [√kram + nis.]

niṣṭha, *a.* resting upon. [√sthā + ni, 333.]

niṣphala, *a.* fruitless, 63[10]; vain, 68[11]. [nis + phala.]

nís, *adv. prep.* –1. out, forth; –2. *in cpds* [1305[2] end], having · · away, without · ·, *e.g.* nirantara; –3. *in cpds,* not, *e.g.* niçcala.

√ **nī** (náyati, -te; ināya [800b], ninyé; ánāiṣit, áneṣṭa [882]; neṣyáti, -te; nītá; nétum; nītvā́; -nī́ya; nīyáte; nāyáyati [1042b]). lead, 24[15]; guide; conduct, 85[20]; carry, 39[19], etc.; carry off, 36[15], 43[17]; vyāghratām̐ nī, bring to tiger-ness, change into a tiger; vaçam̐ nī, bring into one's power.

+**anu**, (draw along toward one, *i.e.*) try to win *or* conciliate by friendly words.

+**abhi**, bring hither to.

+**ā**, bring to, 29[14]; bring, 31[9]; bring (one liquid) into (another, *loc.*), mix, 101[14]; *caus.* cause to be fetched, 50[5].

+**ud**, bring up; rescue (as a drowning man from the water), 90[10].

+**upa**, take unto one's self, of the teacher who receives a youth of one of the three free castes as pupil, and at the same time invests him with the sacramental cord, thus conferring spiritual rebirth, and making him a full member of his caste; *see* upanāyana; upanīta, invested with the sacramental cord.

+**pari**, lead around (a cow, steer), 91[14], 105[22]; *esp.* lead a bride around the fire (as wedding ceremony), *page* 99.

+**pra**, –1. bring forward; –2. *as liturgical terminus technicus,* convey the sacrificial fire and water to their places on and near the altar; praṇītās (*sc.* āpas), holy water; –3. bring forward (one's feelings), *i.e.* come out with *or* manifest one's affection, 9[15].

+**vi**, lead; guide; train; discipline.

nī́ [352], *vbl.* bringing, *in* vaçanī́. [√nī.]

nīcá, *a.* low, not high; morally and socially low. [inorganic transfer-form (1209a) fr. nīc-ā́, q.v.]

nīcā́, *adv.* down, low. [adverbially accented instr.—instead of nī́c-ā, 1112e—fr. ny-àñc.]

nīcā́-vayas [418], *a.* whose strength is low; exhausted. [1306.]

nīḍá, *Vedic* nīḷá, *m. n.* –1. (place for settling down, *i.e.*) resting-place; –2. *esp.* bird's nest. [for ni-zd-a, i.e. ni-s(a)d-a —198b[3]—√sad + ni: cf. Lat. *nidus,* Ger. *Nest,* Eng. *nest:* for ḷ, see Whitney 54.]

nīḍa-garbha, *m.* nest-interior.

nīti, *f.* –1. cónduct, *esp.* right and sagacious conduct; the knowledge of all that governs virtuous and discreet and statesman-like behavior; political and social ethics; –2. leading. [√nī, 'condúct.']

nīti-jñá, *a.* knowing how to conduct one's self discreetly.

nīti-vidyā, *f.* knowledge of nīti *or* political and social ethics, *esp.* as it concerns princes.

nīti-çāstra, *n.* doctrine *or* science of political and social ethics.

nītha, *m.* a leading; nīthá, *n.* (way, *and so, like the German* Weise) a musical air, song. [√nī, 1163a.]

nīrá, *n.* water.

nīrasa, *a.* sapless, dried up; tasteless; insipid, 54[11]. [nis + rasa, 174, 179.]

nīruj, *a.* without disease; healthy, 22[3]. [nis + rúj, 174, 179.]

nīla, *a.* dark-colored, *esp.* dark blue; *as n.* indigo; nīlī, *f.* indigo. [hence, through the Arabic *an-nīl,* for *al-nīl,* 'the indigo-plant,' come Eng. *anil* and *aniline.*]

nīla-paṭa, *m.* dark garment.

nīla-varṇa, *a.* blue-colored.

nīlasaṁdhāna-bhāṇḍa, *n.* vat for the mixing, *i.e.* preparing of indigo.

nīlībhāṇḍa-svāmin, *m.* indigo-vat-proprietor.

nīvā́ra, *m.* wild rice; *sing.* the plant; *pl.* the grains.

nīḷá, *see* nīḍá.

√ **nu** (**návate**; **nunā́va**; **ánūṣṭa**; **nutá**; **-nútya**). cry aloud; shout; exult; praise.
+pra, murmur; hum; *esp.* utter the sacred syllable om.

nú, *adv.* —**1a.** now, at once, *temporal*; —**1b.** now, *continuative*; **adhā nu**, so now, 79[8]; —**1c.** now, *introductory*, 70[1]; —**1d.** so then, *in encouraging or summoning*; —**1e.** now, pray, *in questions*, 5[21], 7[18], 51[20], 74[8], 78[12]; —**2.** *asseverative*: **nakir nu**, surely no one *or* nothing, 73[20]; **mā́ nú**, in order that surely not, 86[10]; —**3.** *w. relatives*: **yā nu**, whatsoever, 74[2]; **yān nu**, *i.e.* **yāt nu**, as long soever as, 79[13]. [in V. often **nū́**: cf. *νύ*, *νῦν*, Lat. *nun-c*, Ger. *nu*, *nun*, AS. *nu*, *nū*, Eng. *now*: see also **náva**, **nū́tana**, **nūnám**.]

√ **nud** (**nudáti**, **-te**; **nunóda**, **nunudé**; **ánutta** [881]; **notsyáti**, **-te**; **nuttá**, **nunná**; **-núdya**). push; thrust.
+parā, thrust away; move from its place.
+pra, push forward; set in motion.
+vi, drive asunder *or* away; turn away, *esp.* from cares, *like the Eng.* di-vert; amuse. [for mg, cf. also *dis-port* and *s-port*.]

nuda, *a.* dispelling, *in cpds.* [√nud.]

nū́tana, *a.* of now; recent; young. [nú, 1245e.]

nūnám, *adv.* now. [nú, 1109.]

nṛ́ [370, 371[5, 9, 10]], *m.* man; hero; *used also* of gods: of the Maruts, 74[4], 77[18]. [cf. *ἀνήρ*, stem *ἀνερ*, 'man'; Old Lat. *nero*, stem *nerōn*, 'manly, strong'; Lat. *Nero*.]

nṛ-cákṣas, *a.* men-beholding. [1296[3].]

√ **nṛt** (**nṛ́tyati**, **-te**; **nanárta**; **ánartīt**; **nartiṣyáti**; **nṛttá**; **nártitum**; **nartitvā́**). dance.

nṛtí, *f.* dance. [√nṛt, 1155.1.]

nṛ-pa, *m.* protector of men, *i.e.* prince, king.

nṛ-páti, *m.* lord of men, *i.e.* prince, king. [acct, 1267a.]

nṛmṇá, *n.* virtus, manliness, courage, strength. [fr. nṛ (1224c), as *virtus* fr. *vir*.]

nṛ-çaṅsa, *a.* man-cursing; malicious.

netavya, *grdv.* to be carried. [√nī.]

netra, *n.* eye. ['leader,' √nī, 1185a: for mg, cf. nayana.]

néd, *adv.* lest, in order that not, *w. accented verb* (595d) *in the subjunctive* (581c), 84[17]. [ná + íd, 1111a[2].]

nedya, *grdv.* to be blamed. [√nid, 963d.]

nemí, *f.* felly, rim. [nam, 1155.]

nāirukta, *a.* pertaining to the Nirukta; *as m.* an etymologist. [nírukta, 1208f.]

nāiṣadha, *a.* pertaining to Nishadha; *as m.* prince of the Nishadhans, *i.e.* Nala. [niṣadha, 1208f.]

nó, *adv.* and not, 21[14]; no ced, and if not, *see* ced. [ná + u.]

nāu, *see* 491.

nāú [361a], *f.* boat; ship. [cf. *ναῦς*, Lat. *nāvis*, 'ship'; perhaps AS. *naca*, 'skiff': perhaps 'the swimmer,' √snū, cf. √snā.]

nyag-ródha, *m.* Ficus indica, banyan tree. ['downwards-growing': nyañc (1249a) + rodha.]

nyàñc [409b], *a.* directed downwards. [ni + añc, 407.]

nyāyá, *m.* —**1.** (that to which a thing goes back, *i.e.*) rule, norm; —**2.** (that in which a thing goes, *i.e.*) way; —**3.** *esp.* the right way, propriety. [√i + ni, 1148.2.]

nyāyya, *a.* regular, normal, right; **-am**, *adv.* rightly; properly. [nyāyá, 1211.]

nyāsa, *m.* a putting down, commitment. [√2 as + ni, 'throw down.']

---

1 pá, *vbl.* drinking, *in cpds.* [√1 pā, 333.]

2 pá, *vbl.* keeping, keeper, *in cpds.* [√2 pā, 333.]

pakṣá, *m.* —**1.** wing, 93[2]; —**2.** side, of a door *or* of the hair of the head; —**3.** half, *esp.* of a lunar month, 27[1], 57[19], *cf.* kṛṣṇa-, çukla-; —**4.** side, *i.e.* party, 37[18].

pakṣa-bala, *n.* strength of wing.

pakṣín, *a.* winged, 92[19]; *as m.* bird, 2[23]. [pakṣa.]

pakṣimṛgatā, *f.* condition of bird or of beast. [fr. pakṣin + mṛga: 1237, 1252.]

pakṣi-çāvaka, *m.* young of a bird; birdling. [pakṣin.]

páñka, *n.* mud, mire.

paṅktí, *f.* set *or* series *or* row of five; row *in general*. [páñca, 1157. 4.]

paṅkti-krama, *m.* order of a row; -eṇa, in a row, 39[14].

√ **pac** (pácati, -te; papáca, pecé [794e]; ápākṣīt; pakṣyáti, -te; páktum; paktvā́). cook, by baking *or* boiling *or* roasting; ripen. [cf. πέσσω, 'cook'; πέπ-ων, 'ripe'; Lat. *coquo*, 'cook'; borrowed AS. noun *cōc*, Eng. *cook*.]

+**vi**, cook thoroughly; *pass.* be brought to maturity; ripen (of an action), *i.e.* come to its consequences *or* issue.

páñca [483[3]], *num.* five. [cf. πέντε, Aeolic πέμπε, Lat. *quinque*, Goth. *fimf*, AS. *fīf*, Eng. *five*.]

pañca-tantra, *n.* Panchatantra, name of a collection of fables. ['having five divisions *or* books.']

pañca-tapas, *a.* having five fires, of an ascetic who sits between four fires, one at each cardinal point, and with the burning sun above.

pañcatva, *n.* fiveness; *esp.* dissolution of the body into the five elements (earth, water, fire, air, ether, *see* bhūta *and* 66[5]N.), *i.e.* death; *w.* gam, die. [pañca, 1239.]

páñca-pada, *f.* -ī, *a.* having (taken) five steps. [acct, 1300.]

pañcamá, *f.* -ī, *a.* fifth. [pañca, 487[6].]

páñca-yāma, *a.* having five courses. [acct, 1300.]

pañca-çīrṣa, *a.* five-headed. [çīrṣan, 1315a.]

√ **paṭ** (pāṭáyati, etc.). split, slit.

+**ud**, open out.

paṭa, *m.* woven stuff; cloth; garment.

paṭala, *n.* veil; cover. [cf. paṭa.]

paṭu, *a.* —1. sharp; *and so* —2. *fig.* (*nearly like Eng.* sharp), clever.

√ **paṭh** (páṭhati; papā́ṭha; paṭhitá; paṭhitvā́; pāṭháyati). read aloud, 54[23], 55[9]; recite, 17[11]; repeat to one's self, study, 22[11]; *caus.* teach to talk, 19[15].

√ **paṇ** (páṇati, -te; paṇitá). —1. bargain; buy; —2. bet, wage, stake, play. [prob. for *paln: cf. πέρνημι and πωλέω, 'sell'; Ger. *feil*, 'for sale, venal.']

+**ā**, *in* āpaṇa, 'market.'

+**vi**, sell.

paṇa, *m.* —1. bargain, stipulation, 45[14]; —2. wage, gage, prize; —3. a certain coin, 47[16]. [√paṇ.]

paṇí, *m.* —1. bargainer, who gives nought without return; chafferer, haggler, *and so* —2. niggard; *esp.* one who is stingy towards the gods, an impious person; —3. a malicious demon. [√paṇ.]

paṇḍitá, *a.* learned; *as m.* learned man, *Anglo-Indian* pandit.

paṇḍita-sabhā, *f.* assembly of pandits.

páṇya, *grdv.* to be bargained for *or* bartered; *as n.* article of trade. [√paṇ, 963.]

√ **pat** (pátati, -te; papā́ta, petús [794e]; ápaptat; patiṣyáti; patitá; pátitum; patitvā́; -pátya; pātáyati, -te). —1. fly; move swiftly through the air; —2. descend, let one's self down; cast one's self at, 26[8]; —3. fall down, tumble down, 34[8], 40[2, 5]; fall (morally), fall from one's caste; fall down (dead); —4. fall upon, be directed to, 13[6]; —5. fall *or* get into, 22[8, 9]; —*caus.* cause to fly; hurl (a curse), 49[11]. [cf. πέτομαι, 'fly'; πί-πτω, 'fall'; Lat. *peto*, 'fall upon, make for, seek': see also pattra.]

+**anu**, fly after, pursue.

+**ud**, fly up.

+**sam-ud**, fly *or* spring up together, 3[6], 8[14].

+**ni**, fly down; light, 3[8]; tumble into, 36[13]; *caus.* cause to fall; kill, 32[11], 33[17].

+**saṁ-ni**, fall together, 99[20]; come together; *caus.* bring together *or* convene, 9[19].

+**parā**, fly off, 93[1].

pátatra, *n.* wing. [√pat, 1185d.]

patatrín, *a.* winged; *as m.* bird. [patatra.]

pátana, *n.* fall. [√pat.]

páti [343b], *m.* —1. master, possessor; lord; ruler, 4[2]; —2. *then* (*like Eng.* lord), husband, 9[7], 89[5], 86[19], 64[13]. [cf. πόσις, 'husband'; Lat. *impos*, stem *im-pot*, 'not master of'; Goth. *faþs* in *bruþ-faþ-s*, 'bridegroom.']

pati-ghnī, *a. f.* husband-slaying. [formally a fem. to pati-han, 402.]

patitvá, *n.* condition of spouse; wedlock. [pati.]

pati-loká, *m.* husband's place, abode of the husband in the future life.

pati-sthāna, *n.* husband's place.

patisthānīya, *a.* belonging to *or* in the husband's place; *as m.* husband's representative. [patisthāna, 1215.]

páttra, *n.* —1. feather; wing; —2. (plumage of a tree, *i.e.*) leaf —*for mg, cf.* parṇa; —3. a leaf for writing on; a written leaf, 54[19]. [√pat: cf. πτερόν, 'wing'; Lat. *penna* and Old Lat. *pesna* (for **petna*), 'wing'; Ger. *Fed-er*, Eng. *feath-er*.]

pattra-çāka, *n.* leaf-vegetable, a vegetable consisting chiefly of leaves.

pátnī, *f.* —1. mistress, lady; —2. *then* (*like Eng.* lady), wife. [fem. to páti, just as πότνια, 'lady,' is to πόσις.]

patsutaḥ-çí [352], *a.* lying at the feet.

patsutás, *adv.* at the feet. [fr. patsú, loc. pl. of pád, 1098b.]

path [433], *same as* panthan.

patha, *for* path *in cpds* [1315c].

pathí [433], *same as* panthan.

pathi-rákṣi, *a.* guarding the paths. [panthan, 1249a: acct, 1276.]

pathya, *a.* (pertaining to the way, course, *or* progress of a thing, *and so*) suitable, wholesome; pathyà, *f.* pathway. [path, 1212d 1.]

√ **pad** (pádyate; papáda, pedé [794e]; ápatta [882]; patsyáte, -ti; panná [957d]; páttum; -pádya; pādáyati). —1. go, step, tread, *only w. prepositions and in derivatives;* —2. fall, sink down (from fatigue), perish. [connection between 1 and 2 not clear: uncompounded verb very rare: see under pád and padá.]

+**ā**, come unto; get into (a condition); *esp.* get in trouble.

+**vy-ā**, fall away, perish; *caus.* destroy; kill.

+**ud**, go forth *or* out of; come into existence; be produced; **utpannam annam**, food (not cooked for the occasion, but) already on hand, 104[1]; **utpanne kārye**, when the emergency has arisen, 38[14]; —*caus.* engender, 23[8]; produce; get, 42[17].

+**praty-ud**, *in ppl.* pratyutpanna, ready *or* on hand to meet an emergency.

+**upa**, fall upon; happen, take place, 100[10]; come to, get at, reach; **upapanna**, (having gotten at [952[2]], *i.e.*) in possession of, endowed with, 1[4], 2[3].

+**prati**, —1. step to; enter upon, 66[18]; —2. get into (a condition), 49[15]; get at, acquire, attain, 98[10]; get back again, 60[17]; —3. go to meet, *and so* (*like the Lat.* ac-cēdere), accede, yield; say yes to; consent, 48[12].

+**vi**, fall asunder, 93[9]; come to nought, get into trouble.

+**sam**, —1. turn out well, succeed, prosper; —2. become, 45[12], 47[18]; —3. fall together, be united with; **sampanna**, endowed with, 2[10].

pád [391], *m.* foot. [√pad: cf. πόδ-α, Lat. *pĕd-em*, Eng. *foot*.]

padá, *n.* —1. step, 17[21], 99[23]; —2. footstep; —3. foot, 86[6]; —4. standing-place, stead, place; home, 56[4]; station, position, 41[1]. [√pad: cf. πέδον, 'ground'; Lat. *op-pedum, op-pidum*, 'town, (on *or* over the field)'; *peda*, 'footprint'; AS. *fæt*, 'step, going, journey,' whence *fetian*, 'go for,' Eng. *fetch*.]

padma, *m. n.* lotus, Nelumbium speciosum (not the plant, but the flower, which closes at evening).

padma-garbha, *a.* containing lotuses; Lotus-filled, name of a lake. [see garbha 2.]

padma-rāga, *a.* having the color of a lotus; *as m.* ruby. [1296.]

pánthan [433], *m.* road, path, way. [cf. πάτος, 'path'; Lat. *pont-em*, 'path, bridge': Eng. *path* and Ger. *Pfad*, if they belong here at all, must be regarded as very early borrowings, fr. the Greek πάτος, or poss. from the Scythian.]

pánthā [433[5]], *same as* panthan.

páyas, *n.* milk. [√pī.]

payo-mukha, *a.* having milk on the face *or* surface. [payas, 1303.]

pára [525[4]], *a.* —1. far, distant, more distant, further off, 86[4]; —2. following, later, future; —3. being beyond, surpassing, summus; chief, 68[7]; best, 36[10]; utmost, 1[13]; greatest, 44[17]; highest, 103[11]; *at end of cpds* [1302b], having ·· as chief thing, given over to ··, devoted to ··; —4. *a. and subst.* other, 64[13]; eka ·· para, the one ·· the other, 53[19]; another, 30[22]; strange, hostile; stranger, 24[6]; foe, 29[10], 37[19]. [√2 pṛ, 'bring across'; cf. *πέρα*, 'beyond'; Lat. *peren-die*, 'the day after,' *i.e.* 'day after to-morrow'; Eng. *far* and *fore.*]

para-dāra, *m. pl.* another's wife.

para-dravya, *n. pl.* another's property.

para-pakṣa, *m.* party of the foe.

para-patnī, *f.* wife of a stranger.

param, *adv.* beyond; *w. abl.* [1128], after, 60[20]. [pára, 1111c.]

paramá [525[3]], *a.* —1. farthest, extreme, last; of heaven, highest, 83[13]; *so* 85[3]; —2. chiefest, 29[1]; supreme; most excellent, 15[17]; *at end of cpds* [1302b], having ·· as supreme object, devoted to ··; —3. *advly in cpds, before an adj.* [1279], highly, exceedingly. [pára, 474.]

parama-çobhana, *a.* exceedingly beautiful.

paramāñganā, *f.* most excellent woman. [añganā.]

parameçvara, *m.* supreme lord. [īçvara.]

parame-ṣṭhín, *a.* standing in the highest place; supreme, as epithet of Prajāpati. [parame (1250c) + sthin, 186.]

para-loka, *m.* the other *or* future world.

parás, *adv.* far; in the distance; beyond; *w. advly used instr.* [1127] enā́, beyond here, *i.e.* beyond, RV. x. 125. 8. [see pára.]

parástāt, *adv.* beyond; afterwards, at the end. [parás, 1100b.]

paras-para, one another; parasparam *and* parasparatas, *adv.* with one another; mutually. [an agglomeration (1314c) of paras (nom. s. m. of para) and para: the syntactical forms sometimes correspond to the logical relation of the two parts—so, *e.g.*, in parasparaṁ nindanti, 'they scold, the one the other'—but have come to be stereotyped and used often where the logical relation would require other case-forms: cf. anyonya.]

parasparādin, *a.* devouring one another. [ādin.]

párā, *adv.* to a distance, away, forth. [cf. *παρά*, w. gen., 'away from, from beside'; Lat. *per-* in *per-ire* and Ger. *ver-* in *ver-gehen*, 'pass away, perish'; Eng. *for-* in *for-bear*, 'hold off from.']

parākrama, *m. s. and pl.* bold advance; courage; strength. [√kram + parā.]

parāñ-mukha, *a.* having the face averted; turning the back upon, avoiding. [parāñc, 1249a, 217, 161.]

párāñc [409a], *f.* párācī, *a.* directed away; averted; turning the back. [parā + añc, 407.]

parārtha, *m.* the sake of others; -am, -e, *adv.* for others. [artha, 1302c 4.]

parāvát, *f.* the distance. [parā, 383d 1, 1245f.]

pári, *adv.* around; *prep. w. abl.:* from around, 87[8]; from, 75[15]. [cf. *περί*, 'around.']

parigha, *m.* iron bar for locking a gate. [√han + pari, 1143c, 333: for mg, cf. Ger. *Schlag*, 'coach-door,' and *schlagen*, 'strike': force of prep. unclear.]

parighopama, *a.* like iron bars. [upamā, 334[2].]

pari-jana, *m.* the surrounding folk, *περίπολοι*; retinue. [1289a.]

pari-jāta, *a.* completely grown. [1289a.]

pariṇeya, *grdv.* to be led around. [√nī + pari.]

parityāga, *m.* relinquishment. [√tyaj + pari.]

paridevita, *n.* lament. [√2 dīv, 'lament,' + pari, 1176a.]

paridhí, *m.* (a put-around, *i.e.*) enclosure, fence, protection, 86[10]; *in the language of the sacrifice*, the three green sticks laid about the altar fire and supposed to hold it together, 105[13, 8]. [√1 dhā, 'put,' + pari, 1155. 2e.]

paripanthín, *a.* besetting the path; *as m.* waylayer. [pari + panthan, 1310a and c end.]

paribhú [352], *a.* being around, encompassing. [√bhū + pari, 323.]

pari-vatsará, *m.* a full year. [1289.]

parivartin, *a.* turning round, circling, constantly returning into itself. [√vṛt + pari.]

parivāra, *m.* that which surrounds, *i.e.* retinue. [√1 vṛ, 'cover,' + pari.]

pariçrít, *f.* (encloser, *i.e.*) one of the little stones by which the sacrificial altar is surrounded. [√çri + pari, 'enclose': 383b.]

parisaṁkhyā, *f.* complete tale *or* enumeration; sum. [√khyā + pari-sam.]

paruṣá, *a.* knotty, rough, harsh. [parus, 1209b.]

párus, *n.* knot; joint, of a plant *or* of the body. [perhaps 'a fullness,' √1 pṛ, 'fill': cf. párvan.]

paróksa, *a.* beyond the eye, out of sight, invisible; -e, *adv.* [1116], behind one's back. [for paro 'kṣa, *i.e.* parás + akṣá, 'eye': 1310a.]

parokṣārtha, *m.* invisible thing, the invisible. [artha.]

parkaṭī, *f.* waved-leaved fig-tree, Ficus infectoria.

parṇá, *n.* —1. wing; plume, feather; —2. leaf — *for mg, cf.* pattra. [√*spṛ (1177a), see under √sphur: cf. Lithuanian *spárna*, 'wing'; Ger. *Farn*, Eng. *fern*, so called (like πτερίς, 'fern,' — cf. πτερόν, 'feather,') from its feathery fronds.]

paryālocana, *n.* deliberation; -ā, *f.* plan, consilium. [√loc + pary-ā, 1150. 2a[2].]

párvata, —1. *a.* consisting of knots *or* ragged masses, *used* of a mountain, giri; *as m.* —2. mountain, 27[6], 92[19]; hill; —3. cloud-mountain, 70[2]; —4. rock *or* bowlder, 86[11]; —5. Parvata, name of a Rishi, companion of Nārada (*q.v.*), 5[9]. [fr. párvan, cf. 1245c: cf. Παρϝασία (*παρϝατια), sc. πόλις, i.e. 'Hil-ton.']

parvata-kandara, *n.* mountain-cave.

parvata-çikhara, *m. n.* hill-top.

parvatopatyakā, *f.* mountain-lowland, lowland by a mountain range. [upatyakā.]

párvan, *n.* knot, joint. ['fullness,' √1 pṛ, 'fill,' 1169. 1a: cf. párus.]

párçu, *f.* rib; sickle.

√ **palāy** (pálāyate; palāyáṁ cakre; ápalāyiṣṭa; palāyiṣyáti, -te; pálāyita; palāyitum; palāyya). flee; depart, cease, 40[19]. [quasi-root fr. √i, 'go,' + parā, 'away,' see 1087c and c[2]: quite different is √pālaya, 'protect.']

palāyana, *n.* flight. [√palāy.]

pávana, *n.* instrument for purifying; winnowing-fan. [√pū, 1150.]

√ **1 paç**, *orig.* spaç (páçyati, -te; *in Veda:* paspaçé; áspaṣṭa [834c]; spaṣṭá; *later:* dadárça, etc.). —1. see; —2. perceive; behold; —3. look; —4. look on, 39[7]; gaze, 13[7]; —5. (see, *i.e.*) experience, 20[16], 35[1]; —6. look upon, 21[23], 40[15]; consider as; —7. see with the spiritual eye (as seers and poets), 94[9]. [for the initial s, see the perfect and vi-spaṣṭa: cf. σκέπ-τ-ομαι, 'look about'; Lat. *specio*, 'behold'; Ger. *spähen*, 'spy,' Old High Ger. *spehōn*, whence, through Old French *espier*, the Eng. *espy*, and shortened *spy*.]

+ anu, look along *or* spy out (*e.g.* a path for some one, *i.e.*), disclose *or* show, 83[7].

+ vi, see in places apart, distinguish, see clearly; víspaṣṭa, clear.

√ **2 paç**, fasten, bind, *in derivs, see* paçú, pāça. [cf. πάσσαλος, *πακ-jαλος, 'peg'; Lat. *pac-iscor*, 'bind myself, agree'; *pax*, 'agreement, peace'; *pang-ere*, 'make fast,' *pac-tum*, 'agreed upon'; Goth. *fah-an*, AS. *fōn*, **fōh-an*, 'fasten on, take hold of'; Eng. verb *fang*, 'seize,' noun *fang*, 'seizing-tooth'; connection of *fing-er* ('grasper, holder'?), doubtful: cf. also Goth. *fagrs*, 'fitting,' AS. *fægr*, Eng. *fair*; AS. *ge-fēgan*, Eng. *fay*, Ger. *fügen*, 'fit together,' trans., and Eng. *fadge*, 'fit together *or* agree,' intrans.]

paçú, *m.* cattle, 90[2] — a single head *or* a herd; domestic animal (*opp. to* mṛga, 'wild beast'), 67[2]; *esp.* beast for sacrifice, 101[6]. [prop. 'tethered (beasts),' √2 paç, 'fasten': cf. Lat. *pec-u*, Ger. *Vieh*, 'cattle,' AS. *feoh*, 'cattle, property,' Eng. *fee*, orig. 'property,' then 'payment.']

paçu-ghna, *a.* slaying cattle; *as m.* cattle-slayer.

paçu-tṛ́p, *a.* cattle-stealing. [vbl of √2 tṛp.]

paçu-bandhá, *m.* animal sacrifice. ['binding of beast' to sacrificial post.]

paçumánt, *a.* rich in cattle. [paçu, 1235 and b.]

paçu-roman, *n.* a hair of an animal.

paçu-vadha, *m.* slaughter of animals.

paçcá, *a.* hinder; later; west; paçcā́t, *as adv.* [1114c]: —1. behind; after, 39^{23}; —2. later, afterwards, 29^{17}, 38^{4}; thereupon, 36^{13}, 39^{17}, 40^{12}; paçcā́t, *as prep. w. gen.* [1130]: —3. after, 51^{2}; —4. to the west of, 98^{17}, 100^{17}, 105^{10}. [paçcá is an inorganic transfer-stem (1209a) fr. paçcā́, q.v.]

paçcā́, *adv.* behind; later; west. [adverbially accented instr. — instead of páçc-ā, i.e. pás-(a)c-ā, 1112e — fr. *pás-añc (407): with pas cf. Lat. *pos-terus*, 'later,' etc.]

paçcā́t, *see* paçca.

paçcima, *a.* last, 52^{16}; westerly. [paçca: cf. 1224a and b.]

√ 1 pā (píbati, -te [671, 749]; papāú, papé; ápāt; pāsyáti, -te; pītá [954c]; pā́tum; pītvā́; -pā́ya, -pī́ya). drink. [cf. *πέ-πω-κα*, 'have drunk'; *Πῖ-σα*, 'The Burn, The Fountain'; Lat. *pō-tus*, 'drunk'; *bibo*, **pi-b-o*, 'drink.']

√ 2 pā (pā́ti; ápāsīt; pā́tum). protect; keep; *for so-called caus., see* pālaya. [cf. *πέ-πᾱ-μαι*, 'have kept, possess'; *πῶ-υ*, 'herd'; Lat. *pa-sc-o*, 'keep, pasture'; see go-pā́.]

+**pari**, protect around.

1 **pā́**, *vbl.* drinking, *in cpds.* [√1 pā.]

2 **pā́**, *vbl.* keeping, keeper, *in cpds.* [√2 pā.]

pāṅsú, *m. pl.* dust.

pā́ka, *a.* —1. of a calf, young; —2. simple. [lit. 'sucking,' √1 pā, 'drink.']

pāka-dūrvā́, *f.* young millet-grass. [pā́ka + dū́rvā: acct, 1280^{2}.]

pāṭala, *a.* pale red; *as m.* Bignonia suaveolens.

pāṭali, *f.* Bignonia suaveolens *or* trumpet-flower. [cf. pāṭala.]

pāṭali-putra, *n.* Pātaliputra, capital of Magadha, at the old confluence of the Sone (çoṇa) and Ganges, the *Παλίβοθρα* of Ptolemy, 17^{9} N.

pāṭavá, *n.* sharpness; cleverness. [paṭu, q.v.: 1208c.]

pāṇí, *m.* hand. [prob. for *palni: cf. *παλάμη*, Lat. *palma*, AS. *folm*, 'palm, hand': radically akin is AS. *fēl-an*, Eng. *feel.*]

pāṇi-grāha, *m.* hand-grasper, *i.e.* (*see* 89^{5} N.) husband.

pāṇḍava, *m.* descendant of Pāndu. [pāṇḍu, 1208c.]

pāṇḍitya, *n.* learning, erudition. [paṇḍitá.]

pāṇḍú, *a.* whitish, pale; *as m.* Pāndu, name of a prince of the Lunar Race.

pāṇḍu-nandana, *m.* son of Pāndu.

pāṇḍu-varṇa, *a.* pale-colored.

pāta, *m.* fall. [√pat.]

pātaka, *a.* causing one to fall (from caste); *as n.* crime. [fr. caus. of √pat.]

pā́tra, *n.* —1. instrument of drinking, cup; vessel; —2. *in general,* utensil (*cf.* bhāṇḍa), 102^{11}; —3. *fig., as in Eng.* (*cf.* sthāna 5), a fit vessel *or* worthy person, 22^{5}; pātrī́ [364], *f.* sacrificial vessel. [√1 pā, 'drink,' 1185a; cf. $362b^{2}$.]

pā́da, *m.* —1. foot; leg, 26^{16}; —2. limb of a quadruped, *i.e.* quarter (*as, conversely, in Eng.,* quarter *means* 'fourth part of a quadruped, including a leg'); *then* quarter (of anything); —3. *esp.* quarter of a (four-versed) stanza, verse; *then* verse (even of a three-versed stanza), 60^{12}; —4. (foot of a heavenly body, *i.e.*) ray, beam — *see* 2 kara. [transition-stem (399) fr. pád, acc. pā́d-am, to which, as if it were pā́da-m, is formed the nom. pā́da-s, etc.]

pāda-pa, *m.* plant, *esp.* tree. [lit. 'drinking with its foot, *i.e.* root.']

pāda-rajas, *n.* foot-dust.

pādika, *a.* amounting to *or* lasting one fourth (of a time). [pāda.]

pādukā, *f.* shoe, slipper. [cf. pád, 'foot.']

pā́na, —1. *n.* the drinking (*esp.* of strong drink); —2. *perhaps as vbl adj.* drenching, *i.e.* tränkend. [√1 pā, 'drink,' 1150.]

pānīya, *grdv.* to be drunk, for drinking; *as n.* drink; water. [√1 pā, 'drink,' 965: prop. fr. pāna, 1215b.]

pānīya-varṣa, *m.* water-rain, downpour of water.

pāntha, *m.* wayfarer; viātor. [pánthan, 1208a² end.]

pāpá, *a.* bad; evil; *as m.* bad fellow, 46¹⁹; *as n.* trouble; harm, 26⁸; evil (deed), 27².

pāpa-karman, *a.* of evil deeds; *as m.* villain.

pāpa-çīla, *a.* having evil as one's nature, prone to evil.

pā́pīyāṅs, *a.* worse; very bad. [pāpa, 466.]

pāpmán, *m.* evil; sin, 93¹¹. [cf. pāpa.]

pārá, *n.* the further bank *or* bound. [√2 pṛ, 'bring across.']

pārameçvara, *a.* of the supreme lord (Çiva). [parameçvara.]

pā́ruṣya, *n.* harshness, *esp.* of speech. [paruṣá.]

pā́rthiva, *a.* of *or* belonging to the earth; *as m.* king. [pṛthivī́, 1208d.]

pārthiva-sutā, *f.* king's daughter.

pārthivendra, *m.* most excellent of kings. [indra.]

pārçvá, *n.* —1. side; *and so* —2. *as in Eng.*, immediate neighborhood. [párçu, 'rib,' 1208c: so French *côté*, 'side *or* ribbed part,' Medieval Lat. *costatum*, fr. Lat. *costa*, 'rib.']

pāla, *m.* protector. [√2 pā, 'protect,' 1189.]

√ **pālaya** (pāláyati). be protector; protect; keep. [pāla, 1042f: acct, 1067: quite different is √palāy, 'go away.']
  + **pari**, protect around.

pāvaká, *a.* pure; clear; bright. [√pū, 1181b and a: cf. çvāpada.]

pāvana, *a.* purifying; freeing from sin. [√pū, 1150b.]

pā́ça, *m.* bond; snare; trap. [√2 paç, 'fasten.']

√ **pi**, *same as* pī.

piñga, *a.* reddish brown.

piñgalá, *a.* reddish brown. [piñga, 1227.]

piñjūla, *n.* tuft of stalks; grass.

píṇḍa, *m.* —1. lump; ball; lump (of earth), 98⁸; —2. *esp.* lump *or* cake of meal offered to the Manes; —3. mouthful, 65⁵; piṇḍī, *f.* meal-cake.

pitāmahá, *m.* father's father, grandfather; great father. [pitā (nom. s. of pitṛ) + maha, 1314c and d.]

pitṛ́ [373], *m.* —1. father; —2. *pl.* father and his brothers (*cf. French* parent, 'relative'), 61¹⁷; —3. *pl.* the fathers, spirits of the forefathers, the Manes, 67¹⁶, 83¹⁸, etc. [origin unknown, see 1182d: cf. *πατήρ*, Lat. *pater*, Eng. *father*.]

pitṛtas, *adv.* on the father's side. [pitṛ, 1098b.]

pitṛ-mitra, *n.* father's friend.

pitṛ-yajñá, *m.* sacrifice to the Manes. [yajñá.]

pitṛvya, *m.* father's brother, patruus. [pitṛ, 1228c: cf. *πάτρως*, Lat. *patruus*, AS. *fædera*, 'father's brother.']

pítrya, *a.* of one's father; of (our) fathers, 78¹⁸; of *or* belonging to *or* sacred to the Manes. [pitṛ́, 1212b: cf. *πάτριος*, Lat. *patrius*, 'of one's father.']

√ **pinv** (pínvati; pipínva; pinvitá). cause to swell *or* stream. [√pī or pi: 749, 749b, 716.]

pipāsā́, *f.* desire to drink, thirst. [fr. desid. (1026) of √1 pā, 'drink': 1149⁴.]

pipīlá, *m.* ant. [perhaps for *pipīḍa, 'pressed in *or* constricted in the middle,' √pīḍ.]

√ **piç** (piṅçáti, -te [758]; pipéça, pipiçé; piṣṭá). adorn. [cf. *ποικίλος*, AS. *fāh*, 'many-colored'; Lat. *pic-tor*, 'painter.']

piçáñga, *a.* reddish brown. [√piç.]

piçācá, *m.* one of a class of demons (*perhaps* personifications of the ignis fatuus); goblin.

píçuna, *a.* backbiting, slanderous. [cf. *πικρός*, 'bitter.']

√ **piṣ** (pináṣṭi; pipéṣa, pipiṣé; ápiṣat; pekṣyáti; piṣṭá; péṣṭum; piṣṭvā́; -píṣya). crush; grind, 47⁵; mill. [cf. Lat. *pinsere*, *pisere*, 'crush': of doubtful kinship is *πτίσσω*, 'pound, husk.']
  + **sam**, crush together *or* to pieces.

piṣṭá, *ppl.* milled; *as n.* meal. [√piṣ: for the mgs, cf. piṣ, piṣṭa, and *molere*, *mola*, with *mill*, *meal*.]

piṣṭa-paçu, *m.* effigy of a sacrificial beast made of meal.

√ **pī** *or* **pyā** (pyā́yate [761d 1]; pīpā́ya [786[8]], pipyúṣ; ápyāsīt; pītá, pīná). swell; overflow. [hence pí-van, πί-ων, 'fat.']

pīṭha, *n.* –1. seat; –2. pedestal (of an image of a god).

pīṭha-cakra, *n.* seat-wagon; wagon with a seat.

√ **pīḍ** (pīḍáyati [1041[2]]; pīḍayā́m āsa; pīḍitá; pī́ḍayitum; pīḍayitvā́; -pī́ḍya). press; oppress, pain. [for *pizd, *pisd, 198b[3]: cf. √piṣ.]

+ā, press out, 103[20].

pīḍā, *f.* pain, ache. [√pīḍ, 1149[3].]

pīná, *a.* thick, brawny. ['swollen,' ppl. of √pī, 957a.]

pī́vas, *n.* fat. [√pī: cf. πῖαρ, i.e. πῖ-Fαρ, 'fat.']

púṅs, *same as* púmāṅs.

puṭa, *m. n.* fold; cavity; nose (of a basket). [for *pl̥ta: cf. -πλασιος, *πλrjos, in δι-πλάσιος or δί-παλτος, Eng. *two-fold*.]

púṇya, *a.* prosperous; happy; lucky, faustus, auspicious, 12[13], 59[1,10]; right, good; *as n.* good work; *sing. collectively*, good works, 28[17]; merit (from good works). [perhaps fr. √puṣ.]

púṇya-gandha, *a.* of good *or* pleasant smell.

puṇya-pāpa, *n. pl.* good and bad deeds. [1253a.]

puṇya-çloka, *a.* of good fame; *as m.* Punyaçloka, epithet of Nala.

puttikā, *f.* white ant. ['the doll-like insect': for putrikā.]

putrá, *m.* –1. son; child, 98[20]; –2. whelp; –3. shortened form for Putraka as proper name.

putraka, *m.* –1. little son (as term of endearment), boy; –2. Putraka, *otherwise* Putra, name of the founder of Pātaliputra-pura, 45[2]; –**putrikā**, *f.* [1222d], daughter; doll (of wood or lac). [putra.]

putra-dāra, *n.* son and wife. [1253b.]

púnar, *adv.* –1. back; home; *w.* ā-gam, go back, 4[8], 41[18]; *so* ā‿i, 83[14]; *w.* vac, reply, 19[19]; –2. again, 8[3], 40[20]; anew; punaḥ punar, again and again, 2[17]; punar, *equiv. to* punaḥ punar, 4[13]; –3. *continuative*, again, further, 29[11]; moreover, 16[8], 57[21]; besides *or* in turn, 10[10]; kim punas tu, but what besides, how much more, a fortiori, 17[15]; longer, 84[8]; –4. but, 46[2,19]; on the other hand, 20[17]. [cf. the similarly connected notions of iteration and opposition shown by πάλιν, Eng. *again* and *against*, Ger. *wieder* and *wider*.]

punar-garbhavatī, *a. f.* again pregnant.

punar-janman, *n.* re-birth.

punaḥ-sará, *a.* coming back (as a ghost from the other world—*exactly like the French* revenant), *and so* ghostly, uncanny. [punar, 178.]

púmāṅs [394], *m.* man; a male, 59[7]; *opp. of* strī, *e.g.* 104[9]; pumāṅsaḥ putrās, male children, 98[20].

1 **púr**, *f.* fullness. [√1 pr̥, 'fill.']

2 **púr** [392], *f.* stronghold; castle; fortified town. [cf. πόλις, 'city.']

pura, *n.* stronghold; fortified town; city. [2 púr, 399.]

puraṁdhi, –1. *a.* courageous, high-spirited, exalted; –2. *as m.* *perhaps as name of a god*, Purandhi; –3. *as f.* exaltation.

purás, *adv.* in front, forward, before; at first, 54[18]; *compounded* [1078[6]] *esp. w.* kr̥ *and* dhā: *w.* kr̥, put in front, appoint; *w.* dhā, put in front *or* in charge, *esp.* of the priestly duties. [see pra: cf. πάρος, 'before.']

puras-kārya, *grdv.* to be appointed *or* commissioned, praeficiendus. [see puras + kr̥: also 963b and 171[8].]

purástāt, *adv.* –1. before; in the front, 85[18]; –2. previously, afore, 98[6], 101[11,13]; –3. before, *i.e.* (*see* prāñc) eastward; –4. *prep. w. gen.* [1130], before, in the presence of, 20[1]. [puras, 1100b.]

puraḥ-sará, *a.* going before; *as m.* forerunner; *at end of cpds* [1302c 2], having · · as forerunner, *i.e.* accompanied by · ·; · · -puraḥsaram, *adv.* with · · *or* after · ·.

purā́, *adv.* formerly, 46[2], 79[14]; once upon a time, 38[9], 48[20]; *prep. w. abl.* [1128], before, 95[17], 104[19]. [see prá.]

purāṇá, *a.* former, belonging to old times; *as n.* things of the past; tale of old times, λόγος *and* μῦθος. [purā, 1245d.]

púrīṣa, *n.* crumbling earth, *as opp. to* fluids; rubble; loose earth. ['fillings *or* heaps,' fr. √1 pṛ, in the sense 'fill, *i.e.* heap': 1197b.]

purú, *a.* much, many. [√1 pṛ, 'fill,' q.v.: cf. πολύ, AS. *fela*, 'much, many.']

purutrā́, *adv.* in many places. [puru, 1099.]

púruṣa, *m.* —1. man; —2. (*as in Eng.*, man, *i.e.*) servant; —3. the personal and life-giving principle in man and other beings, soul, spirit; *then* —4. *personified as* The Supreme Spirit, Soul of the Universe, 57[8].

puruṣa-kāra, *m.* deed of a man, human effort, *as opp. to* dāiva, 'fate.'

puruṣa-siṅha, *m.* man-lion, stout-hearted man.

purūcī́, *a.f.* many, abundant; long. [formally fem. to a stem *puru-áñc, 'directed *or* reaching in many ways, abundant': cf. 407.]

puro-gama, *a.* going before; *as m.* leader; *at end of cpds* [1302c 2], having ·· as leader, accompanied by ··. [puras.]

puro-gavá, *m.* fore-bull, *and so, generalized* (*see* gó 4), leader; purogavī́, *f.* leader. [puras.]

puró-hita, *ppl.* set before *or* in charge (*esp.* of priestly service); *as m.* priest, house-priest of a prince. [see puras with dhā.]

pulkasa, *m.* one of a despised mixed caste.

√ **puṣ** (púṣyati, -te; pupóṣa; ápuṣat; puṣṭá). —1. thrive; bloom; —2. *trans.* cause to thrive; develop; unfold, display, 78[4].

puṣka, bloom, *a word assumed as probable on account of* púṣpa, 'bloom,' púṣkara, 'lotus blossom,' *and* puṣkalá. [√puṣ, 1186[2].]

puṣkalá, *a.* abundant. [prob. 'blooming,' fr. *puṣka, 1227.]

puṣṭá, *ppl.* having thrived; strong; fat. [√puṣ, 955[2].]

puṣṭāñga, *a.* fat-limbed. [áñga.]

puṣṭi, *f.* thrifty growth; prosperity. [√puṣ.]

púṣpa, *n.* bloom; flower. [poss. for *puṣka, q.v.: cf. 1201[2] end.]

puṣpa-danta, *m.* Pushpadanta *or* Flower-tooth, name of an attendant of Çiva, *see* 53[3] N.

puṣpāmoda, *m.* fragrance of flowers. [āmoda.]

pustaka, *m. n.* manuscript; book.

√ **pū** (punā́ti, punīté; pávate; pupā́va; ápāvīt; pūtá; -pū́ya). —1. make clear *or* bright; purify; καθαίρειν; pūtá, pure; —2. *mid.* clear itself, flow clear. [cf. πῦ-ρ, Eng. *fire* (τὸ πῦρ καθαίρει): w. pūtá, cf. Lat. *pūtus*, 'clear,' *pūrus*, 'pure.']
 \+ **sam**, purify, clean.

pū́, *vbl.* purifying, *in cpds.*

pūga, *m.* betel-palm, Areca Catechu; *as n.* betel nut.

√ **pūj** (pūjáyati, -te; pūjayiṣyáti; pūjitá; -pū́jya). honor.
 \+ **abhi**, do honor to.

pūjanīya, *grdv.* to be honored. [√pūj, 965.]

pūjā, *f.* honor.

pūjya, *grdv.* to be honored. [√pūj, 963d.]

pūrṇá, *ppl.* filled; full. [√1 pṛ, 'fill,' 957b: cf. Goth. *fulls*, Eng. *full.*]

pūrṇá-māsa, *m.* full moon *and* the full-moon sacrifice.

pūrtá, *ppl.* filled; bestowed, fulfilled; *as n.* [1176a], fulfilment; reward; merit. [√1 pṛ, 'fill,' 242.]

pū́rva [525[4]], *a.* being before in place *or* time: —1. east (*cf.* prāñc); —2. prior; preceding, 86[13]; pūrva ·· uttara, former ·· latter, 21[8]; ancient, 57[6]; of old time, 69[3], 83[10]; first spoken, 60[2]; *w. past pass. ppl.* [1291]: dṛṣṭa-pūrva, seen before; pūrvam, *adv.* before; beforehand, 60[9]; previously, already, 7[21], 25[17]; in former times, 48[1]; long ago, 46[8]; first, 103[6]; pūrvam ·· uttaram, first ·· last, 104[12]; —3. *at end of cpds*, (having ·· as preceding thing, *i.e.*) accompanied by ··, *or simply* with ··, 8[21]. [connected w. puras and pra.]

pūrvaka, *f.* [1222d] -ikā, *a.* —1. preceding; —2. *used like* pūrva 3. [pūrva, 1222c and 1307.]

pūrva-janman, *n.* former birth, previous state of existence.

pūrvākṣara, *a.* with the preceding letter. [akṣara.]

pūrvyá, *a.* ancient. [pūrva, 1212c.]

pūṣán [426a], *m.* Pūshan, a Vedic divinity, keeper of flocks and herds, and bringer of prosperity. [√puṣ, 1160c.]

√ **1pṛ** (pṛṇáti; pū́ryate; pūrṇá [957b]; *pass.* pūryáte; pūráyati, -te; etc.). fill; bestow abundantly; sate; pū́ryate, becomes sated [*see* 761b]; *caus.* [1041²], fill; make a thing (*acc.*) full of (*gen.*), 102¹⁸. [for treatment of root-vowel, see 242: cf. -πί-πλη-μι, Lat. *plēre*, 'fill'; *po-pul-us*, 'folk'; Eng. *fol-k* (doubtful): see also pūrṇá and √prā.]

+**pra**, *intrans.* prapūryate, becomes sated.

+**sam**, *intrans.* sampūryate, becomes full; sampūrṇa, full.

√ **2pṛ** (píparti; pāráyati, -te; etc.). pass, *trans.*; bring across. [cf. περάω, 'pass over, cross'; πόρος, 'passage, *i.e.* ford, ferry, bridge'; Lat. *por-ta*, 'gate'; Eng. *fare*, 'get on'; *ferry*, *for-d*; Avestan peretu, 'bridge,' and Εὐ-φράτης, 'the well-bridged (stream)'; also Βόσ-πορος and *Ox-ford*.]

+**ati**, bring across.

√ **3pṛ** (pṛṇóti; pṛtá; priyate; pāráyati). be busy; *only w.* ā, *see* 773.

+**ā**, *in* ā́pṛta, busied.

+**vy-ā**, *in* vyāpriyate, is busied.

√ **pṛc** (pṛṇákti, pṛṅkté; papárca; áprākṣīt, ápṛkta [882]; pṛktá; pṛcyáte). fill; mix; put in connection with. [perhaps connected w. √1pṛ, 'fill.']

+**upa**, put one's self close to, be near.

pṛ́t, *f.* fight, battle.

pṛ́tanā, *f.* battle. [cf. pṛ́t.]

√ **pṛtanāya** (pṛtanāyáti). fight; *present ppl.* fighting; *as subst.* enemy. [pṛtanā, 1060.]

√ **pṛtanya** (pṛtanyáti). fight; attack; *present ppl.* fighting; *as subst.* enemy. [pṛtanā, 1059d.]

√ **pṛth**, *collateral form of* prath, *in derivs.*

pṛthá, *m.* the flat of the hand, πλατεῖα. [√prath, 241.]

pṛ́thak, *adv.* separately, 105¹⁶; severally, 65⁴; for one's self, 64⁸. [perhaps 'directed widely (apart)': cf. pṛth and see 1111d.]

pṛthivī́, *f.* the earth *as* the wide and broad. [fem. to pṛthú, 344², and standing for pṛthvī, as the metre shows it is to be pronounced at 92¹⁰: for mg, cf. mah-í, s.v. máh.]

pṛthivī-kṣit, *a.* earth-ruling; *as m.* prince.

pṛthivī-pati, *m.* lord of the earth, king.

pṛthivī-pāla, *m.* keeper of the earth, king.

pṛthú, *f.* pṛthvī́, *a.* wide, broad. [√prath, 241: cf. πλατύς, 'wide': akin are Old Eng. *flaþe*, Ger. *Fladen*, 'broad, thin cake,' Old High Ger. acc. s. *fladon*, 'sacrificial cake,' whence, through French *flan*, 'flat cake,' comes the Eng. *flawn*, 'flat custard *or* pie': √prath has no connection w. AS. *brād*, Eng. *broad*.]

pṛ́çni, *a.* speckled; dapple, *esp.* of kine; *as f.* Priçni, mother of the Maruts. [cf. περκνός, 'dark colored'; Old High Ger. *forhana*, whence Ger. *Forelle*, 'trout.']

pṛṣad-ājyá, *n.* speckled butter, ghee clotted with curds. [pṛ́ṣant.]

pṛ́ṣant, *a.* speckled. [450c.]

pṛṣṭhá, *n.* —1. back, of an animal; —2. the upper side, surface; —3. top, of a hill *or* palace. [cf. Ger. *First*, 'ridge of a house'; AS. *first-hrōf*, 'ridge-pole': observe that νῶτος has mgs 1, 2, and 3, that Lat. *tergum* has mgs 1 and 2, and that Eng. *ridge* has mgs 1 and 3.]

pṛṣṭhatás, *adv.* a tergo, from behind; with the back, with averted face, 30¹⁷. [1098c³.]

pṛṣṭha-māṅsa, *n.* back-flesh; *w.* khād, *in double sense*, bite the back-flesh *and* back-bite.

peya, *n.* a drinking. [√1pā, 'drink,' 1213c.]

pāiçāca, *f.* -ī, *a.* of the goblins. [piçācá, 1208f.]

pāiçunya, *n.* slander. [píçuna, 1208f.]

póṣa, *m.* thriving, development; welfare. [√puṣ.]

pāúṁsya, *n.* manliness; manly deed. [puṁs, 1211².]

pāuruṣá, *n.* manliness; manly deed. [púruṣa, 1208f.]

√ **pyā** (pyā́yate [761d1]; ápyāsīt [882]; pyātá). swell; overflow. [a collateral form of √pī, q.v.]

+ **ā**, become full of *or* rich in.

prá, *prep.* forward, onward, forth, fore. [cf. πρό, 'before'; Lat. *prŏ*, later *prō*, 'before'; Eng. *fore:* see also the following articles, and purás, purā́, and pū́rva.]

prakaraṇa, *n.* treatment; discussion; subject of discussion, what's being talked about. [√1kṛ, 'do, put,' + pra.]

prakarṣa, *m.* (preference, advantage, *i.e.*) superiority. [√kṛṣ, 'draw,' + pra: for mg, cf. Eng. *pre-ference;* also Ger. *Vor-zug*, 'preference, advantage,' with *vor-ziehen*, 'draw forward, prefer.']

prakāçá, *a.* shining out, clear; open; -am, *adv.* openly, aloud. [√kāç + pra.]

prakṛti, *f.* that which one pre-supposes (voraus-setzt), *i.e.* the original *or* natural form *or* condition; nature. [√1kṛ, 'do, set,' + pra.]

prakopa, *m.* a boiling with rage; anger. [√kup + pra.]

prage, *adv.* early in the morning.

pracṛtta-çikha, *a.* with loosened braids *or* flowing hair. [çikhā.]

prácetas, *a.* knowing, wise. [√cit + pra, cf. 1151. 2b.]

√ **prach** (pṛccháti, -te; papráccha [794c]; áprākṣīt; prakṣyáti; pṛṣṭá; prā́ṣṭum; pṛṣṭvā́; -pṛ́cchya). ask; ask after, inquire about; ask some one (*acc.*) about something (*acc.*), 61⁷. [true root-form praç (see 220, 241, and √vṛçc), orig. *pṛk: cf. θεο-πρόπ-os, 'asking the gods'; Lat. *prec-es*, 'prayers,' *proc-us*, 'suitor'; Old High Ger. *frāh-ēn*, Ger. *frag-en*, 'ask': pṛccháti is a sk-formation (*pṛk-sketi), cf. Lat. *poscit*, **porc-scit*, Old High Ger. *forskōt*, **forh-skōt*, 'asks for,' Ger. *forscht*, 'inquires into.']

+ **pari**, ask.

+ **vi**, find out by inquiry.

+ **sam**, *mid.* consult with, converse *or* talk with.

prajā́, *f.* —1. procreation; —2. offspring, children, descendants; —3. creatures, 57¹; *esp.* —4. folk, subjects, of a prince, 16⁵. [√jan or jā + pra, 1147.]

prajā-kāmá, *m.* desire for offspring. [prajā́ + kā́ma, 1264: acct, 1267.]

prajā́-kāma, *a.* possessing prajākāmá, *i.e.* desirous of offspring, 93⁶, 1¹². [1296, 1295.]

prajā́-pati, *m.* —1. lord of creatures; —2. genius presiding over procreation, 89¹⁹; —3. lord of creatures, *i.e.* creator *or* Prajāpati, 60¹⁰, *see note.* [acct, 1267a.]

prajārthe, *adv.* for the sake of offspring. [artha, 1116, 1302c4.]

prajñā́, *f.* understanding. [√jñā + pra.]

prajñāta, *ppl.* well-known. [√jñā + pra.]

praṇaya, *m.* manifestation of one's affection. [√nī + pra: for ṇ, see 192a.]

praṇayana, *n.* —1. a fetching; —2. means for fetching, vessel. [do.]

praṇava, *m.* the sacred syllable om. [√nu + pra, q.v.]

praṇāma, *m.* bow, reverent salutation. [√nam + pra.]

práṇīta, *ppl.* see √nī + pra; -ās, *f. pl.* holy water.

praṇītā-praṇáyana, *n.* the fetching of the holy water. [1250e.]

pratarám, *adv.* further, longer. [pra, 473², 1111c: cf. πρότερον, 'before.']

práti, *prep.* in reversed direction, back to, back against, against, in return; —1. to, towards, *w. acc.*, 2¹⁹, 23¹⁴; —2. with reference to, in respect to, *w. acc.*, 4⁷·¹⁷, 13²⁰; —3. over against, *i.e.* like; —4. *in cpds* [1313a]: before; on, *w. idea of constant repetition;* at; (back-, *i.e.*) reflected; *see the following words.* [cf. προτί, 'to'; Lat. *por-* (*port) in *por-rigere*, 'reach out to.']

pratijñā, *f.* promise. [√jñā + prati.]

prati-dinam, *adv.* on (each) day, daily. [1313a, 1310a and d: cf. pratyaham.]

pratipatti, *f.* the acquiring. [√pad + prati.]

prati-bimba, *n.* reflected disk (of sun or moon in the water); image.

pratimā́, *f.* match; image; likeness. [√1 mā + prati, 'make (so as to be a match) against': for mg, cf. Eng. *counterfeit*, 'imitated,' fr. French *contre-fait*, whose elements go back to Lat. *contra* and *facere*.]

pratimā́na, *n.* that which is made *or* put over against, a match, equal. [√1 mā + prati.]

pratiṣṭhā́, *f.* stead; standing-place; *then* (*like Eng.* standing), position, *i.e.* celebrity. [√sthā + prati.]

pratiṣṭhā́na, *n.* stead; *then* (*like Ger.* Stadt, 'place, town'), The Town, name of a town on the Godāvarī, the Παίθανα of the Greeks. [√sthā + prati, 1150: cf. *Hamp-stead*.]

pratihastaka, *m.* proxy. ['person at one's hand,' prati + hasta, 1310a, 1222c.]

pratīkāra, *m.* counter-action, remedy. [√1 kṛ, 'do, act,' + prati, 'against': 1087b.]

pratīcīna, *a.* backward; being behind; following, *i.e.* future. [pratyañc, 1223d.]

pratīta, *ppl.* *see* √i + prati.

pratīpá, *a.* (against the stream, *i.e.*) contrary; -ám, *adv.* contrarily, frowardly. [prati + ap, 1310a, 1315c, cf. samīpa: for mgs, cf. Eng. *contrary*.]

prátta, *see* 1087e.

pratyakṣa, *a.* before the eyes, plainly visible; -e, *adv.* before one's face. [prati + akṣa, 1310a.]

pratyakṣa-darçana, *n.* a seeing before one's eyes; the ability to see any one (*e.g.* a god) bodily, 15[13].

pratyag-dakṣiṇā, *adv.* (west-southerly, *i.e.*) southwesterly. [pratyañc, 1249a.]

pratyaṅ-mukha, *a.* having the face westward, turned to the west. [pratyañc, 1249a, 161: 1306.]

pratyáñc [408], *f.* [410] pratīcī́, *a.* —1. (directed back, *i.e.*) turned backwards; moving in reverse direction *or* away, 87[11]; —2. turned westward (*see* prāñc), westerly; —3. (being to-ward, *i.e.*) with the face towards, *w. acc.*, 71[18]. [prati + añc, 407: see añc.]

praty-abhivādana, *n.* return-salutation, Gegen-gruss. [1289b.]

praty-aham, *adv.* on (each) day, daily. [1313a, 1310a and d: 1315a: cf. pratidinam.]

pratyākhyāna, *n.* refusal. [√khyā + praty-ā.]

pratyutthāna, *n.* rising up to meet (a person), respectful reception. [√sthā + praty-ud, 233a.]

pratyutpanna-mati, *a.* having wits ready to meet an emergency; *as m.* Ready-wit, name of a fish. [√pad + praty-ud.]

pratyṛcam, *adv.* at *or* with each stanza. [prati + ṛc, 1313a, 1310a and d: 1315c.]

√ **prath** (práthate, -ti; paprathé; áprathiṣṭa; prathitá; pratháyati; ápaprathat). broaden, *intrans.*; *caus.* broaden, *trans.*; spread out, 78[11]. [see under pṛthu.]

+ **vi**, *caus.* spread out wide, 75[8].

prathamá, *a.* first; primal; -am, *adv.* at first. [lit. 'fore-most,' for *pra-tama, superl. of pra, 487[3], 473[2].]

prathama-jā́ [352], *a.* first-born. [1286.]

prada, *a.* giving; furnishing. [√1 dā + pra, 333.]

pra-dakṣiṇa, —1. *a.* moving to the right; —2. -ám, *adv.* to the right, so that the right side is towards an object (a sign of respect), 60[1], 99[1]; *w.* kṛ, put (an object) to the right; —3. *adj.* standing on the right, 62[19]. [perhaps the use as adv. (mg 2) is the primary one, lit. 'forward to the right.']

pradā́na, *n.* a giving. [√1 dā + pra.]

pradíç, *f.* intermediate region (between the cardinal points — *see* díç). [pra + díç, 'fore-point.']

pradeça, *m.* direction; *and so,* place. [√diç + pra.]

pradoṣa, *m.* evening, nightfall. ['fore-dark,' pra + doṣa.]

pradhána, *n.* prize of the contest; the contest therefor; battle. [√1 dhā + pra: cf. dhana.]

pradhāna, *n.* (that which is put forward) the important *or* chief thing; *at end of cpds* [1302], having · · as chief thing, devoted to · ·. [√1 dhā + pra.]

13*

prá-patha, *m.* (forth-path, *i.e.*) onward way, 85[18]; journey in the distance *or* distant journey, 86[2].

prabandha, *m.* uninterrupted connection; continued series. [√bandh + pra.]

prabhavá, *m.* origin; *at end of cpd* [1302], having · · as origin, originating with · · [√bhū + pra.]

prabhā́, *f.* splendor; radiant beauty. [√bhā + pra.]

prabhāta, *ppl.* begun to be light; *as n.* [1176a], day-break. [√bhā + pra.]

prabhāva, *m.* superior might, of gods, of ascetics, of asceticism. [√bhū + pra.]

prabhú, *a.* being before *or* superior to others; *as m.* ruler; master; lord; husband, 52[14]. [later form (354) for Vedic prabhū: √bhū + pra.]

prabhutva, *n.* lordship, power. [1239.]

prábhṛti, *f.* —1. *lit.* a carrying forward *or* on, *i.e.* continuance; *used esp. at end of cpds* [1296], having continuance from · ·, *i.e.* continuing from · ·; —2. *then in such cpds used in acc. s. n. adverbially* [1311], continuing from · ·, beginning with · ·, from · ·; —3. *then as an adv. uncompounded,* prabhṛti, *w. abl.*, from · · on; tataḥ prabhṛti, from then on. [√bhṛ + pra, 1157. 1d.]

pramada, *m.* pleasure. [√mad + pra.]

pramada-vana, *n.* pleasure-grove (of a prince).

pramadā-vana, *n.* pleasure-grove (of the wives of a prince). [a quasi feminine to the preceding.]

pramāṇa, *n.* measure, extent (57[23]), scale, standard; something by which to judge, 54[11]; norm, rule of action, 21[21]; authority, 12[10], 19[22]. [√1mā, 'measure,' + pra, 192a: hence, through the Persian *farmān,* the borrowed Eng. *firman,* 'an authority *or* decree,' esp. of the Sublime Porte.]

√ **pramāṇaya** (pramāṇayati). regard as an authority; take a person (*acc.*) as authority in a matter (*loc.*). [pramāṇa, 1058.]

pramāṇābhāva, *m.* lack of anything to judge by. [abhāva.]

pramāthin, *a.* stirring; agitating. [√math + pra, 1183[3].]

pramṛṣṭa-maṇi, *m.* polished *or* bright gem. [√mṛj + pra.]

pramṛṣṭamaṇi-kuṇḍala, *a.* possessing bright-gem ear-rings.

prayatna, *m.* effort, pains; -ena, -āt, *adv.* carefully. [√yat + pra, 1177a.]

prayā́ṇa, *n.* a going forth (from home), journey. [√yā + pra, 1150, 192e.]

prayotṛ́, *m.* remover. [√2yu, 'keep off,' + pra.]

pralaya, *m.* dissolution; *esp.* dissolution of the universe. [√lī + pra.]

pralāpá, *m.* unintelligible *or* childish *or* lamenting talk; chatter. [√lap + pra.]

pravaṇá, *a.* prone; sloping. [pra, 1170 (cf. 383d 1): cf. πρηνής, Doric πρᾶνός, Lat. *prōnus,* 'inclined forward.']

pravát, *f.* slope, of a mountain; height, 83[7]. [pra, 383d 1.]

prá-vayas, *a.* having (forward, *i.e.*) advanced age; aged. [1305[2].]

pravartaka, *a.* causing to roll onward (as a wheel), setting in motion, promoting; *as m.* promoter, prompter. [caus. of √vṛt + pra.]

pravāda, *m.* a saying *or* an on dit. [√vad + pra.]

pravibhāga, *m.* division. [√bhaj + pra-vi.]

pravīṇa, *a.* clever.

pravīṇatā, *f.* cleverness. [pravīṇa.]

pravṛtta, *ppl.* —1. having turned forward; directed forward (to a specific object), *esp.* of an act performed with a view to the attainment of some advantage, *i.e.* interested, *opp. of* nivṛtta, *q.v.*; —2. engaged in. [√vṛt + pra.]

pravṛtti, *f.* a moving forward *or* taking an active step, 20[15]; advance into *or* exposure of one's self to (danger, *loc.*), 20[12]. [√vṛt + pra.]

pravṛddha, *ppl.* grown up, great. [√vṛdh + pra.]

praveça, *m.* entrance. [√viç + pra.]

pravrājin, *a.* going forth *or* after, *in cpd* dvi-. [√vraj + pra, 1183[3]: for mg, cf. (γυνή) περίδρομος, 'lewd woman.']

praçís [392], *f.* command. [√çās + pra, 639, 225[1,2]: cf. āçís.]

praçraya, *m.* respectful demeanor. ['an inclining forward,' fr. √çri + pra.]

pra-savya, *a.* moving to the left; -am, *adv.* to the left — *cf.* pradakṣiṇam.

prasāda, *m.* grace; favor; prasādaṁ kṛ, do favor, be gracious. [√sad + pra, q.v.]

prásiti, *f.* continuation; extended path (of life, *for example*). [√sā + pra, 250.]

prasiddhi, *f.* success; celebrity; a being known; ato me çaçāñka iti prasiddhis, therefore I am known as "Ç.", 36[8]; *cf.* prasiddha. [√2 sidh, 'succeed,' + pra.]

prastará, *m.* —1. stramentum, straw; —2. rock, 33[10]. [√stṛ, 'strew,' + pra: for mg 1, cf. Eng. *straw* w. *strew:* connection of mg 2 unclear.]

prastāva, *m.* beginning, introduction. [√stu + pra, 1148. 2.]

prastuta-yajña, *a.* having one's sacrifice begun; *as m.* Prastutayajna, name of a Brahman. [√stu + pra.]

prastha, *m. n.* table-land on a mountain. ['that which stands forth from the surrounding country,' fr. √sthā (333) + pra.]

prá-svādas, *a.* (*lit.* having advanced agreeableness, *i.e.*) highly pleasing. [1305[2].]

prahara, *m.* a stroke (on a gong, announcing the lapse of a watch), *and so* a watch (of about three hours). [√1 hṛ + pra.]

prahartavya, *grdv.* to be struck; *impers.* one must strike. [do.]

prahṛṣṭa-manas, *a.* having a delighted heart. [√hṛṣ + pra.]

√ **prā** (prā́ti; paprāú; áprās [889]; prātá). fill. [Vedic collateral form of √1 pṛ, 'fill,' q.v.: cf. πλή-ρης, Lat. *plē-nus*, 'full.'] + ā, fill.

prā́k, *see* prāñc.

prā́kṛta, *a.* natural; usual; common; vulgar; *as n.* the vulgar (language), language of the vulgus, the Prākrit. [prakṛti, 1208d: for mg, cf. Ger. *deutsch*, Old High Ger. *diut-isk*, '(language) of the people (*diot*), *i.e.* German' (as contrasted with the Latin of the Church and with the neighboring Romance tongues); cf. also ἡ κοινή (sc. διάλεκτος), 'the Common (dialect),' as opp. to Doric, etc.]

prāg-grīva, *a.* having the neck directed eastward. [prāñc (1249a) + grīvā.]

prāg-dakṣiṇā, *adv.* east-southerly, south-easterly. [prāñc, 1249a.]

prāñgaṇa, *n.* fore-court, Vor-hof; courtyard. [pra + añgana, 1289a, 193.]

prāñ-mukha, *f.* -ī, *a.* having the face directed eastward. [prāñc, 1249a, 149, 161.]

prājñá, *a.* wise; *as m.* wise man. [prajñā, 1208e.]

prā́ñc [408], *f.* prā́cī, *a.* —1. directed forwards; *w. verb of motion*, onward, 86[9]; —2. east, eastern (since the Hindus, in naming the cardinal points, began with the east, as we do with the north, and conceived it as before them, as we do the north); prācī diç, the eastern quarter, 101[8]; —3. prāk, *acc. s. n. as adv.* before: (in place) before one's face, 26[8]; (in time) formerly, 20[20], 51[7]; (in order) before, *w. abl.* [1128], 59[7]. [pra + añc, 407.]

prāñjali, *a.* having an añjali (*q.v.*) before one, *i.e.* in a posture of reverent salutation. [pra + añjali, 1305.]

prāṇá, *m.* breath; vital breath, 60[16]; vital spirit, 63[21]; *then* (*like Eng.* breath), life; *esp. in pl.* prāṇās, life, 15[5], 21[18], 29[8]. [√an + pra, 192b.]

prāṇín, *a.* having life; *as m.* living being. [prāṇa, 1230.]

prātár, *adv.* —1. early in the morning; *then* —2. (*like the Ger.* morgen *and Eng.* morrow) on the next morning, on the morrow, to-morrow. [pra, 1109: cf. πρω-ί, Ger. *früh*, 'early.']

prādús, *adv.* forth to view; *w.* as [1078[6]], be visible, appear, reveal one's self.

prāntara, *n.* a long and lonely road. ['an advanced interval *or* long distance,' pra + antara, 1289.]

prāpaṇīya, *grdv.* to be brought to. [caus. of √āp + pra, 965, 192e.]

prāpta-kāla, *m.* arrived time, favorable moment. [√āp + pra.]

prāpta-yāuvana, *a.* possessing attained adolescence, having reached a marriageable age. [see 1308.]

prāptavya, *grdv.* to be obtained, about to be got. [√āp + pra, 964.]

prā́pti, *f.* a reaching, arriving at. [√āp + pra.]

prāyá, *m.* —1. a going forth *or* out; —2. that which sticks out *or* is prominent; the principal part of a thing; the most part; *at end of cpds* [1302], having · · for the most part, having · · for its predominant characteristic, like · ·, 22[16]. [√i + pra, 1148. 1a.]

prāyaças, *adv.* for the most part. [prāya, 1106.]

prāyas, *adv.* for the most part, almost, 50[22]. [prop. acc. s. n. (1111d) of a neuter noun *prāyas, 'that which is predominant' (see prāya), √i + pra, 1151. 1.]

prāví, *a.* attentive, heedful, zealous. [√av + pra, 1156[3], 355b end.]

prāçana, *n.* —1. the eating; —2. the giving of food, feeding. [in mg 1, fr. √2aç, 'eat,' + pra; in mg 2, fr. caus. of the same.]

prāçitṛ́, *m.* eater. [√2aç, 'eat,' + pra, 1182a.]

prāçitrá, *n.* the portion of ghee to be eaten by a Brahman at a sacrifice. ['that which belongs to the prāçitṛ,' 1208b.]

prāçitra-háraṇa, *n.* vessel for holding the prāçitra. ['prāçitra-holding,' 1271.]

prāsāda, *m.* lofty seat; building on high foundations, palace, 20[1]. [√sad + pra, perhaps in the sense 'sit forward *or* in a conspicuous place': see 1087b.]

priyá, *a.* —1a. dear, 79[16]; beloved of, *w. gen.* (296b), 84[18]; —1b. priyā, *f.* the beloved, the wife, 32[6], 33[10]; —2a. desired, pleasant; agreeable, 58[22]; priyaṁ kṛ, do a favor, 3[2]; —2b. *as n.* that which is desired, one's wish, 89[17]; —3. (*like Homeric* φίλος) to which one is attached *or* wonted, 76[8], 86[3]; own, 78[9]; wonted; —4a. loving, devoted to; —4b. *as m.* friend. [√prī, q.v., 1148.3: cf. πρᾷος, 'gentle'; Goth. *freis*, acc. s. m. *frijana*, AS. *frī*, Ger. *frei*, Eng. *free*: although the modern mg 'free' is common also to the Goth. and AS. words, yet the orig. mg must have been 'loving *or* loved, kindly treated, spared' (and so 'free'), as is shown by the Goth. abstract *frija-þva*, AS. *freōd*, 'love': for mg 1b, cf. AS. *freō*, 'woman': cf. also Old High Ger. *Frīa*, 'The Loving One,' in *frīā tag*, Eng. *Fri-day*, 'dies Veneris.']

priya-vādín, *a.* saying pleasant things.

priyāpriyá, *n.* comfort and discomfort. [apriya: 1253b.]

√ **prī** (prīṇā́ti, prīṇīté; prī́yate; piprā́ya, pipriyé; ápraīṣīt; prītá; prītvā́). —1a. prīṇā́ti, gladden, show favor to, propitiate; —1b. prīṇā́ti, have pleasure in; —1c. prīṇīté, be glad *or* content; —2. prī́yate, be glad *or* content; have pleasure in; love, be favorably inclined to; —3. prītá: glad, pleased, satisfied; loved, dear. [cf. Goth. *frijon*, 'love'; *frijonds*, AS. *freōnd*, 'loving, *i.e.* friend,' Eng. *friend*; also AS. *freo-þo*, 'a sparing *or* indulgence, favor, grace, peace,' Ger. *Friede*, 'peace'; Goth. *Friþa-reiks*, Eng. *Frede-rick*, 'grace-ruler, gracious prince': see also under priyá.]

prīti, *f.* —1. pleasure; prītyā, with pleasure, gladly; —2. friendship. [√prī.]

prīti-vacas, *n.* friendship-talk, friendly words.

preñkhá, *a.* rocking, pitching; *as m. n.* unsteady boat, skiff. [√iñkh + pra.]

préta, *ppl.* gone onward, *i.e.* departed, dead; *as m.* —1. dead man; —2. ghost. [√i + pra.]

prétya, *grd.* after dying, *i.e.* in the other world (*opp. to* iha). [√i + pra, 992.]

préṣṭha, *a.* very pleasant. [√prī, 470[4]: serves as superl. to priya.]

preṣya, *grdv.* to be sent; *as m.* servant. [√2iṣ, 'send,' + pra.]

prāiṣyá, *n.* servitude. [preṣya, 1208f.]

próṣṭha, *m.* bench *or* couch.

proṣṭhe-çayá, *a.* lying on a couch. [1250c, 1270.]

plavá, *a.* swimming; *as m.* swimmer, name of a kind of duck. [√plu: cf. πλόος, *πλοϝος, 'a sailing.']

√ **plu** (plávate, -ti; puplā́va, pupluvé; áploṣṭa; ploṣyáti, -te; plutá; -plútya, -plū́ya). float through water *or* air:

—1. swim; —2. bathe; —3. sail; —4. hover; fly; —5. fly off; hasten away; —6. spring; —pluta, floating, *and so* (*see* Whitney 78), protracted, of a vowel.

[cf. πλέω, *πλεϝω, 'float, sail'; Lat. *pluere*, 'rain': for mg of *pluere*, cf. the Eng. intrans. *float*, 'swim,' w. trans. *float*, 'cover with water,' and the intrans. *bathe* w. trans. *bathe*:

closely connected w. √plu is the extended form plud as seen in Lithuanian *plud-iti*, 'swim, float': w. this, cf. AS. *fleōt-an*, 'swim *or* float about,' Eng. verb *fleet*, 'float, sail, hasten,' Ger. *fliessen*, sometimes 'swim,' but usually 'flow'; further, AS. *fleōt*, 'raft, ship, fleet,' Eng. *fleet*, 'ships'; also AS. *flota*, 'ship,' Eng. *float*, 'a thing that swims on the surface of a fluid, *e.g.* a raft' (verb *float* is a denom. of this), Ger. *Floss*, 'raft'; finally Eng. *fleet*, 'streamlet *or* bay,' whence *The Fleet*, as name of a small affluent of the Thames at London and of a famous prison thereon, and *Fleet Street*, which crossed The Fleet.]

+ **ā**, bathe, *intrans*.

+ **sam-ā**, —1. bathe, *intrans*.; —2. bathe, *trans*.; inundate; suffuse, 10[19].

+ **ud**, spring up.

+ **upa**, hover unto.

+ **vi**, float asunder; drift in different directions; be dispersed; be lost; be ruined *or* dishonored.

√ **phal** (phálati; paphā́la; phalitá; phullá [958]). burst, split, *intrans*. [prob. for *spal, of which √sphaṭ (i.e. *sphalt), 'split, break,' is an extension: cf. Ger. *spalten*, Eng. *split*.]

+ **ud**, burst out *or* open; utphulla [958], expanded, wide open.

√ **phala** (phalati). bear fruit; fruit; phalitám, *impersonally*, it is fruited, fruit is borne (by a thing, *instr*.), 24[20]. [denom. of phála, 1054.]

phála, *n*. —1. fruit; —2. *then* (*like Eng*. fruit), the good *or* evil consequences of human deeds; result; reward *or* punishment. [perhaps 'the ripe and bursting fruit,' fr. √phal.]

phálavant, *a*. fruitful; yielding good results. [phála, 1233a.]

phulla, *a*. burst open, expanded, blooming. [see √phal and 958.]

phullotpala, *a*. having blooming lotuses; *as n*. Blooming-lotus, name of a lake. [utpala.]

phéna, *m*. foam.

√ **baṅh** *or* bah (bāḍhá [223[3]]; *caus*. baṅháyate). be thick, firm, strong; *caus*. make strong. [perhaps for *bhagh: see bahú and bāhú.]

baka, *m*. heron, Ardea nivea.

baka-mūrkha, *m*. heron-fool, fool of a heron. [1280b.]

baddha-maṇḍala, *a*. having constructed-circles, *i.e.* ranged in circles. [√bandh.]

√ **bandh** (badhnā́ti, badhnīté [730]; babándha, bedhé; bandhiṣyáti, bhantsyáti; baddhá; bándhitum, bánddhum, báddhum; baddhvā́; -bádhya). —1. bind; fasten; catch; *esp*. bind (a victim for the gods, *i.e.*), sacrifice; —baddha: bound; caught; fastened; —2. bind together, join; *and then* (*w. a specialization of mg like that seen in the Eng*. joiner), construct, *e.g.* a bridge; compose (verses, *cf. Lat*. serere). [for *bhandh: cf. πενθερός, 'connection (by marriage)'; πεῖσμα, *πενθμα, 'rope'; Lat. *of-fend-ix*, 'knot'; *fīd-es*, 'string'; *foed-us*, 'league'; Eng. *bind, band*: for mgs, cf. Eng. *connection* and *league* w. Lat. *con-nectere* and *ligāre*, 'bind together.']

+ **ni**, —1. bind; fasten; —2. (bind down together, put down connectedly, *i.e.*) put into written form, write down, 53[6].

+ **pra**, bind on; connect onward, form an advancing connection, form a continued series.

+ **sam**, bind together, con-nect; sambaddha, con-nected, co-herent (*w. the same fig. mg as in Eng*.).

bandhá, *m*. —1. a binding; *esp*. a binding to the sacrificial post (*see* bandh 1), sacrifice; —2. band, string. [√bandh: cf. Eng. *band*.]

bándhana, *a.* binding; *as n.* bond *or* bonds. [√bandh.]

bándhu, *m.* —1. connection *or* relationship; —2. (*concrete, as in Eng.*) a connection, relative; friend; one who belongs to (a certain caste, *for example*). [√bandh, 1178.]

barbara, *a.* stammering, balbutiens; *as m.* —1. *pl.* foreigners, οἱ βάρβαροι, name applied by Aryans to non-Aryan folks (*as* Welsh *and* Wälsch *by English and Germans to folks that speak a strange tongue*); —2. *sing.* a man of lowest origin; a wretched wight, wretch, 30^{19}. [cf. βάρβαρος, 'foreign, outlandish'; Lat. *balbus*, 'stammering,' whence Spanish *bobo*, 'blockhead,' Eng. *booby*.]

barha, *m. n.* tail-feather. [prop. 'pluckings,' √1 bṛh, 'pluck': cf. the no less arbitrary specialization of mg in Eng. *pluck*, 'that which is plucked out after killing a beast, its liver, lights, heart,' and, fig., 'courage.']

barhiṇa, *m.* peacock, 68^{2}. [transition-stem fr. barhin, 1223f, 1209c.]

barhin, *m.* (having tail-feathers, *i.e.* the tail-feathered bird κατ' ἐξοχήν,) the peacock. [barha.]

barhís, *n.* grass *or* straw of Kuça-grass, spread over the sacrificial ground to serve as a place for the oblations and as a seat for gods and offerers. [prop. 'that which is torn up, vulsum, pluckings,' √1 bṛh, 'tear, pluck': for mg, cf. Eng. *hay*, 'cuttings,' from *hew*, 'cut.']

bála, *n.* —1. might, power, strength, force; balāt, forcibly; —2. *then, as in Eng.*, force (for making war); forces, troops, 5^{4}. [for *vala: cf. Lat. *valēre*, 'be strong, well.']

bala-dā́ [352], *a.* strength-giving. [1269.]

bálavant, *a.* powerful. [1233a.]

balādhika, *a.* superior in strength. [adhika: 1265.]

balānvita, *a.* connected with power; suggestive of power. [anv-ita, √i.]

balí, *m.* —1. of-fering, tribute; —2. *esp.* portion of a daily meal *or* sacrifice offered as tribute to gods, semi-divine beings, men, animals, *esp.* birds, and even inanimate objects, 65^{2}. [perhaps fr. √bhṛ: if so, cf., for the mg, φόρος, 'tribute,' w. φέρω, 'bear, bring.']

balín, *a.* mighty, 1^{3}. [bála, 1230a.]

báliṣṭha, *a.* most mighty; very strong. [balin, 468^{2}.]

balonmatta, *a.* frenzied *or* crazed with power. [unmatta, √mad + ud.]

√ bah, *see* baṅh.

bahiṣ-kārya, *grdv.* to be put outside, to be banished. [bahis and kṛ, 'do, put,' 1078^{7}.]

bahiṣ-kṛta, *ppl.* put out, expelled. [bahis and kṛ, 'do, put,' 1078^{7}.]

bahiḥ-paridhí, *adv.* outside the enclosure (*see* paridhi). [1310a.]

bahís, *adv.* [1111d], outside; *as prep.* outside of, *w. abl.* [1128].

bahú, *a.* much, many; bahu man, consider as much, think much of, esteem. [√baṅh or bah: cf. παχύς, 'thick.']

bahudhā́, *adv.* many times. [bahu, 1104.]

bahumāna, *m.* esteem, respect. [√man + bahu.]

bahumāna-puraḥsaram, *adv.* with respect. [1302c 2, 1311.]

bahulá, *a.* —1. thick; —2. abundant; much. [in mg 1, perhaps directly fr. √bah, 1189, and in mg 2, fr. bahu, 1227.]

bahulāuṣadhika, *a.* having abundant herbs. [oṣadhi, 1307.]

√ bādh (bā́dhate; babādhé; ábādhiṣṭa; bādhiṣyáti, -te; bādhitá; bā́dhitum; -bā́dhya). press hard; distress; beset. [see √vadh: cf. Lat. *de-fend-ere*, 'press *or* ward off'; *of-fend-ere*, 'press hard upon, hurt.']

+**ni**, press down heavily.

bādhá, *a.* distressing; *as m.* distress. [√bādh.]

bāndhava, *m.* (having connection *or* relationship, *i.e.*) a relative; friend. [bándhu, 1208c.]

bāla, *a.* young, not grown; *as subst. m. and f.* —1. child (*distinguished from* yuvan, 'young man,' 28^{12}); boy; girl; —2. *applied to a grown person* (*cf. Eng.* childish, puerile), child *or* booby, *w. double mg*, 61^{21}.

bālaka, *a.* young; *as m.* child. [bāla.]

bālāpatya, *n.* young offspring, of men and of animals. [apatya.]

bāṣpa, *m.* tears.

bāṣpākula, *a.* agitated by tears. [ākula.]

bāhú, *m.* arm; *esp.* fore-arm; of beasts, the fore-leg, *esp.* the upper part thereof, 101[19]. [for *bhāghú: cf. πῆχυς, Doric πᾶχυς, *φαχυς, 'fore-arm'; AS. *bōg*, 'arm' and 'arm of a tree, *i.e.* branch,' Eng. *bough*, 'arm of a tree,' Ger. *Bug*, 'shoulder, hip'; also Dutch *boeg*, Eng. *bow*, 'shoulder of a ship,' *bow-sprit*, 'bow-spar.']

bāhu-yuddha, *n.* arm-fight, wrestling.

bāhulya, *n.* abundance; commonness, state of being usual; *concretely*, usual order of things; -āt, from *or* in accordance with the usual order of things, in all probability, 24[21]. [bahula, 1211.]

bā́hya, *a.* being outside, external; *at end of cpds, equiv. to Eng.* extra- *at beg. of cpds.* [bahís, 1211: cf. 1208a[2] end.]

biḍāla, *m.* cat.

bimba, *m. n.* disk of sun *or* moon.

bíla, *n.* cleft; hollow. [perhaps fr. √bil or bid, collateral forms of bhid, 'cleave.']

bī́ja, *n.* seed, of plants and animals.

buddhá, *ppl.* awakened; illuminé; enlightened; —*esp., as m.* The Enlightened One, epithet of Gautama of the Çākya tribe. [√budh: for budh-ta (160), the formal equivalent of -πυθ-το- in ἄπυστος, 'not having learned.']

buddhi, *f.* —1. insight, understanding, intellect; mind, 13[13]; wit, wits; —2. mind *in the sense of* opinion (*as in Eng.*); belief; *at end of cpds:* vyāghra-buddhyā, with tiger-belief, (mistakenly) thinking that it was a tiger, 34[15]; —3. mind *in the sense of* purpose, resolve (*as in Eng.*); buddhiṁ kṛ, make up one's mind, 58[12]; buddhim pra-kṛ, *mid.*, put a plan before one's self, decide, 9[11]. [√budh, 1157: for budh-ti (160), the formal equivalent of πύστις, *πυθ-τι-ς, 'an inquiring.']

buddhi-jīvin, *a.* living by one's mind, employing one's intelligence, intelligent.

buddhimant, *a.* possessing understanding; intelligent.

√ budh (bódhati, -te; búdhyate; bubódha, bubudhé; ábuddha [160]; bhotsyáti, -te; buddhá; bóddhum; buddhvā́; -búdhya). —1. be awake; —2. come to consciousness; *hence* —3. notice; give heed to, *w. gen.*, 76[12]; —4. notice, *i.e.* perceive; *and so*, become acquainted with; understand; —5. *rarely*, (*like Eng.* remember a person, *i.e.*) present a person with a thing (*instr.*); —*caus.* —6a. cause to notice *or* understand; —6b. teach; announce to.

[for *bhudh, orig. 'be awake,' cf. Church Slavonic *bŭd-ĕti*, 'be awake': the cognate words of the related languages agree closely in form, but show considerable diversity of mgs: mg 4 mediates the transition to the idea of the Greek √πυθ, *φυθ, in πυθέσθαι, 'find out': mgs 5 and 6 form the bridge to the principal Germanic mgs, 'offer' and 'command': cf. Goth. *ana-biud-an*, (prob. 'give notice to,' and so) 'command,' AS. *beōd-an*, 'announce, offer, command,' Eng. *bid*, 'announce, offer in words, offer *in general*, *esp.* at an auction, declare, proclaim, command, invite,' Ger. *biet-en*, 'offer'; (from an entirely different root is Eng. *bid*, AS. *biddan*, Ger. *bitten*, 'pray,' as in *bid beads*, 'pray prayers';) cf. also Eng. noun *bode*, 'announcement,' whence denom. verb *bode*, 'foretell': for mg 5, observe the analogy of Ger. *Jemand bedenken*, 'remember *or* take notice of a person *esp.* in one's will, *i.e.* make a bequest to.']

+ ni, attend to, 58[1]; understand, know, 7[9].

+ pra, come forth (from sleep) to consciousness; awake, *intrans.*

+ prati, awake, *intrans.*; awake, *trans.*, 76[8].

budha, *a.* awake; intelligent; wise; *as m.* wise man. [√budh.]

bubhukṣā, *f.* desire to eat, hunger. [fr. desid. of √2 bhuj, 'frui,' 1149[4].]

√ 1 bṛh, *collateral form of* √vṛh, 'pluck,' *q.v.*

√ 2 bṛh (bṛṅhati, -te; babárha; bṛḍhá; *caus.* bṛṅháyati, -te). be thick, great, strong, *in* bṛhánt, *q.v.*; *caus.* make great, strengthen.

bṛ́h, *f.* prayer, *conceived as a* swelling and filling of the heart in devotion. [√2 bṛh.]

bṛhat-kathā, *f.* Great-Story, title of a collection of stories ascribed to Gunādhya (guṇāḍhya), and abridged by Somadeva under the name Kathāsaritsāgara. [bṛhant, 1249a, 1279.]

bṛhád-açva, *a.* possessing great *or* powerful horses; *as m.* Brihadaçva, name of the sage who narrates the story of Nala to Yudhishthira. [bṛhánt (1249a) + áçva, 1298: cf. *Μεγάλ-ιππος, which is similarly compounded and of like meaning.]

bṛhánt [450a], *a.* great; mighty; lofty. [present ppl. of √2 bṛh, 'be great.']

bṛ́has-páti, *m.* Brihaspati, name of a divinity in which the activity of the pious in their relations towards the gods is personified, the mediator between gods and men, and the type of the priest and of the priestly dignity; *later*, god of wisdom and eloquence. ['lord of prayer,' bṛ́has + páti: for cpd, see 1250 and d, and 1267d; for acct, Whitney 94b; for euphony, 171 2.]

bāijika, *a.* pertaining to the semen; of guilt, inherited from one's father. [bīja, 1222e and e 2.]

brahma-cárya, *n.* life of holiness (bráhman), walk and conversation of a Brahman student (brahmán), *esp.* chastity; religious studentship, the first of the four periods of a Brahman's life, *see* āçrama. [bráhman (1249a 2) or brahmán (probably both) + carya, equiv. of caryā: acct, 1272, 1213c.]

brahma-cārín, *a.* (busying one's self with, *i.e.*) studying sacred knowledge; *as m.* Brahman student, 65 3; *as adj. esp.* observing chastity, 64 14, 100 21. [bráhman, 1249a 2.]

brahmaṇyà, *a.* pertaining *or* attached to the holy life and study (bráhman), *i.e.* pious; attached *or* friendly to Brahmans (brahmán). [1212d 1.]

brahma-dāya, *m.* sacred-word heritage, heritage consisting of the sacred word. [bráhman, 1249a 2.]

brahmadāya-hara, *a.* receiving the sacred word as a heritage.

brahma-dvíṣ, *a.* devotion-hating, godless. [bráhman, 1249a 2: acct, 1269.]

bráhman, *n.* –1. devotion (conceived as a swelling and filling of the soul with adoration for the gods), worship, *in general*, any pious expression in the worship of the gods; hymn of praise, praise, 73 6, 10, 74 4, 11; prayer, 76 15; –2. sacred word, word of God (opp. to the profane), 60 8; –3. divine science, 57 13; sacred learning, theology, theosophy; –4. holy life, *i.e.* chastity; –5. the (impersonal) spirit that pervades the universe. [√2 bṛh, 1168. 1c: bráhman (n.) is to brahmán (m.) as *prayer* ('supplication') is to *pray-er* ('supplicant').]

brahmán, *m.* –1. pray-er, 76 18; worshipper; priest, 88 9, RV. x. 125. 5; pray-er by profession, Brahman; –2. the impersonal universe-pervading spirit (bráhman 5), personified as a god, *i.e.* Brahmán, the Supreme All-soul, 57 4, 8; *in the theological system,* the Creator of the world, 67 17. [√2 bṛh, see bráhman.]

brahmarṣi, *m.* priest-sage, priestly sage, *see* 1 14 N. [brahmán (1249a 2) + ṛ́ṣi, 127, 1280b.]

brahmavarcasá, *n.* pre-eminence in sacred learning *or* holiness. [for brahmavarcas, which occurs only in derivs: bráhman (1249a 2) + várcas, 1315c.]

brahmavarcasvin, *a.* eminent in divine knowledge. ['possessing brahmavarcasa,' q.v.: 1232.]

brahma-vedin, *a.* knowing divine knowledge. [bráhman, 1249a 2.]

brahma-hán [402], *a.* Brahman-slaying; *as m.* murderer of a Brahman. [brahmán, 1249a 2.]

brāhmá, *f.* -ī, *a.* –1. pertaining to bráhman, divine; holy, 59 6; spiritual, 61 15; –2. pertaining to brahmán, *in both its senses, i.e.:* –2a. of Brahmans; –2b. of Brahmán *or* (*anglicized*) Brahma, the Creator, 57 23, 58 9. [bráhman and brahmán, 1208a 2 end.]

brāhmaṇá, *m.* (having to do with bráhman *or* prayer and praise and divine science, *i.e.*) priest, 84 15; theologian, Brahman, 57 16; –*f.* brāhmaṇī, woman of the priestly caste, Brahmanee. [bráhman, w. usual shift of acct, 1208a.]

brā́hmaṇa, *n.* (of a brahmán, of a priest *or* Brahman, *i.e.*) the dictum of a priest on matters of faith and cultus; *esp.* a Brāhmana, *as* designation of one of a class of Vedic writings which contain these dicta. [brahmán, w. usual shift of acct, 1208a.]

brāhmaṇa-vāda, *m.* a statement of the Brāhmanas. [brā́hmaṇa.]

√ **brū** (brávīti [632], brūté: *the second clause of* 632 *should read* "before the initial *consonant* of an ending"). –**1.** *act.* say; *w. dat. of person and acc. of thing,* 10[21], 96[14]; *w. acc. of person and either oratio recta* (12[5], 60[7, 23], 98[11]) *or else acc. of thing* (95[18]); speak to, *w. acc. of person,* 3[14]; speak of, *w. acc. of person,* 11[18]; say, *i.e.* announce, tell; *w.* vacas, ἔπος εἰπεῖν, 10[18]; *w.* punar, answer, 8[3]; –**2.** *middle,* brūté (*used esp. to introduce oratio recta and without designation of the person addressed*), says, inquit, 20[18], 28[1], 30[5, 10, 12], 35[18].

+**apa**, remove (the thought *or* recollection of a thing *or* person, *acc.*, from a person, *abl.*) by speaking, *i.e.* try to console a person (*abl.*) for the loss of a thing *or* person (*acc.*), 92[14]. [this locution is apparently like the Eng. colloq. phrase "I'll *talk* it (his opinion) *out of* him."]

+**pra**, tell forth, proclaim, 75[13]; announce, 88[7]; *then* (*like the Eng.* tell of, *bad and colloquial* tell on), inform against, betray, 93[17].

+**prati**, speak back to (*acc.*), answer.

√ **bhakṣ** (bhákṣati, -te; bhakṣitá; bhákṣitum; -bhákṣya; bhakṣáyati [1041[2]]) (partake, enjoy, *i.e.*) eat; consume; devour. [old desid. of √bhaj, 108g end: cf. bhikṣ, and for mg, √2 aç, 'eat.']

bhakṣá, *m.* the enjoying, eating *or* drinking; food; *at end of adj. cpds,* having · · as food, living on · ·. [√bhakṣ.]

bhakṣaka, *m.* eater. [√bhakṣ: see 1181a end.]

bhakṣitavya, *grdv.* to be eaten. [√bhakṣ, 964[2].]

bhakṣin, *a.* eating. [√bhakṣ, 1183[3].]

bhakṣya, *grdv.* to be eaten, eatable; *as n.* proper food. [√bhakṣ, 963.]

bhága, *m.* –**1.** (he who deals out, *i.e.*) dispenser; rich *or* kind master; lord, *frequent epithet of* Savitar—*so* 74[17]; –**2.** *esp.* Bhaga, name of an Aditya, from whom welfare is expected and who brings about love and institutes marriage, 89[6]; –**3.** portion; lot (*w.* dur-, su-); fortune; *esp.* (*as in Eng.*), good fortune, happy lot; –**4.** loveliness. [√bhaj, 216. 1: –**1.** cf. Old Persian *baga,* 'God'; Βαγαῖος· Ζεὺς Φρύγιος; Slavonic *bogŭ,* 'God'; for mg, cf. Eng. *lord,* AS. *hlāf-ord* (**hlāf-weard?*), 'loaf-ward, loaf-keeper'; –**3.** for mg, cf. the relation of μόρος, 'lot, fate,' to ἔμ-μορ-ε, 'gat a share.']

bhágavant, *a.* –**1.** fortunate, possessing a happy lot, blessed; *then* –**2.** (*like Eng.* blessed) heavenly, august, lordly, *applied to* Indra, Brahma, The Self-existent, the Wood-deity, Sun, Moon, Earth, etc.; *used, esp. in voc., as a form of address, so* 94[8], 26[4]. [bhága.]

bhagín, *a.* fortunate; happy; splendid; –**bhaginī**, *f.* sister (the happy one—*so far forth as she has a brother*). [bhága.]

bhagīratha, *m.* Bhagīratha, name of an ancient king, who brought the Ganges down from heaven. [perhaps fr. bhagin + ratha, 'having a splendid chariot.']

bhagna, *see* 957c.

bhagna-bhāṇḍa, *a.* having broken pots *or* [1308] who broke the pots.

bhagnāça, *a.* having broken hopes, disappointed. [āçā, 334[2].]

bhaṅgá, *m.* a breaking. [√bhañj, 216. 1.]

√ **bhaj** (bhájati, -te; babhā́ja, bhejé [794e]; ábhākṣīt, ábhakta [883]; bhajiṣyáti, -te; bhaktá; bháktum; bhaktvā́; -bhájya; *caus.* bhājáyati). –**1.** deal out; apportion; divide; *then* (*as Eng.* share *means both* 'give a part of' *and* 'have a part of') –**2.** *middle,* have as one's part, receive; have *or* take part in; –**3.** give one's self up to; –**4.** (choose as one's part, *i.e.*) declare one's self for, prefer, 15[8]; –**5.** betake one's self to; turn to; go to, 20[10]; –**6.** belong to, be attached to; revere;

love, 9[20]; —*caus.* cause to have a share, *w acc. of person and gen. of thing,* 83[8].

[cf. φαγ-εῖν, 'get one's portion, eat,' w. a specialization of mg like those seen in Eng. *partake* and *take* as used with the implied object *food* or *drink*, in bhakta, 'thing divided, portion, food,' and in bhakṣ: akin are the names of the two food-trees yielding eatable nuts (acorns, buck-mast), φᾱγός, φηγός, 'oak,' Lat. *fāgus*, 'beech,' AS. *bōc*, Eng. *buck-*, 'beech-,' in *buck-mast*, beech-nuts,' and *buck-wheat* (so called from the likeness of the kernels to beech-nuts), AS. *bēce*, Eng. *beech:* with *bōc*, 'beech,' is ident. *bōc*, 'book,' orig. 'runes scratched on branches of a fruit-bearing tree,' see Tacitus, Germania, x.; such a branch was called by a name which became in Old High Ger. *puah-stap* or *buoh-stab*, and meant orig. 'beech-staff'; but the word came to be used for the significant thing on the branch, 'the rune *or* letter,' AS *bōc-stæf*, Ger. *Buch-stabe.*]

+ **ā**, *act., sometimes mid.*, deal out to, give a person (*acc.*) a share in a thing (*loc.*).

+ **vi**, part asunder; divide.

+ **pra-vi**, divide.

+ **saṁ-vi**, —1. divide a thing (*acc.*) with a person (*instr.*); give a share; —2. present a person (*acc.*) with a thing (*instr.*).

√ **bhañj** (bhanákti; babháñja; ábhāñkṣīt; bhañkṣyáti; bhagná [957c]; bhañktvā́; -bhájya). break. [opinions are divided as to whether √√bhañj, 2 bhuj, and bhām (see these) orig. began w. bhr-; cf giri-bhrā́j, 'breaking forth from the mountains': if bhañj does stand for *bhrañj, then Lat. *frangere*, 'break,' *nau-frag-a*, 'ship-breaking' (*tempestas*), and Ger. *brechen*, Eng. *break* are akin.]

bhaṭṭāra, *m.* lord. [a transition-stem (399) fr. bhartṛ: corresponding to the strong acc. s. form bhartār-am, taken as if it were bhartāra-m, is made the nom. s. bhartāra-s, etc.; both transition to the a-declension, and assimilation of rt to ṭṭ are regular in Prakrit.]

bhaṭṭāraka, *m.* lord, applied to gods and learned men. [bhaṭṭāra, 1222c 1.]

bhaṭṭāraka-vāra, *m.* lord's day, Sunday.

bhadrá, *a.* —1. praiseworthy, pleasing; gladsome, 76[4], 90[17]; —2. good, happy, 84[8]; *voc. f.*, good lady, 9[10]; bhadram, *adv.*, *w.* kṛ *or* ā-car, do well, 22[17], 23[19]; —3. favorable, auspicious, 86[8]; —*as n., sing. and pl.*, welfare, prosperity, 20[16]; *w.* kṛ, grant welfare to a person (*dat.*), bless, 69[11]. [√bhand, 1188a.]

bhadra-kṛ́t, *a.* granting welfare; blessing. [1269.]

√ **bhand** (bhándate). receive jubilant praise.

bhándiṣṭha, *a.* most loudly *or* best praising.

bhayá, *n.* —1. fear, anxiety; *in composition w. the thing feared,* 10[12], 31[9], 46[5]; fear of a thing (*abl.*), 40[14]; bhayāt, from fear, 20[10], 36[4], 41[17]; *then, as conversely in Eng.*, fear (*orig.* 'danger,' *so* Job 39.22) *has come to mean* 'anxiety,' —2. danger, peril, 25[19], 42[3,4]. [√bhī, 1148.1a: for mg 2, cf. saṁdeha.]

bhayārta, *a.* stricken with fear. [ārta.]

bhára, *m.* —1. a bearing, carrying; —2. burden; weight, 50[1]; —3. mass, quantity; —4. (*w. specialization as in Lat.* pondus, 'weight,' *then also* 'pound') a particular quantity *or* measure, *in* nir-. [√bhṛ: cf. φωσ-φόρο-s, Lat. *luci-fer(u-s)*, 'light-bringing'; AS. *horn-bora*, 'horn-bearing, trumpeter': for mgs 2–4, cf. Eng. *weigh*, orig. 'bear up, lift,' as in *weigh anchor*, AS. *wegan*, 'carry, bear,' and *weight*, 'burden,' then 'mass,' then 'definite mass.']

bharatá, *a.* to be supported *or* maintained; *esp.* to be kept alive by the care of men, as epithet of the god Agni; *as m.* Bharata, name of a patriarchal hero. [√bhṛ, 1176e.]

bhárgas, *n.* radiant light; glory. [√bhṛj or bhrāj, q.v., 216.1[3]: cf. φλέγος, n., 'flame'; Lat. *fulgur*, 'lightning.']

bhartṛ, *m.* —1. bearer; —2. supporter, maintainer; lord; husband, 10[21]. [√bhṛ, 1182b: cf. Lat. *fertor*, 'bearer.']

bhavá, *m.* the coming into existence. [√bhū.]

bhavat-pūrva, *a.* having bhavant as first *or* preceding; -am, *adv.* [1311], in a way having bhavant first, *i.e.* with the voc. s. f. of bhavant at the beginning of one's begging formula.

bhavadāhārārtham, *adv.* for your food. ['in a way having your food as object,' 1311, 1302c4 : **bhavant + āhāra** and **artha.**]

bhavaduttaram, *adv.* with bhavant as last (word of one's begging formula). [acc. s. n. of adj. ***bhavad-uttara**, 1311.]

bhavana, *n.* dwelling, abode, house. [prop. 'an existing,' then 'place of existing,' √**bhū**, 1150. 1a. so Eng. *dwelling* and *abode* and Lat. *man-sio* meant 'a waiting, an abiding,' and then 'abiding-place, maison': cf. also **mandira** and **asta.**]

bhávant [456], *a.* lordly; *—used in respectful address as substitute* [514] *for pronoun of the second person, and translatable by* your honor, thou (*e.g.* 6[23]), ye (*e.g.* 7[6], 12[10]); *used in the pl. of a single person to express greater courtesy*, 19[22], 28[4,5]; *used in the voc. s. m.* (**bhavas**, *contracted*) **bhos**, *f.* **bhavati**, *as word of address,* (lord, master, mister,) sir, lady. [prob. a contraction of **bhágavant**: cf. 61[10] N.]

bhavan-madhya, *a.* having bhavant as middle (word); -am, *adv.* [1311], with the voc. s. f. of bhavant as the middle (word of one's begging formula).

bhavitavyà, *grdv.* deserving to become, destined to be, about to be; *impers.* [999], **mayā bhavitavyam**, *sc.* **asti**, I must be, 23[13]; **bhavitavyam**, it must be, 27[14]. [√**bhū**, 964.]

√ **bhas** (**bábhasti** [678]; **bhasitá**). chew, bite; crush; devour, consume; **bhasita**, consumed to ashes. [cf. φάμ-μη, *φασ-μη, 'barley-groats': w. the 3d pl. **bá-ps-ati** cf. the collateral form **psā** and ψά-μα-θος, 'sand.']

bhásman, *n.* ashes. ['consumed': see √**bhas.**]

√ **bhā** (**bhā́ti**; **babhāú**; **bhāsyáti**; **bhātá**). be bright, shine; appear. [cf. φη-μί, Lat. *fā-ri*, 'make appear, reveal, say'; Eng. *ban*, 'public proclamation, mandatory *or* prohibitory,' 'notice (of marriage),' etc.: cf. √√**bhāṣ**, **bhās.**]

+ **ā**, shine upon; illumine.

+ **ud**, shine out, become manifest, 56[20].

+ **nis**, shine forth from (*abl.*), *fig.*

+ **pra**, shine forth; begin to be light (of the night).

+ **vi**, shine far and wide.

bhāgá, *m.* part: —1. allotted part, 96[20]; share, 84[10]; lot; *esp.* happy lot; —2. *in post-Vedic*, portion (*not* lot), 64[22]; —3. place, spot (*cf. Eng.* parts, 'regions'). [√**bhaj.**]

bhāga-dhéya, *n.* (bestowal *or* allotment of a part, *i.e.*) portion, 88[7]; *esp.* bestowal of a goodly lot, blessing, 82[4]. [1213c.]

bhāgaças, *adv.* part by part; gradually. [**bhāga**, 1106.]

bhāgīratha, *a.* of Bhagīratha; -ī, *f.* the stream (**nadī**) of Bh., the Ganges. [**bhagīratha**, 1208f.]

bhāgya, *n.* lot; fate; *esp.* happy lot; luck; **bhāgyena**, luckily. [**bhāga**, 1211.]

bhā́jana, *n.* vessel, dish. [lit. 'receiver,' √**bhaj**, mg 2: 1150. 1b.]

bhāṇḍa, *n.* —1. vessel, pot; vat; dish; —2. *generalized* (*like* **pātra**), utensil; wares *or* ware.

bhāṇḍa-mūlya, *n.* capital consisting of wares; stock in trade.

bhānú, *m.* light; beam. [√**bhā**, 1162.]

√ **bhām** (**bhāmitá**). rage, be angry. [orig., perhaps, 'be agitated,' and so, a Prakritic form of **bhram**, q.v.: for loss of **r**, see under √**bhañj.**]

bhā́ma, *m.* rage, fury. [√**bhām.**]

bhārá, *m.* burden. [√**bhṛ.**]

bhā́rata, *a.* descended from Bharata; *as m.* descendant from Bharata, epithet of Yudhishthira, to whom Brihadaçva tells the story of Nala. [**bharatá**, 1208f.]

bhārika, *m.* carrier. [**bhāra.**]

bhāryà, *grdv.* to be supported *or* maintained; -**ā̀**, *f.* wife. [√**bhṛ**, 963b.]

bhāryātva, *n.* condition of being wife *or* (among animals) mate. [**bhāryā.**]

bhāva, *m.* —1. the becoming, 61[2]; existence, 15[18]; being; *in cpds, used as equiv. to the suffix* **tva** *or* **tā**, condition of being · ·, 35[21], 49[12]; —2. (way of being, *i.e.*) condition; —3. (way of being, *i.e.*) nature; —4. natural disposition; feeling; —5. feelings; heart, 30[18]; —6. the existent; existent thing, 66[9]. [√bhū, 1148.2.]

bhāvin, *a.* becoming, coming into existence; about to be, destined to be, 18[9]; future, 38[18]; -inī, *f.* a beautiful woman. [√bhū, 1183[3] end.]

√ **bhāṣ** (bhā́ṣate; babhāṣé; ábhāṣiṣṭa; bhāṣitá; bhā́ṣitum; bhāṣitvā́; -bhā́ṣya). speak; talk; say. [perhaps for *bhāsk, a sk-formation fr. √bhā: 182a.]

+**abhi**, speak unto, address, *w. acc.*; speak, *without object.*

+**prati**, speak back, answer.

bhāṣā, *f.* speech, language. [√bhāṣ.]

bhāṣita, *ppl.* spoken; *as n.* [1176a], what is spoken, the words. [√bhāṣ.]

√ **bhās** (bhā́sati, -te; babhāsé; bhāsitá). shine. [cf. √bhā.]

+**prati**, shine over against, make a show, appear well.

bhā́s, *n.* light. [√bhās: but cf. 1151.1c[2].]

bhās-kará, *m.* the sun. ['light-making': 171[3].]

√ **bhikṣ** (bhíkṣate; bibhikṣé; bhikṣiṣyé; bhíkṣitum; bhikṣitvā́). desire to have a share for one's self, wish for; *then* (*like the Eng.* desire, 'express a wish for'), request; beg; *esp.* go begging for food. [old desid. of √bhaj, 108g[1] end: cf. bhakṣ.]

bhikṣā́, *f.* —1. the act of begging, begging; —2. that which is got by begging, alms. [√bhikṣ, 1149[4]: w. the relation of 1 to 2, cf. that of Eng. *getting*, 'act of getting,' to *getting*, 'that which is got.']

√ **bhid** (bhinátti, bhintté; bibhéda, bibhidé; ábhet [832]; bhetsyáti, -te; bhinná [957d]; bhéttum; bhittvā́; -bhídya). cleave, cut asunder; break in twain, 102[14]; smite sore (in battle), 81[5]; pound, bruise, crush (as a reed), 70[15]; pierce. [orig. 'split, crush': cf. Lat. *findo*, 'cleave,' perfect *fidi*; Ger. *beissen*, Eng. *bite*; also *bit*, 'morsel,' and *bit*, 'part of a bridle'; *bitter*, used of a sword, w. a trace of the orig. mg, Beōwulf, 2705; caus. *bait*, in *bait a bear*, 'make dogs bite him,' and *bait a horse*, 'let him eat.']

+**pra**, split forth *or* open.

+**vi**, split asunder; break to pieces, destroy.

bhiyás, *m.* fear. [√bhī, 1151.2c.]

√ **bhiṣaj** (bhiṣákti). heal.

bhiṣáj, *a.* healing; *as m.* healer. [√bhiṣaj, 1147.]

√ **bhī** (*V.* bháyate; *V. and later*, bibhéti; bibhā́ya; ábhāiṣīt; bheṣyáti; bhītá; bhétum; *caus.* bhīṣáyate [1042f]). fear; be afraid of (*abl.*); bhīta, having feared, frightened; *caus.* affright. [w. bi-bhé-ti, cf. Old High Ger. *bi-bē-t*, 'trembles,' whose *bi-* is syllable of reduplication, Ger. *bebt*, AS. *beofað*, 'trembles': the connection of these words with φέ-β-ομαι, 'am afeard, flee in fright,' and φόβος, 'fear,' is still a moot-point.]

bhī́ [351], *f.* fear. [√bhī, 348.1.]

bhītá, *ppl.* feared; *as n.* [1176a], fear.

bhīmá, *a.* fearful, terrible; *as m.* Bhīma, name of a Vidarbhan king. [√bhī, 1166b.]

bhīma-parākramá, *m.* terrible strength *or* courage. [1264, 1267.]

bhīmá-parākrama, *a.* possessing bhīma-parākramá, 1[11], 2[3]. [1293.]

bhīma-çāsana, *n.* command *or* summons of Bhīma. [1264, 1267.]

bhīrú, *a.* timid. [√bhī, 1192.]

√ **1 bhuj** (bhujáti; bhugná; -bhújya). bend; turn; make crooked. [so far as the meaning goes, the following words may well be taken as cognate: φυγ-εῖν, Lat. *fug-ere*, 'turn about, flee'; AS. *būg-an*, 'bend, turn about' (intrans.), sometimes also 'flee,' Eng. verb *bow* (as in *bow down*), 'bend'; AS. *boga*, Eng. *bow*, 'arcus,' *el-bow*, *rain-bow*; Ger. *bieg-sam*, 'pliable,' Old Eng. *būh-sum*, 'pliable, yielding,' Eng. *buxom*, 'lithe, lively, vigorous': but the Germanic *g* raises phonetic difficulties which are not yet satisfactorily cleared up.]

√ **2 bhuj** (bhunákti, bhuñkté; bubhója, bubhujé; ábhujat; bhokṣyáti, -te; bhuktá; bhóktum; bhuktvā́). —1. enjoy; *in Veda*, (have use with, *i.e.*) have the use of a thing (*and so w. instr.*); —2. *in later Skt.* (*like Ger.* geniessen, *cf. also* bhoga *and* bhojana), enjoy *esp.* food, *w. acc.*; —3. *without object*, take one's meal; *then* —4. enjoy (things that are not food), *w. acc.*, 10 9; —5. reap the fruit (of sin) at the hands of a person (*gen.*), 79 17; —6. *caus.* cause to take food, feed. [if for *bhruj (but this is doubtful—see √bhañj), then cf. Lat. *frui*, **frugvi*, 'have use with' (a thing, hence instr.-abl.), 'enjoy'; *frug-es*, 'fruit'; AS. *brūcan*, 'enjoy' (food or drink), 'use,' Eng. *brook*, orig. 'use,' now 'put up with.']

+**anu**, reap the fruit (of good *or* evil deeds).

+**upa**, —1. enjoy, *esp.* (enjoy food, *i.e.*) eat; —2. reap the fruit (of good *or* evil deeds).

bhujaṁ-gama, *m.* serpent. ['going with bending *or* with crooking': bhujam, grd of √1 bhuj, 995: for mg, cf. khaga.]

√ **bhur** (bhuráti). make short and quick motions, twitch, jerk, kick, struggle, stir. [cf. *φύρω*, 'stir around, mingle'; *φλύω*, 'bubble'; Lat. *fur-ere*, 'be agitated, rage'; *de-fru-tum*, 'boiled off'; Eng. *brew*, 'boil'; *bro-th*, 'bouillon.']

bhuraṇa, *a.* (*like the Eng.* stirring, *i.e.*) *both* —1. moving quickly *and* —2. active, busy. [√bhur, 1150. 2c.]

√ **bhuraṇya** (bhuraṇyáti). be stirring, busy. [bhuraṇa, 1059d.]

bhúvana, *n.* —1. being, existence; —2. world; —3. *with* viçva: *sing.*, tout le monde; *pl.*, all beings. [√bhū, 1150. 2c.]

bhuvana-traya, *n.* world-triad, *i.e.* heaven and atmosphere and earth.

bhúvas, *the second of the so-called "utterances"* (*see* vyāhṛti), bhuvas!, *interpreted as* air *or* atmosphere, *on account of its position between* bhūr *and* svar. [prob. nothing more than the voc. pl. of bhū, 'O ye spaces.']

√ **bhū** (bhávati, -te; babhū́va [789a]; ábhūt; bhaviṣyáti, -te; bhūtá; bhávitum; bhūtvā́; -bhū́ya; *caus.* bhāváyati, -te). become, 93 3, 40 21, 57 3, 67 21, 3 17; come into being, 92 17; arise, happen, take place; exist; *very often to be rendered simply by* be, 2 15, 3 18, 22, 7 1; —pūrvam abhūd rājā, once there was a king, 48 1; tathā bhavatu, so be it, 27 14; *so* 32 17; prāñjalir bhūtvā, (having become prāñjali, *i.e.*) assuming suppliant posture, 13 22; —*w. possessive gen.*, become (the property) of a person; ādhipatyaṁ tasya babhūva, lordship became his, he attained lordship, 37 1; *seldom w. dat.*, 96 20; —*imperative*, bhavatu: (be it, *i.e.*) good; enough; what's the use of talking, 30 16, 42 2; the thing is clear, 23 7, 31 5; tad bhavatu, never mind that, 34 6; —bhūta, *see s.v.*; —*in self-explaining periphrases w. ppls*, 49 19, 52 17, 99 21; —*desid.* búbhūṣati [1027], desire to be, 70 14. [w. ábhūt cf. *ἔφυ*, 'became, grew'; cf. Lat. *fu-it*, 'was'; Old Lat. *fu-at*, 'may be'; AS. *beōm*, 'am'; Eng. *be*.]

+**anu**, —1. (*perhaps* be along after, *and so*) come up with, attain; —2. experience; enjoy, 24 9; —3. (experience, *i.e.*) make practical acquaintance with, come to understand; perceive; hear, 4 21.

+**abhi**, be against [1077 8], oppress, *and so* overpower.

+**ud**, arise up, make itself perceptible.

+**pari**, —1. be around, surround, encompass; —2. (*like the Eng. colloq.* get around, *i.e.*) get the better of, prove superior to; be superior to, *and so* —3. treat with contempt, 37 5.

+**pra**, —1. come forth into being; arise; —2. be before (others), have the power; have power, be strong.

+**vi**, (become asunder, *i.e.*) expand, develop; pervade; —*caus.* cause to expand *or* open; discover; vibhāvita, discovered, found out.

+**sam**, —1. (unite [*intrans.*] together, *and so* take form, *i.e.*) be shapen *in its old sense*, be created; be born, 97 2; come into being; become; originate; sambhūta, sprung from, 19 12; —2. exist, 39 2; be, 39 5; sambabhūva, am, RV. x.125.8; —3. happen, 20 12; occur; pass current, 52 7; —*caus.* —1. (cause to be together, bring into form, *i.e.*) make, accomplish; —2. honor, 30 12; —3. (bring together, *and so*, *like Eng.* con-jecture) suppose. [development of caus. mg 2 unclear.]

\+ **abhi-sam**, (*lit.* become unto, *i.e.*) attain (*e.g.* a condition) by a process of change, enter into (*e.g.* wifehood), 86[19]; be born unto (immortality), 97[3].

bhū́ [351–2], *a. at end of cpds*, becoming, being, existent; *as f.* —1. a becoming, being; —2. the place (*for mg, cf.* bhavana) of being, the world, space; *pl.* worlds, spaces (*cf.* bhuvas); —3. the earth, as distinguished from heaven and atmosphere; bhuvi, on earth; —4. the land, lands. [√bhū, 347.]

bhūtá, *ppl.* —1. become, been, *i.e.* past; real; —2. having become, being, *used in composition w. its predicate as a grammatical device to give the predicate an adj. form w. number and gender* [1273c], 6[7], 19[4], 29[4], 56[15]; —3. *as n.* (that which has become, *i.e.*) a being, divine (90[19]) *or* human *or* other; creature *in general*, 21[18, 23], 57[18], 63[12]; created thing, 58[10]; world, 91[16]; —4. *as m. n.* uncanny being, ghost, goblin, 55[19]; —5. *as n.* element; pañca bhūtāni, five elements (earth, water, fire, air, ether, of which the body is composed and into which it is dissolved), 66[5], 68[9]; *so* 66[1, 8]. [√bhū: cf. *φῠ-τό-ν*, 'plant, creature.']

bhūta-grāma, *m. sing. and pl.* community of creatures.

bhūta-bhāṣā, *f.* language of the goblins *or* Piçāchas.

bhū-tala, *n.* earth-surface, ground, earth. [cf. tala.]

bhūti, *f.* being, *esp.* well-being. [√bhū: cf. *φύσις*, 'a being, nature.']

bhū-pa, *m.* protector of the earth *or* land, king, prince.

bhū́-pati, *m.* lord of the land, king, prince.

bhū-bhāga, *m.* spot of the earth, place.

bhū́man, *n.* earth; world. [√bhū, 1168. 1d: for mg, cf. bhū́.]

bhū́mi, *f.* —1. earth, 57[11]; ground, 43[13]; —2. land; —3. place, 23[14]; *esp.* fit place, proper vessel (*cf.* sthāna, pātra), 21[5], 28[3]. [√bhū, 1167: for mg, cf. bhū́.]

bhūmi-pati, *m.* lord of the land, king, prince.

bhūmi-bhāga, *m.* spot of ground.

bhūmi-ṣṭha, *a.* standing on the ground. [stha.]

bhū́yāṅs, *a.* more; greater. ['becoming in a higher degree, increasing,' √bhū, 470[2].]

bhū́r, *the first of the three "utterances"* (*see* vyāhṛti), bhūr!, O earth. [crystallized voc. sing. of bhū́.]

bhū́ri, *a.* abundant; much. [√bhū, 1191: cf. bhūyāṅs.]

bhūri-kāla, *m.* long time.

bhū́ri-sthātra, *a.* having many stations, being in many places.

bhū́rṇi, *a.* stirring, *and so* vigilant, jealous (of a god). [√bhur, 1158.2, 245b.]

√bhūṣ (bhū́ṣati; bhūṣáyati [1041[2]]). —1. bhūṣati, be busy for; —2. bhūṣayati, (make ready for, *i.e.*) adorn.

bhūṣaṇa, *n.* ornament. [√bhūṣ, mg 2: 1150.]

√bhṛ (bíbharti [645]; bhárati, -te; *V.* jabhā́ra, jabhré [789b]; *later*, babhā́ra; ábhārṣīt; bhariṣyáti; bhṛtá; bhártum; -bhṛ́tya). bear (*cf. the various senses of* bear *in Eng.*): *thus*, —1. hold, *and so* possess; —2. bear (in the womb); abharat, she bare, 85[15]; —3. endure; —4. carry, convey; —5. (bear, *i.e.*, *as in Latimer*) win; —6. bring (as an offering, *cf.* of-fer), 69[14], 82[14]; *w.* ūdhar, offer the breast, suckle, 78[3]; —7. (bear, *i.e.*) support; *and so* (*like Eng.* support), furnish sustenance to, 22[2]; maintain, RV. x. 125. 1; *so also*, keep (on hire); —8. wear (*as Ger.* tragen *means* 'bear' *and* 'wear'); *w.* nakhāni, wear the nails, keep them untrimmed, 64[19]. [cf. *φέρω*, Lat. *fero*, Eng. *bear*, 'bear' in its various mgs, Ger. *gebären*, 'bring forth': AS. *bear-n*, Eng. *bairn*, 'child,' is an old ppl., lit. 'that which is borne *or* born'; cf. also *φώρ*, Lat. *fūr*, 'carrier off, thief': see also under the derivs, bhara, bhartṛ, and bhṛti; cf. bhāra and the following.]

\+ **apa**, carry off, take away, *ἀποφέρω*.

\+ **ava**, bear down (an assailing weapon), ward off.

\+ **ā**, bear unto, bring to.

\+ **upa**, bring unto.

\+ **ni**, *only in ppl.*, nibhṛta, (borne down, lowered, *i.e.*) hidden.

+ **pra**, *act. mid.* bring forward; offer; prabhṛta, brought forward, made ready. [cf. προφέρω, Lat. *prōfero*, 'bring forward.']

√ **bhṛjj** (bhṛjjáti; bhṛṣṭá; bhṛṣṭvā́). roast; parch, *esp.* grain. [cf. φρύγω, Lat. *frīgere*, 'roast': akin w. √bhrāj.]

bhṛtí, *f.* the supporting, maintenance. [√bhṛ, 1157.1a: cf. Ger. *Ge-bur-t*, Eng. *bir-th.*]

bhṛtya, *m.* (one who is to be maintained, *i.e.*) servant. [grdv. of √bhṛ, 963b.]

bhṛça, *a.* powerful.

bhṛça-duḥkhita, *a.* (powerfully, *i.e.*) exceedingly pained.

bhetavya, *grdv.* to be feared; bhetavyam, *impers.* [999], timendum est, one should fear, 42³; na bhetavyam, never fear. [√bhī, 964.]

bhedá, *m.* fissure, split, breach; a creating of divisions. [√bhid.]

bheṣajá, *f.* -ī́, *a.* healing; *as n.* healing (*subst.*). [bhiṣáj, 1209i.]

bhāikṣa, *n.* begging; bhāikṣaṁ car, go a-begging. [bhikṣā́, 1208e.]

bhāima, *a.* descended from Bhīma; *f.* -ī, Bhīma's daughter, Damayantī. [bhīmá, 1208f.]

bhāirava, *a.* fearful, *i.e.* awful; *as m.* Terrible, name of a hunter. [bhīrú, 1208c.]

bho, *see* 176a.

bhóga, *m.* enjoyment; use; *esp.* use of food, *i.e.* eating. [√2 bhuj, 'enjoy,' 216.1.]

bhogin, *a.* enjoying *or* having enjoyment; *esp.* enjoying food, well-fed. [not directly fr. √2 bhuj, but fr. bhoga, on account of the g, 1230c end.]

bhójana, *n.* the enjoying, *esp.* of food; the eating; *then* (*like Eng.* eating), food. [√2 bhuj, 'enjoy,' 1150.1a.]

bhojyà, *grdv.* to be eaten; *as n.* food, supply of food. [√2 bhuj, 'enjoy, eat,' 963d.]

bhobhavat-pūrvaka, *a.* accompanied [1302c2] by bhos or bhavant; -am, *adv.* [1311], with bhos or bhavant.

bho-bhāva, *m.* the becoming bhos; *w.* nāmnām, the becoming bhos of names, *i.e.* the use of bhos instead of a person's real name.

bhos, *excl. of address.* thou, sir!, O!, ho!, halloo!; *often repeated, e.g.* 6²³. [for origin, see bhavant: for euphonic combination, see 176a.]

bhoḥ-çabda, *m.* the word bhos.

√ **bhraṅç** *or* bhraç (bhráṅçate; bhráçyati [767]; ábhraçat; bhraṣṭá). fall.

+ **apa**, fall off; *see* apabhraṣṭa.

bhraṅça, *m.* fall; ruin; loss. [√bhraṅç.]

√ **bhram** (bhrámati, -te; bhrā́myati, -te [763]; babhrā́ma; bhramiṣyáti; bhrāntá [955a]; bhrámitum, bhrā́ntum; bhrāntvā́; -bhrámya, -bhrā́mya). —1. move unsteadily *or* without aim; wander; roam, 36¹², 23⁵; flutter, of insects, etc.; —2. move in a circle, rotate; —3. *fig.* be wandering (of the mind); be agitated *or* confused.

[the orig. meanings seem to have included irregular and aimless and rotary motion as applied to water, wind, and fire, and also to have been transferred to the sound thereof: cf. the derivs bhṛ́mi, 'whirlwind,' bhramá, 'whirling flame' and 'whirlpool,' and bhramara, 'bee': cf. βρέμ-ειν, 'rage,' 'roar' (of storm and wave), βρόμος, 'rage, roar'; Lat. *frem-ere*, 'rage, roar'; Ger. *brummen*, 'hum, rumble'; AS. *brim*, 'surf, surge,' Eng. *brim*, 'place of surf, edge, margin'; Old Eng. *brim*, 'flame, fire,' preserved in Eng. *brimstone*, 'fire-stone': see also √bhām.]

+ **pari**, wander around.

+ **sam**, be much confused; sambhrānta, agitated, perplexed, in a flutter.

√ **bhrāj** (bhrā́jate, -ti; babhrā́ja; ábhrāṭ [890 *or* 833?]; bhrājiṣyáte). shine; be radiant; flame; *fig.* be radiant (with beauty *or* glory). [cf. φλέγ-ω, 'flame, burn'; φλέγ-μα, 'flame'; Lat. *flam-ma*, **flag-ma*, 'flame'; *fulg-ēre*, 'shine, lighten'; AS. *blāc*, 'shining, splendid' (of fires and flames), then 'white' (of the dead), Eng. *bleak*, 'pale'; *bleach*, 'whiten.']

+ **vi**, shine.

bhrā́tṛ [373], *m.* brother. [origin unknown, cf. 1182d: cf. φρά-τηρ, 'brother, *esp.* one of a brotherhood *or* clan,' and

14

so, 'clansman'; Lat. *frā-ter*, 'brother'; Eng. *brother*.]

bhrātṛ-sthāna, *a.* (having, *i.e.*) taking the brother's place; *as m.* representative of a brother.

bhruva, *for* bhrū *at end of cpds*, 1315c.

bhrū́ [351], *f.* brow. [cf. ὀ-φρύ-ς, 'eye-brow'; AS. *brū*, 'eye-lid'; Eng. *brow*.]

---

ma [491], *pron. root, see* ahám. [cf. μέ, Lat. *me*, AS. *mē*, Eng. *me*.]

√ **maṅh** (máṅhate). make great *or* abundant a thing (*acc.*) for a person (*dat.*), grant abundantly to. [for *magh, cf. magha: orig. 'be great,' and trans. 'make great *or* high,' and essentially ident. w. √mah: see under √mah: for mg, cf. Lat. *largus*, 'large, liberal,' w. *largīri*, 'give liberally,' and Eng. *large* with *largess*.]

máṅhiṣṭha, *a.* granting most abundantly, most generous. [√maṅh, 467.]

ma-kāra, *m.* the letter m. [Whitney 18.]

makhá, *a.* jocund. [cf. √mah.]

magádha, *m. pl.* Magadhans, name of a people; Magadha, name of their country, Southern Behar.

magadha-deça, *m.* the land of Magadha.

√ **magh**, *see* maṅh.

maghá, *n.* liberal gift; bounty. [√magh, *i.e.* maṅh.]

maghávan [428], *a.* —1. abounding in liberal gifts, generous; *esp., as m.*, generous (patron), designation of the rich lord who institutes a sacrifice and pays the priests, 88[1]—*cf.* sūri; *applied in particular to* Indra, *as* Rewarder (of priests and singers), 70[6], 71[5], 73[20], 75[10]; —2. *in the Epos*, The Generous One, standing epithet of Indra, 5[11]. [maghá, 1234.]

mañgalá, *n.* —1. welfare, luck; —2. anything lucky, auspicious, *or* of good omen; —3. old *or* traditional usage, 59[18].

mañgalya, *a.* lucky, auspicious, of good omen. [mañgalá, 1212d 4.]

mac-chiṣya, *m.* pupil of me, my pupil. [mad + çiṣya, 159, 203.]

√ **majj** (májjati, -te; mamájja; ámajjīt; maṅkṣyáti, -te; majjiṣyáti; magná [957c]; májjitum; -májya). sink under; dip one's self; dive; duck *or* sub-merge, *intrans.* [perhaps orig. *mazgh, 'get into': cf. madgu, 'duck'; Lat. *merg-ere*, 'duck'; *merg-us*, 'diver' bird: for the phonetic relations, cf. majjan, Avestan mazga, Church Slavonic *mozgŭ*, AS. *mearg*, Eng. *marrow*, Ger. *Mark*, all meaning 'marrow,' and, as meaning originally 'the inmost part *or* pith,' prob. from this root: see rajju.]

+**ud**, e-merge.

+**ni**, sink down; dip one's self, bathe.

majjāo, *Prakrit for* mārjāra-s ('cat') *and for* maj-jāra-s ('my paramour').

maṭhara, *a.* *perhaps* persistent; *as m.* Mathara, name of a man.

maṇí, *m.* —1. pearl; jewel; —2. water-jar.

maṇika, *m.* large water-jar. [maṇi.]

maṇḍapa, *m. n.* open hall *or* pavilion.

maṇḍapikā, *f.* small shed *or* shop. [maṇḍapa, 1222 and d.]

máṇḍala, *n.* disk, circle, ring.

maṇḍū́ka, *m.* frog; *f.* maṇḍūkí [355b], female frog.

matí, *f.* —1. (thinking upon, *i.e.*, *like the Ger.* An-dacht, *see* dhī́ 2) devotion; pious hymn *or* song of praise, 73[10], 79[6]; —2. thought; thoughts, 49[8]; purpose, 73[5]; mind; intention; —3. opinion; —4. understanding, 19[9]; intelligence. [√man, q.v.: cf. Lat. *mens*, stem *men-ti*, 'mind'; AS. *ge-myn-d*, 'mind,' Eng. *mind*.]

mati-prakarṣa, *m.* wit-superiority, *i.e.* a fine dodge.

mátsya, *m.* fish. ['the lively one,' √mad.]

√ **math** *or* **manth** (mathnā́ti, mathnīté; mánthati; máthati [746]; mamátha, mamathús, mamanthús, methús; ámathīt; mathiṣyáti, -te, manthiṣyáti; mathitá; máthitum; mathitvā́; -máthya). —1. stir *or* whirl; *w.* agnim, produce fire by whirling the stick of attrition in a dry piece of wood; —2. shake, agitate, distress.

+**pra**, agitate.

√ **mad** (mádati; mā́dyati; mamáda; ámādīt; maditá, mattá; máditum; mādáyati, -te). —1. bubble, undulate, of water, and as a type of joyousness; apām ūrmir madann iva stomas, praise (joyous) as a bubbling water-wave, 81[10]; boil, be agitated; —2. *fig.* be (pleasantly excited, *i.e.*) glad; rejoice; *w. instr.*, 83[12]; be exhilarated *or* intoxicated with joy; —3. *esp.*, as describing the life of the gods and the blessed, be in bliss; *w. cognate acc.*, 83[18]; —4. *trans.* gladden, rejoice, 75[12]; intoxicate; matta, drunk; —*caus.* —1. *act.* gladden; —2. *mid.* take delight, 84[19].

[the rather rare physical mg (1) is prob. the orig. one, w. a transfer to fig. use, as in Eng. *bubble over with joy or mirth:* cf. *μαδ-άω*, 'be moist'; Lat. *mad-ēre*, 'be soaked, full, drunk'; mat-ta-s (mg 4) and Lat. *mat-tu-s*, 'drunk': see the collateral form √1 mand, and √mud.]

+**ud**, be out (of one's senses) with excitement; be frantic.

+**pra**, take pleasure.

mad, *so-called stem of* 1st *pers. pron.*, 494.

máda, *m.* excitement, inspiration, intoxication, 81[4]; *pl.* intoxicating drinks, *esp.* Soma-draughts, 81[11]. [√mad.]

madīya, *a.* mine. [mad, 494[3], 1215d.]

madgú, *m.* a water-fowl. ['diver,' √majj, q.v.]

mádhu, *a.* sweet; *as n.* sweet food and drink: *esp.* Soma; milk and its products; *oftenest* honey, 26[18]. [cf. *μέθυ*, 'wine'; AS *medu*, Eng. *mead.*]

madhura, *a.* sweet; of speeches, honeyed. [mádhu, 1226a.]

mádhya, —1. *as n.* middle; *w.* nabhasas, middle of heaven, mid-heaven; madhye: in the middle, 57[12]; *w. gen.* [1130] *or at end of cpd*, in the midst of · ·, in · ·, 18[7], 2[9]; —2. *m. n.* (the middle, *i.e.*) the waist; —3. *as adj., used like Lat.* medius: samudram madhyam, in medium mare. [cf. *μέσσος*, **μεθ-jo-s*, Lat. *medius*, Goth. *midjis*, AS. *mid*, Eng. *mid-*, 'middle.']

madhya-ga, *a.* situated in the middle of, tarrying among.

madhya-cārin, *a.* moving in the middle of (*w. gen.*, 1316[2]), *i.e.* moving among.

madhyamá, —1. midmost, situated between; —2. of middling quality, size, etc.; —3. *as m. n.* the middle (of the body), waist; —4. *as n.* the middle (of anything). [mádhya, 474: cf. 525[3].]

√ **man** (mányate; mené [794c]; ámaṅsta; maṅsyáte, -ti; matá; mántum; matvā́; -mánya, -mátya; *desid.* mīmāṅsate). be minded: —1. think, believe, imagine, 34[18], 43[16]; conjecture; yadi nānyathā manyase, if thou art not otherwise minded, if thou art agreed, 25[8]; manye, *inserted parenthetically*, methinks, 51[13]; expect, 52[11]; —2. consider something (*acc.*) as something (*acc.*), 13[12], 37[7], 55[20], 79[8]; prāptakālam amanyata, considered (*sc.* it) an arrived time, thought that the time had come, 13[20]; bahu man, consider as much, esteem, honor; —3. think fit *or* right, 10[16]; —4. think upon, set the heart on, 3[4]; —5. have in mind *or* view, 88[6]; —*caus.*, *see* mānaya; —*desid.* consider, examine, call in question. [cf. *μέ-μον-α*, 'mind, *i.e.* fix the thoughts on, wish, strive' (see man 4); Lat. *me-min-i*, 'keep in mind'; AS. preterito-present *man*, 'am mindful,' and the indirectly connected *mǣnan*, Eng. *mean*, 'have in mind, intend.']

+**anu**, (be minded after another, *i.e.*) follow another in opinion, assent, approve; consent; give leave, *w. acc. of person*, 49[4]; permit, 62[6].

+**abhi**, —1. put one's mind upon, desire; abhimata, desired, agreeable; —2. have intentions against [1077[8]], plot against.

+**ava**, (mind, *i.e.* regard downwards, *i.e.*) regarder de haut en bas, look down upon, *like the Lat.* de-spicere, despise, treat with contempt.

mánas, *n.* mind, *in its widest sense as applied to the* powers of conception, will, and emotion: *thus*, —1. the intellect; the thoughts, 8[16], 10[5], 66[7]; understanding, 82[17]; mind, 10[16], 15[10], 65[12, 13]; —2. reflection; excogitation; *perhaps* the thing excogitated, praise, *or* (*like* dhī 2) devotion, 73[7]; —3. wish, inclination towards; —4. desire; —5. feelings; disposition;

heart, 78[7]. [√man: cf. *μένος*, 'mind, spirit'; Lat. *Miner-va*, the goddess 'gifted with understanding.']

manīṣā́, *f.* —1. thought; understanding; *instr.* manīṣā́, *adv.* wisely; —2. expression of thought and wisdom in saw, prayer, and hymn (*cf.* dhī́ 2). [√man, 1197b.]

manīṣín, *a.* —1. having understanding, wise; —2. prayerful, devout. [manīṣā́, 1230a.]

mánu, *m.* —1. man; *collectively* (*as in Eng., and like Hebrew* adam), man, mankind, 73[19]; —2. (*like Hebrew* Adam) The Man *κατ' ἐξοχήν*, Manu, father of mankind; Manu, as originator of prayer, praise, and sacrifice, 89[2]; Manu, as type of piety and majesty, 1[10]; Manu, suppositious author of the law-book of the Mānavas. [cf. Goth. *manna*, Ger. *Mann*, AS. *man*, Eng. *man*: the noun is generalized to a quasi pronoun in AS. *man*, Ger. *man*, like Lat. *homo* in French *on*, but retains a distinct form as noun in Ger. *Mann* (as *homo* does in French *homme*): cf. also *Mannus*, mythical ancestor of the West-Germans (Tacitus, Germania, ii.): perhaps related are Μίνυ-ς and Μίνως, mythical Greek forefathers: the derivation of manu fr. √man, 'think,' is unobjectionable so far as the form goes (1178b), but the usual explanation of manu as 'the thinker' defies common sense.]

manu-ja, *m.* man. [prop. adj., 'Manu-born, sprung from Manu,' 1265.]

manujendra, *m.* (prince of men, *i.e.*) prince, king, 1[5]. [manuja + indra, 1264.]

manuṣyà, —1. *a.* human; —2. *as m.* man. [manus, 1212d 1: cf. mānuṣa: for mg 2, see mānava.]

manuṣyatvá, *n.* condition of being man. [manuṣya, 1239.]

manuṣya-devá, *m.* human god [1280[1]] *or* man-god [1280b] *or* god among men [1264], *i.e.* Brahman, 95[1].

manuṣya-loká, *m.* world of men.

mánus, *m.* man. [cf. mánu and 1154.]

mano-ratha, *m.* wish. [lit. 'heart's joy,' manas + 2 ratha.]

mano-hara, *a.* (heart-taking, *i.e.*) captivating.

mántu, *m.* counsel, *i.e.* deliberation; *then* (*like Eng.* counsel), result of deliberation, plan, intent. [√man, 1161a.]

mántra, *m.* —1. thought; *esp.* thought as uttered in formal address, in prayer *or* song of praise (*see* dhī́ 2), *or* in pious text; —2. *usual designation of* the hymns and texts of the Vedas; —3. *later* (when these Vedic texts came to be used as magic formulas), spell, charm; —4. *like* mántu, deliberation, plan. [√man, 1185b: for mg 3, cf. Lat. *carmen*, 'solemn utterance' (see √çaṅs), then 'magic spell,' whence Eng. *charm*.]

mantra-da, *a.* giving, *i.e.* imparting the sacred texts, *i.e., as m.*, Veda-teacher.

√ **mantraya** (mantráyate [1067]). —1. speak with solemn *or* formal utterance; —2. deliberate. [denom. of mantra — see its various mgs.]

+ **anu**, follow with a mantra, accompany with a sacred text, *like Lat.* prosequi vocibus.

+ **abhi**, address a spell unto; charm *or* conjure.

+ **ā**, speak unto; *esp.* bid farewell to, 56[8].

+ **ni**, invite. [for mg, cf. (under √budh) Eng. *bid*, 'make formal announcement of,' and then 'invite.']

+ **saṁ-ni**, invite together, 4[20].

mantravant, *a.* accompanied by sacred texts. [mantra, 1233.]

mantra-varṇa, *m.* the wording of a sacred text.

√ **1 mand** (mándati; mamánda; ámandīt). gladden, 74[4]. [collateral form of √mad.]

√ **2 mand** *or* **mad** (mamátti; mádati). tarry, loiter. [amplification of *man, 'remain,' the congener of *μέν-ειν*, Lat. *man-ēre*, 'remain.']

manda, *a.* —1. tarrying, slow; —2. (sluggish, *and so*) weak; insignificant; little; —3. (*like Eng. colloq.* slow) stupid. [√2 mand, 'tarry.']

manda-bhāgya, *a.* having little luck, unlucky.

mandara, *m.* Mandara, a sacred mountain.

mandādara, *a.* having little regard for (*w. loc.*, 303a), careless about. [**manda** + **ādara.**]

mandāra, *m. n.* —1. coral tree, Erythrina indica; —2. *m. used, perhaps, as name of a man*, Mandāra.

mandira, *n.* dwelling; house; palace. [√2 **mand**, 'tarry,' 1188e: prop. 'a waiting, an abiding,' and then 'abiding-place, mansion': cf. *μάνδ-ρα*, 'fold, stable,' later 'monastery': for mg, observe that Lat. *mansio*, stem *man-si-on-* (fr. *man-ēre*, 'tarry'), meant first 'a tarrying,' and then 'a stopping-place, mansion,' French 'maison'; see also **bhavana.**]

manmatha, *m.* love; the god of love. ['the agitator, distresser,' intensive formation fr. √**math** or **manth**, 1148. 4, 1002b.]

mánman, *n.* thought; *esp.* (*like* **dhī́** 2) An-dacht, devotion, prayer *or* praise. [√**man**, 1168.1a.]

man-mā̃sa, *n.* my flesh. [**mad**, 494.]

manyú, *m.* —1. mood, *i.e.* temper of mind; *then* —2. (*like Eng.* mood) anger, heat of temper. [√**man**, 1165a.]

máma, *see* 491 *and* **ma.**

maya, —1. *called a derivative suffix* (*see* 1225, 161[3]), *but really a nomen actionis meaning* formation, make, *used as final element of a cpd*, having · · as its make, made of · ·, consisting of · ·, containing · · in itself; —2. *nomen agentis*, maker, former; *esp.* Maya, The Former, name of an Asura, artificer of the Daityas, and skilled in all magic, 45[6]. [fr. **mi**, weak form (cf. 954c, 250) of √1 **mā**, 'measure, arrange, form,' 1148. 1a and b: so the Eng. deriv. suffix *-hood*, *-head*, Ger. *-heit*, was once an independent noun, see under **ketu.**]

máyas, *n.* invigoration, refreshment, cheer, gladness, joy. [prop. 'a building up,' fr. √1 **mi**, 'establish,' or fr. the weak form **mi** (cf. 954c, 250) of the kindred and partly equivalent √1 **mā**, 'measure, arrange, form, build,' 1151. 1a.]

mayo-bhū́ [352], *a.* being for *or* conducing to **mayas**, *i.e.* refreshing, gladdening.

mara, *m.* death. [√**mṛ**, 'die.']

marakata, *n.* smáragd *or* emerald. [cf. *σμάραγδος*, whence Lat. *smaragdus*, Old French *esmeralde*, French *émeraude.*]

maraṇa, *n.* death. [√1 **mṛ**, 'die.']

márīci, *f.* —1. mote *or* speck in the air, illuminated by the sun; —2. *later*, beam of light. [cf. **marút.**]

marīci-mālā, *f.* garland of rays.

marīcimālin, *a.* having a garland of rays. [**marīcimālā**, 1230a.]

marú, *m.* a waste; desert. [perhaps 'the dead and barren' part, whether of land or water, √1 **mṛ**, 'die': cf. *'Αμφί-μαρος*, son of Poseidon; Lat. *mare*, 'sea'; AS. *mere*, 'sea, lake, swamp,' Eng. *mere*, 'lake, pool,' *Winder-mere*, *mer-maid*; AS. *mōr*, Eng. *moor*, 'marshy waste, heath.']

marút, *m. pl.* the Maruts *or* gods of the storm-wind, Indra's companions, *selections* xxxv., xlii., xlvii., lxvii. [perhaps 'the flashing ones,' as gods of the thunder-storm, and connected w. a √***mar** seen in *μαρ-μαίρ-ω*, 'flash.']

maru-sthalī, *f.* desert-land, desert.

martavya, *grdv.* moriendum; *impersonally*, *see* 999. [√1 **mṛ**, 'die,' 964.]

mártya, *m. like Eng.* a mortal, *i.e.* a man; *as a.* mortal.

mardana, *m.* crusher; *fig.*, *as in Eng.*, subduer. [√**mṛd**, 1150. 1a.]

marma-jña, *a.* knowing the weak spots. [**marman.**]

márman, *n.* mortal part, vulnerable *or* weak spot, *lit. and fig.* [cf. √1 **mṛ**, 'die.']

márya, *m.* man, *esp.* young man; *pl.* (*like Eng.* men, *Ger.* Mannen), servants, attendants, henchmen.

marṣa, *m.* patient endurance. [√**mṛṣ.**]

mála, *n. m.* smut; impurity, physical and moral. [cf. *μέλ-αν*, 'dark'; Lat. *mălu-s*, 'bad.']

malla, *m.* —1. *pl.* the Mallas, a people; —2. professional boxer and wrestler; one who engages in the *παγκράτιον*, pancratiast.

maçáka, *m.* biting and stinging insect, gnat.

maṣī, *f.* —1. bone-black; —2. ink, made of lac *or* of almond-charcoal boiled in cow's urine.

maṣy-abhāva, *m.* lack of ink.

√ **mah** (máhate; māmahé [786]; mahitá; mahitvā́; *caus.* maháyati, -te). *orig.* be great *or* high, *and so* —1. *mid.* be glad, rejoice; *then* (*trans.* make great *or* high, *and so*) —2. *act.* elate; gladden; exalt (*mid.*), 74[8]; —3. esteem highly, honor.

[for *magh, cf. magha, also √maṅh: for orig. mg, cf. participial adj. mahánt, 'great': for mgs 1 and 2, cf. American colloq. use of *high* as 'high in spirit, elated, *esp.* intoxicated':

—with orig. √*magh in the mgs 'be great, mighty, *i.e.* powerful *or* able,' trans. 'make able, help,' cf. *μοχ-λός*, 'helping-bar, lever'; *μηχ-ανή*, 'means'; Goth. *mag*, AS. *mæg*, 'am able,' Eng. *may:*

—with the collateral form *mag, whose deaspiration is prob. Indo-European, cf. *μέγ-ας*, Lat. *mag-nus*, AS. *mic-el*, Eng. *mickle*, 'great.']

máh, *f.* mahī́, *a.* great; mighty, 78[3]; strong; —mahī́, *as subst.* the great, *i.e.* the earth; *for mg, cf.* pṛthivī. [cf. √mah: see 400[2].]

mahá, *a.* great. [√mah.]

mahánt [450b], *f.* mahatī́, —1. *a.* great (in space, time, quantity, *or* quality, *and so*), large, long, mighty, important; significant, 6[11]; *as m.* great *or* noble man, 19[21], 36[10]; —2. *m.* (*sc.* ātman), the intellect, 66[9], 67[17]. [orig. ppl. of √mah, q.v.]

maharṣi, *m.* great Rishi. [mahā + ṛṣi.]

máhas, *n.* greatness; might; glory; gladness; mahobhis, *adv.:* with power, 79[12]; joyfully, 73[13]. [√mah, see its various mgs.]

mahā́, *used as prior member of a cpd, instead of* mahánt, 1249b, 355a. [√mah.]

mahā-kathā, *f.* great tale.

mahā-kavi, *m.* great poet.

mahā-kula, *n.* (great, *i.e.*) noble family.

mahā-guru, *a.* exceedingly reverend [1279]; *as m.* person worthy of unusual honor.

mahā-tapas, *a.* (having, *i.e.*) practising great austerity; *as m.* Great-penance, name of a sage.

mahātman, *a.* having a (great, *i.e.*) noble nature, noble; magn-animus. [mahā + ātman.]

mahā-dhana, *a.* having great wealth, very rich.

mahā-paṅka, *m. n.* (great, *i.e.*) deep mire.

mahā-paṇḍita, *a.* exceedingly learned [1279].

mahāparādha, *m.* great crime. [mahā + aparādha.]

mahā-prājña, *a.* very wise [1279].

mahā-bāhu, *a.* great-armed [1294], *i.e.* stout-armed.

mahā-bhūta, *n.* grosser element, *i.e.* earth, air, fire, water, *or* ether (as distinguished from a subtile element or rudimentary atoms).

mahā́-manas, *a.* great-minded.

mahā-muni, *m.* great sage.

mahā-yajñá, *m.* great sacrifice, 59[6] N.

mahā-yaças, *a.* having great glory, famous.

mahā-rājá, *m.* great prince. [rājan, 1315a.]

mahā-rāva, *m.* great howl.

mahā-vikrama, *a.* having great might *or* courage; *as m.* Great-might, name of a lion.

mahā-vīrá, *m.* great hero.

mahā-vratá, *n.* great vow. [1267.]

mahā́-vrata, *a.* having a mahāvratá, having undertaken a great vow. [1295.]

mahā-siṅha, *m.* great lion.

máhi, *a.* great. [√mah.]

mahitvá, *n.* greatness, might. [1239.]

mahimán, *m.* might; *instr.* mahinā́, *see* 425e. [√mah, 1168. 2b.]

mahiṣá, *a.* mighty; mahiṣo mṛgas, the powerful beast, *i.e.* buffalo, RV.; *as m.*, *without* mṛga, buffalo, 55[3]; —máhiṣī, *f.* [*acct, cf.* 362b[2]], the powerful one, *as designation: of a* woman of high rank; *of* the first wife of a king, 1[16]; *sometimes of any* queen of a king, 50[1]. [√mah, 1197b.]

mahī́, *see under* máh.

mahī-kṣít, *m.* earth-ruler, king.

mahī-pati, *m.* earth-lord, king.

mahī-pāla, *m.* earth-protector, king.

√ **mahīya** (mahīyáte). be glad, happy, blessed. [prop. 'be great, high,' denom. of mahi (1061), with the modification of mg mentioned under √mah, q.v.]

mahendrá, *m.* —1. Great-Indra; —2. great chief, 10^{15} (*w. mg* 1 *also*). [mahā́ + índra.]

mahendratva, *n.* the name *or* dignity of Great-Indra. [1239.]

maheçvara, *m.* great lord; *esp., as pl., designation of* the four lokapālās, Indra, Yama, Agni, and Varuna. [mahā + īçvara.]

mahāujas, *a.* having great strength, mighty. [mahā + ojas.]

√1mā (mímīte [660–3]; mamāú, mamé; ámāsta; mitá [954c]; mā́tum; mitvā́; -mā́ya). —1. measure; —2. measure with, compare; —3. mete out; —4. arrange, form; build; make, 72^{2}. [for 1, cf. μέ-τρον, 'measure'; Lat. *ni-mi-us*, 'not to be measured, excessive'; for 4, cf. μά-ρη and Lat. *mă-nu-s*, 'former, *i.e.* hand'; εὐ-μαρής, 'handy, easy': see also the collateral form √1mi, 'build, set up,' and under mātṛ́ and mā́s.]

+**anu**, (form after, *i.e.*) re-create in imagination, conceive.

+**upa**, measure with, compare.

+**nis**, fashion *or* make out of (*abl.*); construct.

+**vi-nis**, lay out (garden).

+**pari**, measure around, limit.

+**pra**, measure.

+**prati**, make (so as to be a match) against, *cf.* pratimā.

+**vi**, measure out; *then* (*like Eng.* measure), pass over, traverse (the sky).

√2mā *or* mī (mímāti [660–3]; mimā́ya). bellow.

+**vi**, bellow *or* cry aloud.

mā́, *adv. and conj.* not, *mostly in prohibitions* [1122b]: —1. *regularly w. subjunctive, i.e. augmentless form of a past tense* [579–80], 76^{16}, etc.; in order that not, 53^{7}; —2. *w. imperative*, 22^{2}, 35^{11}, 50^{4}; —3. *rarely w. optative*, 79^{17}; —4. *w.* evam, not so, 38^{5}; —5. *w.* u, mo, *see* u. [cf. μή, Elian μά, 'not, that not.']

mā́ṅs *and* mā́ṅsá [397], *n.* meat, flesh; *used also in pl.* [cf. Church Slavonic *męso*, Prussian *mensa*, 'flesh': cf. 64^{7} N.]

mā́ṅsatva, *n.* the being meat, the etymological meaning of mā́ṅsa. [1239.]

mā́ṅsa-ruci, *a.* having pleasure in meat, greedy for meat.

mā́ṅsa-lubdha, *a.* desirous of meat. [√lubh.]

māñgalya, *a.* bringing happiness, pleasant. [mañgalá.]

māciram, *adv.* (not long, *i.e.*) shortly, straightway. [mā́ + cirám, $1122b^{4}$.]

māṭhara, *m.* Māṭhara, name of a man. [maṭhara, 1208f.]

māṇava, *m.* boy, youngster. [not akin w. manu, 'man': perhaps for,*malnava: cf. Prussian *malnyx*, 'child.']

māṇavaka, *m.* manikin, dwarf. [māṇava, 1222b.]

mātariçvan, *m.* Mātariçvan, mystic name of Agni.

mātula, *m.* mother's brother. [mātṛ, 1227^{2}: cf. μήτρως, Doric μάτρως, 'mother's brother.']

mātṛ́ [373], *f.* mother; applied also to the earth, the Dawn, the sticks of attrition (82^{9}). [perhaps 'the one who metes out' food to the household, or else 'the former' of the child in the womb, √1mā, 'measure *or* mete,' 'form,' 1182d: cf. μήτηρ, Doric μάτηρ, Lat. *māter*, AS. *mōder*, Eng. *mother*; also μαῖα, 'mother.']

mātṛtas, *adv.* from the mother, on the mother's side. [mātṛ, 1098b.]

mātṛvat, *adv.* as one's mother.

mā́trā, *f.* —1. measure; *at end of adj. cpds* [*see* 1302c 3], having · · as its measure, so and so long *or* high *or* large, etc.: jānu-mātra, knee-deep; vyāma-mātra, a fathom broad; —2. the full measure, *i.e.* limit; *at end of adj. cpds*, having · · as its limit, not more than · ·; *and then, these adj. cpds being used substantively* (1247 III^{4}), · · merely, · · only, mere · ·, 27^{20}, 50^{9}; *such a cpd as first member of another cpd*, 34^{8}, 37^{6}; *hence* —3. *from this frequent use of* mātrā *at end of cpds in the form* mātra (334^{2}), *the quasi-stem*, mātra, *n.* measure, *i.e.* height, depth, length, breadth, distance (43^{12}). [√1mā, 'measure,' 1185c: cf. μέ-τρον, 'measure.']

māda, *m.* revelry. [√mad.]

1 **māna**, *m. n.* —1. opinion; —2. (*like the Eng.* opinion) estimation, *esp.* good esteem; —3. honor. [√man, 1148.2.]

2 **mā́na**, *m.* *like the Eng.* building, *and so* structure, castle. [√1 mā, 'make, build,' 1150. 1a.]

3 **mā́na**, *m.* —1. *like the obs. Eng.* maker, ποιητής, poet; —2. as name of Agastya's father, Māna. [do.]

māna-da, *a.* (giving, *i.e.*) showing honor (to others); *as m.* honor-giver, *address of a woman to her lover.*

√ **mānaya** (mānáyati). honor. [denom. of 1 māna: cf. 1067.]

mānavá, —1. *a.* human; descended from man *or* Manu (*see* manu); —2. *as m.* one of the sons of men, a man; —3. *m.* Mānava, name of a school of the Yajurveda. [mánu, 1208c: for mgs 1 and 2, observe that Old High Ger. *mennisch*, though prop. an adj. fr. *man*, 'homo,' and meaning 'humanus,' is used also as a subst. meaning 'man,' and used in its Ger. form *Mensch*, 'man,' as subst. only: cf. also nāra, manuṣya, mānuṣa.]

mānava-dharmaçāstra, *n.* law-book of the Mānavas *or* Mānava-school.

mānasá, *a.* sprung from the mind; of the mind. [mánas, 1208a.]

mā́nuṣa, *f.* -ī, *a.* pertaining to man, human; *as m.* man (*cf.* mānava). [mánus, 1208a end: cf. manuṣyà.]

mānuṣa-dāivika, *a.* of men and of gods. [1257.]

māndāryá, *a.* descended from Mandāra; *as m.* descendant of M. [mandāra, 1211.]

mānyá, *a.* descended from a poet *or* from Māna; *as m.* the poet's son *or* Māna's son. [3 mā́na, 1211.]

māma, *a.* *lit.* of mine; *voc. s. m., as word of address of a dog to an ass,* uncle. [mama (491), 1208f.]

māyā́, *f.* —1. (a working, *and so*) a power; *esp., in Veda,* supernatural *or* wonderful power; wile; —2. *later,* trick; illusion. [√1 mā, 'make, *i.e.* have effect, work,' 1149, cf. 258.]

māyā-kapota, *m.* illusion-pigeon.

māyākapota-vapus [418], *a.* having the form of a phantom-pigeon.

māyín, *a.* wily. [māyā.]

māyobhavya, *n.* gladness, happiness. [mayobhū́, 1211, cf. 1208c.]

māra, *m.* a killing, murder. [√1 mṛ, 'die.']

mārakata, *f.* -ī, *a.* smarágdine, emerald (*adj.*). [marakata, 1208f.]

māraṇa, *n.* a killing; *w.* pra‿āp, incur killing, get killed. [caus. of √1 mṛ, 'die,' 1150. 1b.]

mārātmaka, *a.* having murder as one's nature, murderous. [māra + ātmaka, 1302.]

mārga, *a.* of *or* pertaining to game *or* deer; *as m.* track of wild animals, slot; *then, in general,* track, way, path. [mṛga, 1208f.]

mārja, *adj. subst.* cleaning, a cleaner, *in cpds.* [√mṛj, 627[1,2].]

mārjāra, *m.* cat. ['the cleaner,' so called from its habit of cleaning itself often: fr. mārja: formed like karmāra, 1226b.]

mālava, *m.* Malwa, name of a country in west-central India.

mālava-viṣaya, *m.* the land of Malwa.

mālā, *f.* crown, wreath, garland.

mālin, *a.* crowned, wreathed. [mālā.]

mālya, *n.* crown, wreath. [mālā, 1210.]

mā́s [397], *m.* —1. moon, *see* candra-mās; *then* (*as in Eng.*), a moon, *i.e.* month. ['the measurer,' √1 mā, 1151. 1c[2]: cf. μή-νη, 'moon'; Lat. *Mēna*, 'menstruationis dea'; Goth. *mena*, AS. *mōna*, Eng. *moon*; AS. *mōnan dæg*, 'dies Lunae,' Eng. *Monday*; also μήν, stem μενς, Lat. *mens-i-s*, 'month'; AS. *mōnað*, prop. 'a lunation,' Eng. *month*.]

mā́sa, *m.* —1. moon, *see* pūrṇa-māsa; —2. month. [transition-stem fr. mā́s, 399.]

māsa-traya, *n.* month-triad, three months.

māsa-ṣaṭka, *n.* month-hexade, six months.

mā́hina, *a.* glad, blithe. [√mah, 1177b.]

√ **1 mi** (minóti, minuté; mimā́ya; mitá; -mítya). build; establish; set up (a post, pillar). [collateral form (250a) of √1 mā, 'make, build,' q.v.: cf. mít and Lat. *mē-ta*, 'post'; *mū-rus*, 'wall.']

√ 2 **mi** *or* **mī** (**mināti, mīnāti; mimā́ya, mimyé; ámeṣṭa; meṣyáte; mītá; -mī́ya**). minish, lessen; minish, bring low; bring to nought. [cf. *μι-νύ-ω*, Lat. *mi-nu-o*, 'lessen'; AS. positive *min*, 'small'; Old High Ger. comp. *minniro*, **minv-iro*, Middle High Ger. *minre*, Ger. *minder*, 'less'; *μείων*, **μη-ίων*, 'less'; Lat. *min-or*, 'less'; *per-mi-t-ie-s*, 'ruin': fr. AS. *min* comes perhaps Eng. *minnow*, 'very small fish.']

+**pra**, bring to nought; *pass.* come to nought, perish.

√ **migh**, *see* **mih**.

mít, *f.* post, pillar, prop. [√1 mi, 'set up,' 383b[3]: for mg, cf. Eng. *post*, Lat. *postis*, with *pōnere*, 'set up.']

mitrá, —1. *m.* friend, comrade (*Vedic only*); *esp.* —2. Mitra, name of an Aditya; —3. *n.* friendship (*rare and Vedic only*); —4. *n.* friend (*commonest meaning and gender*).

mitrabandhu-hīna, *a.* destitute of friends and relatives. [1265, 1252.]

mitra-lābha, *m.* Friend-acquisition, as title of the first book of the Hitopadeça.

mitrātithi, *m.* Mitrātithi, name of a man. ['having Mitra as his guest' or else 'guest of M.': the mg of the cpd depends on its accent (see 1302[1] and 1267[1]), and this is not known: mitrá + átithi.]

mitrā́-váruṇā, *nom. du. m.* Mitra and Varuna. [see 1255 and a, and Whitney 94a.]

√ **mith** (**méthati; mimétha; mithitá; mithitvā́**). —1. meet together as friends, associate with, pair; —2. meet as rivals, dispute, wrangle, altercari. [observe that Eng. *meet* is just such a vox media and means both 'harmonize' and 'have a conflict.']

mithás, *adv.* together, mutually, among each other; in turns. [√mith, 1111d.]

míthu, *a.* wrong; false; *used only in the adv. acc. s. n.* **míthu** (1111d), *and instr. s. f.* **mithuyā́** (1112e), wrongly, falsely. [√mith: for mg, observe that Ger. *verkehren* means both 'to turn the wrong way' and 'to associate with,' whence *Verkehr*, 'intercourse,' and *verkehrt*, 'wrong.']

mithuná, —1. *a.* paired, forming a pair; —2. *m.*, *later n.* pair (consisting of a male and female), pair of children; pair (of anything). [√mith, 1177c.]

mithuyā́, *adv.* falsely. [see míthu: acct!]

mithyā́, *adv.* wrongly, falsely. [younger form of mithuyā́.]

mithyopacāra, *m.* false service *or* simulated kindness. [mithyā + upacāra, 1279, mithyā being used as a quasi-adj.]

√ **mil** (**miláti; miméla; miliṣyáti; militá; militvā́; -mílya**). meet; assemble. [cf. Lat. *mille*, 'assemblage, host, thousand,' pl. *mīl-ia*, whence the borrowed Eng. *mile*, 'a thousand (paces), mīlia passuum'; perhaps *mīl-it-es*, 'going in companies *or* troops' and so, like Eng. *troops*, 'soldiers.']

√ **miç**, mix, *in the desid.* **mimikṣ** (*see* 1033), *and the deriv.* **miçra** *or* **miçla**. [cf. *μίγνυμι*, **μικ-νυ-μι*, Lat. *misceo*, **mic-sc-eo*, 'mix'; Old High Ger. *misken*, Ger. *mischen*, 'mix'; AS. *miscian*, **mih-sc-ian*, whence Eng. *mix* for *misk* (like *ax*, formerly good English for *ask*); also Eng. *mash*, 'mixture' esp. of grains, whence verb *mash*, 'mix, *and esp.* make into a confused mass by crushing.']

miçrá, *a.* mixed. [√miç, 1188.]

miçrībhāva, *m.* the becoming mixed, the mingling (*intrans.*). [miçrībhū.]

miçrībhāva-karman, *n.* mingling-action, process of becoming mixed.

miçrībhū, become mixed. [miçra, 1094.]

miçla, *same as* **miçra**. [1189.]

√ **miṣ** (**miṣáti; miméṣa; ámīmiṣat; miṣitá; -míṣya**). open the eyes, have the eyes open.

+**ni**, close the eyes; fall asleep; wink.

√ **mih** *or* **migh** (**méhati; ámikṣat; mekṣyáti; mīḍhá** [222[3]]). make water. [fr. migh (223[3]) come ppl. méghamāna, and noun meghá, 'cloud': cf. *ὀ-μιχ-έω*, Lat. *ming-ere*, AS. *mīg-an*, 'make water': orig. mg, 'pour out,' whence on the one hand 'mingere' and on the other 'rain, drip, drop' (cf. noun míh); then, fig. 'drop fatness, bestow richly' (see under mīḍhvā́ṅs).]

míh, *f.* mist. [√mih: cf. ὀ-μίχ-λη, 'mist'; AS. *mist*, **mig-st*, Eng. *mist.*]

mīḍhvā́ṅs, *a.* bestowing richly, bountiful. [said to be perfect ppl. of √mih, 222[3], 790b, 803[2].]

mīmāṅsya, *grdv.* to be called in question. [fr. desid. of √man, 1028e, 963.]

mīḷhúṣe, *see* mīḍhvā́ṅs *and* Whitney 54.

mukta-çāpa, *a.* having a laid aside curse, leaving his curse behind him. [√muc.]

múkha, *n.* —1. mouth, 39[8], 40[10], 51[12]; jaws, 18[23]; —2. visage, countenance, face, 13[3]; snout *or* face of an animal, 44[12]; *at end of cpds, esp. w. an adj.* [1298a], *or adjectively used prep.* [1305], *or adv.* [1306] *denoting direction:* udañ-mukha, having a northward face, turning northward; abhi-mukha, having the face towards; —3. (*like Eng.* face) surface, 25[21]; —4. (*like Eng.* head, *and like* chief *from* caput) the head, *i.e.* chief, best, most excellent, 51[22].

múkhya, *a.* (at the mouth *or* front, *and so*) chief, most excellent. [múkha, cf. mg 4: 1212a.]

√muc (muñcáti, -te [758]; mumóca, mumucé; ámucat; mokṣyáti, -te; muktá; móktum; muktvā́; -múcya; mocáyati, -te [1041[2]]). release; free; let go; let loose, 34[14]; lay aside; release *esp.* from the bonds of sin (93[13]) *or* existence; (let go, *i.e.* emit *or*) utter, *e.g.* sounds; shed (tears); discharge (phlegm, urine, ordure, smells). [orig. mg, 'to free *or* clear': specialized in Greek and Latin—'to clear the nose, to snot': cf. ἀπο-μύσσω, **-μυκ-jω*, Lat. *e-mung-o*, 'snot'; μυκ-τήρ, 'snout, nose'; Lat. *mūc-us*, 'snot': for mg, cf. relation of *snout* to the cognate verbs *snot* and *snite.*]

+nis, let out; release.

+pra, let go forth from, release from, *w. abl.*

+vi, loosen, *e.g.* a bond (*acc.*) from (*abl.*), 79[18]; untie; free; *pass.* be freed *or* separated from, be deprived of, *w. abl.*, *but also w. instr.* (283[2]). [for last mg, cf. Eng. *loose* with *lose.*]

múñja, *m.* sedge; *esp.* Saccharum Munja.

√mud (módate; mumudé; modiṣyáte; muditá). be glad, rejoice; mudita, glad, happy. [cf. √mad and √1 mand.]

+ā, *in* āmoda.

múni, *m.* —1. pressure, the pressing onward, impetus, 78[7]; —2. a man driven on by inward pressure *or* impulse, person in a (religious) ecstasy, enthusiast; *later* —3. *any* distinguished sage *or* seer *or* ascetic, *esp.* one who has taken a vow of silence (*cf.* māuna); hermit, 40[9], etc.

mumūrṣu, *a.* wishing to die, about to die, moribund. [fr. desid. of √1 mṛ, 1028b, 1178f.]

√muṣ (muṣṇā́ti; mumóṣa; ámoṣīt; muṣitá; muṣitvā́; -múṣya). rob; steal. [cf. mū́ṣ, 'the thief, *i.e.* mouse'; μῦς, 'mouse,' and from the shape, 'muscle'; Lat. *mūs*, 'mouse,' whence diminutive *mus-culus*, 'muscle'; AS. *mūs*, 'mouse' and 'muscle,' Eng. *mouse;* Ger. *Maus*, 'mouse' (whence denom. *mausen*, 'steal,' in which we are brought back again to the orig. mg of the primitive), and also 'muscle of the thumb'; further, μυῖα, **μυσια*, Lat. *mus-ca*, 'fly': see also muṣka.]

muṣká, *m.* —1. testicle; —2. pudenda muliebria. [from noun muṣ, *i.e.* (383a[2]) mū́ṣ, 'mouse': for mgs, see under √muṣ: cf. μύσ-χον· τὸ ἀνδρεῖον καὶ γυναικεῖον μόριον: w. muṣka, cf. also Persian *mushk*, Eng. *musk*, 'perfume got from a bag behind the navel of the musk-deer.']

muṣka-deça, *m.* region of the testes, groin.

muṣṭi, *m.f.* fist.

músala, *m. n.* pestle. [1181c.]

√muh (múhyati, -te; mumóha, mumuhé; ámuhat; mohiṣyáti; mugdhá, mūḍhá). be confused; err; lose one's senses; mūḍha, foolish, *and as subst.*, fool, simpleton. [cf. Lat. *mūg-er*, 'false player.']

múhus, *adv.* suddenly; in a moment; muhur muhus, at one moment—at another, *i.e.* repeatedly. ['in a bewildering way,' √muh, 1111d.]

muhūrtá, *m. n.* —1. moment; —2. thirtieth of a day, an hour (of 48 minutes), 59[10]. [muhus.]

mūḍha, *see* √muh.

mū́tra, *n.* urine.

mūrkhá, *a.* stupid, foolish; *as m.* fool. [√mūrch, mg 3.]

mūrkha-çata, *n.* fool-hundred.

√mūrch (mū́rchati; mumū́rcha; mūrchitá, mūrtá [220²]). become rigid: —1. coagulate, acquire consistency; *and so* —2. take shape, be formed; —3. (become stiff, numb, torpid, *and so*) become stupid, senseless. [for mg 3, cf. Eng. *torpid*, 'numb,' and then 'dull, stupid': see mūrti and mūrkha.]

mū́rti, *f.* firm body, definite shape, embodiment. [√mūrch, 220².]

mūrtimant, *a.* having bodily form, incarnate. [mūrti, 1235.]

mūrdhán, *m.* forehead, skull; head; *oftenest figuratively*, highest part; mūrdhni, at the head.

mū́la, *n.* root; *fig.* (*like Eng.* root), that from which a thing grows *or* proceeds, root, basis; capital.

mūlya, *n.* price, 47⁸·¹¹; capital, 46¹⁴. [properly, perhaps, adj. 'pertaining to the root, radical, basal,' and then, as subst., 'basis' of a transaction: fr. mūla, q.v.]

mū́ṣ, *m. f.* mouse. ['the thief,' √muṣ, q.v.: see 383a².]

mūṣaka, *m.* thief; mouse, 46¹⁷; Mousey, as name of a man, 47²¹. [√muṣ, q.v.]

mūṣakākhyā, *f.* the name Mousey. [ākhyā: 1280b.]

mūṣika, *m.* mouse, rat. [√muṣ, q.v.]

mūṣika-nirviçeṣa, *a.* undistinguished from a mouse.

√1 mṛ (mriyáte [773]; mamā́ra; ámṛta; mariṣyáti; mṛtá; mártum; mṛtvā́). die; mṛtá, dead. [w. mṛtá, cf. βροτός, *μροτος, 'mortal'; cf. φλὸξ ἐ-μαρ-άν-θη, 'flame died away'; Lat. *mor-i*, 'die'; *mors*, stem *mor-ti-*, 'death'; Goth. *maur-þr*, AS. *morðor*, Eng. *murther*, *murder*: see amṛta.]

+**abhi**, (*lit.* die against, *i.e.*) affect unpleasantly by dying; guruṇā‿abhimṛta, (affected by a teacher by dying, *i.e.*) bereaved by the death of a teacher.

√2 mṛ (mṛṇā́ti; mṛṇáti [731]; mūrṇá). crush; smash. [cf. μάρ-να-μαι, 'fight,' used of "bruisers," Odyssey 18. 31; μύλ-η, 'mill'; Lat. *mol-a*, 'mill'; Eng. *meal* (for mg, cf. piṣṭa); AS. *mol-de*, Eng. *mol-d*, 'fine earth' (for mg, cf. mṛ́d): cf. also √mṛd.]

√3 mṛ, *exists perhaps in* marut. [cf. μαρμαίρω, *μαρ-μαρ-jω, 'flash'; Lat. *mar-mor*, 'marble.']

mṛgá, *m.* —1. (*like AS.* deōr) wild animal, beast of the forest, *as opp. to* paçu, 'cattle,' 67²; *then* —2. (*w. the same specialization of mg as in Eng.* deer) animal of the genus Cervus, deer, gazelle. [perhaps 'the ranger, rover,' √mṛj, q.v.: for 2, observe the use of *deer* in the more general sense in King Lear, iii. 4. 128, "rats and such small deer."]

√mṛj (mā́rṣṭi [627]; mamā́rja; ámārjīt, ámārkṣīt; mārkṣyáte; mṛṣṭá; mā́rṣṭum; mṛṣṭvā́; -mṛ́jya; *also* mā́rjitum, mārjitvā́, -mā́rjya). rub off; wipe away; clean; polish.

[original meaning 'move hither and thither over': then, on the one hand, —1. 'range, rove, streifen,' as in Avestan mĕrĕgh, and Skt. mṛga; and, on the other, —2. 'go over with the hand, *i.e.* rub, wipe, strip (a tree, a cow), milk': for 2, cf. ὀ-μόργ-νυμι, 'wipe off'; ἀ-μέργ-ω, 'strip off, pluck'; ἀ-μέλγ-ειν, Lat. *mulg-ēre*, 'to milk'; AS. noun *meolc*, Eng. *milk*.]

+**apa**, wipe away; *also fig.*, of guilt. [cf. ἀπομόργνυμι, 'wipe away.']

+**pra**, wipe off, polish.

√mṛḍ (mṛḷáti, mṛḷáyati [1041²]). be gracious; forgive. [for ḷ, see Whitney 54.]

mṛḷīká, *n.* grace, mercy. [√mṛḍ, 1186⁴, Whitney 54.]

mṛtá, *ppl.* dead; *as n.* [1176a], death. [√1 mṛ, 'die.']

mṛtavat, *adv.* as if dead. [mṛta, 1107.]

mṛtyú, *m.* death. [√1 mṛ, 'die,' 1165a: see 95¹⁶.]

√mṛd (mṛdnā́ti; márdati, -te; mamárda; mardiṣyáte; mṛditá; márditum; mṛditvā́; -mṛ́dya). press *or* rub hard, squeeze, crush, smash, destroy.

[extension of √2 mṛ, 'crush': cf. *ἀ-μαλδ-ύνω*, 'destroy' e.g. a wall: w. **mṛdú**, 'soft, weak,' cf. Lat. *mollis*, **molvis*, **moldv-i-s*, 'soft, weak,' and *βραδύς*, **μραδυ-s*, 'slow' (for mg, cf. Ger. *weich*, 'soft,' w. Eng. *weak*, and Lat. *lēn-is*, 'soft,' w. *len-tus*, 'slow'):

with √**mṛd** in **hima-mardana**, 'melting of the snow,' we might compare *μέλδω*, 'melt,' Eng. *melt*; but the *s* of the collateral form *smelt* makes this doubtful: see also **mradas**.]

\+ **vi**, destroy.

mṛ́d, *f.* earth; loam; clay; mound of earth, 62^{18}. [prop. 'crumbled earth,' √**mṛd**: similar specializations of mg are frequent: thus AS. *mol-de*, 'crumbling earth, dust,' Eng. *mol-d*, come fr. a √*mal*, the cognate of √2 **mṛ**, 'crush, crumble'; Ger. *Grand*, 'sand,' is fr. the same root as Eng. *grind*; Ger. *Scholle*, 'clod,' and *zer-schellen*, 'break to pieces,' go back to the same root; **logá** and **loṣṭá**, 'clod,' are derivs of √**ruj**, 'break.']

mṛdú, *a.* soft; weak. [√**mṛd**, q.v.]

mṛnmáya, *a.* made of earth; *w.* **gṛha**, house of clay, the grave. [**mṛ́d** + **maya**: see **maya**.]

√ **mṛç** (**mṛçáti**, **-te**; **mamárça**, **mamṛçé**; **ámṛkṣat**; **mṛṣṭá**; **márṣṭum**; **-mṛ́çya**). —1. touch, mulcēre, stroke; grasp, take hold of; —2. take hold of mentally, consider. [cf. the Hesychian *βρακεῖν*, √**μρακ*, 'grasp, understand'; Lat. *mulcēre*, 'stroke.']

\+ **abhi**, touch.

√ **mṛṣ** (**mṛ́ṣyate**, **-ti**; **mamárṣa**, **mamṛṣé**; **ámarṣiṣṭa**; **-mṛ́ṣya**; *caus.* **marṣáyati**). —1. forget, 92^{16}; —2. (*like Eng.* not mind) disregard, treat as of no consequence, bear patiently.

meka, *a* setting up, *in* **su-méka**. [√1 **mi**, 'establish.']

mékhalā, *f.* girdle, *see* 59^{3} N.

meghá, *m.* cloud. [√**migh**, see **mih**.]

médas, *n.* fat. [√**mid** or **med** (761a), **médyati**, 'be fat.']

médha, *m.* —1. juice of meat, broth; —2. sap and strength, essential part, *esp.* of the sacrificial victim; —3. sacrificial victim; animal sacrifice. [cf. √**mid** under **médas**.]

medhas, wisdom, *in* **su-medhas**. [equiv. of **medhā́**.]

medhā́, *f.* wisdom.

melaka, *m.* assembly; *w.* **kṛ**, assemble. [√**mil**, 1181.]

modaka, *m.* small round comfit, sweetmeat. [prop. 'gladdener,' √**mud**, 1181: so Eng. *cheer* and *refreshment* are applied esp. to eatables.]

māuñjá, *a.* made of Munja-grass; —*f.* **-ī**, *sc.* **mekhalā**, girdle of Munja-grass. [**múñja**, 1208f.]

māuñjī-nibandhana, *n.* ligation of the Munja-girdle.

māuná, *n.* silence. [**múni**, 1208d.]

mna, *uncertain verbal.* minded; *assumed on account of* **sumná**. [√**mnā**.]

√ **mnā** (**mánati**; **ámnāsīt**; **mnātá**). *collateral form of* √**man**, 'be minded,' 108g. [see √**man**: cf. *μι-μνή-σκω*, 'keep in mind.']

√ **myakṣ** (**myákṣati**; **mimyákṣa** [785]; **ámyak**). be fixed in *or* on; be present.

\+ **sam**, keep together, 73^{4}.

mradas, *n.* softness. [√**mrad**, collateral form of √**mṛd**, q.v.]

√ **mlā** (**mlāyati**; **mamlāú**; **ámlāsīt**; **mlāná**). wither. [collateral form of √1 **mṛ**, 'die,' and so 'perish, decay, fade.']

mlāna-sraj, *a.* having a withered garland.

√ **mluc** (**mlócati**; **mumlóca**; **mluktá**). go.

\+ **apa**, go off, retire; **apamlukta**, retired, hidden.

mlecchá, *m.* barbarian. [√**mlech**.]

√ **mlech** (**mlécchati**). speak unintelligibly *or* barbarously. [root *****mlĕk**: **mlécchati** is for *****mlĕk-sketi**, like **pṛcchati**, q.v., for *****pṛksketi**: cf. *ἀ-μ(β)λακ-εῖν*, √*μλακ*, 'err, miss'; *βλάξ*, *βλακ-ός*, 'stupid.']

---

yá [509], *relative pron.* —1. who, which; *sometimes following its correlative:* 7^{6}, 17^{18}, 29^{5}, 30^{15}, 33^{16}, 52^{7}, 73^{9}, 78^{10}, 79^{7}; **evambhūto vidvān, yas · · samarthas,**

tam doctus · · qui possit, 19[4]; —2. *but much oftener preceding its correlative:* ya · · ta, 77[12], 69[7], 3[13], 17[13], 21[23], 22[4], 30[11], 32[10]; yā́ni · · eṣām, 74[8]; yac ca‿ucyate · ·, etad ālasyavacanam, and (what is said, *i.e.*) as for the saying · ·, that is [fatalists'] sloth-talk, 18[8, 11];

—3. *converting the subject or object of a verb into a substantive clause:—sometimes, perhaps, merely for metre:* 29[8], 38[7], 58[6]; *but often for emphasis:* 9[18], 56[19], 57[7]; yé pakṣā́ ā́saṅs, té jīmū́tā abhavan, what were wings, those became clouds, *for* té pakṣā́ abhavan jīmū́tās, 93[3]; ayáṁ yó hótā, kír u sá yamásya, who this priest [is], is he also that of Yama, 88[10]; *so* yad, *even w. words of different gender and number, as,* prajā́pater vā́ etáj jyeṣṭháṁ tokáṁ, yát párvatās, of P. that [was] the first creation, what the mountains are, 92[19]; *so* 95[15], 97[1];

—4. which, what, *as adj. pron. agreeing w. incorporated antecedent:* ná‿asmāi vidyút siṣedha, ná yā́m míham ákirad dhrādúnim ca, not for him did the lightning avail, not what mist he scattered abroad, and hail, 71[4]; *so* 71[20] *to* 72[2], 74[4], 79[9]?, 83[8], 88[7]; *as subst. pron., the antecedent not being expressed,* 74[1, 2], 78[18];

—5. ya *in special connections:* ya ya [511], whoever, whichever, whatever, whosoever, etc., 13[12], 45[18]; *so* ya ka ca, 68[10]; ya ka cid, 60[22], 68[12]; ya ka cana, 9[16]; ya ka cid, anyone soever, no matter who, quīlibet, 21[11]; *so* ya ta, 18[4]; —6. *two or more relatives in the same clause:* yo 'tti yasya yadā māṅsam, when (who) someone eats the flesh of (whom) someone, 29[7]; *so* 37[11], 66[18]; —7. ya, if anybody, si quis (*really an anacoluthon*)*: so* 79[16]; —8. ya, and · · he, 74[15]; —9. *for further illustration, see* 512, 511; *for derivatives,* 510; *for influence on the accent of the verb,* 595; *cf.* yad, yasmāt, yāt, yena.

[orig. and primarily a demonstrative (like Eng. *that* and Ger. *der*)*:* cf. ὅς, 'he,' in ἦ δ' ὅς, 'said he'; ὥς, 'so,' in οὐδ' ὥς, 'not even só'; —secondarily a relative (like Eng. *that* and Ger. *der*)*:* cf. ὅς, ἅ or ἥ, ὅ for *ὅδ, 'who, which'; hence yát, with which cf. ὡς, 'as'; —but these comparisons are rejected in toto by some.]

√ **yakṣ** (yákṣate). *perhaps an extended form of* *yah (*yagh), 'stir, move quickly': *and so, on the one hand,* pursue, *esp.* pursue avengingly, avenge, *and on the other,* dart swiftly (as a suddenly appearing light). [see the following three words and √*yah: kinship of Ger. *jag-en,* 'pursue, hunt,' is doubted.]

yakṣá, *n.* spirit *or* sprite *or* ghost; *as m.* a Yaksha, one of a class of fabulous genii, attendants of Kubera. [perhaps 'a restless one,' √yakṣ: for connection of mgs of root and deriv., cf. the converse relation of Eng. *spirit* or *sprite* to *sprightly,* 'brisk, stirring,' and cf. Scott's "restless sprite."]

yakṣín, *a.* avenging. [√yakṣ.]

yákṣma, *m.* disease. [perhaps, the sin-avenging Varuna's 'avenger,' √yakṣ, 1166.]

√ **yaj** (yájati, -te; iyā́ja, ījé [784[3]]; áyākṣīt, áyaṣṭa; yakṣyáti, -te; iṣṭá; yáṣṭum; iṣṭvā́; *caus.* yājáyati). honor a god (*acc.*), 99[12]; worship; worship with prayer and oblation (*instr.*)*; and so* consecrate, hallow, offer; sacrifice; *in Veda, active, when one honors or sacrifices* (*e.g., as a paid priest*) *on account of another, and middle, when one sacrifices on one's own account;* yájamāna, *as m.* one who institutes *or* performs a sacrifice and pays the expenses of it; —*caus.* cause *or* help *or* teach a person (*acc.*) to worship with a certain sacrifice (*instr.*)*;* serve a person as sacrificing priest. [cf. ἅγ-ος, 'worship, sacred awe, expiatory sacrifice'; ἅζομαι, *ἁγ-jομαι, 'stand in awe of,' e.g. gods; ἁγ-νός, 'worshipped, hallowed'; w. yajya, 'colendus,' cf. ἅγ-ιος, 'to be worshipped, holy': different is ἄγος, see āgas.]

\+ ā, get as result of sacrifice a thing (*acc.*) for a person (*dat.*), einem etwas er-opfern.

yájatra, *a.* venerable, holy. [√yaj, 1185d.]

yájīyāṅs, *a.* excellently sacrificing, right cunning in the art of sacrifice. [√yaj, 1184, 468.]

yajur-vedá, *m.* the Veda of sacrificial texts, Yajurveda. [see yajus.]

yájuṣmant, *a.* (possessing, *i.e.*) accompanied by sacrificial texts; *—f.* -matī (*sc.* iṣṭakā), Yajushmatī, name applied to certain bricks used in building the sacred fire-pile, and so called because each was laid with the recitation of a special text of its own. [yajus, 1235.]

yájus, *n.* —1. sacred awe; worship; —2. sacrificial text, as distinguished from stanza (ṛc) and chant (sāman); —3. the collection of such texts, the Yajur-veda. [√yaj, 1154.]

yajñá, *m.* worship, devotion (*so in Veda*); *later, esp.* act of worship, sacrifice, offering (*these the prevailing mgs*). [√yaj, 1177a, 201.]

yajña-kratú, *m.* sacrifice-ceremony, *i.e.* rite. [1280b.]

yajña-cchāga, *m.* sacrifice-goat. [chāga, 227.]

yajña-pātrá, *n.* sacrificial utensil.

yajñārtham, *adv.* for a sacrifice. [artham, 1302c4.]

yajñíya, *a.* —1. worthy of worship *or* sacrifice, reverend, holy, divine; —2. active *or* skillful in sacrifice, pious; *as m.* offerer. [yajña, 1214.]

yajñopavītá, *a.* the sacrifice-cord, sacred cord worn over the left shoulder. [upavīta.]

yájvan, *m.* worshipper, sacrificer. [√yaj, 1169.1a.]

√yat (yátati, -te; yeté; áyatiṣṭa; yatiṣyáti, -te; yatitá, yattá; yátitum; -yátya). —1. *act.* join, *trans.;* —2. *mid.* join, *intrans.;* range one's self in order, proceed in rows, 86[14]; —3. *mid.* try to join, strive after; take pains; —4. *caus.* (cause to attain, *i.e.*) requite with reward *or* punishment. [perhaps orig. 'reach out after' and akin w. √yam.]

+**ā**, reach to, attain, get a foot-hold.

+**pra**, (reach out, *i.e.*) make effort, take pains.

yátas, *adv.* from what (time *or* place *or* reason): —1. where, 6[14]; —2. because, for, 28[23], 38[5]; *esp. common as introducing a proverb or the first* (*only*) *of a series of proverbs motivating a preceding statement or action, e.g.* 19[7]; yatas · · tena, since · · therefore, 30[7]; *so* yatas · · atas, 36[2]; yatas · · tad, 37[6]; *cf.* tatas. [pron. root ya, 510, 1098.]

1 **yáti** [519], *pron.* as many, quot. [pron. root ya, 510, 1157.4.]

2 **yáti**, *m.* ascetic, man who has restrained his passions and abandoned the world; *see* āçrama *and* 65[8] N. ['striver, one who takes pains, one who castigates himself,' √yat, 1155: its mg was perhaps shaded towards that of 'restrainer' by a popular connection of the word with √yam, 1157[1], cf. 954d.]

yatna, *m.* a striving after; effort; pains; *w.* kṛ: take pains; bestow effort upon (*loc.*), have a thing (*loc.*) at heart, 1[13]; yatne kṛte, pains having been taken. [√yat, 1177.]

yátra, *adv.* where, *e.g.* 11[10]; whither; *—correl. w.* tatra, 24[4], 85[19]; *w.* enā, 83[10]; yatra yatra, where soever; catuṣpathe, yatra vā, at a quadrivium, or somewhere (else), 104[21]. [pron. root ya, 510, 1099.]

yáthā, *rel. adv. and conj.* —1. in which way, as; *sometimes following its correlative:* tathā · · yathā, 22[14], 43[20], 44[20]; evam · · yathā, 37[8]; —2. *but much oftener preceding its correlative:* teṣāṁ saṁ hanmo akṣāṇi, yathā‿idaṁ harmiaṁ, tathā, of them we close the eyes, as (we close) this house, so, 77[13]; *so* 61[6], 27[14], 21[16, 18], etc.; yathā · · evam, 18[18], 95[7, 9]; yathā · · eva (*Vedic*), 86[12, 18];

—3. *correlative omitted:* buddhim prakuruṣva, yathā‿icchasi, decide (so), as thou wishest, 9[11]; 5[20], etc.; *so with verbs of saying, etc.:* tad brūhi, yathā · · upadadhāma, this tell us (*viz.* the way) in which we are to put on · ·, 96[14]; *so* 88[6, 7];

—4. *without finite verb, as mere particle of comparison,* as, like, *e.g.* 6[19]; *so enclitic at end of a* pāda, 71[12, 15], 87[11], 1[5], 2[9], 31[1], 43[4]; *in solemn declarations:* yathā · ·, tena satyena, as surely as · ·, so, 13[23]ff.;

—5. *combinations* (*cf.* ya 5); yathā yathā · · tathā tathā, according as · · so, the more · · the more, 48[18]; yathā tathā, in some way or other (*cf.* **ya** 5 end), at any rate, 62[9];

—6. in order that, so that, ut, (so) that: *in Veda, w. subjunctive,* 88[14], 89[5,10,12], 90[19]; *later, w. opt.,* 14[9]; *w. fut. ind.,* 3[4]; *w. pres. ind.,* **yathā svāmī jāgarti, tathā mayā kartavyam,** I must act so, that the master wakes, 30[16]; *so* 37[5,7], 38[22], 39[1]; —7. that, *w. verbs of saying, knowing, etc.,* 30[7]; —*for influence on accent of verb, see* 595. [pron. root ya, 510, 1101: cf. article ya.]

yathā-kartavya, *a.* requiring to be done under given circumstances; *as n.* the proper course of action, 41[11].

yathākāmám, *adv.* according to wish, agreeably, 16[2]; in an easy-going way, slowly, 49[14]. [yáthā + kā́ma, 1313b.]

yathā-kārya, = yathākartavya.

yathākramam, *adv.* according to order, in regular series. [yathā + krama, 1313b.]

yathāgata, *a.* on which one came; -am, *adv.* by the way by which one came. [yathā + āgata, √gam, 1313b.]

yathāñgám, *adv.* limb after limb *or* limb on limb; membrātim. [yathā + añga, 1313b.]

yathātatham, *adv.* as it really is, accurately. [yathā + tathā, 1313b, 1314a.]

yathābhimata, *a.* as desired, that one likes. [yathā + abhimata, √man.]

yathābhimata-deça, *m.* desired place, place that one likes. [1280[1].]

yathāyogyam, *adv.* as is fit, according to propriety. [yathā + yogya, 1313b.]

yathārtha, *a.* according to the thing *or* fact, true; *as n.* the pure truth. [yathā + artha.]

yathārha, *a.* according to that which is fit; -am, *adv.* suitably, according to one's dignity. [yathā + arha, 1313b.]

yathāvat, *adv.* according to *le comment, comme il faut,* duly. [yathā, 1107.]

yathāvidhi, *adv.* according to prescription *or* rule. [yathā + vidhi, 1313b.]

yathā-vṛtta, *a.* as happened; -am, *w. verb of telling: either* the actual occurrence *or* circumstances (*as nom. or acc. s. n.*), *or* as it really happened (*as adv.,* 1313b).

yathāçraddhám, *adv.* according to inclination, as you will. [yathā + çraddhā, 1313b, 334[2].]

yathepsita, *a.* as desired; -am, *adv.* according to one's wish. [yathā + īpsita, √āp.]

yathokta, *a.* as (afore-)said; -am, *adv.* as aforesaid. [yathā + ukta.]

yád, —1. *as nom. acc. s. n. to* **ya,** *see* **ya**; *used in cpds and derivs, see* 510; —2. *as conjunctive adv.* that; **tan na bhadraṁ kṛtaṁ, yad viçvāsaḥ kṛtas,** therefore it was not well done (herein), that trust was reposed, 22[17]; **niṇyā ciketa, pṛçnir yad ūdho jabhāra,** he knoweth the secret, that P. offered her udder, 78[8]; *introducing oratio recta,* 38[1]; **yad · ·, tad,** as for the fact that · ·, therein, 36[1]; *so* 94[16]; **yad vāi tad abruvan,** as for the fact that they said thát, indeed, 96[23];

—3. *in causal connections: like Eng.* that (*i.e.* on account of which), 78[16]; **yad · · tad,** since · · therefore, 17[5]; **yad · · tasmāt,** inasmuch as · · therefore, 15[8]; since (*i.e.* considering that), 79[14]; *purpose:* in order that, 78[9], 72[12,14]; *result:* that, 71[6,7]; **etādṛçā dharmajñā, yan māṁ hantum udyatās,** so understanding the law, as to undertake to slay me, 28[5];

—4. *temporal:* as, 86[5]; **tad · · yad,** then · · when, 71[2]; **yad · · tatas,** when · · then, 92[12]; *so* **yad · · tādītnā,** 70[7]; *correl. often lacking:* **yad · ·, · ·,** when · ·, (*sc.* then), 75[12]; *so* 80[3], 81[17]; while, 71[5]; —*hence, the temporal use passing insensibly* (*cf.* **yad vaçāma,** when *or* if we will, 73[17], *and Eng.* when *w. Ger.* wenn) *into the conditional,* —5. if, 80[9,10,11]; —**yad** *placed within the dependent clause,* 78[8] (*quoted under* 2), 79[14]; —*for influence on acct of verb, see* 595. [pron. root ya, 510, 1111a.]

yadā́, *adv.* when; **yadā · · tadā** *or* **tatas,** when · · then; **yadā · · atha,** *Vedic,* 84[5,6,7]; **yadā yadā,** quandocunque, *see* **tadā.** [pron. root ya, 1103a.]

yádi, *adv.* if; —1. *w. pres. ind. in protasis: apodosis has pres. ind.,* 20[17], 37[12], 42[14], 43[7], 65[23], 99[21]; *has fut.,* 39[20], 44[4]; *has im-*

perative, 10^{16}; *has no finite verb*, 18^{17}, 25^{8}, 28^{9}, 40^{1}; —2. *w. fut. in protasis and apodosis*, 9^{20}, 11^{8}; —3. *w. pres. opt. in protasis and apodosis*, 3^{17}, 98^{20}; —4. *w. no finite verb in protasis: apodosis has imperative*, 32^{17}, 48^{11}, 84^{9}; *has no finite verb*, 27^{18}, 28^{12}, 63^{9}; —*alternative conditions:* · · vā, yadi vā · ·, · · vā, whether · ·, or · ·, or · ·, 28^{12}; —*apodosis introduced by* tadā (*e.g.* 25^{8}), tad (37^{12}), tarhi (32^{17}), *or without adv.* (*e.g.* 3^{17}). [pron. root ya, 1103d.]

yadbhaviṣya, *a.* who says yad bhaviṣyati, (tad) bhaviṣyati *or* "What will be, will be"; *as m.* fatalist; Yadbhavishya *or* Whatwillb', name of a fish. [1314b.]

√ **yam** (yácchati, -te [747]; yayā́ma, yemé; áyāṁsīt, áyaṁsta; yaṁsyáti; yatá; yáṁtum; yamitvā́; -yámya). hold; hold up, sustain, support; hold back, restrain; hold out, offer, grant, furnish; show (the teeth), 77^{4}. [cf. ζημία, 'restraint, *i.e.* punishment.']

+**ā**, hold out, *i.e.* extend, *and so* (*like Eng.* extend), lengthen; ā́yata, extended, long.

+**ud**, —1. raise (the arms, weapons), 35^{20}; —2. (*like Eng.* take up, *i.e.*) undertake *or* set about (a thing); udyata, having undertaken, *w. inf.*, 28^{6}.

+**sam-ud**, *like* ud-yam [1077b]: —1. raise; —2. set about; samudyata, having set about, *w. inf.*, 40^{20}.

+**upa**, hold on to, take hold of; *esp., middle*, take to wife, marry, 98^{8}.

+**ni**, hold, restrain; niyata, having restricted one's self (to a certain thing), all intent upon one definite object.

+**pra**, hold *or* reach out, offer, give; give in marriage (as a father his daughter), 98^{7}.

+**prati-pra**, offer in turn, pass (food), *w. gen.*, 100^{20}.

+**vi**, hold asunder, stretch out.

+**sam**, hold together, co-hibēre, hold in check; saṁyata, restrained.

yáma, —1. *a.* holding, restraining; —2. *m.* (holder, *i.e.*) bridle. [√yam.]

yamá, —1. *a.* paired, twin, geminus; *as m.* a twin; —2. The Twin, Yama, who, with his sister Yamī, constituted the first human pair, *selection* lxiii.; honored as father of mankind (*cf. also* manu) and as king of the spirits of the departed fathers (pitaras), *see* 83^{8}N.; *in later times*, regarded as the 'Restrainer' (√yam) or 'Punisher,' and ruler of death and of the dead in the under-world, 7^{11}; —**yamí**, *f.* Yamī, twin sister of Yama. [so *Thomas*, Hebrew *tᵉom*, means 'twin.']

yamá-rājan, *a.* having Yamá as their king; *as m.* subject of Yama. [1302a.]

yayā́ti, *m.* Yayāti, a patriarch of the olden time, son of Nahusha. [perhaps 'The Striver,' √yat, cf. 1155.2c: or from √yā, 1157.1c.]

yáva, *m. orig. prob.* any grain *or* corn, yielding flour; *later*, barley-corn, barley. [cf. ζειά, *ζαϝ-ιά, 'corn.']

yava-madhyama, *a.* having a barley-corn middle, *i.e.* big in the middle and small at the ends, like a crescendo-diminuendo sign; *as n.* the Yavamadhyama, name of a cāndrāyaṇa or lunar penance. [1297, 1280b.]

yáviṣṭha, *a.* youngest; *esp.* of a fire just born of the sticks of attrition *or* just set on the altar. [superl. to yúvan, q.v., but from the simpler *yu, 468.]

yáviṣṭhya, *a.* = yaviṣṭha, *but always at the end of a* pāda *and as diiambus.*

yávīyāṅs, *a.* younger. [comp. to yúvan, q.v., but from the simpler *yu, 468.]

yáças, *n.* fame, honor. [1151.2a.]

yaçás, *a.* honored, splendid. [1151.2a.]

yaṣṭí, *f.* staff. [perhaps 'a support,' fr. yacch, quasi-root of the present system of yam: cf. 220, 1157.]

√ **yah**, stir, move quickly, *inferred fr.* yakṣ, q.v., *and* yahva, 'continually moving, restless.'

√ **yā** (yā́ti; yayāú; áyāsīt [911]; yāsyáti; yātá; yā́tum; yātvā́; -yā́ya). —1. go, 39^{1}; yātas, avasitasya, of him that journeys (and) of him that rests, 71^{8}; *w.* astam, 62^{14}, *see* astam; —2. go to, *w. acc.*, 43^{17}, 91^{6}; *w. dat.* 49^{14}; —3. go to, *i.e.* attain to (a condition): *e.g.* devatvaṁ yā, attain to godhead, *i.e.* become divine,

19[21]; *so* 17[22], etc.; —4. yātu, let it go, no matter, 44[8].

[collateral form of √i, 'go,' 108g: hence yāna, 'passage, way,' w. which cf. Lat. *jānus*, 'passage, archway,' and the god thereof *Jānus*: fr. √yā comes also yā́-ma, 'period *or* watch of the night'; *ὥ-ρα*, 'time, season,' Eng. *year*, show a development of mg like that of yā́ma, q.v., but their connection w. √yā is doubtful (see 2 vāra).]

+anu, go after, follow.

+ā, come hither *or* to *or* on.

+sam-ā, come hither together; assemble; samāyāta, come.

+ud, go forth *or* out.

+upa, go *or* attain unto.

+pra, go forth; set out.

√ yāc (yā́cati, -te; yayācé; áyāciṣṭa; yāciṣyé; yācitá; yā́citum; yācitvā́; -yā́cya). make a request; ask a person (*acc.*) for a thing (*acc.*), 46[14]; ask a thing (*acc.*) of a person (*abl.*), 55[21].

yā́t, *adv.* as; *temporally*, so long as, 79[18]. [abl. of pron. root ya, 1114a, 510: see under ya.]

yātanā, *f.* requital; *esp.* punishment, pains of hell. [√yat, 1150.]

yātṛ́, *m.* avenger. ['pursuer,' √yā, 1182.]

yā́na, *m.* way; *as n.* wagon. [√yā, 1150.]

yāmá, *f.* -ī, *a.* of *or* coming from Yama. [yamá, 1208f.]

yā́ma, *m.* —1. course *or* going, 78[5]; —2. *as in Eng.*, course (of a feast); —3. watch of the night. [√yā, 1166: for mg 2, cf. *περί-οδος*, 'way around, circuit, course at dinner,' and Ger. *Gang*, 'course': for mg 3, cf. *περίοδος*, 'time of circuit.']

yā́vant [517], —1. *a.* as great, 101[9]; as many, 64[4], 105[4]; as much; *preceding its correl.* tāvant; —2. yā́vat, *adv.* as long, while; tāvat · · yāvat, so long · · as, 19[2], 42[3]; yāvat · · tāvat: as long as · ·, so long, 15[5], 32[2], 40[18]; as soon as *or* the moment that · ·, then, 44[15], 22[7]; —3. yāvat, *as quasi-prep. w. acc.*: during; up to (in space *or* time); sarpavivaraṁ yāvat, as far as the serpent's hole, 39[13]; adya yāvat, until to-day, 24[2]. [pron. root ya, 517. cf. tāvant.]

yāvayád-dveṣas, *a.* driving away foes. [√2yu, 'keep off': see 1309.]

√ 1yu (yaúti [626], *3rd pl.* yuvánti, *mid.* yuté; yuváti, -te; *finite forms Vedic only*; yutá; -yū́ya). fasten, hold fast; draw towards one, attract; join, unite.

+sam, unite; saṁyuta, connected with, *i.e.* having reference to, 59[14].

√ 2yu (yuyóti; yúcchati [608[2]]; áyāuṣīt; yutá; -yū́ya; *caus.* yāváyati). repel, keep off *or* separate, *trans.*; *sometimes* keep off *or* separate, *intrans.*; *a Vedic word.*

+pra, remove; prayucchant, removing (*intrans.*), moving away, *and so* (*like Eng.* absent), heedless.

yu, *root of* 2d *pers. pronoun*, *cf.* 494. [cf. *ὑμεῖς*, Lesbian *ὔμμες*, 'ye': kinship of Eng. *ye*, doubtful.]

yukti, *f.* —1. a yoking, harnessing; —2. yoke, team. [√yuj, 1157, 219: cf. *ζεῦξις*, **ζευγ-σι-ς*, 'a yoking.']

yugá, *n.* —1. yoke; —2. couple, pair; —3. *esp. w.* mānuṣa, a human generation (*as* that which is united by common descent), *γένος ἀνθρώπων*; —4. *and so, in a temporal sense*, an age of the world, *see* 58[1] N. [√yuj, q.v., 216. 1: cf. yugma.]

yugapat-prāpti, *f.* simultaneous reaching *or* arriving at. [1279 and a.]

yugapad, *adv.* simultaneously. [apparently acc. s. n. of an adj. *yuga-pad, 'pair-footed, even-footed, side by side,' a possessive form (1301) of a descriptive cpd (1280b) *yuga-pad, 'pair-foot.']

yugmá, *a.* paired, even; *as n.* pair, couple. [√yuj, 1166, 216. 5: for mg, cf. *couple*, Lat. *cōpula*, **co-ap-ula*, √*ap* + *co-*, 'fit *or* join together.']

√ yuj (yunákti, yuñkté; yuyója, yuyujé; áyukta; yokṣyáti, -te; yuktá; yóktum; yuktvā́; -yújya; yojáyati). —1. yoke; harness; make ready for draught, *used* of wagon (101[17]) as well as of steed (72[6]); *then, generalized*, —2. make ready, set to work, apply; use, *e.g.* the Soma-press-stones, 76[18]; yukta, engaged upon (*loc.*), busied with, 62[11]; —3. unite; *middle*, unite one's self with (*instr.*); yujāná, in company with, 73[12]; —4. *passive*, be united with (*instr.*), *i.e.* become possessed of, 60[15]; yukta: possessed of (*instr.*), 1[12]; having · ·, *at end of cpd*, 65[12]; — 5. *pass.* be joined *or* made ready, *and so* be fitted, suited; yukta, fit, suitable, right, proper, 23[19]; yuktam, *adv.* fitly, rightly, etc., 36[2]; — 6. yojayati [1041[2]], apply; lay on, 102[11]. [cf. *ζεύγ-νυμι*, Lat. *jung-o*, 'yoke, harness, join'; w. yugá, 'yoke,' cf. *ζυγόν*, Lat. *jugum*, Ger. *Joch*, Eng. *yoke:* for euphony, see 219.]

+**ud**, *mid.* make one's self ready, set to work, exert one's self.

+**upa**, *mid.* harness, put to, 73[18]; apply, use.

+**ni**, *mid.* — 1. fasten to; — 2. put (a task) upon, commission; — *caus.* [1041[2]], set, lay, *e.g.* snares, 24[17]. [for mg 2, cf. niyoga; also Eng. *en-join* w. its Lat. predecessor *in-jungere.*]

+**pra**, apply, use; *w.* namaskāram, employ, *i.e.* do adoration.

+**sam**, join together, unite; saṁyukta, *at end of cpd:* joined with, *i.e.* endowed with, 34[4]; connected with, *i.e.* having reference to, 59[12, 14].

yúj [389, 219, 386b], — 1. *a.* yoked together; *as m.* yoke-fellow, *and so* comrade, 88[8]; — 2. *a.* paired, even. [√yuj: see ayuj and ayuja.]

yújya, *a.* united, combined. [√yuj, 1213e.]

yuddhá, *ppl.* fought; *as n.* [1176a], fight, battle, contest. [√yudh, 1176, 160.]

yuddha-varṇa, *m.* a sort of battle; a battle, so to speak.

√ **yudh** (yúdhyate; yuyudhé; áyuddha; yotsyáte; yuddhá; yóddhum; -yúdhya). fight. [cf. *ὑσμίνη*, **ὑθ-μίνη*, 'battle.']

+**ā**, fight against.

yúdh, *f.* fight. [√yudh.]

yudhi-ṣṭhira, *m.* Yudhishthira, son of Pāndu and Kuntī, to whom Brihadaçva tells the story of Nala; *see* 1[14] N. ['firm in battle,' yudh-i (1250c) + sthira.]

√ **yup** (yuyópa; yupitá; yopáyati [1041[2]]). set up an obstacle, block *or* bar the way; hinder, thwart, 80[10]; obstruct *or* clog, *see* 86[6] N.

yuvá, *pron. stem, 2d pers. dual*, 491.

yuvatí, *serving as a feminine to* yúvan. young woman; maiden. [1157.3 end: perhaps pres. ppl. of √1 yu, 'attract.']

yúvan [427], *a.* young; *as subst.* young man (*distinguished from* bāla, 'child,' 28[12]); youth (used even of youthful gods). [perhaps fr. √1 yu, 'attract,' suffix an, not van, 1160: see yavīyāṅs, yaviṣṭha, yuvati: cf. Lat. *juven-i-s*, 'young'; w. *juven-cu-s*, 'young,' cf. Germanic **yuvunga*, *yunga*, Eng. *young;* also Old Eng. *yung-þe*, Spenser's *youngth*, Eng. *youth.*]

yuṣmá, *see* 491.

yūthá, *m. n.* herd. [prop. 'a union,' √1 yu, 'unite,' 1163: for mg, cf. also Ger. *Bande*, 'gang *or* set of men,' and Eng. *band*, 'company,' both indirectly fr. the root of *bind.*]

yūtha-nātha, *m.* protector *or* leader of the herd.

yūtha-pa, *m.* keeper *or* protector of the herd; *esp.* the elephant that leads the herd.

yūtha-pati, *m.* lord of the herd; *esp.* the elephant that leads the herd.

yū́nas, *see* 427.

yūyám, *see* 491.

yena, *adv.* — 1. wherefore, 6[2]; — 2. yena · · tena, because · · therefore, 64[9]; — 3. that, ut, *introducing a result and corresponding to a* 'such' *or* 'so' *expressed* (21[10]) *or implied* (11[8]). [pron. root ya, 1112a.]

yéṣṭha, *pronounced* yaïṣṭha, *a.* (best going, *i.e.*) swiftest. [√yā, 470[8], 468.]

yóga, *m.* — 1. a setting to work; use; appliance (act of applying); — 2. appliance (thing applied), *and so* means; *esp.* supernatural means, magic, 56[8]; — 3. (the applying one's self to a thing, *and so*) pursuit *or* acquisition (of a thing), *cf.* kṣema; — 4. connection, relation; -yogāt, *at end of cpd*, from connection with · ·, *i.e.* in consequence of · ·. [√yuj, 216. 1.]

yógya, *a.* of use, suited for use, fit, fitting. [yóga, 1212a.]

yoddhṛ, *m.* fighter. [√yudh, 1182, 160.]

yodhin, *a. at end of cpds*, fighting. [√yudh, 1183[3].]

yóni, *m.f.* —1. lap; womb *or* birth-place; —2. place of origin; origin, 93[4]; —3. birth-place, *i.e.* home; place of abiding; place, 80[17], 89[8], RV. x.125.7; —4. (*like Eng.* origin *or* birth) family, race; form of existence (as man, Brahman, beast, etc., in the system of transmigrations) as this form is determined by birth, 67[20]. ['the holder' of the born or unborn babe, √1yu, 'hold,' 1158.2[2]: cf. the analogous metaphors in Lat. *con-cipere*, 'take, hold, conceive'; and in *volva*, 'cover, envelope,' and so 'womb,' fr. a root cognate with 1vṛ, 'cover.']

yonitas, *adv.* from birth, by blood. [yoni, 1098b.]

yoṣít, *f.* young woman, maiden. [perhaps 'the attractive one,' fr. √1yu, 'attract,' 1200a, 383.3 (through the intermediate form yó-ṣā, 1197, of the same mg): cf. yuvatí.]

yāuvaná, *n.* youth, period between childhood and maturity, adolescence (of man or maid). [yúvan, 1208a.]

yāuvana-daçā, *f.* time of youth.

√ raṅh (ráṅhati, -te). —1. make to run; hasten, *trans.*; —2. *mid.* run; hasten, *intrans.* [for *raṅgh: cf. the forms laṅgh and raghú, and see under laghú.]

raktá, *ppl.* colored; *esp.* red; *as n.* blood. [√rañj, 954a.]

√ 1rakṣ (rákṣati, -te; rarákṣa; árakṣīt; rakṣitá; rákṣitum; -rákṣya). de-fend, protect; keep, *i.e. both* retain *and* maintain; take care of (as a sovereign), *i.e.* govern; guard, ward; save. [a desid. extension of √*rak or ark: cf. ἀλέξ-ω, 'ward off,' which bears a similar relation to √ἀλκ or ἀρκ in ἄλ-αλκ-ε, 'warded off,' ἀρκ-έω, 'ward off, protect'; cf. also Lat. *arc-eo*, 'ward off,' *arx*, 'stronghold of defence, citadel'; AS. *ealh-stede*, 'defence-stead, strong-hold'; *ealgian*, 'protect': for the two chief mgs of √rakṣ, cf. Lat. *de-fendere*, 'ward off, protect.']

+**pari**, protect around; save.

√ 2rakṣ, harm, *in* rákṣas. [perhaps only another aspect of 1rakṣ, 'ward off,' *i.e.* 'beat away.']

rakṣaka, *m.* keeper; warder; protector. [√1rakṣ, 1181.]

rákṣaṇa, *n.* protection; preservation. [√1rakṣ, 1150.]

rákṣas, *n.* —1. harm; —2. *concrete*, harmer, name of nocturnal demons who disturb sacrifices and harm the pious. [√2rakṣ, 1151.2a.]

rakṣā, *f.* protection; watch. [√1rakṣ, 1149.]

rakṣi, *a.* guarding, *at end of cpds.* [√1rakṣ, 1155.]

rakṣitṛ́, *m.* protector; watcher. [√1rakṣ, 1182a.]

raghú, —1. *a.* running, darting, swift; *as m.* runner; —2. *m.* Raghu (The Runner, Δρομεύς), name of an ancient king. [√raṅh, q.v.: older form of laghú, q.v.]

rañga, *m.* —1. color; —2. theatre, amphitheatre. [√raj or rañj, 216.1: connection of mg 2 unclear.]

√ raj *or* rañj (rájyati, -te; raktá; -rájya; *caus.* rañjáyati). —1. be colored; *esp.* be red; rakta: red; dyed; *as n.* blood; —2. *fig.* be affected with a strong feeling (*cf.* raj + vi); *esp.* be delighted with, have pleasure in, be in love with; —*caus.* —1. color; redden; —2. delight, please, make happy.

[orig. 'be bright *or* white' (whence rajaka); then 'glow, be red': see the ident. √3ṛj and its cognates ἄργυρος, etc.; and cf. √ῥεγ in aor. ῥέξαι, 'dye,' and ῥεγεύς, 'dyer': w. this root may be connected the root rāj in its mgs given under 2.]

+**anu**, —1. be colored after, take the tinge of; —2. feel affection towards.

+**vi**, —1. lose color; —2. be cold *or* indifferent towards (*loc.*), 45[8]. [for mg 2, cf. the senses of the simple verb: the metaphor may be either 'not glowing,' and so, as in Eng., 'cold,' or else 'colorless,' and so, 'indifferent.']

rajaka, *m.* washerman, who is also a dyer of clothes. ['whitener' or else 'dyer,' √raj, 1181.]

rájas, *n.* —1. atmosphere, air, region of clouds, vapors, and gloom, clearly distinguished from heaven (dyāus, 72[2]) or the ethereal spaces of heaven (rocanā divas, 81[8], or svar), "where the light dwelleth," these being beyond the rajas, just as the αἰθήρ is beyond the ἀήρ; *used loosely in pl.*, the skies, 71[7]; the sky conceived as divided into an upper and a lower stratum, *and so dual*, rajasī, 75[5, 12]; *so far Vedic;*

—2. *post-Vedic: like the Greek* ἀήρ, the thick air, mist, gloom, darkness; —3. dust, *e.g.* 14[13]; —4. *in the philosophical system*, darkness (*cf.* 2), the second of the three qualities (*see* guṇa), soul-darkening passion (popularly connected with rāga, 'passion'), 66[8, 16].

[since the orig. mg, as indicated by usage, is 'the cloudy (region), region of gloom and dark' as distinguished from the everlasting light beyond, the word is prob. to be derived fr. √raj in the sense 'be (colored, *i.e.*) not clear': cognate are ἔ-ρεβος, 'darkness, Erebus,' and Goth. *riqis*, neut., 'darkness': for connection of mgs 2 and 3, cf. Ger. *Dunst*, 'vapor,' and Eng. *dust*.]

rájju, *f.* cord; rope. [√*razg, 'plait': cf. Lithuanian *rezgis*, 'plaited work, basket'; Lat. *restis*, **resctis*, **rezg-ti-s*, 'rope': see √majj.]

√ **rañj**, *see* raj.

ráṇa, *m.* pleasure, gladness. [√ran.]

raṇvá, *a.* pleasant, lovely. [√ran, 1190.]

ráti, *f.* —1. rest, quiet; —2. comfort, pleasure. [√ram, 1157, cf. 954d.]

rátna, *n.* —1. gift; blessing, riches, treasure, *as something* bestowed *or* given (*cf.* ratna-dhā́); *so far Vedic;* —2. *post-Vedic:* precious stone, jewel, pearl; *fig.*, *as in Eng.*, jewel, *i.e.* the most excellent of its kind. [√1 **rā**, 'bestow.']

ratna-dhā́ [352], *a.* bestowing blessings.

1 **rátha**, *m.* wagon, *esp.* the two-wheeled battle-wagon (lighter and swifter than the anas, 'dray'); car *or* chariot of gods (72[4, 6], 89[11]) as well as of men (87[14]). [√ṛ, 'move,' 1163: for mg, cf. Lat. *currus*, 'chariot,' and *currere*, 'run.']

2 **ratha**, *m.* pleasure, joy. [√ram, 1163, cf. 954d.]

√ **ran** (ráṇati; raráṇa; árāṇīt). be pleased; *Vedic.* [ident. w. √ram.]

rápas, *n.* bodily injury; disease.

√ **rabh** (rábhate; rebhé; árabdha; rapsyáte; rabdhá; rábdhum; -rábhya). grasp; take hold of. [prob. a collateral form of √grabh, and ident. w. labh, see these: cf. τὰ λάφ-υρα, 'spoils, booty'; εἴ-ληφ-α, 'took'; Lat. *lab-or*, 'undertaking, labor'; perhaps ἦλφ-ον, 'gat, earned.']

+**ā**, —1. take hold upon; touch, RV. x.125.8; —2. take hold of, *i.e.* undertake, 14[6]; *w.* yatnam, undertake an effort, *i.e.* exert one's self, 11[2]; —3. (*like Ger.* an-fangen *and Lat.* in-cipere) begin; ārabhya: *w. abl.*, beginning from · ·, *or simply* from · ·, 39[13]; *w.* adya, from today on, 36[19].

+**anv-ā**, take hold of from behind, hold on to.

+**sam-anv-ā**, hold on to each other (said of several); sam-anv-ārabdha, touching.

+**sam-ā**, undertake (*see* ā-rabh) together.

+**sam**, take hold of each other (for dance, battle, etc.), hold together; take hold (of a thing) together.

√ **ram** (rámati, -te; raráma, remé; áraṁsīt, áraṁsta; raṁsyáte; ratá; ráṁtum; raṁtvā́; -rámya; rāmáyati). —1. *act.* stop, *trans.* —2. *mid.* stop, *intrans.*; rest; abide; stay gladly with; —3. *mid.* (rest, take one's ease *or* comfort, *and so*) find pleasure in; rata, *w. loc.*, *or at end of cpds*, taking pleasure in, devoted to; —4. *caus.* bring to a stand-still, stay, 73[7]. [cf. ἠ-ρέμ-α, 'quietly'; Goth. *rimis*, 'quiet'; ἔραμαι, ἔραται, *ἐ͜m̲-μαι, *ἐ͜m̲-ται, 'love, loves'; ἐ-ρατό-ς, 'lovely,' formally ident. w. ratá: for mgs 2 and 3, cf. √2 çam.]

+**abhi**, *mid.* —1. stop, *intrans.*; —2. find pleasure; please, *intrans.*, 106[1].

+**ā**, *act.* stop, *trans.*

+**upa**, stop; uparata, ceased, (of sounds) hushed.

+**vi**, *act.* stop, *intrans.*; pause.

ramaṇīya, *grdv.* enjoyable, pleasant. [√ram, 965, 1215.]

ramyà, *grdv.* enjoyable, pleasant. [√ram, 963.]

rayí, *m.* wealth, treasure. [prop. 'bestowal' (cf. 76[11]), fr. ri, a weaker form of √1 rā, 'bestow,' 1155.1: cf. ratna and rāi.]

ravi, *m.* the sun.

raçanā́, *f.* cord; strap; rein. [cf. raçmi.]

raçmí, *m.* –1. line, cord; –2. *fig.* (line, *i.e.*) ray, of light; beam. [so Eng. *ray* involves a metaphor, its Lat. predecessor *radius* meaning orig. 'staff' and then 'spoke': cf. raçanā́ and rā́çí.]

rása, *m.* –1a. the sap *or* juice of plants (36[18]), *and esp.* of fruits; fruit-syrup, 68[1]; –1b. *fig.* the best *or* finest *or* strongest part of a thing, its essence *or* flos, 44[7], 83[3]; –1c. sap, *generalized*, fluid, liquid; drink, 15[17]; –2a. taste (*regarded as* the chief characteristic of a liquid); –2b. taste, *i.e.* relish for, 97[6]; –2c. object of one's taste, *esp.* that which pleases one's taste, *e.g.* the beauties (of a story), 56[11].

rasā́, *f.* –1. moisture; –2. Rasā, a mythical stream supposed to flow round the earth and atmosphere. [cf. rása.]

rasika, *a.* tasty; *as m.* connoisseur. [rasa, 1222.]

√ **rah** (rahitá; ráhitum). leave, give up, abandon.

+**vi**, abandon, separate from, *in* viraha.

rahas, *n.* solitude; lonely place; *as adv.* [1111b], secretly. [√rah.]

√ **1 rā** (rárāte; rarā́ú, raré; árāsta; rātá). give, grant, bestow. [see rā́i: cf. rayí.]

√ **2 rā** (rā́yati [761d1]). bark; bark at. [cf. Lat. *in-rī-re*, 'growl at.']

rākṣasa, *a.* demoniacal; *as m.* a demoniacal one, a Rakshas. [rákṣas, q.v., 1208a.]

rāga, *m.* –1. coloring, color; –2. affection, feeling, passion. [√raj, 216.1.]

rāghava, *m.* descendant of Raghu, *i.e.* Rāma. [raghú, 1208c.]

√ **rāj** (rā́jati, -te; rarā́ja, rejé [794e[2]]; árājit).

–1. direct; rule; be first; be master *or* king of, *w. gen.*;

–2. shine; be illustrious; distinguish one's self; –*caus.* cause to shine.

[orig., perhaps, two distinct roots, but no longer distinguished in form, and with the two sets of mgs partly coincident: w. rāj 1, cf. √1 ṛj, 'reach out'; w. rāj 2, cf. √3 ṛj, 'be bright,' and √raj: see under rājan.]

+**vi**, –1. become master of, master (*gen.*), 81[11]; –2. shine out; –*caus.* adorn, 12[17].

rā́j [*nom.* rā́ṭ], *m.* king. [√rāj.]

rāja, *at end of cpds for* rājan, 1249a[2].

rāja-kula, *n.* –1. royal family; *in pl.*, *equivalent to* princes; –2. (*as conversely in Eng.*, The Sublime Porte, *lit.* 'the high gate,' *is used for* the Turkish government) the royal palace. [1280b.]

rāja-dvāra, *n.* king's door, door of the royal palace.

rā́jan, *m.* –1. king, prince, 1[3], etc.; applied also to Varuna, 83[12], 75[3], 76[17], 78[19], 80[1]; to Indra, 71[8]; to Yama, 83[12,8], 84[20]; –2. *equiv. to* rājanya, a kṣatriya *or* man of the military caste, 59[13,22]; –3. *at end of cpds: regularly* rāja; *sometimes* rājan, 6[8], 84[20]. [√rāj, 1160c: cf. Lat. *rēg-em*, 'king'; Keltic stem *rīg-*, 'king': from the Keltic was borrowed very early the Germanic **rīk-*, 'ruler'; of this, Goth. *reiki*, AS. *rīce*, 'dominion,' are derivs; so also Goth. *reiks*, AS. *rīce*, 'powerful,' Eng. *rich: rīce*, 'dominion,' lives in Eng. *bishop-ric*.]

rājanyà, *a.* royal, princely; *as m.* one of royal race, a noble, *oldest designation of* a man of the second caste; *see* kṣatriya. [rā́jan, 1212d 1.]

rāja-putrá, *m.* king's son, prince. [acct, 1267.]

rā́ja-putra, *a.* having princes as sons; -trā, *f.* mother of princes. [1302: acct, 1295.]

rāja-puruṣa, *m.* king's man, servant of a king, royal official.

rājasa, *f.* -ī, *a.* pertaining to the second of the three qualities (*see* rajas 4), passionate, *as terminus technicus.* [rajas, 1208a.]

rājendra, *m.* best *or* chief of kings. [rāja + indra.]

rā́jñī, *f.* queen, princess, *Anglo-Indian* rannee; ruler. [rā́jan, 1156.]

rājya, *n.* kingship. [rāj, 1211.]
rātí, *a.* ready to give *or* bless; gracious; *as f.* grace. [√1 rā, 'give.']
rātra, *n. for* rātri *at end of cpds.* [1315b.]
rátrī, *later* rátri, *f.* night. [perhaps fr. √ram, 'rest.']
√ **rādh** (rādhnóti; rádhyate [761a], -ti; rarádha; árātsīt; rātsyáti; rāddhá; rāddhvá; -rádhya; rādháyati). —1. be successful; prosper, have luck; be happy, 103[7]; —2. *trans.* make successful *or* happy; gratify; —*caus.* accomplish; make happy, satisfy. [akin w. √ṛdh.]
+**apa**, —1. hit away (from the mark), miss (the mark), fail; —2. be at fault, be to blame; offend, sin; aparāddha, guilty, to blame, 33[1]. [for 1, cf. the simple verb, 'succeed,' i.e. 'make a hit': for 2, cf. the relation of Eng. *fail* and *fault*.]
+**ā**, *caus.* make happy, satisfy.
rádhas, *n.* gracious gift, blessing. [√rādh, 'gratify': for mg, cf. French *gratification*, 'gift.']
rāmá, *a.* dark; *as m.* Rāma, hero of the epos Rāmāyana; *cf.* rāghava.
rāyas-poṣa, *m.* development, *i.e.* increase of wealth. [gen. s. of rāi, 1250d: 171[2].]
rāva, *m.* cry; yell; howl. [√ru, 1148.2.]
rāçí, *m.* troop, host; heap. [perhaps akin w. raçmí, q.v.: for connection of mg, cf. Eng. *line* and French *cordon*, as applied to soldiers.]
rāṣṭrá, *n.* kingdom; sovereignty. [√rāj 1: see 219[5], 1185a.]
rā́ṣṭrī, *f.* directrix, sovereign. [√rāj 1: see 219[5], 1182[2].]
rāṣṭríya, *a.* belonging to the sovereignty; *as m.* sovereign, ruler. [rāṣṭra, 1215.]
rāhú, *m.* The Seizer, Rāhu, who is supposed to seize and swallow sun and moon, and thus cause eclipses. [prob. fr. √rabh, 1178[2].]
√ **ri** *or* **rī** (riṇáti; ríyate [761c]). —1. *act.* cause to run *or* stream, let loose; —2. *mid.* flow; run; dissolve. [cf. Lat. *rī-vus*, 'stream, brook'; provincial Eng. *run*, 'brook,' as in *Bull Run; Ger. rinnen*, Eng. *run:* see also √lī + pra.]
√ **ric** (riṇákti; rícyate [761b]; riréca, riricé; árāikṣīt, árikta; rekṣyáti; riktá; *pass.* ricyáte; *caus.* recáyati). —1. leave; —2. let go, let free; —3. *very rarely* (*like Eng. colloq.* part with), sell.
[w. riṇákti cf. Lat. *linquit*, 'leaves': cf. ἔ-λιπ-ε, 'left'; Lat. *lic-et*, 'it is left, *i.e.* permitted' (Eng. *leave* means 'permission'); AS. *leōn*, **lih-an*, Ger. *leih-en*, 'leave a thing to a person for a time, einem etwas überlassen, *i.e.* lend'; AS. *lǣn*, 'gift, loan,' Eng. noun *loan*, whence denom. verb *loan;* fr. *lǣn* comes *lǣnan*, 'give, loan,' Old Eng. *lēn-en*, preterit *lēn-de*, whose *d* has become part of the root in Eng. *lend* (though good usage has not sanctioned the precisely similar blunder in *drownd-ed*).]
+**ati**, *mid.* (*through pass. sense* be left over) surpass; predominate; —*caus.* cause to be in surplus; overdo, 96[12].
√ **rip** (rirépa; riptá). —1. smear; stick; smear, *and so* —2. *as in Eng.*, defile; —3. (*with the same metaphor as in the Ger.* an-schmieren) cheat, impose upon. [the old form of √lip: see under √lip.]
ripú, *m.* impostor, cheat; *later* foe. [√rip, 1178b.]
riprá, *n.* defilement; impurity. [√rip, 1188c.]
ripra-vāhá, *a.* carrying off *or* removing impurity. [acct, 1270.]
√ **riç** (riçáti, -te; riṣṭá). —1. pull; —2. pull *or* bite off, crop. [older form of √liç.]
√ **riṣ** (réṣati; ríṣyati, -te [761a]; riṣṭá; *caus.* reṣáyati; árīriṣat). be hurt; receive harm; *caus.* harm.
√ **rī**, *see* ri.
√ **ru** (rāúti [626]; ruváti; ruráva; árāvīt; rutá; rótum). cry; yell; howl; hum, 26[9]. [cf. ὠ-ρύ-ομαι, 'howl'; Lat. *raucus*, 'screaming, hoarse'; AS. *rȳn*, 'a roaring.']
rukmá, *m.* ornament of gold; *as n.* gold. [√ ruc, 1166, 216.5.]
√ **ruc** (rócate, -ti; rurucé, ruróca; árucat, árociṣṭa; rociṣyáte; rucitá; rócitum). —1. shine; be bright *or* resplendent; —2. appear in splendor; —3. appear beautiful

or good, please. [cf. ἀμφι-λύκ-η, 'twilight'; λευκ-ός, 'bright'; Lat. *lūx, lūmen,* for **lūc-s, *luc-men,* 'light'; *lūna, *luc-na,* 'moon'; AS. *leōh-t,* Eng. *light;* cf. also Lat. *lūc-us* (*a lucendo,* after all!), 'a clearing (Eng. of U.S.) *or* Lichtung (Ger.) *or* glade *or* grove'; AS. *leāh,* Eng. *lea,* 'field, meadow'; *-ley* in *Brom-ley,* 'broom-field,' and *-loo* in *Water-loo.*]

+**prati**, appear good unto, please, 74⁶.

rúci, *f.* pleasure. [√ruc, 216.2.]

rucira, *a.* splendid; beautiful.

rucirānana, *a.* fair-faced. [ānana: 1298.]

√ **ruj** (rujáti; rurója; rugṇá; ruktvā́; -rújya). —1. break, break to pieces; —2. injure, pain. [cf. λυγ-ρός, 'painful, sad'; Lat. *lūg-eo,* 'grieve.']

rúj, *f.* pain, disease. [√ruj: for mg, cf. Ger. *Ge-brechen,* 'infirmity,' w. *brechen,* 'break'; also roga.]

rujā́nā, *f. perhaps* breach, cleft, rift (of the clouds). [√ruj.]

√ **rud** (róditi [631], rudánti; ruróda; rodiṣyáti; ruditá; róditum; ruditvā́; -rúdya). —1. cry, weep; —2. weep for, lament. [cf. Lat. *rud-ere,* 'roar'; AS. *reōt-an,* 'weep.']

rudrá, *a. connected by Hindus w.* √rud, 'cry,' *and so* howling, roaring, terrible, applied to Agni and other gods; *true meaning uncertain;* — *as m.* —1a. *sing. in the Veda:* Rudra, leader of the Maruts *or* Storm-gods, 77¹⁸, RV. x. 125. 6; —1b. *in pl.* The Rudras, a class of storm-gods, RV. x. 125.1; —2. *sing.* Rudra, *received into the Hindu Trinity in the later mythology, and known by the name* Çiva, *q.v.*

√ **1rudh** (ruṇáddhi, runddhé; ruródha, rurudhé; árāutsīt, áruddha; rotsyáti, -te; ruddhá; róddhum; ruddhvā́; -rúdhya). —1. hold back; obstruct; hold; —2. keep off; hinder; suppress; —3. shut up; close.

+**anu**, *as pass., or mid. intrans., i.e. as of the* yá- *or* ya-*class,* anurudhyate, *also* -ti, be held to, keep one's self to; be devoted to, practice, 10¹³; have regard for.

+**ava**, —1. hold off; —2. *mid.* (hold apart for one's self, lay up, *and so*) obtain; —*desid. mid.* desire to obtain, 96¹¹.

+**ni**, hold; stop; shut up.

+**vi**, hinder *or* disturb.

√ **2rudh** (ródhati). grow. [collateral form of √ruh, q.v.: cf. Lat. *rud-is,* fem., 'rod, staff': for mg, cf. w. √rudh and Ger. *wachsen,* 'grow,' the nouns vī-rudh and *Ge-wächs,* 'a growth, *i.e.* plant': kinship of Eng. *rod,* 'a growing shoot, rod, measure of length,' older *rood,* 'measure of length *or* surface,' is improbable on account of the *ō* of AS. *rōd.*]

√ **ruṣ** (róṣati; rúṣyati; ruṣitá, ruṣṭá). be cross *or* angry. [cf. λύσσα, **λυσ-ja,* 'rage.']

rúṣ [ruṭ, ruḍbhyām], *f.* anger. [√ruṣ.]

√ **ruh** (róhati, -te; ruróha, ruruhé; áruhat, árukṣat; rokṣyáti, -te; rūḍhá; róḍhum; rūḍhvā́; -rúhya; rúrukṣati; roháyati, *later* ropáyati [1042e]). —1. rise, mount up, climb; —2. spring up, grow up; —3. grow, develop, thrive; —*caus.* —1. raise; —2. place upon. [see √2rudh: for euphony, see 222³.]

+**adhi**, *caus.* cause (*e.g.* one's body, *acc.*) to rise to (*e.g.* the balance, *acc.*), *i.e.* put (one's body) upon (the balance), 48¹⁶.

+**ā**, mount *or* get upon (a stone); seat one's self upon; climb (tree); ascend to (the head, hill-top, life, place); embark upon (boat, ship); *fig.* get into (danger); —*caus.* cause to get upon (stone, pelt) *or* into (wagon, boat), *w. acc. of person and acc. or loc.* (105¹¹) *of thing;* — *desid.* desire to climb up to.

rūpá, *n.* —1. outward look *or* appearance, *as well* color *as* form *or* shape; *Lat.* forma; form, 48¹⁷, 77², 96¹²; rūpaṁ kr̥, assume a form, 14⁸, 49⁶; (reflected) image, 62¹⁷; —2. (*like Lat.* forma, *and Eng.* shape *in* shape-ly) good form, *i.e.* beauty, 2⁴, etc.; —3. appearance, characteristic mark, peculiarity. [cf. varpas: see also varcas.]

√ **rūpaya** (rūpáyati [*cf.* 1056, 1067]). *used esp. in theatrical language* (to have the look *or* appearance of, *i.e.*) act. [rūpá, 1058.]

+ni, —1. *like Eng.* look into — *tentatively, i.e.:* investigate, 20[18]; seek, 29[17]; search, 33[12]; —2. look into — *successfully, i.e.:* find out, 44[17]; discover, 26[10]; —3. act, *see simple verb.*

rūpa-jitāpsaras, *a.* surpassing the Apsarases in beauty.

rūpavant, *a.* *like Eng.* shape-ly *and Lat.* formosus; beautiful, handsome, 1[4]. [rūpa, 1233.]

rūpa-sampad, *f.* beauty of form, *i.e.* beauty.

rūpa-sampanna, *a.* endowed with beauty, beautiful. [√pad.]

re, *word of address.* O; ho. [cf. are.]

√ rej (réjati, -te). —1. *act.* shake, *trans.;* —2. *mid.* shake, *intrans.;* tremble. [perhaps akin w. √λιγ in ἐ-λέ-λιξε, 'caused to tremble, shook.']

reṇú, *m.* dust. [perhaps connected w. √ri, 'dissolve, go to pieces,' just as Ger. *Staub,* 'dust,' w. *stieben,* 'fly asunder': 1162.]

revā, *f.* Revā, a river, the same as the Narmadā, *q.v.*

rāí [361b], *m., rarely f.* possessions; wealth; prosperity. [stem strictly rā́: prop. 'bestowal,' √1rā, see 361b and rayí: w. acc. rā́-m, cf. Lat. nom. *rē-s,* 'property.']

roká, *m.* brightness, light. [√ruc.]

róga, *m.* infirmity, disease. [√ruj, 216.1: for mg, see noun rúj.]

rocaná, *a.* shining, light; *as n.* light; the place of the light, ethereal space *or* spaces, 71[17], 81[4,8]; *see* rájas *for further description.* [√ruc, 1150.]

rocisṇú, *a.* shining, bright; *fig.* blooming. [√ruc, 1194a: or rather perhaps fr. rocís, 1194c.]

rocís, *n.* brightness. [√ruc, 1153.]

ródasī, *dual f.* the two worlds, *i.e.* heaven and earth.

ródha, *a.* growing. [√2rudh, 'grow.']

ropaya, *see* 1042e end.

róman, *n.* hair on the body of men and beasts (usually excluding that of the head and beard and that of the mane and tail); *later* loman, *q.v.*

romānta, *m.* *loc.* -e, in hair-vicinity, *i.e.* on the hairy side (of the hand). [roman (1249a[2]) + anta.]

rāukma, *a.* golden, adorned with gold. [rukmá, 1208f.]

---

lakṣá, *n.* —1. *rarely,* mark, token; —2. a hundred thousand, an Anglo-Indian lac; —3. (*like Eng.* mark) mark which is aimed at. [√lag, 'be fastened to,' 1197a: for mg 1, cf. connection of Eng. verb *tag,* 'fasten,' w. noun *tag,* 'attachment, appendage,' and so, esp. as used in modern shops, 'a mark *or* label-tag'; for 2, cf. the specialization of Eng. *marc* or *mark* as 'a weight' (of gold or silver) and as 'a money of account'; also that of Eng. *token* as 'a coin' and as 'ten quires printed on both sides.']

lakṣaṇá, *n.* —1. mark, token; characteristic; attribute, 66[11]; character, 101[12]; essential characteristic, 41[14]; special mark; *esp.* lucky mark, mark of excellence, 62[7], 98[7,8]; mark *in the sense of* determinant *at* 58[23]; —2. (*like Eng.* designation) name, 57[14]; —3. form, kind, 65[12]. [fr. the denom. lakṣaya (1150.2a), or rather fr. the simpler but very rare form of the same denom. (1054), √lakṣa.]

√ lakṣaya (lakṣáyati [1056]). mark, note, notice. [lakṣa, 1053: so Lat. *notare* fr. *nota.*]

+upa, mark, notice; see; *pass.* appear.

lakṣasaṁkhya, *a.* having lacs (*see* lakṣa) as their number, numbered by hundred-thousands. [lakṣa + saṁkhyā.]

lakṣmī́ [363[2]], *f.* —1. mark, sign; —2. *with or without* pāpī, bad sign *or* omen, something ominous, bad luck; —3. *oftenest* a good sign, *in the older language usually with* puṇyā; good luck; prosperity, 18[14]; wealth, 46[2]; (royal) splendor, 51[19]. [fr. lakṣ (1167), the quasi-root of lak-ṣa, which is a deriv. of √lag: for connection of mg 1 w. √lag, see lakṣa: as for 2 and 3, observe that Eng. *luck* sometimes means 'bad luck,' but oftener 'good luck.']

lakṣya, *grdv.* to be noticed *or* seen; to be looked upon *or* considered as, 41[14]. [derivation like that of lakṣaṇa.]

√ **lag** (lágati; lagiṣyáti; lagná [957c]; lagitvā́; -lágya). attach *or* fasten one's self to; lagna, attached to, put upon. [cf. lakṣa, lakṣmī, liñga.]

laguḍa, *m.* cudgel.

laghú, *younger form of* raghú, *a.* —1. swift, quick; —2. light, *i.e.* not heavy; —3. (light, *i.e.*) insignificant; small; contemptible; low.

[for derivation, see raghú and √raṅh: cf. ἐ-λαχύ-ς, 'small,' ἐλάχιστος, 'smallest'; Lithuanian *lèngvas*, 'light'; Lat. *lĕvis*, **lenhu-i-s?*, '1. swift, 2. light, not heavy, 3. insignificant, small' (mgs quite parallel w. those of laghu); AS. *lung-re*, 'quickly'; Eng. *lungs*, 'lights': kinship of AS. *leōh-t*, Eng. *light*, 'not heavy,' *lights*, 'lungs,' not certain: for connection of mgs 1 and 2, observe that *swift* and *light*, just as *slow* and *heavy*, name qualities naturally associated: for *light*, 'not dark,' see √ruc.]

laghu-krama, *a.* having a quick step; -am, *adv.* [1311], quickly.

laghu-cetas, *a.* small-minded.

√ **lañgh** (lañgháyati; lañghitá; -láñghya). spring over. [see √raṅh, and under laghú.]

√ **lajj** (lajjáte; lalajjé; lajjitá; lájjitum). be ashamed.

+**vi**, be ashamed.

lajjā, *f.* shame. [√lajj, 1149.]

lajjāvant, *a.* having shame; embarrassed. [1233.]

√ **lap** (lápati; lalā́pa; lapiṣyáti; lapitá, laptá; láptum; -lápya). chatter; talk; lament. [cf. ὀ-λοφ-ύ-ς, 'a lamenting'; ὀλοφύρομαι, 'lament'; perhaps Lat. *lāmenta*, 'laments.']

+**ā**, talk to, converse with.

+**pra**, talk out heedlessly *or* lamentingly.

+**vi**, utter unintelligible *or* lamenting tones.

+**sam**, talk with; *caus.* (cause to talk with one, *i.e.*) address, 26[1].

√ **labh**, *younger form of* rabh (lábhate; lebhé; álabdha; lapsyáte; labdhá; labdhvā́; -lábhya). —1. catch; seize; —2. receive; get. [see under √rabh.]

+**pra**, —1. seize; take; —2. dupe; fool. [for 2, cf. Eng. colloq. *take in*, 'gull,' and *catch*, 'ensnare.']

+**vi-pra**, fool, 37[6]. [see √labh + pra.]

√ **lamb** (lámbate; lalambé; lambiṣyáti; lambitá; lámbitum; -lámbya). —1. hang down; —2. sink; —3. hang upon, hold on to; cling to; *and so* —4. (*like Eng.* stick) tarry, lag. [younger form of √ramb, 'hang down limp': cf. λοβ-ός, 'lobe *or* pendent part' (of ear, liver); Lat. *lāb-i*, 'sink, fall'; *limbus*, 'fringe, border'; AS. *læppa*, 'loosely hanging portion,' Eng. *lap* (of coat, apron); Eng. *limp*, 'hanging loosely, flaccid'; *lop*-ears, 'hanging' ears (of a rabbit).]

+**ava**, —1. hang down; —2. sink; —3. hang upon, hold on to.

+**vi**, lag, loiter. [see √lamb 4: for mg, cf. also Eng. *hang*, in *hang fire*.]

√ **lal** (lálati, -te; lalitá). sport, dally, play; behave in an artless and unconstrained manner; lalita, *see s.v.*

lalā́ṭa, *n.* forehead.

lalita, *a.* artless, naive; lovely. [prop. 'unconstrainedly behaved,' ppl. of √lal, 952[2]: so Eng. *behaved* has rather adjectival than verbal coloring.]

lavaṇá, *n.* salt, *esp.* sea-salt; *as a.* salt.

√ **las** (lásati; lalā́sa; lasitá). gleam, glance. [orig. 'glance,' but, like Eng. *glance*, with the subsidiary notion (see lasa), 'move quickly hither and thither,' and so, 'play' (see the cpds w. preps.): conversely, Eng. *dull* means 'slow,' and then, 'not glancing': cf. Lat. *lasc-ivus* (through **las-cu-s*), 'wanton.']

+**ud**, —1. glance; —2. play; —3. be overjoyed, 24[23].

+**vi**, —1. glance; —2. play; —3. be joyful *or* wanton.

lasa, *a.* moving quickly hither and thither; lively. [√las.]

lājá, *m. pl.* parched *or* roasted grain. [perhaps akin w. √bhṛjj.]

lābha, *m.* the getting, acquisition. [√labh.]

√ **likh** (likháti; lilékha; álekhīt; likhiṣyáti; likhitá; likhitvā́; -líkhya). —1. scratch; furrow; slit; draw a line; —2. write; write down; delineate. [younger form of √rikh: cf. ἐ-ρείκ-ω, 'furrow' (χθόνα, 'ground'); ἐ-ρέχ-θω, 'tear, rend'; Lat. rīma, *ric-ma, 'slit, crack': for mgs, observe that Eng. *write* is fr. the same root as Ger. *ritzen*, 'scratch.']

liñga, *n.* mark (by which one knows *or* recognizes a thing), Kenn-zeichen, characteristic. [connected w. √lag in the same way as lakṣa, q.v.]

liñga-dhāraṇa, *n.* the wearing of one's characteristic marks.

√ **lip** (limpáti, -te [758]; lilépa; álipat, álipta; liptá; -lípya). —1. besmear *or* rub over a thing (*acc.*) with a thing (*instr.*); —2. smear a thing (*acc.*) over *or* on a thing (*loc.*); stick (*trans.*) on to; *pass.* stick *or* stick to, *intrans.*

[younger form of √rip: orig. mg 'smear, stick': cf. τὸ λίπος, 'grease'; ἀ-λείφ-ω, 'anoint'; Lat. *lippus*, 'blear-eyed'; λῐπαρός, 'greasy, shiny': further akin are the following words, but with curious divarication of mg: λῐπαρέω, like Eng. *stick to*, i.e. 'persist'; AS. *be-līf-an*, Goth. *bi-leib-an*, Ger. *b-leib-en*, (lit. 'stick,' i.e.) 'remain'; AS. *libban*, Eng. *live*, Ger. *leben*, 'be remaining *or* surviving, superstitem esse'; AS. *līf*, Eng. *life*; finally AS. *lǣf-an*, Eng. *leave*, 'cause to remain.']

+**anu**, smear over, cover with.

+**vi**, besmear.

lipi, *f.* —1. a rubbing over; —2. writing. [√lip, 1155. 1.]

√ **liç** (liçáte; liliçé; áleçiṣṭa; liṣṭá). tear, break. [younger form of √riç.]

liça, tearing, breaking, *and so* cutting, in ku-liça. [√liç.]

√ **lī** (láyate; líyate; lilyé; áleṣṭa; līná; -líya). —1. cling to; —2. stick; —3. (stay, *i.e.*) of birds and insects, light upon, sit upon; —4. slip into; disappear.

+**ni**, —1. cling to; —2. light upon (of birds); —3. slip into; disappear; hide.

+**pra**, go to dissolution. [cf. √ri.]

līlā, *f.* —1. play; —2. (*like Eng.* child's play) action that can be done without serious effort; līlayā, without any trouble.

√ **luṭh** (luṭháti; lulóṭha; luṭhitá). roll.

√ **lup** (lumpáti [758]; lulópa; luptá; lóptum; luptvā́; -lúpya). —1. break; harm; —2. attack; pounce upon; —3. rob, plunder. [younger form of √rup: cf. Lat. *rumpere*, 'break'; AS. *reōf-an*, 'break'; *reāf*, 'spoil of battle, booty, armor, etc., *esp.* clothing, garments,' Ger. *Raub*, 'robbery, booty'; AS. *reāfian*, 'despoil, rob,' whence Eng. *reave*, ppl. *reft*, and *be-reave*: fr. Old High Ger. *roubōn*, 'rob,' through Old French *rober*, 'rob,' comes French *dé-rober*, Eng. *rob*, and fr. Old High Ger. *roub*, 'robbery, booty, *esp.* pillaged garment,' in like manner, French *robe*, 'garment,' Eng. *robe*.]

lubdhaka, *m.* hunter. [lubdha, √lubh.]

√ **lubh** (lúbhyati; lulóbha, lulubhé; lubdhá; lóbdhum). —1. go astray; —2. be lustful; have strong desire; lubdha, longing for. [cf. ἡ λίψ, *λιφ-s, 'longing'; λίπ-τ-ομαι, 'long for'; Lat. *lub-et*, *lib-et*, 'is desired *or* agreeable'; *libens*, 'willing, glad'; *libīdo*, 'desire'; AS. *leōf*, 'dear,' Eng. *lief*, 'dear, gladly'; Ger. *lieb*, 'dear'; also Eng. *love*.]

√ **lul** (lólati; lulitá). move hither and thither.

√ **lū** (lunā́ti [728]; luláva; lūná). cut (*e.g.* grass, hair); cut off; gnaw off. [cf. λύ-ω, 'separate, *i.e.* loose'; Lat. *so-lū-tus*, 'loosed.']

lekha, *m.* a writing; letter. [√likh.]

√ **lok** (lókate; luloké; lókitum; *caus.* lokáyati [1056]; lokitá; -lókya; *only caus. forms are in common use, and these only with* ava, ā, *and* vi). get a look at; behold; —*caus.* [1041²] —1. look, look on; —2. get a look at, behold. [on account of the guttural k, prob. a secondary root fr. roká (√ruc, 216.1): for connection of mg, cf. λευκ-ός, 'bright,' and λεύσσω, *λευκ-jω, 'see'; Lat. *lūmen*, 'light,' then 'eye' (see under √ruc); also locana: no connection w. Eng. *look*.]

+**ava**, *caus.* —1. look; —2. look at *or* upon; —3. behold, see, perceive.

+**ā**, *caus.* —1. look at; —2. see, perceive.

+vi, *caus.* —1. look; —2. look at, inspect, 25[6]; —3. behold.

loká, *perhaps a younger form of* uloká *(which appears regularly in the oldest texts, but divided as* u loká, 84[11]), *m.* —1. open space; free room; place, 83[15]; —2a. the vast space; the world, 103[8]; any imaginary world *or* worlds, 15[16]; *cf.* antarikṣa-, indra-, jīva-, pati-, pára-, manuṣya-, svarga-loka; —2b. *used of heaven:* svargo lokas, the world situate in the light, 103[5, 14, 16]; *so* sukṛtām ulokas, the world of the righteous, 84[11]; *later,* sukṛtasya lokas, world of virtue, 89[8]; *so* 5[20]; —2c. *of earth:* loke kṛtsne, in the whole earth, 5[15]; asmin · · loke, in this world (*cf.* iha), 66[12]; *in same sense,* loke, 57[8], 63[7]; —2d. *with senses merging imperceptibly into those given under* 3, *e.g.,* in the world *or* among men, 26[2], 36[3], 47[21]; —3. (*like Eng.* world *and French* monde) people; folks; men *or* mankind; *sing.* 6[7], 21[18]; *pl.* 2[5, 14], 39[19], 57[15]. [etymology uncertain: no connection with Lat. *locus,* Old Lat. *stlocus,* 'place.']

loka-kṛ́t, *a.* world-making, world-creating. [1269.]

loka-pālá, *m. pl.* world-protectors, either four in number (regents of the four quarters of the world), or eight (regents of the cardinal points and four points mid-way between).

loka-pravāda, *m.* world-saying, common saying.

lokam-pṛṇá, *a.* world-filling; *f.* -ā (*sc.* iṣṭakā), Lokamprinā, name applied to the common bricks used in building the sacred fire-pile, and so called because all laid with the recitation of the one general formula, lokám pṛṇa, 'fill thou the world.' [1314b: for pṛṇa, √1 pṛ, see 731.]

logá, *m.* clod (of earth). [√ruj, 'break,' 216.1: for mg, see under mṛ́d.]

√ **loc** (locayati; locitá; -lócya). *used only with* ā. [derived fr. √ruc; just how, is unclear: see √lok.]

+ā, —1. *rarely,* cause to appear *or* be seen; —2. *usually,* bring to one's own sight *or* mind, consider, reflect; matsyāir ālocitam (*impers.*, 999), the fishes reflected; ity ālocya, thus reflecting.

+pary-ā, *see* loc + ā; reflect, deliberate.

+sam-ā, *see* loc + ā; reflect.

locana, —1. *a.* enlightening; —2. *as n.* eye, *usual mg.* [√loc: for mg, cf. *lūmen,* under √lok.]

lobha, *m.* strong desire; greed, avarice. [√lubh.]

lobha-viraha, *m.* freedom from avarice.

lóman, *n.* hair on the body of men and beasts (usually excluding that of the head and beard and that of mane and tail). [prop. 'clippings, shearings,' √lū, 'cut,' 1168. 1a: cf. roman.]

lola, *a.* —1. moving hither and thither, uneasy; *and so* —2. anxious for, desirous of; greedy. [√lul.]

loṣṭá, *m. n.* clod (of earth). [√ruj, cf. 222[4]: for mg, see under mṛ́d.]

lohá, *a.* reddish; coppery; *as m. n.* reddish metal, copper. [cf. lóhita, róhita, and rudhirá, all meaning 'red': with the last, cf. *ἐ-ρυθ-ρός,* Lat. *ruber, rūfus,* Eng. *ruddy, red.*]

lohāyasá, *n.* coppery metal, any metal alloyed with copper. [āyasá.]

lāulya, *n.* greediness. [lola, 1211.]

lāuhāyasa, *a.* metallic; *as n.* metallic ware. [lohāyasa, 1208f.]

vaṅçá, *m.* —1. cane *or* stock *or* stem, *esp.* of the bamboo; —2. (*like Eng.* stock, *and* stem [*rarely*], *and Ger.* Stamm) lineage, family, race.

vaṅça-viçuddha, *a.* —1. made of perfectly clear *or* unblemished bamboo; —2. of pure lineage. [lit. 'vaṅça-pure, pure in its *or* his vaṅça,' 1265: √çudh.]

√ **vak** (vāvakré [786, 798a]). roll. [akin w. √vañc, q.v.]

vaktavyà, *grdv.* to be said *or* spoken; *see* 999 end. [√vac, 964.]

vakrá, *a.* —1. crooked; —2. *fig.* (*nearly like Eng.* crooked) disingenuous, ambiguous. [√vak, 1188.]

vakṣáṇā, *f. pl.* belly; bellies (of cloud-mountains).

√ vac (vákti; uvā́ca, ūcús [784, 800c]; ávocat [847 end, 854]; vakṣyáti, -te; uktá; váktum; uktvā́; -úcya; ucyáte; vācáyati). say *or* speak (*w. acc. of person*, 10[22]; *or w. acc. of person and acc. of thing*, 7[19]); announce *or* tell, 66[19], 98[17]; name *or* call, 58[7]; **punar uvāca**, replied, 19[19]; **ity uktvā**, with saying so, *i.e.* with the words "..," saying "..," 4[2]; so saying, 19[23], etc.;

—**uktá**, —1. spoken, said; *impers. pass.* [999 mid.], **kākena‿uktam**, the crow said, 24[18], etc.; **uktam**, *introducing a proverb*, 't is said, 19[9], 20[15], etc.; —2. spoken unto; **evam ukta**, thus addressed, 3[5], etc.

—*caus.* —1. *mid.* cause *or* ask (*e.g.* the Brahmans) to pronounce for one's self (*e.g.* a benediction), 101[2], 106[4]; —2. cause (a written leaf) to speak, *i.e.* read, 54[20].

[cf. *ὄσσα*, **Fοκ-ja*, 'voice, rumor'; Lat. *vŏc-āre*, 'call'; Ger. *er-wäh-nen*, 'mention': w. vác-as, 'word,' cf. *ἔπος*, stem **Fεπ-εσ*, 'word,' w. labialization: w. ávocam, **a-va-uc-am*, cf. *ἔειπον*, **ἔ-Fε-ιπ-ον*, 'said': w. nom. vā́k, **vā́k-s*, stem vā́c, 'voice,' cf. Lat. *vox*, **vōc-s*, 'voice,' and *ὄψ*, for **ὤψ*, i.e. *Fωπ-s*, 'voice.']

+**anu**, —1. repeat *or* say (sacrificial prayers, etc.) for some one (*gen.*); —2. *mid.* say after (the teacher), *i.e.* learn, study; **anūcāná**, *perf. mid. ppl.*, who studies, studied, learn-ed.

+**abhy-anu**, say with regard to *or* with reference to something; describe (an occurrence) in (metrical and Vedic) words.

+**nis**, speak out *or* clearly; explain.

+**pra**, —1. tell forth, proclaim; tell, announce, mention; *and so* —2. (*as conversely* laudāre, 'praise,' *comes to mean* 'mention') praise; —3. tell of, *colloq.* tell on, *i.e.* betray, 93[18]; —4. say, 45[9]; —5. declare to be; name, 57[5].

+**prati**, say in return, answer.

+**sam**, say together.

vacana, *n.* —1. speech; words, 9[18], etc.; dictum; —2. (*like Lat.* e-dictum *and Eng.* edict *and* word) command; injunction, 26[18]. [√vac, 1150.]

vácas, *n.* —1. speech, 4[6], etc.; words; word; counsel; —2. language, 54[11]; —3. (*like Eng.* word) order; request, 53[8]. [√vac, 1151. 1a: cf. *ἔπος*, 'word.']

√ vaj (vājáyati). *probable root, with the meaning* be strong *or* lively, *inferred from* ugrá, ójas, vájra, vā́ja; *see these words;* vājáyant, hastening, 75[9]: *cf.* √vājaya. [cf. *ὑγ-ιής*, 'strong, healthy'; AS. *wac-ol*, 'awake'; Eng. *wake*, 'not to sleep'; perhaps Lat. *vig-ēre*, 'be lively *or* strong,' *vig-il*, 'awake.']

vájra, *m.* *Indra's* thunderbolt, 70[8], 88[15]. [orig., perhaps, a mere epithet, 'The Mighty' (√vaj), like *Miölnir*, 'The Crusher,' name of Thor's hammer.]

vájra-bāhu, *a.* having the thunderbolt on his arm (of Indra), lightning-armed. [1303.]

vajrín, *a.* having the thunderbolt (of Indra). [vajra, 1230.]

√ vañc (váñcati; vañcáyati; vañcitá). totter; go crookedly; *caus.* (cause to go astray, *i.e.*) mislead, deceive; cheat. [cf. Lat. *vacillare*, 'totter, be unsteady'; AS. *wōh*, 'crooked, wrong,' whence Eng. *woo*, 'incline to one's self, court.']

+**upa**, totter unto.

vañcaka, *m.* deceiver. [√vañc, caus.]

vañcayitavya, *grdv.* to be deceived; *as n.* a to-be-practised deceit, *w. objective gen.* (296b beg.), 26[2]. [√vañc.]

vaṭa, *m.* Ficus indica; *cf.* nyag-rodha.

vaṇik-putra, *m.* merchant's son. [vaṇij.]

vaṇíj, *m.* merchant. [√paṇ, 383.5.]

√ vat (vátati; vātáyati). *only with* api. understand; *caus.* cause to understand *or* know, reveal, inspire (devotion). [cf. Lat. *vāt-es*, 'wise seer': see under vā́ta.]

vatsá, *m.* young; *esp.* young of a cow, calf. [prop. 'yearling,' from a not quotable **vatas*, 'year': with **vatas*, cf. *Fέτος*, 'year,' Lat. *vetus-* in *vetus-tu-s*, 'bejahrt, in years, old': akin are Lat. *vit-u-lu-s*, 'yearling, *i.e.* calf,' and Eng. *weth-er*: for mg, cf. *χίμαρος*, 'goat,' prop. 'winter-ling' (see hima): see vatsara.]

vatsará, *m.* year; *personified*, 67[15]. [cf. vatsa; also pari- and saṁ-vatsara.]

√ **vad** (vádati, -te; uvā́da, ūdé [784]; ávādīt, ávadiṣṭa; vadiṣyáti, -te; uditá; váditum; uditvā́; -údya; vādáyati). —1. speak, 95[7, 9]; say, 20[10], etc.; speak to, *w. acc., or w. loc.* (4[1]); —2. communicate; announce, RV. x. 125. 5; speak of; udita, stated (authoritatively), 58[16]; —3. tell, *i.e.* foretell, predict, 103[12]; —4. designate as, 55[5]; name.

+**abhi**, speak to, salute; signify, *in the derivs* abhivādin, abhivāda; *caus.* speak to; salute.

+**praty-abhi**, *caus. mid.* salute in return.

+**ā**, speak to; vidatham ā-vad, give orders to (the household), rule (as master *or* mistress).

+**pra**, —1. speak forth; say; —2. declare to be.

+**vi**, *mid.* contradict.

+**sam**, *mid.* talk *or* take counsel with one's self.

vádana, *n.* —1. mouth; —2. face. ['organ of speaking,' √vad, 1150: for mg, cf. nayana.]

vaditavya, *grdv.* to be spoken. [√vad.]

vadya, *grdv.* to be spoken of, worthy of (favorable) notice, *and so* praiseworthy. [√vad, 963[3] c.]

√ **vadh** (ávadhīt, ávadhiṣṭa; vadhiṣyáti, -te). —1. strike; harm; —2. (*just as AS.* sleān *meant first* 'strike' *and then* 'slay, *i.e.* kill') slay, kill. [see √bādh: cf. ὠθ-έω, 'push': see vadhar.]

vadhá, *m.* —1. murderer; —2. weapon of death, *esp.* Indra's bolt; —3. slaying, slaughter. [√vadh.]

vádhar, *n.* weapon of death, *i.e.* Indra's bolt. [√vadh.]

vadhasná, *only in instr. pl.* weapons of death, *i.e.* Indra's bolts. [vadhá, 1195.]

vadhū́, *f.* —1. bride; —2. woman. [prop. 'the one fetched home' by the bridegroom, √vah, q.v.]

vadhū-vastra, *n.* bride's garment.

vádhya, *grdv.* —1. to be struck, *i.e.* punished, 27[21]; to be harmed; —2. to be slain, 27[18]. [√vadh, 963[3] c.]

vádhri, *a.* whose testicles have been crushed; emasculated, *opp. of* vṛṣan. [√vadh, 1191.]

√ **van** (vanóti, vanuté; vavā́na, vavné; vātá). —1. hold dear, love; desire, seek, beseech, 79[19]; —2. get; —3. win. [cf. Lat. *ven-ia*, 'favor'; *Ven-us*, 'The Lovely One'; AS. *winnan*, 'exert one's self, strive,' Eng. *win*, 'gain by striving'; AS. *wēn*, 'hope, expectation, supposition,' whence *wēn-an*, Eng. *ween*, 'suppose': see √vāñch.]

vána, *n.* wood; forest.

vanánā, *f.* desire. [√van, 1150. 2b[2].]

vánanvant, *a.* having desire, desiring. [perhaps fr. vanánā, 1233, w. irreg. loss of final ā: both mg and derivation are doubtful.]

vana-prastha, *m. n.* forest-plateau, wooded table-land. [1280b.]

vana-vāsa, *m.* the living in a wood; -tas, owing to (his) forest-life.

vánas-páti, *m.* tree. ['lord of the wood': see 1267 and a and d: perhaps vanas stands for vanar, a subsidiary form of vana, cf. 171[3].]

√ **vand** (vándate; vavandé; vanditá; vánditum; vanditvā́; -vándya). —1. praise; —2. salute reverentially. [orig. ident. w. √vad, 108g.]

+**abhi**, make reverent salutation unto; salute.

vanditṛ́, *m.* praiser. [√vand.]

√ **1vap** (vápati, -te; uptá; -úpya; vāpáyati). shear (hair, beard); trim (nails); *caus.* cause to be clipped, *or simply* [1041[2]], clip.

√ **2vap** (vápati, -te; uvā́pa, ūpé [784, 800e]; ávāpsīt; vapsyáti; uptá; uptvā́; -úpya). —1. strew; scatter, *esp.* seed, sow; —2. (*like* χόω) throw *or* heap up, *i.e.* dam up.

+**apa**, cast away; *fig.* destroy.

+**abhi**, bestrew.

+**ā**, throw upon, strew.

+**ni**, throw down.

+**nis**, throw out, *esp.* deal out (from a larger mass) an oblation to a god, *dat.*; offer.

vapā́, *f.* caul, omentum.

vápus, *a.* —1. wondrous, admirabilis; —2. (*like Eng.* admirable) exciting wonder mixed with approbation, *esp.* wondrous fair;

—*as n.* —1. a wonder; wonderful appearance; vapur dṛçaye, a wonder to see, θαῦμα ἰδέσθαι, 79[9]; —2. beautiful appearance; beauty, 8[8]; —3. appearance; form, 48[3,4]. [for 2 and 3, cf. the converse transition of mg in rūpa, 1, 2.]

vayám, we, *see* 491. [cf. Ger. *wi-r*, Eng. *we.*]

1 **váyas**, *n.* —1. fowl, *collective;* —2. bird. [see ví, 'bird.']

2 **váyas**, *n.* food, meal. [prop. 'enjoyment,' √1 vī, 'enjoy': for analogies, see √2 bhuj, 'enjoy,' and √1 vī.]

3 **váyas**, *n.* —1. strength, of body and of mind; health; —2. the time of strength, youth; marriageable age, 2[6]; —3. *generalized*, any age *or* period of life; years (of life). [akin w. vī-ra, q.v.]

vayā́, *f.* strengthening.

1 **vára**, *m.* choice; wish; a thing to be chosen as gift *or* reward, *and so* gift, reward; varaṁ vṛ, wish a wish, make a condition, 94[1]; varaṁ dā, give a choice, grant a wish, 1[17]; práti váram *or* váram ā́, according to one's wish. [√2 vṛ, 'choose': cf. Eng. *well*, lit. 'according to one's wish.']

2 **vara**, *a.* (*like Eng.* choice *or* select) most excellent *or* fair, best, *w. gen. or loc.*, 16[2], 3[21]; *w. abl.*, most excellent as distinguished from · ·, *i.e.* better than · ·, 68[14]; varam · ·, na ca · ·, the best thing is · ·, and not · ·, *i.e.* · · is better than · ·, 17[2]. [√2 vṛ, 'choose': for mg, cf. AS. *cyst*, 'a choice,' and then 'the best,' with *ceōsan*, 'choose.']

varaṇa, *n.* a choosing. [√2 vṛ, 'choose.']

vara-varṇa, *m.* most fair complexion.

varavarṇin, *a.* having a fair complexion; -inī, *f.* fair-faced woman. [varavarṇa, 1230.]

varāñganā, *f.* most excellent woman. [añganā.]

varāroha, *a.* having fair hips *or* buttocks; καλλίπυγος. [āroha.]

varāhá, *m.* boar.

várivas, *n.* breadth; *fig.* freedom from constraint, ease, gladness, *w.* kṛ. [belonging to urú, 'broad': see 1173[3], 467[2].]

várīyāṅs, *a.* very broad, wide extended. [√1 vṛ, 'cover, extend over': see 467[2] and 1173[3].]

váruṇa, *m.* The Encompasser (of the Universe), Varuna, name of an Aditya; *orig.* the supreme god of the Veda (*see selection* xxxvii. *and notes*), and so called king as well as god, 83[12]; omniscient judge who punishes sin and sends sickness and death, *selections* xliii., xliv., xlv.; *later*, god of the waters, 7[10]. [a personification of the 'all-embracing' heaven, √1 vṛ, 'cover, encompass,' 1177c: cf. οὐρανός, 'heaven,' and Οὐρανός, 'Heaven,' personified as a god.]

várūtha, *n.* cover; *and so, as in Eng.*, protection. [√1 vṛ, 'cover,' 1163c.]

varūthyà, *a.* protecting. [varūtha, 1212d 4.]

váreṇya, *grdv.* to be desired; *and so*, longed for, excellent. [√2 vṛ, 'choose,' 1217[1,2,3], 966b.]

varga, *m.* group. [√vṛj, 'separate,' 216.1: for mg, cf. Eng. *division*, 'a separating into parts,' and then 'the part separated, group.']

várcas, *n.* vitality, vigor; the illuminating power in fire and the sun; *and so*, splendor; *fig.* glory. [perhaps akin with ruc: cf. varpas with rūpa.]

várṇa, *m.* —1. outside; external appearance; color, 36[19], 37[6], etc.; complexion; —2. (color, *and so, as in Eng.*) kind, species, sort, 98[2]; —3. (sort of men, *i.e.*) caste, 28[18]; —4. letter; sound; vowel, 59[16]; syllable; word, 98[3]. [√1 vṛ, 'cover,' 1177a: for mg 1, cf. Eng. *coating*, and *coat* (of paint), and Lat. *color*, prop. 'cover *or* coating,' cognate w. *oc-cul-ere*, 'cover over.']

√ **varṇaya** (varṇayati). —1. color, paint; —2. *fig.* (*like Eng.* paint), depict, describe; tell about; *pass.* 12[3]. [varṇa, 1058.]

vartana, *n.* *prop.* an existing, *and so* (*like Eng.* living), means of subsistence. [√vṛt, mgs 3, 5: cf. vṛtti.]

vartṛ́, *m.* restrainer, stayer. [√1 vṛ, 'cover,' mg 3, 'restrain': 1182.]

vártman, *n.* wheel-track; path, 43[9]; vartmanā, *at end of cpds:* by way of, 39[14]; *or simply* through; ākāça-vartmanā, through the air, 39[1]. [√vṛt, 1168. 1a.]

vártra, *a.* warding off, holding back; *as n.* a water-stop, dam, weir. [√1 vṛ, 'cover,' q.v.]

1 **várdhana**, *a.* –1. increasing, *trans.*; *as m.* increaser; –2. delighting in. [√1 vṛdh, 'increase,' q.v.]

2 **vardhana**, *n.* the cutting. [√2 vṛdh, 'cut.']

várpas, *n.* assumed appearance; image, form. [akin with rūpá: cf. varcas.]

várman, *n.* énvelope; coat of armor; protection; at end of Kshatriya-names, 59[18] N. [√1 vṛ, 'envélop,' 1168. 1a.]

varṣá, *n.* –1. rain; –2. (rainy-season, *i.e.*) year; –varṣā́, *f. pl.* –1. the rains, *i.e.* the rainy season; –2. *very rarely*, rain-water, 104[14]. [√vṛṣ: cf. ἔ-ερσαι, 'rain-drops': for mg 2 of varṣa, cf. Eng. "girl of sixteen *summers*," "man of seventy *winters*," abda and çarad.]

varṣa-karman, *n.* the action of raining.

varṣa-ṣaṭka, *n.* year-hexade, period of six years.

varṣmán, *m.* height; top; crown of the head. [see 1168. 1c[2] and 2b.]

valá, *m.* *prop.* an encloser, *and so* –1. (enclosure, *i.e.*) cave; –2. *personified*, Vala, name of a demon who shuts up the heavenly waters to withhold them from man and is slain by Indra, 81[5,7]. [√1 vṛ, 'enclose.']

vala-vṛtra, *m.* Vala and Vritra. [1252.]

valavṛtra-niṣūdana, *m.* destroyer of Vala and Vritra, *i.e.* Indra. [1264.]

valavṛtra-han [402], *a.* slaying Vala and Vritra; *as m.* slayer of Vala and Vritra, *i.e.* Indra. [1269.]

valmíka, *m.* ant-hill.

vavrí, *m.* *prop.* cover, *and so* –1. place of hiding *or* refuge; –2. corporeal tegument (of the soul), *i.e.* body. [√1 vṛ, 'cover,' 1155. 2c.]

√ **vaç** (váṣṭi, uçánti [638]; uvā́ça [784]). –1. will, 73[17]; –2. desire, long for; –*ppls, pres.* uçánt, *perf.* vāvaçāná [786]: willing *or* (*when qualifying subject of verb*) gladly, 83[4], 85[6]; longing, 78[9]; –3. (*like Eng.* will *in its rare or obsolete sense* 'order') order, command. [cf. ἑκών, stem *ϝεκ-οντ, 'willing.']

váça, *a.* willing, submissive; *as m.* –1. will; –2. command; *and so* controlling power *or* influence. [√vaç.]

vaça-ní [352], *a.* bringing into one's power; *as m.* controller.

vaçā́, *f.* –1. cow, *esp.* farrow cow; –2. female elephant, Elephanten-kuh. [perhaps 'the lowing' beast, fr. √vāç: cf. Lat. *vacca*, 'cow': usual name for 'cow' is gó.]

vaçín, *a.* having command *or* control; *as subst. m. or f.* master, mistress. [vaça.]

vaçī-kṛ, make submissive, enthrall, ensnare. [vaça and √1 kṛ, 'make,' 1094.]

vaçya, *grdv.* to be commanded *or* ordered, *and so* obedient, submissive, yielding. [vaç, 963[3] c.]

vas, *encl. pron.* you, 491. [cf. Lat. *vōs*, 'ye, you.']

√ 1 **vas** (uccháti [753, 608]; uvā́sa [784]; vatsyáti [167]; uṣṭá). grow bright; light up (of the breaking day), dawn. [for cognates, Lat. *us-tu-s*, 'burned,' *east*, *Easter*, etc., see the collateral form uṣ, 'burn,' and the derivs uṣas, usra, vasanta, vasu, vāsara: cf. also ἦμαρ, *ϝεσ-μαρ, 'day'; ἔαρ, *ϝεσ-αρ, Lat. *vēr*, *ve-er, *ves-er, 'dawn of the year-light, *i.e.* spring'; *Ves-uv-ius*, 'the burning' mountain.]

+ **vi**, shine abroad, 75[15]; light up, 97[13].

√ 2 **vas** (váste [628]; vavasé; ávasiṣṭa; vatsyáti; vasitá; vásitum; vasitvā́; -vásya). put on (as a garment), clothe one's self in. [cf. ἕννυμι, *ϝεσ-νυ-μι, 'put on'; ἕ-εσ-το, 'had on'; εἷμα, 'garment'; Lat. *ves-tis*, 'garment'; Goth. *ga-vas-jan*, 'clothe'; AS. *wer-ian*, Eng. *wear*.]

√ 3 **vas** (vásati; uvā́sa [784]; ávātsīt [167]; vatsyáti; uṣitá; vástum; uṣitvā́; -úṣya; vāsáyati). stay in a place; *esp.*

stay over night, 38^2, 100^8 (*with* rātrīm); dwell, abide; live. [cf. ἄστυ, *Ϝασ-τυ, 'dwelling-place, town'; Lat. *ver-na*, 'one who lives in the house, *i.e.* slave' or 'one who dwells in the land, *i.e.* native,' like Eng. *domestic*, 'servant,' and *domestic*, 'not foreign'; AS. *wes-an*, 'be'; Eng. *was, were.*]

+**ā**, take up one's abode in (a place), occupy; enter upon, 62^8.

+**ud**, *caus.* (cause to abide out, *i.e.*) remove from its place, 97^{14}?.

+**upa**, —1. stay with; wait; —2. (*with a specialization of mg like that in Eng.* abs-tain, 'hold off, *esp.* from food *or* drink') wait, *and so* stop (eating), fast.

+**ni**, dwell (of men and of beasts).

+**prati**, have one's dwelling.

√ **4 vas** (vāsáyati; vāsitá). cut. [cf. Lat. *vōmis, *vos-mis, vōmer*, 'plow-share, colter.']

+**ud**, cut away *or* off, 97^{14}?.

vasantá, *m.* spring. ['the dawning *or* lighting-up' year-time, √1 vas, $1172^{3,4}$: see 1 vas: cf. ἔαρ, *Ϝεσ-αρ, Lat. *vēr, *ve-er, *ves-er*, 'spring.']

vásiṣṭha, *a.* most excellent, best; —*as m.* Vasishtha, name of one of the most famous Vedic seers, 78^{19} N. [formed as superl. to vasu, fr. √1 vas as a verbal (467), the verbal having the same transferred sense as the adj. vasu, q.v.]

vásu, *a.* excellent, good; —1. *as m.* good (of gods), 76^{11}; —2. *as m. pl.* The Good Ones, the Vasus, a class of gods, RV. x. 125.1; —3. *as n. sing. and pl.* good, goods, wealth. [prop. 'shining, *i.e.* splendid,' √1 vas, 'shine,' but w. a transfer of mg like that in the Eng. *splendid* as used by the vulgar for 'excellent': connection w. ἠύς, ἐύς, 'good,' and εὖ, 'well,' is improbable, see āyu.]

vasu-dhā́ [352], *a.* yielding good; vasudhā [364], *f.* the earth; the land.

vasudhādhipa, *m.* (lord of the earth, *i.e.*) king, prince. [adhipa.]

vasuṁ-dhara, *a.* holding good *or* treasures; -ā, *f.* the earth. [vasum + dhara, 1250a: we should expect vasu (acc. s. neuter, or stem), not vasu-m (masculine!), 341.]

vásu-çravas, *a. perhaps* [1298a] having good fame, *or else* [1297 and 1280b] having wealth-fame, *i.e.* famed for wealth.

vasu-sampūrṇa, *a.* treasure-filled. [√1 pṛ, 'fill.']

√ **vasūya** (vasūyáti). crave good. [denom. of vasu, 1058^1, 1061.]

vasūyā́, *f.* desire for good; longing. [√vasūya, 1149^6.]

vastṛ, *m.* illuminer; *or, as adj.*, lighting up. [√1 **vas**, 'shine,' 1182, 375^3.]

vástra, *n.* garment, piece of clothing; cloth. [√2 vas, 'clothe,' 1185a.]

vastra-veṣṭita, *a.* covered with clothes, well dressed.

vastrānta, *m.* border of a garment. [anta.]

√ **vah** (váhati, -te; uvā́ha, ūhé; ávākṣīt; vakṣyáti; ūḍhá [222]; vóḍhum; ūḍhvā́; -úhya; uhyáte). —1. conduct, 84^{11}; carry, *esp.* the oblation, 85^1, 93^{14}, 94^1; bring with team, 73^{11}, 81^{14}, *or* car, 72^4, 87^{14}; draw (wagon), guide (horses); —2. *intrans.* travel; proceed (in a wagon); —3. *pass.* be borne along; —4. flow, carry with itself (of water); —5. (*like Ger.* heimführen) bring home to the groom's house, wed; —6. carry, $43^{11,16}$, 52^9; bear, 26^4; carry far and wide, *i.e.* spread (a poem, fragrance), 54^2.

[for *vagh: cf. ὄχος, *Ϝοχος, 'wagon'; ὀχέομαι, 'ride'; Lat. *veh-ere*, 'carry'; *vehiculum*, 'wagon'; AS. *weg-an*, 'carry, bear,' whence Eng. *weigh*, 'lift' (as in *weigh anchor*), 'find weight of by lifting' (cf. bhara); AS. *wægn* or *wǣn*, Eng. *wain*, Dutch *wagen* (whence the borrowed Eng. *wagon*), 'that which is drawn, *i.e.* wagon'; further, Lat. *vi-a, ve-a, *veh-ia*, 'that which is to be travelled over, way'; AS. *weg*, Eng. *way*, 'that which carries' one to a place.]

+**ā**, bring hither *or* to.

+**ud**, —1. bear *or* bring up; —2. *esp.* lead out (a bride from her father's house), wed.

+**pari**, —1. lead about; —2. *esp.* lead about (the bride *or* the wedding procession), wed.

+**pra**, carry onward.

+vi, lead away, *esp.* the bride from her parents' house, *and so* wed, marry; *mid.* get married.

+sam, carry together; carry.

váh, *vbl.* carrying, drawing, *in cpds.* [√vah.]

vahatú, *m.* wedding procession; wedding. [√vah, 1161c.]

vahyá, *n.* portable bed, litter. [√vah, 1213: for mg, cf. Eng. *bier* and verb *bear.*]

vahye-çayá, *a.* lying on litters. [vahya, 1250c: acct, 1270.]

√ **1vā** (vā́ti; vavāú; ávāsīt [882]; vāsyáti; vātá; vā́tum; vāpáyati [1042d]). blow. [cf. ἄημι, *ἀ-ϝη-μι, 'blow'; Goth. *va-ian*, Ger. *weh-en*, AS. *wāwan*, 'blow'; αὔ-ρα, 'breeze'; ἀήρ, *ἀϝηρ, 'air'; Lat. *ventu-s* (a participial form which has made a transition to the vowel-declension — cf. vasanta and 1172[3,4]), 'wind,' Eng. *wind;* AS. *we-der*, Eng. *wea-ther*, 'wind (e.g. in *weather-cock*), condition of the air': see vā́ta and vāyú, 'wind.']

+ā, blow hither.

+nis, —1. (blow out, *intransitively, i.e.*) go out, be extinguished; —2. *intrans.* (blow till one gets one's breath, *and so*) cool off; —*caus.* —1. extinguish; —2. cool off, *transitively, i.e.* refresh.

+parā, blow away.

+pra, blow *or* move forward, *intrans.*

+vi, blow asunder, *i.e.* scatter to the winds.

√ **2vā** (váyati [761d2]; uvā́ya [784[2]]; vayiṣyáti; utá; ótum; ūyáte). weave, interweave, *both lit., and also* (*like Lat.* serere), *fig.*, of hymns and songs; plait. [orig. idea perhaps 'wind' or 'plait': root-forms are u, vā, and vi: cf. ἰτέα, *ϝιτεα, 'willow'; οἶσος, 'osier'; Lat. *vi-ēre*, 'plait'; *vī-men*, 'plaited work'; οἴνη, 'vine'; οἶνος, 'wine'; Lat. *vīnum*, 'wine'; *vī-tis*, 'vine,' Eng. *withy* or *withe*, 'pliant twig,' Ger. *Weide*, 'withe, willow.']

vā, *enclitic particle, following its word.* —1. or; · · vā, · · vā, 50[17], 64[10], 96[12,23], 97[18,19]; ·, · · vā, 77[6], 24[6], 59[9,20], 64[18], 97[2,8,16], 104[21]; *similarly*, 35[6], 59[18], 84[9]; ·, ·, · · vā, 20[4], 91[9]; —*further:* · · vā, yadi vā · ·, · · vā, 28[12]; · ·, · · vā, · · vā‿api, 62[2]; · ·, · · (vā *omitted*), · · vā, · · vā, 61[23], 62[1]; *finally*, · · na, · · vā‿api, · · ca, neither · ·, nor · ·, nor · ·, 63[4]; —atha vā, *see* atha 6; uta vā, *see* uta; —2. vā, *for* eva, 59[10]N.; —3. *with interrogatives:* kiṁ vā, what possibly, 17[19]; *so* 18[1]. [cf. Lat. *-ve*, 'or.']

vākya, *n.* —1. speech, words; —2. *as technical term*, periphrasis, *e.g.* vīrasenasya sutas *for* vīrasena-sutas. [√vac.]

vāg-doṣāt, by *or* as a bad consequence of his voice, *i.e.* because he was fool enough to let his voice be heard. [vāc: see doṣa.]

vāghát [*like* dā́sat, 444[2]], *m.* the pledging one, *i.e.* institutor of a sacrifice, not the priest, but the yajamāna. [perhaps akin are εὔχ-ομαι, Lat. *vovēre*, **vogv-ere*, 'vow.']

vāṅmáya, *a.* consisting of voice *or* utterance. [vā́c: see 1225[2] and maya.]

vā́c [391], *f.* —1. speech, voice, word, utterance, sound; vācaṁ vy-ā-hṛ, utter words, 3[1], *and* vācaṁ vad, speak words, 94[9], *verb-phrases, used like a simple verb of speaking, and construed w. the acc. of the person* (*see* 274b); *perhaps* (utterance, *i.e.*) sacred text, 91[2]; —2. *personified*, The Word, Vāch, Λόγος. [√vac, q.v.]

vācaṁ-yamá, *a.* restraining *or* holding one's voice, silent. [1250a, 1270[1] and b.]

vācaka, *a.* speaking; *as m.* speaker. [√vac, 1181.]

vācika, *a.* verbal, consisting of words. [vā́c, 1222e.]

vācya, *grdv.* —1. to be spoken; —2. to be spoken to. [√vac, 1213a.]

vā́ja, *m.* —1. swiftness; courage, *esp.* of the horse; —2. race, struggle; —3. prize of race *or* contest; booty; reward *in general;* treasure, good. [prob. akin w. √vaj, q.v.: orig. 'strength and liveliness,' 'that in which strength and courage show themselves,' and then 'the result of quick and brave struggle.']

√ **vājaya** (*only in ppl.*, vājayánt). crave treasure; seek good, 74[16]; *cf.* √vaj. [denom. of vā́ja, 1058.]

√ **vāñch** (vā́ñchati; vāñchitá). wish. [for *vānsk, orig. inchoative (cf. √1 iṣ) to √van, q.v.: cf. Ger. *Wunsch*, 'a wish'; AS. *wūsc*, 'a wish,' whence verb *wȳscan*, 'wish,' whence Eng. verb *wish*, whence noun *wish*.]

vāṇijya, *n.* merchant's business, trade. [vaṇíj, 1211.]

vā́ta, *m.* —1. wind; air; —2. Vāta, god of the wind. [√1 vā, 'blow': acct, 1176c: cf. Icelandic *Óð-inn*, AS. *Wōd-en*, Old High Ger. *Wuot-an*, names of the highest Germanic god, Odin: the name still lives in the Eng. *Wednes-day*, AS. *Wōdn-es dæg*: some connect *Wōden* w. √vat, 'inspire, excite.']

vā́ta-svanas, *a.* having the roar of the wind, *i.e.* blustering, exhibiting noisy violence, tumultuous.

vātāikabhakṣa, *a.* having wind as sole food, *i.e.* fasting. [vāta + ekabhakṣa.]

vāda, *m.* speech, expression, statement. [√vad.]

vāda-yuddha, *n.* speech-fight, *i.e.* controversy.

vādayuddha-pradhāna, *a.* devoted to controversy; *as m.* eminent controversialist.]

vādin, *a.* speaking. [√vad, 1183[3].]

vānaprastha, *m.* a Brahman of the third order, who has passed through the stages of student and householder (*see* āçrama) and dwells in the woods, 65[3] N.; hermit. [vanaprastha: for mg, cf. ἐρημίτης, Eng. *hermit*, and ἐρημία, 'solitude, desert.']

vānara, *m.* monkey, ape.

vāpī, *f.* oblong pond; lake. [√2 vap, 'heap up, dam up,' and so, perhaps, orig. 'a dam' (cf. χῶμα, 'dam,' from χόω, 'throw *or* heap up'), and then, by metonymy, 'the pond made by the dam.']

vāpī-jala, *n.* lake-water. [perhaps the first element is here to be taken in its orig. sense of 'dam,' so that the whole means prop. 'dam-water,' and so 'pond-water.']

vām, *see* 491.

vāmá, *a.* lovely, pleasant; *as n.* a lovely thing, a joy. [√van: cf. dhūma and √1 dhvan.]

vāyasá, *m.* —1. bird; —2. *esp.* crow; -sī, *f.* crow-hen. [1 váyas, 'bird,' 1208a.]

vāyú, *m.* wind. [√1 vā, 'blow,' 1165.]

vā́r, *n.* water. [cf. οὖρ-ο-ν, orig. 'water,' and so, as in Eng., 'urine'; Lat. *ūrīnāri*, 'stay under water'; *ūr-īna*, 'urine'; *Ur-ia*, 'Water-town,' a port in Apulia; prob. akin is AS. *wær*, 'sea.']

1 **vā́ra**, *m.* tail-hair, *esp.* of a horse. [prob. akin w. οὐρή, 'tail.']

2 **vāra**, *m.* —1. choice treasure; —2. moment chosen *or* determined for any thing, appointed time, turn; —3. time (*as used with numerals*); vāraṁ vāram, time and again; —4. the time *or* turn (of one of the planets which rule in succession the days of the week), *and so*, day of the week, day. [√2 vṛ, 'choose': identified by some w. ὥρα, 'time, season,' see under √yā.]

vāraṇá, *a.* warding off (those that attack it), *and so* strong *or* ungovernable (of wild beasts); *as m.* elephant. [√1 vṛ, 'cover, ward off,' 1150. 1b.]

vārāṇasī, *f.* Vārāṇasī, the modern Benares.

vāri, *n.* water. [see vā́r.]

vāri-stha, *a.* situated in the water, *i.e.* (of the sun's disk) reflected in the water.

vā́vá, *particle, emphasizing the word which it follows.* surely, just. [for double acct, see Whitney 94.]

√ **vāç** (vā́çyate [761c]; vavāçé; ávīvaçat [861]; vāçitá; vāçitvā́). bleat; low; cry (of birds). [see vaçā, Lat. *vacca*, 'cow,' and vāçrá.]

vāçrá, *a.* lowing (of kine). [√vāç, 1188a.]

vāsá, *m.* —1. *prop.* a staying over night; —2. an abiding, 32[5]; —3. abiding-place, 23[20]. [√3 vas, 'dwell': for mg, cf. bhavana.]

vāsa-bhūmi, *f.* dwelling-place.

vāsará, —1. *in Veda, as adj.* of the dawn; ἠέριος; —2. *in classical Skt., neuter, used as subst., also masculine,* (*prop.* time of dawn, as distinguished from night, *and so*) day *in general.* [prop. a secondary deriv. (1188d) fr. an obsolete *vas-ar, 'dawn,' √1 vas, 'dawn'; see

1 vas: and for the form vas-ar, cf. ἔαρ and *vēr*, there given, and ah-ar, ūdh-ar, 430.]

vāsa-veçman, *n.* chamber for spending the night, sleeping-room.

vā́sas, *n.* garment. [√2 vas, 'clothe.']

vāsin, *a.* dwelling. [√3 vas, 'dwell,' 1183[3].]

vāstavyà, *a.* belonging to an abode; *as m.* inhabitant. [vā́stu, 1212d 2.]

vā́stu, *m. n.* dwelling. [√3 vas, 'dwell,' 1161a.]

vā́stoṣ-páti, *m.* lord *or* Genius of the dwelling, 77[2]N. [vā́stos, gen. of vā́stu (1250d) + páti: acct, 1267a and d.]

vāhá, *a.* carrying; carrying off. [√vah.]

vā́hana, *a.* carrying off; *as n.* —1. beast of burden, 56[8]; beast for riding; team; vehicle; —2. the carrying, 34[18]. [√vah, 1150. 1b.]

1 **ví** [343e], *m.* bird. [cf. οἰωνός, *ὀϝι-ωνος, Lat. *avi-s*, 'bird.']

2 **ví**, *preposition.* apart, asunder, away, out; *denoting intensity in descriptive cpds* (1289), *cf.* vicitra, vibudha; *denoting separation or non-agreement in possessive cpds* (1305), *cf.* vimanas, *etc.*; *similarly in the prepositional cpd* (1310a), vipriya.

viñçatí [485], *f.* twenty. [cf. εἴκοσι, Boeotian ϝίκατι, Lat. *viginti*, 'twenty.']

vikaṭa, *a.* —1. exceeding the usual measure; *and so* —2. (*like Eng.* enormous) monstrous, hideous; —*as m.* Hideous, name of a gander. [cf. 1245g.]

vikramá, *m.* a stepping out, appearance; *esp.* bold *or* courageous advance, courage, might. [√kram + vi.]

vigata-saṁkalpa, *a.* with vanished purpose, purposeless. [√gam + vi: 1299.]

vigulpha, *a.* abundant. [origin unclear.]

vigraha, *m.* —1. separation; *and so* —2. division; *and so* —3. discord, quarrel, war. [√grah + vi.]

√ **vic** (vinákti; viktá; véktum; -vícya). separate, *esp.* grain from chaff by winnowing; separate, *in general.*

+**vi**, separate out *or* apart; vivikta, isolated, *and so* lonely.

vicakṣaṇá, *a.* appearing far and wide, conspicuous; *or*, far-seeing. [√cakṣ + vi.]

vi-citra, *a.* —1. very variegated; —2. differently colored, varied; —3. (full of variety and surprises, *and so*) entertaining, beautiful. [in mg 1, vi- has perhaps intensive force; in 2, perhaps variative.]

√ **vij** (vijáte; vivijé; ávikta [834c]; vijiṣyáti; vigná). move with a quick darting motion, ἀίσσειν; (*like Eng.* start) move suddenly from fear. [cf. AS. *wīc-an*, 'give way'; Eng. *weak*, 'yielding, soft, feeble.']

+**ud**, start up; be affrighted; udvigna, terrified.

vijayá, *m.* victory; *personified*, Victory, name of a rabbit. [√ji + vi.]

víjiti, *f.* conquest. [√ji + vi.]

vijitendriya, *a.* having the organs of sense subdued. [vijita + indriya.]

vijñéya, *grdv.* to be known *or* considered as. [√jñā + vi, 963[3]a.]

viṇ-mūtra, *n.* faeces and urine. [viṣ, 226b, 161: for cpd, 1253b.]

vitatha, *a.* false. ['differing from the so,' vi + tathā, 1314a.]

vitathābhiniveça, *m.* inclination towards that which is false. [abhiniveça.]

vítasti, *f.* a span, about nine inches *or* twelve fingers. [prob. fr. √tan + vi, and so 'a stretch' from the tip of the thumb to that of little finger: for mg, cf. Eng. noun *span* and verb *span*, 'extend over,' and see vyāma.]

vitāna, *m. n.* —1. spreading out, extension; —2. canopy. [√tan + vi: for mg 2, cf. Eng. *expanse* (of heaven) and *expand.*]

vittá, *ppl.* gotten; *as n.* (*like Lat.* quaestus) gettings, that which is got, property. [√2 vid, 'get.']

√**1 vid** (vétti; véda [790a]; ávedīt; vediṣyáti, -te; vetsyáti, -te; viditá; véditum, véttum; viditvā́; -vídya; vedáyati). —1. know; understand; perceive; ya evaṁ veda, who knoweth thus, who hath this knowledge, *frequent formula in the Brāhmanas*, 97[8]; vidyāt, one should know, it should be known *or* understood; —2. recognize as; nalam māṁ viddhi, recognize me as N., know that I am N.; —3. notice; be mindful of, 75[13]; bethink one's self, 94[6, 10]; —4. believe; assume; consider a person (*acc.*) to be · · (*acc.*), 43[19]; —*ppl.* vidváṅs, *see s.v.*

[with **véda**, **vidmá**, cf. *οἶδα*, *ἴδμεν*, AS. *ic wāt, wē witon*, 'I know, we know'; Eng. *I wot*, gerund *to wit*, noun *wit*, 'understanding': cf. also *εἶδον*, **ἔϝιδον*, 'saw'; Lat. *vidēre*, 'see'; AS. *witan*, 'see'; whence *wit-ga*, 'seer, soothsayer, wizard' (Icelandic *vit-ki*, 'wizard'), *wicca*, 'wizard,' *wicce*, 'witch,' Eng. *witch*, masc. and fem.: **véda** is an old preterito-present, 'have seen *or* perceived,' and so, 'know'—see √2vid: the forms of the other tense-systems are comparatively modern.]

+**anu**, know along, *i.e.* from one end to the other, know thoroughly.

+**ni**, *caus.* cause to know; do to wit; announce; communicate.

√ 2vid (**vindáti, -te** [758]; **vivéda, vividé; ávidat, ávidata; vetsyáti, -te; vittá; véttum; vittvā́; -vídya**). —1. find, 4[12], etc.; get, 74[13]; obtain (children), 100[5, 9]; —2. get hold of, 80[7]; —3. *pass.* **vidyáte**: is found; *later, equiv. to* there is, there exists, *ppl.* **vídāna** [619[3]], found, 73[21]; —*ppl.* **vitta**, *see s.v.*

[orig. ident. w. √1vid, of which this is only another aspect, namely that of 'seeing *esp.* an object looked for, *i.e.* of finding': see 1vid.]

+**anu**, find.

vid, *vbl.* knowing, *at end of cpds.* [√1vid.]

vida, *a.* knowing, *at end of cpds.* [do.]

vidatra, *a.* noticing, *in cpds.* [√1vid, 1185d.]

vidátha, *n.* directions, orders. [prop. 'knowledge given, *i.e.* instructions,' √1vid, 1163b.]

vidarbha, —1. *m. pl.* the Vidarbhans, Vidarbha, name of a people, and of their country, which was south of the Vindhya mountains, and is now called Berar; —2. *m. sing.* Vidarbha, *i.e.* a king of Vidarbha, 4[2]. [for mg 2, cf. "*Norway*, uncle of young Fortinbras," Hamlet, i.2.28.]

vidarbha-nagarī, *f.* city *or* capital of Vidarbha, *i.e.* Kundina (**kuṇḍina**). [**vidarbha-** does not stand in the relation of a gen. of appellation: see 295[1].]

vidarbha-pati, *m.* lord *or* king of Vidarbha.

vidarbha-rājan, *m.* king of Vidarbha.

vidāsin, *a.* becoming exhausted, drying up. [√das + vi, 1183[3].]

vidyā́, *f.* —1. knowledge; a discipline *or* science; *esp.* **trayī vidyā**, the triple science *or* knowledge of the holy word, as hymn, sacrificial formula, and chant, *or* the Rigveda, Yajurveda, and Sāmaveda; —2. *esp.* the science *κατ' ἐξοχήν*, *i.e.* magic; a magic formula, spell. [√1vid, 1213d: for mg 2, observe the equally arbitrary specialization in Eng. *spell*, which in AS. meant 'a saying.']

vidyā-dhara, *a.* keeping *or* possessed of knowledge *or* the magic art; *as m.* a Vidyādhara, one of a class of genii, who are attendants on Çiva, and reputed to be magicians.

vidyā-mada, *m.* knowledge-intoxication, *i.e.* infatuated pride in one's learning.

vidyāvayo-vṛddha, *a.* grown old in knowledge and years, distinguished for learning and age. [**vidyā** + 3**vayas**, 1252.]

vidyút, —1. *a.* lightening; *and so, as in Eng.*, —2. *f.* lightning. [√dyut + vi, 'lighten'.]

vidvaj-jana, *m.* wise man. [**vidvāṅs**, 1249a, 202.]

vidvā́ṅs [461], *ppl.* knowing; wise, 17[18], etc.; learned; **tvaṣṭā vidvān**, a cunning workman (*cf. Eng.* cunning *and Old Eng.* cunnen, 'know'), 75[6]. [√1vid, 'know,' 790a, 803[2].]

√ 1vidh (**vidháti**). worship a god (*dat.*) with (*instr.*); honor (*acc.*) with (*instr.*). [cf. **vedhas**.]

√ 2vidh (**vindháte**). lack *or* be without a thing (*instr.*), viduāri; be bereft *or* alone. [see **vidhavā**.]

√ 3vidh, *see* √vyadh.

vidh, *vbl.* boring through, wounding, *at end of cpds.* [√3vidh or vyadh, 252, cf. 785.]

vidhávā, *f.* widow. [√2vidh, 'be bereft,' 1190; cf. *ἠ-ίθεος*, 'youth without a wife, bachelor'; Lat. *viduus*, *vidua*, 'widower, widow'; AS. *widwe*, *wuduwe*, Eng. *widow*.]

vidhā́, *f.* proportion, measure; way; *and so* kind, sort; *esp. at end of cpds* [*see* 1302c 5]: *e.g.* **tri-vidha**, of three kinds, three-fold. [prop. 'dis-position, arrangement, order, method,' see √1 dhā + vi.]

vidhātavya, *grdv.* to be shown. [√1 dhā + vi, mg 5.]

vidhātṛ́, *m.* dis-poser, arranger. [√1 dhā + vi.]

vidhā́na, *n.* a dis-position, ordering, ordinance; **vidhānatas**, according to (established) ordinance. [√1 dhā + vi, 1150.]

vidhi, *m.* —1. a dis-position, ordinance, prescription, rule (65[7]), method; —2. (method, *i.e.*) way, 38[23]; procedure; —3. (the supreme disposition *or* ordaining, *i.e.*) destiny, fate. [√1 dhā + vi, 1155. 2e, 345[2]: for mg 3, cf. Lat. *destinâre*, 'establish, ordain,' and Eng. *destiny*.]

vidhivat, *adv.* according to rule; *equiv. to Lat.* rite. [vidhi, 1107.]

vidhú, *a.* lonely (of the moon that wanders alone among the star-hosts); *as m.* moon. [prob. fr. √2 vidh, 1178.]

vidhura, *a.* —1. alone, bereft; —2. suffering lack, miserable; —3. disagreeable; *as n.* trouble. [prob. fr. √2 vidh, through the intermediate vidhu, 1188f.]

vidhura-darçana, *n.* sight of adversity.

vidheya, *grdv.* to be done. [see √1 dhā + vi, mg 5: also 963[3]a.]

vinayá, *m.* —1. training, breeding, *i.e.* formation of manners; *and so* —2. *transferred* (*like the Eng.* breeding), manners, good breeding, politeness. [√nī + vi.]

vínā, *prep.* without, *w. instr. or acc.* [1127, 1129.]

vinīti, *f.* (good breeding, *esp.*) modesty. [√nī + vi: see vinaya.]

vinoda, *m.* *exactly like Eng.* di-version; amusement. [see √nud + vi.]

√ vind, *see* √2 vid.

vindhya, *m.* Vindhya, name of the mountain-range crossing the Indian peninsula and separating Hindustan from the Deccan.

vindhyāṭavī, *f.* the Vindhya-forest. [aṭavī.]

√ vip (**vépate**; **vivipé**; **ávepiṣṭa**; **vepáyati**). be in trembling agitation; tremble *or* shake; *caus.* shake, *trans.* [cf. Lat. *vibrāre*, 'shake, brandish,' from **vib-ru-s*, **vip-ru-s*, 'shaking'; AS. *wæfre* (formed like **vip-ru-s*), 'moving this way and that,' whence Eng. *waver*; Eng. frequentative *whiffle*, 'veer about, blow in gusts'; *whiffle-tree*, so called from its constant jerky motion (*-tree* means 'wooden bar,' see dāru).]

vipaṇa, *m.* trading-place, shop; **-ī**, *f.* shop. [√paṇ + vi, 1156.]

vipatti, *f.* a coming to nought, destruction. [√pad + vi, 1157.]

vipad, *f.* misfortune, trouble. [√pad + vi, 383a.]

vípāka, *m.* the ripening, *esp.* of the fruit of good *or* bad deeds, *and so* the consequences; the issue, *in general*. [√pac + vi, 216. 1.]

vípra, —1. *a.* agitated, inspired; *as subst.* he who gives utterance to pious emotion at the altar, poet, singer, 74[11, 18]; —2. *a.* (inspired, *i.e.*) gifted with superior insight, wise, of a god, 79[13, 17]; —3. *as m.* a Brahman, 60[15], etc. [√vip, 1188a: mg 3 is to be taken directly from 1.]

vípriya, *a.* not dear, unpleasant; *as n.* something disagreeable, an offense. [2 vi + priya, see vi and 1310a end.]

vi-budha, *a.* very wise (vi- *is intensive*, 1289); *as m.* a god.

vibudhānucara, *m.* attendant of a god. [anucara.]

vibudheçvara, *m.* a lord of the gods. [īçvara.]

vibhava, *m.* —1. development *or* growth; —2. (the result of growth, *i.e.*) power, *and so* lordship, majesty, high position; —3. *sing. and pl.* (*like Ger.* Vermögen) property, possessions. [√bhū + vi: cf. vibhu and vibhūti.]

vibhā́van, *f.* **-varī**, *a.* shining far and wide. [√bhā + vi, 1169. 1b and 2[2], 1171b.]

vibhī́daka, *m. n.* the large tree Terminalia Bellerica; one of the nuts of this tree, which were used for dicing; a die, dice. [perhaps 'the destroyer,' fr. √bhid

+vi: if so, we must suppose that the name was first given to the die as die, and applied secondarily to nut and tree.]

vibhú, *a.* –**1.** pervading, far-reaching; unlimited, 74[2]; –**2.** powerful, mighty, of Indra, 5[12, 15]; *as subst.* lord *or* ruler. [√bhū + vi, 354: for 2, cf. **vibhava** 1 and 2, and **vibhūti**.]

víbhūti, *f.* –**1.** development *or* growth; –**2.** (the result of growth, *i.e.*) power, *esp.* of a lord *or* ruler. [√bhū + vi, 1157d: cf. **vibhava** and **vibhu**.]

ví-manas, *a.* (having an away-removed mind *or* heart, *i.e.*) out of one's senses *or* disheartened. [1305.]

vimarda, *m.* destruction; (of sleep) disturbance. [√mṛd + vi.]

vimā́na, *a.* traversing, *esp.* the sky; *as m. n.* a palatial car of the gods that moves through the air, sky-chariot. [√1 mā + vi, 'measure,' q.v.: 1150.]

vi-mukha, *a.* having the face away; vimukhā yānti, they go (with averted faces, *i.e.*) homewards. [1305.]

vi-rajas, *a.* having dust away, dustless, pure. [1305.]

viraha, *m.* –**1.** abandonment, separation from; –**2.** absence, freedom from. [√rah + vi.]

virāma, *m.* stop, end, pause. [√ram + vi.]

virodhin, *a.* hindering, disturbing. [√rudh + vi, 1183[3].]

vilāsa, *m.* joy. [√las + vi.]

vivará, *m. n.* opening; hole (of creatures that live in the ground). [√1 vṛ + vi, 'uncover, open.']

vi-varṇa, *a.* having the color away, colorless, pale. [1305.]

vivarṇa-vadana, *a.* pale-faced. [1298a.]

vivásvan, *a.* lighting up; vivásvabhis, *as adv.* [1112c], so that it lights up; *as n.*, *perhaps*, flash, spark. [√1 vas + vi, 'light up,' 1169b.]

vívasvant, *a.* lighting up; *as m.* Vivasvant, name of a god of the dawning daylight *or* morning-sun, father of the twins Yama and Yamī and of the Açvins, 85[13, 14]. [√1 vas + vi, 'light up,' see 1233e.]

vivāhá, *m.* fetching home of the bride, wedding, marriage. [√vah + vi.]

vivāha-catuṣṭaya, *n.* marriage-quaternion, *i.e.* the marrying of four wives.

vivāhāgni, *m.* wedding-fire. [agni.]

vividha, *a.* having different kinds, *i.e.* of different sorts, various. [2 vi + vidhā, 334[2], 1305.]

vivṛddhi, *f.* growth; increase in size; increase. [√vṛdh + vi, 1157.1d.]

viveka, *m.* –**1.** a separating apart; –**2.** discrimination, discernment, good judgment. [√vic + vi, 216.1: for mg 2, cf. *discrimination* w. Lat. *discrimināre*, 'separate,' fr. *discrīmen* of the same root as *discernere*, 'separate'; cf. also *discernment* with *discernere*.]

√ **viç** (viçáti, -te; vivéça, viviçé; ávikṣat; vekṣyáti, -te; viṣṭá; véṣṭum; -víçya; veçáyati). settle down; go in; go into, enter. [with **veçá**, 'house,' cf. οἶκος, 'house' (analogous to *entry* from *enter*); Lat. *vīcus*, 'settlement, village,' whence the borrowed AS. *wīc*, 'village'; Goth. *veihs*, 'village'; Lat. *villa*, **vic(u)la*, 'small settlement, farm': see further **víç** and **veçá**.]

+**ā**, go into, enter; pervade, RV. x. 125. 6; **āviṣṭa**: *actively*, having entered; *passively*, entered by, filled with; –*caus.* cause to go into, put into, communicate.

+**upa**, settle down upon; sit down; **upaviṣṭa**, seated.

+**ni**, *mid.* go in; go home (to house *or* nest); settle down to rest.

+**abhi-ni**, settle down to; be inclined towards, *fig., as in Eng.*; be bent upon.

+**pra**, enter, get into; *w. acc.*, 85[2]; *w. loc.*, 18[23]; *without expressed object:* enter, 8[4]; go in, 33[14]; go home, 103[21]; penetrate, pierce; –*caus.* cause to enter.

+**sam-pra**, go in; *w.* **gṛham**, go home; *w.* **niveçanam**, go to bed; enter, *w. loc.*

+**sam**, enter together, *i.e.* make their appearance together *or* come hither together, 86[16]; –*caus.* cause to enter upon, put *or* set upon.

víç (víṭ, víçam, viḍbhís [218[3]]), *f.* –**1.** a settlement, *i.e.* dwelling-place; *and so* house; –**2.** a settlement, *i.e.* the community, clan, folk; viçām patis, lord of peoples, *i.e.* *simply* prince; tribe *or* host (of gods), 71[18], 78[4]; —3. the folk, as distinguished from the Brahmans and Kshatriyas, the third caste, later called vāiçya; a man of the third caste, 59[22]. [√viç, q.v.: cf. *Δωριέες τριχά-ικ-ες*, 'three-tribed Dorians'; also Keltic *vic* in *Ordo-vīc-es*, people of North Wales, and *Lemo-vīc-es*, people of modern Limoges.]

viçaṅkā, *f.* hesitation. [√çaṅk + vi, 1149.]

víçākha, *a.* having spread-asunder branches, *i.e.* forked; -e, *dual f.* Viçākhe, name of an asterism. [2 vi + çākhā, 1305, 334[2].]

viçākhila, *m.* Viçākhila, name of a merchant. [viçākha, 1227: perhaps named after the asterism because various green-grocer's commodities belonged to it.]

viçālá, *a.* capacious, spreading, broad.

viçiṣṭatā, *f.* condition of being distinguished, distinction, superiority. [viçiṣṭa, 1237: see çiṣ + vi.]

viçeṣa, *m.* —1. that which separates *or* distinguishes one thing from another, distinction *or* difference; *and so* —2. (*like Eng.* distinction) eminence, excellence; viçeṣeṇa, *as adv.* [1112b], to an eminent degree, *i.e.* very much, especially, *like French* par excellence. [√çiṣ + vi.]

viçeṣatas, *adv.* —1. *at end of a cpd*, according to the difference of · ·, 66[23]; —2. (*like* viçeṣeṇa, *see above*) especially. [viçeṣa, 1098b.]

viç-páti, *m.* master of the house. [euphony, 218[5]: acct, 1267a: cf. Old Prussian *wais-patti-n*, 'house-mistress'; Lithuanian *vësz-pat-s*, 'lord.']

viçrabdham, *see* √çrambh.

viçrambha, *m.* confidence. [√çrambh + vi.]

viçrambhālāpa, *m.* confidence-talk, familiar conversation. [ālāpa.]

víçva [524], *pron. adj.* —1a. all, every; every one; *common in Veda, but replaced in the Brāhmana and later by* sarva, *q.v.*; —1b. víçve devā́s: all the gods, 82[1]; *or* the All-gods (as a class, *see* deva 2b), 88[6, 8], 90[8]; —1c. víçvam, *as n.* The All, *τὸ πᾶν*, 92[12]; —2. *sometimes*, entire, whole; *so* 71[17].

viçvá-cakṣas, *a.* all-beholding. [see 1296[8]: acct, 1298c.]

viçvátas, *adv.* from *or* on all sides, everywhere. [víçva, 1098b: acct, 1298c.]

viçváto-mukha, *a.* having a face on all sides, whose face is turned every-whither. [1306.]

viçvá-darçata, *a.* to be seen by all, all-conspicuous. [acct, 1273, 1298c.]

viçvá-deva, *m. pl.* the All-gods (*see* deva 2b), RV. x. 125. 1. [víçva + devá: acct, 1280a, 1298c.]

viçvá-bheṣaja, *a.* all-healing. [víçva + bheṣajá: acct, 1280a, 1298c.]

viçvá-çcandra, *a.* all-sparkling. [víçva + çcandrá: acct, 1280a, 1298c.]

viçva-sṛ́j, *a.* all-creating; *as m. pl.* All-creators, name of certain creative beings.

viçvád, *a.* all-consuming. [víçva + ád.]

viçvā́yu, *assumed as stem of* viçvā́yos, 75[1], *prop. a form of transition to the* u-*declension of the stem* viçvā́yus, *and meaning either* friendly to all, all-friendly (*if taken with* mama, *i.e.* varuṇasya), *or else* all living creatures (*if taken with* rāṣṭram, 'lordship over'); *see* viçvā́yus 1 *and* 2.

viçvā́yus, —1. *a.* belonging to *or* appearing to all life *or* living creatures, *i.e.* *either* friendly to all *or* all-known (applied to gods), *or else* dwelling in all (of the Genius of Life), 85[18]; —2. *as n.* all-life, *i.e.* all living creatures, men and beasts. [víçva + ā́yus, acct, 1280a, 1298c: for mg 1, see 1294[2].]

viçvāsa, *m.* confidence. [√çvas + vi.]

viçvāsa-kāraṇa, *n.* reason for confidence.

viçvāsa-bhūmi, *f.* proper vessel for confidence, one who may safely be trusted.

viçvā́hā, *adv.* always, for evermore. [víçva, see 1100a and cf. 1104[2, 3]: acct, cf. 1298c.]

√ viṣ (viveṣṭi; vivéṣa; vekṣyáti, -te; viṣṭá; -víṣya). work, be active, accomplish.

víṣ (víṭ, víṣam, viḍbhís), *f.* excrement, faeces.

viṣá, *n.* poison. [prop. 'the potent *or* overpowering,' √viṣ: no less arbitrary is the specialization in Eng. *poison*, fr. Lat. *potionem*, 'draught': cf. *ἰός*, *ϝίσος*, Lat. *vīrus*, 'poison.']

viṣa-kumbha, *m.* jar of poison.

viṣaya, *m.* —1. *prop.* working, *and so* sphere of activity *or* influence; —2. one's department *or* line *or* peculiar province; *and so, generalized* —3. province, field, domain, empire, country; —4. field of activity of one of the sense-organs (*e.g.*, sound is the viṣaya of the ear), *a mere specialization of* mg 1; object of sense, pleasure of sense; —5. object *in general.* [√viṣ: but the formation of the stem is not clear.]

viṣāda, *m.* despondency, dejection. [√sad + vi.]

viṣu, *adv.* on both sides.

viṣuvat-saṁkrānti, *f.* equinox-passage (of the sun from one zodiacal sign to the next); the time of equinox-passage, the equinox. [viṣuvant.]

viṣuvánt, —1. *a.* having *or* taking part on both sides, *i.e.* keeping *or* being in the middle; —2. *m.* middle day (*e.g.* of a long sacrifice); —3. *m. n. esp.* middle day between the solstices, the vernal *or* autumnal equinox. [viṣu, 1233c and b end.]

√ **viṣṭ** (véṣṭate; viṣṭitá; -véṣṭya; veṣṭáyati). wind one's self about; *caus.* wind around, envelope, wrap up, dress.

víṣṇu, *m.* Vishnu, name of a god, whose chief work in the Veda is the measuring of the sky in three paces, and who became one of the Hindu Trinity, and extremely important in the later sectarian development of India; *cf.* brahmán 2 *and* çivá. [prob. 'the mighty worker,' √viṣ, 1162.]

viṣṇu-çarman, *m.* Vishnuçarman, name of a sage. ['having V. as his protection' or else 'the delight of V.': the mg of the cpd depends on its accent (see 1302[1] and 1267[1]), and this is not known.]

viṣṇuçarma-nāman, *a.* possessing viṣṇuçarman as name, named V. [1249a[2].]

víṣvañc [408], *a.* directed in both ways *or* parted asunder. [viṣu + añc, 407.]

visárjana, *n.* the letting go; evacuation. [√sṛj + vi.]

víspaṣṭa, *see* √1 paç + vi.

vispaṣṭārtha, *a.* having clear *or* intelligible meaning. [artha.]

vismaya, *m.* astonishment. [√smi + vi.]

vismayānvita, *a.* filled with astonishment. [anvita, √i + anu.]

vi-hasta, *a.* —1. having the hands away, handless; *and so* —2. (*like Eng.* unhandy) awkward; *and so* —3. perplexed, confounded. [1305.]

vihārin, *a.* wandering about. [√1 hṛ + vi, 1183[3].]

√ **1 vī** (véti; vivā́ya, vivyé; vītá). —1. seek eagerly; —2. accept gladly; enjoy; —3. strive to get; —4. fall upon.

[cf. Lat. *vēnāri*, 'hunt,' a denom. of **vē-na*, 'hunt'; AS. *wā-ð*, 'hunt'; Old High Ger. *weida*, '1. the seeking, *esp.* of food, *i.e.* hunting, fishing, *and then* 2. place for getting food, pasture, *and* 3. food, fodder'; *weida* appears w. mg 1 in Ger. *Waid-mann*, 'hunter' (also as family name, *Weidmann*, 'Hunter'), and w. mgs 2 and 3 in *Weide*, 'pasture, food': perhaps 2 váyas, 'food,' q.v., comes fr. √vī in mg 1, 'seek for, hunt,' and in this case the development of mg is like that of *weida* 3 and like that of Lat. *vēnātiōn-em*, 'hunting, game,' whence Eng. *venison*.]

+upa, seek after.

√ **2 vī**, *see* vyā.

vī́ṇā, *f.* lute.

vīta, *see* √i + vi; *also referable to roots* vī *and* vyā.

vīta-darpa, *a.* having one's pride departed; humbled. [√i + vi.]

vīta-rāga, *a.* having one's passions departed, *i.e.* having conquered one's passions. [do.]

vīrá, *m.* —1. man; *esp.* man of might, hero; *in pl.* Männer; —2. hero, applied to gods; —3. *pl.* (*like Eng.* men) retainers, Mannen, 86[5]. [cognate with 3 vayas, 'strength': cf. Lat. *vir*, AS. *wer*, 'manly *or* heroic man'; Eng. *were-wolf*, 'man-wolf.']

√ **vīraya** (vīráyate [1067]). be a hero, show one's self brave. [vīra, 1058.]

vīrávant, *a.* having *or* rich in men *or* heroic sons. [vīrá, 1233a.]

vīra-sū́ [352], *a.* bringing forth heroes (as sons).

vīrásena, *a.* possessing a vīrasenā́ *or* hero-army; *as subst. m.* Vīrasena, king of Nishadha, *like the Greek* 'Ἡρό-στρατος *in formation and mg.* [vīra-senā́, 334[2], 1297: acct, 1295.]

vīrasena-suta, *m.* Vīrasena's son, 1[3]. [1264.]

vīra-senā́, *f.* hero-army, army of heroes. [vīrá + sénā, 1280b: acct, 1280[2].]

vīryà, *n.* —1. manliness, courage; strength; —2. *concrete,* heroic deed. [vīrá, 1212 d 4.]

vīhasta, *for* vihasta, *q.v.*, 52[12]. [see 1087 b.]

√ **1 vṛ** (vṛṇóti, vṛṇuté; vavára, vavré; ávārīt; vṛtá; váritum, vártum; vṛtvā́; -vṛ́tya; vāráyati). —1. cover, enclose, encompass; surround, *i.e.* guard, 11[21]; —2. *offensively,* keep in, hold back *or* captive; vṛta, pent up, 75[14]; —3. *defensively,* hold back, keep in check (75[11]), ward off, hinder, restrain; —*caus.* [1041[2]], keep back, hinder, stop.

[cf. ἐ-ελ-μένος, 'enclosed' and 'held in check,' referred to εἴλω, Aeolic ἔλλω, *Ϝελ-νω; εἶλαρ, *Ϝελ-αρ, 'cover, defense'; Lat. *ver-ēri,* 'be on one's guard, fear'; *vellus,* '(cover, *i.e.*) pelt, fleece'; *vallum,* 'defense, palisaded rampart, wall,' whence the borrowed Eng. *wall;* Eng. *ware, wary,* 'on one's guard, cautious'; Ger. *wehren,* 'check, ward off'; *Wehre,* 'defense'; with vártra, 'stopping,' and then 'a dam,' cf Ger. *Wehr,* AS. *wer,* Eng. *weir,* '(water-) stop, dam': for other cognates, see **uru**, **ūrṇa**, **varuṇa**: cf. the derivs **vala**, **vṛtra**, **varūtha**, **varṇa**, etc.]

+**anu**, cover over.

+**apa**, uncover, open. [cf. the relation of Ger. *decken,* 'cover,' and *auf-decken,* 'uncover.']

+**abhi**, cover.

+**ā**, cover; —āvṛta: covered, 33[20]; concealed; encompassed, surrounded, 3[9]; (covered with, *i.e.*) filled with, provided with, 66[1].

+**sam-ā**, cover; samāvṛta, surrounded.

+**ni**, keep down, suppress, ward off; *caus.* [1041[2]], stop, 98[4].

+**nis**, *in ppl.* nirvṛta, pleased, contented, free from care. [prop. 'uncovered, not covered over, *i.e.* not dark *or* gloomy,' and so 'clear, bright': cf. √1 vṛ + vi, which shows a similar metaphor.]

+**pari**, surround.

+**pra**, cover.

+**sam-pra**, *mid.* cover completely.

+**vi**, uncover, open; make open *or* clear, illume. [cf. √1 vṛ + nis.]

+**sam**, —1. cover over; —2. keep together *or* in order, *and so* put in order, gather up, 26[20].

√ **2 vṛ** (vṛṇīté; vavré; ávṛta; variṣyáte; vṛtá; várītum [254[3]]; varitvā́; *caus.* varáyati, -te [1042b[3]]). choose; prefer; desire, wish; choose for one's self, make one's portion, 70[5], 86[14]; varaṁ vṛ, wish a wish, make a condition, 94[1]; —*caus.* [1041[2]], choose.

[cf. Lat. *volo,* 'will'; Old Eng. *wol, wul,* 'will,' still living in *I won't,* 'I wol not'; Ger. *Wahl,* 'choice, selection,' whence *wählen,* 'select,' Chaucerian *wail,* 'select'; Ger. *wohl,* Eng. *well,* 'according to one's wish' (see under 1 vara): perhaps akin are βούλομαι, *βολνομαι, Epic βόλομαι, 'will,' and βέλ-τερος, 'choicer, better,' but this is disputed.]

+**ā**, choose, desire.

vṛ́ka, —1. *a.* tearing, harming, *in* a-vṛka; —2. *m.* (the tearer, *i.e.*) wolf. [√*vṛk or *vrak, simpler form of √vraçc: cf. λύκος, *Ϝλυκος, Church Slavonic *vlŭkŭ,* Lat. *lupus,* Eng. *wolf.*]

vṛkka, *dual m.* the kidneys.

vṛkṣá, *m.* tree. ['that which is felled,' √*vṛk (1197) or *vrak, simpler form of √vraçc: for mg, cf. barhís.]

vṛkṣa-traya, *n.* tree-triad, three trees.

vṛkṣatraya-tale, under three (separate) trees, *see* tala.

vṛkṣopari, on the tree. [upari: see 1314f.]

√ vṛj (vṛṇákti, vṛñkté; vavárja; ávark [832]; varkṣyáti, -te; vṛktá; -vṛ́jya; varjáyati). —1. turn; twist off; —2. turn *or* set aside; —3. (turn aside, *i.e.*) di-vert *or* keep away *or* alienate something from some one;

—*caus.* [1041 2] —1. (set aside, *i.e.*) abandon, shun; avoid, 25 21, 104 3; —2. (set aside, take out, *and so, like* ex-cipere) except; varjayitvā, with an excepting, *i.e.* with exception of, 54 22; leave out, exclude, separate.

[orig. 'bring out of its original direction *or* position, by bending *or* diverting *or* keeping in' (in this last sense, cf. vṛjáṇa, 'enclosure,' and ἐ-έργ-νυ, 'shut in'), and so the opposite of √1ṛj, 'stretch *or* reach straight out,' q.v.: cf. also Lat. *vergere*, 'bend, turn'; Eng. *wrick*, 'to twist,' and *wriggle*; prob. cognate is *wring*, 'twist'; also Eng. *wrong*, 'twisted, crooked' (as in *wrong-nosed*, Wyclif), 'bad,' which shows the same metaphor as vṛjina and French-Eng. *tort*, from Lat. *torquēre*, 'twist.']

vṛjána, *n.* enclosure, *esp.* enclosed settlement, *and so, either* dwelling-place (74 13) *or* the dwellers. [√vṛj, q.v.: 1150. 2c.]

vṛjiná, *a.* crooked, wrong, *opp. of* ṛju, 'straight, right.' [√vṛj, 1177b: for the mg, see √vṛj.]

√ vṛt (vártate, -ti; vavárta, vāvṛté [786]; ávṛtat; vartiṣyáti, -te; vartsyáti, -te; vṛttá; vártitum; -vṛ́tya; vartáyati, -te). —1. turn *or* roll *or* move as does a wheel; *in general,* move *or* come from (*abl.*), 76 14; —2. (*like Eng.* take its course) go on, take place; happen; ekāpāyena vṛt, go with a diminution-by-one, *i.e.* decrease by one, 58 5; —3. (move one's self about in a place, *and so*) abide, exist, be, be present; mūrdhni vṛt, stand at the head, be chief in importance, 22 21; —4. be in a certain condition, case, occupation; be concerned with (*loc.*), 10 5; —5. live; live by (*instr.*), *i.e.* live upon, 104 2; —6. proceed, behave; —7. *attenuated in mg from sense* 3 *to that of a simple copula,* be, 51 4; —vṛttá, *see s.v.*

[cf. Lat. *vert-ere*, 'turn'; AS. *weorðan*, 'become,' Eng. *worth*, 'become, be to' (in *wo worth the day*), Ger. *werden*, 'become'; for transition of mg in Eng. and Ger., cf. Eng. *turn*, which also means 'become' (as in *turn traitor*): —cf. also Eng. *-ward*, as in *go south-ward*, i.e. 'turned to the south,' *fly up-ward*, i.e. 'directed up,' etc. (see añc); also Ger. *Wirt-el*, 'spindle-ring'; Church Slavonic *vret-eno*, 'spindle':

—further akin is, prob., AS. *wrīðan*, 'twist,' whence come: Eng. *writhe*; AS. *wræð*, 'a twisted band,' Eng. *wreath*; *wrist*, earlier *hand-wrist*, **-wrið-st*, 'hand-turner':

—with vṛttá, cf. Lat. *versus*, 'turned,' whence *versāre*, 'turn much': for mgs 3–6 of vṛt, cf. Lat. *versāri*, whose senses are quite parallel, and the Eng. phrase "in whom we live and *move* and have our being."]

+anu, roll after; follow; *and so,* continue.

+ā, *act.* turn hither (*trans.*), 73 6; *so at* 74 11 (*sc.* rátham vas, 'your car'); *mid.* turn (*intrans.*), roll back, 63 8.

+upa‿ā, turn hither unto, 93 19.

+abhi-pary-ā, turn around unto.

+vy-ā, turn away, *intrans.*; separate from *or* part with (*instr.*), 86 8, 96 22.

+sam-ā, turn back to meet; go home, *used esp.* of a religious preceptor's pupil who has finished his studies.

+ud, turn out (centrifugally), *intrans.*, fly asunder; *caus.* burst asunder *or* open.

+ni, —1. turn back; —2. flee; —3. turn away; —4. turn from, abstain; —nivṛtta, *see s.v.*

+prati-ni, turn back from (*abl.*).

+nis, roll out, *intrans.*, *and so* (*with a metaphor like that in the Eng.* e-volve itself *and Ger.* sich ent-wickeln) develop, come into being, 92 13; *caus.* e-volve from, *i.e.* create from (*abl.*), 57 16.

+pari, turn around; move in a circle.

+pra, —1. turn *or* move forward; —2. set out; —3. begin, set about; —4. engage in; —pravṛtta, *see s.v.*; —*caus.* set in motion.

+vi, turn away; part with (*instr.*), 88 8; *caus.* whirl about, *trans.*

+sam, unite, *intrans.*, *and so* take shape, form itself, come into being.

vṛ́t, *vbl.* turning, *in cpds.* [√vṛt.]

vṛttá, *ppl.* —1. happened (√vṛt 2); tad **vṛttam**, that took place; —2. existing (vṛt 3); —*as n.* —1. thing happened, occurrence (vṛt 2); —2. life, behavior (vṛt 5, 6).

vṛttānta, *m.* occurrence, adventures, story. [anta: force of anta not clear.]

vṛtti, *f.* *prop.* an existing, *and so* (*like Eng.* living) means of subsistence, support. [√vṛt 3, 5: cf. vartana.]

vṛtti-nibandhana, *n.* means of support.

vṛttāujas, *a.* possessing existing strength, *i.e.* mighty. [ojas.]

vṛtrá, —1. *n.* that which wards off *or* holds in check, *i.e.* the enemy, 75[14]; —2. *m.* coverer, encloser; *personified*, Vritra, demon of drought and darkness, principal personification of the malign power that covers *or* darkens the sky and encompasses (70[16]) *or* withholds the heavenly waters, *selections* xxxii. *and* lxvii.; slain by Indra, 73[18]; *see* 82[1] *and* 97[19]. [√1 vṛ, 'cover,' 1185b.]

vṛtratára, *comparative to* vṛtra (*see* 473[1]). the arch-withholder. [acct irregular, 471, 1242a[2].]

vṛtrá-putra, *a.* having Vritra as son; **-ā**, *f.* the mother of V. [1302.]

vṛ́thā, *adv.* at will, at pleasure; for pleasure, *i.e.* not for the sake of the gods. [√2 vṛ, 'choose, will,' 1101.]

vṛthā-paçughna, *a.* slaying cattle for pleasure; *as m.* one who slays cattle for pleasure, *i.e.* not for sacrifice. [1279.]

vṛddhá, *ppl.* —1. grown, become great; increased (of wealth), 42[16]; —2. *as adj.* grown up, *opp. of* young; old, aged; *as subst.* old man, 28[12]; —3. (grown great, *and so, like Lat.* altus) eminent, distinguished. [√vṛdh, 160.]

vṛddhatva, *n.* condition of being old, old age. [1239.]

vṛ́ddhi, *f.* —1. growth, increase; —2. interest (on money lent), 46[20]; —3. the (second) increment of a vowel, *see* 235-6. [√vṛdh, 1157. 1a, 160.]

√ **vṛdh** (várdhati, -te; vavárdha, vavṛdhé; ávṛdhat, ávardhiṣṭa; vartsyáti; vṛddhá; várdhitum; vardháyati, -te). *act. trans.*: —1. elevate, make to grow, make greater, strengthen; —2. *fig.* elevate inwardly, excite pleasantly, cheer, inspire (*cf. the metaphor in slang Eng.* high, 'slightly intoxicated'), *used* of the effects which the homage and sacrifices of men are supposed to have on the gods;

—*mid. intrans.*: —3. grow, 24[8]; thrive, 69[16]; **vardhate**, he thrives, *i.e.* it goes well with him, 65[2]; grow strong *or* greater *or* mighty, 81[2], 82[8]; increase, 8[11], 60[19]; —4. *fig.* be pleasantly excited, take delight in; be inspired;

—*caus.* —1. make to grow; make strong; bring up (a child), 46[8]; increase, *trans.*, 64[21]; —2. *fig.* excite pleasantly, cheer, inspire; — *distinction between the physical and fig. mgs not always to be made, so* 80[19].

[cf. βλάστη, *ϝλαθ-τη, 'growth, a shoot,' βλαστάνω, 'grow'; ὀρθός, *ϝορθος, 'upright'; Lat. *verb-er*, 'a shoot, rod'; *verbēna*, '(sacred) twig.']

+**pra**, grow on, grow up; **pravṛddha**, (*like Lat.* altus) exalted.

+**vi**, grow, increase, 2[19].

+**sam**, grow; *caus.* make to grow; bring up; nourish, feed.

vṛ́dh, *vbl.* being pleased, rejoicing. [√vṛdh.]

√ **vṛṣ** (várṣati, -te; vavárṣa, vavṛṣé; ávarṣīt; varṣiṣyáti, -te; vṛṣṭá; várṣitum; vṛṣṭvá, -vṛ́ṣya). rain; **várṣati** [303b], ὕοντος, while it is raining. [orig., perhaps, more general, 'to pour down,' esp. either the fructifying water of heaven (masc.) upon the earth (fem.), or semen of the bull or male animal upon the female: with varṣa, 'rain,' cf. ἕ-ερσαι, 'rain-drops'; with vṛṣan and vṛṣabha, 'bull,' cf. Lat. *verres*, **vers-es*, 'boar,' so named from his great generative power, just as the sow (see sū) from her fecundity.]

vṛṣa, *used only at end of cpds* [1315a] *in Veda, but later independently, instead of* **vṛṣan**.

vṛ́ṣan [426b], *adj. and subst.* *describing or denoting* all that was distinguished for its strength and virility: —1. man, as opposed to a castrated person, 70[14]; —2. of animals: stallion; bull; boar; —3. of gods: manly, mighty, great; of Indra, 74[5]; of the Maruts, 73[5]; of the Sun *or* Sun-horse, 79[7]. [√vṛṣ, q.v., 1160c: cf. ἄρσην, stem *ϝαρσεν, 'male.']

vṛṣabhá, *essentially the same as* vṛṣan, *q.v.: esp.*. —1. bull; *with* sahasra-çṛṅga, the thousand-horned steer, *i.e.* the sun *or* (77[14]) the moon; —2. bull, as type of greatness and might; most mighty one, of Indra, 73[16]. [√vṛṣ, 1199.]

vṛṣalá, *m. prop.* manikin, *i.e.* little man, *and so, as term of contempt*, a low person, *esp.* a Çūdra. [vṛṣa, 1227.]

√ **vṛṣasya** (vṛṣasyáti). desire the male, be lustful. [vṛṣa, 1059e, 1058.]

√ **vṛṣāya** (vṛṣāyáte). act as a vṛṣa, *i.e.:* show one's manly strength *or* courage; be lustful; *or simply*, be eager. [vṛṣa, 1059b, 1058.]

vṛṣṭi, *f.* rain. [√vṛṣ, 1157.]

√ **vṛh** *or* **bṛh** (vṛháti; vavárha; ávṛkṣat; vṛḍhá [224a]; -vṝhya). pluck, tear.

veṇu, *m.* reed, *esp.* bamboo-reed.

véda, *m.* —1. understanding, knowledge; —2. *esp.* the sacred knowledge, handed down in triple form of ṛc, yajus, and sāman, *see these, and cf.* (trayī) vidyā; —*later*, the well-known collections called Rigveda, Yajurveda, and Sāmaveda (63[5,6]), the holy scriptures, held to be a revelation and so called çruti, 58[18]. [√1 vid.]

vedá, *m.* tuft of strong grass (kuça *or* muñja) tied so as to form a broom, 62[18].

veda-traya, *n.* the three Vedas.

veda-nindaka, *m.* one who scoffs at the Veda, infidel.

veda-puṇya, *n.* Veda-merit, sanctity acquired by Veda-study.

veda-bāhya, *a.* being outside of the Veda, *i.e.* extra-Vedic, differing from *or* conflicting with the Veda. [1265, veda-being in an abl. relation.]

veda-víd [391], *a.* Veda-knowing. [1269.]

1 **védas**, *n.* knowledge; *possibly adj.*, knowing, *cf.* na-vedas. [√1 vid, 'know': cf. 1151. 2a, b.]

2 **védas**, *n.* (*like Lat.* quaestus) gettings, property, *cf.* vitta. [√2 vid, 'get.']

vedādhyayana, *n.* Veda-study, scripture-reading. [adhyayana.]

védi, *f.* sacrificial bed, *i.e.* a spot of ground excavated two or three inches and covered with straw and serving as a kind of altar.

vedin, *a.* knowing. [√1 vid, 1183[3].]

vedi-purīṣa, *n.* loose earth of the vedi.

vedhás, *subst. adj.* —1. worshipper of the gods, worshipping, pious, devoted; —2. *generalized*, faithful, true, *used* of Indra, 75[18]. [√1 vidh, 'worship a god,' 1151. 2b.]

vélā, *f.* —1. end-point, limit; —2. *esp.* limit of time, point of time, hour.

veçá, *m.* —1. settler; neighbor. —2. (settlement, *i.e.*) dwelling, house. [√viç: cf. οἶκος, 'house,' Old Lat. *veicus*, Lat. *vīcus*, 'houses, quarter of a town, village': hence the borrowed AS. *wīc*, 'town,' as in *Eofor-wīc*, Eng. *York*, prop. 'Eber-stadt' or 'Boar-town,' and perhaps in *Nor-wich*, 'Nor-ton.']

véçman, *n.* (settlement, *i.e.*) dwelling, house, abode, chamber. [√viç, 1168.1a.]

vāí, *postpositive particle, emphasizing the preceding word, e.g.* 3[17], 96[13]; *rare in the* saṁhitā, 90[2?], 103[4] (*in a quoted* mantra); *excessively common in the* brāhmaṇa (92[14,19], 93[6], 94[4,13,18], 95[6,15]) *and Epos* (7[6], etc.); *in* brāhmaṇa *often marking the preceding word as the first of its clause* (*cf.* atha, *near end of mg* 3): *so* 94[6], 95[12], 96[12], *and in the examples just given; often used, esp. in Epos, as a mere expletive* [*see* 1122a[4]], *so at end of a* pāda, 3[9], 10[9], 68[9].

vāicitrya, *n.* variety, diversity. [vicitra, 1211.]

vāiṇavá, *f.* -ī, *a.* of reed, *esp.* of bamboo. [veṇu, 1208c.]

vāidarbha, *f.* -ī, *a.* belonging to Vidarbha; *as m.* the Vidarbhan, *i.e.* king of V.; *as f.* the princess of V., *i.e.* Damayantī, 8[7], etc. [vidarbha, 1208f.]

vāidika, *a.* Vedic, prescribed by *or* conformable to the Vedas. [veda, 1222e 2.]

vāidyá, —1. *a.* having to do with science, learned; *and so* —2. *as m.* (*with a tran-*

sition like that from Lat. doctor, 'teacher, learned man,' *to Chaucer's* doctour of phisik) physician, doctor. [vidyā́, 1211.]

vāimānika, *a.* riding in a sky-traversing car called vimāna, *q.v.* [vimāna, 1222e 2.]

vāivasvatá, *a.* descended from Vivasvant; *as m.* son of V., *i.e.* Yama. [vívasvant, 1208 and a and a².]

vāíçya, *adj. subst.* man of the viç *or* folk *or* third caste, 57[16]. [víç, 1211.]

voc, *quasi-root, see* 854 *and* √vac.

vyàṅsa, *a.* having the shoulders apart, *i.e.* broad-shouldered; *as m.* Viansa, Broad-shoulder, name of a demon, slain by Indra. [vi + aṅsa, 1305.]

√ **vyac** (vivyakti [682]; vivyā́ca [785]). embrace, encompass, extend around. [cf. 1087f², 108g.]

vyácas, *n.* compass, extent.

vyatikara, *m.* a mixing, confusing; confusion, disaster. [√3kṛ, 'scatter,' + vi.]

√ **vyath** (vyáthate; vivyathé [785]; ávyathiṣṭa; vyathitá). —1. move to and fro, rock, reel; —2. *fig.* (*like Eng.* be restless) be disturbed in mind, be pained.

vyáthā, *f.* feeling of painful unrest, discomfort, sorrow.

√ **vyadh** *or* vidh (vídhyati; vivyā́dha [785]; vetsyáti; viddhá; véddhum; viddhvā́; -vídhya). bore through, pierce, hit (with a weapon). [akin w. √vadh: cf. Lat. *di-vid-ere*, 'part asunder, divide.']

vyapadeça, *m.* the making a false show of, an unauthorized referring to *or* using the name of (a person of high position). [√diç + vy-apa.]

vyaya, *a.* going asunder *or* to pieces, perishing, *w.* a-. [√i + vi, 1148. 1b.]

vyàlkaçā, *f.* Vialkaçā, a certain plant.

vyavasāya, *m.* determination, resolve. [√sā + vy-ava.]

vyavasāyin, *a.* determined, resolute. [vyavasāya.]

vyavahāra, *m.* —1. procedure, conduct, way of acting; —2. (way of acting with others, *i.e.*) intercourse, 24[12]. [√1hṛ + vy-ava.]

vyasana, *n.* *prop.* a throwing one's self away (upon a thing), *and so* —1. passionate devotion to a thing (whether good or bad, *e.g.* alms-giving, scripture-study, gambling); hobby; —2. an overpowering passion, *esp.* for something bad; vice, 20[4]; —3. (a throwing one's self away, *i.e.*) misfortune, adversity, 25[3,4]. [√2as + vi.]

√ **vyā** *or* vī (vyáyati, -te [761d 2]; vivyā́ya [785], vivyé; vītá; -víya). *mid.* envelope *or* hide one's self. [orig. 'wind around' as with robe or girdle, and so a a doublet of √vi, i.e. √2vā, 'weave,' q.v.]

+**upa**, hang about, *esp.* wind the sacred cord over the left shoulder and under the right arm; upavīta, *see s.v.*

+**ni**, wind about, hang (*e.g.* garland, cord) about (*e.g.* neck, shoulders); nivīta, *see s.v.*

+**pari**, *act.* envelope around *or* completely; *mid.* wind something as cover around one's self, envelope one's self in; *perhaps in sense of act.*, 84[16].

vyākaraṇa, *n.* the putting asunder, *and so* analysis, grammar. [√1kṛ, 'do, put,' + vy-ā.]

vyākhyātṛ, *m.* explainer. [√khyā + vy-ā.]

vyāghrá, *m.* tiger; *like* çārdūla *and* siṅha, as type of noble manliness, *in cpds, see* nara-vyāghra. [perhaps fr. √1ghṛ, 'besprinkle,' + vy-ā, 'the sprinkled *or* spotted one.']

vyāghra-çarman, *n.* tiger-skin.

vyāghratā, *f.* tigerhood, condition of being a tiger. [1237.]

vyādha, *m.* hunter. [√vyadh.]

vyādhi, *m.* disease. [√1dhā, 'put,' + vy-ā, 1155. 2e.]

vyādhita, *a.* diseased. [vyādhi, see 1176b.]

vyāpāda, *m.* destruction. [√pad + vy-ā.]

vyāpādayitavya, *grdv.* to be destroyed *or* killed. [caus. of √pad + vy-ā.]

vyāpāra, *m.* —1. business, *i.e.* occupation; —2. (*as in Eng.*) business, *i.e.* concern, 30[4]; —3. activity, exertion. [√3pṛ + vy-ā, 'be busied.']

vyāpāra-çata, *n.* exertion-hundred, a hundred attempts.

vyāmá, *m.* *prop.* a stretch-out, the distance covered by the stretched-out arms, a fathom, about six feet. [for vi-yāma, √yam + vi: for mg, cf. the precisely parallel Eng. *fathom* w. AS. *fæðm*, 'the extended arms'; ὀργυιά, 'fathom,' and ὀρέγω, 'stretch'; French *toise*, Medieval Lat. *tesa*, 'fathom,' from Lat. *tensa*, ppl. of *tendere*, 'stretch.']

vyāma-mātra, *a.* having a fathom as its measure, *see* mātrā. [mātrā, 334².]

vyā́hṛti, *f.* —1. utterance; —2. *esp.* one of the three sacred and mystical exclamations, bhū́r, bhúvas, and svàr, *which see.* [√1 hṛ + vy-ā.]

vyòman, *n.* heaven, sky.

√ **vraj** (vrájati; vavrā́ja; ávrājīt; vrajiṣyáti; vrajitá; vrájitum; vrajitvā́; -vrájya). march, proceed, go.

+ **ā**, come hither, go unto.

+ **praty-ā**, march *or* go back.

+ **pari**, march round about; wander around.

+ **pra**, march forth; go unto; wander; *esp.* leave one's house to wander about as an ascetic, 65².

vratá, *n.* —1. will; devānām ati vratam, beyond the will of the gods, 88²—*cf.* ὑπὲρ Διὸς αἶσαν; decree, command *or* Gebot, statute; *and so* —2. (*as Eng.* command *is applied to the forces under one's command*) that over which one exercises command, domain, Gebiet; —*further, directly from the root again* —3. choice, determination; firm resolution, 14⁶; —4. *esp.* resolve (to keep a religious or ascetic observance); vow *or* holy work (*e.g.* of chastity, fasting, etc.), 28²³, 59⁵, 61²³, 64⁸, 65⁸; —5. religious duty, duty *in general.* [√2 vṛ, 'will, choose': for mg 2, observe that Ger. *Gebiet* formerly meant 'command' and now means 'domain.']

√ **vraçc** (vṛçcáti; vṛkṇá [957e]; vṛṣṭvā́; -vṛ́çeya). hew off; fell (a tree); cut to pieces. [orig. form is vṛk, as in vṛ́k-a, vṛk-ṇá, vṛk-ṣá, which see: vṛçc is prop. only a quasi-root of the present stem vṛçca, for *vṛk-ska, formed like the present of √√prach and mlech, which see: see 221² and cf. 220.]

+ **vi**, cut asunder *or* to pieces.

√ **çaṅs** (çáṅsati, -te; çaçáṅsa, çaçaṅsé; áçaṅsīt; çaṅsiṣyáti; çastá; çastvā́; -çásya). *orig.* say in a loud and solemn way, *and so:* —1. recite, *esp.* a sacred hymn *or* text to a god by way of praise; *and so* —2. *generalized*, praise; çasta, *see s.v.*; —3. *rarely*, make a solemn wish, whether blessing *or* curse (*see* çaṅsa), *like* imprecāri; —4. announce; communicate, 52¹³. [cf. Lat. *carmen*, **cas-men*, 'an utterance in solemn, measured, *or* melodious way, *i.e.* song, oracle, magic charm'; *Camēna*, **casmenja*, name of the goddess of song; *cens-ēre*, 'declare, pass judgment on'; AS. *herian*, 'praise.']

+ **ā**, —1. wish, *esp. in the noun* āçás *or* āçā́, 'wish,' *q.v.*; *and so* —2. hope in, put one's trust in (*acc.*); —3. pronounce a blessing upon, wish good to (*acc.*), 101⁴. [mg 1 may be a mere specialization of the mg 'speak solemnly unto' (cf. √çās + ā), and mg 2 a further development of mg 1; for mg 3, cf. the simple verb, mg 3.]

+ **pra**, tell forth; praise, 2¹⁶. [cf. simple verb.]

çáṅsa, *m.* —1. solemn utterance; —2. imprecatio, blessing *or* curse; *as adj.* —3. cursing. [√çaṅs.]

√ **çak** (A. çaknóti; çaçā́ka, çekús [794e]; áçakat; çakṣyáti, -te; çaktá; —*pass.* çakyáte, çakitá;

—B. *desid.* çíkṣate [1030, 108g¹ end]; *caus. of desid.* çikṣáyati; *pass. of desid. and of caus. of desid.* çikṣyáte, çikṣitá).

—A. *simple verb:* —1. be strong; be able, 8¹⁹; *in pass.: impersonally*, it is possible; *with infin.* [988], be able, by the instrumentality of some person *or* thing (*instr.*), to become the object of an action; mayā nītiṁ grāhayituṁ çakyante, they are able to be caused by me to get hold of nīti, 19¹³; —2. *rarely* (be strong for a person, *i.e.*) be serviceable *or* helpful, help, *w. dat.*;

—B. *desiderative:* —1. *desid. to* A. 1, (strive to be able, *i.e.*) practice; learn; *caus.* cause a person (*acc.*) to learn a thing (*acc.*), 51[23], 52[8]; *pass. of caus.:* çikṣita, caused to learn *or* taught a thing (*acc.*), 46[10]; *without noun,* taught, 52[5]; çikṣyamāṇa, instructed, 51[17]; —2. *desid. to* A. 2, be willing to help; aid; (of gods) bestow blessing upon (*dat.*), 80[13]; grant, give.

[cf. Lat. *cac-ula,* 'servant' (like *help* as sometimes used in America for 'servant'); w. çagmá, *çak-ma, 'helpful, friendly,' cf. Lat. *cōmis, *coc-mi-s,* 'friendly': prob. akin is Ger. *be-hag-en,* AS. *on-hag-ian,* 'suit, please' (cf. çak, A. 2).]

+**upa,** (bring unto one's self by giving, *i.e.*) attract, 70[18]. [for mg, see the uncompounded verb, B.-2.]

çákala, —1. *m. n.* chip; piece; —2. *n.* half (of an egg-shell).

çakuná, *m.* bird.

çákti, *f.* ability, power.

çakya, *a.* —1. possible, practicable, 33[16]; *common with the infinitive:* **çakya** *being used* —2. *impersonally; or* —3. *in agreement with the subject, in which case the inf.* [988] *is to be translated as a passive,* 29[10]. [√çak, 1213.]

çakrá, —1. *a.* powerful, mighty, standing epithet of Indra; —2. *as m.* The Mighty One, *i.e.* Indra (*just as we use* The Almighty *as a name for* 'God'). [√çak, 1188a.]

√ çañk (çáñkate; áçañkiṣṭa; çañkitá; çáñkitum; -çáñkya). —1. be anxious *or* suspicious; —2. hesitate.

+**vi,** hesitate.

çañká, *f.* hesitation. [√çañk, 1149[3].]

çácī, *f.* —1. might *or* help (*esp.* of the helping deeds of Indra); —2. Çachī *or* Might, as wife of Indra (*derived from the misunderstood* çacī-pati, *q.v.*), 2[7]. [√çac, collateral form of çak.]

çácī-páti, *m.* —1. *Vedic,* lord of might *or* of help, epithet of Indra, 80[13]; —2. *later* (páti, *q.v.*, *being misunderstood as* 'husband'), husband of Might *or* Çachī, name of Indra, 15[14], 49[4]. [acct, 1267a and d, Whitney 94b.]

çaṭha, *a.* false.

√ çat (çātáyati; çātitá). cut in pieces; make to fall off.

çatá [485[2]], *n.* hundred; *also as expression of* a large number; *for construction, see* 486b. [cf. ἑ-κατόν, 'one-hundred'; Lat. *centum,* AS. *hund,* neut., 'hundred'; Eng. *hund-red.*]

çatā́tman, *a.* having a hundred lives. [çatá + ātmán: acct, 1300a.]

çátru, *m.* —1. (victor, *i.e.*) victorious opponent; —2. foe, enemy, *in general.*

[if mg 1 is the orig. mg, we may take the word fr. √çad and as standing for *çat-tru, 1185e, 232:

if mg 2 is the orig. mg, we may analyse thus, çat-ru (1192), and compare Church Slavonic *kot-ora,* Irish *cath,* 'battle'; AS. *heaðo* in cpds, as *heaðo-weorc,* 'battle-work,' Old High Ger. *had-u* in names, as *Hadu-brant,* 'Battle-flame,' *Hadu-wīch,* 'Battle-strife,' Ger. *Hedwig;* Ger. *Hader,* 'strife'; cf. also the Keltic proper name *Catu-rig-es* (*rig* under rājan), 'The Battle-kings.']

çatru-nandana, *a.* causing joy to one's enemies.

çatru-saṁkaṭa, *m.* danger from the foe.

√ çad (çacáda, çāçadé [786]). distinguish one's self; get the upper hand, prevail; *Vedic only.* [cf. κεκασμένος, Doric κε-καδμένος, 'distinguished.']

çanakāis, *adv.* quietly; gently; slowly. [instr. (1112c) of an unused stem *çanaka, diminutive to *çana, see çanāis.]

çanāis, *adv.* quietly; gently; slowly; gradually. [instr. (1112c) of an unused stem *çana, which is prob. connected w. √2 çam, 'be quiet.']

çáṁtāti, *f.* benefit. [çám, 1238.]

√ çap (çápati, -te; çaçā́pa, çepé; çapiṣyáte; çaptá; çápitum; çapitvā́). —1. curse, *usually act.*, 93[17]; —2. *mid.* (curse one's self, *i.e.*) assert with an oath, swear, vow, *w. dat. of person,* 97[7].

çapátha, *m.* curse; oath. [√çap, 1163b.]

çabála, *a.* brinded.

çábda, *m.* —1. sound; cry; noise; çabdaṁ kṛ, make a noise, raise one's voice; —2. word, 50[9], 61[1].

çabda-çāstra, *n.* word-theory, word-compendium, *i.e.* grammar.

√ **1çam** (çámyati; çaçamé; áçamiṣṭa; çamitá). get weary by working, work. [cf. κάμ-νω, 'get weary by working.']

√ **2çam** (çā́myati [763]; çaçā́ma, çemús; áçamat; çāntá [955a]; çamáyati). be quiet *or* still *or* content; stop; *for these senses, cf.* √ram; çāntá, *see s.v.*; *caus.* quiet, still; *euphemistically*, kill.

+**upa**, be quiet; stop.

+**pra**, come to rest; stop; go out; praçānta, extinguished.

√ **3çam** (çamnīté). harm.

√ **4çam** (çānta; -çámya; çamáyati, çāmáyati). *used only with* ni. observe; perceive; hear.

çám [384²], *n.* welfare; happiness; blessing.

çáma, *a. word of doubtful mg at* 71⁸: *perhaps* tame (*cf.* √2çam, *caus.*) *or* industrious (*cf.* √1çam).

çamayitṛ, *m.* slayer. [√2çam, caus.]

çamí, *f.* a fabaceous plant, *either* Prosōpis spicigera *or* Mimōsa Suma; a tree from which the sticks of attrition (araṇi) were taken.

çamīmáya, *f.* -ī, *a.* of *or* made of Çamī-wood. [see maya.]

çamī-çākhā, *f.* Çamī-branch.

çamī-sumanas, *f.* Çamī-flower.

çamīsumano-mālā, *f.* garland of Çamī-flowers.

çámyā, *f.* staff, 102¹⁶.

çaya, *a.* lying, sleeping, *at end of cpds.* [√çī, 1148. 1a.]

çayana, *n.* a lying, sleeping. [√çī, 1150. 1a.]

çayanīya, -1. *a.* serving for lying; -2. *n.* bed, couch. [çayana, 1215.]

çayyā, *f.* -1. bed; -2. a lying, sleeping. [√çī, 1213d, cf. 963³b.]

çará, *m.* -1. reed, *esp.* of the Saccharum Sara, used for arrows; -2. arrow. [observe that Lat. *arundo* means 'reed' and 'arrow.']

çaraṇá, -1. *a.* protecting, affording refuge, 87⁷; *as n.* -2. shed, that gives cover from the rain; καλιά, hut; -3. protection; refuge, 50¹⁷.

[çaraṇá presupposes a root *çṛ or *çl, 'cover, protect'; w. such a root agree well in form and mg as derivs, çárīra, çárman, and çā́lā, see these:

further agree as cognates καλιά, 'hut, barn'; AS. *heal*, Eng. *hall*; κάλ-υξ, 'husk, pod'; Ger. *Hülle*, 'covering'; Eng. *hull*, 'covering' of grain; AS. *hel-m*, 'protector' (used of God and Christ), 'head-protector, helmet,' Ger. *Helm*, Eng. *helm*; Lat. *oc-cul-ere*, 'cover'; *color*, 'color' (see varṇa); *cēl-āre*, Ger. *hehl-en*, Chaucer's *hel-en*, later *hele*, 'conceal'; further, κᵃλύπ-τ-ω, 'cover,' and the ident. κρύπ-τ-ω, 'hide.']

çaraṇāgata, *a.* come for refuge, seeking protection with any one. [āgata.]

çarád, *f.* autumn; *pl. poetic for* years (*cf.* varṣa).

çárāva, *m. n.* flat earthen dish.

çárīra, *n.* the body, as distinguished from the vital breath or from the immortal soul (*so* 96²¹, ²², 29⁶) and from the soft viscera and inward fluid secretions, of which things the body, or the firm red flesh with the bones, forms as it were the hollow cover (57¹), tegument, or Hülle; *used also in pl.*, 84⁹; body *in general*; mṛtaṁ çarīram, corpse, 63¹⁷; *so* 84⁴. [prop. 'the corporeal tegument' of the soul, √*çṛ, 'cover' (1188e²), see under çaraṇa: for mg, cf. the cognate Ger. *Hülle* (under çaraṇa) in *sterbliche Hülle*, 'mortal envelope, *i.e.* body': cf. 97¹⁶ N.]

çarīra-ja, *a.* (born of, *i.e.*) performed by the body.

çarīrāntakara, *m.* destroyer of the bodies. [anta-kara.]

çáru, *f.* missile, *either* spear *or* arrow. [cf. çara.]

çarkara, *m.* brown sugar. [fr. the Prakrit form sakkara comes on the one hand, through Arabic *sokkar* and Medieval Lat. *zucara*, the Eng. *sugar*, and on the other σάκχαρον, Lat. *saccharum*, all borrowed words: cf. khaṇḍa.]

√ **çardh** (çárdhati). be strong *or* defiant.

çárdha, *m.* troop, host. [cf. Ger. *Herde*, Eng. *herd*.]

çárman, *n.* —1. cover; protection; shelter; refuge; —2. comfort, joy; —3. common at the end of Brahman-names, 19[11], 42[11], 59[13]N. [see under çaraṇa.]

çarmavant, *a.* containing (the stem) çarman. [1233.]

çarvá, *m.* Çarva, name of an arrow-slaying god; *later*, a common name for the god Çiva. [çáru, 1209, cf. 1209g.]

çarvara, *a.* variegated; *f.* çárvarī, the night (as variegated with stars). [cf. çabala.]

çarva-varman, *a.* having Çiva as his protection; *as m.* Çarvavarman, name of a man.

çalá, *m.* —1. staff; —2. prickle (of a hedge-hog). [cf. çará.]

çalyá, *m. n.* point of spear *or* arrow; thorn; prickle. [cf. çalá, çará: cf. κῆλον, 'missile.']

çályaka, *m.* hedge-hog. [cf. çalya.]

çávas, *n.* superior might; heroic power; *also pl.* [√çū, 1151. 1a.]

çáviṣṭha, *a.* most mighty. [√çū, 468.]

çaçá, *m.* hare; the Hindu sees, not "a man in the moon," but rather, a hare or a gazelle. [for *çasa (see √çuṣ and çvaçura): cf. Ger. *Hase*, Eng. *hare*.]

çaçaka, *m.* hare, rabbit. [çaça, 1222b.]

çaçāñka, *m.* the moon. [prop., adj., 'having a rabbit as its mark,' çaça (*q.v.*) + añka, 1302a.]

çaçin, *m.* the moon. [prop., adj., 'having the (picture of a) rabbit,' çaça, 1230.]

çáçvant, *a.* ever repeating *or* renewing itself.

√ças (çásati; çaçása; çasiṣyáti; çastá; -çásya). cut to pieces; slaughter. [see çastra.]

çastá, *a.* praised, esteemed as good *or* lucky; *equiv. to* happy, cheerful, 52[11]. [prop. ppl. of √çaṅs.]

çastrá, *n.* knife; sword; weapon. ['instrument of cutting,' √ças, 1185: ças-tra is ident. in form and mg w. the Lat. stem **cas-tro*, which appears in the denom. *castrāre*, prop. 'cut,' and so, like Eng. *cut*, 'castrate.']

çastra-pāṇi, *a.* having a sword in the hand. [1303.]

çastra-vṛtti, *a.* having weapons as one's means of subsistence, living by military service. [1302a.]

çāka, *n.* an edible herb; vegetable food.

çákhā, *f.* branch.

çātayitṛ, *m.* one who cuts in pieces, destroyer, 97[19]. [caus. of √çat, 1182c.]

çāntá, *a.* quiet; still; stopped. [ppl. of √2 çam, 'be quiet.']

çánti, *f.* a ceasing, stopping; *esp.* the absence of the evil results of some word *or* thing of evil omen. [√2 çam, 'be quiet,' cf. 955a.]

çānti-karman, *n.* a ceremony for averting the results of something ominous.

çāpa, *m.* curse. [√çap.]

çāpādi, *a.* having the curse as its first; *as n.* curse and so forth. [1302c 1.]

çāpādi-ceṣṭita, *n.* curse-and-so-forth doings, *i.e.* adventures including the curse et cetera. [1280b.]

çāpānta, *m.* end of the curse *or* period during which the curse has effect. [anta.]

çāyin, *a.* lying, sleeping. [√çī, 1183[3].]

çārīrá, *a.* corporeal, of the body. [çárīra, 1208f.]

çārdūlá, *m.* tiger; *at end of cpds, like* vyāghra, the best of · ·.

çálā, *f.* hut; house; room; stable. [see under çaraṇa: cf. the derivs καλιά and Eng. *hall*, there given.]

çālin, *a.* —1. possessing a house; —2. *at end of cpds, attenuated in mg so as to signify merely* possessing · ·. [çālā.]

çālmalī, *f.* Salmalia malabarica, the silk-cotton tree.

çāva, *m.* the young of an animal. [see √çū.]

çāvaka, *m.* the young of an animal. [çāva.]

çāçvatá, *a.* continual; eternal. [çáçvant, 1208a, a[1].]

√çās *or* çiṣ (*Vedic*, çásti, çáste [639]; *Vedic and Epic*, çásati; çaçása; áçiṣat [854[3]]; çāsiṣyáti, -te; çāsitá, çāstá, çiṣṭá [954c]; çásitum, çástum; çāsitvá; -çásya, -çíṣya). —1. chasten, correct; —2. instruct, teach; direct; —3. (*like Eng.* direct) give order to, rule, govern.

[perhaps reduplicated form of çaṅs, 675: for the weak form çiṣ, cf. 639.]
+ā, *mid.* wish *or* pray for, *cf.* āçis *and* √çaṅs + ā; make supplication, 73[11].
+pra, instruct; direct; command, *cf. simple verb, and* praçis.

çā́sana, *n.* —1. government, way of ruling; —2. command. [√çās.]

çāsitṛ, *m.* teacher. [√çās.]

çāstrá, *n.* —1. instruction; —2. rule; theory; compendium (of an art *or* science); a scientific *or* canonical work; science, 17[13]. [√çās.]

√ **çikṣ**, *see* 1030 *and* √çak.

çikhara, —1. *a.* peaked; —2. *m.n.* peak. [çikhā, 1226.]

çikhā, *f.* —1. tuft *or* braid of hair; —2. (*like Eng.* crest) top *in general*, peak.

çithirá, *a.* loose; flaccid; unsteady, 93[2]; *opp. of* dṛḍha, 'firm, hard.' [perhaps fr. √çrath, 1188e: for loss of r, cf. √bhām.]

çibi, *m.* Çibi, name of a king.

çíras, *n.* head. [cf. κάρα, 'head'; Lat. *cerebrum*, **ceres-ru-m*, 'brain': w. the collateral form çīrṣán, q.v., cf. Ger. *Hirn*, Old High Ger. *hirni*, **hirsni*, 'brain': akin is also κρανίον, 'skull.']

çirīṣa, *m.* the tree Acacia Sirissa; *as n.* the blossom.

çiro-mukha, *n.* head and face. [1253b.]

çilā́, *f.* stone; crag.

çilā-bhāva, *m.* condition of being stone; -am āp, turn into stone.

çilī, *f.* the beam under a door.

çilī-mukha, *m.* Block-snout, name of a hare.

çiloccaya, *m.* crag-pile, *i.e.* craggy hill. [uccaya.]

çivá, —1. *a.* kind, 90[2]; friendly; gracious; agreeable, lovely; *opp. of* ghora; —2. *m.* The Friendly One, name euphemistically applied to the horrible god Rudra, who under this name (Çiva) becomes the third person of the Hindu Trinity. [for mg 2, cf. Εὐμενίδες, 'The Gracious Ones, *i.e.* the Furies,' and nandi.]

çíçu, *m.* young; child. [see √çū, and 1147b and b[2].]

√ **1 çiṣ** (çináṣṭi; çiçiṣé; áçiṣat; çekṣyáti, -te; çiṣṭá; çiṣṭvā́; -çíṣya). leave, leave remaining.
+ud, leave remaining.
+vi, (leave apart *or* by itself, *i.e.*) separate, distinguish; viçiṣṭa, (separated, *and so, like Eng.* distinguished) eminent, excellent.

√ **2 çiṣ**, *subsidiary form to* √çās, *q.v.*

çiṣya, *grdv.* to be taught; *as m.* pupil. [√çās, weak form çiṣ.]

√ **1 çī** (çéte [*see* 628–9]; çiçyé; áçayiṣṭa; çayiṣyáte, -ti; çeṣyáte, -ti; çayitá; çáyitum; çayitvā́; -çáyya). —1. lie still; lie; —2. sleep. [w. çé-te, cf. κεῖ-ται, 'lies': cf. also κοί-τη, 'bed.']
+adhi, lie in *or* on; dwell in.
+anu, lie down after another.
+ā, lie in.
+upa, lie by.
+sam, be undecided *or* in doubt. [lit. 'lie together': metaphor unclear.]

√ **2 çī**, *simpler form of* √çyā, *q.v.*

çí, *vbl.* lying. [√çī.]

çītá, *a.* cold; *as n.* cold. [ppl. of √çyā *or* 2 çī.]

çítaka, *f.* çītikā, *a.* cool. [çita: cf. 1222d.]

çītala, *a.* cool. [çīta, 1227.]

çītārta, *a.* distressed with the cold. [ārta.]

çītikāvant, *a.* cool. [as if from fem. of çītaka: 1233, cf. b.]

çípāla, *m. n.* Blyxa octandra, a common water-plant.

çīrṣán, *n.* head. [çīrṣ-án is to çiras (q.v.), as īrṣ-yā́ is to iras-yā́, see these.]

çíla, *n.* —1. natural *or* acquired way of being; character, 23[20]; habit *or* habits, 58[14]; *in composition* [1302] *with that to which one is inclined or accustomed*, 21[4], 60[18]; —2. (character, *i.e., as in Eng.*) good character, 98[7].

çīvan, *a.* lying. [√1 çī, 1169. 1a.]

çúka, *m.* parrot. [prop. 'the bright one,' on account of its gaudy colors, √çuc: cf. 216. 1, 1[2].]

çukavat, *adv.* like a parrot. [çuka, 1107.]

çukrá, *a.* clear, bright, 76[9]. [√çuc, 1188a, 216.7.]

çuklá, –1. *a.* clear; bright; white; *with* pakṣa, the bright lunar half-month, from new to full moon; –2. *as m.* (*sc.* pakṣa), the bright lunar fortnight, 65[5]. [see 1189 and [2].]

çukla-pakṣa, *m.* fortnight of the waxing moon.

çuklapakṣādi, *a.* having the bright lunar fortnight first, beginning with the bright lunar fortnight. [ādi, 1302c 1.]

çuklāmbara, *a.* having a white garment. [ambara.]

√ **çuc** (çócati, -te; çuçóca; áçocīt; çociṣyáti; çócitum; çocitvā́). –1. flame, light, beam; glow, burn; –2. *fig.* suffer burning pain; grieve; grieve at (*loc.*), 66[18]; –*intens.* flame brightly. [for mg 2, cf. √tap, dagdha and √dah.]

+**apa**, *intens.* [1002a], drive away by flaming brightly, 72[8].

+**abhi**, burn, *trans.*

+**ā**, bring hither by flaming, 72[8].

çúci, *a.* –1. flaming, beaming; *fig.* beaming (of a smile); light, bright; –2. *fig.* clear, pure; holy (of a god), 80[6]; honorable (in business), 25[2]; pure (in a ritual sense), 62[10]. [√çuc, 1155.2a, 216.2.]

çuci-smita, *a.* having a beaming smile, bright-smiling.

çuddhá, *a.* pure. [ppl. of √çudh, 160.]

çuddha-mati, *a.* pure-minded.

çudh *or* çundh (çúndhati, -te; çúdhyati; çuddhá). –1. çúndhati, -te: *act.* purify; *mid.* become pure; –2. çúdhyati, become pure. [orig., perhaps, 'to clear,' and akin w. √çcand, q.v.]

+**vi**, viçudhyati, become entirely pure; viçuddha, perfectly clear.

çuná, *a.* grown, prosperous, fortunate; *as n.* [*cf.* 1176a], growth, prosperity; luck. [perhaps fr. √çū, 1177a.]

√ **çundh**, *see* çudh.

çundhyú, *f.* -yū́ [355c], *a.* pure; unblemished; fair. [√çundh, 1165b.]

√ **1çubh** *or* çumbh (çúmbhate). glide along lightly; move onward, 73[9]. [perhaps akin w. κοῦφος, 'light, nimble.']

√ **2çubh** *or* çumbh (çóbhate; çúmbhate; çumbháti; çuçubhé; çobhiṣyáti). *act.* adorn; *mid.* adorn one's self, 73[12]; look beautiful, appear to advantage, shine (*fig.*).

1 **çúbh**, *f.* a gliding onward, *esp.* through the sky; onward progress; *so, perhaps,* 78[6]; course, 73[4]; *dat., infinitivally* [982], so as to glide onward, 79[11]. [√1çubh.]

2 **çúbh**, *f.* beauty; *so, perhaps,* 78[6]. [√2çubh.]

çubha, *a.* –1. fair, 9[11]; beautiful, agreeable to the eyes, 15[13], 45[18], 62[13]; –2. agreeable (to other senses than the eyes); çubhān gandhān, perfumes; –3. agreeable *in general*, 20[13]; –4. of good quality, 64[12]; –5. fortunate, auspicious, 12[13]. [√2çubh, 'adorn.']

çubhānana, *a.* fair-faced. [ānana.]

çubhāçubha, *a.* agreeable and disagreeable, agreeable or disagreeable; good and bad, good or bad, *in ethical sense*, 65[19]. [açubha, 1257.]

çubhāçubha-phala, *a.* having agreeable or disagreeable fruit, resulting in weal or woe.

çubhrá, *a.* beautiful; clear (of sounds). [√2çubh, 'adorn,' 1188a.]

√ **çuṣ** (çúṣyati; -çúṣya). be dry, dry up. [for *suṣ (see çaça), as shown by Avestan √hush, 'dry': cf. *αὔω*, 'dry'; Syracusan *σαυ-κός*, 'dry'; AS. *seārian*, 'dry up,' denom. of *seār*, Eng. *sear*.]

çúṣka, *a.* dry. [√çuṣ, 1186[2]: see 958.]

çúṣma, *m.* –1. whistling, 73[6], 78[7]; –2. exhalation, *i.e.* (fragrant) odor (of the Soma), 73[10]; –3. (exhalation, breath, *and so, like Eng.* spirit) courage, impetuosity, 82[4]. [√çvas, 252, 1166.]

√ **çū** *or* çvā *or* çvi (çváyati; çūçā́va [786[4]]; çūná [957a]; çváyitum). swell; be greater *or* superior *or* victorious.

[orig. sense of root, 'swell,' but with two diverse ramifications:

–1. negatively, 'be swollen, *i.e.* hollow, empty'; cf. çūna, 'vacuum'; *κύ-αρ*, 'hole'; Lat. *cavus*, 'hollow'; *caelum*, **cav-i-lu-m*, 'heaven's hollow vault'; *κοῖλος*, 'hollow';

–2. positively, 'be swollen, *i.e.* full, strong'; with special reference: (*a*) to the womb and its fruit; cf. çi-çu and çāva, 'young'; κύω, 'be pregnant'; Lat. *in-ciens*, 'pregnant'; (*b*) to strength and growth in general; cf. çūra, 'man of might'; çavas, çaviṣṭha, çuna; κῦρος, 'might'; κῦμα, 'swell, billow.']

çūdrá, *m.* a man of the fourth caste, a Çūdra.

çū́na, *n.* emptiness. [√çū, 1177a.]

çū́ra, *a.* mighty, bold; *as m.* man of might, hero. [√çū, 1188c: çūra is parallel w. *κυ-ρο-ς, 'mighty,' whence τὸ κῦρ-ος, 'might' (cf. αἰσχ-ρό-ς w. τὸ αἶσχ-ος).]

çū́rpa, *n.* a plaited basket for winnowing grain.

√ **1 çṝ** (çṛṇā́ti; çaçré; áçarīt; çariṣyáti, -te; çīrṇá [957b]; -çī́rya; çīryáte). crush; break; tear. [cf. Eng. *har-m*, which answers to a Skt. *çar-ma.]

+ **vi**, *pass.* be broken to pieces; perish, 60[9].

+ **sam**, break (a bow); *like* zusammenbrechen.

√ **2 çṛ**, *see* çrā, 'boil.'

çṛ́ñga, *n.* horn.

çṛñgín, *a.* horned; *as m.* horned beast.

çṛtá, *see* √çrā.

çéva, *a.* kind; dear. [cf. çivá.]

çeṣa, —**1.** *m. n.* rest, remainder, 68[17]; çeṣe, *like Ger.* im Uebrigen, for the rest, 12[10]; —**2.** *a.* remaining, 55[15]. [√1 çiṣ, 'leave.']

çéṣas, *n.* offspring. ['those whom one leaves behind him, one's relicts,' √1 çiṣ, 'leave.']

çóka, *m.* pain, grief. [√çuc, 216. 1.]

çoka-ja, *a.* grief-born; çokajaṁ vāri, grief-born water, *i.e.* tears, 10[19].

çokārta, *a.* sorrow-stricken. [ārta.]

çocíṣ-keça, *a.* having flame-locks, with locks of flame. [çocis, 187: 1297, cf. 1280b.]

çóciṣṭha, *a.* most *or* bright flaming. [√çuc, 468.]

çocís, *n.* flame; beam; heat. [√çuc, 1153.]

çóṇa, —**1.** *a.* red, deep-red; —**2.** *m.* Sone *or* Red River, affluent of the Ganges. [prop. 'flame-colored': cf. ἔ-καυ-σα, 'burned,' καῦ-μα, 'heat.']

çoṇita, *n.* blood; *also pl.* [çóṇa, 1176d.]

çobhaná, *a.* beautiful. [√2 çubh, 'adorn,' 1150. 2a.]

çóbhiṣṭha, *a.* most swiftly moving onward *or* most beautiful, 78[5], *according as the word is referred to* √1 çubh *or to* √2 çubh — *see these.* [468.]

√ **çcand** (*intens. ppl.* cániçcadat [1002c]). shine, glance. [for *skandh: cf. ξανθ-ός, 'gold-yellow'; καθαρός, Doric κοθ-αρός, 'clear, clean, pure'; κάνδ-αρος, 'coal'; Lat. *cand-ēre*, 'glow.']

çcandrá, *a.* shining. [√çcand, 1188a: cf. viçvá-çcandra, and candrá.]

√ **çcut** (çcótati; cuçcóta; ácuçcutat; çcutitá). drip.

çcút, *vbl.* dripping. [√çcut.]

çmaçāná, *n.* the place for burning the corpses and for burying the bones, cemetery.

çmáçru, *n.* beard.

√ **çyā** *or* **çī** (çyā́yati, -te [761d 1]; çītá, çīná, çyānā́; çīyáte). freeze; coagulate.

çyená, *m.* eagle; falcon; hawk. [cf. ἰ-κτῖνο-ς, 'kite.']

√ **çrath** (çrathnītḗ; çaçrathé; áçiçrathat; çṛthitá). become loose.

çrád, *indecl. meaning perhaps orig.* heart; *used w.* dhā ('grant, give,' *see* √1 dhā 4) *and dat. of person, thus,* çrád asmāi dhatta, (your) heart to him give ye, *i.e.* trust ye him, have faith in him, RV. ii. 12. 5; *ppl.* çrad-dadhat, trusting, trustful, 26[2]; *cf.* 1079[2].

[cf. καρδία, κῆρ, *κηρδ, Lat. *cor*, gen. *cord-is*, Lithuanian *szirdìs*, Ger. *Herz*, Eng. *heart*: further, w. çrad-dhā, cf. Lat. *crēdĕre*, **cred-dere*, 'trust': — the regular Skt. word for 'heart' is hṛ́d, and this can not be connected w. the above words, since they require in the Skt. an initial ç, *çṛd or çrad.]

çraddhā́, *f.* trust, faith; desire. [see çrád: 1147.]

çraddhivá, *a.* credible. [çraddhā́, 1228a.]

√ **çram** (çrā́myati [763]; çaçrā́ma; áçramīt; çrāntá; -çrámya). be weary; take pains; *esp.* castigate one's self, 96[10].

+ā, *in* āçrama, 'hermitage.
+pari, weary one's self exceedingly; pariçrānta, tired of, disgusted with.

çráma, *m.* weariness. [√çram.]

√ **çrambh** (çrámbhate; çrabdhá; -çrábhya). *used only with* **vi.** put confidence in; **viçrabdha**: confiding, 26[8]; -am, *adv.* confidently, without distrust *or* hesitation, 9[17].

çrávaṇa, —1. *m.* ear; —2. *n.* hearing; —3. *n.* fame. [√çru, 1150. 1a: for mg 3, cf. çravas and esp. under √çru.]

çrávas, *n.* —1. sounds; *esp.* loud praise, 91[15]; —2. glory, 74[6]; fame. [√çru, 'hear,' 1151. 1a: the precise equiv. of κλέος, stem κλεϝ-ες, 'fame': for mg, see √çru.]

√ **çrā** *or* **çrī** *or* **çṛ** *or* **çir** (çrīṇā́ti, çrīṇīté; çiçriyé; çrātá, çrītá, çṛtá, çīrtá). cook; boil; çṛtá, cooked, done.

çrāddha, *n.* an oblation to the Manes, accompanied by a funeral meal and gifts to Brahmans. [çraddhā́, 1208e: according to the Scholiast, 'a thing of trust,' because the gift for the Manes is as a matter of fact entrusted to Brahmans.]

çrāntá, *ppl.* wearied; *as n.* [1176a], weariness. [√çram, 955a.]

çrāntāgata, *a.* wearied and arrived, *i.e.* arriving wearied. [āgata: 1257.]

√ **çri** (çráyati, -te; çiçráya, çiçriyé; áçiçriyat; çrayiṣyáti, -te; çritá; çráyitum; çrayitvā́; -çrítya). —1. *act.* lean, *trans.; lay against or on; rest on, *trans.* —2. *mid.* lean upon, *intrans.; rest upon, or, simply,* be lying *or* situated upon, 70[3]; —3. *mid., act.* betake one's self to, *esp.* for help *or* protection, 48[5]. [cf. κλί-νω, 'lean'; κε-κλί-αται, 'rest on'; Lat. *clināre*, 'lean'; AS. *hlinian*, Eng. *lean; κλῖ-τύς*, 'incline, slope, hill'; Lat. *cli-vus*, 'hill'; AS. *hlǣw, hlāw*, Eng. *-law, -low*, 'hill,' in *Mood-law, Lud-low; κλῖ-μαξ*, 'ladder'; AS. *hlǣ-der*, Eng. *ladder*.]

+ā, lean upon, *intrans.; seek support* and protection with *or* from; **āçrita**: depending upon (another); *as m.* a dependent *or* subordinate, 30[13].

+upa, *mid.* lean against; brace one's self, 87[6]; **upaçrita**, (leaned upon, *equiv. to*) laid upon *or* in, *w. loc.*, 79[4].

+pari, *act.* lay about; enclose.

+pra, lean forward.

çrí [351], *f.* —1. beautiful appearance; beauty, 78[5], 2[4], 8[8]; —2. welfare; —3. *personified*, Çrī, goddess of beauty and welfare, 2[10]; —4. *as honorific prefix to proper names*, the famous *or* glorious · ·, 54[1]. [cf. çreyāṅs, çreṣṭha.]

√ **çru** (çṛṇóti, çṛṇuté [243]; çuçráva, çuçruvé; áçrāuṣīt; çroṣyáti, -te; çrutá; çrótum; çrutvā́; -çrútya; çrūyáte; çúçrūṣate; çrāváyati). —1. *act.* hear, 86[5]; know by hearing; *w. gen. of person*, 6[2]; listen; give heed to, 25[14]; hear (a teacher), *i.e.* learn, study; **çuçruvā́ṅs**, having studied, *i.e.* learned, 94[18]; —2. *mid., in Veda, with pass. sense*, be heard of (as subject of talk), *i.e., like Lat.* cluere, be called, be famed as, 75[14];

—3. *pass.:* be heard; **çrutá**: heard; heard of, 2[12]; *impers.:* **çrūyatām**, let it be heard, *i.e.* hear ye; evaṁ çrūyate, thus it is heard, there is this saying, 31[6]; çrutam mayā, I've heard (your story), 33[9]; —4. *caus.* cause (hearers, *acc.*) to hear (a thing), *i.e.* proclaim to; recite to, 54[20]; —5. *desid.* be willing to hear, *and so* (*cf. Eng.* obedient *and Lat.* ob-oediens *with* audīre), obey, 64[9].

[with çru-dhí, 'hear thou,' cf. κλῦ-θι, 'hear thou'; Lat. *clu-ere*, 'be called'; *cluens, cliens*, 'who hears *or* obeys, *i.e.* a dependent'; with çru-tá, 'heard, heard of,' cf. κλυ-τός, 'famed,' Lat. *in-clu-tus, inclitus*, 'famed,' Old High Ger. *hlu-do* in *Hludo-wig*, 'Loud-battle,' Ger. *lau-t*, AS. *hlū-d*, Eng. *lou-d*;

with the subsidiary form çruṣ, as in çruṣ-ṭi, 'a listening to, compliance,' cf. AS. *hlos-nian*, 'listen,' *hlys-t*, 'the hearing,' whence *hlyst-an*, Eng. *listen:* —for the mg 'famed' of çruta, etc., cf. çravaṇa, çravas, and çloka.]

+prati, answer, say yes to; make a promise to (*gen.*). [prop., like Eng. *hear*, 'give a hearing in return to what is said,' i.e. 'not turn a deaf ear to,' and so 'answer.']

+vi, *pass.* be heard of far and wide, be famous; viçruta, known as, named, 6[3].

+sam, —1. hear; —2. *like Eng.* hear, accede to the request of, make a promise to (*loc.*). [cf. çru + prati.]

çrutá, *ppl.* heard; heard of; *as n.* that which is heard from the teacher, that which is learned; learning. [√çru.]

çrutavant, *a.* possessing learning, learn-ed. [çruta.]

çrúti, *f.* —1. a hearing; —2. ear; —3. the thing heard; sound; —4. report, hearsay; —5. utterance; *esp.* a sacred utterance handed down by tradition, a religious prescription, a sacred text, the Veda, 58[18] N.; —6. learning; *prob. incorrect for* çruta. [√çru, 1157. 1a.]

çrutimant, *a.* possessing learning; *prob. incorrect for* çrutavant, *q.v.* [çruti.]

çrútya, *a.* worthy to be heard (of a hymn), goodly. [√çru, 1213a.]

çreyasa, *for* çreyas (çreyāṅs) *in cpds*, 1315c.

çréyāṅs, *a.* fairer; more beautiful *or* excellent; better; *as n.* (the better, *i.e.*) welfare, prosperity, 35[1]. [from an unused root çrī corresponding to the noun çrí, 470[4]: cf. κρείων, 'superior, ruler.']

çréṣṭha, *a.* fairest; most excellent; best: *w. gen.*, 1[10]; *w. loc.*, 58[10]; *at end of cpd*, 11[9]; best as distinguished from (*abl.*), *equiv. to* better than, 68[14]. [see çreyāṅs.]

çrāíṣṭhya, *n.* supremacy, precedence. [çréṣṭha, 1211[2] end.]

çrótra, *n.* ear; hearing. [√çru, 1185a.]

çrótriya, *a.* studied, learned (in sacred tradition); *as m.* a Brahman versed in sacred lore. [çrotra, 1214c: for mg, cf. √çru, mg 1, and çrutá, s.v.]

çlakṣṇá, *a.* slippery; smooth. [cf. 1105.]

√ **çlāgh** (çlā́ghate; çaçlāghé; çlāghitá). —1. have confidence in; —2. talk confidently; brag, praise one's self; —3. praise.

çlāghya, *grdv.* to be praised, praiseworthy; honorable. [√çlāgh.]

çlóka, *m.* —1. (thing heard, *i.e.*) sound; —2. fame, *for mg, cf.* √çru; —3. strophe; *later, esp.* the anuṣṭubh-strophe, the epic çloka, in which, for example, the story of Nala is composed. [√çru, 1186[2].]

√ **çvañc** (çváñcate). open itself; receive in open arms (as a maid her lover).

+ud, open itself out, open, 87[4].

çván [427], *m.* dog. [cf. κύων, Lat. *can-i-s*, AS. *hun-d*, Eng. *hound*, 'dog.']

çváçura, *m.* father-in-law. [for *svá-çura: cf. ἑκυρός, Lat. *socer*, *socerus*, Church Slavonic *swekrŭ*, AS. *sweor*, *sweohor, Ger. *Schwäher*, 'father-in-law': for ç in place of s, cf. çaça and √çuṣ.]

çvaçrū́ [355c], *f.* mother-in-law. [çváçura, 355c: cf. ἑκυρά, Lat. fem. *socrus*, AS. *sweger*, Ger. *Schwieger*, 'mother-in-law.']

√ **çvas** (çvásiti [631]; çvásati; çaçvā́sa; çvasiṣyáti; çvasitá, çvastá; çvásitum; -çvásya; çvāsáyati). —1. blow, bluster, whistle, snort; —2. breathe; —3. sigh. [cf. AS. *hweōs*, preterit to *hwǣsan, Eng. *wheeze*.]

+ā, get one's breath, become quiet; *caus.* quiet, comfort.

+nis, breathe out, sigh.

+pra, blow forth.

+abhi-pra, blow forth upon, *acc.*, 94[7].

+vi, have confidence, be unsuspecting; *caus.* inspire confidence.

çvás, *adv.* to-morrow, on the next day; çvaḥ çvas [1260[2]], from day to day.

çvasátha, *m.* a snorting. [√çvas, 1163b.]

çvástana, *a.* of the morrow; *as n.* the morrow, 92[17]. [çvás, 1245e.]

çvā́pada, *m.* a beast of prey, 84[14]. [to be pronounced çvapāda (cf. pāvaka, 1181a): prop., perhaps, 'having the feet of a dog,' çvan + pāda.]

çvāvídh [*nom.* -vít], *m.* porcupine. [çván + vídh, 'dog-wounding.']

ṣaṭka, —1. *a.* consisting of six; —2. *as n.* a whole consisting of six, a hexade. [ṣaṣ, 1222a, 226b.]

ṣáṭ-triṅçat [485], *f.* six and thirty. [ṣaṣ.]

ṣáṭ-pada, *f.* -ī, *a.* having (taken) six steps. [ṣaṣ: 1300a.]

ṣaṇ-māsa, *n.* semester, six months. [ṣaṣ: prop. 'that which has six months,' see 1312.]

ṣáṣ [483[3]], *num.* six. [see 182b[2], 146[8]: cf. ἕξ, Lat. *sex*, Eng. *six*.]

ṣaṣṭí, *f.* sixty. [ṣaṣ, 1157.4.]

ṣaṣṭhá, *a.* sixth. [ṣaṣ, 487[5]: cf. ἕκ-τος, Lat. *sex-tus*, AS. *six-ta*, Eng. *six-th*.]

---

1 **sá**, *pron.* *see* ta *and* 495.

2 **sa**, *inseparable prefix denoting* similarity, community, *or* connection — *numerous examples on the pages following; esp. common w. an adj. value in possessive cpds* [*see* 1304c], having an accompanying · ·, with · ·. [1121b: prob. ident. ultimately w. 3 sa.]

3 **sa**, one, *in* sa-kṛt, sa-hasra. [for *sm (vocalic m), root *sem: cf. εἷς, *σεμ-ς, μία, *σμ-ια, 'one'; ἑ-κατόν, 'one-hundred'; ἁ-πλόος, 'one-fold'; Lat. *sem-el*, 'once'; *sim-plex*, 'one-fold'; ἄ-λοχος, 'having one (*i.e.* one and the same) bed, spouse'; ὅ-πατρος, 'having one (*i.e.* one and the same) father'; ἀ-δελφός, see under garbha.]

sáṁyatendriya, *a.* having restrained senses, self-controlled, 1[9]. [sáṁyata (√yam, 1085a) + indriyá, 1298.]

saṁyama, *m.* restraint, control, 68[6]. [√yam + sam.]

saṁvatsará, *m.* year. [sam + vatsara, q.v.]

saṁçaya, *m.* —1. doubt; na saṁçayas, (there is) no doubt; —2. danger, 20[16]. [√çī + sam.]

saṁsád, *f.* *like Lat.* consessus, a sitting together *and* those who sit together, *i.e.* assembly. [√sad + sam.]

saṁsarga, *m.* mixture, union; contact. [√sṛj + sam, 216.1.]

saṁsāra, *m.* the wandering of the soul from one existence to another, metempsychosis; transmigration, 66[18]; the cycle *or* round of existence, 18[1]. [√sṛ + sam.]

saṁskāra, *m.* —1. a working over, a preparing *or* purification; *esp.* a technical proceeding with a thing; an adorning *or* adornment, 17[5]; —2. a domestic religious rite to be performed upon *or* observed by every member of the three upper castes, *prop.* his preparation *or* purification; sacrament, consecration, 59[2] N.; —3. impression; an impression produced on the mind *or* a disposition formed in the mind by something past (*e.g.* deeds of a former existence, a past conversation, etc.), but which has ceased to work on the mind, 40[4]. [√1 kṛ, 'do,' + sam, 1087d.]

saṁskṛta, *ppl.* —1. prepared; adorned, fine, cultivated; *as n.* the cultivated language, as opposed to the low vernaculars, Sanskrit, 52[6]. [√1 kṛ, 'do,' + sam, 1087d.]

sáṁhita, *ppl.* put together; -ā, *f.* a putting together; a text whose sounds and words are put together according to grammatical rules. [√1 dhā + sam, 954c.]

sa-kacchapa, *a.* having tortoises along with them, *i.e.* along with tortoises. [1304c.]

sakala, *a.* having its parts together, *i.e.* all, entire; *as n.* everything, one's entire property, 46[4]. [sa + kalā, 1304c, 334[2].]

sakāça, *m.* presence; tasya sakāçaṁ gaṁ, go to the presence of him, *i.e.* go to him; -sakāçe, *at end of cpd*, in the presence of · ·, before · ·, 3[8]. [sa + kāça: orig., perhaps, 'having visibility, present,' and then 'presence.']

sakṛ́t, *adv.* for one time, a single time, once. [3 sa + 2 kṛt.]

sa-kopa, *a.* angry; -am, angrily. [2 sa, 1304c.]

sáktu, *m.* coarsely ground parched grains, grits, *esp.* barley grits.

sakha, *for* sakhi *at end of cpds* [1302], having · · as attendant, accompanied by · ·. [1315b.]

sákhi [343a], *m.* attendant, companion, 82[1]; comrade; friend, 23[16], etc.; *in connection with a fem.*, 75[18, 19], 100[4]. [√sac: for mg, cf. ἐπ-έτης and *soc-ius*, under √sac.]

sakhí [364], *f.* female companion, friend (of a woman). [sákhi: cf. 362b[2].]

sakhī-gaṇa, *m.* (friend-crowd, *i.e.*) friends.

sakhī-jana, *m.* (friend-persons, *collectively, i.e.*) friends.

sakhyá, *n.* friendship. [sákhi, 1212c.]

sá-gaṇa, *a.* with (their) troops (of attendants). [2 sa.]

ságara, *m.* —**1.** the atmosphere, Luftmeer; —**2.** Sagara, name of a mythical prince.

saṁkaṭa, —**1.** *a.* narrow, strait; —**2.** *m.* Slender, name of a gander, 37[21]; —**3.** *n.* narrow passage, a strait; —**4.** *fig.*, *like Eng.* strait, a difficulty, 52[14]; danger, 25[4]. [cf. 1245g.]

saṁkalpá, *m.* a decision of the mind; the will *or* wish *or* purpose proceeding from such decision, a definite intention. [√kḷp + sam, 1148.1, 236.]

saṁketa, *m.* agreement; *esp.* a meeting agreed upon with a lover, a rendezvous. [prop. 'co-intention,' sam + keta.]

saṁkrānti, *f.* an entering, *esp.* entering of the sun upon a new zodiacal sign. [√kram + sam, cf. 1157[1] w. 955a.]

saṁkhyā́, *f.* the tale *or* number. [√khyā + sam.]

sañga, *m.* —**1.** a sticking to *or* hanging upon; —**2.** *fig.* an attachment (of the mind) to anything, desire for a thing; sañge, in case of desire, 64[2]; *pl.* lusts. [√sañj, 216.1.]

saṁgamá, *m.* a coming together, union. [√gam + sam.]

saṁgámana, *f.* -ī, *a. subst.* causing to assemble, gatherer. [caus. of √gam + sam.]

saṁgará, *m.* agreement, promise. [√1 gṛ + sam, 'chime in with.']

saṁgha, *m.* (a combination, *i.e.*) company, crowd. [√han + sam, 333, cf. 216.9 and 402.]

√ **sac** (síṣakti; sácate; saçcús, saçciré [794d[2]]). —**1.** be with, be united with; be together, have intercourse together, 70[14]; —**2.** accompany a person (*acc.*) to a thing (*dat.*), *i.e.* help him to it, 60[18]; —**3.** be attached to; *fig.* follow (a commandment), 75[2]; follow up, *i.e.* attend to, 82[17].

[orig. 'accompany,' *i.e.* 1. 'go at the side of, with help *or* favor,' and 2. 'go after, seek, follow': cf. ἕπ-ομαι, 'accompany,' ἑ-σπ-όμην, 'followed'; Lat. *sequ-or*, 'follow'; *sec-undus*, 'following, second'; also ἐπ-έτης, 'attendant,' Lat. *soc-ius*, 'comrade': further, AS. *seōn*, **seh(w)on*, Eng. *see*, Ger. *seh-en*, '(seek, look for, follow with the eyes, *i.e.*) see.']

saciva, *m.* attendant, supporter. [√sac, 1190, with union-vowel i.]

sa-jóṣas, *a.* (of like pleasure, *i.e.*) unanimous, harmonious; kindly disposed, 86[15]. [1304c[3].]

sajja, *a.* —**1.** *as used* of a bow, having its string on, strung, ready for use (the string being wound around the bow when this is not in use); —**2.** *generalized*, ready, *as used* of persons and things. [for sajya, q.v., with assimilation as in sajyate, sajjate — see √sañj.]

sajjī-kṛ (-karoti). —**1.** make strung, string (a bow); —**2.** make ready, 34[17]. [sajja, 1094.]

sajya, *a.* having its string on, strung. [2 sa + 2 jyā, 'bow-string.']

saṁcaya, *m.* a piling together, accumulation, *esp.* of wealth; supply (of food). [√1 ci, 'pile up,' + sam.]

saṁcayana, *n.* the gathering (of the bones of the dead). [do.]

saṁcayavant, *a.* possessing an accumulation (of wealth), rich; *with* arthāis, rich with money, *i.e.* having capital. [saṁcaya.]

saṁcārin, *a.* wandering. [√car + sam, 1183[3].]

saṁciti, *f.* a piling; pile. [√1 ci, 'pile up,' + sam.]

√ **sañj** *or* saj (sájati; sasáñja; ásāñkṣīt; saktá; sáktum; -sájya; *pass.* sajyáte *or* sajjate). stick to, be attached to; saktá, attached (of a glance), immovable. [cf. Lat. *seg-nis*, 'sticking, *i.e.* slow, lazy.']

+**pra**, be attached to; prasakta, addicted to.

satata, *only in acc. s. neut.*, -am, *as adv.* continuously, constantly, always. [for saṁtata, see √tan + sam: for mg, cf. Lat. *con-tinens*, 'con-tinuous.']

sat-kṛ, *see* sant 6.

satkāra, *m.* good treatment, *esp.* kind reception of a guest, hospitality. [satkṛ.]

sáttama, *a.* best. [sant, 471.]

sattvá, —1. *n.* condition of being, beingness, being, existence, essent-ia; —2. *n.* condition of being good, absolutely good being, goodness, the highest of the three qualities (*see* **guṇa**), 66[8] N.; —3. *m. n.* a living being, creature, 28[14], 48[2]. [formed from sant (1239), just as the artificial Lat. *essent-ia*, 'being-ness, that on which a thing depends for being what it is,' from *essens*, a quasi-ppl. of *esse*.]

sátpati, *m.* strong ruler; master. [sánt + páti, 1280, cf. 1267a.]

satyá, —1. *a.* real; true; existing in reality, 45[12]; truthful, trusty, faithful, 69[9]; —2. *n.* the real; the true; reality; truth, 95[6] end of line; truthfulness, 21[6], 95[6] near mid. of line; faithfulness, 69[12]; **yathā** · ·, **tena satyena**, as · ·, by this truth, as truly as · ·, so truly, 14[1] ff.; —3. *n.* vow, promise, oath; **satyam brū**, swear, 10[21], 15[6]; **satyaṁ cikīrṣamāṇas**, desiring to keep his promise, 8[12]; —4. **satyam**, *adv.* truly, indeed, 49[10]. [sánt, 1212c: radically akin w. ἐτεό-ς, 'true,' but of different formation, since the Cyprian shows that ἐτεός stands for *ἐτεϝο-ς.]

satyá-rādhas, *a.* having real blessings, bestowing real blessings. [1298.]

satya-vādín, *a.* truth-speaking, truthful. [1275.]

satya-vratá, *n.* vow of truthfulness. [1264, acct 1267.]

satyávrata, *a.* having, *i.e.* keeping a satyavratá, always truthful, 6[23]. [1296, acct 1295.]

satya-saṁgara, *a.* having, *i.e.* keeping a true agreement, *i.e.* true to his promise.

satyásaṁdha, *a.* having, *i.e.* keeping a true agreement, *i.e.* faithful. [satya + saṁdhā.]

satvara, *a.* with haste; **-am**, *adv.* quickly, immediately. [2sa + tvarā.]

sat-saṁnidhāna, *n.* a being near to the good, intercourse with the good. [sant.]

√**sad** (**sídati**, **-te** [748]; **sasáda**, **sedús** [794e]; **ásadat**; **satsyáti**; **sattá**, **sanná**; **sáttum**; **-sádya**; **sādáyati**, **-te**). —1. sit; seat one's self; —2. settle down, sink beneath a burden; be overcome; get into trouble; be in a desperate predicament, 18[7]; despair; not know what to do, be unable to help one's self; —*caus.* set. [w. sīdāmi, *si-zd-āmi, si-s[a]d-āmi, cf. ἵζω, *σι-ζδ-ω, *σι-σ[e]δ-ω, 'sit,' Lat. *sīd-ere*, 'settle down'; cf. also *sed-ēre*, 'sit'; Eng. *sit*, caus. *set*; **sad-as**, ἕδ-ος, ἕδ-ρα, Lat. *sella*, **sed-la*, AS. *set-l*, Eng. *settle*, 'a seat.']

+**ava**, sink down, get into trouble, be in distress.

+**ā**, —1. sit upon; —2. lie in wait for, 80[13]; —3. get to, reach (a place); **ásanna**: approached; near, neighboring, 33[10]; —*caus.* —1. set upon; —2. get to, arrive at, reach; find, obtain, gain, 23[11], 46[2]; —3. **āsādya**, *often so attenuated in mg as to be equiv. to a mere preposition:* **nimittaṁ kiṁcid āsādya**, (having obtained some cause or other, *i.e.*) by *or* in consequence of some cause or other, *cf.* √**diç** + **ud**.

+**ni**, —1. sit down; take one's seat, *esp.* of the hotṛ at the sacrifice, 88[6, 8]; —2. *act. and mid.* set, install as, *trans.!*, 82[12]; —*caus. act. and mid.* set, install as, 88[17].

+**pra**, be favorable *or* gracious; **prasanna**, kindly disposed, 1[17]; —*caus.* make kindly disposed, propitiate, 36[6]. [behind the mg 'be gracious' lies doubtless the physical mg 'settle forward, incline towards, *e.g.* a suppliant.']

+**vi**, sink, *used* (*like the Eng.* be depressed) of the spirits, be dejected; despond, 35[11]; come to grief, 31[1]; **viṣaṇṇa**, dejected.

+**sam**, sit together.

sadadí, *adv.* always, 93[8]. [cf. sadā.]

sádana, *n.* seat; *generalized, like Eng.* seat *and Lat.* sēdes, place (75[7]), dwelling. [√sad.]

sádas, *n.* seat. [√sad: cf. ἕδος, 'seat.']

sadasat, *n.* existence and non-existence. [sat + asat, the subst. used neuter stems of sant and asant, 1252.]

sadasad-ātmaka, *a.* having existence and non-existence as its nature, whose nature it is to exist and also not to exist at the same time. [sadasat.]

sádā, *adv.* always. [cf. 1103a [2].]

sad-ācāra, *m.* the conduct *or* practices of the good. [sant.]

sa-dṛ́ça, *a.* of like appearance; equal, *used* (296b) *w. gen.* [518.]

sadyás, *adv.* on the same day; immediately. [see 1122f.]

sadha, *adv. equiv. of* 1 sahá, *see* 1104 [3].

sadha-máda, *m.* co-revelry, *συμπόσιον*, common feast; sadhamādam mad, revel in bliss with, *w. instr.* [1290.]

sadhá-stha, *n.* (*orig., perhaps,* co-place, *i.e.* place of union, *but generalized to the simple mg of*) place.

sána, *a.* old. [orig. 'of long standing, long continued': cf. *ἕνο-s*, 'old'; Lat. *sen-ex*, 'old man'; Goth. *sin-ista*, 'oldest'; AS. *sin-ceald*, 'perpetually *or* extremely cold'; AS. and Old Eng. *sin-grēne*, 'evergreen,' Eng. *sen-green*, '(extremely green, *i.e.*) house-leek': from a not quotable Goth. **sina-skalks*, Medieval Lat. *siniscalcus*, 'oldest house-servant,' through intermediate Romance forms, comes Eng. *seneschal*; Ger. *Sünd-flut*, 'sin-flood,' is a popular interpretation of Old High Ger. *sin-vluot*, 'the long-continued flood, the Noachian deluge.']

sánā, *adv.* of old, always. [instr. of sána, 1112c, not a.]

sanā́t, *adv.* from of old, always, forever. [sána, acct 1114d.]

sanātána, *a.* everlasting, eternal. [sanā, 1245e.]

sá-nīḷa, *a.* having a common nest *or* origin, affiliated, united. [1304c.]

sánemi, *adv.* always. [perhaps from sana.]

sánt, —1. *ppl.* being; *otiose*, 24 [16], *see* √1 as; existing; —2. *a.* real, genuine; true, good; —3. of people, good, noble, excellent, 19 [8, 20], 28 [11]; —4. satí, *f.* a true, good, virtuous wife (*hence Anglo-Indian* Suttee); —5. *n.* the existent; existence; —6. sat-kṛ, make good, treat well, receive kindly. [present ppl. of √1 as, 'be,' q.v.: cf. *ἐών*, stem *ἐοντ*, 'being'; Lat. *absens*, stem *ab-sent*, 'being off'; *sons*, stem *sont*, 'the real doer,' 'the guilty one'; Danish *sand*, AS. *sōð*, 'true,' Eng. *sooth*, 'true, truth': for mg 2, cf. the mg of satya, of *τὸν ἐόντα λόγον*, 'the true story,' and of Eng. *sooth*.]

sáṁtati, *f.* —1. continuation; —2. *esp.* continuation of one's race *or* family, *i.e.* offspring.

saṁtāpá, *m.* —1. heat; —2. pain, sorrow. [√tap + sam.]

saṁtāpavant, *a.* sorrowful. [1233.]

saṁdṛ́ç, *f.* a beholding; sight. [√dṛç + sam.]

saṁdehá, *m.* —1. doubt; -āt, from (by reason of) uncertainty [291 [2]]; —2. danger, 20 [15]. [√dih + sam: for mg 2, cf. bhaya.]

saṁdhā́, *f.* —1. covenant, agreement; —2. promise. [√1 dhā, 'put,' + sam: for mg 1, cf. *συνθήκη*, 'covenant,' and *συντίθημι*, the counterpart of saṁdadhāmi.]

saṁdhā́na, *n.* a putting together, *σύνθεσις*, mixing. [√1 dhā, 'put,' + sam: paroxytone, 1150. 1c.]

saṁdhí, *m.* —1. a putting together, *σύνθεσις*; —2. *like* saṁdhā, compact, alliance, 41 [18]; peace, 17 [7]; —3. the putting together of sounds in word and sentence (*see* Whitney 109b [2]), euphonic combination, 50 [9]; —4. junction (of day and night), *i.e.* morning *or* evening twilight. [√1 dhā, 'put,' + sam, 1155. 2e.]

sáṁdhya, *a.* pertaining to saṁdhi *or* junction; saṁdhyā, *f.* —1. time of junction (of day and night), morning *or* evening twilight; *du.* morning and evening twilight; —2. morning twilight (of a yuga), 58 [8]. [saṁdhí, cf. 1212b.]

saṁdhyāñça, *m.* (*lit.* twilight-portion) evening twilight of a yuga. [añça.]

saṁdhyā-samaya, *m.* twilight-time, evening.

saṁnidhāna, *n.* (a putting down together, juxta-position, approximation, *and so*) a being near; contiguity; presence; neighborhood, 40 [9]. [√1 dhā, 'put,' + sam-ni, 1150: cf. saṁnidhi.]

samnidhi, *m.* presence. [√1dhā, 'put,' + sam-ni, 1155.2c: for mg, cf. samnidhāna.]

√ **sap** (sápati, -te; sepús). follow after; be attached *or* devoted to. [identified by some with √sac.]

sáp, *vbl.* following after, *in cpds.* [√sap.]

sapátnī, *a. f.* having a common husband; *as subst.* one of two or more wives of the same man, co-wife, fellow-wife, concubine. [sa + pati, but in the fem. form, since the masc. would not be used: 1304c: cf. supatnī.]

√ **saparya** (saparyáti). pay devotion to, worship. [denom. of a not quotable *sapar, 'devotion,' from √sap.]

sa-piṇḍa, *a. subst.* having the piṇḍa (*q.v.*) in common, said of persons who have a common ancestor not more than six generations back to whom they offer a piṇḍa together, persons related in the sixth generation. [1304c.]

saptá [483[4]], *num.* seven, 53[6], 99[23]; *also*, *as* a favorite sacred number, *the expression of* an indefinite plurality, *e.g.* 71[8], 72[4, 6]. [cf. ἑπτά, Lat. *septem*, AS. *seofon*, Eng. *seven.*]

saptakathāmaya, *f.* -ī, *a.* consisting of seven narrations. [sapta-kathā: see maya.]

saptá-tantu, *a.* having seven courses.

saptá-pada, *f.* -ī, *a.* —1. being for seven, *i.e.* many *or* all, steps (*see* 1294[2]), *i.e.* being at every step, constant; —2. having (taken) seven steps; *see* 100[4] N. [1300a.]

sa-praçraya, *a.* with respectful demeanor; -am, *adv.* respectfully.

sa-phala, *a.* fruitful, fruit-bearing.

sá-bandhu, *a.* having a friend.

sa-bāṣpa, *a.* tearful.

sa-brahmacārin, *m.* fellow-student.

sa-bhaya, *a.* fearful; -am, *adv.* in terror.

sabhā́, *f.* house *or* hall for public meetings, *esp.* gambling-house; assembly, 19[8]; society, 19[1]. [orig., perhaps, 'family': cf. Goth. *sibja*, 'relationship,' AS. *sibb*, 'relationship, related'; Old Eng. *god-sib*, 'related in God,' *i.e.* 'a sponsor in baptism,' Eng. *gossip*, 'sponsor, familiar friend, tattler'; Ger. *Sipp*, masc., 'relative,' *Sippe*, fem., 'relationship, kindred.']

sabhārya, *a.* having his wife with him, *i.e.* with his wife, 1[17]. [2 sa + bhāryā, 1304c, 334[2].]

sám, *prep.* along, with, together. [cf. 2sa.]

1 **sama** [525[4]], *encl. pron.* any; every, 70[12]; *cf.* samaha. [cf. ἀμό-θεν, 'from some place or other'; οὐδ-αμός, 'not any'; οὐδ-αμῶς, 'in not any wise'; AS. *sum*, 'some one,' Eng. *some.*]

2 **samá**, *a.* —1. even; —2. like, 63[17]; equal, 48[11]; *w. gen.* (296b), 3[16]; -am, *adv.* equally with, along with, with, *w. instr.*, 29[6], 26[5]; —3. like *or* equal (to the usual), *i.e.* not distinguished, common, mediocre, 19[10]. [cf. ἅμα, Doric ἀμᾶ, 'at the same time'; ὁμός, 'one and the same, common'; ὁμα-λός, 'even, equal'; Lat. *simi-lis*, 'like'; AS. *same*, 'in like manner'; Eng. *same.*]

samátā, *f.* equality; mediocrity, 19[10]. [2sama, 1237.]

samád, *f.* fight, contest. [sam, 383d[4]: cf. ὅμαδ-ο-ς, 'confused voices of men, din of battle, throng.']

sam-adhika, *a.* having a surplus with it; māsatrayam samadhikam, three months and more. [1305.]

sam-anantara, *a.* with a non-interval, immediately adjoining; -am, *adv.* immediately thereupon. [1305.]

samayá, *m.* —1. (a coming together, *i.e.*, *like Eng.* con-vention) agreement; —2. (*like Eng.* juncture) a point of time; *and so* time *or* season, 49[16]; occasion; —3. a con-currence (of circumstances), *i.e.* a case—*see* iha. [√i + sam.]

samayocita, *a.* suitable to the occasion; -am, *adv.* as the occasion demands. [ucita, √uc.]

samáraṇa, *n.* battle; Treffen. [prop. 'a coming together,' √ṛ + sam, 1150.1a: just so, Eng. verb *meet* sometimes means 'come together with hostile purpose,' and Eng. noun *encounter* is used mostly of 'a hostile meeting.']

sam-artha, *a.* (having an agreeing *or* accordant object [1305], *i.e.*) suiting its object, *and so* suitable; capable; able, *w. inf.*

sam-alaṁkṛta, *a.* well adorned. [see alam: sam intensive, 1077b end.]

samavatta-dhā́na, *a.* containing gathered pieces. [see 1087e.]

samaha, *accentless adv.* somehow, 80^{5}. [1 sama: cf. 1100a and 1104^{3}.]

samāgama, *m.* —1. a coming together, meeting; —2. meeting with, *i.e.* intercourse. [√gam + sam-ā.]

samānā́, *f.* -ī́, *a.* —1. like; one and the same, 78^{15}; -am, *adv.* in the same way, 103^{13}; —2. common (to different persons *or* countries), 73^{4}, 98^{17}; united, 73^{16}. [2 samá, 1245d.]

samāna-grāma, *m.* the same village.

samānagrāmíya, *a.* belonging to the same village. [samāna-grāma, 1215.]

samāsa, *m.* —1. a putting together; *and so* (*cf. Lat.* con-trahere, 'draw together,' then 'abridge') —2. a condensation; abridgment; -ena *and* samāsatas, succinctly. [√2 as, 'throw,' + sam.]

samídh, *f.* (*like Eng.* kindlings) fuel. [√idh + sam, 'kindle.']

samīpa, —1. *a.* near; —2. *as n.* nearness, neighborhood, presence; *used like* antika, *q.v.*; —2a. samīpam, *w. gen. or in cpd*, (to the presence of, *i.e.*, *simply*) to, *w. verbs of going*, 6^{10}, 27^{14}, 33^{4}, 44^{11}; —2b. samīpe, *w. gen. or in cpd* (in the presence *or* neighborhood of, *i.e.*, *simply*): before, 2^{16}; near, 25^{9}; hard by, 34^{14}; by, 40^{3}. [cf. pratīpá.]

samīpa-stha, *a. in cpd*, situated in the neighborhood of, near.

samutsarga, *m.* an ejecting, discharge. [√sṛj + sam-ud, 216. 1.]

samudrá, *m.* a gathering of waters, a sea, an ocean. ['a con-fluence,' √ud + sam, 1188b.]

samunnati, *f.* a rising; elevation, *i.e.*, *fig.*, distinction. [√nam + sam-ud, 1157 and d.]

sámṛti, *f.* (a coming together, *and so*) col-lision, shock. [√ṛ + sam, 1157d: cf. samaraṇa.]

sampatti, *f.* success; prosperity; abundance, 17^{14}. [√pad + sam, 1157d.]

sampád, *f.* —1. success; —2. (a falling together, co-inciding, *and so* a fitting of the parts to each other, *i.e.*) correct proportion, beauty. [√pad + sam.]

sampuṭa, *m.* hemispherical bowl *or* dish; round casket (for jewels); sampuṭe likh, write a thing (*acc.*) in the strong-box of a person (*gen.*), *i.e.* credit it to him. [sam + puṭa, 'a together-fold,' 1289a.]

samprati, *adv.* —1. just opposite; *and so* —2. (to the same limit) even, exactly; —3. (*like Eng.* even) at the very time; *and so* just now. [sám (intensive, 1077b end) + práti, 1314a.]

sám-priya, *a.* mutually dear. [priyá, 1289a.]

sambandha, *m.* con-nection; *and so, as in Eng.*, relationship. [√bandh + sam.]

sambhava, *m.* origin; *at end of adj. cpds*, having · · as its origin, originating in · ·. [√bhū + sam.]

sambhāvya, *grdv.* to be supposed, supposable. [caus. of √bhū + sam.]

sambhrama, *m.* extreme agitation, haste arising from excitement. [√bhram + sam.]

sám-miçla, *a.* com-mixed, mixed with, united with. [1289a.]

sam-rā́jñī, *f.* complete, *i.e.* sovereign ruler; mistress. [for sam, see 1289b end, and 1077b end: for m instead of ṁ, see $213a^{2}$.]

sa-yatna, *a.* (having, *i.e.* taking pains to, *i.e.*) trying to, *w. inf.*; engaged in, *w. inf.*

sará, *a.* running, moving, going, *in cpds.* [√sṛ.]

saraṇa, *a.* running; *as n.* a running. [√sṛ, 1150. 1a.]

√ **saraṇya** (saraṇyáti). run, hasten. [saraṇa, 1059d.]

saraṇyú, *a.* hastening, swift; -yū́ [355c], *f.* Saranyū, daughter of Twashtar, and spouse of Vivaswant, to whom she bare Yama and Yamī, 85^{15} N. [√saraṇya, 1178h: cf. Ἐρῑνύ-ς, 'the swift' goddess of vengeance.]

sarámā, *f.* the bitch of Indra *or* of the gods; *cf.* 83^{17} N. ['the runner' *or* 'messenger,' √sṛ, cf. 1166.]

sáras, *n.* lake, pool. [orig. 'fluid, *i.e.* water,' from √sṛ, 'run,' just as *fluidus* from *fluere*, 'flow, run.']

saras-tīra, *n.* bank of a pool.

sárasvant, —1. *a.* rich in waters; -vatī, *f.*: —2. Saraswatī, name of a mighty stream, probably the Indus; —3. Saraswatī, a small stream in Madhyadeça, to which the name and attributes of the great stream were transferred; —4. Saraswatī, the goddess of voice and speech, learning and eloquence. [sáras.]

sarít, *f.* stream. [√sṛ, 'run, flow,' 383.3: for mg, cf. Ger. *Fluss*, 'stream,' w. *fliessen*, 'flow,' and Eng. *stream* under √sru.]

sárga, *m.* —1. shot; —2. stream *or* spurt *or* jet; —3. a letting loose; —4. that which is let loose, *esp.* a herd let loose from the stall, 76[4]; —5. chapter of an epic poem, *a fig. use of the word in mg* 1 *or* 2. [√sṛj, 216.1.]

sarpá, *m.* (*like* serpent *from* serpere, 'creep') the creeper, snake, serpent, 84[14]. [√sṛp, q.v.]

sarpís, *n.* clarified butter, *either* warm and still fluid *or* cold and hardened, *and so not differing from* ghṛta, 'ghee.' [orig. 'fluid' butter, or 'the slippery, fat' stuff, from √sṛp, 'creep, move gently, slip,' 1153: see √sṛp and sṛpra: akin are Hesychian ἔλπ-ος, 'olive oil, fat,' and ἔλφ-ος, 'butter'; Ger. *Salbe*, AS. *sealf*, Eng. *salve*.]

sárva [524], *pron.* —1. entire *or* complete, 50[20], 95[18], 96[2]; salvus, integer, unharmed; —2. *adj.* all, every; —2a. *subst.*: *sing. m.*, everyone; *sing. n.*, everything; *pl.*, all; —2b. *common at beg. of cpds instead of an adj.*: *thus* sarva-guṇāir yuktas, *for* sarvāir guṇāir yuktas, 1[12], *cf.* 2[3]; *so cf.* 10[15] *w.* 10[20], 32[15] *w.* 32[14], 51[22] *w.* 52[23]; *similarly* 6[4], 17[1,9], 21[23], etc.; —2c. idaṁ sarvam, 63[21], *see* idam; *so for* 66[19];

—*observe that both mgs,* 1 *and* 2, *are common to the post-Vedic literature; that in the oldest parts of the Veda,* sarva *occurs only in mg* 1, *while for mg* 2 *the proper Vedic word is* viçva, *q.v.*; *but see* 77[11] N.

[cf. ὅλος, Epic οὖλος, *ὄλλος, *ὄλϝο-ς, 'whole, entire'; Lat. *salvus*, 'whole, unharmed, well'; Oscan *sollu-s*, 'entire'; Lat. stem *sollu-* in cpds, e.g. *solli-ferreum*, 'all-iron (weapon),' *soll-ennis*, 'of every year, annual,' used of religious ceremonies: no connection w. Eng. *(w)hole*, see also kalya.]

sarvaṁ-saha, *a.* patiently bearing all things. [sarvam, 1250a, 1270b.]

sarva-gata, *a.* (gone to all, *i.e.*) universally prevalent.

sarvátas, *adv.* —1. from all sides; on all sides, 93[12]; in every direction, 3[11], 101[12]; —2. omnino, altogether, 56[16]. [sárva, 1098b: acct, cf. 1298c.]

sarvátra, *adv.* —1. everywhere *or* in all cases, 21[19]; —2. at all times; always, uninterruptedly, 5[14]. [sárva, 1099: acct, cf. 1298c.]

sarvathā, *adv.* —1. in every way; —2. by all means. [sárva, 1101.]

sarvadā́, *adv.* always; constantly; for ever. [sárva, 1103.]

sarva-deva, *m. pl.* all the gods.

sarvadevamaya, *a.* containing in himself all the gods, *i.e.* representing *or* being in the name of all the gods, 28[19]. [sarva-deva: see maya.]

sarva-dravya, *n. pl.* all things.

sarva-bhāva, *m.* the whole heart.

sarvabhūtamaya, *a.* containing in himself all beings, 56[20]. [sarva-bhūta: see maya.]

sarva-yoṣit, *f. pl.* all women.

sarva-loká, *m.* the entire world.

sárva-vīra, *a.* with unharmed heroes *or* with all heroes, *i.e.* having lost none. [1298.]

sarvaçás, *adv.* wholly, altogether; all together, 6[6]; together, 65[15]. [sarva, 1106.]

sarvānavadya, *a.* entirely faultless. [anavadya, 1279[1].]

sarvānavadyāñga, *a.* having an entirely faultless body. [āñga, 1298.]

sávana, *n.* a pressing, *esp.* of Soma. [√1 su, 'press out.']

sá-vayas, *a.* of like strength *or* age; *m. pl.* (*like* ἥλικες, ἡλικιῶται, 'equals in age, comrades') comrades. [3 vayas.]

sá-varṇa, *a.* —1. having the same external appearance, exactly similar, 85[14]; —2. of the same caste, 62[7]. [for mgs, see varṇa.]

sa-vitāna, *a.* having a canopy, with a canopy.

savitṛ́, *m.* —1. (*with the two mgs of Eng.* quickener) impeller, enlivener; —2. The Enlivener, Savitar, name of a god, *selection* xxxvi.; —3. the sun, 23[18]. [√2su, 'impel.']

sa-vinaya, *a.* with politeness; -am, *adv.* politely.

sa-viçeṣa, *a.* possessing distinction, distinguished; -am, *adv.* in a distinguished way, especially.

savyá, *a.* left, 101[19], 102[11], 103[2]; *as m.* the left hand *or* foot, 60[5]. [prob. for *syavya (as would appear fr. the Church Slavonic form *šuj*, 'sinister'), and so perhaps akin with σκαιός, *σκαϝιο-ς, Lat. *scaevus*, 'left.']

savyatha, *a.* with sorrow *or* trouble. [sa + vyathā.]

savyāvṛt, *a.* with a turn to the left, *i.e.* turning to the left. [āvṛt.]

sa-çiṣya, *a.* with his pupils.

√ **sas** (sásti). sleep, slumber.

sasá, *m. or n.* herbs; grass.

sasaṁdhya, *a.* with the morning twilight. [saṁdhyā.]

sa-saṁdhyāñça, *a.* with the evening twilight.

sa-sambhrama, *a.* with excited haste.

sa-sarpa, *a.* with a serpent.

sasyá, *n.* standing crop; produce of the field, grain. [cf. sasa.]

sasya-kṣetra, *n.* field of grain.

sasya-rakṣaka, *m.* keeper *or* watcher of the standing crop.

√ **sah** (sáhate; sasā́ha, sasahé; ásahiṣṭa; sahiṣyáte; soḍhá [222[3]]; sáhitum, sóḍhum; -sáhya). —1. overpower, 90[8]; be victorious, 78[4]; —2. hold out against, withstand; *and so* bear; endure patiently, 32[7].

[orig. 'be powerful, withstand, hold back, hold': cf. the collateral √sagh, 'take on one's self, bear': cf. ἴσχω, *σι-σχ-ω, 'hold back'; ἔχω, ἔ-σχ-ον, 'hold *or* have, had': — w. sahas, *sagh-as, cf. the Germanic stem *seg-oz*, as it appears in Goth. neut. *sigis*, AS. *sigor*, prob. neuter, all meaning 'victory'; the stem appears also in *Seges-tes*, name of a Cheruscan prince (Tacitus, Annals), and in *Sigismund:* cf. also AS. *sige*, Ger. *Sieg*, 'victory.']

+**ud**, —1. hold out, endure; —2. be able, *w. inf.*; kathaṁ svārtham utsahe, how can I (*sc.* do, prosecute) my own object.

1 **sahá**, —1. *adv.* together; saha na etad, in common ours (is) that, *i.e.* we'll own that together, 97[10]; —2. *prep.* with, along with, *w. instr.*, 1[16], 89[8]. [cf. 2sa, and 1104[8].]

2 **sahá**, *a.* —1. powerful; —2. enduring, patiently bearing. [√sah.]

saha-cārin, —1. *a.* going together, accompanying; —2. *as m.* comrade. [for 2, cf. sahāya.]

saha-já, *a.* born together, con-nate, inborn, natural.

saha-bhasman, *a.* with the ashes.

sahá-vatsa, *a.* with the calf. [1304c.]

saha-vāhana, *a.* having their teams along, with their teams. [1304c.]

sáhas, *n.* superior power; might, 75[11]; victory; sahasā, *adv.* (with violence, *i.e.*) suddenly, straightway. [see under √sah.]

sa-hasta, *a.* having hands.

sahasyà, *a.* powerful. [sáhas, 1212d1.]

sahásra, *n.* a thousand; *esp.* a thousand kine; a thousand, *in the sense of* a great many, 87[6]; *for constructions, see* 486. [prop. 'one-thousand,' 3sa + hasra: with hasra, cf. -χῑλο-, *χειλο, *χεσλο (in δεκά-χῑλοι), and χίλιοι, 'thousand.']

sahásra-ṇītha, *a.* having a thousand songs, rich in songs. [nītha, 193, 1300a.]

sahásradakṣiṇa, *a.* having a thousand kine as his gift *or* as its reward; *as m.*, *sc.* yajña, a sacrifice at which such reward is given, 87[15]; of persons who offer such gifts, 91[9]. [dakṣiṇā, 1300a.]

sahásra-dvār [388c], *a.* thousand-doored.

sahásra-çṛṅga, *a.* thousand-horned.

sahasrāñçu, *a.* thousand-rayed; *as m.* the sun. [añçu.]

sahasrāñçu-sama, *a.* sun-like.

sahásrā-magha, *a.* having thousand gifts. [247.]

sáhasvant, *a.* mighty. [sáhas.]

sahāya, *m.* companion, attendant. [lit. 'going together *or* with,' saha + aya: for mg, cf. Lat. *comes*, stem *com-i-t*, √*i*, lit. 'going with, *i.e.* companion,' and also sahacārin.]

sahāyatana, *a.* along with the fire-place. [āyatana.]

sahita, *a.* united; *pl.* in company, all together. [quasi-ppl. from 1 saha, like Eng. *downed* from *down*.

sahela, *a.* with levity; -am, *adv.* playfully. [2 sa + helā.]

√ **sā** *or* si (syáti [761d 3]; sinā́ti; siṣā́ya; ásāt; siṣyáti; sitá; sítum; -sā́ya; sāyáyati). bind; *used almost exclusively with* ava *and* vi. [cf. ἱμάς, stem *σι-μαντ, 'strap, thong'; AS. *sī-ma*, 'bond'; Church Slavonic *sě-tĭ*, Lithuanian *së-tas*, AS. *sā-da*, Ger. *Sai-te*, 'string'; Church Slavonic *si-lo*, AS. *sā-l*, Ger. *Sei-l*, 'rope': see also √sīv and snā́yu.]

+**ava**, —1. unbind *or* unharness (a team); *and so* turn in; go to rest; go home, 101[6]; ávasita, having turned in, at rest; —2. come to a stop at, *i.e.* decide upon (*e.g.* a dwelling-place).

+**adhy-ava**, *caus.* bring one's self to a stop at, *i.e.* decide upon, undertake, 28[28].

+**ud-ava**, set out, *esp.* from the place of sacrifice, *cf.* sā + ava, 1; betake one's self, *w. loc.*, 101[4].

+**vy-ava**, decide, determine, *cf.* sā + ava, 2.

+**pra**, *in* prasiti, 'continuation.'

sākūta, *a.* having a (definite) intention; -am, *adv.* significantly, impressively. [ākūta.]

sākṣa, *a.* having *or* with the eyes; —*used only in abl.* sākṣā́t, *as adv.* —1. with the eyes; —2. plainly, actually, 51[14]; exactly, 58[23]; —3. (in reality, *i.e.*) in propria persona, embodied, in person, 1[10], 6[18]. [akṣa: 1114c.]

sāgara, *m.* ocean. [cf. sagara: according to the legend, a basin hollowed out by the sons of Sagara, and filled by Bhagīratha with the water of the Ganges.]

sāgnika, *a.* having Agni with them, with Agni. [sa + agni, 1304c: for -ka, see 1222c 2[2] and 1307.]

sāñguṣṭha, *a.* with the thumb. [añguṣṭha.]

sāta, *m.* Sāta, name of a Yaksha.

sāta-vāhana, *a.* having Sāta (in the form of a lion) as his beast of burden, riding on Sāta; *as m.* Sātavāhana, name of a king, 49[17].

sāttvika, *f.* -ī, *a.* —1. (really existent, *i.e.*) real, 22[5]; —2. standing in relation to the quality sattva (*q.v.*), proceeding from sattva, governed by sattva, good. [sattvá, 1222e 2.]

sā́dana, *n.* dwelling. [√sad: for mg, cf. sadana.]

sādara, *a.* with respect; -am, *adv.* respectfully. [ādara.]

√ **sādh** (sā́dhati, -te; sā́dhitum; sādháyati). —1. come straight to one's aim, attain one's object; —2. bring straight to one's object; —*caus.* —1. bring to its object *or* end; accomplish; —2. attain, win. [cf. √2 sidh, 'succeed.']

sādhú, *f.* sādhvī́, *a.* —1. leading straight to the goal; straight (path), 83[17]; —2. good *or* noble (of people); faithful (wife), 64[10]; *as m.* noble man, 21[19]; *as f.* excellent woman, 46[7]; —3. *as adv.* right; regularly, 86[12]; well; *as excl.* bravo! 14[22], 48[16]. [√sādh, 1178a.]

sādhuyā́, *adv.* straight, directly. [sādhú, 1112e end.]

sādhyá, *grdv.* to be won; *as m. pl.* Sādhyas, a class of deities. [√sādh.]

sā́nu, *n. m.* top; surface; ridge; back. [cf. snu.]

sānuçaya, *a.* full of repentance. [anuçaya.]

sāma-dhvani, *m.* sound of the sāman. [1249a[2].]

sā́man, *n.* song; *as technical term, esp.* a Vedic stanza as arranged for chanting, a sāman; the collection of sāman's, the Sāmaveda.

sāmarthya, *n.* ability; -aṁ kṛ, do one's utmost; strength, 41[4]. [samartha, 1211.]

sāma-vedá, *m.* the Veda of sā́man *or* chants, 63[6]. [1249a[2].]

sāmprata, *a.* of now, present; -am, *adv.* at present, now. [samprati, 1208d.]

sāmya, *n.* equality. [2samá, 1211.]

sāmyatā, *f.* condition of equality *or* likeness. [sāmya.]

sāyá, *n.* —1. a turning in, going to rest; —2. evening; sāyám, *adv.* at evening.

sā́yaka, *a.* suitable for hurling, missile. [√2si, 'hurl,' 1181a.]

sāraṅga, *a.* dappled; *as m.* antelope.

sārameyá, *m.* descendant of the bitch Saramā, name of certain dogs, 77[4], 83[17]. [sarámā, 1216a.]

sārdha, *a.* with a half; dve çate sārdhe, two hundred and fifty; sārdhám, *adv.*, *generalized*, together; *as prep.* along with, *w. instr.* [ardha: the generalization of mg is paralleled by that seen in çālin.]

sāvitrá, *f.* -ī, *a.* belonging to Savitar; *with or without* ṛc, a verse to Savitar, *esp.* Rigveda iii. 62. 10 (=74[14, 15]), regarded as the most sacred in the Veda, and called also gāyatrī, 60[13]. [savitṛ, 1208b.]

sāçru, *a.* tearful; sāçru, *adv.* [1111c], tearfully, with tears in (their) eyes, 54[19]. [açru.]

sāṣṭāṅgapāta, *a.* having *or* with an aṣṭāṅgapāta, *q.v.*; -am, *adv.* with profoundest obeisance.

sāsūya, *a.* with impatience; -am, *adv.* impatiently. [asūyā.]

sāhasrá, *a.* consisting of a thousand, milliarius. [sahásra.]

sāhāyya, *n.* office of attendant, *and so* (*like Eng.* attendance) service, aid. [sahāya, 1211.]

√ 1si, bind, *see* √sā.

√ 2si, hurl, *in* prá-sita, 'darting along,' sā́yaka, 'missile,' *and* sénā, 'weapon.'

siṅhá, *m.* lion; *at end of cpds*, the best of · ·, noble *or* brave · ·, *cf.* vyāghra. ['the powerful' beast, √sah.]

√ sic (siñcáti, -te [758]; siṣéca, siṣicé; ásicat, -ata; sekṣyáti, -te; siktá; séktum; siktvā́; -sícya; sicyáte). —1. pour out; sprinkle, 49[20]; —2. *esp.* semen infundere feminae; —3. (*like Eng.* found) cast, *e.g.* molten metal; phenaṁ vajram asiñcan, they cast the foam into (the shape of) a thunderbolt, 97[12]. [cf. ἰκ-μάς, 'moisture'; AS. *seōn*, **sīh-an*, 'filter, flow,' Ger. *seih-en*, 'strain'; Church Slavonic *sĭc-ati*, Ger. *seich-en*, 'mingere': cf. also Swedish *sila*, **sih-la*, 'strain,' whence Eng. *sile*, 'drain, strain,' whence *sil-t*, 'drainings, sediment.']

+**abhi**, —1. pour upon, sprinkle; —2. sprinkle in token of consecration, *and so* (*like Eng.* anoint) consecrate.

+**ava**, pour upon.

+**ā**, pour into.

+**ni**, pour down *or* in; semen infundere feminae.

síc, *f.* hem of a garment *or* robe.

siddha, *a.* perfected; *as m. pl.* the Siddhas, a class of demi-gods, with supernatural powers, *esp.* that of flying through the air. [see √2sidh, 'succeed.']

siddhi, *f.* —1. success, 36[10]; accomplishment (of a wish), 24[21]; successful performance, 57[14]; attainment of an object, 52[11]; —2. (perfection, *i.e.*) magic power. [prop. 'the reaching an aim,' √2sidh, 'hit the mark,' 1157. 1a.]

siddhimant, *a.* possessing magic power. [1235.]

√ 1sidh (sédhati; siṣédha; setsyáti; siddhá; séddhum; -sídhya). drive off; scare away.

√ 2sidh (sídhyati, -te; siṣédha; setsyáti, -te; siddhá). —1. reach an aim, hit the mark; —2. succeed, 18[17]; be accomplished, 18[22]; become realized, 18[19]; be of advantage, boot, avail, 71[4]; —siddha, having reached one's (highest) aim, having attained perfection; *esp.* perfect *in the sense of* having attained supernatural *or* magic powers; *as m.* a Siddha, *q.v.* [cf. √sādh.]

+**pra**, succeed; prasiddha, known, *cf.* prasiddhi · aham prasiddho mūṣakākhyayā, I go by the name of M., 47[21].

síndhu, —1. *in V.*, *m.* stream; —2. *in V. and later*, *f.* The Stream, *i.e.* the Indus (incolis Sindus appellatus — Pliny); —3.

the land on the Indus and its inhabitants (*pl.*). [cf. the Old Persian form *hindu* (in an inscription of Darius Hystaspis at Persepolis), as name of the land on the Indus: hence, w. loss of aspiration, the classical form Ἰνδό-ς; hence also Persian *Hind*, 'India,' and *Hind-u-stan* (*stan* = sthāna, 'abode, land').]

sisṛkṣu, *a.* desirous to create. [fr. desid. of √sṛj, 1038, 1178f: euphony, 184c².]

√ **sīv** (síivyati; syūtá; -síivya). sew. [prop. siū (765): cf. √sā, si, 'bind,' sū́tra, 'thread,' sūcí, 'needle': cf. κασ-σύω, *κατα-σύω, 'sew down, stitch together, cobble'; Lat. *su-ere*, 'sew,' *sū-tor*, 'shoemaker'; AS. *siw-ian*, *seowian*, Eng. *sew*; AS. *seām*, Eng. *seam*, Ger. *Saum*, 'hem, border.']

√ **1 su** (sunóti, sunuté; suṣā́va; saviṣyáti, soṣyáti; sutá; -sútya). press out, extráct, *esp.* the Soma *or* éxtract; sunvánt, *as m.* the Soma-presser; — sutá, extracted; *as m.* the éxtract, *i.e.* Soma-juice, 70⁵; draught of Soma, 73¹⁰.

√ **2 su** *or* sū (suváti; suṣuvé; ásāvīt; sutá, sūtá; -sútya). impel, set in motion; bring about; occasion; give authorization to; *w. loc.*, *perhaps* set, *at* RV. x. 125. 7. [cf. ἐάω, *σεϝ-άω, 'let go, permit'; αἷμα σύ-το, 'the blood shot *or* spurted.']

+ **ud**, impel upwards; set a-going, begin, *in* utsava.

+ **parā**, drive away.

√ **3 su**, generate, bear, *see* √sū.

sú, — 1. *adv.* [1121d], well; *with* sthā, stand well, *i.e.* firmly, 87⁶; *asseverative or emphatic, and to be rendered variously:* we pray, 79⁴; ni ṣu svapa, sleep in peace; *with* u, 'now,' just now, right soon, 80¹, 74¹¹; — 2. *inseparable prefix* [1304b, 1288b], *with force of either adv. or adj.*, well *or* good; *sometimes intensive, as*, su-dustara, 'very bad-to-cross.' [no prob. connection w. εὖ, 'well'; see āyú.]

sukumāra, *a.* very delicate. [cf. kumāra.]

sukumārāñga, *f.* -ī, *a.* having very delicate limbs. [áñga.]

su-kṛ́t, *a.* well-doing, righteous; *as m. pl.* the righteous ones κατ' ἐξοχήν, *i.e.* the departed fathers (85¹⁹), who enjoy the reward of their works in the world of the pious — sukṛ́tām u loké, 84¹¹.

su-kṛtá, *n.* a good deed, good works, 63¹⁶; sukṛtásya loká, world of righteousness, 89⁸, *modernized substitute for the old phrase* sukṛ́tām u loká. [1288 and b: acct, 1284a.]

su-keçānta, *a.* fair-locked. [1304b.]

su-kṣatrá, *a.* having a good *or* kind rule; *as m.* kind *or* gracious ruler. [kṣatrá, 1304b.]

su-kṣétra, *n.* fair field. [kṣétra, 1288b.]

√ **sukṣetriya** (*sukṣetriyáti). to desire fair fields — *denom.*, *found only in the following word.* [sukṣetra, 1059c and c².]

sukṣetriyā́, *f.* desire for fair fields. [√sukṣetriya, 1149⁶.]

sukhá, *a.* pleasant; comfortable; *as n.* pleasure; comfort; joy; bliss, 58¹⁷, 66¹; sukham, -ena, *adverbially*, pleasantly, with pleasure, in comfort, happily, well *or* easily, 24⁹, etc. [cf. duḥkha.]

sukha-duḥkha, *n.* weal or woe. [1253b.]

sukhin, *a.* having comfort, being in comfort. [sukha.]

sukhocita, *a.* accustomed to ease. [ucita, √uc.]

sukhodya, *a.* easily pronounceable. [udya.]

sukhopaviṣṭa, *a.* comfortably seated. [upaviṣṭa, √viç.]

su-gá, *a.* having the going *or* approach easy; easy to attain; *as n.* good path.

su-gata, *a.* well-conditioned, *i.e.* having had a good time.

su-gātuyā́, *f.* desire for welfare. [presupposes a noun *su-gātu, 'wel-fare' (see gātu), whence the denom. verb-stem *sugātuya, 'desire welfare' (1061), whence this noun — 1149⁶.]

su-cira, *a.* very long; -am, *adv.* very long.

su-jániman, *a.* having good productions *or* creations; skillfully fashioning.

1 sutá, *ppl.* extracted; *as m.* éxtract; *see* √1 su, 'extráct.'

2 suta, *m.* son; sutā, *f.* daughter. [prop. 'generated, born,' ppl. of √3su, see √sū: for mg, cf. sūnú, and Eng. *bairn* (under √bhṛ).]

su-tṛ́p, *a.* easily satisfied. [vbl. fr. √1 tṛp.]

su-darçana, *a.* having a beautiful appearance, handsome, εὐ-φανής; *as m.* Sudarçana, name of a king, Εὐφάνης.

su-dāman, *a.* having good gifts, bestowing blessings; *as m.* cloud, as source of rain and therewith connected blessings, blessed rain-cloud.

su-dína, *a.* very bright *or* clear; *as n.* (*like Lat.* serenum) clear weather.

sudinatvá, *n.* (*like Lat.* serenitas) clear weather; *fig.* auspicious *or* blessed time, *always in the phrase* -tvé áhnām, in der Glückszeit der Tage, in the happy days. [1239.]

su-dītí, *f.* beautiful flaming *or* flame.

su-dustara, *a.* very hard-to-cross, hard to get over; (of a promise) hard to perform.

1 sudhā́, *f.* (good place *or* position, *i.e.*) well-being. [sú + 1 dhā́.]

2 sudhā, *f.* (good drink, *i.e.*) drink of the gods, nectar. [sú + 2 dhā́.]

su-nāsākṣibhruva, *a.* having beautiful noses-and-eyes-and-brows. [for nāsākṣibhrū (1315c), *i.e.* nāsā + akṣi + bhrū, 1253.]

su-niçcaya, *a.* having a very firm resolve, very resolute.

sundara, *f.* -ī, *a.* beautiful.

sunva, *a.* Soma-pressing. [√1 su, 'press': see 1148. 3b and 716.]

supátnī, *a. f.* having a good husband. [su + pati, but in the fem. form, since the masc. would not be used: 1304b: cf. sapatnī.]

su-parṇá, *a.* with good wings; *as m.* bird of prey; eagle, vulture; mythical bird. [parṇá, 1304b.]

su-putrá, *a.* having good sons. [putrá, 1304b.]

sú-pratiṣṭhita, *a.* properly set up.

su-prāví [355b], *a.* very zealous. [1288b.]

sú-prīta, *a.* well pleased. [1288b and 1284.]

su-baddhá, *a.* well *or* fast bound. [1288b and 1284a.]

su-buddhi, *a.* having good wits; *as m.* Bright-wits, Good-wits, name of a crow.

su-bhága, *a.* having a goodly portion, fortunate, happy; *esp.* loved (by one's husband), 89[10]; charming; amiable, 61[12]. [bhága, 1304b.]

súmakha, *a.* jocund. [perhaps sú + makhá.]

su-mañgála, *f.* -galí [355b], *a.* having *or* bringing good luck. [mañgalá: acct irregular, cf. 1304b[2] end.]

su-madhyama, *a.* fair-waisted.

su-mánas, *a.* —1. good-hearted, well-disposed, 90[2]; kind; —2. (having good, *i.e.* happy feelings, *i.e.*) cheerful; glad, 78[18]; —3. *as f. pl.* (the cheerful ones, *i.e.*) the flowers; *in cpd*, 19[20]. [cf. the second part of εὐ-μενής, stem εὐ-μενες, 'well-disposed.']

√ sumanasya, *only in ppl.* sumanasyámāna, being cheerful; joyous. [sumanas, 1063.]

sú-mahant [450b], *a.* very great *or* important. [1288b.]

sumahākakṣa, *a.* having very-great (enclosures, *i.e.*) halls *or* rooms. [sumahā + kakṣā, 1298a, 334[2].]

su-méka, *a.* (having a good setting-up, *i.e.*) firmly stablished.

su-medhás, *a.* having good insight *or* wisdom, wise.

sumná, *n.* favor, grace; welfare. [perhaps neuter of an adj. su-mna, 'kindly minded'—see mna: but cf. 1224c.]

súra, *m.* a god. [a pendant to asura, formed by popular etymology from asu-ra, as if this were a-sura, 'non-god'—see asura.]

su-rakṣita, *a.* well-guarded.

su-rátna, *a.* having goodly treasures. [rátna, 1304b.]

surabhí, *a.* sweet-smelling, fragrant.

surabhisrag-dhara, *a.* wearing fragrant garlands. [surabhi-sraj.]

sura-sattama, *m. pl.* the best of the gods.

súrā, *f.* spirituous, *and esp.* distilled, liquor; brandy; liquor. [√1 su, 'express': cf. 1 suta and soma.]

su-rā́dhas, *a.* having goodly blessings, bounteous.

surottama, *a. subst.* chief of gods. [uttama.]

su-lalita, *a.* very lovely; (of meat) delicious.

su-locana, *a.* fair-eyed.

su-várcas, *a.* having good varcas, *i.e.*: full of life, 83[14]; blooming, 90[2]; fiery, 2[2]; glorious, 1[16].

su-várṇa, *a.* having a beautiful color; *as n.* gold.

suvarṇa-kañkaṇa, *n.* gold-bracelet. [1280b.]

su-vidátra, *a.* kindly noticing, *i.e.* taking kind notice, kindly. [1288b.]

suvidatríya, *a.* kindly. [suvidatra, 1214a.]

su-vī́ra, *a.* having good heroes; rich in retainers, 87[1]; heroic, 78[4], 88[14]. [vīrá: acct, 1304b[2] end.]

suvṛktí, *f.* excellent praise, goodly hymn. [su + ṛkti, with euphonic v.]

su-çéva, *a.* very kindly. [çéva, 1288b.]

su-çlakṣṇa, *a.* very smooth.

su-saṁcitạ, *a.* well-gathered; -am, *adv.* susaṁcitaṁ saṁcitya, having gathered (in a well-gathered way, *i.e.*) carefully.

sú-samāhita, *a.* very intent, entirely concentrated upon one thing. [√1 dhā, 'put': acct, 1284[2].]

su-stha, *a.* (well situated, *i.e.*) safe and well.

su-hṛd, *m.* friend. [prop. adj., 'having a good heart, kindly disposed.']

suhṛd-bheda, *m.* a creating of divisions among friends, separation of friends.

suhṛd-vākya, *n.* (speech, *i.e.*) words of a friend.

√ sū *or* su (sū́te [628]; suṣā́va, suṣuvé; ásoṣṭa; saviṣyáti, -te; soṣyáti, -te; sūtá, sutá; sūtvā́; -sū́ya). generate; bring forth; bear; *so perhaps at* RV. x. 125.7. [cf. 2 suta, 'bairn'; *υἱός*, **συ-ιο-ς*, 'son'; for pronunciation as trisyllable, *ὑ-ι-ός*, cf. Boeotian *οὑιός*: see also under sū́ and sūnú.]

+**pra**, bring forth; prasūta, born of (*gen.*).

sū́ [351], *vbl.* bearing, *in* vīrasū; *as f.* mother. [√sū, q.v.: with sū́-s, cf. *σῦ-ς*, *ὗ-ς*, Lat. *sū-s*, AS. *sū*, Eng. *sow* (qua pecude nihil genuit natura fecundius — Cicero, cf. *verres* under √vṛṣ); also AS. *swīn*, **su-ina*, Eng. *swine*, prop. a diminutive of *sū*.]

sūkará, *m.* swine, boar. [origin uncertain.]

sūkṣma, *a.* fine, small; subtile, intangible, atomic, 56[19].

√ sūcaya (sūcayáti). indicate; sūcita, made recognizable. [sūci, mg 3: 1061[2].]

sūcí *and* sūcī́, *f.* —1. needle; —2. *generalized*, a pointed object; *and so* —3. (*like Eng.* pointer) indicator; index. [prob. fr. √sīv, siū, q.v.]

sū́tra, *n.* —1. thread; cord; —2. brief rule *or* book of such rules (so called, perhaps, because each rule was a short 'line' or because the collection was a 'string' of rules), *cf.* Whitney xvii. [√sīv, q.v.]

√ sūd (sūdáyati). —1. lead straight on, keep a-going; —2. bring about, finish; —3. finish (*in its colloquial sense*), put an end to, destroy.

+**ni**, destroy, *see simple verb.*

sūnára, *f.* -ī, *a.* gladsome, joyous. [cf. sūnṛ́tā.]

sūnú, *m.* son; *once* (*at* 57[5]), *as f.* daughter. [√sū: cf. Church Slavonic *synŭ*, AS. *sunu*, Eng. *son*: for mg, cf. 2 suta.]

sūnṛ́ta, *a.* joyous, gladsome, kind; -ā, as *f.* joy. [sūnára: see 1237[3].]

sūnṛtāvan, *f.* -varī, *a.* joyous. [sūnṛ́tā, 1234 and [3]: for fem., 1169.2[2].]

sū́pa, *m.* soup. [despite the identity of mg, no etymological connection has as yet been discovered.]

sūpa-kāra, *m.* soup-maker, cook.

sūpavañcaná, *a.* (having an easy faltering-approach, *i.e.*) to which one easily *or* gladly totters (of the grave), *i.e.* easy of approach *or* not repulsive. [upavañcana, 1304b[2].]

sūpāyaná, *a.* (of easy approach, *i.e.*) easy of access. [upā́yana, 1304b[2].]

sū́ra, *m.* the sun. [cf. svàr, gen. sū́r-as, 'sun': perhaps a transfer to the a-declension, 399.]

sūrí, *m.* (*prop.* impeller, inciter, *i.e.*) he who engages priests to perform a sacrifice for his own benefit and pays them for it, a sacrifice-master; the same as **maghavan** (*q.v.*) and the later **yajamāna**. [√2 su, 'impel,' 1191.]

sū́rya, *m.* the sun, *selection* xl.; the Sun, *personified*, *selection* xxxiii.; **sūryā́**, *f.* —1. the Sun, *personified as a female;* —2. the hymn of Sūryā's wedding, RV. x. 85, *selection* lviii. [fr. svàr (sū́r), 1212a.]

sūryā-vid, *a.* knowing the Sūryā-hymn, RV. x. 85.

√ **sṛ** (sísarti; sasā́ra, sasré; ásarat; sariṣyáti; sṛtá; sártum; sṛtvā́; -sṛ́tya; sāráyati, -te). run swiftly, glide, flow; *caus. act.* set in motion. [cf. ὁρ-μή, 'rush, onset, spring,' whence ὁρμάω, 'rush on'; ἅλ-μα, 'spring'; ἅλλομαι, 'spring'; ἁλ-το, 'leaped'; Lat. *salīre*, 'spring'; cf. saras, 'pool,' sarit, 'stream,' and, for the root with l, sal-ila, 'flowing' and 'fluid, *i.e.* water.']

+**anu**, run *or* go after.

+**apa**, go off; *caus.* remove; take out.

+**ava**, go down, *in* avasara.

+**ā**, run unto; run.

+**upa**, go unto, approach.

+**nis**, go out; *caus.* drive out *or* away.

+**pra**, go forth; *caus.* stretch forth *or* out.

+**sam**, —1. flow together; —2. go about, wander, sam *intensive*, 1077b end; *esp.* wander from one existence to another (of the soul).

sṛká, *m. perhaps* missile, lance.

sṛgālá, *m.* jackal.

√ **sṛj** (sṛjáti, -te; sasárja, sasṛjé; ásrākṣīt; srakṣyáti, -te; sṛṣṭá; srásṭum; sṛṣṭvā́; -sṛ́jya; sísṛkṣati). —1. let loose (from the hand), dart, hurl; throw; —2. let go, pour out (streams, rain), discharge; —3. let loose (herds); —4. spin *or* twist (cord *or* garland); —5. (discharge from one's self, *cf.* 57¹, *and so*) procreate, engender; create.

+**ava**, —1. shoot off (arrows); throw *or* put in, 57²; —2. let loose (streams); loose (from a bond), 78¹⁹; deliver over, 84¹²; —3. (*like Eng. colloq.* let slide) let pass unnoticed, forgive, 78¹⁸.

+**ud**, —1. cast; hurl (a bolt); —2. pour out, 103¹⁸; —3. cast off; lay down (a corpse); —4. let go, 3⁵.

+**sam-ud**, let go, discharge.

+**upa**, (hurl at, *and so*) plague, distress, vex; **āditya upasṛṣṭas**, *sc.* **rāhuṇā**, the sun vexed by Rāhu, *i.e.* eclipsed.

+**vi**, —1. throw away, 105¹⁷; —2. discharge; (let go from the hand, *i.e.*) lay down, 103²¹; *mid.*, *w.* **vācam**, let go the voice, *i.e.* break silence by saying · ·, 100⁸; —3. create, 57⁸, *cf. simple verb.*

+**sam**, (let go together) mix, unite.

sṛ́j, *vbl.* creating. [√sṛj.]

√ **sṛp** (sárpati, -te; sasárpa; ásṛpat; sarpsyáti, srapsyáti; sṛptá; sárpitum; sṛptvā́; -sṛ́pya; sísṛpsati). creep, crawl; glide; *used* of gentle and cautious motion. [cf. ἕρπω, 'creep, go'; Lat. *serp-ere*, 'creep'; *rēpere*, **srep-ere*, 'creep,' *rep-ti-lis*, 'creeping'; AS. *sealf*, Eng. *salve*, so named from its slipperiness, like sarpis and sṛpra, see these; cf. also ἑρπ-ετόν and Lat. *serpens*, 'snake': no connection w. Eng. *slip*.]

+**ud**, creep out *or* up; rise; *desid.* wish to rise.

+**upa**, go gently unto, approach gently.

+**vi**, —1. move asunder, disperse; —2. move about.

sṛprá, *a.* slippery, fatty; smooth. [√sṛp, 1188a.]

1 **sénā**, *f.* a missile; weapon. [√2 si, 'hurl,' 1177a.]

2 **sénā**, *f.* line of battle; acies; army. [akin with sī́tā, 'furrow,' sīmán, 'parting of the hair': from these a root *sī, 'draw a straight line,' may perhaps be inferred.]

serṣya, *a.* with jealousy; **-am**, *adv.* with jealousy. [sa + īrṣyā́.]

√ **sev** (sévate; siṣéva, siṣevé; seviṣyáti; sevitá; sévitum; sevitvā́; -sévya). —1. stay by (*loc.*), *the opp. of* tyaj; —2. stay by, *and so* (*like Eng.* wait upon) serve *or* reverence, 30¹⁷; —3. devote one's self to; practice, 21⁸, 66², 68⁹. [no connection w. σέβομαι, 'reverence,' see √tyaj.]

+**upa**, reverence; be devoted to.

+**ni**, be devoted to, *i.e.* cohabit with.

+**sam**, practice.

sevana, *n.* practice. [√sev.]

sevā, *f.* a serving *or* reverencing. [√sev, 1149.]

sāinika, *a.* belonging to an army; *as m.* soldier; champion *or* fighter. [2 senā, 1222e 2.]

sódaka, *a.* with water, containing water. [udaká, 1304c.]

sóma, *m.* —1. éxtract, *esp.* of certain species of the Asclepias family, *see* 70⁵ N.; Soma, *both literally, and also personified as a god; as pl.* Soma-draughts; —2. the moon, *see* 70⁵ N. [√1 su, 'extráct,' 1166.]

soma-pā́ [352], *a.* Soma-drinking; *as m.* Soma-drinker.

soma-péya, *n.* a drinking of Soma; *dat.* in order to drink the Soma, *see* 1213c, 982. [acct, 1272a.]

somyá, *a.* having to do with Soma, *i.e., as m.:* Soma-offerer; *pl.* the Manes, 84[18]. [sóma, 1212c.]

sāudāmanī, *f.* lightning; *prop., f. of an adj.* *sāudāmana, 'of the rain-cloud, cloud-born,' *and to be taken in its adj. sense, as epithet of* vidyut, *at* 2[9]. [see sudāman and 1208a.]

sāúbhaga, *n.* happiness. [subhága, 1208f.]

sāubhagatvá, *n.* condition of happiness; weal and blessing. [sāúbhaga, 1239.]

sāúbhāgya, *n.* happiness, *esp.* conjugal felicity, 89[16]; charmingness, 2[5]. [subhága (1211, 1204c) — see its mgs.]

sāumyá, *a.* —1. of *or* relating to Soma; Soma-, 96[6]; —2. (moon-like, *i.e.*) having a mild and kindly influence on senses and feelings, *and so* mild, gentle; —3. *voc. sing.* sāumya, O gentle sir, 61[8]. [sóma, 1211.]

sāuryá, *a.* pertaining to the sun; *neut. pl., sc.* sūktāni, hymns to Sūrya. [sū́rya, 1211.]

sāuvarṇa, *a.* golden. [suvarṇa, 1208f.]

√ skand (skándati; caskánda; áskāntsīt; skantsyáti; skanná; -skándya, -skádya). *intrans.* dart, spring, spurt; drop, be spilled; fall. [cf. *σκάνδ-αλον*, 'trap-stick' (cf. Ger. *Falle*, 'trap, pit-fall,' w. *fallen*, 'fall'), and 'stumbling-block'; Lat. *scand-ere*, 'climb,' *de-scend-ere*, 'climb down'; *scāla*, **scad-la*, 'ladder.']

skandhá, *m.* shoulder.

skandha-deça, *m.* region of the shoulder, *i.e.* shoulder.

skándhas, *n.* ramification; branches of a tree, tree-top.

stána, *m.* the breast of a woman.

stabdha, *a.* immovable, rigid, stiff. [√stabh, 954, 160.]

stabdha-locana, *a.* having immovable, *i.e.* unwinking eyes.

stabdhī-kṛ, make rigid *or* stiff (as if dead). [stabdha, 1094.]

√ stabh *or* **stambh** (stabhnā́ti; tastámbha, tastambhé; ástambhīt; stabdhá; stábdhum; stabdhvā́; -stábhya). —1. make firm *or* steady, prop *or* uphold (heaven *or* earth); —2. *mid.* become firm *or* immovable *or* rigid; — stabdha, immovable, rigid. [cf. *στέμφ-υλον*, 'olives pressed hard, oil-cake'; *στέμβ-ειν*, 'maltreat,' collateral form of *στείβ-ειν*, 'stamp on, tread'; Eng. *stamp:* for connection of mgs, cf. *ἐρείδω*, 'make steady *or* firm, fix firm, plant.']

+**ud**, prop up.

+**vi**, —1. prop asunder, 78[10]; —2. (make immovable, *i.e.*) bring to a standstill, stop, 6[21].

stambha, *m.* prop, post, column. [√stambh.]

√ stā (stāyánt). be stealthy. [see stená, stāyú.]

stāyú, *m.* thief. [√stā, 1165: cf. tāyú.]

√ stigh (stiññóti). proceed, stride; *esp.* proceed against, attack. [cf. *στείχω*, 'proceed, march, go in line,' rarely 'mount up'; Church Slavonic *stignąti*, 'hasten': the root is wide-spread in Germanic, but often shows a specialization of mg, 'proceed upward, ascend, climb'; cf. AS. *stīg-an*, which often means simply 'proceed, go,' but also 'ascendere,' and even 'descendere'; Ger. *steig-en*, 'mount up'; AS. *stǣg-er*, 'a step to climb by,' Eng. *stair;* AS. *stigel*, 'step *or* steps for climbing over a fence,' Eng. *stile;* AS. *stig-rāp*, *stī-rāp*, 'mounting-rope,' Eng. *stirrup;* Ger. *Steg-reif*, 'stirrup'; AS.

stīgend, 'rising *or* sty,' Eng. *sty*, 'swelling (on eye-lid)': for change of gh to ñ in present, cf. 161[1] and [4].]

+**pra**, get ahead in attacking, succeed in one's attacks, 93[5,10,11].

√ **stu** (stāúti [626], stuté; tuṣṭháva, tuṣṭhuvé; ástāuṣīt, ástoṣṭa; ástāvīt; staviṣyáti, -te; stoṣyáti, -te; stutá; stótum; stutvā́; -stútya, -stū́ya; stūyáte). praise; extol (a god); stuvánt, (praising, *as subst.*) worshipper.

+**pra**, —1. praise; —2. bring forward as object of mention *or* subject of conversation (*cf. Lat.* laudare, *prop.* 'praise,' *but also* 'mention'), *and so* —3. *generalized*, introduce, begin.

stúkā, *f.* lock *or* tuft (of wool *or* hair). [see stoká.]

√ **stṛ** (stṛṇā́ti, stṛṇīté, *in mg* 1 *in Veda;* stṛṇóti, stṛṇuté, *in mg* 2; tastā́ra, tastaré; ástarīt [900]; stariṣyáte; stṛtá, stīrṇá [957b]; stṛtvā́, stīrtvā́; -stṛ́tya, -stī́rya). —1. strew, *esp.* the sacrificial straw, 88[17]; spread out; —2. (*like Lat.* sternere) overthrow (an enemy).

[cf. *στόρ-νυ-μι*, Lat. *ster-n-ere*, 'strew, spread out'; *στρῶ-μα*, (like Eng. *spread*) 'bedding,' *στρω-μνή*, 'bed,' Lat. *strā-men*, 'straw,' *storea*, 'straw mat,' *torus*, **stor-u-s*, 'bed'; AS. *strea-w*, *streo-w-ian*, Eng. *straw*, *strew*; *στρω-τός*, Lat. *strā-tus*, 'bespread'; (*via*) *strata*, '(way) bespread' with stones, *i.e.* 'paved,' whence borrowed AS. *strǣt*, Eng. *street*; Old Lat. *stlā-tus*, Lat. *lātus*, 'spread out, spreading, *and so* broad, wide'; see also under noun stṛ́.]

+**anu**, cover over.

+**ā**, spread out.

+**upa**, spread upon, spread as a cover; *as technical term of the ritual, with or without* ājya, pour the sacrificial butter over (*e.g.* the hand) so as to make a coating, 99[9].

+**pra**, spread out.

stṛ́ [371[12], tā́ras, stṛ́bhis], *m.*, *plural only.* the stars. [if fr. √stṛ, we may interpret the name as meaning either (*a*) 'the light-strewers,' *or* (*b*) 'the scattered' ones, those that are 'spread out' over the vault of heaven; but the connection w. √stṛ is very uncertain: cf. *ἀστήρ*, stem *ἀ-στερ*, Avestan **star**, Lat. *stella*, **ster-la*, Ger. *Stern*, AS. *steorra*, Eng. *star:* see also **tārā**.]

stená, *m.* thief. [√stā.]

stoká, —1. *m.* drop; —2. *as adj.* small, insignificant. [akin with stúkā, 'tuft': from these, a root **stu*, 'drop, dribble, run together, be compacted into a round mass,' may perhaps be inferred: for mg 2, cf. Eng. *dribble* w. *driblet.*]

stotṛ́, *m.* praiser (of a god), worshipper, singer. [√stu, 1182a.]

stóma, *m.* praise, song of praise. [√stu, 1166a.]

stoma-várdhana, *a.* delighting in praise. [acct, 1271.]

strī́ [366], *f.* woman, female individual, wife, *opp. of* pumāṅs, *e.g.* 104[9]. [prob. for **sūtrī́*, 'generatrix,' √sū, 1182[2].]

strī́-kāma, *a.* having desire for female (children). [1296.]

sthá, —1. *vbl in cpds.* standing; *and so, generalized* (*like Eng.* stand, 'be situated'), situated, staying, being; —2. *sometimes, perhaps, substantively*, place (*like Eng. noun* stand, 'place'), *in* go-ṣṭha, sadha-stha. [√sthā, 333: sometimes -ṣṭha, 186.]

sthála, *n.* dry land (*as opp. to* water), terra firma, Fest-land; sthalī, *f.* place. [prob. akin w. √sthā, 'that which stands firm.']

sthávira, *a.* —1. firm, thick, massy, sturdy; —2. full-grown, old; *as m.* old man. [from sthū, collateral form of √sthā, 1188e: for mg 1, cf. Eng. *steady*, cognate w. *stand*, and cf. sthira; for 2, cf. Eng. *of long standing.*]

√ **sthā** (tíṣṭhati, -te [671, 749a]; tasthāú, tasthé; ásthāt, ásthita [884]; sthāsyáti, -te; sthitá; sthā́tum; sthitvā́; -sthā́ya; sthīyáte; sthāpáyati, -te [1042d]).

—1. stand, 13[18], 25[16], 47[6], 80[7], 87[6], 98[18]; stand still, 70[19,21]; remain standing; —2. stand by (a friend); hold out faithfully, 25[5], 63[13,14]; —3. remain, 64[16]; wait, 54[6]; abide, 39[19], 46[6]; *pass., impers.:* sarvāiḥ sthīyatām, let all remain, 24[10]; atra sthīyatām, stay here, 39[21]; —4. remain *or* be in a condition, continue in an action [1075c]: *w. adj. or ppl.*, 28[3], 30[3]; vyāpāditas tiṣṭhati, lies dead, 44[16]; *w. gerund*, 26[16]; *w. instr.*, 41[6];

—5. exist; be present, 10[3], 45[13]; —6. be situated, be, 1[5], 26[13], 33[4]; —7. (remain standing, *i.e.* unmoved *or* untouched, *and so, like Ger.* dahingestellt bleiben) remain unconsidered *or* unmentioned; *thus*, dūre tiṣṭhatu tadvṛddhis, (let the interest of it stand afar off, *i.e.*) to say nothing of the interest of it, 46[21]; —8. sthitá, *see s.v.*; —9. *caus.* cause to stand, set; put, 41[19].

[for *stā: cf. Doric inf. *στᾶ-μεν*, Epic *στῆ-ναι*, Church Slavonic *sta-ti*, Lat. *stā-re*, Old High Ger. *stā-n*, Ger. *steh-en*, 'stand': this old form of the root appears also in Ger. *Statt*, AS. *stede*, Eng. *stead*, 'place': the prevailing form of the root in Germanic is *stand*; cf. AS. *stond-an*, Eng. *stand*; Ger. preterit *stand*, 'stood': —with á-sthā-t, cf. *ἔ-στη*, 'stood'; w. tí-ṣṭhā-mi, cf. *ἵ-στη-μι*, 'set,' Lat. *si-sti-t*, 'sets': —for mgs of √sthā, cf. in general those of Eng. *stand*.]

+**adhi**, stand upon.

+**anu**, —1. (stand along by, *i.e.*) take one's place along by, *and so* support, help; —2. devote one's self to a thing, *e.g.* virtue, 58[16]; devote one's self to (an undertaking), *and so* carry out (a plan), 33[14]; accomplish; *pass. impers.*: evam anuṣṭheyam, it must be done so, 37[8]; *so* 38[15]; tathā‿anuṣṭhite, it having been thus accomplished, this being done, 33[14]; *see* 303b[4] *and cf.* 35[16], 37[13], 39[15, 22].

+**abhi**, set the foot upon, vanquish; withstand.

+**ava**, —1. stand off, 105[20]; —2. stand; —3. remain, abide; —**avasthita**: standing; posted, 43[12]; situated; abiding, dwelling; —*caus.* (cause to stand apart, *i.e.*) leave behind, 44[2, 9].

+**ā**, take one's place at; resort to, 10[1].

+**ud**, stand up; rise up (from sleep *or* inactivity), 30[20]; spring up, 26[17]; get out of (*abl.*), 36[13]; *caus.* cause *or* bid to rise, 102[7]; pull out (of a mire, a vat), 22[9], 36[14]. [s lost, 233a.]

+**praty-ud**, rise up to meet (in token of respect).

+**sam-ud**, rise up, spring up.

+**upa**, —1. stand by, 94[9]; set one's self near; stand opposite, 59[23]; —2. approach, *esp.* with reverence *or* supplication; —**upasthita**: (having) approached *or* appeared; near at hand, 41[8].

+**anu‿upa**, *mid.* approach one after another; *w.* mā (*the pronoun*), come to my side, 94[4].

+**sam-upa**, approach; fall to one's lot; **samupasthita**, on hand.

+**ni**, stand in, rest on.

+**pari**, stand round about, encompass; restrain.

+**pra**, *mid.* arise, *and so* set out to go; go off; prasthito 'bhavat, profectus est; *caus.* send away, dismiss, 36[9].

+**prati**, stand; be established; get a place *or* foot-hold, 84[9]; **pratiṣṭhita**: established, resting upon; set up; —*caus.* set.

+**vi**, *mid.* (stand asunder, *i.e.*) spread itself.

+**anu-vi**, spread one's self over, pervade (*acc.*), RV. x. 125. 7.

+**sam**, *mid.* —1. remain with; —2. *in the ritual*, come to a stand-still (sam, *intensive*), *i.e.* get through, finish; saṁsthite, *loc. absolute*, if he (end, *i.e.*) die, 101[6].

sthātrá, *n.* station, place. [√sthā, 1185: for mg, cf. Eng. *stead* w. root sta under √sthā.]

sthā́na, *n.* —1. a standing; —2. a remaining, abiding; —3. standing, *i.e.*, *as in Eng.*, rank; —4. an abode (*see* bhavana); place, 35[5], etc.; —5. *pregnantly* (*cf.* pātra), a proper place; —6. a proper occasion; *concrete*, a proper object for giving occasion to anything; tatkāvyasya‿arpaṇa-sthānam ekaḥ s-, of this poem S. is the sole consignment-occasioner, *i.e.* the only one worthy of having this poem entrusted to him, 54[1]. [√sthā, 1150. 1.]

sthāna-bhraṅça, *m.* abode-ruin, loss of abode.

sthāvará, *a.* standing; not endowed with the power of locomotion, *and so*, *as collective n. sing.*, the plants, 63[22]; *as m. pl.* plants, 67[1]. [√sthā, 1171a.]

sthāvaratā, *f.* condition of being a plant. [1237.]

sthitá, *a.* —1. standing (*as opp. to* going, lying), 14[13]; —2. (of animate and inanimate beings) standing in a place; abiding; sthitas (*supply, as is often necessary, some form of* √as, 'be'), was abiding, *i.e.* abode, 29[13]; situated; bhūtale sthitam, being on the earth, *i.e., simply,* on the earth, 6[17]; *impers.:* sthitam, it was waited by (*instr.*), *i.e.* (he) waited, 34[18]; —3. existing; present, 6[18];

—4. being *or* remaining in a situation *or* condition (*cf.* √sthā 4), *which is expressed: by an adj. in the same case,* 13[10]; *by an adv.;* tathā, 26[18]; kaḥ sthito 'tra, who (is) being here, *i.e.* who is here, 49[7]; *by a gerund;* ātmānam ācchādya sthitas, after concealing himself (was) remaining, *i.e.* kept hidden, 25[10]; *so* 36[14], 38[19], 41[4]; upaviçya sthitās, waited sitting, 43[9]; yāir vyāpya bhāvān sarvān sthito mahān, with which the intellect, pervading all beings, stands, *i.e.* with which it constantly pervades all beings, 66[9].

[ppl. of √sthā, 954c: cf. στα-τό-ς, Lat. *sta-tu-s*, 'standing, set': for mgs above, cf. √sthā.]

sthíti, *f.* —1. a standing; —2. a remaining by a thing; *and so* —3. devotion to (*loc.*), 15[17]; —4. (*like Lat.* status) condition; *and so* —5. way, method of procedure, 26[7]. [√sthā, 1157. 1a, cf. 954c.]

sthin, *vbl.* standing, *in cpds.* [√sthā, 1183[3].]

sthirá, *a.* steady; steadfast, 81[9]; firm; *also of persons,* 99[7]; enduring (of might), 78[6]. [√sthā, 1188[1], cf. 954c: for mg, cf. sthavira.]

√ **sthū**, *assumed as collateral form of* sthā, *cf.* sthávira, *and see under* √snā.

sthū́ṇā, *f.* post, pillar. [for *stul-na, fr. √*stul or *stal, an extended form of √*sta, Skt. sthā: cf. Ger. *Stolle(n)*, Old High Ger. *stollo*, **stol-no*, 'prop, post'; στῦλ-ος, 'post, pillar'; these words, like στήλη, Doric στάλα, 'prop, post,' presuppose the root in causal mgs, 'cause to stand,' i.e. (*a*) 'keep from falling, prop up,' and (*b*) 'set up,' as a pillar: the root appears also in Ger. *Stall*, Eng. *stall*, 'stand, *i.e.* standing-place,' and in Ger. *still*, Eng. *still*, 'standing, not moving.']

√ **snā** (snā́ti; sasnāú; snāsyáti, -te; snātá; snā́tum; snātvā́; -snā́ya). bathe; perform a religious ablution, *esp.* at the end of religious studentship (62[6]) *or* of a vow. [orig. snā or snū (so sthā, sthū): cf. √σνυ in ἔννεον, *ἔ-σνεϝ-ον, 'swam'; Lat. *nā-re*, 'swim': see also under nāú.]

snā́taka, *a.* who has performed the ablution customary at the end of religious pupilage. [snātá, 1222.]

snāna, *n.* a bathing, religious ablution. [√snā, 1150.]

snāna-çīla, *a.* (having bathing as a habit, *i.e.*) practicing religious ablutions. [1302.]

snāyin, *a.* performing religious ablutions. [√snā, 1183[3], 258.]

snā́yu, *f. n.* —1. sinew, 25[7]. [perhaps 'ligament,' from √sā or si, 'bind, ligāre,' *q.v.:* if so, it is formed from the present-stem sinā (see 1148. 3b and cf. sunva), abbreviated to snā, with suffix u (1178b) and interposed y (258): cf. Old High Ger. *sënawa*, Ger. *Sehne*, AS. *sinu*, Eng. *sinew*, which point to a Goth. **sinava:* that snā́-yu and its older equiv. snā́-van are abbreviated forms (for sinā-) would appear from the Germanic cognates.]

snāyu-bandha, *m.* sinew-band, *i.e.* bow-string.

√ **snih** (sníhyati; snigdhá). —1. be supple, greasy, moist; *and so* —2. stick to, *i.e., as in Eng.,* be attached to, be fond of.

snú, *n. collateral form of* sānu. surface.

sneha, *m.* —1. stickiness; —2. viscid and smooth stuff; oil; fat; —3. attachment, love, friendship. [√snih: for connection of 1 and 3, see snih.]

√ **spaç**, *older form of* √1 paç, *q.v.*

√ **spṛdh** (spárdhate; paspṛdhé; spardhitá; spárdhitum). contest the precedence among one another; emulate; strive.

spṛ́dh, *f.* rival; opponent; foe. [√spṛdh.]

√ **spṛç** (spṛçáti, -te; paspárça, paspṛçé;

áspräkṣīt, áspṛkṣat; sprakṣyáti; spṛṣṭá; sprâṣṭum; spṛṣṭvā́; -spṛ́çya). touch.

+upa, —1. touch, 103[22]; reach to, RV. x. 125. 7; —2. w. apás, touch water, *technical term for* symbolical purification, by dipping the hand in a dish, by rinsing the mouth, *or* by washing, 104[17, 22]; *word for water to be understood*, 65[6].

spraṣṭavya, *grdv.* to be touched. [√spṛç, 241.]

√ sphur *or* sphṛ (sphuráti, -te; ásphariṭ; sphuritá). make a quick *or* jerky motion: —1. dart, *trans.*; with the foot, kick; —2. dart, *intrans.*; twitch (of the eye, arm); —3. (of the lightning) flash.

[for *spṛ, 'quiver, jerk, kick, flutter': cf. ἀ-σπαίρ-ω, 'struggle convulsively' (as a fish just out of water); Lat. *spernere*, 'kick away, reject'; Eng. *spur*, 'goad with the heel'; *spurn*, 'kick away': see also under parṇa.]

+pra, shake, tremble.

sphyá, *m.* wooden splinter, shaped like a knife and as long as the arm, for use at the sacrifice.

sma, *enclitic and slightly asseverative particle*, 79[17], 6[8]; *accompanying a verb which is in the present tense but has the value of a past*, 2[8], 8[19], 12[21]; *explained at* 778b *and* b[2].

√ smi (smáyate; siṣmiyé; ásmayiṣṭa; smitá; smitvā́; -smítya). smile; smile bashfully; blush. [cf. φιλο-μμειδής, 'fond of smiles,' stem σμειδες, as in Hesychian μεῖδος, 'smile'; μειδάω, 'smile'; Lat. *mī-ru-s*, 'wonderful,' *mīrāri*, 'wonder' (for mg, cf. smaya, 'wonder'); Middle High Ger. *smie-r-en*, *smie-l-en*, 'smile'; Eng. *smile, smirk.*]

+vi, be astonished.

smita, *a.* smiling; *as n.* [1176a], a smile. [ppl. of √smi.]

smita-pūrva, *a.* previously smiling, with a smile. [for irreg. order, see 1291.]

√ smṛ (smárati; sasmā́ra; smariṣyáti; smṛtá; smártum; smṛtvā́; -smṛ́tya). —1. remember, *both* keep in mind *and* call to mind; —2. call to mind, *i.e.* hand down by memory, hand down by tradition, hand down—*see the important word* smṛti;

—smṛta: —1. remembered; —2. handed down by smṛti *or* taught by tradition; *and so* —3. declared to be · ·, 61[2]; passing for · ·; regarded by tradition as · ·, 63[6]; *to be variously paraphrased;* mārgo 'yaṁ smṛtas, this is, we are taught, the path, 21[7]; called, 22[5], 57[6].

[cf. μέρ-μερ-α ἔργα, 'memorable works'; μέριμνα, 'anxious thought, care'; μάρ-τυρ, 'rememberer, witness'; μέλειν, 'care for'; μέλλειν, 'hesitate, delay, be going to do'; Lat. *me-mor*, 'mindful'; *memoria*, 'memory'; *mor-a*, 'hesitation, delay.']

+vi, forget.

smṛti, *f.* —1. remembrance; —2. tradition (*see* √smṛ 2); tradition which is handed down and accepted as authoritative (*except* çruti, *q.v.*); *defined*, 58[18], *see note;* a work based on such tradition; a law-book. [√smṛ.]

smṛti-çīla, *dual n.* tradition and habits (habits *in collective sense, i.e.* usage). [1253a.]

syá [499a], *pron.* that; *cf.* tyá.

√ syand *or* syad (syándate; sasyandé; ásyān [890[2]]; syantsyáti; syanná; syánttum; syattvā́; -syádya). run (of animate beings and of fluids); flow.

+abhi, flow unto.

+pra, flow forth *or* away.

syoná, *a.* soft; mild; tender.

srákva, *m.* corner of the mouth; mouth, jaws.

sragvín, *a.* wearing a wreath. [sráj, 1232.]

sráj, *f.* wreath, garland. [√sṛj, mg 4, 'twist,' just as AS. *wræð*, Eng. *wreath*, fr. AS. *wrīðan*, Eng. *writhe*, 'twist' (under √vṛt).]

srávantī, *f.* flowing (water), stream. [ppl. of √sru.]

√ sru (srávati; susrā́va; ásrāvīt; sraviṣyáti; srutá). —1. flow, stream; —2. flow *or* trickle away, waste away, become lost, 60[9]. [cf. ῥέω, *σρεϝ-ω, Lithuanian *srav-j-ù*, 'flow,' Irish *sruth*, 'stream'; cf. also Church Slavonic *stru-ja*, 'stream,'

Ger. *Stro-m*, Eng. *strea-m*, with *t* between *s* and *r* (see under usra and svasṛ): further ῥεῦ-μα, 'stream'; Lat. *Rū-mo*, 'The River,' old name of the Tiber: w. á-srav-a-t, cf. ἔρρεε, *ἐ-σρεϝ-ε-τ.]

srúc, *f.* one of the large sacrificial ladles (as long as the arm), of which there are three, juhū, upabhṛt, and dhruvā, *see* 102[11] N.; used for pouring ghee in the fire. [akin w. √sru.]

sruvá, *m.* a small sacrificial ladle (a cubit long), used for dipping from the pot and pouring into the sruc. [akin w. √sru.]

srótas, *n.* stream. [√sru, 1152a.]

svá [525[4]], –1. *pron. adj.* own; my own, 73[18], 78[12,20]; thy own, 69[16], 86[4]; his own *or* his, 4[17], 45[8], etc.; her, 8[10]; their own *or* (each) his own, 14[8]; *indef.*, one's own, 58[22], 66[6]; *very often at the beginning of cpds:* my, 10[23], 21[10]; his, 31[9], etc.; their, 27[9]; our, *etc.*, *see following words;* –2. *m.* kinsman, friend; –3. (*like* ātman) one's self, *see* 513[2]; one's natural self *or* condition; –4. *n.* (*like Goth.* sves) possessions, property. [cf. ἑός, *σεϝό-ς, and ὅς, ἥ, ὅν, and σφός, 'own'; Old Lat. *sovo-s*, Lat. *suu-s*, 'own'; Goth. *sve-s*, AS. *swǣs*, 'own'; also ἕ, σφέ, Lat. *sē*, Goth. *si-k*, Ger. *si-ch*, 'self.']

svaka, *a.* own; his own, *etc.; equiv. to* sva. [sva, 1222a.]

svá-kṣatra, *a.* (having self-rule, *i.e.*) free.

sva-cchanda, *m.* own will. [chanda, 227.]

svacchanda-vanajāta, *a.* (by its own will, *i.e.*) spontaneously wood-grown, *i.e.* growing wild in the wood.

√ svaj (svájate; sasvajé; svajiṣyáte; svaktá; sváktum; svajitvā́; -svájya). embrace.

+**pari**, embrace.

√ svad (svádati, -te; sasvadé; svāttá; svadáyati, svādáyati). –1. *act.* make savory, season; *fig.* make agreeable; –2. *mid.* be savory, relish, *intrans.;* –3. *mid.* relish, *trans.;* take pleasure in. [cf. ἁνδ-άνω, 'please,' aorist εὔαδε, *ἐ-σϝαδ-ε, 'pleased'; ἥδομαι, 'rejoice'; see also under svādu.]

sva-dharma, *m.* own duty.

1 **svadhā́**, *f.* –1. wont, habit, custom, 76[7]; rule; ἔθος; –2. accustomed place, home, ἦθος; –3. (wonted condition, *i.e.*) comfort; joy; bliss, 83[12]; pleasure, 73[14]; svadhā́m ánu nas, according to our pleasure, *i.e.* exactly to our wish, 73[18]; svadháyā *and* svadhā́bhis: in wonted wise; with pleasure, gladly; (gladly, *i.e.*) willingly, freely, 84[12]. [cf. ἔθος, 'custom,' ἦθος, 'wonted place, haunt,' εἴ-ωθ-α, 'am accustomed'; AS. *sidu*, Ger. *Sitte*, 'custom.']

2 **svadhā́**, *f.* sweet drink; *esp.* a libation of ghee to the Manes. [perhaps for 2 sudhā: for the etymology, cf. svadhā́ adhayat, 'he drank the sweet drinks,' RV.]

svadhā́vant, *a.* –1. (having his wont, *i.e.*) keeping to his custom, faithful, constant; –2. (having bliss, *i.e.*) blessed, 78[17], 79[4,15]. [1 svadhā, 1233: see mgs 1 and 3.]

svádhiti, *m. f.* axe.

√ svan (svánati, -te; sasvā́na; ásvanīt, ásvānīt; svanitá). sound, resound, roar. [cf. Lat. *sonus*, 'sound'; Old Lat. *son-it*, 'sounds'; AS. *swinsian*, 'sound'; Eng. *swan*, so named from its song; similarly in Ger. the cock is called *Hahn*, a name akin w. Lat. *can-ere*, 'sing' — cf. Hamlet i.1.160, "the bird of dawning singeth."]

svaná, *m.* sound; roar (of wind). [√svan.]

svanas, *n.* roar. [do.]

√ svap (svápiti [631]; suṣvā́pa [785[3]]; ásvāpsīt; svapsyáti; suptá [954b]; sváptum; suptvā́; svāpáyati). sleep; fall asleep; suptá, sleeping; *caus.* put to sleep. [cf. Lat. *sop-or*, 'sleep'; w. caus., cf. Lat. *sōpīre*, 'put to sleep'; see also under svapna.]

+**ni**, go to sleep; *caus.* put to sleep.

+**pra**, fall asleep; prasupta, fallen asleep, asleep, sunk in sleep.

svápas, *a.* having good works, *i.e.* wonder-working. [sú + ápas, 1304b.]

svapū́ [352], *f.* *perhaps* besom. [perhaps for su-pū, 'cleaning well': for va in place of u, cf. 2 svadhā: for mg, cf. pavana.]

svápna, *m.* —1. sleep; —2. dream. [√svap, q.v.: cf. ὕπ-νο-ς, Lat. *som-nu-s*, 'sleep'; AS. *swef-n*, 'sleep, dream'; Chaucerian *swefn*, 'dream'; Lat. *somnium*, 'dream': for connection of 1 and 2, cf. 51[9], where either sense fits.]

svapna-māṇavaka, *m.* the Dream-manikin, name of a certain magic whose performance brings dreams that become realized, 51[8].

sva-bhāva, *m* own way of being, inherent nature, ingenium, as distinguished from acquired qualities, *see* **guṇa** 2, *and* 22[21]; **svabhāvāt**, by nature [291[2]], naturally.

svabhāva-dveṣa, *m.* natural hatred. [1280b.]

svayaṁ-vara, *m.* self-choice; *esp.* free choice of a husband, which was allowed to girls of the warrior (**kṣatriya**) caste, a Swayamvara.

svayám [513], *pron.* own self, self; himself, *etc.; referring to subject*, 48[8], etc , all by itself, of its own accord, 93[9]; *referring to predicate*, 1[10]. [from **sva** with nom. case ending **-am** (cf. **tv-am**, **a-y-am**), and interposed **y**, cf. 258.]

svayam-bhū́ [352], *a.* self-existent; *as m.* epithet of Brahma.

svayam-mṛta, *a.* dead of himself.

svá-yukti, *f. pl.* own team [acct, 1274: for mg, cf. the Dutch and the American Eng. *span* (of horses) w. AS. *spannan*, 'join.']

√ **svar** (**svárati**; **ásvārṣīt**; **ásvārīt**). sound. [cf σῦρ-ιγξ, 'pipe, flute'; Lat. *su-sur-ru-s*, 'a humming'; Eng *swar-m.*]

svàr [388d], *pronounced* **súar** *in the Veda*, *n.* —1. the sun, 71[19]; —2. sunlight, sunshine; light, 79[9], —3. (the place of the light, *cf.* **rajas**) heaven, 91[6], 92[8]; —4. one of the three "utterances," *see* **vyāhṛti**.

[cf. Σείρ-ιος, Σείρ, 'sun, dog-star'; σέλ-ας, 'light'; σελ-ήνη, 'moon'; Lat. *ser-ēnus*, 'bright'; *sōl*, AS. *sōl*, 'sun'; AS *swel-an*, Eng. *sweal*, 'burn, glow, waste away by heat'; and the kindred *swelter*, 'be overcome by heat,' whence *sweltry* or *sultry:* if the forms with *r* and *l* are fr. extended forms of a root ***su**, 'to light,' and if **svàr** is a direct deriv. of the same √***su** (**sú-ar**), we may compare Ger. *Sonne*, AS. *su-nne*, Eng. *sun*, AS. *sunnan dæg*, Eng. *Sun-day.*]

sva-rūpa, *n.* own form *or* shape; true nature, 40[19].

svarūpa-bhāva, *m.* the becoming *or* being the true form (of names), *i.e.* the use of the true form (of a person's name). [1280b: **svarūpa** is used predicatively.]

svar-gá, —1. *a.* going *or* leading to the light *or* to heaven; situate in the heavenly light, heavenly; *esp. w.* **loka**, **svargo lokas**, the heavenly world, heaven, 103[5, 14, 16] —*also as one word, see* **svargaloka**; —2. *m. without* **loka**, heaven, 64[9], 66[1].

svarga-gāmin, *a.* going to *or* attaining heaven.

svarga-loka, *m.* the heavenly world, heaven, 103[7].

svàr-bhānu, *m.* Suarbhānu, name of a demon causing the eclipse of the sun, *cf. the later* **rāhu**. [poss. 'having, *i.e.* withholding the sun's rays.']

svaryà, *pronounced* **svaría**, *a.* sounding; of a thunderbolt, whizzing. [√**svar**, 1213.]

svalaṁkṛta, *a.* well adorned. [**su** + **alaṁkṛta**: see **alam**.]

sváçva, *a.* with goodly horses. [**sú** + **áçva**, 1304b.]

svásṛ [373], *f.* sister. [cf. Lat. *sŏror*, AS. *sweoster*, *swuster*, Eng. *sister:* cf. 369[2] and 1182f: for *t* between *s* and *r*, cf. *Easter*, under **usra**, and *stream* under √**sru**.]

svastí, *pronounced* **suasti** *in Veda*, —1. *f.* (*like the Eng.* well-being, *i.e.*) welfare; blessing; —2. **svastí**, *instr.* [336[3] end], with luck, happily; *hence* —3. *the indeclinable nom.-acc. neut.* **svasti**, luck, happiness, 84[1]; **svasty astu te**, a blessing on thee. [**sú** + an unused **asti**, 'be-ing,' fr. √1 **as**, 'be,' 1157 1a. acct, 1288b.]

svasti-dā́ [352], *a.* bestowing welfare.

svastyáyana, *n. sing. and pl.* (luck-progress, *i.e.*) wel-fare, prosperity; blessing; *and so* benediction, 101[2], 106[4]; *pl.* the blessings, *i.e.* Vedic hymns containing the word svasti, 106[8]. [svastí + áyana: acct, 1271: with -ayana, cf. *-fare* in *wel-fare.*]

sva-stha, *a.* being in one's natural condition, self-contained, healthy, well.

svādas, *n.* agreeableness, *in* prá-svādas. [√svad, 1151. 1b: cf. ἦδος (sic), Doric ἆδος, 'pleasure.']

svādú, *a.* tasting good, savory; sweet. [√svad, q.v., 1178a: cf. ἡδύς, Doric ἁδύς, *σϝᾱδυ-ς, Lat. *suāvis*, **suadv-i-s*, AS. *swēte*, Eng. *sweet.*]

svādhyāyá, *m.* the reading *or* repeating to one's self, study (of the Veda). [adhyāya.]

svāmi-kārya, *n.* master's business.

svāmi-kumāra, *m.* the Lord Kumāra, name of Skanda, god of war, *see* **kārttikeya** *and* **kumāra.**

svāmi-guṇa, *m.* ruler-virtue.

svāmin, *m.* owner, proprietor, master, lord; *opp. of* servant, subject, wife. [sva, 'own,' 1231.]

svāmi-sevā, *f.* the serving one's master.

svāmi-hita, *n.* master's welfare.

svārtha, *m.* own affair *or* cause. [artha.]

sváhā, *excl. used when making oblations,* hail, *w. dat.*, 103[3]; *at the end of an invocation, like* Amen, 99[13].

√ **svid** (svédate; svídyati, -te; siṣvidé; svinná). sweat. [svídyāmi = ἰδίω, 'sweat'; cf. ἶδος, ἰδ-ρώς, 'sweat,' ἱδρόω, 'sweat'; Lat. *sūdā-re*, 'sweat,' denom. of **sūdu-s*, 'sweat'; *sūd-or*, 'sweat'; Lettish *swidrs*, 'sweat'; AS. noun *swāt*, Eng. *sweat*: observe that though there is a word for 'sweat' common to most Indo-European tongues, there is no such common word for 'be chilly.']

svecchā, *f.* own will; **svecchayā**, according to one's inclination, at will. [icchā.]

svéda, *m.* sweat. [√svid.]

---

ha, *enclitic and slightly asseverative particle,* 64[4]; *in the Veda,* 78[15], 79[12], 92[12]; *in the Brāhmanas,* 94[8], *and very often (so pages* 95–6), 103[15] *(quotation from a Brāhmana); in the Sūtras,* to be sure, of course, *designating that the author agrees with the view or method mentioned,* 99[19], 101[5], 103[14.16]; —*very common at end of half-çloka,* 7[15]; *esp. after a 3d sing. perf.* (◡—◡), 9[4], 10[2]; *so* iti ha, 12[8]; —*combinations:* · · iti hovāca, "· ·," he said, 61[18]; *so* hovāca, hocus, 95[18], 96[18]. [this word appears also as gha in the Veda: cf. γε, Doric γα, enclitic asseveratives.]

haṅsá, *m.* goose, gander; *perhaps applied also to the* swan and like water-fowl. [prob. a consonantal stem, transferred (399) to the a-declension, and so orig. *ghaṅs: cf. χήν, Lat. *ans-er*, Lithuanian *żąsì-s*, Irish *goss*, Ger. *Gans*, AS. *gōs*, Eng. *goose*: even the s of *ghaṅs may be derivational; cf. AS. *gan-d-ra*, **gan-ra*, Eng. *gander*; Old High Ger. *gan-azzo*, 'gander'; AS. *gan-et*, Eng. *gannet*, 'sea-fowl.']

hatá, *see* 954d.

hatya, *n.* slaying. [√han, 1213c and a (middle), cf. 954d.]

√ **han** (hánti [637]; **jaghā́na** [794d]; **haniṣyáti**; **hatá** [954d]; **hántum**; **hatvā́**; **-hátya**; **hanyáte**; **jíghāṅsati** [1028f]). —1. strike; strike down; smite *or* slay, 70[2], etc.; kill, 28[6], 35[14], etc.; overcome; —2. destroy, 37[19]; bring to nought; (of darkness) dispel, 18[3]; —*desid.* wish to smite *or* afflict, 78[16];

—**hatá**, —1. smitten, slain, 98[4]; killed, 23[21]; —2. destroyed, ruined; lost, 27[13], 42[1]; —3. pounded.

[with **hán-mi**, cf. θείνω, *θεν-jω, 'smite'; w. **ja-ghn-ús**, cf. ἔ-πε-φν-ον, 'slew'; w. **hatá**, ***ghata**, cf. φατός, 'slain'; w. **ghaná**, q.v., 'a slaying,' cf. φόνος, 'slaughter'; w. **ha-ti**, 'a smiting, slaying,' cf. Old High Ger. *gun-d*, AS. *gūð*, **gun-ð*, 'battle'; AS. *gūð-fana*, Old High Ger. *gund-fano*, 'battle-flag'; fr. the last form (not fr. the AS.), through the French, comes Eng. *gonfanon*, *gonfalon*; for mg of *gūð*, cf. Ger. *schlagen*, 'smite, slay,' with *Schlacht*, 'battle': for senses under 1, observe that AS. *sleān* (whence Eng. *slay*) means 'smite' and then also 'slay.']

+ **ava**, strike down; bring to nought.

+ **ā**, strike upon; hurl (a bolt) upon (*loc.*

w. adhi); *mid.* strike (one's thigh with one's hand).

+**ud**, force up; uddhata [163], raised.

+**ni**, strike down; slay.

+**pari**, strike around; encompass.

+**prati**, strike back at (*acc.*); strike against so as to transfix, to broach (on a lance, *loc.*).

+**sam**, strike together; (of the eyes) close; unite, combine.

hán [402], *vbl.* slaying, slayer, *in cpds.* [√han.]

hánta, *interjection.* come! go to!

hantavya, *grdv.* to be slain, occidendus. [√han, 964.]

hantṛ́, *m.* slayer, destroyer. [√han.]

√ **har** (háryati, -te). be gratified, take pleasure; take pleasure in (*acc.*), *and so,* desire, long for. [perhaps a transfer (see 761a and b) from the yá-class, with change of accent, and so properly an irregular pass. to √1 hṛ, 'take' (reg. hriyáte); for the mg, cf. Eng. *be taken,* i.e. 'be charmed,' and hara 2: some take √har as representing Indo-European **ghel* (*ghwel*), and connect it w. θέλω, 'will,' Eng. *will;* cf. also √2 vṛ.]

+**prati**, long for, entice.

hara, *a.* —1. taking, receiving; —2. (*like the Eng.* carrying away, taking) charming; —3. carrying off, removing, destroying; *as m.* Hara, the Destroyer, a name of Çiva, 55[21]. [√1 hṛ, see its mgs.]

háraṇa, *a.* holding. [√1 hṛ, 'hold.']

háras, *n.* grip; *esp.* the seizing *or* devouring power of fire. [√1 hṛ, 'hold.']

hári, *a.* fallow, pale yellow, yellowish; greenish; *as m. du.* (*cf. Eng.* pair of bays, *i.e.* bay horses) the fallow steeds, *esp.* of Indra, his coursers. [√*ghṛ, *hṛ, 'be yellow,' is inferrible, but not quotable: cf. χλω-ρός, 'greenish-yellow'; χλόη, 'verdure'; Lat. *helus* or *holus* or *olus,* 'greens, vegetables'; *helvus,* 'grayish-yellow'; AS. *geolo,* Eng. *yellow;* also *gol-d* (cf. hiraṇya).]

harít, *a.* fallow, yellowish; *as f.* fallow mare, *esp.* of the Sun-god. [√*ghṛ *hṛ under hari: 383d 3.]

hárivant, *a.* having fallow steeds; *as m.* lord of the coursers, *i.e.* Indra, *see* hari. [hári, 1233.]

harmyá, *n.* a strong building; dwelling.

harṣa, *m.* joy. [√hṛṣ.]

halāhala, *m. n.* a certain deadly poison.

háva, *m.* call. [√hū.]

havanī, *f.* sacrificial ladle. [prop. fem. of a substantival nomen agentis, havana, √hu, 1150d, 'the sacrificing' instrument.]

havíṣmant, *a.* having an oblation; *as m.* offerer. [havís, 1235.]

havís, *n.* oblation, which, as gift for the gods, is offered wholly or partly in the fire; *generally,* grain (parched, boiled, as porridge, or as baked cake), milk in divers forms, fat, and — best of all — Soma. [√hu, 1153.]

havyá, *n.* oblation. [prop. grdv., 'offerendum,' √hu, 1213.]

hávya, *grdv.* invocandus. [√hū, 1213a.]

havya-váh [403], *a.* carrying the offering (to the gods); *as m.* oblation-bearer (used of Agni), *selections* lvi., lxvi.

√ **has** (hásati, -te; jahā́sa, jahasé; hasiṣyáti; hasitá; hásitum; hasitvā́; -hásya). laugh.

+**pra**, laugh out, laugh.

+**vi**, laugh out.

hása, *m.* laughter. [√has.]

hásta, *m.* hand; (of an elephant) trunk; (of a tiger) paw; *at end of cpds* [1303[2] end], having ·· in the hand.

hasta-gṛ́hya, *grd.* taking by the hand.

hasta-grābhá, *a.* grasping the hand. [acct, 1270.]

hastín, *a.* having hands; *w.* mṛgá, the beast with the hand, *i.e.* trunk, Vedic designation of the elephant; *as m.* elephant; Hastin, name of an ancient king. [hasta, q.v.]

hastināpura, *n.* Hastināpura, a town on the Ganges, home of the Kurus, said to have been founded by king Hastin. [cf. pura.]

hasti-rāja, *m.* elephant-king, leader of a herd of elephants.

hasti-snāna, *n.* ablution of an elephant.

√ **1 hā** (jíhīte [664]; jahé; áhāsta; hāsyáte; hāná; hā́tum). move, *intrans.,* run away, yield.

√ **2 hā** (jáhāti [665]; **jahāú**; áhāsīt [913]; hāsyáti; hīná [957a]; hā́tum; hitvā́; -hā́ya; hīyáte, hī́yate). —1. leave, *i.e.*: quit; leave in the lurch, 82[1]; desert, 86[13]; leave behind, 85[15]; abandon, cast off; lay aside, 83[14]; relinquish; —2. hīyate, be forsaken *or* left behind; fall short *or* be deficient; become deficient, decrease; deteriorate, be lowered, 19[9]; —hīná: —1. forsaken; —2. (*like Eng.* abandoned) vicious, low, low-lived, 19[9]; —3. *at end of cpds*, abandoned by · ·, *i.e.* destitute of · ·, free from · ·. [cf. *χῆ-ρο-ς*, '(forsaken) destitute,' *χή-ρα*, 'widow'; Lat. *fa-mes*, 'lack, hunger.']

+**pari**, —1. forsake; —2. *pass.* be lacking, decrease; come to an end, *see simple verb.*

+**vi**, leave; vihāya, passing over.

hā, *excl. of pain or astonishment.* [1135a.]

hā́rya, *grdv.* to be taken away *or* stolen. [√1 hṛ, 'seize,' 963[3]b.]

hāsin, *a.* laughing. [√has, 1183[3].]

hāsya, *grdv.* to be laughed at; *as n.* laughter; ridicule. [√has, 963[3]c.]

√ **hi** (hinóti, hinuté; jighā́ya; áhāiṣīt; heṣyáti; hitá). set in motion, drive, impel.

+**pra**, send off *or* away; deliver over.

hí, *particle.* —1. *asseverative:* surely, verily, indeed, 18[22,23], 22[20], 23[21], 28[15], 35[21], 83[1], etc.; —2. *giving a reason:* because; for, 3[19], etc., 53[2], 70[11]; —3. *w. interrogatives*, pray, 11[1], 13[14]; —*finite verb accented w.* hí [595d], 72[18]; hí *never at beg. of sentence.*

√ **hiṅs** (hinásti [696]; jihíṅsa; áhiṅsīt; hiṅsiṣyáti; hiṅsitá; híṅsitum; hiṅsitvā́; -híṅsya). hurt, harm, slay. [perhaps, orig., desid. of √han, see 696.]

hiṅsā, *f.* a harming, injuring. [√hiṅs, 1149.]

hiṅsrá, *a.* harming; *as m.* a savage *or* cruel man. [√hiṅs, 1188a.]

hitá, *ppl., adj.* —1. put, set; placed; *and so* —2. *pregnantly* (*like Eng.* in place, *i.e.* 'in the right place,' *and Ger.* gelegen, 'lying aright, *i.e.* convenient'), fit, convenient, agreeable; yadi tatra te hitam, if it suits thee there; advantageous, salutary; —3. *as n.* welfare, safety. [√1 dhā, 'put,' 954c: -dhita in Veda: cf. *θετός*, 'set.']

hita-kāma, *a.* wishing one's welfare, well-wishing. [see kāma.]

hitecchā, *f.* desire for the welfare (of another). [icchā.]

hitopadeça, *m.* salutary instruction; Hitopadeça, *name* of a collection of fables. [upadeça.]

himá, *m.* the cold; winter. [the stem **χιμα*, 'winter,' appears in *χίμα-ρο-ς*, lit. 'winter-ling, *i.e.* a one-winter-old *or* yearling goat,' named *χίμαρος* precisely as is the dialectic Ger. *Ein-winter*, 'a one-winter-old goat'; cf. *χίμαιρα*, 'she-goat, chimera'; see similar names under vatsa: cf. further *-χιμο-* in *δύσ-χιμο-ς*, 'very wintry'; Lat. *-himu-* in *bimus*, **bi-himu-s*, 'of two winters *or* years'; also *χιών*, 'snow,' *χειμών*, 'winter'; Lat. *hiems*, 'winter.']

híraṇya, *n.* gold. [akin w. hari, q.v.]

hiraṇya-garbhá, *m.* fruit *or* scion *or* child of the gold (*i.e.* of the golden egg, 57[8]), Hiranyagarbha *or* Gold-scion, name of a cosmogonic power, the personal Brahmán, 91[16].

√ **hīḍ** (*Vedic forms* [Whitney 54, 240[3]]: héḷant, héḷamāna; jihīḷa, jihīḷé; hīḷitá; *Epic*, hélamāna). be angry; be inconsiderate *or* careless.

hīná, *see* √2 hā.

√ **hu** (juhóti, juhuté; juhā́va, juhvé; áhāuṣīt; hoṣyáti; hutá; hótum; hutvā́). pour into the fire, cast into the fire; *and so* offer; make oblation even of things not cast into the fire; hutá: offered; *as n.* oblation.

[orig. **ghu*: cf. *χέω*, **χεϝ-ω*, 'pour'; *χυ-λό-ς*, 'liquid, juice'; w. hu-tá, cf. *χυ-τό-ς*, 'poured'; w. ā-hu-ti, cf. *χύ-σι-ς*, 'a pouring,' Lat. *fū-ti-s*, 'water-pot'; further, *fons*, stem *font*, **fov-ont*, 'pouring,' *i.e.* 'fountain':

with the extended form **ghud*, cf. Lat. √*fud* in *fund-ere*, 'pour,' AS. *geōt-an*, Ger. *giessen*, 'pour'; provincial Eng. *gut*, 'water-course'; and Eng. *gut*, w. like sense, in *Gut of Canso*.]

+**ā**, offer in (*loc.*); ā́huta: offered; laid

in the fire (of a corpse), 84[12]; *as n.* oblation.

hu ta-homa, *a.* having offered oblation.

hutāça, *m.* fire; the fire-god, Agni. [prop. 'having the oblation as his food,' āça: 1302.]

hutāçana, *m.* fire; the fire-god, Agni. [prop. 'having the oblation as his food,' açana: 1302.]

√ **hū** *or* **hvā** (hávate *and* huváte, *Vedic; classical,* hváyati, -te [761d 2]; juhā́va, juhuvé; áhvāsīt [912]; hvayiṣyáti, -te [935c]; hūtá; hvā́tum, hváyitum; hūtvā́; -hū́ya). call; call upon; invoke, *esp.* a god. [orig. *ghū: w. hū-tá, 'called upon, invoked,' some identify the Goth. stem *gu-þa, gu-da,* 'God,' AS. and Eng. *God.*]

+**ā**, —1. call to *or* hither; summon, invite; —2. *mid.* challenge.

+**upa**, *mid.* —1. call *or* summon to one's self; —2. call encouragingly unto.

hūti, *f.* invocation. [√hū.]

√ **1 hṛ** (hárati, -te; jahā́ra, jahré; áhārṣīt, áhṛṣṭa; hariṣyáti, -te; hṛtá; hártum; hṛtvā́; -hṛ́tya; hriyáte; jíhīrṣati). —1. carry, 102[5], 104[21]; hold; —2. carry unto, bring; offer, 105[9]; —3. carry away; remove, 85[3]; —4. *esp.* take away by violence *or* unlawfully, 46[4], 53[7]; steal, 30[2], 67[23], 68[4], 97[6, 9]; seize; —5. take lawfully, receive (a gift); come into possession of (as heir), 45[8, 15]; —6. get hold of, 96[22]; become master of; —7. (*like Eng.* take) charm, captivate; —8. (carry off, *i.e.* remove, *and so*) destroy. [cf. χείρ, dialectic χέρ-ς, 'hand'; εὐ-χερής, 'easy to handle'; Lat. *hir,* 'hand'; *hērēs,* 'heir,' see root, mg 5.]

+**ava**, (carry down, *i.e.*) move down.

+**vy-ava**, move hither and thither, go to work, proceed, act.

+**ā**, —1. bring hither, 34[3]; fetch; fetch *or* get back, 97[10, 11]; —2. receive, 47[12]; accept; —3. *used* (*like Eng.* take) *esp.* of food, take, eat; —*desid.* be willing to get back, 97[10].

+**ud-ā**, bring out, *and so* utter, say, tell.

+**praty-ā**, get back again; *at* 11[6], *incorrect reading for* pra-vy-ā-.

+**vy-ā**, bring out, *and so* utter; *with* vācam, speak words to a person (*acc.*), 3[1]; *similarly,* 8[19].

+**pra-vy-ā**, utter; speak.

+**ud**, take out.

+**pari**, carry around.

+**pra**, —1. (bring forward, *i.e.* reach out, *e.g.* feet, fists, *and so*) strike, attack, deal blows; —2. throw, *esp.* into the fire.

+**anu-pra**, throw into the fire *or* on a fuel-pile.

+**vi**, —1. take apart, divide; —2. pass (part of one's life), 64[22]; —3. pass one's time, *esp.* pleasantly; wander about for pleasure, enjoy one's self, 16[9, 12], 49[18]; —4. wander about.

+**sam**, bring *or* draw together, contract; withdraw.

+**upa-sam**, bring *or* draw together to one's self, *mid.*; withdraw.

√ **2 hṛ** (hṛṇīté). be angry.

hṛcchayá, *a.* lying *or* abiding in the heart [1265]; *as m.* love, 2[19]. [hṛd + çaya, 159, 203: acct, 1270.]

hṛcchaya-pīḍita, *a.* love-pained, love-sick.

hṛcchaya-vardhana, *a.* increasing *or* arousing love.

hṛcchayā́viṣṭa, *a.* entered by *or* filled with love. [ā́viṣṭa, √viç, 1085a: acct of cpd, 1273.]

hṛcchayā́viṣṭacetana, *a.* possessing a love-filled mind. [hṛcchayā́viṣṭa + cétanā, 1298a, 334[2].]

hṛ́d [397], *n.* heart; *esp. as* seat of the emotions and of mental activity in general; *also, properly,* region of the heart. [see under çrad.]

hṛ́daya, *n.* heart; —1. *prop.* heart, as an organ of the body, 100[21]; —2. *fig.* heart, as seat of the feelings. [see hṛd and 397.]

√ **hṛṣ** (hṛ́ṣyati, -te [761a]; jahárṣa, jahṛṣé; hṛṣitá, hṛṣṭá; -hṛ́ṣya; harṣáyati, -te). be excited, *esp.* with pleasure *or* fear; (of the hair) bristle *or* stand on end by reason of fright *or* pleasure; be impatient; —hṛṣṭa, delighted; —hṛṣitá: (of the hair) standing on end; (of flowers) not drooping, unwithered, fresh; —*intens.* be very impatient, 84[17]; —*caus.* excite pleasantly, gladden. [for ghṛṣ: cf. Lat. *horr-ēre*, **hors-ere*, 'bristle, shudder'; *hirsūtus*, 'bristly, rough'; *hor-deum*, Ger. *Gers-te*, 'barley,' so called from its bristly ears.]

+pra, give one's self up to joy, exult; **prahṛṣṭa**, delighted, glad.

hṛṣitasragrajohīna, *a.* having unwithered garlands and free from dust. [hṛṣita-sraj + rajo-hīna, 1257.]

hetú, *m.* —1. *prop.* an impeller, *and so* occasioner, causer, occasion, cause; hetos, (*like Lat.* causā) on account of; trāsa-hetos, from fear; —2. reason, argument, proof; —3. means, 41[16]. [√hi, 1161a.]

hetu-çāstra, *n.* reason-book, rationalistic work; dialectics.

hema *or* heman, *n.* gold.

hemantá, *m.* winter. [cf. hima: 1172[4].]

helā, *f.* carelessness; levity. [for heḷā, from √hīḍ, q.v.]

hāima, *a.* golden. [hema, 1208f.]

hótṛ, *m.* —1. priest, chief priest, whose assistant in oldest times was the adhvaryu; Agni, as the chiefest hotṛ, 69[2], 88[6]; —2. *in the highly developed ritual*, the first of the four chief priests, *see* ṛtvij. [prop. 'offerer,' from √hu, 'offer': but the sense of 'invoker,' naturally suggested by his function in the ritual, was popularly associated with it and the word thus connected with √hū, 'invoke.']

hotrá, *n.* offering, sacrifice, *both* the action *and* the thing offered. [√hu, 1185a.]

hóma, *m.* a pouring into the fire; oblation; sacrifice; *observe that the older word is* āhuti. [√hu, 1166.]

hradá, *m.* pool, lake. [cf. √hlād.]

√hras (hrásati, -te; hrasitá, hrastá; hrāsáyati). become less; *caus.* diminish. [w. hrás-īyāṅs, 'less,' cf. χείρων, *χέρσjων, 'worse,' and for the mg, cf. Lat. *dētero*, 'lessen,' w. *dēterior*, 'worse.']

√hrād (hrā́date; hrāditá; hrādáyati). sound (of drums); rattle (of stones *or* dry bones). [for *ghrad: cf. καχλάζω, *κα-χλάδ-jω, 'sound' (of liquids, breakers, rain), κε-χλαδ-ώς, 'resounding' (song of victory); AS. *grǣt-an*, obsolete Eng. *greet*, 'cry, lament'; χαράδ-ρα, 'noisy mountain torrent': see hrāduni.]

+sam, strike (*intrans.*) together so as to rattle; *caus.* cause to rattle.

hrādúni, *f.* hail-stones, hail. [so called from its rattling sound, √hrād: cf. χάλαζα, *χαλαδ-jα, Church Slavonic *gradŭ*, Lat. *grando*, stem *grand-in*, 'hail.']

√hlād (hlā́date; hlādáyati, -te). cool off, *intrans.*, refresh one's self; *caus.* cool *or* refresh, *trans.*

hlādaka, *f.* -ikā, *a.* cooling, refreshing. [√hlād, 1181 and a[3].]

hlādikāvant, *a.* rich in cooling. [from fem. of hlādaka, substantively?]

√hvṛ (hvárati, -te; áhvārṣīt; hvṛtá; hvāráyati). go crookedly; bend over, fall.

+vi, fall; *caus.* overturn.